LEVIATHAN

Also by David Scott

Politics and War in the Three Stuart Kingdoms, 1637–49

LEVIATHAN

The Rise of Britain as a World Power

DAVID SCOTT

Harper
Press

Harper*Press*
An imprint of HarperCollins*Publishers*
77–85 Fulham Palace Road,
Hammersmith, London W6 8JB
www.harpercollins.co.uk

Published by Harper*Press* in 2013

1

David Scott asserts the moral right to
be identified as the author of this work

A catalogue record for this book
is available from the British Library

ISBN 978-0-00-724080-7

Maps by HL Studios

Set in Minion by Palimpsest Book Production Limited,
Falkirk, Stirlingshire

Printed and bound in Great Britain by
Clays Ltd, St Ives plc

MIX
Paper from
responsible sources
FSC
www.fsc.org   **FSC** C007454

For Sarah

CONTENTS

The Tudor Territories, 1485–1558

Kingdom of
Scotland

Edinburgh

North Sea

Ulster

**Gaelic
Ireland**

Connacht

Dublin

Irish Sea

Leinster **Gaelic
Ireland**

**Lordship of
Ireland**

Munster

**Gaelic
Ireland**

(Boundaries
as at 1525)

Wales
Principality

Marches

**Kingdom of
England**

Pale of
Calais
(Eng.
1347–1558)

Antwerp

**Spanish
Netherlands**

London

Boulogne
(Eng.
1544–50)

Tournai
(Eng.
1513–19)

English Channel

Paris

Brittany
(Annexed to
France 1532)

France

Key

Land over 700ft/200m

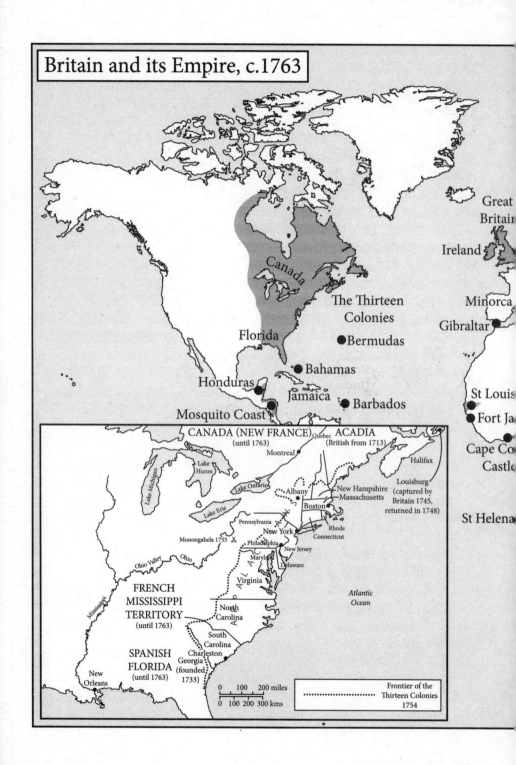

Britain and its Empire, c.1763

Canada

The Thirteen
Colonies

Florida

Bermudas

Bahamas

Honduras

Jamaica

Barbados

Mosquito Coast

Great
Britain

Ireland

Minorca

Gibraltar

St Louis

Fort Ja

Cape Co
Castle

St Helena

CANADA (NEW FRANCE)
(until 1763)

ACADIA
(British from 1713)

Quebec

Montreal

Halifax

Lake
Huron

Lake Michigan

Lake Ontario

Albany

Lake Erie

New Hampshire
Massachusetts

Louisburg
(captured by
Britain 1745,
returned in 1748)

Boston

Pennsylvania

Monongahela 1755

Philadelphia

New York

Rhode
Connecticut

New Jersey

Maryland

Delaware

Ohio Valley

Ohio

Virginia

Atlantic
Ocean

Mississippi

FRENCH
MISSISSIPPI
TERRITORY
(until 1763)

North
Carolina

South
Carolina

SPANISH
FLORIDA
(until 1763)

Charleston

Georgia
(founded
1733)

New
Orleans

| 0 | 100 | 200 miles |
| 0 | 100 200 | 300 kms |

Frontier of the
Thirteen Colonies
1754

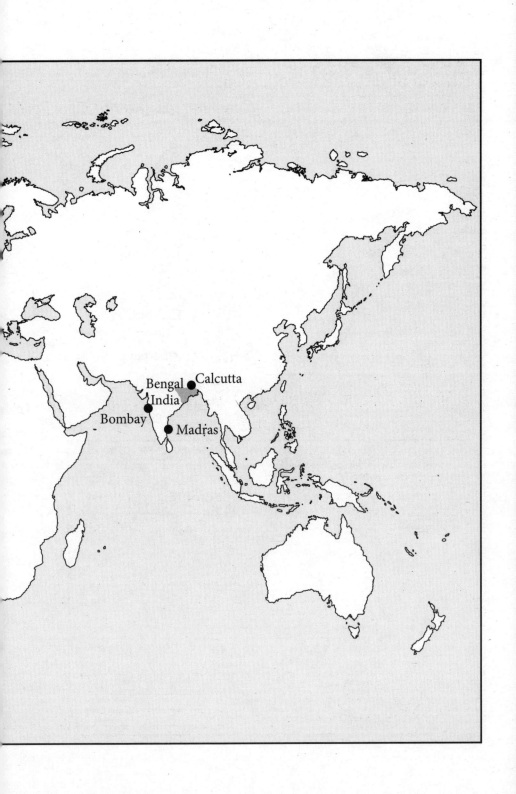

LIST OF ILLUSTRATIONS

1. King Henry VII by unknown Flemish artist, 1505 (© *National Portrait Gallery, London. NPG 416*)
2. From *The Image of Irelande* by John Derrick, 1581 (*Courtesy Edinburgh University Library*)
3. Armada playing cards, 1588 (© *National Maritime Museum, Greenwich, London. PU0214; PU0183; PU0181; PU0179*)
4. From *Narratio regionum indicarum per Hispanos quosdam devastatarum verissima*, 1598 (*Courtesy Bibliothèque Nationale de France. BNF C43328*)
5. Equestrian portrait of Charles I by Anthony Van Dyck, 1633 (*Supplied by Royal Collection Trust / © HM Queen Elizabeth II 2013. RCIN 405322*)
6. The *Tiger* by William Van de Velde the elder, *c.*1681 (© *National Maritime Museum, Greenwich, London. PZ7304*)
7. View of the beheading of Charles I by unknown artist (*Private Collection / © Look and Learn / Peter Jackson Collection / The Bridgeman Art Library*)
8. East India Company Ships at Deptford by unknown artist, *c.*1660 (© *National Maritime Museum, Greenwich, London. BHC1873*)
9. Duke's plan of New York, 1664 (© *The British Library Board. Maps K.Top.CXXI.35. 008318*)
10. Engraving of London before the Great Fire by Pieter Hendricksz Schut, mid-17th century (*Courtesy Guildhall Library, City of London*)
11. *A Representation of the Popish Plot in 29 figures*, *c.*1678 (© *The Trustees of the British Museum. All rights reserved. 1871,1209.6512*)
12. *The Common wealth ruleing with a standing Army*, 1683 (© *The Trustees of the British Museum. All rights reserved. 1868,0808.3297*)
13. *Emblematical Print on the South Sea Scheme* by William Hogarth, 1721
14. *Excise in Triumph*, *c.*1733 (*Courtesy of The Lewis Walpole Library, Yale University*)

While every effort has been made to trace the owners of copyright material reproduced herein, the publishers would like to apologise for any omissions and would be pleased to incorporate missing acknowledgements in future editions.

PREFACE

As Britain entered upon another global war with her old enemy France in the mid-1750s, the Royal Navy took timely delivery of the largest warship in the world. Built at Woolwich Dockyard and launched in 1756, the three-decker *Royal George* was a vast and intricately designed killing machine. Her construction had taken almost ten years and had consumed the wood of more than 5,000 oak and elm trees. She carried the tallest masts and the greatest spread of canvas of any ship in the navy. A crew of 867 men and boys was needed not only to sail her but also to work the hundred guns she mounted, which included twenty-eight massive 'full cannon' – the heaviest pieces of ordnance afloat – each firing a hull-smashing 42-pound ball. One broadside alone would throw over 1,000 lb weight of metal. Two broadsides were enough to sink the French 74-gun *Superbe* at the battle of Quiberon Bay in 1759 – the decisive naval engagement of the Seven Years War. Nelson's flagship at Trafalgar in 1805, named *Victory* to commemorate Britain's 'year of victories' in 1759, would be modelled on the *Royal George*. Ships of the line such as these were the ultimate expression of Britain's determination to stamp her naval superiority on every European rival, or indeed combination of rivals. The British would tolerate no balance of power at sea as they would on the Continent. But the Georgian navy served a larger purpose than engaging enemy fleets, for it kept the sea lanes open to the stream of goods to and from Britain that invigorated its industries, powered its economy towards the industrial revolution, and sustained the military expenditure of an altogether deadlier war machine: the British imperial state.

This book is partly about how and why the British and Irish peoples acquired the kind of state that could outdo the French and every other European power; that could build the *Royal George* and keep her, and hundreds more warships, at sea around the globe for months on end. It is a story that grew to encompass all of Britain and Ireland, and many other lands besides. But it began life in England. And here I must pause to make the familiar confession of English historians writing supposedly 'British' history. It was said of Georgian Britain's longest-serving prime minister, Sir Robert Walpole, that his political genius consisted in 'understanding his own country, and his foible, inattention to every other country, by which it was impossible he could thoroughly understand his own'.[1] Though I do not lay claim to Walpole's superlative mastery of his art, there is no doubt that I share his foible. In my own defence I would argue that in writing a narrative history that covers (if only loosely) Britain and Ireland, it is almost impossible to avoid focusing on England. There is no ignoring the fact that England was the largest, the most populous and the most aggressive of the states that occupied the British Isles during the period covered by this book. Events in London and lowland England were bound to exert a greater influence over Scotland and Ireland than the other way round.

This unavoidable Anglocentrism is also apparent in the period I have chosen to cover – that is, from 1485 to 1783. Henry Tudor's victory at Bosworth in 1485 was, or would become, an event of immense significance in English history, but it looks rather less of a turning-point when viewed from a Scottish or Irish perspective. The capacity of the English to throw their weight around in the British Isles was unusually weak at the end of the fifteenth century – a legacy of the Wars of the Roses. Henry's seizure of the crown took some time to disturb the pattern of English rule in Ireland, and longer still to make any great impact on the Stuart kingdom of Scotland. By contrast, the cataclysm of the American War of Independence, with which this book ends, reverberated immediately and powerfully across the British Isles. Yet although Bosworth itself was more of an Anglo-French event than a British or Irish one, the year 1485 is of larger significance than simply as a boundary marker between the Plantagenets and the Tudors. Henry VII's reign (1485–1509), it is now recognised, did much to reshape and reinvigorate the English monarchy – which was, after all, the most powerful political institution in the British Isles. Moreover, the decades around 1500 have often been taken to mark the end of the Middle Ages in Britain and the beginning of a new era, the 'early modern period'. Although historians (myself included) are vague about the timing and nature of this transition, the early modern period is generally assumed to have included the sixteenth and seventeenth centuries, and some, or most, of the eighteenth century – in other words, roughly the period covered by this book.

Writing history entails the risk of imposing order and meaning where none existed. Whether the early modern period has themes and trends that are peculiarly its own, or is merely a convenient label for the centuries between the end of the Middle Ages and the first stirrings of the industrial revolution, is too large a question for a preface, and too abstract for a narrative history. What is certainly true is that this period covers some very important historical territory for a proper understanding of modern Britain. The Reformation in England and Scotland in the sixteenth century wrought perhaps the most profound and enduring transformation in British and Irish society – for Catholics as well as Protestants – of anything that has happened in these islands since the Norman Conquest. The consequences of Britain's traumatic break with medieval Christendom are still with us today, as are those of another innovation closely associated with the Reformation, and the early modern period more generally: printing. Britain's first printing press was set up by William Caxton in 1476. The print revolution changed the way people read and wrote, thought and communicated, and how they perceived their nation and their relationship to the crown. Print was a vital medium by which London in particular, but also Edinburgh and Dublin, extended their authority and influence across the British Isles to create at least some of the attributes of a single political and cultural system. The partial incorporation of Ireland and Scotland by a London-dominated British state took place largely during the early modern period. And running through this story of the forging of modern Britain are the plot-lines, the dramatic twists and the heroes and villains of a true epic: the rise and fall of the 'first' British empire across the Atlantic.

These themes will carry the burden of my story, but there are also significant subplots that I thought worth unravelling. The development of representative institutions in the British Atlantic; the deepening and widening commitment to ideas of freedom and the rule of law (which ultimately enabled the colonial American cubs to defy the parental British lion); the consolidation of a political culture built around ideas of rights and the answerability of monarchs to their subjects – a process that was fitful, occasionally bloody, and at various times highly uncertain of outcome – and the emergence, by the late seventeenth century, of a degree of religious tolerance that had no parallel in any major European state.

Yet if the history of early modern Britain is not devoid of overarching themes, nor is it without deep fissures. Two are central to my narrative. The first and most obvious is the Reformation of the sixteenth century and, in particular, the way Protestantism altered how people in Britain related to the rest of Europe. From the 1550s there was a growing number of British Protestants who recognised no greater cause than fighting alongside their co-religionists in Europe in the great cosmic struggle against 'popery' – Catholicism understood as political and spiritual tyranny. Mere national security by means of a strong navy was the very least of their demands. They continually urged their monarchs to send armies to the Continent, and fleets to the New World, to uphold the Protestant cause. A few would be bolder still, and embrace the idea of the new and massively enlarged state that the British would have to build if they were properly to challenge the might of Catholic Europe.

The second great fissure in the history of early modern Britain occurred in the 1640s, and would see precisely that: the construction of a monstrous, militaristic state. And yet the circumstances surrounding the birth of this Leviathan would frustrate the dreams of a Protestant crusade abroad for half a century. In the end it would require a Dutch invasion to put Britain firmly and unstoppably on the path to global ascendancy. That ascendancy, both real and imagined, would frequently be challenged by the Dutch themselves, the French, the Spanish, and by Britain's own colonial subjects. What was special about the state that emerged in Britain in the mid-seventeenth century was not so much its power as its resilience. One of my aims has been to explain how the growth of such a state enabled the British not simply to win an empire, but to survive and indeed flourish after losing more than half of it – a setback that would have overwhelmed a lesser imperial power.

There are many ways of telling this story of wars and empire, and of the fears and dreams that made them. I have chosen to look more closely at those pursuing and exercising power than at the instruments and victims of their ambition. If this too is a foible on my part, it also has some grounding in historical fact. In our democratic society, the wishes and opinions of the majority are constitutive of the political order. Until the 1800s, however, democracy was merely a polite word for mob rule, and barely a thought was given to empowering women. The social, economic and intellectual structures that prevailed in early modern Britain allowed small groups of men to exercise a disproportionately large influence over the affairs of their communities. This book reflects that reality. It is about monarchs and their courts; about Parliament-men and religious reformers; and about those who observed

and anatomised these worlds, or whose convictions and learning transformed them. The constraints of time and space inevitably make this
a highly select cast. I am particularly conscious that I all but ignore,
for example, Britain's great experimental scientists and inventors of the
seventeenth and eighteenth centuries. Men such as John Harrison
(1693–1776), whose 'sea clock' for determining longitude, first successfully tested in 1761, ensured that the *Royal George* was far less likely to
run aground than its French or Spanish rivals. I also have relatively
little to say about the lives of ordinary men and women, or the squalor
and deprivation that often accompanied them. I take it largely for
granted that a society with rudimentary sewerage and welfare systems
was disease-ridden and very hard on the poor who made up the vast
majority of the population.

Another constant across the period that I *do* make much of, but
which is worth emphasising from the outset, is a matter of simple
topography. To the east and west, England and Wales were separated
from their neighbours by water. The observation of the Italian
philosopher Giovanni Botero in the 1590s holds true throughout the
early modern era: 'In strength of situation no kingdome excelleth
England: for it hath these two properties . . . one is, that it be difficult
to besiege; the other, that it be easie to convey in and out all things
necessarie: these two commodities hath England by the sea, which to
the inhabitants is a deep trench against hostile invasions, and an easie
passage to take in or sende out all commodities whatsoever.'[2] Here was
the starting-point for England's and, later, Britain's rulers as they sized
up the world beyond their shores.

The aim of this book is first and foremost to provide a clear narrative
and explanation of events. With that in mind, I have tried not to fill
my canvas with too many figures. Similarly, I have opted for a traditional
rendering of places and names – thus Bombay rather than Mumbai;
Philip II of Spain, rather than Felipe II, and so on. The most significant
exception to this rule has been French kings named Henry, who have
been given their native 'Henri' in order to distinguish them more clearly
from their English counterparts. I have employed the words 'Britain'
and 'British' generously, usually with reference to the Protestants of
England, Wales, Scotland and Ireland, but also as a shorthand for the
British and Irish peoples as a collective political unit. 'The Irish' I generally reserve for Ireland's Catholics, whether Gaelic or of Anglo-Norman
extraction. There is no single word that accurately denotes the islands
of Britain and Ireland as a geographic whole. I have used the phrases

'the British Isles', or simply 'Britain and Ireland'. Neither is entirely
satisfactory, but they are preferable to the recently in vogue 'Atlantic
Archipelago' – a designation that can be claimed, with equal entitle-
ment, by more than two dozen island groups fringing the Atlantic from
the Canaries to the Bahamas.

The realm over which successive Tudor, Stuart and Hanoverian
monarchs imposed their rule was a composite of many overlapping,
and often conflicting, communities. To combine such disparate
elements, and then to erect on this shifting base the superstructure of
a global empire, would be a fraught and lengthy process. Taking the
long view, as I have in this book, has distinct advantages in trying to
understand the forces that have shaped modern Britain. Issues and
tensions that took centuries to resolve can be traced with a clarity that
is sometimes missing when the analysis is confined to a shorter time-
frame. A three-centuries viewpoint is particularly revealing of the
shifting patterns in Britain's relations with the rest of Europe, and of
the frequent and often substantial impact of European events and ideas
on domestic developments. Britain was in many ways an 'exceptional'
state in the early modern period. But equally it was an integral part
of Europe. If the peoples of Britain and Ireland clung more tenaciously
to their particular locality than we generally do today, they were also
much more likely to see themselves as part of transnational communities of faith and political culture that were centred on the Continent.
Many of their greatest exploits during the early modern period – from
the Henrician Reformation to the forging of an empire – were under-
taken with conscious reference to this European dimension. 'The
utmost rational aim of our Ambition', declared one Georgian
pamphleteer, 'ought to be, to possess a just Weight, and Consideration
in *Europe*.'[3] What follows is an exploration of why, how, and with what
success that ambition was pursued.

1

Lost Kingdoms, 1485–1526

But what miserie, what murder, and what execrable plagues this famous region hath suffered by the devision and discencion of the renoumed [sic] houses of Lancastre and Yorke, my witte cannot comprehende nor my toung declare nether yet my penne fully set furthe . . . All the other discordes, sectes and faccions almoste lively florishe and continue at this presente tyme, to the greate displesure and preiudice of all the christian publike welth. But the olde devided controversie betwene the fornamed families of Lancastre and Yorke, by the union of Matrimony celebrate and consummate betwene the high and mighty Prince Kyng Henry the seventh and the lady Elizabeth his moste worthy Quene, the one beeyng indubitate heire of the hous of Lancastre, and the other of Yorke was suspended and appalled in the person of their moste noble puissant and mighty heire kyng Henry the eight, and by hym clerely buried and perpetually extinct.

Edward Hall, *The Union of the Two Noble and Illustre Famelies of Lancastre [and] Yorke* (London, 1548), fo. 1

The men who would be king

On 22 August 1485 the grandson of an obscure Welsh squire seized the throne of England after a brief and relatively bloodless battle. He was a mere twenty-eight years of age, and had spent all of his adult life in exile on the Continent. His invasion force had consisted of a few thousand French and Scottish mercenaries, whose services he had paid for by mortgaging all he owned. And he was acclaimed king on the field of a battle – Bosworth – in which his opponent's army had outnumbered his own by perhaps two to one. How had Henry Tudor, this unlikely king, this foreigner almost, succeeded? And what does his success tell us about the state of late medieval England, the most powerful territory of his new realm?

An important clue to this seemingly bizarre twist of fate that had
put Henry on the throne lies in the manner of Richard III's defeat.
There is much that we do not know about the battle of Bosworth,
including where exactly it took place – beyond the fact that it was in
the vicinity of the Leicestershire village of Market Bosworth. But one
thing is clear: many of Richard's soldiers either did not fight for him
or they switched sides. His headlong charge at Henry's standard was
probably intended to settle the issue quickly before his army disintegrated entirely. In the event, it was the cue for his supposed ally, Sir
William Stanley, to bring his sizeable contingent of troops over to
Henry's side. Unable to penetrate the phalanx of French pikemen that
protected Henry, the royal guard, surrounded and outnumbered, was
cut down. Scorning the opportunity of escape or surrender, Richard
was killed 'fyghting manfully in the thickkest presse of his enemyes' –
the last king of England to perish in battle.[1]

For Shakespeare, writing over a hundred years later, Bosworth
provided a fitting conclusion to Richard III – man and play – and to
the Wars of the Roses. 'The bloody dog is dead . . .' declares Henry after
killing Richard, supposedly in single combat. 'Now civil wounds are
stopp'd; peace lives again.'[2] But in fact the battle resolved very little.
The hesitation and treachery that marked many of Richard's followers
at Bosworth were symptomatic of a malaise that had afflicted the English
monarchy since the 1450s. Admittedly, Richard had been a peculiarly
unpopular king. Even in an age accustomed to over-mighty subjects
challenging under-mighty kings, his *lèse-majesté* following the death of
his brother, Edward IV, in 1483 had appeared peculiarly monstrous.
For rather than be satisfied with the role of lord protector during his
nephew Edward V's minority, he had seized the young prince and his
brother, imprisoned them in the Tower, declared himself king, and had
then had them murdered. An uncle killing his nephews, defenceless
children, in a naked bid for power was as shocking then as now.

Yet neither Edward V's fate nor Richard's was exceptional. The mental
and physical feebleness of Henry VI (1421–71), in the context of a
deep and prolonged economic recession, and military humiliation
abroad, had profoundly weakened the monarchy as an institution.
Between 1461 and 1485 the crown had changed hands violently on five
occasions – six, if we take the story back to Henry Bolingbroke (the
future Henry IV) toppling Richard II in 1399. Nor was there any
certainty, in the aftermath of Bosworth Field, that the series of noble
revolts, battles and executions for treason that had intermittently

convulsed England since 1455 would come to an end any time soon. Not until 1485 did anyone think of these events as part of a single narrative, with Bosworth its final denouement; indeed, the term 'the Wars of the Roses' was not popularised until 1829, when it was taken up by the romantic novelist Sir Walter Scott. Henry was fortunate in that Richard III had died without an heir, and that in disposing of the rightful claimants to the throne (the princes in the Tower) he had alienated many of his subjects. But Henry was aware how much he owed to the god of battles, and how weak his title to the crown remained. The vulnerability of the English monarchy by 1485 was plain for all to see, and Bosworth merely raised the question of who was Henry Tudor anyway? To most of his subjects he was merely the latest in a series of royal usurpers, and a largely unknown one at that.

The future Henry VII was born in Pembroke Castle, in southern Wales, in 1457. His father was a half-brother (on his mother's side) of Henry VI, and his mother was the great-great-granddaughter of Edward III (1312–77). This gave him royal blood, to be sure, but by no means made him Richard III's presumptive heir. Much of his boyhood was spent in Wales; and, as king, he would play up his Welsh background, although he neither spoke Welsh nor showed much concern for those who did. His lineage put him on the Lancastrian side in the Wars of the Roses, and when the Yorkist king Edward IV (1442–83) resumed the throne in 1471, Henry and his uncle Jasper Tudor fled to the (then independent) duchy of Brittany. They spent the next fourteen years as the guests or political pawns of the duke of Brittany and the French king; and it had seemed that all Henry could look forward to was a precarious life in exile. But in 1483 his prospects were transformed by the death of Edward IV and its aftermath. For Richard's usurpation, and the 'disappearance' of the young princes in the Tower, gave Henry not only a moral basis for claiming the throne but also won him vital support from senior figures in the Yorkist camp to add to that of his Lancastrian followers.

Yet only the most creative of genealogists could depict Henry Tudor as the head even of the House of Lancaster. Going by the strict rules of inheritance, perhaps a dozen men were more legitimate heirs presumptive than he was. To strengthen his candidacy, therefore, Henry vowed to marry Edward IV's eldest surviving child, Princess Elizabeth, and thereby to unite the Yorkist claim with his own. And briefly, in 1484–5, it seemed that the French court would back him in his ambition – only for the French to lose interest as their various domestic and international crises resolved themselves. Desperate to launch his invasion, but strapped for cash, Henry was forced to take out a private loan with a French nobleman. This would be an invasion on credit. The French did at least allow Henry to hire some of their ships and demobilised troops, and this investment in expert pikemen may well have saved his life at Bosworth.

Henry landed in his native Pembrokeshire on 7 August 1485. His army of French and Scottish mercenaries was swelled on its march to Bosworth by Welsh recruits and disaffected Yorkists who had turned opponents of Richard. But it was the defection of the beleaguered king's commanders on the field of battle that proved decisive. Henry was keen to depict his victory as a triumph for the Lancastrian *and* Yorkist causes, but the real winners at Bosworth, in the short term anyway, were the French. The kings of England had by no means relinquished their claim to the crown of France, despite the loss of all their French possessions, save Calais, by 1453. But Henry's accession gave the French a few years' freedom from English hostility and meddling in which to advance their designs of annexing the duchy of Brittany.

The Tudor dominions

Henry headed south after Bosworth, making for London. On his march through southern Wales and into England he would have passed through a variety of half-remembered landscapes and communities. The Wales of his youth had not changed much since its conquest by Edward I two centuries earlier. Its population of about 200,000, most of them monoglot Welsh-speakers, was concentrated in the villages and small towns of the coastal lowlands. The interior was mainly moorland and mountains, fit only for sheep and cattle farming. Agriculture of one sort or other was the predominant source of livelihood, as it was in England. The social and political landscape of Wales still bore the marks of its violent past. The west of the country was dominated by the Principality, the area that Edward had conquered, and brought under English rule, where a mixture of native Welsh and English laws were in force. To the east, along the border with England, were 130 or so 'marcher' lordships, that had once formed a military frontier between the two nations. The king's writ did not run in these semi-autonomous feudal franchises, and they were therefore a haven for criminals, with an unenviable reputation for violence and lawlessness.

Henry's progress from Bosworth to London would have taken him through the economic heartland of his new realm: the rich fields and pastures of lowland England. This was the wealthiest and most populous of Henry's territories. Well over half his subjects lived in this fertile countryside, and yet Henry's human resources were meagre compared with those of the largest states on the Continent. England's population of about 2.3 million was dwarfed by the 16 million of France, for example, and was itself less than half of what it had been before the Black Death had struck in 1348. Average living conditions in England were also unimpressive by continental standards. The vast majority of people belonged to tiny farming communities made up largely of cramped, window- and chimneyless one-room cottages. Only about 5 per cent of the population lived in towns, which was well below the urban density in the Low Countries or northern Italy. And though London had around 50,000 inhabitants by 1500 – or more than double that of any other English city – it was still only a quarter the size of Paris.

Henry entered London on 3 September 1485 'like a triumphing general'.[3] The city was his new kingdom's financial centre, the hub of England's overseas and domestic mercantile network, but the seat of royal power lay in nearby Westminster. The Palace of Westminster was the monarch's principal royal residence, and the usual location of Parliament, when sitting. A stone's throw to the west of the palace was the great Benedictine monastery of Westminster Abbey, where Henry was crowned on 30 October 1485 (it would be here, too, that in January 1486 he honoured his promise to marry Princess Elizabeth). After prostrating himself before the high altar, as the coronation ceremony required, he swore before England's senior churchman, the archbishop of Canterbury, to 'kepe . . . to the Church of God, to the clergie, and the peple, hoole [whole] peace, and goodly concord', and to preserve the laws and privileges of 'holy churche'.[4] Nothing deterred, Henry spent the rest of his reign mulcting the clergy for money, trying (unsuccessfully) to force the papacy to end the monasteries' jurisdictional privileges, and encouraging his lawyers to undermine ecclesiastical law. It was no thanks to him that the Church in England was one of the best-run and most flourishing in all of Catholic Europe.

At the heart of medieval piety was the miracle of the Mass and its saving power for both the living and the dead. The increasing use of printed books of prayer among England's educated, mostly town-dwelling, literate minority may have encouraged a more inward-looking, intellectual kind of devotion, but very few people questioned the idea of constant supernatural intervention in human affairs. Nor had there been any significant challenge to the Church's teachings since the early fifteenth century. There was no effective movement of religious dissent in England – only the Lollards, or 'mumblers', who were a highly amorphous group, with no agreed agenda or political influence. Most of them lived unobtrusively in the villages of southern England, attending church like their orthodox neighbours, but also meeting secretly to read their illicit vernacular bibles (the church authorities in England had banned all translations of the Scriptures save those in Latin) and to criticise and ridicule priestly authority, transubstantiation, and any clerical teachings for which they could find no warrant in the Scriptures.

If late fifteenth-century England was small and relatively poor compared with its continental rivals, it was nevertheless precocious in terms of its political culture. Lowland England – roughly the southern and home counties and the Midlands – was unusual in its administrative and cultural uniformity. It was an area of mostly gentle terrain, with reasonably good access to London (at least in the warmer months, when travel on the unpaved roads was relatively easy), where the Anglo-Norman monarchy had created a complex and integrated central administration by 1250, complete with national courts of law and financial institutions, all operating through proper forms and channels. By 1485, therefore, lowland England had formed the core of the English state for centuries, and respect for crown, Parliament and the common law – England's traditional, precedent-based legal code – was strong. In addition, the great majority of the people spoke the same language, albeit with a variety of distinctive regional accents. The nobility had switched from French to English long before the Tudor period – a process of linguistic colonisation that was picking up speed by the late fifteenth century. English was replacing Latin and legal French in a growing range of political, administrative and ecclesiastical contexts, and as it did so its vocabulary expanded and became ever more nuanced. The increasing sophistication and application of the English language encouraged, in turn, greater participation in public affairs and a wider sense of shared knowledge and assumptions. At the same time, there were strongly centralising forces at work in the growth of this participatory political culture. The trade in printed books that emerged following the introduction of the printing press to England by William Caxton (c.1415–92) in the mid-1470s was dominated by London. It was the London dialect that would become the standard for written

English in Anglophone Britain and Ireland, and it was the political and cultural interests that clustered around the crown's metropolitan centre that did much to set the intellectual agenda and shape public opinion throughout the Tudor realm.

Royal authority operated with little hindrance in southern England, reaching – through a variety of officials – from London to the shires and down to the meanest parish. Of course, there were parts even in the lowlands where simple topography rendered the structures of government comparatively weak – the East Anglian fens, for example, which were largely undrained in this period, or densely wooded areas, where settlements were often scattered and subject to fewer social and economic controls than the more arable regions, with their networks of manors and manorial courts. Generally, however, lowland England set the standard for civility and orderliness by which English monarchs judged their domains as a whole.

Yet beyond this centralised core, England was fragmented both ethnically and politically. For a start, it shared three major cultural borders: in the south-west with the Cornish – a distinct ethnic grouping with its own language; with their Celtic cousins the Welsh, who had settlements in the English counties adjoining the marcher lordships; and with the Scots. The Welsh lived more or less in harmony with the English. The Cornish could be more troublesome, as Henry VII would discover in 1497 (see below). But the real problem area in England, at least from the crown's perspective, was its northern border with Scotland, where the two British kingdoms met and clashed. Even on the English side of that frontier there were considerable obstacles to exerting royal authority, for the rugged Pennine terrain and its scattered communities did not favour centralised control. Moreover, the threat of Scottish invasion and cross-border raids had promoted forms of administration that were geared to the needs of local defensive warfare, not to maintaining law and order. Between 1333 and 1502 (save for a brief period in the 1470s) there was no formal peace between England and Scotland, only a series of temporary truces. English monarchs generally had better things to do with their time and money than defending this remote region, so they devolved this duty, and the powers that went with it, upon their northern magnates. This, in turn, meant creating special offices and feudal franchises that lay outside the normal structures of English government. An unstable international frontier and weak civil authority were a recipe for lawlessness. The Anglo-Scottish borderlands were like Welsh marches, therefore, only very much worse.

For even when England and Scotland were not at open war, the northern marches were prey to cattle rustling and feuding by clans from both sides of the border.

Henry had another vulnerable frontier to worry about besides the northern marches, and that was in Ireland. English monarchs had claimed lordship over Ireland since the Anglo-Norman invasion of the twelfth century. Ireland, so royal rhetoric would have it, was a dependency of the English crown. Yet by the late fifteenth century the full exercise of royal authority was limited to the hinterland surrounding Dublin, the seat of English administration in Ireland. This area, known as the maghery, formed the core of a larger and more amorphous territory, the Pale, which covered much of Leinster and Munster, the provinces closest to England and Wales. The Pale contained most of Ireland's towns, ports and fertile land, and over half the island's population of about half a million people. English customs and common law generally prevailed here, and leading Palesmen, who claimed descent from the Anglo-Norman settlers, considered themselves English. It was largely down to these 'Old English' lords to defend the Pale, which was under constant threat of raiding by the native (Gaelic) Irish. The Pale, therefore, was another unstable marcher society, just like the northern marches in England, and the crown's solution to the problem had been virtually identical. Short of money, and with pressing concerns elsewhere, it had delegated the maintenance of war and justice to Old English nobility, ensuring that the Pale outside the maghery was at least under English influence, if not direct crown rule.

Beyond the Pale was a landscape dominated by mountains, woodland and bogs. This was the Gaedhealtacht: an area of Gaelic language, law and culture that stretched across most of the western and northern provinces of Connacht and Ulster and into the western Highlands of Scotland. The Irish in the Gaedhealtacht generally lived in loosely formed clans, leading a semi-nomadic existence based upon raising and raiding cattle. To the English they appeared 'savage, rude, and uncouth', the 'wild men of the woods'.[5] An early Tudor report on the state of Ireland divided Irish Gaeldom into over sixty territories, each of which was ruled by a clan chief who 'makeyth warre and peace for hymself . . . and hathe imperiall jurysdyction within his rome [room], and obeyeth to noo other person, Englyshe ne Iryshe, except only to such persones, as maye subdue hym by the swerde'.[6]

In short, Henry had succeeded to a disparate collection of territories on the periphery of Europe. The idea that this small and vulnerable realm, along with the even smaller kingdom of Scotland, would one day form the heart of a great, transoceanic empire would have seemed preposterous to contemporaries. Even welding England, the least fragmented of Henry's dominions, into a uniform state would be a major challenge. Moreover, his subjects were menaced by the Gaels in Ireland, and – more worryingly – by the Scots in northern England. Scotland may have been poorer and weaker than England, with a population of only about 600,000, but politically it was more stable; and the Scots' 'auld alliance' with France – designed to preserve both kingdoms from English aggression – made them a potentially formidable enemy. Commercially and culturally the Scots were oriented more towards the French and the Baltic states than towards the English. Faced with a fragmented realm and hostile neighbours, and uncertain that the Wars of the Roses were truly over, Henry had no alternative but to make dynastic security his long-term priority. But in the short term, as he well knew, the best way to gain his subjects' confidence, and quell 'inward troubles and seditions', was an honourable war against the only worthy foe in English eyes: the French.[7]

Warlike Harry

In a century in which Henry VII's predecessors had struggled to make their authority felt, the personal qualities of the king mattered more than ever. To the Tudor poet Edmund Spenser, the monarch stood in the very breach between order and chaos. Without 'the continuall presence of their King', he doubted whether the English would ever have outgrown 'civil broiles'.[8] The royal court (which, technically speaking, was wherever the monarch happened to be in residence), not Parliament, was the institutional heart of the realm. The monarch was 'the Sunne of the Court, from whose glorie, all Courtiers, as starres, borrowe theire attracting splendor'.[9] So what kind of man was Henry VII? The fullest description we have of him is by his own court historian Polydore Vergil, who was hardly the most impartial of royal biographers. Nevertheless, Vergil seems to have been accurate in two of his observations: that Henry's presence of mind never deserted him, 'even in moments of the greatest danger'; and that he 'well knew how to maintain his royal majesty and all which appertains to kingship at every time and in every place'.[10]

Medieval monarchs could display their 'royal majesty' in a variety of ways, but nowhere more impressively than in conducting foreign policy and the successful waging of war – and Henry was to have numerous opportunities for both during the early years of his reign. His own success in wresting the crown from Richard had demonstrated to foreign powers and potential rivals just what could be achieved with experienced foreign soldiers and a big slice of luck. So it came as no surprise to anyone that less than two years after the battle of Bosworth a new royal pretender had emerged: Lambert Simnel, the teenage son of an Oxford carpenter. Simnel was the front-man for a powerful group of Yorkist exiles backed by Edward IV's sister Margaret of York and her nephew the earl of Lincoln. These would-be kingmakers connived in Simnel's impersonation of Edward IV's nephew, Edward, earl of Warwick – a man with an even stronger claim by royal lineage to be Richard III's successor than Henry Tudor (and for which reason the real earl was a prisoner in the Tower). Late in 1486, Simnel landed in Ireland, where many of the nobility hailed him as king and had him crowned as 'Edward VI'. The following year this 'counterfeit Plantagenet' invaded England with an army of 4,000 Irish light infantry, together with 2,000 German mercenaries from the army of Archduke Maximilian (who in 1493 would succeed his father, Frederick III, as Holy Roman Emperor and head of the House of Habsburg). The real leader of this invasion, the earl of Lincoln, had resolved 'to try the fortunes of war, recalling that two years earlier Henry with a smaller number of soldiers had conquered the great army of King Richard'.[11] But there would be no rerun of Bosworth. When the two armies met near Stoke on 16 June 1487, Lincoln's troops fought bravely, but they were outnumbered by the king's, who made short work of the lightly armed Irish, before dealing with the German mercenaries. Lincoln was killed in the battle; Simnel was captured and later put to work in the royal kitchens as a scullion. He was still alive when Vergil wrote his history of Henry VII in 1534.

Stoke was a painful warning that the Wars of the Roses might not yet be over. The birth of Henry's first son Arthur in 1486, followed by Henry (the future Henry VIII) in 1489, did little to deter plots and foreign-backed imposters intriguing against his throne. In 1491 the Yorkists persuaded the son of a Flemish artisan, Perkin Warbeck (the Anglicisation of Pierrechon de Werbecque), 'a youth of fine favour and shape', to pose as the younger of the two princes who had been murdered in the Tower after Richard III's usurpation.[12] Warbeck was taken up at various times and for various reasons by Charles VIII of France,

Emperor Maximilian, James IV of Scotland, the Irish magnate the earl of Desmond, and Margaret of York. Three times in as many years (1495, 1496 and 1497) Warbeck and his backers attempted to mount invasions of England – from the Continent, from Scotland, and from Ireland – only to fail on each occasion for lack of popular support. In the final attempt, Warbeck himself was captured and, after further intrigues, was executed in 1499. By then there were few, if any, noblemen left in England with the appetite or the landed power to disturb Henry's throne. Nevertheless, the death of Prince Arthur in 1502, and Henry's own poor health, left the crown vulnerable, if not to royal pretenders and 'kingmakers', then possibly to a succession crisis should the king die while the second and younger of his two sons, Prince Henry, was still a boy.

What made Yorkist conspiracies so dangerous to Henry VII was not their popularity in England – they had little – but the support they received from foreign princes, few of whom had reason to want a strong monarchy in England. The crown's traditional claims to dominion throughout the British Isles had soured its relations with the Scots and large sections of the Irish elite. Here was one reason why Dublin and Edinburgh were receptive to such obvious frauds as Simnel and Warbeck. The French, too, had good cause to prefer a weak and divided England. For if the English had been pushed out of Scotland in the fourteenth century, and had gradually lost ground in Ireland, it was only because they had been too busy building a new empire for themselves in France. Of course, the English had been pushed out of France too (Calais excepted) in 1453 – and the 150 years between defeat in the Hundred Years War and the death of the last Tudor monarch, Elizabeth I, would prove one of transition between the Anglo-French 'dual monarchy' of the later Plantagenets and the British multiple monarchy of post-1603. But these lost territories in France exerted an almost magnetic pull on English monarchs well into the sixteenth century. The battles of Crécy, Poitiers and Agincourt were the stuff of English legend; indeed, were woven, thinly but conspicuously, into the fabric of national identity. 'Warlike Harry' and the Agincourt campaign would be the inspiration for perhaps Shakespeare's greatest history play, *Henry V*. In the 1480s the wounds of defeat in France were still fresh and smarting, and hopes of recovering 'the world's best garden' still very much alive.[13] Losing the last parts of the once extensive Plantagenet empire in France seemed to signal England's relegation to second-tier status in Europe, and the English elite was to expend much blood and treasure in attempting to reverse that defeat. English armies fought in France on at least eight occasions between 1475 and 1558; and in 1475, 1492, 1513 and 1544, kings of England led expeditions to France in conscious emulation of Henry V and other English heroes of the Hundred Years War. England's mental surrender of its continental empire would be a slow and costly process.

Henry VII had been raised on tales of Henry V's military exploits in France, and he tried, throughout his reign, to identify himself with that greatest of Lancastrian kings. He also appreciated, as Henry V had, that a successful war against France would help to legitimise his dynasty and to purge the ill-humours of unrest and rebellion. Fighting the French bound society together against a common enemy, and allowed unruly elements at home to indulge their desire for loot or chivalric glory abroad. French incursions into Brittany in 1488 gave Henry the perfect excuse for renewing hostilities against them, and between 1489 and 1492 he launched numerous military expeditions to support the Bretons in their struggle to preserve their independence. However, the growing power of the French crown meant that Henry could not wage war against the old enemy single-handedly. He was obliged to negotiate alliances with the Habsburg Archduke Maximilian and Spain's husband-and-wife monarchs Ferdinand and Isabella, who had their own claims and grievances against the French. Indeed, it was in an effort to detach Henry from this alliance that the French king Charles VIII supported Perkin Warbeck. Likewise, it was because Maximilian believed that Henry had betrayed him in making peace with Charles in 1492 that he too offered his support to the would-be usurper. In truth, the allies had such differing, indeed contradictory, strategic objectives that there was little chance of them mounting a coordinated offensive against the French.

The minimum that Henry hoped from his Breton wars of 1489–92 was to keep the French out of Brittany. It was clearly not in his or England's interest to allow Charles VIII to annex a territory with so many ports and anchorages that could harbour invasion fleets or pirates who might prey on English shipping in the Channel. Yet policy alone did not dictate that Henry lead his 13,000-strong invasion force – the largest English army that crossed to France during the fifteenth century – in person, as he did in 1492. The terms of his international alliances are also revealing in that they suggest he was at least half-serious about recovering one or more of the French provinces lost at the end of the Hundred Years War. His public pronouncements on the war mingled imperial rhetoric with strategic self-interest, justifying it as an honourable undertaking to assert English claims to 'the crowne and regally of Fraunce', and to counter 'thinsaciable covetise and voluptuous desire' of the French for their neighbours' territory.[14] If all this were merely grandstanding in order to boost royal revenue and domestic support – as many then and since have argued – it was largely successful in its intended objective. English chauvinism and Francophobia helped to loosen Parliament's purse-strings, providing Henry with at least £160,000 in taxes between 1488 and 1492. Moreover, despite losing the war and seeing Brittany annexed by the French crown, he nevertheless came away with the consolation prize of a handsome annual pension from Charles VIII. More importantly, however, Henry may have done just enough to convince most of his subjects that the nation's honour and imperial pretensions were safe in his hands.

Having made an early and plausible showing as a war leader, and put royal finances on a sounder footing, Henry kept his bow unstrung for the rest of his reign. Avoiding another clash with France was made all the easier by Charles VIII's invasion of Italy in 1494. For the next fifty years or so the thrust of French expansionism was directed mainly southwards, and against Europe's new superpower, the German and Spanish empire of the Habsburgs. Neither side in this struggle between Valois and Habsburg cared much what was happening across the Channel. England was no longer France's great rival, merely a potential irritant. From the mid-1490s, therefore, Henry could afford to let matrimony replace warfare as his main method of securing the safety of the Tudor dynasty. In the late 1490s, he negotiated the marriage of his eldest son Arthur to Ferdinand and Isabella's daughter Katherine (1485–1536); and following Arthur's death in 1502, Katherine was promptly betrothed to his younger brother Henry. This Anglo-Spanish (and implicitly anti-French) alliance would endure, with varying degrees of warmth, until Elizabeth I's reign. Henry also agreed – apparently reluctantly, and after a great deal of raiding and marshalling of troops along the Anglo-Scottish border – to the marriage of his eldest daughter Margaret to James IV of Scotland, thereby laying the foundations, if unwittingly, of what would become the union of the English and Scottish crowns under Margaret's great-grandson James VI and I in 1603.

Although these developments would have profound implications for his subjects, it is unlikely that Henry thought in terms of a national interest independent of his own. He was happy, for example, to promote England's lucrative cloth trade with the Low Countries, and yet ruthless in cutting it off when dynastic security and his own princely honour demanded. Overall his actions may have done more harm than good to English commerce. Similarly, his patronage of the Italian maritime explorer Zoane Caboto (or John Cabot as the English called him) was probably driven by dynastic rather than commercial concerns. The king had been among the European monarchs approached by Christopher Columbus to sponsor his voyage across the Atlantic in 1492, and but for a series of accidents the riches of the New World might have fallen to the English rather than the Spanish crown. Cabot, by contrast, proved a poor investment. Sailing from Bristol in 1497, he made landfall on the North American coast, and grandiloquently claimed the 'new isle' for England. In a second voyage the following year he appears to have sailed down the length of the American coast and into the Caribbean. This was impressive seamanship, certainly, but it yielded nothing for Henry by way of wealth or princely reputation. On the contrary, Cabot may have caused him considerable diplomatic embarrassment with the Spanish, who claimed exclusive dominion over the Caribbean. Cabot died either at sea in 1498 or back in England in 1500 – it is not clear which – and for the next fifty years, while the Conquistadores forged an empire in the Americas, the Tudors' imperial sights remained fixed firmly on France.

Fighting lords and civil gentlemen

The Breton wars of 1488–92 brought Henry VII money and a certain amount of prestige, and he would need healthy surpluses of both if he were to maintain the necessary distance between himself and his leading subjects for royal authority to function effectively. Ruling England and its outliers meant, above all else, ruling its aristocracy – that is, the nobility and greatest gentry. Lacking a standing army, a police force or a professional bureaucracy, the crown could not govern without these great landowners and their retinues of hundreds – in some cases, thousands – of tenants and retainers. The power and influence enjoyed by the Tudor titular nobility – the peerage – was all the more remarkable given its size. The number of peers – the dukes, marquesses, earls, viscounts and barons who sat in the House of Lords in English Parliaments – hovered around the fifty mark for most of the Tudor period, although contemporaries in England often regarded the heads of the 200 or so greater gentry families as part of the same political elite as the nobility. Below this aristocracy were the lesser esquires and 'mere gentlemen', who numbered no more than a few thousand in 1485. Together, the nobility and gentry constituted the Tudor ruling class. They comprised a tiny minority, less than 5 per cent of the population, and yet they owned between a third and a half of the land. Their role and defining characteristics would alter over the course of the early modern period, but land ownership generally remained a sure – though by no means the only – ticket to political power.

The landed elite administered the realm under licence from the king. In normal circumstances, a great nobleman and his gentry allies governed their region both on their own authority as landowners and as crown-appointed officers such as justices of the peace (JPs). Just as Henry VII needed the nobility and gentry to help him govern the shires, so they needed his authority, both personal and legal, to protect them against unscrupulous rivals. It was the breakdown of this reciprocal relationship between monarch and nobility that had triggered the Wars of the Roses. Richard Neville, earl of Warwick (1428–71), dubbed 'the Kingmaker', and other supposedly over-mighty subjects had been driven to rebel largely in self-defence – because the weak and, at times, catatonic Henry VI had been incapable of keeping his side of the bargain.

In the long run these rebellious peers did more harm to the nobility than to the monarchy. A combination of natural wastage and the topsy-turvy fortunes of war killed off half of the nobility between the 1440s and 1490s, and left the eventual winner, Henry Tudor, suspicious of noble families and determined to bring them to heel. In consequence he largely excluded noblemen from policy-making, and made their power in the localities more dependent on royal favour. If he encouraged them to attend his court it was not to give counsel but to add much-needed lustre to the new dynasty. His favourite weapon against the nobility, and indeed anyone who was not thought entirely conformable to his rule, was the penal bond: an ancient legal device that enforced good behaviour on pain of severe financial penalties. Most of his noblemen were forced to give one bond or more, and in the case of Prince Henry's mentor, Lord Mountjoy, this number rose to twenty-three. Thousands of Henry's subjects, not just noblemen, would be enmeshed this way in the coils of his distrust. It was the king's desire, admitted one of his most skilled administrators, the London lawyer Edmund Dudley (c.1462–1510), 'to have many persons in his danger at his pleasure'.[15]

This is not to suggest that Henry deliberately set out to break the power of the nobility. In an age when almost everybody regarded the social order as a divinely ordained hierarchy this would have been very unwise. Moreover, the nobility was essential to maintaining royal magnificence, managing Parliament, and supplying suitably impressive commanders in time of war. Henry VII and Henry VIII would execute, imprison and otherwise pull down more than one hundred of their leading subjects, but they also built up the power of those noblemen they trusted. Rather than weaken the influence of the peerage, Henry VII's policies accelerated a process whereby noblemen became more closely tied to the court and their power channelled through the structures of royal government. No Tudor nobleman who wished to dominate the politics of his locality could do so without also acquiring influence on the royal council (the king's consultative body and principal source of advice) at court. This lack of an independent noble power base was particularly marked in England – a consequence of the exceptionally strong centralisation of the English legal system. A Venetian visitor to Tudor England noted that whereas the greatest of the French nobility were 'absolute' in their regions, their English counterparts had 'few castels or strong places . . . neither have they jurisdiction over the people'.[16]

This shift in the Tudor nobility's power away from feudal lordship towards royal service and influence at court was linked to cultural changes that affected the landed elite all over Europe in the fifteenth and sixteenth centuries. The hallmark of the nobility and gentry since Norman times had been prowess in arms and an interest in chivalry – and the mounted knight, fighting for God and feudal overlord, had been the ultimate expression of both. It was once thought that the increasing use of infantry, and particularly archers, in the fourteenth century, and of gunpowder weapons in the fifteenth, had rendered the landowner-turned-knight obsolete by the sixteenth century. In fact, it is now clear that heavy cavalry were an important component of most Tudor armies. In what is sometimes regarded as the first 'modern' battle on British soil, at Pinkie near Edinburgh in 1547, the English destroyed a large Scottish army by a combination of artillery fire, archery, and the repeated charges of the mounted squirearchy of England.

In the same way that the mounted knight adapted to the age of gunpowder, so the martial cult of chivalry that had emerged in the early Middle Ages continued to exert a strong appeal to the Tudor landed elite. That shrewd businessman William Caxton made a good living, it seems, publishing the Arthurian tales of Sir Thomas Malory (*c.*1405–71), in which valiant knights on mettlesome steeds battled for honour, love and the glory of God. Chivalric romances, and histories full of descriptions of jousts and challenges, were the main secular reading matter of the Tudor nobility and gentry. Regardless of whether a gentleman had ever swung a sword in battle – and most had not – he was usually anxious to prove his descent from some hero of the Crusades or the Hundred Years War, and to emblazon his house, his parish church and his tomb with his family coat of arms. Henry VII's lawyer-administrator Edmund Dudley – a man who seemingly had little connection to the world of the knightly warrior – still reckoned himself and his fellow gentlemen part of 'the chivalry': a term he used to distinguish the landed elite from 'the commonalty'.[17] Henry himself valued the chivalric tradition as a prop to royal dignity, using admission to the Order of the Garter – England's highest and most exclusive chivalric order – to flatter and impress (or so he hoped) both his own noblemen and foreign princes. There would be revivals in chivalric culture under Henry VIII, Elizabeth I and Charles I; and the knightly tournament – jousting on horseback with couched lances and full armour – would remain a part of court festivities until the 1620s.

But though most early Tudor noblemen would regard themselves as 'fighting lords', and the recreations, literary tastes and accoutrements of the aristocracy retained a strongly martial flavour, the daily interests of ordinary gentlemen often centred more upon civilian pursuits such as local administration and estate management. The qualities associated with gentlemanly status were also given a more civilised gloss through repeated contact from the early fifteenth century with ideas and men inspired by the Italian Renaissance. At the heart of this cultural revolution was a renewed engagement with the works of classical literature, and with it a turning away from theology towards the more secular preoccupations of the ancient Greeks and Romans. Renaissance scholars by no means rejected Christianity or the Church. Indeed, some were themselves clerics, who devoted themselves to textual analysis of the Bible and the writings of the Church Fathers. But many of the greatest figures associated with the Renaissance, from Dante (1265–1321) onwards, tended to focus on the world of human affairs – hence the contemporary term for their scholarship, the *studia humanitatis* (or Humanism as it was labelled in the nineteenth century). By recovering Cicero and other classical authors in their original purity, and extolling their insights as a fount of political wisdom, humanist scholars were convinced that they could transform European society for the better. The practical applications of their learning – that is, as a manual for Renaissance statecraft – certainly proved popular with elites across Europe, so that by 1600 the politic arts and other 'civil knowledge' were considered just as essential for a gentleman as horsemanship and the punctilio of the *code duello* (another Italian import that served to distinguish men of rank). A clear sign of this shift in cultural values at the top of English society would be the rising number of sons from noble and gentry families who were sent to Oxford and Cambridge universities from the mid-sixteenth century. A military elite was also becoming a learned elite, the civic–legal mentality gradually replacing the chivalric.

The rise of the 'civil' gentleman was welcomed and encouraged by the crown. Distrustful of magnate power, Henry VII and subsequent Tudor monarchs were generally happier promoting gentry and commoners to high office than peers. Men who owed their advancement to royal favour naturally tended to be more grateful and loyal to their sovereign than were great noblemen. The first two Tudors created court offices specially for the gentry, binding them directly to the royal household and cutting out the aristocratic middleman. Moreover, as the size of the crown's landed estate increased under Henry VII, so more and more gentlemen were added to the royal affinity. A similar trend was occurring in local government. The Tudors regarded county JPs – who were mostly gentry – as more reliable servants than the greater nobility, and increased their powers accordingly. It was at some point during the sixteenth century that the JP replaced the 'good lord' as the main pillar of local society. The gentry, therefore, like the nobility, were drawn more closely into royal service under the Tudors, as too were urban elites after 1485. Many Tudor towns acquired noble patrons at court by trading their readiness to do the crown's bidding (which, of course, reflected well on their courtly sponsors) for royal grants of commercial and jurisdictional privileges.

The gentrification of Tudor rule had deep roots in lowland England, but beyond the southern and Midland shires it was a different story. In the northern marches, where the gentry were more thinly scattered and the priority was defence, rather than keeping to the letter of the law, the crown had traditionally governed through the region's magnates, or great territorial overlords. Henry seemed willing at first to let at least one of the leading marcher families – the Percys, earls of Northumberland – retain their influence in the region. But he was distrustful of their tendency to assert their autonomy, and, following the murder of the

4th earl in a tax revolt in 1489, he took the opportunity to spread offices and authority more widely among less powerful peers and leading gentry families. The only great nobleman that he trusted with power in the North was the earl of Surrey, who was a southerner and governed entirely on royal sufferance. Henry's cautious – indeed, suspicious-minded – policy in the North would prove counterproductive, however. His mistrust of the region's most powerful noblemen, combined with his unwillingness to pay for border garrisons and a standing defence force, led to a virtual collapse in law and order in the northern marches; and peace with Scotland between 1502 and 1509 removed what little incentive existed in London to address the problem.

Sidelining the great landed nobility would prove impossible in Henry's most turbulent marcher society: Ireland. Like earlier English kings, Henry VII attempted to maintain Ireland in a semblance of order – and nominal obedience to the English crown – by relying on the most powerful members of the Irish nobility to govern in the king's name. If Henry had one indisputably over-mighty subject it was the 'Old English' magnate Gerald Fitzgerald, 8th earl of Kildare, who, as one Tudor chronicler recalled, was 'without great knowledge or learning' yet 'a mightie man of stature, full of honour and courage', 'a warrior incomparable'.[18] As lord deputy of Ireland – that is, the king's representative in Irish government – Kildare was in theory answerable to Henry. In practice, however, the unsettled state of English affairs from the mid-1480s meant that he was answerable to no one, and indeed entertained ambitions of becoming an Irish version of Warwick the Kingmaker. It was Kildare, as we have seen, who supplied the 4,000 Irish troops for Simnel's invasion in 1487. Yet Henry had little alternative but to acquiesce in Kildare's political dominance in Ireland. Henry tried a variety of tactics in order to strengthen his grip on the territories of the Pale. He built up the power of Kildare's rivals, the Butlers, earls of Ormond, and by 1492 felt confident enough to risk replacing Kildare as lord deputy with an English interloper: the experienced soldier and administrator Sir Edward Poynings. But the English newcomer, with his patent of appointment from the king, was no match for the earl of Kildare, with his extensive estates, regional influence within the Pale, and huge following among the Old English and the Gaels. By the mid-1490s, Henry conceded that he had no alternative but to revert to the well-tried policy of English kings in Ireland: rule through – rather than in rivalry with – the most powerful of the native Anglo-Irish nobility.

This policy of vicarious royal government brought one signal advance: the consolidation of English rule in eastern and central Ireland. Reinstalled as lord deputy in 1496, Kildare endeavoured not merely to defend the 'Englishry' in Ireland but to strengthen his and the crown's authority beyond the frontiers of the Pale. During the late 1490s and early 1500s he mounted military expeditions and conducted progresses deep into the Gaedhealtacht, visiting parts of Ireland that had seldom seen any royal representative. In 1504, his Gaelic allies and Pale levies of billmen (infantry wielding halberds) and archers combined to defeat supposedly the mightiest Gaelic war host for three centuries at the battle of Knockdoe, near Galway, in the far west of Ireland. Kildare's harrying of the Gaels was to come to an abrupt end in 1513 when he was shot by one of them while watering his horse in the River Barrow. But even had he lived longer he would not have been able to bring the Gaedhealtacht under full obedience to the crown. To tame the Gaelic warlords of northern and western Ireland would require human and material resources that were beyond even the most powerful of Tudor magnates.

Henry VII can take some of the credit for the modest resurgence of royal authority in Ireland by the early sixteenth century, from its nadir fifty years earlier. In restoring the Kildare ascendancy he had recognised the necessity of laying aside some of his kingly pride and distrust of his great noblemen. But this decision was made easy for him anyway, because the alternative – bringing Ireland under direct rule from England – was a waste of time and money. Henry's (mostly) benign neglect of his lordship of Ireland reflected a fundamental political truth, which was that the foundation of his power lay at the centre of his realm, not on the peripheries. It was natural therefore that he and his advisers looked to replenish royal authority at its roots, and here they were fortunate in that the great recession that had blighted the reigns of Henry VI and Edward IV had ended by the 1490s. No longer could ambitious magnates like Warwick the Kingmaker foment popular rebellion on the (wholly unkeepable) promise of alleviating hardship and bringing back the good times of old. Although tax revolts continued intermittently under the Tudors, on the relatively rare occasions when the people resorted to organised violence, they did so to restore what they saw as the traditional order, not to overthrow their king, as they had done a generation earlier. And as the economy strengthened so too did the government's military resources, making it harder for dynastic rivals to wage war on anything like equal terms. Henceforth, there

would be room for only one over-mighty power in Tudor England, and
that was the crown itself.

Law state and war state

From the distance of James I's reign, in the early decades of the seventeenth century, the philosopher and royal biographer Francis Bacon
(1561–1626) recounted a 'merry tale' concerning Henry VII's pet
monkey. The king, being 'full of apprehensions and suspicions', kept a
notebook in which he recorded his secret observations about 'whom
to employ, whom to reward, whom to inquire of, whom to beware of'
– and finding this notebook the monkey tore it in pieces, 'whereat the
court which liked not those pensive accounts was almost tickled with
sport'.[19] This story, though probably apocryphal, is nevertheless revealing
of what contemporaries took to be a defining aspect of Henry's style
of kingship. The first of the Tudor monarchs never forgot that he had
usurped the crown from a usurper, and that as fortune and his friends
had raised him up, so fortune and his enemies might cast him down.
If he was 'haunted with sprites', as Bacon termed it – or paranoid, as
we might – it was not without reason.[20]

To retain the throne that he had so fortuitously won, Henry must
invest his rule with such unshakeable authority as to inspire awe and dread
in even his greatest subjects. It was Henry's wish, observed Polydore
Vergil, to make 'all Englishmen obedient through fear';[21] and to Spanish
diplomats, writing home in 1498, it seemed that the king was succeeding:
'Henry is rich, has established good order in England, and keeps the
people in such subjection as has never been the case before.'[22] More
than most monarchs, Henry equated 'subjection' with money. Dudley
put it well when he remarked that his royal master believed that
'security standeth much in plenty of treasure'.[23] Although the king was
legal-minded in the extreme, not to say obsessively bureaucratic – he
scrutinised and countersigned every page of the royal accounts –
the financial devices he employed to exact obedience largely explain
why the monarchy would become more exploitative, tyrannical even,
during his reign than it had been under the mightiest of the Plantagenets.

To appropriate the enormous sums that Henry felt necessary for his
security would involve challenging some of the most deeply held political assumptions in English society. England, as we have already noted,
had acquired a system of government by the mid-thirteenth century

that was deeply rooted in legal forms and observance. This 'law state' provided a stable platform from which Edward I (who reigned from 1272 to 1307) and his successors launched invasions of Wales and Scotland, and then took on France in the Hundred Years War. Warfare became England's staple export from the late thirteenth century and, in the process, law state gave way to 'war state', pushing the crown into ever closer political partnership with the landed classes. Needing money and cooperative subjects to sustain their military ambitions, the Plantagenets granted the nobility and gentry a major role in governing the localities, and agreed to impose direct taxation only with the consent of Parliament. The effect of these various trade-offs was to make government increasingly consensual, an activity that a significant section of the population, from yeomen (the village elite) upwards, participated in and manipulated for their own purposes. Royal authority became public authority inasmuch as it was deployed on behalf of and by an informed and articulate political community that existed alongside the monarch. The monarchy, in turn, became more closely identified with the role of serving and protecting society. Faced with Henry VI's inept kingship in the mid-fifteenth century, this conception of the state as a body devoted to the public good would acquire a new name and language, that of the 'commonwealth'.

The war state of the later Middle Ages had been capable of prodigious military feats. Henry V's conquest of Normandy in the 1410s had dazzled all of Europe. Clearly the partnership between the crown and the political community had created a formidable war machine. But looked at from Henry VII's perspective, the crown had made a Faustian pact with its people. It could tap the wealth of the realm with an efficiency and regularity that some of its European rivals could only envy – but upon two conditions. In England (but crucially, not in France) a consensus emerged during the fourteenth century that direct taxation should only be levied to address an immediate or obvious military need, and on the understanding that such levies required the consent of the political community as represented in Parliament. The taxes voted by Parliament, together with customs revenues and loans, were generally sufficient to meet the crown's military needs; and Parliament's support added greatly to royal authority, especially in time of war. But then came the weakening of the monarchy under Henry VI, defeat in 1453, and France's re-emergence as a European superpower. The English state contained deep-seated forces pushing for prolonged war, and yet geopolitical reality made such a commitment impossible to sustain by

the mid-fifteenth century. France was just too powerful. Once intermittent peace became the normal state of affairs, the crown's dependence
upon parliamentary taxation became a huge liability. Henry VII and
his successors found themselves trapped by the political conventions
of England's imperial past.

Henry VII's reluctance to continue hostilities against France beyond
1492 deprived him of parliamentary taxation while at the same time
doing little to reduce his need for cash. For example, he spent very
large sums of money after 1492 – sometimes in excess of £100,000 (or
roughly his ordinary annual income) – on 'loans' (bribes) to the
Emperor Maximilian and other foreign princes to persuade them to
extradite or cease sheltering Yorkist exiles on the Continent. Not quite
as costly, but still very expensive, was the investment Henry made in
the royal gun-making industry, based at the Tower of London. He was
determined to control the manufacture of heavy artillery in England,
and to ensure that he had more and bigger guns than any of his subjects.
Yet with no war to justify regular parliamentary taxation, his government had to resort to more piecemeal and frowned-upon methods to
meet this expenditure. Informers were employed to spy on the monied
and influential and to nose out hidden wealth; the property of Henry's
Yorkist enemies was seized at every turn; and a concerted effort was
made to exploit the money-raising potential of the royal prerogative
– that is, the reserve and emergency powers which inhered in the king
by virtue of his status as an anointed sovereign.

These sharp financial practices certainly succeeded in increasing
Henry's income, but as the king seems to have realised, to secure a
significant, long-term improvement in royal revenue would require
renegotiating the financial – and, therefore, political – relationship
between crown and subject. The Spanish ambassador reported that
Henry 'would like to govern England in the French fashion'[24] – in other
words, to have fewer constraints upon royal action – but specifically,
perhaps, to be in the position of Francis I of France (1494–1547), who
when asked by a Venetian ambassador how much he could raise from
his subjects replied: 'Everything I need, according to my will.'[25]

The early Tudors made repeated attempts to shift the basis of their
income away from parliamentary taxation to financial sources grounded
upon the royal prerogative. This in part explains Henry VII's reputation
for avarice. It also accounts for his unpopularity. For although his
exploitation of his prerogative rights was perfectly legal, it violated the
spirit of political partnership between crown and people as it had

developed in the preceding two centuries. Henry's resort to prerogative taxation sparked numerous small-scale riots, and contributed significantly to major uprisings in Yorkshire, in 1489, and Cornwall in 1497. The Cornish insurgent army, 15,000 angry taxpayers, got to within a few miles of London before Henry's cavalry cut it to pieces. When Henry VIII's chief minister, Cardinal Wolsey, introduced a non-parliamentary 'benevolence', or forced loan in 1525 – the spectacularly misnamed Amicable Grant – it would provoke unrest not in far-off Cornwall but in London and the home counties, and was hastily dropped. 'All people curssed the Cardinal', claimed one of his critics, 'as subvertor of the Lawes and libertie of England. For thei said if men should geve their goodes by a Commission [royal warrant], then wer it worse than the taxes of Fraunce and so England should be bond and not free.'[26] The English would continue to associate the French monarchy with tyranny for the next three centuries.

Public opinion and the almost religious veneration of common law and custom – enforced and enforceable through the courts – prevented Tudor monarchs from riding roughshod over 'Lawes and libertie' in the manner of French kings. Nevertheless, Henry VII succeeded in making government more regal, and less accountable to the political community – partly because in the absence of long-term military commitments he did not need to call Parliaments as often as his predecessors had. The great struggle against France had required the crown to call Parliaments regularly in order to vote the necessary taxes, and that had given Parliament-men the opportunity to maintain a running check on royal government. Without regular Parliaments it would prove more difficult to hold the monarchy to account. Parliament would not regain the executive power it had enjoyed under the Plantagenets until the British civil wars of the 1640s.

The most powerful instrument of Henry's intensely personal style of government was the royal council – or rather an inner ring of councillors, grouped into committees, who owed their influence entirely to the king and who worked under his supervision. One of these committees – the 'Council Learned in the Law' – was set up specifically to enforce the king's prerogative rights, and was widely feared for its power to summon anyone, at will, on unspecified charges. Henry had no time for the traditional notion that noblemen of ancient lineage were the monarch's natural advisers, his 'born councillors'. His council was dominated by lawyers, royal dependants 'and such other caitifs and villains of [low] birth'.[27] His two most prominent councillors by the end of his reign were Edmund Dudley and his fellow lawyer Sir Richard Empson. These were Henry's most notorious henchmen, 'whom the people esteemed as his horse-leeches [bloodsuckers] and shearers . . . both like tame hawks for their master, and like wild hawks for themselves, insomuch as they grew to great riches and substance'.[28] Empson and Dudley came to symbolise the rapacious and intrusive character of royal government during Henry's final years.

As a lawyer from a prominent London family, the future lord chancellor and Catholic martyr Thomas More (1478–1535) was all too familiar with the inquisitorial practices of Empson, Dudley, and the Council Learned in the Law. If he had any particular monarch in mind when exploring the themes of royal misgovernment and aggrandisement of power in his early works it was surely Henry VII. His great critique of European society, *Utopia*, published just a few years after Henry's death, describes an imaginary land where the office of king is elective and where the ruler can be deposed for 'suspicion of tyranny'. More was one of the first English writers, though by no means the last, to use classical republican texts and arguments about popular sovereignty to criticise the swelling power of Renaissance monarchy.

The ruthless legalism of Henry's kingship was matched by its financial efficiency. In a novel departure from his predecessors, Henry merged his private sources of income, those belonging to the crown, and national taxation into one consolidated (though physically dispersed) treasury, administered mainly from a department of his household, the Chamber, and subject to close royal scrutiny. This chamber system of finance concentrated large amounts of cash in the king's hands – a good deal of which he secretly stockpiled in the Tower and other places – giving him unprecedented political independence, and excluding all but his inner entourage from understanding the true extent of the crown's wealth. In a similar spirit, Henry created a new inner space within the royal household, the privy (or private) chamber, staffed by a corps of hand-picked servants – mostly men of relatively low social status – who alone had access to him during his private hours. The privy chamber, like Henry's specialised council committees, or the royal bodyguard he formed against possible assassination, put further distance between the king and the political community – thus imitating, probably consciously, features of the French and Breton courts where he had spent his formative years. His lavish building projects served the same purpose as his innovations at court: to invest Tudor monarchy with a godlike majesty. Nothing spoke more tellingly of this aspiration than the magnificent chapel in Henry's Thameside palace at Richmond, which was apparently unique in England in having the royal closet, or private pew, placed not at the west end, but to one side of the nave, closer to the altar (probably in deliberate emulation of chapel usage at the court of the dukes of Burgundy).[29] Royal appropriation of sacred space was equally striking in Henry's contribution to the completion of King's College Chapel, Cambridge, with its antechapel made over not to Christian iconography but to massive displays of Tudor heraldic badges and royal arms.

As Henry's health began to deteriorate from the late 1490s, so his obsession with 'treasure' and the control it supposedly conferred grew even stronger. To the victims of his ever-expanding system of financial penalties, it must have seemed that he had succumbed in his declining years to greed, pure and simple. Yet the lavish burial chapel that he commissioned to be built at the east end of Westminster Abbey, at a cost during his lifetime of £34,000, reveals a king who was still willing to spend liberally on affirming his inherited and divine right to rule. The time and money he invested in securing the Tudor dynasty would prove to have been well spent, for when he died in 'grete agony of body & soule' on 21 April 1509, no one challenged the succession of his son, Prince Henry. In his sermon at Henry VII's funeral in St Paul's Cathedral, John Fisher, bishop of Rochester, listed among the late king's worldly accomplishments his success in making Tudor authority 'dredde every where, not onely with in his realme but without also, his people were to hym in as humble subgeccyon as ever they were to kynge'.[30]

The morning after Henry VII's death, Dudley and Empson were arrested and sent to the Tower. The following year, in response to public pressure, the young Henry VIII would have the two men tried and convicted on trumped-up treason charges, and then beheaded. The kingdom had rid itself of these 'horse-leeches', to be sure, but the political conditions that had given rise to an Empson and a Dudley remained. Permanently in need of cash, and in ever-increasing quantities, the crown was dependent for its long-term financial health upon an unwieldy and sometimes fickle institution: Parliament. Resorting instead to prerogative taxation was always an option, but only in emergencies, and even then it ran the strong risk of alienating the political community. The partnership between crown and subject that had formed under the Plantagenets had thus become a love–hate relationship for the Tudors. It helped them govern and yet hindered them financially. Strong monarchs though they were, neither Henry VII,

Henry VIII nor Elizabeth I proved capable of putting royal finances on a fundamentally new and less consensual footing. The kingdom's fiscal system would remain fossilised in its medieval form until the mid-seventeenth century.

Such a king as never before

Of all the prosperous Londoners who had felt the lash of Henry VII's greed and distrust, perhaps the most articulate was Thomas More. It was with relief, therefore, as well as joy that More wrote his 1509 *Coronation Ode of King Henry VIII*: 'What wonder, then, if England rejoices in a fashion heretofore unknown, since she has such a king as she never had before?'[31] With hindsight, of course, More's words are full of irony. For when Henry VIII did finally prove himself such a king as never before, by breaking with Rome, More and many others were very far from rejoicing. But in 1509 there was no hint of the storm to come. Indeed, for the first fifteen or so years of his reign the young king made no radical break with his father's reign, let alone with Catholic Christendom. What was new and dazzling about Henry VIII was his larger-than-life personality and glamorous style of kingship. Optimism abounded at his accession, partly because the people were thoroughly sick of his father, but also because the eighteen-year-old Henry VIII cut such a dashing and graceful figure. When the date of his coronation was announced 'a vast multitude of persons at once hurried to London to see their monarch in the full bloom of his youth and high birth . . . everybody loved him'. At six feet two inches tall, with a 32-inch waist, the young Henry seemed, in the words of the Venetian ambassador,

> the handsomest potentate I ever set eyes on; above the usual height, with an extremely fine calf to his leg, his complexion very fair and bright, with auburn hair combed straight and short, in the French fashion, and a round face so very beautiful, that it would become a pretty woman.[32]

Henry's beauty was complemented by his physical prowess. In his youth he was a fine athlete and tennis-player, and remained an accomplished horseman to the end of his life. Hunting was almost an obsession with him, causing his secretary (a bookish type) to complain that he turned 'the sport . . . into a martyrdom' for those obliged to keep up with him during the chase.[33] As with most princes of the period, Henry was trained in the art of killing men as well as deer, and was proficient in a wide variety of weapons, including sword, lance and longbow. He also liked to practise with firearms and to experiment with artillery, destroying the roof of a nearby house on one occasion. But when it came to martial pursuits his real passion was jousting. Like his father and Edward IV, Henry was fascinated by the culture of pageantry and chivalric machismo that had reached its apogee in the court of the dukes of Burgundy, and which was epitomised in the knightly tournament. No expense was spared in staging these extravagant spectacles at Henry's court. The bill for the 1511 tournament alone came to £4,000, or considerably more than it cost to build the pride of Henry's navy, the 78-gun *Mary Rose*. His father's mantra of 'keeping distance' had confined him to the royal box during tournaments; Henry, on the other hand, was a full-blooded participant. His tournaments showcased not only Tudor magnificence, therefore, but also his own skill in arms to impressionable foreign dignitaries. So spectacular was the tournament he staged in 1517 to mark his alliance with the Emperor Maximilian, so sumptuously were the hundreds of knights and footmen arrayed (Henry's armour and accoutrements alone were valued at 300,000 ducats, or roughly £75,000), that one visiting Italian clergyman among the 50,000 or so spectators was quite overcome:

> In short, the wealth and civilization of the world are here; and those who call the English barbarians appear to me to render themselves such. I here perceive very elegant manners, extreme decorum, and very great politeness; and amongst other things there is this most invincible King, whose acquirements and qualities are so many and excellent that I consider him to excel all who ever wore a crown . . .[34]

Henry's jousting days did not come to an end until 1536, when the 44-year-old king was unhorsed by an opponent and knocked unconscious for two hours.

Henry's personal accomplishments were not confined to the tiltyard or the tennis court. He was educated in a manner befitting a Renaissance prince, according to a classically inspired curriculum of history, poetry, grammar and ethics. Somewhere along the way he acquired a strong grounding in theology – as his later debates with his senior clergy were to show – and an enthusiasm for astronomy and geometry. He was also a fine linguist. According to the Venetian ambassadors, Henry could speak French and Latin, and understood Italian well. He had a particular talent for music, and 'played on almost every instrument, [and] sang and composed fairly'.[35] The celebrated Dutch humanist and church critic Desiderius Erasmus (c.1467–1536) thought him a genius, but that was mere flattery. Henry's intellectual interests were genuine, but not profound. Moreover, his eagerness to attract the Continent's best poets, musicians, painters and architects to his court was rooted in the same desire that fed his passion for chivalric ostentation – that is, to outshine his fellow monarchs. He followed his father, therefore, in commissioning works from some of the most fashionable virtuosi of the day, including the Florentine sculptor Pietro Torrigiano and the Flemish painter Hans Holbein. Torrigiano tried to persuade his fellow Florentine the brilliant Benvenuto Cellini to join him in England, but Cellini had no wish to live among 'such beasts as the English'.[36] Most of Henry's client artists were essentially second-raters. Nevertheless, his patronage of Renaissance talent went some way to dispel the belief at the centres of European culture that the English were little better than barbarians.

Henry's flamboyant kingship certainly made a change from the rapacious authoritarianism of his father's final years. But there would be no fundamental shift in royal policy, at least on the domestic front, until the king's 'great matter' began to trouble the political waters in the later 1520s. One of Henry's first decisions on becoming king was to honour what he claimed was his father's deathbed wish that he marry Prince Arthur's widow Katherine of Aragon. Similarly, Henry inherited his father's determination to extend royal authority at the expense of the Church in England. But he showed no sympathy with the challenge to Catholic orthodoxy and papal authority begun in the late 1510s by the German friar and theology professor Martin Luther (1483–1546) – a confrontation that precipitated the Protestant Reformation. Indeed, in 1521, Henry was given the title 'defender of the faith' by a grateful pope for writing a rebuttal of Luther's ideas, although most of the hard work on it had been done by a small group of scholars that included Thomas More, who was knighted that same year.

Another carryover from the previous reign revealed a darker side to Henry's character: his suspicion of possible Yorkist claimants to the crown. It would be many years before Henry had a son – or at least one that lived beyond a few weeks – and until he did so the Tudor dynasty remained insecure. Like his father, therefore, he used political executions to weed out potential challengers. Among the earliest victims of Henry's suspicious mind were the earl of Suffolk (Lincoln's brother) and the duke of Buckingham. Both men went to the block for the sole reason that they had more Plantagenet blood in their veins than Henry did. Henry executed more of his leading subjects than any English monarch before or since. The death toll would eventually include two wives, the 68-year-old countess of Salisbury (surely a threat to nobody), and six close attendants. It was Henry who introduced the punishment of boiling alive, although this particularly macabre form of death was reserved for poisoners. 'If all the pictures and Patternes of a mercilesse Prince were lost in the World,' thought Sir Walter Ralegh (1554–1618), 'they might all againe be painted to the life, out of the story of this King.'[37] Henry was less distrustful of the nobility in general than his father had been, and its numbers revived during his reign. But though he had the Council Learned in the Law abolished, he continued the use of penal bonds to keep aristocratic troublemakers in line. He also followed his father in exploiting the crown's feudal and prerogative rights to maximise cash-flow, and for the first few years of his reign he stuck with the wise heads of Henry VII's council, minus those of Empson and Dudley. Again like his father, Henry was indifferent to the needs of the merchant community. His wars and the taxation required to fund them depressed rather than promoted trade.

When Henry did stray from his father's style of government it was not to reform or innovate but to free himself from the chores of being king. Following the precedents set by his medieval predecessors, Henry employed able bishops to undertake the major administrative offices of the realm. But one, in particular, rose so high in the king's favour, and took over so many of the day-to-day tasks of kingship, that he came to be known as *alter rex*, 'the second king' – this was Thomas Wolsey (c.1470–1530), archbishop of York from 1514, and lord chancellor and a cardinal from the following year. The son of an Ipswich butcher – hence the jibes about his 'greasy genealogy' – Wolsey had made his name as a gifted and energetic administrator. Above all, he was an acute reader of the royal character. Recognising that Henry was 'disposed all to mirth and pleasure . . . nothing minding to travail in the busy affairs of this realm', he put the king 'in comfort that he shall not need to spare any time of his pleasure for any business . . . in the council, as long as he [Wolsey] being there, having the king's authority and commandment, doubted not to see all things sufficiently furnished and perfected'.[38] Wolsey took great delight in asserting his authority both as Henry's foremost councillor and as cardinal. The public triumph that he organised in London for the receiving of his cardinal's hat was likened by contemporaries to the coronation of a great prince. But Henry liked and trusted Wolsey, confiding to the pope that royal business was impossible without him, and that he valued Wolsey above his closest friends. During his dozen or so years at the height of royal favour, the cardinal would continue the firm rule and centralising policies of Henry VII.

Henry's desire to sweeten the 'time of his pleasure' inspired the only major innovation in government before the late 1520s. In 1518 he followed the French court in creating a series of new positions in the royal household, those of gentleman of the privy chamber. The old king's privy chamber servants had been lowly born valets, menial-status nonentities. Henry's privy chamber would be staffed by handsome, high-spirited young gentlemen, his boon companions in the revels at court. These 'minions' were blamed for Henry's 'incessant gambling', and for taking undue advantage of their familiar attendance upon him. Certainly, their intimacy with the king gave them a head start in the scramble for royal favour, particularly as Henry expanded their budget and remit to take in diplomatic missions and other secret affairs of state. The privy chamber men became Wolsey's main rivals for the king's ear, and though cardinal and council attempted to limit the privy chamber's influence, they were largely unsuccessful, simply because of the personal esteem that these mostly high-born and elegant young men enjoyed in the eyes of the king. When Wolsey fell from power in 1529, he immediately submitted to arrest by the privy chamber man sent to apprehend him, without waiting to examine any formal warrant, since as the messenger was 'oon [one] of the kynges privy chamber' that was 'sufficient warraunt to arrest the greattest peere of this realme'.[39]

Wars of magnificence

The young Henry VIII's positioning of himself on the international stage represented a clear departure from his father's handling of foreign affairs. Henry VII's serpentine dealings with his fellow princes and the papacy were not for Henry VIII. Raised on stories of chivalric derring-do and English conquest in France, he dreamed of emulating his Plantagenet heroes Edward III and Henry V. By the time he became king he was determined to 'create such a fine opinion about his valour among all men that they would clearly understand that his ambition was not merely to equal but indeed to exceed the glorious deeds of his ancestors'.[40]

A century later, when princely politics was guided more by reason of state than questing after chivalric glory, Henry's foreign wars were criticised by Ralegh as 'vaine enterprises abroade'.[41] Yet to judge Henry's foreign policy, as Ralegh and many since have done, in terms of territory gained or against some putative national interest is to miss the point. Although he never seriously troubled the French monarchy – hardly surprising given the disparity in resources between the two kingdoms – Henry certainly achieved his other main aim: to cut a dash as a warrior-king. Moreover, as with Henry VII's Breton wars, there was a domestic rationale for his 'enterprises abroade'. Even that most cynical of political theorists Niccolò Machiavelli (1469–1527) believed that nothing brought a prince more prestige, and therefore loyalty, than 'great exployts, and rare trialls of himselfe in Heroicke actions'.[42] Style counted as much as substance therefore; indeed, style *was* substance. As Henry himself put it: 'the fame, glory reputacion, honnour, and strength of Princes depende upon exterior appearances, and opynyons of the worlde, which many tymes preveyleth and is better than trouthe, or at the lest standeth in more sted'.[43]

Yet Machiavelli also believed that a state's capacity and readiness for war was what created civic virtue, and guarded against decadence. Henry too was well-read in the classical tradition that war was essential to the health of the state, and that long periods of peace could lead to softness and corruption. His enthusiasm for fighting the French may have owed at least something to a princely concern for fostering a properly warlike spirit in the English nation. Belligerence was not the antithesis to the *studia humanitatis* and a taste for classical literature; it was its complement.

Henry's career as a warrior-king began as it would end, with an invasion of France. In 1513 he led a force of 30,000 men over to Calais, where it joined an army led by Emperor Maximilian and advanced towards the emperor's territories in modern-day Belgium. On the way, the English cavalry surprised and routed a French supply column – a minor skirmish that Henry shamelessly extolled as a famous victory. The allied armies then took the French-held towns of Thérouanne and Tournai, and would have marched on Paris if the emperor's Swiss allies had not deserted him.

Yet while Henry was casting greedy eyes over northern France, a more significant war was being fought in northern England. The resumption of hostilities with France, and bluster from Henry about his title to sovereignty over Scotland, had reactivated the 'auld alliance' between the French and the Scots. In August 1513, Henry's brother-in-law, James IV of Scotland, crossed the Tweed at the head of one of the strongest Scottish armies ever to invade England. Facing him was a large English force led by the veteran soldier the earl of Surrey. When the two armies met at Flodden, in Northumberland, James deployed his troops Swiss-style in massed formations of pikemen. But the uneven ground and English artillery fire created gaps in the Scots' ranks that Surrey's billmen exploited to lethal effect. In four hours of carnage, 10,000 Scottish soldiers and virtually an entire generation of Scotland's political leaders were killed. Most catastrophically of all for the Scots, the dead included James IV himself. Queen Katherine, who was leading a reserve army northwards when news of Flodden reached England, sent James's blood-soaked tunic to Henry as a trophy. But Henry, flushed with the conquest of Tournai and obsessed with recovering 'our kingdom of France', failed to follow up on this victory with any urgency, and the chance to entrench English influence in Edinburgh, or to secure England's vulnerable northern border, was lost.

Henry's continental conquests, though meagre, were sufficient to establish him as a player of consequence in European affairs. Having humbled France – or so he imagined – he concluded a peace in 1514 that confirmed what he now regarded as his superiority over the French king, Louis XII. The enormous expense of the 1513 campaign rather took the shine off Henry's 'victory', however, and his decision to retain and fortify the strategically irrelevant Tournai put further strain on crown finances. All the reserves that his father had accumulated over many years had disappeared in the pursuit of a single campaign. The cost of the war amounted to £992,000, as against an annual royal income of well under £150,000. Moreover, this expensively purchased reputation as Europe's *jeune premier* was soon under threat: first by the accession of the young and dynamic Francis I (1494–1547) as king of France in 1515, and then in 1519 by the election of the equally formidable Charles V (1500–58) as Holy Roman Emperor in place of his recently deceased grandfather Maximilian. Charles V's father, Philip the Fair, duke of Burgundy, had married a daughter of Ferdinand and Isabella, and had succeeded to the Spanish throne. Charles's inheritance thus combined the kingdoms of Spain, the Spanish conquests in southern Italy and in the New World, the Habsburg lands in central and eastern Europe, and the Habsburgs' Burgundian territories in eastern France and the Low Countries, in one massive dynastic conglomeration. The rivalry between Charles V and Francis I would dominate European politics for the next thirty years, and leave Henry with seemingly little room for manoeuvre. In effect, he had three choices: he could ally with Francis, ally with Charles, or remain in dangerous isolation. In typically audacious manner, he chose none of these options. If he could not head the league table in waging wars of magnificence, then the next-best thing was to arrange a magnificent peace. Skilfully stage-managed by Wolsey, the 1518 treaty of London – a non-aggression pact between the European powers in response to Ottoman advances in eastern Europe – allowed Henry to pose as the arbiter of all Christendom.

Henry's ostentatious peacemaking climaxed in 1520 on the Field of the Cloth of Gold, near Calais. Anxious to assert the power of their crowns in the face of Charles V's election as emperor, Henry and Francis I revived an idea they had been toying with for several years of a personal meeting between the two monarchs. Following a treaty devised by Wolsey detailing the exact terms of the summit, Henry and Queen Katherine crossed the Channel late in May 1520, accompanied by some 6,000 courtiers, clerics and attendants. For seventeen days that June, Henry and Francis and the flower of English and French chivalry jousted, feasted and exchanged lavish gifts and compliments. Little in the way of hard diplomatic business was conducted amid all this extravagance. Nevertheless, the Field of the Cloth of Gold served a serious political purpose for both parties. Henry was desperate to secure Francis's recognition of his power and international status, while Francis wanted to keep Henry quiescent and well away from Charles V. If nothing else the occasion allowed the two monarchs to put the Anglo-French peace agreed at London in 1518 on a more personal footing. Yet beneath the canopies of 'soo ryche and goodly tentys' the old animosities stirred.[44] One English nobleman was heard to declare: 'If I had a drop of French blood in my body I would cut myself open to get rid of it.'[45] That this was envy as much as disdain is clear from Henry's court, where French fashions and tastes had begun to displace Burgundian and Italian influences. Polydore Vergil was clearly shocked that 'from many most wanton creatures in the company of the French ladies [at the Field of the Cloth of Gold], the English ladies adopted a new garb which, on my oath, was singularly unfit for the chaste'.[46] The vogue for French fashion at court did nothing to change the English people's knee-jerk contempt for the French. 'The best word an Englishman can find to say of a Frenchman', claimed one foreign observer, 'is "French dog"'.[47]

The rivalry between Henry and Francis quickly turned nasty. Within two years of the Field of the Cloth of Gold the glory-hungry Henry was at war with Francis as part of the Emperor Charles V's own, much more deadly, rivalry with the French king. English troops from Calais raided deep into northern France in 1522. And in 1523 an Anglo-Habsburg army under English command marched to within fifty miles of Paris, before retreating in the face of superior French forces. It was only years later that Henry recognised the 1523 campaign for what it was – the final opportunity to revive, however transiently, the 'dual monarchy' of Henry V. The 1523 thrust towards Paris represented the last faint echo of English greatness in the Hundred Years War.

Henry's enthusiasm for war against France faded after 1523 as his cash reserves ran dry. By early 1525, Wolsey was preparing to make peace with the French when news reached England of the Spanish–Imperial victory over Francis I's army at the battle of Pavia, in northern Italy, in which the French king himself had been taken prisoner. A jubilant Henry now proposed to Charles V that they divide Francis's leaderless realm between them. But the emperor had no wish to share the spoils of his victory, and resented what he regarded as the English king's niggardly contribution to the war effort. The tax revolts that greeted Wolsey's Amicable Grant of 1525 – which was designed to raise money for Henry's proposed partition of France – exposed all too clearly the Tudor state's incapacity for sustained warfare. Desperate for money, and fearful of Charles V's intentions, Henry had Wolsey negotiate a treaty with the French regent, Louise of Savoy, by which he promised to work for Francis's release (which was duly secured in 1526) in return for a large French pension. Although Wolsey helped to create the anti-Imperial Holy League of Cognac in 1526, the exhausted state of royal finances was probably one reason why Henry then declined to play an active part in this alliance.

A lack of interest, as well as money, marked Henry's handling of the volatile Tudor borderlands. Following the death of the 8th earl of Kildare in 1513, he appointed the 9th earl, his boyhood companion, as lord deputy of Ireland in his father's place. Henry was at first content to give Kildare a free hand, being no more interested in imposing direct rule or in conquering Gaelic Ireland than Henry VII had been. As long as the Pale was adequately defended and at a minimum cost to the crown, Henry was happy to let Wolsey and Kildare get on with it. To attempt anything more ambitious was, in Henry's own words, 'consumpcion of treasour in vayne' – certainly when that treasure might be better employed winning him great victories in France.[48] Kildare's high-handed style of government landed him in trouble at court, however, and during the 1520s the king and Wolsey experimented with the earl of Surrey and then one of Kildare's rivals among the Butlers as lord deputy. But these alternatives to the Kildare ascendancy proved either too costly or incapable of preventing Gaelic raiding – and usually both. The royal council in Dublin was certainly not up to the job, as a government report of 1526 made clear:

> The Council, being in a corner of the land, are satisfied if the part of four shires called the English Pale be at peace; in which case they report to the King that the land is in good quiet, caring no more for the rest of it than the Venetians do for the Scots. They have thus diminished the King's jurisdiction from a large forest to a narrow park.[49]

The council itself admitted to the king that 'there is none of this land that can or may do for defence of the same so well as [Kildare]'.[50] By the close of 1532, Henry was back at square one, having reappointed a triumphant Kildare as deputy. Henry showed even less imagination when it came to governing England's northern marches, where his distrust of the border nobility, and his belligerence towards the Scots, simply perpetuated the region's endemic state of lawlessness and violence.

Henry's wars of magnificence had made him more enemies than friends by the mid-1520s, for all Wolsey's clever diplomacy. More worryingly, his pretensions to rival Charles V and Francis I in martial greatness, in so far as they required financial expedients like the Amicable Grant to sustain them, threatened the stability of the Tudor realm. With the ideas of the 'heretic' Luther provoking schism and peasant revolts in Germany, and beginning to find a small but receptive audience in London and at Oxford and Cambridge universities, it was no time for Henry to be stirring up domestic unrest. Opposition at home did not reflect well on him abroad, and he would need to project an image of assured authority, of a king who commanded the undivided loyalty of his subjects, if he was to overcome a crisis that was developing within his own family by the mid-1520s: the breakdown of his marriage to Katherine of Aragon. The queen had borne Henry at least five children since 1510, but only one, Princess Mary (b. 1516), had survived infancy. The rest had been stillborn or had died shortly after birth. The king had an acknowledged son, Henry Fitzroy (b. 1519), by one of his mistresses, Elizabeth Blount, a lady-in-waiting to the queen, but he needed to sire a legitimate and healthy male heir to safeguard the Tudor dynasty; and with Katherine in her mid-thirties by 1520, and looking – according to the Venetian ambassador – 'rather ugly than otherwise', the chances of that happening had begun to seem remote.[51] The apparent seriousness of Henry's affair with one of his courtiers' daughters, Mary Carey, née Boleyn, during the early 1520s suggests that sexual relations between the king and queen had ceased, and were not likely to resume. It was now merely a question of time before Henry sought an annulment of his marriage, and began looking for a new wife and queen.

Untying the knot with Katherine would present as great a diplomatic challenge for Henry as any of his 'enterprises abroad'. Matrimonial law relating to princes came under the pope's jurisdiction, and obtaining a papal annulment for a royal marriage could sometimes turn into a power struggle between the princely relations and allies of the parties involved. Katherine's predicament could not be expected to sit well with her nephew (and Henry's enemy by 1526), Emperor Charles V. Yet Henry too had a formidable champion in any contest for papal favour, and that was Wolsey. The great trust reposed in him by Henry, and the almost complete control that he had established over the administration of the Church in England, gave the cardinal considerable influence at Rome. Papal authority in England – the Vatican's power of levying taxes on the English clergy, for example – was exercised, very largely, through Wolsey, and he used that authority in the king's interest. Whether the cardinal's cunning and diplomacy could prevail against the emperor's vast resources was open to question. But Henry had seen his hopes of becoming Christendom's greatest warrior-king dashed. He would not bear lightly the frustration of his other great ambition, that of securing the Tudor dynasty.

2

The Protestant Cause, 1527–1603

To conclude, in Countries, kingdomes, Cities, Townes, and Churches reformed, your errours and superstitious vanities bee so blotted out within the space of these forty yeares in the harts of men, that their children and youth being so long nouseled [i.e. noursled – brought up] in the sound doctrine of Christ, like as they never heard of your ridiculous trumpery, so they wyl never be brought to the same. And if nothing els wyll deface you, yet printing onely wyl subvert your doinges, do what ye can, which the Lord onely hath set up for your desolation.

John Foxe, *Acts and Monuments of These Latter and Perillous Dayes*
(London, 1563), 'To the Persecutors of Gods truth, commonlye
called Papistes, an other preface of the Author'

The king's great matter

The story of the English Reformation was until quite recently a reassuringly familiar one – of a people languishing in spiritual bondage, held captive by a moribund and decadent Church, until Henry VIII's marital problems provided the catalyst for a swift and popular Protestant exodus. It was a tale sealed with the blood of martyrs, illuminated by the fires of Smithfield, and hymned in all its thrilling horror and triumph by England's greatest Protestant hagiographer John Foxe (1516/17–87) in his *Acts and Monuments*. Whether or not we accept this version of events, there is little question that the English and Scottish Reformations have been the most momentous and transformative developments to have occurred in Britain and Ireland for almost a thousand years. The British empire would be conceived and perceived through a haze of ideas and myths that Foxe and the early Reformers inspired. It was Protestantism, patriotism and the lure of plunder – the three became inextricably linked – that propelled the English from their European coastal waters out onto the Atlantic and the sea lanes of empire. And it was commitment to the Protestant cause and the fight against 'popery' at home and abroad that spawned Leviathan – the so-called fiscal–military state – in the mid-seventeenth century. Yet for all their long-term consequences, the British Reformations were among the least likely of contingencies. If Henry VIII had produced a healthy son by Katherine of Aragon the English Reformation, and very likely the Scottish too, would probably never have happened. Similarly, if Elizabeth I had died of the smallpox in 1562, as she very nearly did, England might well have been plunged into religious civil war just as France was that very year, and emerged, as France would do, a Catholic kingdom.

The problem with the old-school version of Reformation history, based as it was on the assumption that most people were thirsting for Protestantism, is that the English Church on the eve of Henry's break with Rome was in remarkably rude health. In fact, there was something of a religious revival occurring in Europe during the early sixteenth century, driven in large part by the laity's desire to gain remission for their own souls and those of their departed loved ones in purgatory. Prayers and Masses for the dead lay at the heart of a thriving body of devotional practices that included pilgrimages, veneration of saints and their relics, and all kinds of communal celebrations and festivities associated with the religious calendar. Devout fraternities or religious guilds to raise money for intercessory prayers and Masses were flour- ishing. London alone had at least 150 such fraternities. Donations for the decoration or repair of churches remained popular among the laity. Never was more money spent by ordinary men and women on rebuilding their parish church than in the fifty years before 1530. Monasteries still played a central role in the devotional and social life of northern England, while in the south there was an exuberant parish piety. A few urban sophisticates, particularly those influenced by humanism, might demand a more lively personal faith and an improve- ment in the standards of clerical training, but late medieval Catholicism was generally more responsive to the needs of the laity, more satisfying to the senses (if not necessarily the intellect), more effective at binding local communities, and less open to state interference than much of what followed. The overlap between the average lay person's social and religious life was extensive and generally harmonious; certainly disputes between priests and their parishioners were relatively infrequent. Overall, the pre-Reformation English Church was unusually well run by contemporary standards elsewhere in Europe.

If the Church was vulnerable, it was from the top down rather than the bottom up. Henry VIII was the first king of England whose intellectual resources included the potential for virulent scepticism about the value and godliness of certain aspects of popular worship. Henry VII had been a man of largely conventional piety. He had bullied the Church, to be sure, and created valuable precedents for Henry VIII to do likewise, but there had been no questioning of church doctrine on his watch. Henry VIII, on the other hand, was an admirer of Erasmus and other humanist scholars, some of whom were critical of the mechanical and superstitious elements in traditional religion, particularly those without scriptural foundation. The ideas of these 'orthodox' reformers for religious and social renewal did not necessarily challenge papal authority or the central tenets of Catholicism. The faith that Erasmus and many other humanists put in education and human reason was actually easier to square with the Church's teaching on salvation through good works than was the Protestant emphasis on the uniquely saving power of God's arbitrary grace to a fallen and corrupt mankind. Katherine of Aragon and Sir Thomas More are prime examples of Erasmians who remained committed to orthodox religion. But in the hands of a king who was exceptionally touchy about any perceived challenge to his authority, and who was driven to question 'the bishop of Rome's usurped power', the humanist critique could be a formidable weapon against the Church.[1]

Henry's quarrel with the papacy – the lightning before the storm of Reformation – was provoked not by humanist idealism, however, but by dynastic insecurity. Convinced by 1527 that his ageing wife was incapable of supplying him with a male heir, Henry made a formal request to Pope Clement VII for an annulment of his marriage – not, strictly speaking, a divorce, but a papal declaration that no valid marriage had been contracted. The argument that Henry used to satisfy his own scrupulous conscience in this matter was based upon the question of consanguinity. Katherine had been his sister-in-law, the widow of his elder brother Arthur. In order to marry her in the first place, Henry had needed a papal dispensation, and he had never been entirely convinced that their union was lawful in the eyes of God. The couple's failure to produce a male heir seemed to confirm his worst suspicions. He was minded of Leviticus 20:21: 'if a man shall take his brother's wife, it is an unclean thing . . . they shall be childless' – conveniently ignoring the fact that this passage apparently referred not to a brother's widow but to a brother's wife. By arguing that the dispensation which had been granted to allow his marriage to Katherine had contravened divine and natural law, and had therefore been invalid, Henry was implicitly challenging papal authority itself.

The role of Anne Boleyn (c.1500–36) in Henry's dynastic drama was not initially that of queen-in-waiting. Policy and precedent demanded that Katherine's shoes be filled by another princess from one of Europe's ruling houses. Henry, a practised adulterer, began pursuing Anne early in 1526 as his mistress, having recently discarded her elder sister Mary. The daughter of a leading diplomat, Anne had been brought up in the most fashionable courts in Europe, and like Henry she could speak French and was an accomplished musician. To look at she was no great beauty. 'Madame Anne', observed the Venetian ambassador in 1532, 'is not one of the handsomest women in the world; she is of middling stature, swarthy complexion, long neck, wide mouth, bosom not much raised, and in fact has nothing but the English King's great appetite, and her eyes, which are black and beautiful.'[2] But her vivacious personality and sophisticated French manners made her the most exciting woman at court. Henry was besotted, and her refusal to become maîtresse-en-titre seems to have inflamed 'the great love that he bare her in the bottom of his stomach'.[3] In the summer of 1527 therefore, a few months after deciding to seek an annulment of his marriage to Katherine, he threw policy out of the window and asked Anne to marry him. The couple apparently agreed not to have sex until they were man and wife, for Henry no less than Anne wanted their first child to be legitimate. But it was to be over five years before they could marry and finally consummate their relationship, which to a man of Henry's sexual appetite and dynastic anxieties must have required immense restraint.

The course of British history might have been very different if Henry's request for a papal annulment had not coincided with a decisive moment in the long-running Franco-Habsburg struggle for control of the Italian peninsula. In 1527 Imperial troops sacked Rome, killed almost 50,000 of the city's inhabitants, and left the pope under the power of Katherine's nephew, Emperor Charles V, who was not about to let his aunt's place be usurped by some pro-French upstart like Anne Boleyn. To persuade any pope to grant an annulment on Henry's terms would have been difficult, but with Clement in thrall to the Imperialists it was impossible. Henry's next move was to have the case heard and settled in England. In 1529 a legatine court was convened at Blackfriars in which Henry was confronted by his now estranged queen. Katherine protested on her knees that she had always been a faithful wife; and she may have gone further and insisted that she had never consummated her marriage to Arthur (undermining Henry's argument of consanguinity) and challenged her husband to deny it. What she certainly did do was formally appeal her cause to Rome and walk out of the court. All this while, Cardinal Wolsey had been working tirelessly to secure an annulment at Rome, but his mounting failures lost him first Anne's support and finally the king's. Dismissed as lord chancellor in the autumn of 1529, he died the following year before he could be brought to trial for high treason. For the first time in over fifteen years, Henry was without a chief minister.

The king's 'great matter' portended a major constitutional upheaval. Like most of his royal predecessors, Henry had been keen to manage the Church as far as was prudently possible. He had not denied papal jurisdiction as such. He had simply asserted the traditional right of the temporal authority to circumscribe the spiritual. But the impasse over his annulment led him to consider an altogether more radical approach to Church–state relations. In the autumn of 1530 he informed the Imperial ambassador and the pope that as supreme ruler within his dominions he was answerable to no external authority, and that his annulment could therefore be settled only in England, if necessary by appeal to Parliament. He followed this up in 1531 by demanding that the clergy acknowledge him as 'sole protector and supreme head of the English church' with spiritual care over the souls of his subjects. He felt on firm ground here, having received a dossier from a team of royal scholars that proved to his and their satisfaction that God had granted kings of England 'imperial' authority – that is to say sovereign power, free from any foreign jurisdiction – in spiritual as well as temporal matters. He was also emboldened by the alliance he had formed with Francis I in 1527, believing that he enjoyed the French king's approval in challenging the authority of the pope, although Francis supported Henry only in so far as it served his own interests, particularly in his continuing power struggle with Charles V. Moreover, like most of those watching the unfolding drama in England, Francis was convinced that all Henry wanted was to vindicate his princely authority and honour on the annulment issue. That Henry would take matters to the point of actual schism seemed scarcely credible.

What gave the king's great matter a specifically religious dimension was his receptiveness to the Erasmian critique of traditional worship. The fall of Wolsey cleared the ground for the 'evangelicals' at court (the label 'Protestant' was German in origin and was not applied to English reformists until the late 1540s), a faction headed by Anne and her clients, among them the brilliant scholar Thomas Cranmer (1489–1556) and Wolsey's protégé Thomas Cromwell (c.1485–1540). During the early 1530s the evangelicals gradually persuaded the king of the theological and political merits of adopting at least some of their ideas on church reform. The last thing Henry wanted was to encourage heresy, particularly in doctrinal matters. He detested Luther – a feeling Luther heartily reciprocated – and the Lutheran belief common to most evangelicals that Christians were saved by God's free gift of faith to individual believers. Not that the king's own ideas on how to attain salvation were exactly orthodox. Rather than adhere to the official Catholic line that God's grace was conveyed through the Church, he came to believe that faith (which he understood merely as assent to the creeds) *and* good works were essential. Yet as much as Henry disliked Luther's doctrinal ideas, they had the same practical effect as the humanists' attack on superstitious practices, in that they challenged the Church's emphasis on the saving power of pilgrimages, ritual fasting and other traditional works of penance. Because Henry shared some of the humanists' concerns, and was desperate to believe that in leading England towards schism he was doing God's will, he cautiously backed the evangelicals' call for purifying reform and a return to a more Bible-based faith. Moreover, he was beginning to find one evangelical idea particularly compelling: that for a king to submit to the power of the Church was 'a shame obove all shames . . . one kynge, one lawe, is Gods ordinance in every realme'.[4]

Henry's campaign against the Church became even more direct and aggressive in 1532. His patience was now wearing very thin, to the point where he committed the Parliament he had called in 1529 (later dubbed the Reformation Parliament) to a full-blooded attack on the clergy and papal jurisdiction in England in an effort to bludgeon the pope into submission. The legal theorist Christopher St German had argued in print that 'the king in parliament [is] the high sovereign over the people which hath not only charge on the bodies but also on the souls of his subjects', and Henry evidently agreed.[5] The man largely responsible for turning this doctrine into a legislative programme and steering it through Parliament was Thomas Cromwell, who had emerged by 1534 as the king's principal secretary and new chief minister. A man of wide experience and learning, full of roguish charm and good conversation, Cromwell also possessed all the necessary skills of a brilliant politician and administrator. He was remembered by John Foxe as 'pregnant in wit . . . in judgement discreet, in tongue eloquent, in service faithful, in stomach courageous, in his pen active'.[6]

The switch to a more binding, legislative solution to the problem reflected Henry's confidence that Francis I was firmly in his corner; indeed, in the summer of 1532 an Anglo-French treaty was signed in which Francis promised Henry military support if England was attacked by Charles V. The fact that the Lutheran states of northern Germany and Scandinavia had either rejected papal authority or were moving in that direction must also have given Henry confidence. But he nevertheless regarded Francis as his most powerful ally in defying the pope.

It was while Henry and Anne were at Calais in the autumn of 1532, celebrating their alliance with Francis, that they finally slept together. By December she was pregnant, giving Henry nine months in which to divorce Katherine and marry Anne or have his longed-for son born a bastard. He and Anne were married in secret in January 1533, and in April, Parliament passed the Act in Restraint of Appeals, preventing Katherine or any other subject appealing their case to Rome. Armed with this legislation, the new archbishop of Canterbury Thomas Cranmer pronounced Henry's marriage to Katherine illegal and therefore invalid. Katherine spent the remaining three years of her life in sorrowful seclusion. Anne's delivery of a daughter – the future Queen Elizabeth (1533–1603) – in September 1533 disappointed Henry. But he was sure that Anne would provide him with a male heir at some point (wrongly, as it turned out); and anyway, his great matter had long ceased to be simply a dynastic issue. Francis I, meanwhile, looked on appalled. He had never meant to condone schism. Yet it had been French assurances of support against the pope – or what Henry had chosen to interpret as such – that had persuaded Anne to climb into the royal bed in the first place. And from the moment she became pregnant the die was cast.

The royal supremacy

The legislation that effected the decisive break with Catholic Christendom was the 1534 Act of Supremacy, which pronounced Henry 'the only supreme head in earth of the Church of England'.[7] The king took this to mean that he had the divinely ordained authority, indeed duty, to determine and if necessary reform church government and doctrine, although he stopped short of claiming the sacramental powers of the ordained clergy. At the same time an act was passed that made it treason to deny the royal supremacy or to call the king a heretic, schismatic or tyrant. Only the zealously committed or the foolhardy would now challenge Henry's right to play the Old Testament patriarch. His subjects, if they knew what was good for them, must conform their piety to his own – a shifting, eclectic and theologically unstable blend of orthodox and Erasmian beliefs. It can best be described as Catholicism shorn of the pope and certain unscriptural elements and practices closely associated with Rome, such as belief in purgatory, the intercession of saints, pilgrimages and monasticism. The veneration of images, 'feigned relics' and saints' shrines was denounced as idolatrous, and the objects themselves held up to public ridicule and destroyed. But woe betide anyone who denied the royal supremacy or the miracle of transubstantiation (the turning of the bread and wine during Mass into the body and blood of Christ). The first were deemed traitors, the second heretics, and Henry imposed his 'middle way' upon both with ruthless impartiality. On one notorious occasion in 1540 he had three Lutheran 'heretics' burned while having three papist 'traitors' hung, drawn and quartered. The condemned were never charged with a specific offence, for the government wanted to drum home the message that their ultimate crime was not in holding this or that doctrine but in daring to question Henry's right to tell them what to believe in the first place.

Hardly less violent was the fate of the monasteries during Henry's Reformation. By the early sixteenth century the Church owned one third of all land in England, and had an annual revenue of £270,000, which was substantially more than the crown itself enjoyed. The monasteries alone controlled property worth £136,000 a year, making their confiscation and sale not only immensely profitable to Henry but also an excellent way of binding their purchasers – a great swathe of landed society, from noblemen down to yeomen – to the new religious order. Masterminded by Cromwell, the Dissolution would initiate the most sweeping change in land ownership in England since the Norman Conquest. But this was incidental to its main purpose, which was to endow the crown with a large enough landed income that it could govern and defend the realm without recourse to unpopular prerogative levies such as the Amicable Grant.

Financially and politically the Dissolution made considerable sense; culturally, however, it was the greatest tragedy in modern British history. Between 1536 and 1540 about 800 monasteries and convents in England,

Wales and about half of Ireland were suppressed in what amounted to a campaign of state-licensed vandalism. Religious artworks were plundered; whole libraries, including irreplaceable early English manuscripts, were destroyed or sold for toilet paper; and some of Europe's finest church buildings were auctioned off and demolished. The Dissolution may have begun as a reformist initiative, a campaign to eradicate these hotbeds of traditional worship, opposition to the royal supremacy, and, so it was claimed, 'beastly buggery'.[8] But it ended as out-and-out asset-stripping.

Besides the evangelicals at court and the purchasers of monastic lands, few had cause to welcome the Reformation. The reformist, anticlerical elements in Henrician religious policy appealed to some members of that small, educated elite influenced by humanism, while the evangelicals gained converts among England's medieval dissenting community, the Lollards. The reformists' attack on religious flummery and clerical ignorance, and their skill in using sermons and printed polemic to get their message across, certainly widened their appeal. Nevertheless, the evangelicals and their sympathisers remained firmly in the minority during Henry's reign, and were largely confined to the two universities, the larger towns, and to those parts of the country, notably the south-east, with comparatively high literacy rates and strong commercial contacts with London and the Protestant communities on the Continent.

The prevailing response to the Reformation ranged from bewilderment to outright hostility. Katherine's supporters and the defenders of traditional religion were strongly represented among the clergy, in Parliament, and even on the king's council, and it needed all of Henry's menace and Cromwell's guile to overcome their resistance. In the end, enough people put loyalty to their terrifying yet charismatic king before loyalty to the papacy. But there were notable exceptions. Sir Thomas More, who had replaced Wolsey as lord chancellor in 1529, was executed in 1535 for steadfastly refusing to acknowledge the royal supremacy. Although sometimes seen today as a martyr for freedom of conscience, More had been a determined persecutor of evangelicals. Heresy, he had insisted, bred sedition, and must be ruthlessly cut out to prevent 'infeccyon of the remanaunt'.[9]

The Reformation – and in particular the suppression of the monasteries – provoked the biggest rebellion in Tudor history: the 1536 Pilgrimage of Grace. Wearing badges of the Five Wounds of Christ, and bound by an oath to defend the Catholic Church, the pilgrims mustered more than 30,000 strong in northern England, outnumbering the army that Henry hastily raised to confront them. But anxious to avoid a civil war, the pilgrims agreed to disperse on (false) assurances from Henry that he would reverse his religious policies and show mercy to the rebels – over two hundred of whom were executed. One of the condemned leaders of the rebellion pleaded not to be dismembered before he was dead, and therefore Henry had him hung in chains – in other words, gibbeted until he died of thirst. Subsequent attempts to revive the Pilgrimage were put down by noblemen rewarded with monastic lands and using troops paid for from the proceeds of the Dissolution.

The struggle between reformers and traditionalists divided many parishes in the south-east, while much of northern and western England remained altogether resistant to the new religion. The Reformation was to be greeted with even greater hostility in Ireland, where it represented an extension to the religious sphere of early Tudor efforts to impose English government and 'civility' – that is, English laws and cultural values. Protestantism thus became fatally bound up with the long-standing English attack on Gaelic Irish identity and way of life. Gaelic Wales and Cornwall remained solidly Catholic until well into the Elizabethan period, but Gaelic Ireland would never succumb to Protestant evangelisation.

The Reformation continued apace during the later 1530s despite the loss of its most influential patron at court, Queen Anne (Boleyn), who was executed in May 1536. She had been tried on charges of adultery and incest, although whether she had indeed been unfaithful to Henry or was the victim of court intrigue is not clear. Her racy reputation and the flirtatious behaviour of her entourage had certainly not helped her cause. But it is possible that the king would have been less easily persuaded of her guilt if she had given him a healthy son. Instead she had suffered two miscarriages since the birth of Elizabeth. The day after Anne's execution, Henry was betrothed to the woman that the religious conservatives had been dangling before him as his next queen, Jane Seymour (1508/9–37), and ten days later they were married. She provided Henry with a healthy son at last, Prince Edward, but the king's joy was mingled with grief when she died shortly afterwards of post-natal complications. His fourth wife, whom he married early in 1540, was Anne of Cleves (1515–57), the so-called 'mare of Flanders'. Her brother, the duke of Jülich-Cleves on the lower Rhine, shared Henry's Erasmian reformism, and enjoyed close links with the Schmalkaldic League: the alliance of evangelical princes in the Holy Roman Empire.

Henry was desperately in need of allies on the Continent by the late 1530s, for the spread of Lutheran ideas in France had so alarmed Francis I that he had distanced himself from England's schismatic king and sought a rapprochement with Charles V. Besides strengthening Henry's hand against potential foreign enemies, the marriage to Anne of Cleves may have been part of Cromwell's attempts to consolidate the Reformation by putting another patroness of reform into the royal bedchamber: a second Anne Boleyn. Unfortunately for Cromwell, and for Anne of Cleves, Henry was put off by the 'looseness of her breasts . . . and other parts of her body', and could not consummate the marriage, which was quickly annulled by the obliging archbishop of Canterbury, Thomas Cranmer.[10] Henry consoled himself with one of Anne's maids of honour, the young and flighty Katherine Howard (c.1524–42), and in July 1540 she became his fifth queen. There was no lack of royal ardour this time round; indeed, Henry doted on his teenage consort. Katherine had a sexual history of her own, however, and may have taken another lover after becoming queen. It would be understandable if she had, for after years of over-indulgence the golden youth of 1509 had become a raddled, bloated monster with suppurating ulcers on his once shapely legs. When her indiscretions came to light late in 1541, Henry was overcome with self-pity, and lamented 'his ill-luck in meeting with such ill-conditioned wives'.[11] Katherine, like Anne Boleyn, paid for her alleged infidelity with her head. Henry's sixth and final marriage was in 1543 to the graceful, intelligent and evangelically-minded Katherine Parr (1512–48). She had the unenviable task of comforting the uxoricidal Henry in his declining years, and only narrowly avoided execution herself.

As wives came and went and the pressures – dynastic, sexual and political – that had pushed Henry into schism abated, he shifted back towards religious orthodoxy. The Pilgrimage of Grace had troubled him greatly, highlighting the unpopularity of his reformist policies, while the rapprochement between Francis I and Charles V in the late 1530s had left him dangerously isolated on the Continent. One casualty of Henry's efforts to appease the Catholic powers was Thomas Cromwell, who fell terminally from royal favour for having promoted the Anne of Cleves marriage. Charged with treason and heresy, he begged Henry for his life, ending one letter with the plea: 'Most gracyous prynce I crye for mercye mercye mercye' – though he, of all people, should have known that he was wasting his time.[12] He was beheaded on 28 July 1540, the day before Henry's wedding to Katherine Howard. For the next five years or so the religious conservatives held the upper hand in Henry's counsels, and leading evangelicals either kept quiet or went into exile. Yet the reformers remained well placed in London, the universities and at court to contend for the kingdom's future religious identity. Henry allowed 'reforming' humanists to dominate the household of the young Prince Edward, and put measures in place to prevent the religious conservatives from attacking what he regarded as his crowning achievement: the royal supremacy.

British Reformations

Henry's reign would end where it had begun, with costly and largely futile wars that satisfied his vainglory while heaping misery on the peoples of England and Scotland. The resumption of his 'enterprises abroad' in the 1540s, and his failure before his death to give his idiosyncratic Reformation greater coherence and stability, were major errors of judgement. The great strengthening of the crown's authority and income during the 1530s might have been used to stabilise the realm and to safeguard it against the worst effects of rising inflation and, more ominously, the break-up of Catholic Christendom. Instead, Henry's failure to use his new resources wisely would leave a debilitating and divisive legacy for his successors.

The Dissolution netted the king some £1.3 million in the decade after 1536, the kind of money he had not been able to lay his hands on since inheriting his father's huge cash reserves in 1509. His first thought then had been to wage war against France; and his new-found wealth in the early 1540s, and perhaps a desire to restore his pride after he had been cuckolded by Katherine Howard, rekindled this ambition. When Charles V fell out with Francis I in the early 1540s, therefore, and started bidding for English support, Henry abandoned what had largely been Cromwell's policy of an alliance with the German evangelical princes – which Henry had privately considered beneath his dignity as king of England – and prepared to resume his wars of magnificence against the French. Before invading France again, however, he thought it prudent to neutralise Francis's allies, the Scots. Late in 1542 a small English army routed a poorly led Scottish force five times its size, and then two weeks later the Scottish king James V died of cholera. James was succeeded by an infant daughter Mary – the future Mary Queen of Scots (1542–87) – the granddaughter of Henry's sister.

Henry now saw an opportunity to end England's Scottish problem once and for all by marrying his heir, Prince Edward, to Mary. But the Scots were understandably hostile to this Tudor takeover bid, and with French help resisted Henry's scheme for a dynastic union. Henry then reverted to Plan A: to use military force to keep the Scots quiescent while he was in France. In May 1544, an English army under Edward Seymour, earl of Hertford (c.1500–52) sailed up the Firth of Forth, sacked Edinburgh, and then ravaged its way back to the English border, leaving a resentful, humiliated but temporarily impotent Scotland in its wake.

The army that Henry assembled at Calais in July 1544 for a new invasion of France would be larger than any to be fielded by the crown for the next 150 years. Six thousand of his 42,000 troops were mercenaries supplied and paid for by his one-time and now current ally Charles V on the understanding that Henry's army would rendezvous with an equally large Imperial force for a joint attack on Paris. But Henry opted instead to expand the English enclave around Calais by seizing the nearby port of Boulogne. Left to bear the full brunt of French military power on his own, Charles concluded a separate peace with Francis in September 1544. It was now Henry who had to soldier on alone, but he was too proud of his tiny French conquests to make terms, and therefore England was dragged into a prolonged war against both France and Scotland. The defence of Boulogne, another slash-and-burn raid into Scotland, and fighting off a huge French invasion fleet[13] – bigger even than the Spanish Armada of 1588 – required the crown to maintain over 150,000 troops for much of 1545. The strains upon England's manpower and economy were enormous, and in 1546 Henry was forced to conclude a peace with the French by which he agreed to return Boulogne in 1554 for a mere £600,000 (the siege of the town alone had cost £586,000). It had taken all of the crown's resources just to take and hold one minor French port. Once again, the inability of the Tudor state to wage prolonged war on the Continent had been exposed – as had the royal army's obsolete combat tactics. The English still relied on longbows, which were effective against the latest armour only at very close range. 'We who were accustomed to fire our arquebuses [handguns] at a great distance', wrote one French officer, 'thought these near approaches of theirs [the English] very strange, imputing their running on at this confident rate to absolute bravery.'[14]

Henry could have used the Dissolution to endow the crown with a landed income that would have left it wealthier and more powerful than it had ever been before. But instead he chose to sell off the bulk of former religious property in a last futile bid for chivalric glory, and that was not all he squandered. During the mid-1540s taxes were raised to their highest levels since the fourteenth century, and the currency was debased (by reducing the gold and silver content of the coinage) for short-term profit, although at the cost of destabilising the economy and exacerbating inflation. From an economic point of view, Henry's death in January 1547 did not come soon enough.

Anxious not to leave the royal supremacy at the mercy of religious conservatives, Henry had made sure, by the terms of his will, that the council which would govern during the minority of his successor, the nine-year-old Edward VI (1537–53), was dominated by evangelicals. The most powerful of these regency councillors was Edward's uncle the earl of Hertford, created lord protector and duke of Somerset. An experienced soldier, who had scored victories against the French and the Scots, Somerset was committed to the aggressive foreign policy that the crown inherited from Henry, and therefore the military and financial overreach of Henry's final years would continue under Edward. But whereas defeating Scotland had been a sideshow for Henry, for Somerset it was his highest priority. His ambition was to forge a greater England, and a Protestant Britain, by reviving Henry's policy of using military force to secure a marriage between Edward and Mary Queen of Scots. By establishing garrisons at strategic points in Lowland Scotland, Somerset aimed to create a new English 'Pale' north of the border in which the evangelical (and pro-English) minority there might flourish and become the dominant force in Scottish politics.

Somerset's Scottish war began well with a resounding English victory at the battle of Pinkie in September 1547. But his very success encouraged France's new king, Henri II, to send a 12,000-strong army to the Scots' assistance. Worse still, Mary Queen of Scots was betrothed to Henri's heir, Francis, threatening to turn Scotland into a virtual satellite of France. French power was growing and yet the Protestantism of the Edwardian government ruled out an alliance with the devoutly Catholic Charles V. England again found itself fighting the French and Scots single-handedly, and with the same desperate financial expedients: currency debasement, sale of ex-religious lands, and massive loans on the international money-market. One of Somerset's advisers warned him early in 1549 that to continue the war would bring 'certayn and undoubted ruyne and destruction to the hole realme and to your selfe ioyned with an infamy'.[15] That summer there were rebellions and riots in many English counties in response to a toxic combination of rising unemployment and inflation, declining wages, and Somerset's insensitive economic policies. The rebellions, although bloodily suppressed, damaged the lord protector's authority beyond repair, and in October he was removed from power by a court faction, and replaced as chief minister by John Dudley, earl of Warwick. The following year a treaty was concluded by which England withdrew its garrisons from Scotland and Boulogne. English ambitions in France and Scotland had ended in a humiliating defeat that would leave royal finances crippled for years to come.

Henry VIII's unstable and ill-defined middle way in religion did not satisfy Edward and his leading councillors. The young king had been raised largely by Katherine Parr and educated by evangelical tutors, and although most of his subjects still clung tenaciously to the tattered fabric of traditional religion, he and his mentors were determined to move the realm towards fully formed Protestantism, to finish what Henry had begun. New and much larger waves of iconoclasm struck England's parishes, destroying many stained-glass windows as well as carved images. Traditional religious plays and processions were banned, and religious guilds, often the mainstay of parish festivities and charitable work, were abolished. Within a few years of Edward's accession much of the remaining devotional heritage of medieval Catholicism had gone. It was his reign, not his father's, that most people came to regard as the true 'tyme of Scysme when this Realm was devyded from the Catholic Churche'.[16]

In one of the few more positive initiatives of the Edwardian Reformation, Archbishop Cranmer replaced the Latin liturgy with the first vernacular book of common prayer in 1549. Yet this too proved deeply unpopular in some quarters, provoking major uprisings in Devon and Cornwall that required German and Italian mercenaries and much killing to suppress. Undeterred, Cranmer brought out an even more uncompromisingly Protestant prayer book in 1552. The theology of many leading evangelicals was also moving further away from Catholicism – breaking with Lutheranism as it did so – in embracing the idea of the Eucharist as a service of commemoration, a symbol of Christ's sacrifice for sinful mankind and of the true believer's membership of the community of the faithful. This radicalisation was accelerated by the arrival in England in the late 1540s and early 1550s of eminent Protestant theologians, fleeing Catholic victories on the Continent.

Edward's death from tuberculosis in June 1553 came as a double blow to England's Protestants, depriving them of a godly prince, and bringing his 37-year-old and devoutly Catholic half-sister Mary (1516–58) to the throne. An attempt by Edward's leading councillors to divert the succession to his Protestant cousin, Lady Jane Grey, which occasioned a sermon by Bishop Ridley of London denouncing Mary and her half-sister Elizabeth as bastards, quickly collapsed in the face of strong popular resistance. Mary's courage in rallying the people against the Edwardian Protestant establishment demonstrated that England's first female ruler in her own right was also every bit Katherine of Aragon's daughter. Her callous treatment by Henry during the break with Rome had weakened her health, but had strengthened her attachment to the old religion. Indeed, she saw herself as an instrument of God's will to restore Catholicism in her realm, and she duly returned England and Ireland to papal obedience and had the act of royal supremacy repealed by Parliament. She accepted, if reluctantly, that any attempt to recover the church property that had been sold into private hands since the 1520s would be successfully resisted by the landed elite. But her concern was not so much to turn back the clock to the days before the Henrician Reformation as to reform Catholicism along broadly Erasmian lines. With her support, the new archbishop of Canterbury, Cardinal Reginald Pole, set about trying to raise standards of education among the clergy, and to use sermons and printed works of religious instruction to improve the laity's grasp of Christian fundamentals.

Mary's Catholic restoration was welcomed by the majority of her subjects, despite the fact that Henry VIII's propaganda had generated widespread disdain for papal authority both among Catholics and Protestants. Nevertheless, she committed two major errors that undermined her popularity and that of her religious programme. The first, and most serious, was in marrying Charles V's eldest son, the future Philip II of Spain (1527–98), who would shortly inherit his father's Spanish crown and empire (which, besides Spain and its possessions in the Americas, included the Netherlands, Milan and Naples), while his Habsburg uncle, Ferdinand, would succeed Charles V as Holy Roman Emperor. Mary had a duty to her faith and to her realm to produce an heir, and was obliged by the lack of a suitable English candidate to select a foreign consort. Nevertheless, Philip was a particularly unpopular choice with the English public. Although the marriage treaty denied him regal authority, in private he repudiated its terms, and it was widely anticipated, and feared, that he would turn England into another

Habsburg dependency. In marrying Philip, therefore, the queen coloured perceptions of her religious settlement by linking it with the threat of foreign subjugation.

The mere prospect of Mary marrying Philip had provoked a major rebellion early in 1554, its leader Sir Thomas Wyatt claiming that his 'hole intent and styrre was agaynst the comyng in of strangers [foreigners] and Spanyerds and to abolyshe theym out of this realme'.[17] There was no substantial linkage as yet between Protestantism and English national identity. Anti-Spanish xenophobia was felt across the religious divide. Nevertheless, Protestants played a leading role in the reaction against England's Spanish 'captivity', publishing anti-Habsburg pamphlets and helping to widen participation in debates on foreign policy. It was in Mary's reign that the seeds of the 'Black Legend' were sown. Hatred of all things Spanish intensified after Mary committed England to the Habsburgs' long-running struggle against Valois France. She had been warned by her privy council that the English economy could not sustain another major war, and that 'the common people [were] . . . many ways grieved and some pinched with famine . . . some miscontented for matters of Religion and generally all yet tasting of the smart of the last wars [of the 1540s]'.[18] But Mary allowed herself to be overruled by Philip, only to see Calais fall to a surprise attack by 27,000 French troops early in 1558. The first line of England's defences against French aggression, the last outpost of its Plantagenet empire in continental Europe, had gone. The English had regarded the town as so thoroughly theirs that it had been given seats in Parliament. Its sudden loss shocked the whole country, and dealt a huge blow to national pride. Overlooked in the gloom of losing Calais was the Marian government's refurbishment of the fleet and overhaul of naval administration. Without these reforms the navy would not have been equal to its many and formidable challenges in the years ahead.

Mary's second major mistake was countenancing a high-profile campaign of persecution against Protestant heretics. Although conventional wisdom decreed that heresy was a social cancer that must be excised, the Marian burnings aroused more revulsion than rejoicing. About 285 men and women refused to recant their Protestantism and were burned at Smithfield in London, and other sites. Most of these 'martyrs' were relatively obscure figures, but they also included three of Edward's reforming bishops: Cranmer, Hugh Latimer and Nicholas Ridley. Latimer and Ridley were burned together – Latimer with the rousing exhortation: 'Be of good comfort Master Ridley, and play the man: we shall this day light such a candle by God's grace in England, as (I trust) shall never be put out.'[19] Yet had Mary reigned as long as her father had done, and continued to burn Protestants at the rate she was doing, England would have remained Catholic. Her death, childless, in November 1558 did not alter the fact that the candle of Tudor Protestantism flickered in a very dark place. The new religion had yet to win hearts and minds in Ireland and Wales, and even where Protestantism had proved most popular – in London and southern England – its adherents remained a minority.

England's new monarch, Elizabeth I, was as much her mother's daughter as Mary had been, possessing all of Anne Boleyn's quick intelligence and imperious nature, her petulance and sharp tongue, and her talent for music and languages. Like her half-brother Edward VI, Elizabeth had been educated by humanist evangelicals, and was a Protestant too, of sorts. Her piety was based upon the Bible and, probably, the foundational Protestant doctrine of salvation by faith alone. But in style it was closer to that of the Henrician evangelicals than to the more dogmatic Protestants of Edward's reign. Her decision to establish some form of Protestantism in her realm was consistent with her conscience, many of her friendships, and the desire of the landed elite for security in its title to former church property. Nevertheless, it threatened to leave her kingdoms a prey to the Catholic powers, or as one government adviser put it, 'a bone thrown between two dogs'.[20]

Peace with France, and between the houses of Habsburg and Valois, was concluded at the treaty of Cateau-Cambrésis in April 1559, which ended almost seventy years of Franco-Spanish warfare for control of northern Italy. With the great powers now free to turn their attention elsewhere, the treaty looked ominously like the prelude to a pan-Catholic onslaught against the rapidly growing Protestant communities in England, Scotland, France and the Netherlands. The threat to England was particularly acute, for the Catholic powers had never recognised the marriage between Henry VIII and Anne Boleyn. As far as they were concerned Elizabeth was illegitimate, and Mary Queen of Scots was the rightful heir to the throne. Soon after Elizabeth's accession, Henri II and his heir Francis II suggested to Philip II that they join forces to invade England. But the heretical and illegitimate Elizabeth looked less alarming to Philip than the prospect of his Valois rivals gaining control of both sides of the Channel and cutting the sea route between Spain and the Netherlands, and he therefore offered to assist Elizabeth against French aggression.

Elizabeth inherited essentially the same predicament that had faced Edward VI ten years earlier: a weakened economy, a people divided in religion, and the threat of French invasion from Scotland. But two fortuitous developments would give respite to her beleaguered and cash-strapped government. The first was the outbreak of a major rebellion by Scotland's Protestants in 1559, which allowed the queen's chief minister, William Cecil (c.1520–98) – created Lord Burghley in 1571 – to persuade her to send English military assistance to the rebels. With the help of an English fleet and army, Scotland's Protestant nobles and lairds were able to expel the French and to establish a Protestant regime under the Catholic but politically incompetent Mary Queen of Scots. Given that the Protestant party in Scotland was in a minority at this stage, albeit with powerful aristocratic leadership, the outcome might have been very different had not the 'Protestant wind' made its debut by destroying a relief expedition that sailed from France during the winter of 1559–60. Death also intervened in timely fashion for the English and their Scottish allies by carrying off Scotland's formidable regent, Mary of Guise (Mary Queen of Scots' mother), in June 1560. At a stroke, or two, the centuries-old Franco-Scottish alliance had been sundered, to be replaced by an uneasy, indeed sometimes very strained, friendship between England and Scotland based upon a common commitment to Protestantism. The northern marches remained violent and lawless, and the unsettled state of Scottish politics until the mid-1580s would give repeated cause for alarm at Whitehall. But from 1560 the border with Scotland no longer constituted England's vulnerable back door – that role would now be reserved for Ireland.

The second development – the accidental death of Henri II in 1559 and of his sickly heir Francis II a year later – largely explains French impotence at their expulsion from Scotland, and France's descent into a civil war between Catholics and Protestants in 1562. In the space of a few years Europe's most powerful kingdom would implode.

In the two decades that followed Elizabeth's succession in England and the victory of Scotland's Protestants in 1560, the British Reformations would effect the greatest transformation in England's foreign relations since the start of the Hundred Years War in the 1340s. They would make an ally of England's medieval enemies the Scots, and an enemy of its medieval allies the Burgundians. They would make English foreign policy acutely sensitive to public opinion at home, and, astonishingly, to the fate of ordinary (Protestant) men and women abroad. The advancement of the 'Protestant cause' in Europe, and, more specifically, the survival of the Protestant communities in France and the Netherlands, became of vital concern to the Elizabethan government, for as one English diplomat put it in 1568: 'now when the general design is to exterminate all nations dissenting with them [Europe's Catholic powers] in religion . . . what shall become of us, when the like professors with us shall be destroyed in Flanders and France?'[21] What indeed?

The imperial crown

'This realm of England is an empire,' asserted the 1533 Act of Restraint of Appeals, 'and so hath been accepted in the world, governed by one supreme head and king having the dignity and royal estate of the imperial crown of the same.'[22] Henry VIII's claim to 'imperial' dominion – the supreme form of jurisdictional authority – was not without precedent in English history, as the Act itself made clear. But just as Henry's Reformation would help to transform England's relations with its neighbours, so it would lend substance to the imperial pretensions of the Tudor monarchy and magnify the authority of the English state.

Ever since the mid-fourteenth century, the crown had been preoccupied with imperial adventures in France or civil war at home, and had therefore neglected its border regions in Ireland and northern England. While the Plantagenet empire had frayed around the edges, however, at its centre it had grown ever stronger. Lowland England, its cloth industry nurtured by easy access to the rich markets of Flanders, had become more prosperous and heavily populated than anywhere in the British Isles. Here was a power base – a dynamic economy and a lucrative source of taxes – from which the 'new monarchy' of the early Tudors might extend royal authority over all of Ireland and perhaps northward into Lowland Scotland. Yet for the first fifty years of Tudor rule there had been no interest in such a project. The lure of conquests in France remained strong, and the crown's policy towards its borderlands had been poorly funded and short-sighted. It was not until the 1530s, and the need to enforce obedience to the new religious order, as formulated in London, that the crown began to make a concerted effort to create a larger, more centralised and more powerful English state within the British Isles.

The legislation of 1533–4 asserting unilateral independence from Rome and the untrammelled power of the English monarchy was the spur for what was apparently a deliberate government drive towards the creation of a sovereign unitary state. The first architect of this restructuring of the Tudor realm had been Thomas Cromwell, using his favoured instrument of policy: parliamentary statute. In 1536 the Reformation Parliament passed an act for dissolving all 'franchises' in England – that is, private lordships where legal jurisdiction was still exercised by noblemen or bishops, rather than crown officials. Then between 1536 and 1543 statutes were passed for integrating Wales and England into one consolidated kingdom. The Principality and the old Welsh marcher lordships were divided up into English-style counties and given parliamentary representation at Westminster; and English common law and administrative structures were introduced throughout Wales so that 'Welsh rudeness would . . . be framed to English civility'.[23] The Tudors' Welsh ancestry made this process of integration easier, as did grants of monastic lands to the native gentry.

The incorporation of Wales was seen as a blueprint for dealing with Ireland. The need to address the Irish situation became urgent in 1534, when Henry VIII's removal of the 9th earl of Kildare as lord deputy sparked a major insurrection under the earl's son and vice-deputy, Lord Offaly. In an ominous sign for the future, Offaly presented the rebellion as a Catholic crusade against Henrician heresy in the hope of winning support from Charles V (who sent him armaments) and the opponents of the Reformation in England. An English army was required to return the Pale to obedience. Offaly surrendered in August 1535 on assurances that his life would be spared; he was executed at Tyburn in 1537.

The fall of the Kildares cleared the ground for the only viable alternative to government by local magnates: an English-born lord deputy backed by a standing army. The drawback with this policy was the great expense needed to shore up direct rule. And as Henry remained essentially uninterested in investing time and money in Ireland, so English governors there lacked the resources to fill the gap left by the Kildares. The Ulster Gaels exploited this power vacuum in dramatic fashion, launching a massive raid into the Pale in 1539. The one initiative that offered hope of bridling, and perhaps in time Anglicising, the Irish, and at minimum cost to the crown, was that of 'surrender and regrant', whereby Gaelic chiefs agreed to recognise Henry as their sovereign in return for peerages and common-law title to their lands. In effect, they became subjects of the crown. To help speed this process the Irish Parliament – which sat at Dublin when summoned by the king, and was overseen by his royal council in London – passed legislation in

1541, which he subsequently ratified, that silently dropped his feudal title of 'lord of Ireland' and recognised him instead as 'king of Ireland'. The aim was to provide a constitutional platform from which all the peoples of Ireland could be integrated into a single political entity under English law and government. From 1541 therefore the crown became committed to the Anglicisation not just of Dublin and the Pale but the whole of Ireland.

Under Edward VI the policy of surrender and regrant was replaced by a more aggressive approach to Irish reform. The royal army in Ireland quadrupled in size, and a new method of Anglicising Ireland was introduced: the 'plantation', in which English settlers were granted lands confiscated from the native Irish. The idea of plantations was to replace the 'wild Irish' in frontier areas with English colonists, who would supposedly reform and civilise the remaining natives. A start was also made on introducing a staunchly Protestant church settlement. Although Mary restored Catholicism to the kingdom, she pressed ahead with the plantation programme, setting a policy trend that would poison relations between the various communities in Ireland for generations to come.[24]

The Reformation thus gave new edge to the crown's imperial appetite, although with very mixed results. English law was extended to the Irish and the Welsh, and Wales was effectively 'jointed into' the English state. But efforts at greater centralisation in the northern marches of England foundered for lack of money and government interest, and the region descended into even greater violence and disorder. And although central authority in Ireland was gradually strengthened – a standing army saw to that – it was at a high cost in terms of cash and native good will. Moreover, the enforcement of Protestantism would heighten ethnic and political divisions in Ireland, where it was perceived by the Gaels and Old English as a form of cultural imperialism. Protestantism was at once an impetus and an obstacle to the subjugating of all Ireland.

The incorporation of Wales and direct rule in Ireland were part of a general upgrading of English monarchical power following the break with Rome. The royal supremacy stretched the concept of personal, or 'imperial', monarchy to its limits. The theory that a sovereign state was an 'empire' had been developed most articulately by French royal lawyers in the Middle Ages, and meant that kings who ruled such states recognised no superior except God. All secular power in their realm came from God and through the monarch. In the sixteenth century, therefore, the terms 'empire' and 'imperial' more often referred to the kind of power a ruler exercised rather than the territories over which they exercised it. Most European kings claimed imperial authority, and they signified this status by their adoption of a 'closed crown' – that is, a crown surmounted by two or more intersecting arches of gold – rather than the simply decorated circlet of gold, or 'open crown', familiar from portraits of early medieval kings. The Reformation, however, allowed Henry VIII to do more than simply employ the outward symbols of imperial status. By breaking with Rome he could formally annex to himself the theocratic powers that had long been associated with imperial kingship, and become, as one of his noblemen put it, 'absolute both as Emperor and Pope in his own kingdom'.[25] His reign therefore marked the height of personal monarchy in England, and added considerably to the ideological buttresses that his father had built against rebellion – particularly of the king-deposing kind that had marked the Wars of the Roses.

Yet in investing himself with greater power, Henry simultaneously encouraged the growth of bureaucratic government. The very expansion of royal authority and revenues from the 1530s obliged him to lean more heavily on skilled administrators such as Cromwell and, above all, upon Parliament. Although Henry preferred to rely on his 'imperial' prerogative wherever possible, he recognised that only parliamentary statute was powerful enough to make the break with Rome binding. 'All other knottes being losse [loose] and slippery,' he wrote, 'this knott of acte and statute is by authorite therof permanent and durable.'[26] Statute had long been regarded as the ultimate legal form of authority in England. But the legislation passed by the Reformation Parliament established the novel principle that statute could address doctrinal as well as temporal matters.

The new omnicompetence of statute raised Parliament's standing in the eyes of the nation. Indeed, a powerful body of opinion held that Parliament had not merely 'declared' the royal supremacy – as Henry and later Elizabeth maintained – but created it, and that any major changes in the doctrine or the discipline of the Church depended on parliamentary assent for their validity. Disagreement over whether the law-making authority was vested ultimately in the king-in-Parliament or the monarch alone would become a major source of tension in English politics for the next 150 years. The considerable increase in the number of Commons-men who sat in each Parliament during the sixteenth century, from 296 to 462 (the vast majority of them members of the gentry by 1600), certainly lent credibility to the 'forward' view of Elizabethan Parliaments as a representative council for the debate of royal policy, rather than simply an instrument of regal power. But regardless of such views, Parliament remained a transient institution, called and dissolved at the monarch's whim (or, more precisely, in response to the monarch's financial needs), possessing no executive powers, and unable to enact a single law without royal consent.

Effective management of the Commons by the Tudor monarchs ensured that they never lost control of a Parliament. The main challenge to personal monarchy during the sixteenth century came not from Lords or Commons but from the court. The heart of royal government was usually located from the early 1530s in Wolsey's old residence York Place, soon renamed Whitehall. This sprawling complex of buildings on the north bank of the Thames replaced the nearby medieval Palace of Westminster as the principal royal residence. The political crises of the mid-1530s resulted in an overhaul of the king's council, and by 1541 it had acquired a new meeting-chamber in the king's private apartments in Whitehall, and a smaller, more formal membership comprising the main officers of state. It would also acquire a new name, the privy council, and would form the crown's principal executive agency – in effect a proto-cabinet – until 1640. Henry's VIII's preference for taking advice informally, from trusted intimates, ensured that the privy chamber more than matched the fledgling privy council in political influence. But this dual-centred structure of court politics collapsed following the accession of Mary. The gentlewomen who staffed the privy chamber under Mary and Elizabeth were largely excluded by their sex from political affairs, leaving the council chamber to become the undisputed centre of national politics and government.

But no amount of administrative reform or creative restructuring of royal authority could overcome the fundamental constraint upon the Tudor imperial crown: a relative lack of resources. The Henrician Reformation left England ringed by Catholic states who, in the case of France and the Habsburg empire, were many times more powerful. Attempting to keep on level military terms with either was impossible. By the 1540s the growing cost of warfare was beginning to outstrip Parliament's willingness to fund increases in military expenditure. Customs duties, one of the crown's greatest sources of revenue, were vulnerable to the vagaries of international politics – all the more so as Europe divided into warring religious camps. And, as we have seen, the proceeds from the sale of monastic lands had largely been squandered in reckless wars during the 1540s. Moreover, all these revenue sources had been hit by the marked rise in inflation that had begun during Henry's reign – a process driven partly by the rapid growth in England's population in the century after 1520. Neither Henry's greed for international glory, nor the spoils of the Dissolution, could disguise the fact that England remained a second-rate power.

The Word

If Elizabeth and her councillors feared for the survival of Protestantism abroad it was partly because they were conscious of how weak a plant it remained at home. In marked contrast to the sociable ritualism and oral traditions of medieval Catholicism, Protestantism was an introspective, intellectually demanding religion that stressed the doctrine of salvation through a God-given faith, supported by reading the Bible. Because it was so much a religion of the preached and printed word, it struggled to put down roots beyond its urban seedbeds, for among the rural poor, who made up much of the English population, literacy rates were low. Sir Thomas More had estimated in 1533 that 60 per cent of the population was illiterate, and that was probably an optimistic assessment.

To the extent that a return to Protestantism was a viable political option for Elizabeth at the start of her reign in 1558, it owed much to the tradition of translating the Bible into the vernacular that had begun under her father, Henry VIII. As we have seen, the pre-Reformation church authorities had banned all versions of the Bible in English, leaving the clergy's standard Latin translation as the only authorised edition. To read or hear the Bible in English involved using an inaccurate manuscript translation made by the Lollards, the mere possession of which had been evidence of heresy. In 1530 the bishops had discussed the idea of an English translation of the Bible, but had rejected it on the grounds that access to the Scriptures would encourage people to form their own religious opinions and would thus nurture heresy. It was this want of God's Word that persuaded the Gloucestershire scholar and evangelical William Tyndale (c. 1494–1536) to make and print an English translation of the New Testament from the original Greek. He was inspired in this task by Erasmus, who believed that the Scriptures should be freely available to everyone in their own language. Tyndale believed more strongly than most reformers that the Bible should come first in determining the Church's doctrine and ceremonies.

The urge to bring the Bible to the people had been a defining mark of the evangelicals, and was not felt by Henry VIII until the late 1530s, and then only fleetingly. Tyndale had to leave England for Lutheran Germany in order to complete his translation and have it published. The first copies of his English New Testament – printed in a handy pocket-size edition – were smuggled into England in 1526 and circulated widely. For the first time the English people had easy access to the Gospel, and could read and interpret it for themselves. The Church's monopoly on the Word was broken.

Tyndale's New Testament was more than just a religious phenomenon; it transformed the way English was spoken and written. Tyndale had the literary skills to convey the music as well as the meaning of the Scriptures. His prose style was homespun yet numinous, simple yet profound. The King James or 'Authorized' version of the Bible, published in the early years of the seventeenth century, would largely be Tyndale in fancier clothing, and retained many of his phrases: 'the spirit is willing'; 'a law unto themselves'; 'gave up the ghost'; 'fight the good fight'; 'the powers that be'. If any individual can be credited with enriching the expressive qualities of the English language to the level reached by Shakespeare's day it is William Tyndale. There is some truth in the remark that 'without Tyndale, no Shakespeare', although Shakespeare himself probably used the more trenchantly Protestant Genevan Bible.[27] The translation of the Common Prayer Book and the Bible into Welsh during Elizabeth's reign helped to win the Welsh for Protestantism. But the New Testament and prayer book were not translated into Gaelic Irish until the early seventeenth century, by which time, as we shall see, it was too late.

Tyndale's Bible, Cranmer's *Book of Common Prayer* and Foxe's stridently anti-Catholic *Acts and Monuments* were fundamental in shaping English Protestant identity. Yet they represented merely the peaks in a vast range of works of instruction and controversy that was thrown up during England's 'long' Reformation. The several and conflicting Tudor religious settlements provided a massive stimulus to the publishing industry as first the crown and then various court-backed interests, both Catholic and Protestant, used print and scribal publications to mobilise public opinion in the name of 'true religion' and the common good (the two were deemed inseparable). An unintended consequence of this playing to the gallery – one that was deplored as seditious and divisive by its very practitioners – was a dramatic widening of the discursive space in English society, or what has been termed the 'public sphere'. Moreover, the huge redistribution of land and wealth from Church and crown to the private sector following the Dissolution ensured that the productions on this stage played to an increasingly prosperous and attentive audience.

There were few greater causes of controversy in word and print than Elizabeth I's idiosyncratic piety (the palimpsest of modern-day Anglicanism). Unlike most Protestants, the queen preferred to have ritual and the sacraments at the centre of public worship rather than 'painful' preaching of the Word, and this religious conservatism was reflected in the church settlement that her first Parliament (skilfully purged of its Catholic bishops) enacted in 1559. The royal supremacy in religion was reinstated, and much of the ceremony enjoined in the Edwardian prayer books and canons was retained, along with episcopacy: the Church's government by crown-appointed bishops. This eccentric synthesis was created with one eye on winning approval from Protestant states on the Continent, and was a kind of halfway house between Catholicism and the more rigorous and systematic Protestantism of 'the Reformed': the second-generation Protestants who were now at the cutting edge of the Reformation in Europe. Elizabeth had mixed feelings about these advanced Protestants and their battle against the forces, spiritual and military, of the Counter-Reformation: the great movement of Catholic revival that the papacy had initiated in the mid-1540s. In general, she did not share their visceral hatred of 'popery', which was fast becoming the most highly charged word in the English language. Broadly speaking, popery signified the threat that Catholicism posed to the political and scriptural integrity of Protestantism at home and abroad. Elizabeth, however, worried little about foreign Catholics as such, nor about her own 'popish' subjects. Provided they conformed outwardly she was content to let them believe what they liked.

The most strident opposition to the Elizabethan settlement – this 'leaden mediocrity' as one of her own bishops called it[28] – came not from religious conservatives but from those eager for 'further reformation'. Some of the more devout Protestants had gone into exile under Mary and had experienced at first hand the 'purer', Reformed Protestantism that was beginning to find a spiritual leader in the influential Genevan theologian Jean Calvin (1509–64). Yet while the Elizabethan Church adopted a recognisably Reformed theology – given the generic name of Calvinism – its liturgy and government remained fossilised in their Edwardian form and were regarded by the hotter sort of Protestants as unwarrantable in Scripture and therefore as vestiges of popery. The Elizabethan Book of Common Prayer, declaimed one leading Protestant polemicist, was 'culled and picked out of that popishe dunghill, the Masse', while episcopacy was 'drawne out of the Popes shop . . . Antichristian and devillishe, and contrarye to the scriptures'.[29] Those committed to purging the Church of these Romish 'superstitions' formed a small but vociferous minority, with powerful friends at court. Their shrill denunciations of what to many people seemed harmless customs earned them the derogatory nickname 'Puritans'. Using Parliament and print the Puritans – or 'the godly', as they called them-selves – tried to pressure Elizabeth into further church reform and to pursue a more militantly anti-Catholic foreign policy. A defining feature of Puritanism was the belief that the Church of England was merely one part of a pan-European Calvinist community, the Reformed Church, and should therefore be – as should Elizabeth – attuned to the needs of the Protestant cause. Puritans also subscribed to the very unappealing doctrine (certainly to modern eyes) that God had predestined the vast majority of mankind to eternal damnation, reserving Heaven for the remnant – the 'elect' – that He had decided to save solely through His own inexplicable mercy. All good Calvinists believed in predestination. But what marked out Puritans was their hunger for assurance that they were among the elect, which they satisfied, in part at least, by seeking out the society of the godly and shunning the ungodly. This, again, did not make them very popular. Nevertheless, as Protestantism gradually became bound up with the nation's identity, the Puritans' zeal in the fight against popery gave them the look of over-ardent patriots, and, as such, their message on political issues – national security, for example – carried wide appeal.

The calculated mediocrity of the Elizabethan religious settlement was in stark contrast to the thoroughgoing Calvinist Reformation effected north of the border. Protestantism triumphed in Scotland – as its king from 1567, James VI (1566–1625), would lament – by 'populaire tumulte and rebellion and not proceeding from the princes ordare as it did in Englande'.[30] Slowly but surely after 1560, the majority of Scots were indoctrinated in Calvinist Protestantism and its austere form of church worship. Moreover, the reformers were gradually able to intro-duce Presbyterianism in Lowland Scotland – that is, a hierarchy of clerical governing assemblies, or presbyteries, modelled along Genevan lines. This system of church government limited royal control in matters of religion. Scottish Presbyterians also fostered the idea that Kirk and crown were completely separate jurisdictions, and that the Kirk had the power to discipline the monarch on religious matters. It is not surprising, therefore, that when a pro-Presbyterian group emerged among the English Puritans in the 1570s in opposition to episcopacy, it was suppressed. Yet in spite of the different church structures and national identities that prevailed in England and Scotland, the Elizabethan period saw the emergence of a 'British' Protestant culture based on a sense of shared destiny in the struggle against popery. The Scots did much to encourage this religious bond between the two nations by using English rather than their own language in the devotional literature that circulated between the Protestants of both kingdoms. This linguistic convergence, and the spread of Protestantism among the powerful Clan Campbell and its allies in the western Highlands, helped to widen the already growing cultural divide between the Gaels of Scotland and Ireland.

The Reformation pulled England into, or at least towards, the Calvinist communities on the Continent while at the same time distancing it from Catholic Europe and its cultural fashions. It is telling that although the sale of monastic lands fuelled a building craze among the nobility and gentry that was unprecedented in English history, none of the great houses built between 1560 and 1620 comprehensively applied the neoclassical designs favoured on the Continent. Most of these buildings mingled Gothic, Renaissance and vernacular motifs in an exuberant architectural cacophony. Royal portraiture by the 1590s, with its two-dimensional, almost surrealistic appearance, and encoded propaganda messages in adoration of the Virgin Queen, reveals much the same sense of self-imposed isolation from the fashionable neoclas-sicism of Catholic Europe.

Nowhere was the Reformation's cultural impact felt more deeply than in English church life. The state-sponsored iconoclasm that had begun in the 1530s, and intensified under Edward VI, would continue during the early years of Elizabeth's reign, destroying the rich visual culture of medieval religion. The decorative and devotional art that had once adorned parish churches was replaced by whitewash and biblical texts – paintings and statues giving way to the Word. The first generation of English Protestants had tolerated images in a good cause. Early English bibles, for example, had been copiously illustrated. But the continued use of devotional imagery by Catholics, in the context of the ever-deepening religious divide in Europe, convinced many Elizabethan Protestants that all religious pictures were popish and 'lewd'. The mere hankering after such things, declared the Church of England's homilies, was 'the beginning of whoredom'.[31] By the end of the sixteenth century the material fabric of worship had been reduced to tatters. Having travelled around the country for three months in 1593, the writer Phillip Stubbes claimed that he had found 'in most places, (nay almost in all) the Churches to lye like barnes . . . the windowes all to torne, the wals cleft and rent asunder, the roofes rayning in without measure, and the chauncels . . . eyther pulled quite downe . . . or else ready to fall uppon their heads every day'.[32] One early seventeenth-century survey of parish churches would record mournfully that 'a little small silver chalice, a beaten-out pulpit-cushion, an ore-worne Communion-cloth and a course Surplice: these are all the riches and ornaments of the most of our Churches'.[33]

The Reformation had a particularly devastating effect on church music. The intricate, polyphonic liturgical music of the pre-Reformation Church, which had been admired throughout Europe, all but disappeared from English parishes from the mid-sixteenth century, although it survived in much of its old glory in the cathedrals and the Chapel Royal. Singing of the psalms was the only concession to religious music that most reformers would make, and even then the melody must be subservient to the Word: 'that the same may be as plainly understanded as if it were read without singing'.[34] At least with the singing of the psalms the whole congregation was encouraged to participate. Before the Reformation any singing in the service had been confined to the clergy and choristers.

The reformers' attack upon 'carnal' practices extended well beyond the trappings of formal worship. Corpus Christi plays, St George processions, May games, and a whole host of ceremonial and festive activities that traditional religion had sustained or at least tolerated, either petered out in many places during the reigns of Edward and Elizabeth or were suppressed. It was nostalgia for this vanished world of good cheer that gave rise to the myth of Merry England. All in all, the Reformation left a void at the heart of the English religious and social experience that Protestantism at first found very hard to fill. Beer (like traditional English ale but brewed with hops) and alehouse sociability may have helped plug the gap in some measure. It was said in the 1540s that beer, a 'naturall drynke for a Dutche man', was 'of late . . . moche used in Englande to the detryment of many Englysshe men'.[35]

Yet the triumph of the Word was by no means a total cultural disaster. The Protestant assault on religious art served to channel talent and patronage into more reformer-friendly media, helping to stimulate an artistic renaissance under Elizabeth in which literature held centre stage. Having dropped the curtain on the old religious plays, the reformers eagerly co-opted drama to promote the new religion. Elizabeth and several of her courtiers patronised troupes of players that toured the country during the 1560s spreading the Protestant message. However, as plays became more secular in content during the 1570s, and began competing with sermons and prayer for people's leisure time, so they too became a target for the godly. 'Wyll not a fylthye playe, wyth the blaste of a Trumpette, sooner call thyther a thousande, than an houres tolling of a Bell bring to the Sermon a hundred?', fulminated one godly minister: '. . . I will not here enter this disputatio[n], whether it be utterly unlawfull to have any playes, but will onelye ioyne in this issue, whether in a Christia[n] common wealth they be tolerable on the Lords day, when the people should be exercised in hearing of the worde'.[36] Puritan preachers warned that 'the cause of plagues is sinne, if you looke to it well: and the cause of sinne are playes: therefore the cause of plagues are playes'.[37] This providentialist syllogism might convince London's godly governors, but not the entertainment-hungry court – the show would most definitely go on. In 1576, a hundred years after William Caxton had set up his printing press in Westminster, the London businessman James Burbage built the first commercial play-house: The Theatre, in Shoreditch. Other playhouses soon followed, most of them in London's suburbs, the city council having banned theatres from the capital itself. Denounced by the Puritans as 'a shew place of al beastly & filthie matters', the early theatre was a bit like horse-racing today – slightly downmarket, but a major crowd-pleaser that attracted everyone from lords to labourers.[38] It would not be until the 1620s that plays became respectable literature.

The 1580s through to the 1620s were the golden age of English drama. Settling in London gave the acting companies a huge target audience, for the capital's population had soared to 200,000 by 1600, putting it among the five largest cities in Europe. Playing to the same crowd, however, and competing with other companies, required a constant stream of new and exciting productions to keep the punters happy. This artistic and commercial challenge was answered in particu-larly innovative fashion by Christopher Marlowe (1564–93) and his followers Thomas Kyd (1558–94) and Shakespeare (1564–1616). They broke new literary ground for lesser playwrights, blending classical themes and medieval theatrical forms into something rich and strange. By the 1590s, drama had transcended its traditional, moralistic remit to explore imaginary new worlds, rewrite the nation's history, stir patriotic feeling, and, controversially, to offer thinly veiled political commentary. 'Playing' gave voice to the angst of sixty years of religious turmoil, and a new vocabulary in which to express it. Shakespeare and his competitors and collaborators (Elizabethan and Jacobean plays were often joint efforts) coined many of the thirty thousand new words that entered the English language between 1570 and 1630 – more than in any period before or since. The theatre also challenged foreign perceptions of England as a cultural wasteland, which the Reformation had undoubtedly reinforced. 'Playing', claimed the playwright Thomas Heywood, 'is an ornament to the City, which strangers of all nations, repairing hither, report of in their countries, beholding them here with some admiration.'[39] The coming of the Word, for which Tyndale had been burned at the stake in 1536, had spawned an entertainment industry in which the godless Marlowe could declare: 'I count religion but a childish toy, And hold there is no sin but ignorance.'[40]

Outrageous piracies

The London theatre was not all that foreigners admired about the Elizabethans. In the early 1590s, the Italian political philosopher Giovanni Botero described the English as 'marvellous expert in maritime actions, then whom at sea there is not a valianter and bolder nation under heaven. For in most swift ships, excellent well furnished with ordnance (wherewith the kingdome aboundeth) they goe to sea with as good courage in winter as in sommer, all is one with them . . . Two of their Captaines [Sir Francis Drake and Sir Thomas Cavendish] have sayled round about the world, with no lesse courage then glorie.'[41] Seadogs such as Drake and Cavendish, and their exploits against the Spanish, would convince future generations of English people that it was somehow their God-given right to rule the waves. But in the 1580s this was a very novel feeling indeed. Until the 1560s, English mariners had rarely ventured beyond their coastal waters, and knew little about deep-sea navigation. Meanwhile, of course, the Spanish had been establishing colonies around the world; their ships plying back and forth across the Atlantic, crammed on the homeward journey with bullion from the silver mines of Potosí, in Peru. What changed in the 1560s, above all, was a shift in English relations with the French, or at least with that large Calvinist minority in France known as the Huguenots.

England's ancestral enemies had become endangered fellow Protestants. With technical assistance and encouragement from the Huguenots, the English would take to the high seas in increasing numbers from the 1560s, and turn Protestant piracy into a global enterprise.

England was already a formidable naval power by the time the Huguenots had appeared on the horizon. One of Henry VIII's more sensible reactions to the isolated and precarious position he had found himself in after breaking with Rome had been to build up the royal fleet from seven warships to almost fifty. English shipwrights, borrowing heavily from the Portuguese, the Scottish and other naval innovators, had developed the 'sailing-galley', or galleon, carrying heavy cannon firing through gun ports. But no navy could operate long-term without a complex infrastructure of dockyards, storehouses, victualling industries and administrative machinery. And here too the legacy of the Henrician Reformation had been beneficial, for by leaving England at odds with her Catholic neighbours it had created a powerful incentive for sustained investment in the navy and its onshore facilities as a front-line defence against foreign aggression. This is why Henry's navy had not simply withered away after his death as Henry V's had done a century earlier.

The need for economies after the military overspend of the 1540s had inevitably led to some streamlining of the navy, but Elizabeth was still left with what for the time was an exceptionally well-managed and well-maintained battle fleet of about thirty sail. Most of these warships had been specially built or adapted by the 1580s to fight more as gun platforms than by the traditional methods of grappling and boarding. Smaller than the high-castled galleons of the Spanish and Portuguese, they were also faster, more manoeuvrable and carried heavier guns. They were the best fighting ships of any European navy, provided they stuck to what they had been designed for: defending home waters. On long ocean voyages, where durability and a capacious hold for storing supplies mattered more than speed and firepower, the advantage lay with their lumbering Iberian rivals.

Alongside, and overlapping with, the Elizabethan navy was a pack of pirate and 'trading' vessels that operated mainly out of the West Country ports. Royal experiments with 'reprisals by general proclamation' – in other words, privateering – in 1544, 1557 and 1563 had revitalised the centuries-old pirate trade in the Channel. At the same time, a few of the more intrepid English freebooters had begun to challenge Spanish and Portuguese claims to exclusive dominion over

Africa and the Americas by raiding or trading with the scattered and often poorly defended Iberian colonies. One of the most successful of these interlopers was England's first Atlantic slave-trader, the Devon sea captain Sir John Hawkins (1532–95), whose investors included Elizabeth herself.

By the 1550s there was a growing identification between Protestantism, piracy and deep-sea trading ventures. But it was the arrival of Huguenot privateers, driven to England during the 1560s by Catholic victories in France, that turned English seamen into warriors for the Protestant cause. As early as 1564, Cecil was privately expressing concern to his court colleagues at what he termed 'this matter of resort of pyratts, or if you will so call them, our adventurers, that dayly robb the Spaniards and Flemings'.[42] But the English government had never been very sensitive to such goings-on in the Channel, and – as Cecil's words suggest – there were some at court who were inclined to regard pirates more as anti-Catholic 'adventurers'. With tacit licence from the authorities, a joint English–Huguenot fleet, sailing under French letters of marque (an official licence to act as a privateer), was operating out of ports along the south coast by the late 1560s, preying upon ships of all nations, but especially those of Spain. Scottish and Dutch privateers, many of them Calvinists, also joined this unofficial war. For the English crews involved, piety and piracy ran in happy congruence: 'we cold not do God better service than to spoyl the Spaniard both of lyfe and goodes'.[43] Attacks on foreign merchant vessels in the crowded waters off southern England grew so frequent that the English themselves were forced to admit that 'wee . . . are moste infamous for our outeragious, common, and daily piracies'.[44]

Not content with plundering Spanish shipping in European waters, Huguenot privateers had crossed the Atlantic in the 1550s and 1560s to attack Spanish settlements in the Caribbean. Inspired by the Huguenots' example, and drawing on their maritime experience, the English followed in their wake – the indomitable Hawkins and his protégé Francis Drake (1540–96) at the helm. The luckier or bolder pirates like Drake won fame and fortune seizing Spanish treasure ships and raiding the Spanish Main. Their daring escapades caught the public's imagination, and inspired more and more gentlemen and merchants to follow Drake's example. But it was Huguenot navigators who had helped steer Drake and his like to their targets across the Atlantic, and it was Huguenot and other foreign mapmakers who taught the English to become expert cartographers themselves. Without this

French connection it is doubtful whether English seapower would have spread beyond European waters as rapidly as it did.

But Protestantism and piracy would account only in part for the dramatic increase in English seafaring ventures during the second half of the sixteenth century. At least as important was the relative stagnation after 1550 of English cloth exports, which had made up the bulk of England's trade with Europe since medieval times. Time-honoured trading patterns were then disrupted after the Spanish laid an embargo on English imports into Antwerp – the main entrepôt for English cloth – in 1563–5 in response to English acts of piracy in the Channel. Further obstacles to peaceful trade with the Low Countries were raised in the mid-1560s, as Philip II's authoritarian and anti-Protestant policies – exacerbated by the impact of bad harvests and the activities of Calvinist provocateurs – plunged the Netherlands into rebellion. For the next eighty years or so the Spanish crown would pour troops and colonial treasure into the Low Countries in an effort to reconquer its Burgundian inheritance.

Commercial and political dislocation in the Low Countries encouraged a more venturous spirit among England's merchants. Numerous trading companies were set up during the second half of the sixteenth century to open new trade routes to the Baltic, Africa and the Mediterranean. These 'new' merchants concentrated not on cloth exports but on luxury imports, which in the case of those who traded in the Mediterranean required the development of a new kind of heavily armed merchant vessel to ward off the attentions of Barbary corsairs and other pirates. The struggle for commercial supremacy in the Mediterranean during the later sixteenth century would provide much of the know-how and capital needed to extend England's maritime trading network into the Indian Ocean in the early seventeenth century (see chapter 7).

England's trade with Spain also boomed during Elizabeth's reign, despite the growing tension between the two countries and the danger posed to English traders and seamen by the Inquisition. The example of William Bet, an English ship's carpenter who was burned alive by the Inquisition simply for failing to take off his hat or kneel when a procession bearing the Host (the bread consecrated during the Mass) passed by, was not unique. Undeterred by the occasional victimisation of Protestant traders in Iberian ports, some English merchants defied their own government's injunctions and sold heavy ordnance to the Spanish. Then, as now, England was a leading player in the arms industry, or at least in one vital sector of it: the manufacture of cannon. The relative ease and cheapness of acquiring heavy guns in England compared with the rest of Europe helps to explain the unusual willingness of English ships, however small, to give battle, and the English propensity to steal colonial goods from others rather than go to the trouble of establishing colonies of their own.

The prodigies of skill and courage performed by England's seafarers during the first half of Elizabeth's reign owed little to direct government action. Indeed, it was largely the queen's failure to take a lead in advancing the Protestant cause in Europe or the New World that drew in Huguenots, pirates and merchants to fill the void. The Elizabethan government's fitful involvement in resisting the might of the Spanish empire before the 1580s was entirely understandable. The fearsome Spanish *tercios* (massed infantry formations) were the Roman legions of their day, and Philip II a new Augustus. His annual income from New World silver and taxation at home was at least ten times that of Elizabeth. Moreover, England's traditional commercial ties with the Low Countries, and its growing trade with Spain itself, meant there were sound economic reasons for staying on good terms with Philip and eschewing a militantly anti-Habsburg foreign policy. Philip too was generally anxious to avoid conflict. He gave serious consideration to regime change in England on several occasions between 1559 and the 1580s, but he usually had more pressing demands on his time and money than dealing with what he regarded as a divided and unstable country. Besides, all he or any other Catholic had to do was to wait for England's spinster queen to die and for Mary Queen of Scots to succeed her.

Elizabeth's desire to avoid war with Spain did not mean that she was willing to concede the claims of the Spanish and Portuguese to exclusive dominion in the New World. To make this point clear, as well as make money for the crown, she invested in the kind of buccaneering-cum-business ventures that Drake and Hawkins went in for. These 'trading' expeditions cost her very little, and yet could prove hugely profitable. Even better, as ostensibly private initiatives they allowed Elizabeth to 'dysavowe', as she put it, her subjects' piratical proceedings – what we today would call plausible deniability. Except, of course, that Philip II found such denials anything but plausible.

The most famous Elizabethan maritime venture, and a striking illustration of advances in English seamanship, was Drake's circumnavigation of the globe in 1577–80. Only one ship had achieved this feat before, that of the Portuguese explorer Ferdinand Magellan in 1519–22, and he himself had been killed during the voyage. When Drake's flagship, the *Golden Hind*, dropped anchor back at Plymouth it contained a fortune in Spanish booty. The queen's share alone amounted to £300,000, which was more than the crown's entire annual income. The implications of Drake's voyage for the security of Spain's empire greatly alarmed Philip II and, for that reason, some of Elizabeth's councillors as well. They refused to accept Drake's presents, and tried to persuade Elizabeth to have his treasure returned to the Spanish. But she could not resist such a huge windfall. And nor could she resist flaunting her victory over Philip – knighting Drake in 1581, for example, and wearing plundered Spanish jewellery in full view of Philip's ambassador.

An obvious strategy for challenging the power of Spain in the New World and in Europe was to copy the example of the Conquistadores. English buccaneers, like their Huguenot role models, dreamed of founding colonies that might vie with Spain for the wealth of the Indies. It was the king of Spain's 'Indian Golde', warned Sir Walter Ralegh, 'that indaungereth and disturbeth all the nations of Europe, it purchaseth intelligence, creepeth into Councels, and setteth bound loyalty at libertie, in the greatest Monarchies of Europe'.[45] Until the English themselves embarked upon colonial enterprises, thought Ralegh, the Spanish colossus could not be checked.

In fact, the English state was too weak before the 1640s – and the Spanish too strong – to maintain any considerable military presence in the Caribbean for very long. The penny-pinching Elizabeth was certainly not interested in such a scheme, even supposing she could afford one. She did not want open war with Philip in the New World any more than in the Old. It was left to private enterprise to plant England's first settlement in North America: Ralegh's would-be privateering base on Roanoke Island, in modern-day North Carolina, close to Spanish shipping lanes from the Caribbean. Two expeditions – one in 1585, the other in 1587 – deposited a small number of colonists there, but fighting the Spanish closer to home hampered preparations to supply the colony, and when a ship finally returned to the island, in 1590, the colonists had vanished without trace.

The Elizabethan age would end with an empire nowhere. The privateering war that ruined the Spanish merchant fleet for centuries to come would increase the range and scale of English overseas commerce beyond all recognition. But though it also produced a cadre of ocean-going explorers and would-be colonisers, the only evidence of their activities by 1600 was a scattering of bones and deserted outposts along the western Atlantic seaboard.

The world is not enough

'Assuredlie, there was never heard or knowen of so greate preparac[i] on as the kinge of Spaigne hathe & dailie maketh readie for the invasyon of Englande.'[46] So wrote a triumphant Drake after he had plundered and burned over two dozen ships in the Spanish naval base of Cadiz in April 1587. The recipient of Drake's letter, William Cecil (now Lord Burghley), probably thought this warning a bit rich coming from a man whose repeated attacks upon Spain and its colonies were largely responsible for these ominous preparations in the first place. Despite the confidence of Drake that he and his fellow seadogs were more than a match for the Spanish, the fact that Philip II even contemplated the *Empresa de Inglaterra* – 'the enterprise of England' – was a foreign-relations catastrophe for the Elizabethan government. How was it that the English, with still painful memories of the hardships and dangers they had faced in fighting the French in the 1540s, were again under threat of invasion from a continental superpower?

As we have seen, relations between England and Spain had often been strained since Henry VIII's break with Rome, but they deteriorated markedly during the 1560s. Fear of France, the force that had pushed the two countries together since medieval times, had subsided after 1562 as French Catholics and Protestants had fallen to killing each other rather than annoying their neighbours. English piracy in the Channel, and Spanish embargoes on English trade with Antwerp, had weakened the two countries' common commercial interests. But tension between them would increase dramatically from 1567 with the arrival in the Low Countries of Philip II's ruthless military commander the duke of Alba at the head of ten thousand veteran troops – reinforced by 30,000 German and Italian levies – with orders to crush the rebellion there by whatever means necessary. It was hardly in Protestant England's interest to have a Catholic army stationed just across the Narrow Seas, less than 200 miles from London, or to stand idly by while it destroyed Protestantism in the Low Countries. The Catholic threat was magnified by reports of anti-Protestant atrocities on the Continent, and particularly the St Bartholomew's Day massacre of 1572, when Catholic mobs in Paris and other French cities butchered thousands of Huguenot men, women and children. The queen's conservative political instincts recoiled at the idea of assisting Calvinist rebels against their rightful prince, but even she could see the necessity of sending money and troops to support the Protestant rebellions in the Netherlands and France, although she did so grudgingly and as covertly as possible. She also tried to forge alliances with the Protestant princes of northern Germany and Scandinavia.

It was in this context of war for Protestant survival and Spanish hegemony on the Continent that Elizabeth gave tacit protection to Huguenot privateers and rebels from the Low Countries, and that Philip, in turn, began giving surreptitious aid to Catholic conspiracies against her throne and life. By 1570 a state of cold war could be said to have existed between England and Spain. It was always likely that Philip's devout Catholicism and the equally zealous Protestantism of some of Elizabeth's councillors would strain Anglo-Spanish relations. Paradoxically, however, it was the weakness of English Protestantism rather than its strength that made open war more likely.

The power and unity of the Catholic world were greatly magnified in the minds of English Protestants by their own sense of insecurity. The godly were surrounded and outnumbered by 'cold statute Protestants' and 'church papists' – that is, men and women who attended parish church services, as law required, but had no positive commitment to the new religion. It was not until the 1570s and 1580s, with a rise in the number of university graduates entering the ministry, and sustained effort by Whitehall to remove Catholics from local government and the Church, that Protestantism began to make a decisive impact upon popular piety, at least in lowland England. And even then, much of the old religious sensibility, of fondness for ceremony and communal rites, lingered on and re-formed in attachment to the Book of Common Prayer. Catholicism as an organised religion, which acknowledged the pope as its spiritual head on Earth, had shrunk in most counties into a tiny, gentrified sect by 1600. Among the Protestant majority, however, hatred of popery now vied and overlapped with hatred of foreigners as the English people's defining characteristic. Yet no matter how hard godly ministers tried, they could not persuade most of their parishioners to abandon the pre-Reformation belief in salvation through good neighbourliness, and to accept distinctively Protestant doctrines.

Elizabeth would have calmed Protestant nerves had she heeded the pleas of her councillors and Parliaments and married and produced a son. But Elizabeth did not relish the role of a brood mare. Nor did she want a husband trying to relieve her of the burden of government, as Philip II had very gallantly offered to do at the start of her reign. 'I will have here but one mistress,' she told a would-be consort, 'and no master.'[47]

When she did toy with the idea of marriage she invariably scared her Protestant subjects rather than reassured them. In 1561, for example, she had informed Philip that she would consider restoring links with Rome if he would back her marriage to her favourite, Robert Dudley (1532/3–88), created earl of Leicester in 1564. Nothing came of this proposal. But then in her mid-forties she apparently gave serious consideration to marrying the duke of Anjou, who was the younger brother of the French king Henri III (1551–89), and was possibly the inspiration for the English folk song 'Froggie went a-wooing'. The prospect of having the ambitious and conniving Anjou as king-consort horrified Protestant activists not only in England but also in France and Scotland. They feared that if Elizabeth followed Mary I and married a papist it would be only a matter of time before the court and ultimately the entire kingdom succumbed to popery. In desperation, Leicester and other 'forward' Protestants at court surreptitiously organised a propaganda campaign that effectively forced the queen to abandon whatever marriage plans she may have entertained. But what really terrified Protestants was the prospect of Elizabeth dying (as she had very nearly done in 1562) without an heir, for the person with the best claim to succeed her was her Catholic cousin, Mary Queen of Scots.

The Scottish queen became the focal point for English fears of an anti-Protestant 'holy league', headed by Philip II and Mary's relatives, the powerful Guise family, which dominated France's ultra-Catholic faction.[48] Despite Mary's strong personal commitment to Catholicism she had managed at first to work reasonably well with Scotland's Protestant establishment. But the murder of her husband – the weak and scheming Lord Darnley – in 1567, her marriage to his probable killer the earl of Bothwell, and her evident desire to restore Catholicism and the Franco-Scottish alliance had lost her the support of her Protestant subjects, and in 1568 she had been deposed and fled to England. Kept under house arrest while Elizabeth explored ways of restoring her without endangering the Protestant ascendancy in Scotland, Mary soon became involved in an English court plot to remove the queen's chief councillor, William Cecil, and seek a rapprochement with Spain. When this plot failed, two of Mary's fellow Catholics among England's northern nobility rose in rebellion to put her on the throne and restore the old religion. The Northern Rising of 1569 proved but a faint echo of the Pilgrimage of Grace, however, and quickly collapsed, although it might have attracted greater popular support if the government had not whisked Mary beyond the reach of a rebel rescue party.

Although the events surrounding the Rising would result in the disgrace or execution of her leading supporters at court, Mary continued to dabble in Catholic plots to overthrow Elizabeth. Most of these intrigues interwove schemes for Elizabeth's assassination, an English Catholic uprising, and an invasion of England by the Spanish army in the Netherlands. With Cecil pulling the strings, the English Parliament of 1572 called for Mary's execution, or at least for legislation excluding her from the succession – 'an axe or an acte' as one MP succinctly put it.[49] Another MP charitably wished that Mary might 'have her head cut off and no more harm done to her'.[50] But Elizabeth, with her high sense of the reverence due to anointed sovereigns, angrily forbade any public discussion of Mary's fate or her own dynastic responsibilities.

Plots against Elizabeth's life seemed to confirm Protestant propaganda that England's Catholics took their orders from Rome and Madrid. The pope put his English flock under even greater suspicion from the government in 1570 by issuing a papal bull pronouncing Elizabeth a heretic and usurper and absolving her subjects from allegiance to her. Protestant fears of a Catholic fifth column intensified still further from the mid-1570s as missionary priests and Jesuits began arriving from the Continent to minister to the Catholic community and to work for the reconversion of England. This English Mission produced some of the Counter-Reformation's most effective propagandists, and was seen by men like Cecil as the spiritual vanguard of the Spanish army in the Netherlands. A government crackdown against Catholicism began in the 1570s, and over the next few decades hundreds of priests and their lay abettors would be executed as traitors. Tudor and Stuart England would end up killing more Catholics for their religion than any other European country. Protestant paranoia notwithstanding, the number of professed Catholics was quite small. Furthermore, most of these *dévots* were able to reconcile their religion with their allegiance to the crown. Catholics loudly protested their loyalty even as the Armada sailed up the Channel in 1588; some even offered to fight in the front line against the invaders. But the connection between Catholicism and unEnglishness was too deeply ingrained by this stage. The government ordered the internment of prominent papists, prompting one local official to lock up his own Catholic grandmother.

In trying to exorcise the demon of popery the English effectively conjured it into existence in Ireland. Given Ireland's largely illiterate, Gaelic-speaking population and its poorly funded Church, it was never going to be easy introducing Protestantism there, especially as the crown faced a constant struggle just to defend the Pale, let alone impose its authority on the Gaedhealtacht. Perhaps with more effort and sensitivity the Elizabethan government might have won over enough of Ireland's elite – particularly among the Old English, who accounted themselves true subjects of the crown – to stimulate a grass-roots Reformation. Instead, it prioritised short-term security in promoting English 'civility' – of which Protestantism became the central feature – by force. Elizabeth virtually guaranteed the failure of a political solution in Ireland by farming out Irish affairs to court syndicates composed largely of Protestant hardliners like Cecil and the government spymaster Sir Francis Walsingham (c.1532–90), who tended to see Ireland not as a legally constituted kingdom but as a colony, ripe for exploitation. Their remedy for Ireland's problems was more plantations, more English colonists, and more soldiers to defend them. It was no accident that Ralegh and several others involved in privateering and colonising ventures in the Americas had used Ireland as a test-bed for their money-grubbing and land-grabbing schemes.

The 'New English', as the Elizabethan settlers became known, colonised not only Irish land but also the places in the Dublin administration formerly reserved for the Old English. The effect of this aggressive Anglicisation was to erode some of the historic barriers between the Old English and the Gaelic Irish. Both communities suffered as the crown increasingly equated Catholicism with disaffection and unEnglishness. A wave of rebellions hit Ireland from the late 1560s, unprecedented in the savagery shown by both sides. One notoriously brutal English commander made the Irish who submitted to him walk through 'a lane of heddes' that had been severed from their 'dedde fathers, brothers, children, kinsfolke, and freendes'.[51] Lord Grey, a friend of Walsingham's, admitted that during his two years as lord deputy (1580–2) he had summarily executed almost 1,500 men, and that was 'not accounting . . . killing of churls [Gaelic peasants], which were innumerable'.[52] The draconian methods of Grey and his like were similar to Alba's in the Netherlands, and had much the same effect, transforming specific grievances among the natives into 'faith-and-fatherland' resistance. By the 1590s, Protestantism had become indelibly associated in Irish Catholic eyes with English colonial oppression.

England's Protestant Conquistadores reaped the whirlwind in Ireland, although, typically, they regarded the unfolding tragedy there as further evidence of a Spanish-led design to subjugate all of Christendom. Like their fellow Calvinists on the Continent they were convinced that the Habsburgs and the pope aspired to build a universal tyranny upon the graves of Europe's Protestants. A powerful clique at court – led by Leicester and Walsingham – argued that open war with Spain and her allies was inevitable, and that unless Elizabeth joined with the Dutch and anti-Spanish elements in France in a pre-emptive strike against Philip II, his forces would subdue the Netherlands and then invade England. The decline of France and the growing might of Spain certainly made such counsel sound sensible. Indeed, it may have represented an early formulation of the balance-of-power strategy that would dominate English foreign-policy thinking from the later seventeenth century. But the belief of Leicester and his friends in an international Catholic alliance where none existed (at least formally) before the 1580s, and their ambition for England to champion the Protestant cause, were inspired not by realpolitik but an apocalyptic world-view that saw European politics in terms of a cosmic struggle between Protestantism and the popish Antichrist. Leicester and his like were ideologues, not pragmatists, their political agenda, like that of the pietistical Philip II, driven by religious conviction.

Furthermore, in pressing for full-scale intervention in the Netherlands, the 'forward' party at court was gambling that England had the resources and military capability for a prolonged war against Spain. This was a wager that Elizabeth was very reluctant to make, for besides the costs and dangers of such a strategy she needed convincing that Spain was ultimately more threatening to English interests than France. When the leader of the Netherlands rebels, William of Orange, had concluded an alliance with the French king in 1572 she had even considered sending troops to assist Alba! The queen wanted the Netherlands to regain the semi-autonomous state it had enjoyed under the Emperor Charles V, not to fall under the sway of France.

Was war with Spain inevitable? Certainly the trickle of English volunteers and subventions to the Netherlands rebels, and Elizabeth's connivance in attacks on Spanish shipping and colonies, meant that the risk was always there, especially as she never understood that Philip II put a somewhat different construction on her actions than the one she intended. To her they were warning shots; to him, they were the prelude to an all-out assault upon his dominions – a forgivable mistake, as this was precisely how Leicester and Walsingham preferred to see them as well. Both monarchs, however, were to some extent 'bounced' into war by contingent factors and forces beyond their control. Philip's brilliant new general in the Low Countries, Alessandro Farnese (created duke of Parma in 1586), began to reassert royal authority in the Catholic-dominated provinces of the southern Netherlands from the late 1570s, heightening concern in England that Spanish forces would soon overrun the Protestant provinces in the north. Even more menacing was Philip's conquest of Portugal in 1580 following the extinction of the Portuguese royal line. At a stroke, Spain acquired Portugal's formidable Atlantic fleet and another global empire. A medal struck to commemorate Philip's triumph bore the uncompromising legend *non sufficit orbis*: the world is not enough.

The slide towards war became virtually unstoppable in 1584. With town after town in the Netherlands falling to Farnese's army, the assassination of William of Orange in July 1584 threw the rebels into even greater disarray. In England a majority on the privy council now backed open military intervention to help the Dutch before it was too late. In October 1584, Burghley and Walsingham drew up and disseminated a patriotic 'Bond of Association' by which thousands of loyal Englishmen pledged to hunt down and kill any 'pretended successor' – meaning Mary Queen of Scots – should Elizabeth too be assassinated. The Bond represented the first stage in raising an armed party to fight for a Protestant succession and its supporters at court. It also served as a potent reminder to the vacillating Elizabeth of the strength of Protestant public opinion.[53] Similarly warlike preparations were taking place across the Channel. Having cooperated informally since the mid-1570s, Philip and the Guisards signed a military alliance late in 1584 that not only ended any prospect of Spain's French enemies succouring the Dutch rebels but also threatened France as well as the Netherlands with Spanish domination. The Protestant nightmare of an international Catholic league for what Walsingham believed was 'the ruyne and overthrow of the professours of the Ghospell' had finally become a reality.[54]

The enterprise of England

There was no formal declaration of war between England and Spain. This would be a conflict far removed from the chivalric posturing of Henry VIII's campaigns. Reluctantly, in August 1585, Elizabeth agreed to support the rebels with 7,500 English troops under the command of the earl of Leicester. The long-suffering Philip II had been weighing up the pros and cons of invading England since the early 1570s. Now, faced with Elizabeth's treaty with the rebels, and raids by Drake late in 1585 on the Spanish coast and Indies, he finally made up his mind. Preparations for the *Empresa de Inglaterra*, 'the enterprise of England', went into high gear in February 1587 following the execution of Mary Queen of Scots, which left her Calvinist son James VI of Scotland heir-presumptive to the English throne. Mary had dabbled in one plot too many, giving Walsingham and his agents the chance to arrange her entrapment – her written support for Elizabeth's murder. Under intense pressure from the privy council and Parliament, and convinced that it was a case of kill or be killed, Elizabeth had signed Mary's death warrant, and although she subsequently repudiated the regicide, she had undoubtedly wanted Mary dead. When Philip learnt of Mary's execution he wept for the new Catholic martyr, and then issued a flood of orders to begin assembling the Armada. In the words of his secretary, it was time to put England 'to the torch'.[55]

The question of who would carry that torch into England would prompt perhaps the most fateful decision of the entire Enterprise. Philip could have opted to deploy the Armada in a direct descent on England or Ireland, thereby minimising the time his fleet would be exposed to the elements and to English warships. Instead, he eventually decided on a combined operation. The Armada would sail up the Channel, anchor off Flanders, and then escort Parma's army across to Kent. The advantage of this plan was that it would bring Europe's finest troops to bear on England's ramshackle and ill-prepared land defences; the disadvantage was that it was too complicated, as was only to be expected from an armchair strategist like Philip. His habitual reliance on divine intervention to plug any gaps in his preparations did little to improve the Armada's chances of success, and nor did his choice of the duke of Medina Sidonia to command it. The duke, although a steady man, lacked the initiative or naval experience to depart significantly from his master's inflexible instructions. Nevertheless, the sheer size of the Armada, and the good sailing conditions it enjoyed as it bore down upon England in the summer of 1588, left few in any doubt that the great moment of crisis not only in Elizabeth's reign but also in the fortunes of the Protestant cause throughout Europe had arrived. To the English sailors who first caught sight of the Armada off the Lizard in mid-July 1588, it must have been a daunting sight: about 130 ships spread across the horizon in a crescent formation, carrying almost 19,000 troops, and mounting 138 heavy guns (that is, of 16-pounder calibre or above).

The story of Drake nonchalantly continuing his game of bowls on Plymouth Hoe after receiving news of the enemy's sighting is one of the many fictions that have grown up around the Armada like barnacles on a galleon's hull. Another is that this was a David-and-Goliath contest that the English won against the odds. The fleet that left Plymouth on 20 July to confront the Armada was, in fact, the most powerful in the world. Commanded by Lord Howard of Effingham, it comprised some eighty ships that between them carried 251 heavy guns. Less than half of these vessels belonged to the royal navy, and the rest were provided by port towns, the London merchant companies, and privateer ship-owners such as Leicester and Ralegh. The English ships were faster and handier than the floating fortresses of the Spanish, with crews better practised in standing off and outgunning opponents (although against less formidable opposition than the Armada, such tactics would normally have preceded, rather than replaced, boarding). The one glaring weakness on the English side was that Effingham's captains had no experience of fighting in disciplined formation – in other words, as a fleet – which was the only way to attack the Armada effectively. Drake, for example, abandoned his station after the first day's fighting to do what he knew best – seize a rich Spanish galleon – instead of leading the fleet as he had been ordered. The English made another unwelcome discovery in the heat of battle, which was that even their heaviest guns were incapable of crippling an enemy vessel unless fired at suicidally close range. As long as the Spanish maintained good order, which they did, the English ships had little chance of making their superior fire-power or manoeuvrability tell. By the time the Armada dropped anchor in the Calais roads on 27 July not one Spanish ship had been severely damaged by English gunfire, much less sunk.

Calais, the scene of England's greatest defeat in living memory, was about to witness one of its greatest victories. Medina Sidonia had done what Philip had asked of him: he had brought the Armada intact to its rendezvous point with Parma's army. But this still left the problem of how the two forces were actually to combine. Even if Medina Sidonia had felt secure enough (with the English fleet lurking just to windward) to detach ships from the Armada to clear a way through the Dutch craft patrolling the inshore waters, Parma's troop barges needed calm conditions to cross the Channel safely, and by late July the weather was worsening. While Medina Sidonia waited for something little short of a miracle, his ships – anchored against a lee shore – were sitting ducks. On 28 July the English launched fireships towards the Armada, and at the sight of these most feared of naval weapons many Spanish captains panicked and broke formation. At last the English were able to get in among the enemy and pound them at close quarters. Several Spanish galleons were surrounded by English ships and battered until blood ran from their gunwales. Hundreds of Spaniards were killed or wounded. And although all but half a dozen vessels survived this bombardment, the prevailing winds forced the Armada out into the North Sea and beyond all hope of a conjunction with Parma's army.

The Armada's long and limping journey home (round Scotland and down the west coast of Ireland), battered by autumn gales and low on food and water, took a far greater toll on ships and men than the English had, and only about two thirds of the fleet made it back to Spain. Yet the victorious English seamen fared little better. Having kept his casualties to below sixty during the fighting itself, Effingham watched in anguish during August as his exhausted and malnourished men succumbed to disease by their thousands in the ports of southern England.

The Armada's defeat stirred a cocktail of emotions in the English. Some gloated: 'It came, it saw, it fled' joked the legend on one commemorative medal.[56] But most people mixed righteous jubilation with a profound sense of relief and thankfulness for God's mercy. Yet in spite of the weakness of England's coastal defences, and the fact that the county militia which formed the bulk of its land forces were no match for Parma's *tercios*, the Armada was never really a close-run thing, simply because Philip's plan, which he insisted be adhered to rigidly, was so impractical. In the unlikely event of the Armada succeeding then it is hard to see how Protestantism as an organised political force would have survived in the Netherlands, France and Scotland, let alone in England. But what that would have meant in terms of the broader shape of European history is impossible to say.

The Armada was no more than the opening broadside in the war at sea. English naval expeditions struck at Corunna, Cadiz and other Spanish ports in 1589, 1596 and 1597, while Drake and Hawkins returned to plundering Spain's colonies in the Caribbean, until fatigue and tropical disease claimed both men in 1595–6. Philip II retaliated by sending huge armadas into the Narrow Seas in 1596 and 1597 with the ultimate objective of knocking England out of the war in the Low Countries – only for the 'Protestant wind' to rise up on both occasions and drive the Spanish fleets back to port. The immediate cause of the war, the English expeditionary force to the Netherlands, proved equally ineffective, at least in the short term. The queen wanted Leicester merely to hold his ground until a treaty could be negotiated that would preserve the delicate balance between French and Spanish influence in the Low Countries. Leicester, on the other hand, wanted glorious victories for the Protestant cause, for which he had neither the men, money, nor competence as a general.

Like most of Elizabeth's armies (and in contrast to Henry VIII's semi-feudal war-hosts) the expeditionary force was chronically under-funded and consisted in part of conscripts from the dregs of English society: 'our old ragged roggues' as Leicester called them.[57] Underfunded by Elizabeth and cheated by corrupt officers, the English soldiers were forced to borrow and steal from their increasingly hostile Dutch hosts. Conditions deteriorated so much in one English-held garrison that its commanders handed the town over to Parma and took their starving, unpaid troops into Spanish service. Initially, therefore, the first expe-ditionary army contributed little to the rebel war effort while spurring Philip into launching the Armada. Leicester himself returned home in 1588 an exhausted man, and died shortly afterwards. But from the late 1580s, English troops, operating as part of a reorganised Dutch army, began to make a real difference, helping to retake many of the towns that had fallen to Parma. By the late 1590s the Spanish *reconquista* had stalled, and the northern Low Countries had emerged as a new independent state, the Dutch republic, which was a confederation of sovereign provinces under the semi-hereditary military leadership of the House of Orange.

Parma's all-conquering army was repulsed in the Low Countries because much of it had been diverted to France in 1589 to help the Guisards in the struggle against the Huguenots. The Protestant cause had received a tremendous boost that year with the succession of the Huguenot leader Henri de Bourbon as France's new king, Henri IV (1553–1610). France now replaced the Low Countries as the main battleground in Europe's wars of religion, and with Parma's men digging in just across the Channel, Elizabeth again had no choice but to send thousands of English soldiers to help stave off defeat by the pro-Habsburg French. Although Henri's politically expedient conversion to Catholicism in 1593 infuriated the queen, it eventually enabled him to defeat the Guisards, reunite France (with toleration for its Huguenot minority) and expel the Spanish. Whether they realised it or not, the English had won their first war to maintain the balance of power in western Europe.

Just as it looked as if a Protestant meltdown in north-western Europe had been averted, another rebellion in Ireland revived English fears of Catholic encirclement. There was always an incentive for Irish trouble-makers to stir when the English were preoccupied elsewhere, but the rebellion that broke out in Ulster in 1594 was altogether more serious than its predecessors – largely because of the man who came to lead it, Hugh O'Neill, earl of Tyrone (c.1550–1616). With a vast lordship in Ulster yielding perhaps as much as £80,000 a year, Tyrone was probably the wealthiest man in all of Ireland. As it turned out, he was also a master strategist and a fine general. Add to this winning combination the fact that Philip II and his heir – who would succeed him in 1598 as Philip III – were willing to send troops to Tyrone's assistance, and it looked as if Elizabeth's policy of trying to control Ireland on the cheap by licensing Protestant profiteers and warlords was finally unravelling.

Tyrone's rebellion began unremarkably enough as a reaction against attempts by New English officials to extend their authority, and their greed for Irish land, into Ulster. However, to the government's conster-nation it found itself facing not the usual lightly armed Gaelic levies but a large and well-drilled army that Tyrone had equipped with muskets and pikes. Early successes against scratch English forces, and assurances from Philip's agents that Spanish troops were on the way, encouraged Tyrone to take the momentous step in 1596 of hitching his Ulster 'confederacy' to a Spanish alliance and Philip's war against Elizabeth. Indeed, Tyrone seems to have given serious consideration to handing Ireland over to Spanish rule once the English had been expelled. Certainly Ireland's only hope of enduring as a Catholic state was to help the Spanish topple the Protestant regime in London. Ireland by the mid-1590s had become a second front in the enterprise of England.

To widen support for the rebellion while he waited for Spanish troops, Tyrone appealed to all of Ireland's Catholics, Old English and Gaels, to join what he portrayed as a struggle for religious and national liberation. In 1598, with the rebellion taking hold in Connacht and Munster, Elizabeth sent over an army of 17,000 men – the largest to leave England during her reign – under the command of her favourite Robert Devereux, 2nd earl of Essex (1565–1601). But though brave to a fault, Essex did not have the stomach for a protracted campaign, and after holding private – and possibly treasonous – talks with Tyrone, he returned to England to confront the queen (more of Essex shortly). He was replaced by the resourceful soldier–courtier Lord Mountjoy.

The rebellion reached crisis-point in 1601 with the landing of 3,400 Spanish veterans at Kinsale on Ireland's southern coast. Tyrone marched south from Ulster to link up with the Spanish, who had been bottled up in Kinsale by Mountjoy's army, and on arriving outside the town he decided to risk pitched battle on the understanding that the Spaniards would sally out to support him. Inexplicably, however, the Spanish stayed put, and – as so often in set-piece battles between English and Gaelic forces – the Irish foot were routed by the English heavy cavalry. Even had Tyrone won, it would have needed more Spanish troops to take and hold Ireland against the English. As it was, Mountjoy's victory at Kinsale effectively broke the rebellion. The Spanish surrendered and sailed home, and Tyrone was offered and accepted very generous peace terms shortly after Elizabeth's death in March 1603. The Nine Years War (1594–1603), as it would become known, finally brought all of Ireland under Tudor control, and greatly increased the rate at which the English language, customs and systems of law and government – though not Protestantism – penetrated Irish Gaeldom. Nevertheless, victory in 1603 left a bitter legacy of religious and ethnic hatred. The English had prevailed not by the political arts but by the sword, and neither the victors nor the vanquished would forget it.

The Anglo-Spanish war ended quietly, by treaty, in 1604, with both sides financially exhausted. England had survived through luck and because Spain had succumbed to a classic case of imperial overreach. Successfully defying the Spanish had not transformed England into a major European power. It had, however, fixed the idea of English seapower in the national consciousness. No matter that England's seadogs were every bit as rapacious as their Catholic adversaries, or were in some cases – Hawkins, for example – of doubtful Protestant credentials. They had preserved English liberties and Protestantism against Catholic 'tyranny'. The crises and triumphs of Elizabeth's reign also sealed the bond between Protestantism and patriotism. The defeat of the Armada had been taken, certainly by Calvinists, as clear proof that God had chosen England among His 'elect' nations, with a providential role as a champion and bulwark against the popish Antichrist. The old half-joke that (in Parma's words) 'God is sworne Englishe' seemed a more serious proposition by 1604.[58]

Much of the credit for holding off the Spanish belonged to the private interests that had helped to push Elizabeth into war in the first place – to the pirate grandees and their lordly Calvinist patrons at court – rather than to the crown or to the royal navy. In fact, there was no royal navy as we might understand the term. The 'Navy Royal' was not a national institution but the personal property of the monarch. The bulk of the national fleet was controlled by private shipowners and merchants, who were often able to commandeer the royal ships in their midst for their own privateering ventures. Yet even though Elizabeth's impressive military record against the forces of popery owed much to private initiative, it still became the standard by which her Stuart successors, and their policies, would be judged by the English public. Elizabeth's carefully crafted but fictitious image as a Protestant heroine made her an almost impossible act to follow.

The long struggle against Spain was remarkable on several counts. It had been fought not for territorial gain or dynastic ambition but for national survival and the defence of Protestantism, and on a global scale that would not be rivalled for another century. The stories and debates surrounding the war and its related horrors in France and the Low Countries became the principal stuff of Elizabethan news pamphlets. England's engagement with these various theatres of war gripped readers like almost no other issue. The war also exposed a curious reversal that had occurred in the English psyche in the hundred years since Henry VII's victory at Bosworth. In 1485 the English had still fancied themselves as conquerors with one foot planted firmly in northern France, even though they had been weakened by civil war and were in fact a prey to their neighbours rather than vice versa. A century later, however, and their self-image was much more that of an island race, alone and menaced by mighty enemies, and yet England, on its day, could be a formidable power itself, as the Armada campaign showed. The English would wrestle with this paradox of 'lyttel England['s] great discovered strength' well into the seventeenth century.[59]

Fighting Spain on several fronts and for so many years imposed a terrible strain on the Elizabethan state. The expeditionary force to the Netherlands had cost one and a half million pounds by 1603, perhaps six years' ordinary royal revenue. Defeating Tyrone had drained another two million pounds from the exchequer. And over 100,000 English and Welsh men had been raised for service on the Continent and in Ireland, or about 20 per cent of the available manpower. To meet these huge expenses, the government resumed the sale of crown lands – starving the goose that laid the golden eggs – and used the royal prerogative to sanction oppressive financial expedients, of which the most hated were royal patents granting exclusive commercial rights over trade in a specified commodity. The sale of these monopolies to courtiers and crown creditors certainly put money in the queen's coffers, but the restrictive practices of the patentees – these 'bloodsuckers of the commonwealth' as one MP called them – removed it from the pockets of her subjects.[60] The Commons' debates over monopolies in 1597 and 1601 were among the most acrimonious of any Parliament during the entire Tudor period. At least Elizabeth managed to avoid bankruptcy – Philip II suffered four during the course of his reign – but being equally adept at avoiding difficult issues she also ignored the opportunity the war afforded to develop new sources of revenue and new credit mechanisms. At the very least the crown should have increased customs rates and the value of the main form of parliamentary taxation, the subsidy, in line with inflation. The queen's failure to address the crown's financial weakness, and to end the war with Spain before her death, meant that James VI of Scotland would succeed to a realm in which money and, in consequence, political good will were in short supply.

Commonwealth courses

The pitiful demise from disease and neglect of thousands of English sailors after their heroics in defeating the Armada was symbolic of the fate of Elizabethan England in the fifteen years that followed. The threat of Spanish encirclement and invasion was resisted – if sometimes more by luck than bravery – and all of Ireland was conquered. But although no direct blow was landed upon England itself, the economic impact of prolonged war, combined with the bad harvests and dearth that marked the 1590s, would inflict almost as much hardship upon the lower orders as they had suffered in similar circumstances during the 1540s and 1550s. Local resistance to the government's heavy wartime demands would coincide with, and heighten, an authoritarian reaction among the queen's advisers against Puritanism and other perceived challenges to her 'imperial' authority. At court, too, the war's poisonous influence upon an increasingly sclerotic regime would foment the 'inward broils' of factionalism and aristocratic conspiracy. The very people whose duty it was to stand by the queen in time of war and unrest, her great noblemen, would (as one of them put it) 'repyne that the state value them not at that rate thay prise themselves worthy of'.[61] And some peers would do more than just repine; they would turn upon Elizabeth in violent fashion.

The climate at court by the 1590s was not altogether hospitable for those who fancied themselves the 'ancient nobility' – two or three generations among the peerage usually sufficed in this regard. Thomas Wolsey, Thomas Cromwell and William Cecil – the foremost royal councillors of their generation – were not simply the products of Henry VIII's and Elizabeth's belief that 'new men' made more reliable servants than did great noblemen, for the rise of these administrative master-minds also pointed to the growing complexity of royal government, and of the need for expert bureaucrats and men of letters to make it function effectively. Elizabeth's peers tried, with varying degrees of success, to adapt themselves to the requirement at court for men schooled in the politic arts of government. But the traditional view that what truly defined a nobleman was honour in arms and chivalric glory continued to be widely held. Most peers aspired not only to high office at court but also to command of their county's or the kingdom's armed forces.

Yet if honourable military service for prince and country remained the mark of the true nobleman, it was an increasingly hard-won commodity by the later sixteenth century. Elizabethan peers who sought high command must balance the often conflicting requirements of building a serviceable military following from among their gentry supporters and tenantry, and maintaining the favour of a monarch who, like her father and grandfather, distrusted noblemen with the landed power to retain what were, in effect, their own private armies. Even with the Armada anchored in the English Channel in July 1588, the queen declined the offer of the great territorial magnate the 2nd earl of Pembroke to attend her 'with 300 horse and 500 foote at the leaste of my followers, armed at myne oune coste and with myne oune store'.[62] The growing sophistication of warfare from the 1540s was another disincentive to would-be 'fighting lords'. The profession of arms was becoming just that: a full-time career that demanded expert know-ledge. Few noblemen had the application or inclination to master the latest techniques in deploying pikemen and musketeers, and it is no surprise that some of the positions in Elizabeth's armies that would once have been graced by peers or their younger sons were occupied by relatively low-born professional soldiers. Then there was the problem of adapting to the new age of religious warfare. During the second half of the sixteenth century the ideals of chivalry and military service in the Protestant cause would fuse in England, rendering futile any hopes that Catholic peers might entertain of command in the queen's armies.

The squeeze on lordly preferment and military ambition grew

particularly tight during the 1590s. Not only did Elizabeth make very few new creations to the peerage – which numbered about sixty during the 1590s – she also largely ignored the ancient nobility in appointments to high office. By 1597 her privy council had contracted in size to a mere eleven men, not one of whom was a territorial magnate. 'The nobility are unsatisfied that places of honor are not given them,' complained one peer, 'that ofices of trust are not laid in there handes to manage as thay were wont; that her maiestie is percimonius and sloe to reliefe there wants . . .'[63] Although there was no shortage of soldiering to be had during the 1590s, the queen rarely favoured the kind of ambitious military operations that would satisfy her peers' craving for honour in arms. Her caution, as we have seen, was entirely justified. Royal finances would not sustain warfare on the profligate scale of the 1540s. The only reason she authorised major naval expeditions against the Spanish was that they were cheaper than land campaigns and promised rich pickings by way of plunder.

Her distrust of grand military ventures, and their promoters, was not just financially driven, however, but also reflected her predicament as a female ruler in a patriarchal society, surrounded by egotistical men. To prevent her courtiers uniting and coercing her she allowed herself (in Francis Bacon's words) 'to be wooed and courted, and even to have love made to her', playing her suitors off against each other in competition for her favour.[64] These 'love tricks' generally proved very effective – except, that is, in times of war. Unable to lead her soldiers in person, she had no choice but to delegate command to her court gallants; and once out of their gilded cage and onto a charger or quarter-deck they had the annoying habit of ignoring her orders and seeking glory for themselves. War also brought out the male prejudice that women were constitutionally incapable of acting decisively and should let the men take charge of military matters. Elizabeth had to struggle constantly, and not always successfully, to remind her commanders who called the shots.

Elizabeth's troubles with her military men, and theirs with her, were epitomised in the person of the 2nd earl of Essex: Leicester's stepson and protégé. 'No man was more ambitious of Glory by vertuous and noble Deeds,' wrote one Elizabethan historian, 'no man more careless of all things else' than Essex.[65] His youthful good looks caught the attention of the ageing but still vain Elizabeth, and his military expertise and charismatic leadership were invaluable in time of war. His strategic vision, however, differed profoundly from that of the queen and his main court rival Sir Robert Cecil (1563–1612) – like his father, Lord Burghley, a courtier–bureaucrat par excellence. Essex and his circle longed to make mainland Europe tremble once again at England's military might, though not for mere conquest or dynastic ambition as the Plantagenets and Henry VIII had done, but to defend the 'libertie of Christendome', Catholic as well as Protestant, from the designs of Philip II and his successors for 'universall monarchie'.[66] Elizabeth and the 'Cecilians', by contrast, strove merely to keep the Spanish at bay at minimum expense. Essex vented his frustration with this cautious strategy by repeatedly flouting Elizabeth's orders. During his first outing as a general – in Normandy in 1591 – the queen angrily remarked: 'Where he is, or what he doth, or what he is to do, we are ignorant.'[67] True to his aristocratic ideals he put honour in arms before playing the politician, which is why the hunchbacked Sir Robert Cecil would win their rivalry to succeed Burghley as the queen's chief minister. Essex, unlike Cecil, could not adapt to political realities: to the crown's financial disabilities, and to Elizabeth's chronic indecisiveness and suspicion of 'martial greatness' and grand imperial designs.

The greatest constraint upon Essex was the will of the monarch. Indeed, most of the queen's counsellors, Burghley included, chafed under this restriction, particularly when it came to budging Elizabeth on the succession or military intervention on the Continent. Even after the execution of Mary Queen of Scots in 1587, Elizabeth had refused to name James as her successor, leaving dangerously unsettled the question of who England's next monarch would be. Burghley wrote a long memo to himself entitled 'Certain matters wherein the Queen's Majesty's forbearing and delays hath produced, not only inconveniences and increases of expenses, but also dangers'.[68] The 1584 Bond of Association was just one of several initiatives designed to bend Elizabeth to the will of Protestant public opinion as represented by Parliament and its management team, the privy council. England was envisaged by Burghley and many other leading Protestants as a 'mixed' monarchy in which the queen's 'imperial' power was circumscribed by due process, wise counsel and the interests of the 'commonwealth' – that is, the public good and the institutional and legal structures that sustained civil (i.e. Protestant) society.

For the enemies of Puritanism, however – anxious to appropriate royal authority in their struggle against the godly – England was not a mixed polity at all but a 'right and true monarchy' in which the sovereign's personal power could not be gainsaid or limited.[69] Having grown in number since the 1570s, these zealous upholders of the ecclesiastical order and the queen's imperial prerogative were winning patrons and royal favour at court by the early 1590s. Anti-Calvinist clerics and court careerists of various stripes now insisted that Elizabeth derived her authority directly from God, and therefore that her crown and Church were beyond the reach of the common law or parliamentary statute. The efforts of a group of godly ministers and propagandists to stir up the people against the episcopal hierarchy and in support of Presbyterianism provoked a government crackdown against the Puritan leadership in the early 1590s. In a conscious attempt to fight fire with fire, senior churchmen employed populist hacks – among them that master of satirical wordplay Thomas Nashe – to wage a propaganda war against the godly, who were portrayed as factious and seditious. The court cleric and future archbishop of Canterbury Robert Bancroft published an influential tract in 1593 in which he argued that the Puritans and Jesuits were as bad as each other, since both were 'labouring with all their might by railing, libelling and lying to steal away the people's hearts from their governors, to bring them to a dislike of the present state of our church'.[70]

The Presbyterian movement was driven underground during the early 1590s, and Puritan ministers confined to the great unfinished work of implanting Protestant doctrine among the profane multitude. But by then the damage had been done. Elizabeth's failure to impose religious uniformity meant that she would leave a kingdom that was divided between Puritans, anti-Calvinists, prayer-book Protestants and Catholics; and religious pluralism at that time, even the informal kind tacitly allowed by Elizabeth, was regarded as highly dangerous. The earl of Essex was merely stating the obvious, as contemporaries saw it, when he insisted that 'a pluralitie of religions . . . is against the pollicie of all states, because where there is not unitie in the Church, there can be no unitie nor order in the state'.[71] By failing to stamp out religious dissent, Elizabeth may have spared England a civil war in the sixteenth century, but only perhaps by deferring it until the seventeenth. The dreadful consequences of religious division were all too evident in war-torn France, which was, in Essex's words, 'the theater and stage wheron the greatest actions are acted'.[72] The French wars of religion would provide a rich source of ideological nutrient for both the supporters and opponents of 'imperial' monarchy in Britain.

To the swordsmen and the young, discontented noblemen who flocked round Essex, the ageing Elizabeth and her court seemed increasingly threatening to all but England's popish enemies. How could English honour and liberties be preserved, they asked, when the queen's counsels were full of sycophants and 'base penn clarkes' such as Sir Robert Cecil?[73] The continental vogue for the Roman historian Tacitus (AD 56–117) in the 1590s spoke loudly to the Essexians' concerns. Like most gentlemen of the age they had received a humanist education and turned readily to classical literature for what Essex termed 'not onely precepts, but lively patterns, both for private directions and for affayres of state'.[74] Tacitus' account of the Claudian emperors – a dark tale of princely virtue corrupted by evil counsellors – validated their jaundiced view of Elizabeth and her court. As royal patronage and political access to the queen contracted during the 1590s, so the court's reputation for corruption grew. Cecil was regarded as especially venal. 'You may boldly write for his favour,' a lawyer advised his client concerning Cecil. 'You paid well for it.'[75]

From disillusion with the court and its political culture it was but a short step to more subversive doctrines. Essex's advisers adapted Huguenot arguments that the nobility could legitimately discipline a monarch who had broken their supposed contract to rule by the consent and for the benefit of the people. Essex was apparently the first man in England to refer to himself in print as a 'patriot' – a term that entered the Anglophone world from France, where it was closely associated with a Huguenot reforming agenda. Only a strong and patriotic nobility, the Essexians argued, conscious of its personal honour irrespective of royal favour, and endowed with the formal independent power of the great medieval offices of state such as the earl marshalcy (which Essex was granted in 1597), could preserve the commonwealth against tyranny. Essex and his circle blended several different and seemingly contradictory strands of thinking – Protestant chivalric ideals; medieval baronial constitutionalism; support for Catholic toleration; classical and Renaissance ideas about civic and martial virtue; and concepts justifying resistance to monarchical misrule – into a persuasive political language that could appeal to both Puritans and 'loyalist' anti-Habsburg Catholics. Essex himself used propaganda and his fame as a war-hero to affect 'popularity', appealing to public opinion against what he saw as the fatal timidity of royal policies. What Shakespeare, one of Essex's admirers, called this 'courtship to the common people' was tantamount to rabble-rousing, and was too much for the earl's adviser Francis Bacon, who urged him in 1596 not to abandon his 'commonwealth courses' but yet to 'take all occasions to the Queen to speak against popularity'.[76]

The appeal of (and to) commonwealth courses went far beyond Essex's circle. The huge gap that the dissolution of the monasteries and religious guilds had left in the provision of education and communal welfare had been filled in the decades after 1540 by a multitude of secular 'little commonwealths'. Borough corporations and grammar schools had multiplied rapidly as the crown responded to local requests for greater powers to maintain order and manage public services by granting new charters of incorporation. These 'corporate and politic' bodies had become vehicles for a new sense of communal identity that mingled traditional notions of the 'goodly commonwealth' with humanist ideas about civic virtue, and, as time went on, the moral reformism of godly Protestantism.[77] Civil authority and commonwealth principles had found another important focus after 1540 in England's 9,000 or so parishes. The medieval parish had been primarily a religious body devoted to promoting neighbourly good will. With the retreat of communal religious sociability at the Reformation, however, the parish had been given, or took over, a wide range of secular functions, becoming the fundamental unit of state power. This process reached its climax under the Tudors with parliamentary legislation in 1598 and 1601 for parish poor relief, whereby rates were levied on better-off parishioners to keep their poorer neighbours from starving. These measures not only imitated schemes in towns on the Continent but also built upon many local initiatives for relieving poverty. In fact, the poor laws owed more to local than to central pressures, and are a prime example of how, since the Middle Ages, the English state had been moulded as much by forces from within political society as by the will of successive monarchs.

Economic forces during the 1590s pushed parish communities into the front line of the war against 'sin and enormities'. Harvest failures and government demands for more money and military resources made the last decade of Elizabeth's reign particularly wretched for the poor. The price of basic foodstuffs climbed higher in real terms in 1594–8 than at any time in the sixteenth century, while the death-rate among the poor also jumped alarmingly. Yet the inflation that reduced many smaller landholders to vagrancy – creating a permanent underclass of labouring poor – meant bumper profits for those farmers able to produce a surplus to sell at market. This widening economic divide at parish level during the second half of the sixteenth century assumed a political and cultural dimension as the prospering 'middling sort' came to regard many popular recreations – maypoles, tippling in alehouses

etc. – as licentious, and used commonwealth rhetoric and parish office
to impose civility upon their poorer, increasingly desperate, neighbours.
For conscientious Protestants there was also a moral imperative to join
the fight against popery (which to the godly was synonymous with sin
and disorder) at all levels of public life, from punishing village drunkards and unmarried mothers to supporting parliamentary candidates
who promised to purge the state of papists and 'evil counsellors'.

An important reason for the failure of the commons to rise in rebellion during the 1590s, as they had done in similarly hard times forty
years earlier, was that the prosperous farmers and tradesmen who had
traditionally led such protests now sided with the gentry against their
social inferiors. Like the gentry, the middling sort would be more closely
integrated into crown administration in the localities during the Tudor
period. This high (and rising) level of participation in local government
– both by contemporary European and modern-day standards –
strengthened the English people's already firm commitment to the rule
of law, and their sense of public duty. Political power was not only
more widely diffused by 1600 than it had been a century earlier but it
had also assumed a more civic, less martial, character.

The earl of Essex's last desperate bid for power attempted to trade
upon this commitment to public-spiritedness, or 'active citizenship'.
Henri IV's peace with Philip II at the treaty of Vervins in 1598 had
undermined the earl's policy of an alliance between England, France
and the Dutch republic against Spain. And his disastrous tour as lord
lieutenant of Ireland had ended in 1599 with him storming back to
England and into the queen's bedchamber while she was still half-
dressed and her hair in disarray. Banished from court and facing financial ruin, he and his diehard supporters decided to stage a coup to
'rescue' Elizabeth from the clutches of the Cecilians and other courtiers
eager to end the war with Spain. The Essexians feared that peace would
leave the Spanish free to wipe out Dutch resistance, and then to strike
at England and the German Protestants. Essex was also convinced,
wrongly, that his enemies at court were plotting with the Spanish to
kill him and to have Elizabeth succeeded not by the Protestant James
VI but by a Catholic.

On 8 February 1601, Essex and several hundred 'swagringe companions' – among them three earls, three barons and the younger brothers
of several noblemen – marched through the London streets, trying to
rouse the inhabitants as concerned citizens as well as loyal subjects:
'now or never is the tyme for you to pursue your liberties: which yf

at this tyme you forsake, you are suer [sure] to enduer bondage'.[78] But this half-baked and treasonous resort to 'popularity' met only with stunned surprise; Essex, cornered in his London residence by nightfall, was forced to surrender. After a brief trial he was executed in the courtyard of the Tower on 25 February, his head 'severed from his bodie by the axe at three stroakes'.[79] Among the small party of onlookers was Sir Robert Cecil. And it was Cecil who took over Essex's surreptitious contacts with James VI, and who reaped the rewards after overseeing the Scottish king's succession to the English throne following Elizabeth's death in March 1603.

With the dismal failure of Essex's rebellion, victory in Ireland over the earl of Tyrone, and the peaceful transition to a new ruling dynasty, it seemed that the crown had finally rid itself of over-mighty subjects and dispelled lingering fears of baronial revolt left by the Wars of the Roses. Yet the aristocratic constitutionalism that Essex had honed and levelled, if only briefly, at the court would prove a potent weapon in more capable hands and in a greater cause. The language of common-wealth had emerged at national level in reaction to the failings of the Plantagenet king Henry VI in the mid-fifteenth century. The same commonwealth courses that bound English society together had the potential, should monarch and political nation become estranged, to tear it apart. In the words of one of Essex's later admirers, and himself a reluctant rebel against his prince: 'Thus may wee see that setled governments doe cherish in themselves their owne destructions, and their own subjects are oftentimes cause of their owne ruine, unlesse God of his mercy prevent it.'[80]

3

Free Monarchy, 1603–37

> But the Popular state, ever since the begynnynge of his maiestes gracious and sweete governement, hath growne bygge and audacious. And in every session of Parlement swelled more and more.
>
> Lord Chancellor Ellesmere, 'Speciall observacions touching all the sessions of the last Parliament' (1611)[1]

> Kings walke the heavenly milky-way,
> But you in by-paths goe astray.
> God and King doe pace together,
> But vulgars wander light as feather . . .
> Hold you the publick beaten way,
> Wonder at Kings and them obey.
> For under god they are to chuse,
> Whats rights to take and what refuse:
> Wherto if you will not consent,
> Yet hold your peace, least you repent,
> And be corrected for your pride,
> That Kings designes dare thus deride
> By raylinge rimes and vaunting verse,
> Which your Kings breast shall never peirce.
>
> James I, 'The wiper of the peoples teares' (1622–3)[2]

Dangerous distinctions

A mood of pessimism descended over western Europe during the 1590s. In the face of unabating religious wars and inflation, of massive plague outbreaks and bad harvests, it seemed that humans could merely hope to endure the flux of time rather than participate in God's great redemptive drama. Christian humanist schemes for promoting civil society began to seem hopelessly idealistic, as fashionable opinion shifted towards an increasingly cynical, self-interested view of public life. The French philosopher Michel de Montaigne (1533–92) looked to the narrowing political horizon, insisting that 'a wise man ought inwardly to retire his minde from the common prease [press] . . . Publicke societie hath nought to doe with our thoughts.'[3] Princes were the only legitimate source of public authority. Citizens – those capable of perceiving and acting on the public good, of exercising civic virtue – must learn to be passive subjects once again. Britain's first two Stuart kings were quick to nose out and beat down 'popularity' – that is, the incitement or political empowerment of the people. Unlike Elizabeth, a pragmatist to the core, James Stuart, king of Scotland from 1567 and of England from 1603, and his son and successor Charles I were visionary monarchs. Theirs would be an age of 'projects' – grand designs to increase royal authority and revenues – and they themselves the chief projectors. The trend towards a more peremptory and exacting style of government that had begun during the 1590s would continue after 1603. But the new authoritarianism did not go unchallenged. The nobility and zealous Protestants, groups that had absorbed classical republican ideas from the humanists, developed sophisticated arguments to preserve a political space for the citizen and the patriot. James VI of Scotland had succeeded in taming these disruptive forces in Scotland. Could he do so again as king of England?

James was a man of strong likes and dislikes. His love of hunting, for example, rivalled that of his great-great-uncle Henry VIII. He spent weeks on end enjoying the pleasures of the chase, just he and a few select companions pursuing a stag across miles of country until it died of exhaustion, whereupon the king would dismount, cut it open, and 'blood' his fellow huntsmen. He hunted with hawks too, he even fished in the Thames using cormorants (a technique probably imported from China). This 'perpetual occupation with country pursuits', observed one foreign diplomat, often left government business at a standstill.[4] On one occasion one of James's favourite hounds was abducted and later returned with a note round his neck asking it to speak to the king, 'for he hears you every day, and so doth he not us', and urge him to return to his kingly duties in London.[5] James thought this a great joke, and stayed on to hunt for another fortnight. When he was not out harrying animals himself, he and his courtiers spent many happy hours watching bears, bulls and lions being baited by dogs. Another of his great pleasures was alcohol. Indeed, he was so fond of binge-drinking that his queen, Anne of Denmark (1574–1619), feared for his life. His favourite tipple was 'thick white muscatel', which was diagnosed as the cause of his chronic diarrhoea. His dislikes were equally vigorous. Smoking was a particular bugbear, and he attacked it at length in print.

Yet even 'so vile and stinking a custome' as smoking was not as contemptible in his eyes as popularity.[6] His own aversion to courting the mob was apparent from his very first days in England. As he neared London in May 1603 on the final leg of his journey from Edinburgh to claim the English crown, the common people flocked to see their new monarch, just as they had done during Henry VII's journey down to London after the battle of Bosworth. How Henry responded to this plebeian throng is not known, but James was clearly discomfited by it and would have preferred the crowds to keep their distance. It would not be long before the 'poore sort' started grumbling that on public occasions he treated them 'with a kind of kinglie negligence, nether speakeinge nor lookeinge uppon them'.[7]

Why did James, one of the age's shrewdest political operators, disdain to work the crowd? The answer is complex. In part it was simply because he misread the nature of his welcome in England. James had never been formally acknowledged by Elizabeth as her successor, and he was by no means the only claimant to her crown. At the time it seemed little short of a miracle to the English that the king of one of their most ancient enemies had succeeded to the throne without violent opposition. The 'papists' had certainly been expected to mount some kind of a challenge, and perhaps they would have, had it not been for James's diplomatic skill in persuading the Spanish not to field a Catholic candidate. The crowds that greeted him in England were therefore animated by sheer relief as much as anything else. James, however, attributed his rapturous reception to gratitude; had he not ended the 'curse' of female rule and given England a secure Protestant succession? In other words, he thought he was doing the English a favour, not the other way round. But it was not only James who was mistaken. The people had assumed, quite unreasonably, that he would show the same deft common touch that Elizabeth had, and would grace them with 'well-pleased affection'.[8] They took his aloofness so badly because it contrasted with 'the manner of there laite Queene, whoe when she was publiquely seen abroad would often staye & speake kindlie to the multitud'.[9]

James's churlishness in public – he would often 'bid a p[iss] or a plague on such as flocked to meet him' – was not natural to his character.[10] In less formal surroundings he could be affability itself. Indeed, he was as extravagant and indiscreet with his affections as he was with his money – or as some MPs liked to point out, taxpayers' money. He was a good conversationalist too, and a man of formidable learning – 'they gar [made] me speik Latin ar [before] I could speik Scotis' he recalled of his boyhood tutors.[11] Perhaps afflicted by a mild form of cerebral palsy, and certainly in later life by arthritis, James was none too steady on his feet, which probably did little for his confidence in public. But fundamentally his distaste for crowds was a reflection of his political philosophy.

James brought a new and authoritarian style of kingship to England. He set much greater store than his Tudor predecessors had on the mystical claims of royal blood as a source of political authority, and hence he played up his descent from Henry VII and from the ancient kings of Scotland and Ireland. Hereditary kingship, he argued in his writings, was prescribed by the will of God as revealed in nature and the Bible. Royal authority was conferred by God alone, and in consequence kings were answerable to none but Him. Kings were like gods themselves, said James (taking his cue from the 82nd psalm), or the head of another supposedly divinely ordained institution, the patriarchal household. His intellectual and emotional investment in the divine right of kings far outstripped Elizabeth's, and grew out of his tough political apprenticeship in Scotland, where he had endured the indignity of kidnapping by power-hungry noblemen, and of Presbyterian ministers berating him as 'God's sillie [weak] vassall'.[12] None of these affronts had troubled him as much, however, as the strictures and beatings administered by his principal tutor George Buchanan (1506–82). Buchanan had belonged loosely to a group of Calvinist writers whose arguments for contractual kingship, and the right of the people – or more usually their governors or political representatives – to resist tyrants were to prove hugely influential across Protestant Europe. He had argued for the duty of true citizens to depose and if necessary kill their king if he subverted the civil society he was appointed to preserve, defining these true citizens not in religious terms but as 'Those who obey the laws and uphold human society, who prefer to face every toil, every danger, for the safety of their fellow countrymen rather than grow old in idleness . . .'[13]

The most radical arguments for popular sovereignty had been made by Huguenot writers in the aftershock to the St Bartholomew's Day massacres of 1572, when the French monarchy had become stained with the blood of its own people. Equally, it was French writers who had led the counter-reaction in favour of authoritarian, divine-right kingship, which had gathered pace following the recognition in 1584 of the Huguenot Henri de Bourbon (the future Henri IV), king of Navarre, as heir-presumptive to the French crown. James, in turbulent 1580s Scotland, had eagerly embraced this reaction against the political legacy of his old tutor. In fact the French wars of religion generated useful ideas and lessons for monarchs everywhere in the face of potent new challenges to their authority, whether it be Calvinist resistance theories or Catholic claims for papal superiority over secular rulers. Sixty years of religious war, of theological as well as physical iconoclasm, had turned Europe's rulers into fanatics for order, and James was no exception.

Good order, for James, meant a narrowing of political participation, of subduing the crowd, not exciting it. Obedience to prescribed authority was his recipe for a well-ordered society, not the humanist emphasis on inculculating moral and civic responsibility in ordinary citizens. His dismissive attitude towards the people was reinforced by his conception of who 'the people' – meaning the political classes – actually were. Although Elizabeth had been just as determined as James was to keep the people in their place and to stifle public debate, she had at times relied heavily on the support of 'baser personages'. Moreover, she had generally distrusted her great noblemen. By contrast, James was very indulgent of his nobility, even when they abused his trust, and thought that the only proper actors on the political stage were the great men of the realm. He regarded his people emphatically as subjects, not citizens. Popular participation in Church or state he associated with demagoguery and rebellion. In Scotland he had seen Presbyterian ministers – those 'trumpets of sedition' he called them – as the main agents of popularity.[14] Once in England he broadened this category to include Puritans, lawyers and 'free speakers' in the House of Commons. He referred to a 'vaine popular humour' at work among such men, who 'cannot be content with the present forme of Governement, but must have a kind of libertie in the people . . . and in every cause that concernes [the royal] Prerogative, give a snatch against a Monarchie, through their Puritanicall itching after Popularitie'.[15]

Browbeating 'free speakers' was one way of trying to curb popular humours; another was to expand the claims for the king's imperial or legally unfettered prerogative. The suppression of English Presbyterianism during the early 1590s had encouraged high-fliers at court and in the Church to talk up the idea of imperial sovereignty. However, from 1603 the absolute power of kings was openly espoused by the monarch himself and by those who would later be dubbed the 'Regians': the 'great Dependents upon the Crown, both in Church and State, who swell up the Prerogative, preaching and distilling into the King, the Almightiness of his power'.[16] James and the Regians insisted that where necessity, or 'reason of state', demanded, the king could use his prerogative power to override the common law. James could be alarmingly frank on this subject – 'the King is above the law', and although a good king, in a settled kingdom, would usually abide by existing constitutional arrangements, 'yet is hee not bound thereto but of his good will'.[17] The nature of kingship and the actions of kings were like the ways of God, he insisted, not for ordinary mortals to question. If, God forbid, a king was set on being a tyrant there was nothing his subjects could do to stop him. James was wise enough not to act upon his more 'absolutist' pronouncements, and England remained in practice a mixed monarchy. But he was prepared to resort to prerogative taxation – that is, taxation without parliamentary consent – more brazenly than Elizabeth had, and without her excuse of having a war to fight. To the 'free speakers' in James's first English Parliament (which sat intermittently between 1604 and 1610) it seemed that tyranny was almost upon them, and they questioned whether they had secure legal title in anything, even their own lands.

By investing his office with this godlike aura the first Stuart king of England was trying to emulate the first Tudor king in restoring the monarchy's majesty and mystery, for to foreigners like James it seemed that female rule and Elizabeth's overfamiliarity with her people had diminished the standing of the English crown. This princely desire to preserve a proper distance from the rude multitude was taking hold across Europe. Monarchs were beginning to withdraw from the public gaze into the more private world of their courts, recoiling from anything that smacked of popularity. James's preference for this more intimate style of royal deportment acquired a new institutional form and location at his court: the Bedchamber.

The Bedchamber began life in 1603 as a Scottish outpost at the heart of what was still effectively an English court. Thwarted in his desire to divide all court offices equally between Englishmen and Scotsmen, James settled for creating a new department of the royal household, the Bedchamber, and staffing it almost exclusively with his most trusted Scottish courtiers. The Bedchamber took over control of the monarch's private apartment(s) from the privy chamber, and was off-limits to all but the Bedchamber men – the king's gentleman body-servants. They dressed and undressed him, one slept every night on a pallet at the foot of his bed, and one attended him when he relieved himself on the 'close-stool'. These might seem like menial jobs for a gentleman, but in a personal monarchy a great deal depended upon access and proximity to the king – the fount of all patronage – and a place in the Bedchamber offered both. James returned to his native Scotland just once (in 1617) after becoming king of England, so the Scottish presence in the Bedchamber, and the presents James lavished on its members, helped reassure the Scots that they would not be ignored by their absentee monarch. The Bedchamber therefore buttressed royal authority in Scotland. Nevertheless, to the English, who were largely excluded from this charmed inner circle, the Bedchamber attracted a great deal of suspicion and resentment.

The Bedchamber aroused fears among the English of sinister court intrigues against liberty. These fears had a grain of truth, inasmuch as the Bedchamber became an alternative focus of power to the privy council – as the privy chamber had under Henry VIII – reviving the dual-centred politics of council and entourage that had disappeared during fifty years of female rule. Leicester and the other Protestant heroes on the Elizabethan council, and their success during the 1570s and 1580s in eroding personal monarchy, had created the myth that Elizabeth 'governed by a grave and wise counsell'.[18] Although this brief period of conciliar assertiveness was out of the ordinary, an influential body of opinion in England came to believe that it was the right and proper template for royal government. James more than doubled the size of the Elizabethan council, adding English noblemen and Scottish courtiers, yet many of his English councillors, including his chief minister Sir Robert Cecil (created earl of Salisbury in 1605), struggled to adjust to the normal pattern of politics under an adult male monarch – that is, to having to vie for influence and favour with the king's entourage. They resented the 'base and beggarly' Scots of the Bedchamber for supposedly encouraging James in his various experiments with prerogative finance, and certainly for profiting by them.

James's failure to stick to 'the publick beaten way' did indeed cause wonder, but not necessarily obedience. His rancorous relationship with his English Parliaments owed a lot, as we shall see, to the crown's ramshackle and overstretched finances. But what made this problem intractable was a lack of trust between the king and some of his leading subjects; and this, in turn, can be traced to the emergence during Europe's wars of religion of two competing visions of 'good government'. James and his senior legal adviser Lord Chancellor Ellesmere (1540–1617) championed the authoritarian model, with its emphasis on the unfettered power of kings, or what James called 'free monarchy'. If he were to do his job properly and as God had ordained then James must have discretionary emergency powers that trumped all human laws. In the most advanced versions of this doctrine – which drew heavily on contemporary French writings on divine-right kingship – the monarch actually *was* the nation in a political and legal sense. Ellesmere certainly, and probably James too, distrusted the political models and lessons that the Essexians and other 'popular' politicians drew from classical antiquity. The ancient Greeks might have been 'men of singular learning and wisdome', Ellesmere conceded, but they had lived in 'popular States: they were enemies, or at least mislikers of all Monarchies . . . their opinions therefore are no Cannons to give Lawes to kinges and kingdomes, no more than sir Thomas Moores Utopia, or such Pamphlets as wee have at everie Marte [market]'.[19] Ellesmere probably detected such classical influences in the readiness of popular politicians to suggest that the people's primary allegiance was not to the monarch's person but to the crown.

Elizabeth's long reign had encouraged her ministers to think and act in ways that reinforced this distinction between crown and monarch. They had defied her will on the grounds that they were acting as she would have done had she not been incapacitated by her sex. Obviously this argument would not wash under a competent male monarch such as James, and Ellesmere thought that the 'dangerous distinction betweene the King and the Crowne' was merely a cloak for rebels and extremists.[20] He was convinced that a faction of unscrupulous MPs, sitting in a 'rebellious corner' in the House of Commons, 'kept secrette and privye Conventicles and Conferences, wherein they devised and sett downe speciall plottes' for turning their fellow Parliament-men against free monarchy.[21] From the distinction that some MPs made between king and crown flowed other, more controversial, ideas: that the king possessed no power above or beyond the law; that even in emergencies he could not levy taxes without the consent of Parliament; and that he should govern through the privy council, relegating the Bedchamber to a purely domestic role. There was even talk at Westminster of contractual kingship. This commonwealth agenda overlapped with the combination of aristocratic constitutionalism and belligerent patriotism pioneered by Essex and his circle. Indeed, former Essexians figured prominently in the popular challenge to free monarchy.

With these contending agendas of free monarchy and 'commonwealth courses' went rival demonologies. James equated opposition to his will with puritanical popularity, while his critics came to regard free monarchy as a manifestation of popery. Popularity and popery – although conspiracy theories for the most part – seemed to make sense of the forces that menaced European society, and as solvents of traditional loyalties and constitutional niceties they would have no equals.

New Jerusalem

'First for the countrey I must confesse it is too good for them that possesse it and too bad for others to be at charge to conquer it, the ayre might be wholsome but for the stinckinge people that inhabit it . . .' was how one of James's English courtiers began his *Discription of Scotland*, and he was just warming up.[22] The strain of having to be polite about the Scots soon began to tell on the English. The Gunpowder Plot of 5 November 1605 was only the most extreme example of this disenchantment with England's new Scottish king.[23] Even in James's first English Parliament some MPs attacked his countrymen as beggars and traitors. English contempt for the Scots (as for the Irish) was a combination of xenophobia and chauvinism. Humbling the Spanish had strengthened the English people's belief in the superiority of their laws and national character over those of other nations. Yet their Scotophobia also reflected a fundamental truth about the relative power and wealth of the component parts of the Stuart dynastic union. It was hard for the English to respect a nation five times smaller, and with a crown twenty times poorer, than their own.

The Scots were not only poorer than the English but also, like 'the Irish', had an identity problem. When James transferred his court from Edinburgh to London in 1603 he left behind a kingdom of just 750,000 people, divided ethnically between Anglo-Scots-speaking Lowlanders and Gaelic-speaking Highlanders. The cultural gap between these two groups was growing in the seventeenth century as Lowlanders increasingly embraced notions of Protestant civility and derided their Highland neighbours as lawless savages, given to feuding and raiding. One Lowland poem described how God had created the first Highlander from a horse turd. Similarly, Highlanders tended to think of Lowlanders as a different race, the *Gaill* (non-Gael or foreigner), and resented them for having driven the Gaels from the fertile Lowlands. Another important difference between the two regions of Scotland centred on their relationship to the crown. Lowlanders participated in and attempted to manipulate central government. Most Highlanders, by contrast, although they acknowledged themselves subjects of the Scottish crown, preferred to ignore royal authority altogether.

Significant differences existed within as well as between the two regions of Scotland. Irish Franciscan friars created pockets of Counter-Reformation Catholicism in the western Highlands during the early seventeenth century, particularly among the clan enemies of the zealously Protestant Campbells of Argyllshire in the south-west Highlands. In the Lowlands, Ayrshire and the surrounding region was the heartland of Presbyterianism, whereas Aberdeenshire was noted for its episcopalian sympathies.

Although James extended the reach of his government deep into the Highlands and islands, Scotland remained a highly decentralised kingdom. Even the most powerful instrument of royal authority, the Scottish privy council, relied for local enforcement not upon crown officials but the landed elite. The heads of Scotland's 2,000 or so lairdly families dominated all aspects of public life. The crown could not rule effectively without their cooperation. James had increased royal control over the Scottish national Church – known as the Kirk – by reintroducing bishops in the late sixteenth century, but the Kirk remained more or less Presbyterian in structure, and therefore difficult for him to bend to his will.

Despite the many disparities and differences between England and Scotland, James dreamed of turning the 1603 union of crowns into a union of laws, Parliaments and churches. 'I am the Husband, and all the whole Island is my lawful Wife,' he told his first English Parliament, 'I am the Head, and it is my Body . . . I hope therefore no man will be so unreasonable as to think that I . . . should be a Polygamist, and Husband to two Wives.'[24] His scheme for merging his two British kingdoms into a new monarchy of Great Britain was overambitious, however, and proved unacceptable to both the Scots and the English. There were, admittedly, some Scottish Protestants, and not a few English ones, who got excited by the idea that the dynastic unification of Britain heralded the Apocalypse: the climactic confrontation between 'true religion' and the popish Antichrist supposedly foretold in the Bible. But most Englishmen thought James's union scheme favoured the Scots too much, 'fearing that the Scots (creeping into English Lordships, and English Ladies Beds, in both which already they began to be active) might quickly make their least half the predominant part'.[25] In practice the only kind of union most Englishmen would consider was that of incorporating Scotland into a greater English state, as their Tudor forebears had with Wales. England was constituted essentially by its laws, argued MPs, so that merging them with those of another country was effectively to abolish the kingdom itself. In taking this line, MPs were straying close to Ellesmere's 'dangerous distinction' between king and crown, and it is not hard to see why the union project was an early flashpoint in the running battle between James and the 'popular spirits'. The Scots, more realistically, thought in terms of a federal union that would preserve their own laws and the purity of their reformed Kirk. But the English Parliament had effectively killed the whole idea by 1607. It grudgingly accepted the naturalisation of the king's Scottish subjects, and free trade between England and Scotland, but little else. James had to introduce his new title of 'King of Great Britain' and a new flag for the king's ships, the Union Flag, solely on his own authority.

One king ruling separate kingdoms was not unusual in early modern Europe. The Spanish and Austrian branches of the Habsburg family each ruled composite monarchies, and their experience suggested that unity was best achieved by tolerating a fair degree of diversity. That said, it was widely believed that any prince who failed to impose religious uniformity on his subjects was asking for trouble. It was 'A generall Opinion received by all men' that 'One religion is the author of unitie, but from a confused religion, there alwaies groweth dissention . . . it giveth boldnesse to subiectes not onely to forsake God, but likewise to spurne against the Prince, and to live in contempt of his lawes and proceedinges'.[26] The fact that the Puritans were denied the kind of reformed church government that operated in Lowland Scotland, or that English Catholics did not have the religious leeway that their co-religionists enjoyed in Ireland, seemed to bode disaster. James's plan to bring the established churches – and in the long term, religious loyalties – in his three kingdoms more into line with each other was entirely understandable therefore. In England he turned a blind eye to what the godly got up to at parish level so long as they recognised episcopal authority, which they mostly did, and therefore Puritanism was safely contained within the Church. However, from north of the border, royal policy came to be viewed in a more sinister light, as a process of creeping Anglicisation that threatened to sully the purity of the Kirk and to reduce Scotland to the status of an English province.

James's gradualist approach to religious reform, and his far from empty boast that he could govern Scotland by pen from England, ensured that discontent in his northern kingdom did not get out of hand. It also helped that he had been raised, and remained, a doctrinal Calvinist, as distinct from the 'practical' Calvinism of the Puritans with their inward and outward war against ungodliness. Nevertheless, he had developed a taste for ornate ceremony in his own Chapel Royal even before he had succeeded to the English crown, and once ensconced in London he came to favour the Church of England, with its dutiful bishops and pre-Calvinist liturgy, as a model for reform in Scotland. However, when he tried to foist English church ceremonies upon Scotland in 1618 he encountered bitter opposition from the Kirk and in the 1621 Scottish Parliament. Only the Scottish bishops' quiet non-compliance with his orders kept the Kirk from open division.

James's efforts at 'rooting out of all barbaritie' in the Gaelic Highlands gave him some inkling of the problems he faced in Ireland.[27] Thanks to English victory in the Nine Years War there were no internal frontiers for the crown to defend. On the other hand, of course, the war had left Ireland's huge Catholic majority even more resentful and alienated. The solution as far as James was concerned was essentially more of the same, in particular plantations. When, in 1607, Tyrone and his supporters were either panicked into exile or fled to avoid royal punishment (there are signs they were up to their necks in treasonous intrigues with the Spanish), James authorised a massive plantation in Ulster that involved Scottish as well as English settlers. Besides allowing James to move his 'British' agenda forward in Ireland (if not in Britain itself), the scheme had the advantage from the crown's perspective of driving a Protestant wedge between the Irish and Scottish Gaels, although at the cost of creating a hostile Catholic underclass in Ulster.

Appeasing the Catholics was not a priority for James's longest-serving lord deputy of Ireland, Sir Arthur Chichester (1563–1625), who seems to have suffered from the constitutional schizophrenia common to most English governors of Ireland. When Englishmen thought about their own government they tended to become misty-eyed about its antiquity and legal integrity, but when they thought about government in Ireland they were far more open to schemes for uprooting ancient customs, trampling upon civic liberties and applying extra-legal force. Chichester, one of Ireland's 'wasters and destroyers', was no exception.[28] He made little distinction between the native Irish – 'beasts in the shape of men', he called them – and the Catholic Old English, terrorising both in the name of Protestant civility.[29] The Old English pleaded their loyalty to the crown, but their religion was tantamount to treason in James's eyes, and the New English minority continued to usurp their place in public office. With the English doing little to endear themselves to the Catholic Irish it is not surprising that the established Protestant Church in Ireland proved no match for Counter-Reformation Catholicism. Seminary priests, trained mostly in the Spanish Netherlands, and Franciscan friars revitalised Catholicism in Ireland (especially in the towns) to such an extent that the Dublin administration had no choice but to turn a blind eye to the activities of a Catholic ministry, complete with bishops, operating alongside the official Protestant church establishment. Ironically, this Catholic ministry tried to imbue the native Irish with much the same notions of civility as those demanded by James and Chichester.

British colonisation of Ireland consumed cash and human resources that might otherwise have gone into planting colonies in the Americas. Perhaps as many as 100,000 people (about 30,000 Scots, the rest English or Welsh) migrated from Britain to Ireland in the early Stuart period. Yet by 1640 there were probably less than 30,000 British settlers in North America. The unspectacular pace of transatlantic expansion before 1640 was also in part a by-product of the Elizabethan privateering war. In the long term, certainly, the war helped to fashion the tools of empire – developing the skills, the ships and the investment structures needed for colonisation. But in the short term it encouraged would-be colonial adventurers such as Ralegh to go in for get-rich-quick solutions. Colonial pioneers might have to wait many years to see a return on their investment, which was not an appealing prospect to a generation of English merchants and seafarers accustomed to the quick profits to be had from privateering. Within fifty years of losing the last remnant of their medieval empire in France (Calais), the English had become global seafarers capable of rivalling the Spanish. Yet most of this expansion was commercial, not colonial, and was related to developing markets in Europe or the emerging trade routes with the Far East. It was the smaller traders and planters, men excluded from more profitable markets by the big boys in London, who dabbled in colonial ventures.

Public interest in overseas expansion was equally limited. News from the New World was avidly consumed but soon forgotten, 'as if were nought els, but a pleasing dreame of a golden fancie'.[30] Although the English no longer expected or perhaps even wanted to regain their continental empire, their sights remained firmly fixed on Europe and the unfinished business of stemming the flood-tide of Habsburg popery. Of course the main problem under the early Stuarts, as under Elizabeth, was lack of government support. The crown's only consistent colonial policy during the early Stuart period was to avoid being seen to do anything likely to anger the Spanish or the French. James was more interested in the Ulster plantation than in the settlement established in Virginia in 1607 and named Jamestown in his honour. The kind of men who did see the advantages of a new English empire across the Atlantic were generally not welcome at the courts of James and Charles I. James had Ralegh executed in 1618 after his last voyage to the New World – to find 'El Dorado' on the Orinoco River – had degenerated into a raiding party against Spanish settlements.

Because early colonial enterprises were largely private undertakings they were inspired by a wide variety of motives. Militant Protestants saw the setting up of colonies as a weapon in the war against Spain, hence their focus on the Americas, the source of Spain's great wealth. In 1630 a group of leading English Puritans formed a company to settle Providence Island, off what is now the Nicaraguan coast, as both a godly commonwealth and a privateering base against Spanish shipping. At their head stood Robert Rich, earl of Warwick (1587–1658), the son of a great Elizabethan privateer and himself the operator of England's largest privateering fleet. At its worst, this eagerness to batten on the Spanish Indies was driven by greed 'for golde, for prayse, for glory'.[31] At its best it was inspired by the hope of 'freeing the poor Indians from their devourers' – meaning the Spanish – and spreading 'the grace of Christ among those . . . that yet sit in darkness and in the shadow of death'.[32] Another Puritan colonising project, the Massachusetts Bay Company, founded in the late 1620s with the support of Warwick and his friends, had the nerve to depict on its seal a group of Indians waving a banner with the words 'Come over and Help Us'.[33]

Yet, as in Ireland, the colonists' desire to plant civility and 'true religion' was undermined by their lack of sympathy with the indigenous cultures. Either the 'savages' must submit to English civility for the good of their souls or they must submit to English muskets. In Virginia, for example, relations between the English and the equally proud and ethnocentric Powhatan Indians quickly deteriorated into mutual incomprehension and mistrust, and then into a vicious conflict over territory and resources. The colony's first governor, Lord De La Warr, arrived at Jamestown after the terrible winter of 1609–10, or the 'starving time', when lack of food and a siege by the Indians had reduced the colony's population from 600 to about 90. De La Warr was ready, if necessary, to apply the terror tactics he had learned on campaign in Ireland, where soldiers routinely killed enemy civilians. But his main job was not to fight the Indians but to lick the colonists into shape for confronting the Spanish. He was followed by another officer who had served in Ireland, the sadistic Sir Thomas Dale, and 300 heavily armoured English musketeers, veterans of the fighting in the Low Countries. Dale divided his time between disciplining the colonists, strengthening Virginia's defences against possible Spanish attack, and killing Powhatans. By the 1620s the Virginian colonists talked openly of effecting 'the extirpation of the Indians'.[34] The coastal tribes had been dispersed or subjugated by the English in Virginia long before the end of the seventeenth century. The settlers in New England dealt similarly with the Wessagussets and Pequots – most notoriously when they surrounded and burnt a Pequot village in 1637, killing 400 or more men, women and children. It was a 'fearful sight to see them thus frying in the fire and the streams of blood quenching the same', but the settlers consoled themselves that they were meting out divine retribution on a 'proud and insulting people',[35] and that they had 'sufficient light from the word of God for our proceedings'.[36]

Virginia was joined in the early 1630s by another Chesapeake colony, Maryland, which was founded by the Catholic nobleman Cecil Calvert, Lord Baltimore, and named in honour of Charles I's queen, Henriette Marie (1609–69). The 'Indian Golde' in the Chesapeake would turn out to be tobacco – not the bitter stuff grown locally but the hybrid developed in the early 1610s by John Rolfe, the man who married the Indian princess Pocahontas and was consequently snubbed by James I for presuming too much above his station. Tobacco was easy to grow and required little investment, but it was land-intensive, and here lay the root of the tension between the colonists and the region's Indians. Overproduction of the 'vicious weed' caused a significant drop in the price of Chesapeake tobacco in the mid-1620s. Nevertheless, Virginia and Maryland were attracting about 1,000 colonists a year in 1640, the vast majority of them poor young Englishmen who came over as contract labourers to work on the tobacco plantations that straggled the riverbanks of the Chesapeake. Living mostly in isolated one-roomed wooden shacks, amid the heat and humidity of the coastal plains, one in three of these new arrivals perished of malaria and other diseases well before they had realised their ambition of becoming tobacco planters themselves.

Five hundred miles to the north of the Chesapeake was the more bracing climate (moral as well as meteorological) of the Plymouth colony, founded by the *Mayflower* Pilgrim Fathers in 1620. Today it is famous as the setting for the first Thanksgiving celebrations, but at the time it was overshadowed by its larger neighbour, the Massachusetts Bay colony. The 14,000 or so colonists in New England by 1640 were grouped mainly in small towns near the coast and eked out a living by farming and fishing. Most of the population was made up of Puritan families from England's 'middling sort', eager for the chance not simply to own their own land but to create a godly, disciplined commonwealth, a New Jerusalem in a new world, free of what they saw as the spreading stain of popery back home. This conviction – that England's rulers and churchmen were failing God's cause – would help to build Britain's transatlantic periphery even as it undermined kingly power at the centre.

The crisis of Parliaments

One of the driving forces behind the Puritan exodus to the New World was fear that the rising tide of popery had all but washed away the greatest bulwark of English liberties – England's Parliament. The war against Spain had forged an unbreakable link in popular imagination between Parliament and the defence of Protestantism and national autonomy. But this almost mystical understanding of Parliament's place in national life was lost on James I and his successor Charles I, who held stubbornly to the view that Parliament's main role was to vote them taxes. Money – who should provide it and how it should be spent – was central to the relationship between the early Stuarts and their English Parliaments.

A characteristic of most European states during the early modern period was their governments' drive to build the necessary institutions, industries and political relationships – particularly with their nobilities – to raise money for and to fight wars. This process, as we have seen, had begun in England under the Plantagenets, but had then stalled after defeat in the Hundred Years War and the Tudors' failure to find a politically acceptable way either to levy taxes without parliamentary consent, or to scrap the convention that the crown should ask Parliament for cash only to meet the extraordinary demands of war or national defence. The rise of the fiscal–military state elsewhere in Europe was accelerated by the Reformation – which created new and bitter divisions among Christians – but also by the escalating costs of war itself. The limited range and accuracy of early modern firearms meant that they had to be used in mass formations to be effective, which meant more men, training and equipment, and consequently more cash. Building the latest in artillery-proof fortifications – complex polygonal structures of brick and earth – could bankrupt smaller states, while at sea, the gradual shift in naval tactics during the period 1580–1650 from boarding to broadside fire required specialised, and very expensive, warships. Elizabeth could use the prospect or the fact of war with Spain to wring taxes from her Parliaments. But James I faced the problem that had confronted Edward IV and Henry VII: peace. No war meant little or no money from Parliament.

James brought this problem upon himself to some extent by presenting himself in the role of Europe's peacemaker. The great enemy to European order in his view was religious intemperance, whether Protestant or Catholic. One of his first acts as king of England was to make peace with Spain. The Anglo-Spanish treaty of 1604 ended the privateer war, at least in the Channel, and allowed for the formal restoration of England's lucrative commerce with Spain and its outposts in Europe. But there would be 'no peace beyond the line' – that is, outside of European waters. Indeed, it is a measure of how well the English had performed in the war that the Spanish could not bring them to recognise Spain's claim to exclusive dominion in the Americas. Even so, Elizabeth had done little to carry the fight against Spain across the Atlantic; and James would do nothing at all. As far as his subjects were concerned, he had made peace, and in peacetime they expected him to live largely off his own revenues from crown lands and customs.

What many overlooked, or were not aware of, was that the sale of crown lands to finance war – notably in the 1540s and 1590s – had severely reduced the size and value of the royal estate. Inflation had bitten deep too, so that royal revenue by 1600 was 40 per cent less in real terms than it had been a century earlier. Peace would of course reduce James's outgoings. On the other hand, he had three courts to maintain – his own, his wife's, and his eldest son Prince Henry's – to Elizabeth's one; and royal households were ruinously expensive. James's only way round the resulting financial shortfall was to do as

Henry VII and VIII had done in similar circumstances, and that was exploit the crown's prerogative rights for all they were worth. These financial expedients brought some short-term relief, but were merely 'patchings and plasterings of a ruinous edifice'.[37] And whereas Parliament had just about tolerated Elizabeth's resort to prerogative taxation in wartime, the same practices in time of peace were bound to meet with resistance from a body newly sensitised to the monarchy's financial needs and assertiveness. MPs had only to look at France to see how enfeebled representative assemblies became when kings had the power to raise taxes by their own command.

Any prospect of James living off his own 'proper' revenues, however, was skewered by his utter fiscal incontinence. He thought that balancing the books was a matter for his privy councillors to sort out, and was not really his problem. He had been profligate as king of Scotland, but once he succeeded to the English crown, with its vastly greater revenues, his largesse knew no bounds. Royal debts rose from £387,000 in 1603 to £775,000 by 1606, and by 1610 he had handed out some £90,000 in gifts and £10,000 a year in pensions to his Bedchamber men and other Scottish courtiers. It was generally accepted that kings, and especially newly enthroned kings, needed to splash out on gifts and sweeteners in order to cement the loyalty of their subjects, but there were limits, and James completely overstepped them. On one occasion in 1621 he laid on a feast for his Scottish friend Viscount Doncaster that consisted of 1,600 dishes and was rumoured to have cost £3,000, or 300 times what the average labourer earnt in a year.

The unseemly scramble for the delicacies that tumbled from the royal table did nothing for the court's already unsavoury reputation. The factionalism of the 1590s had destroyed any vestigial notion of the court as a forum for virtuous reform. It was now seen as a place of unbridled ambition and vice, where honest men were corrupted or destroyed. Yet if the late Elizabethan court glowed and shone like rotten wood, to borrow Ralegh's phrase, its Jacobean successor was positively incandescent. It was not only the fact of James's extravagance that drew criticism but also its objects. James's choice of royal favourites was invariably unfortunate. He was probably bisexual, but after he had done his dynastic duty and fathered two sons and a daughter – Henry (1594–1612), Elizabeth (1596–1662) and Charles (1600–49) – his preference was for handsome young men. His first favourite as king of England was a 'comely visag'd' Scottish pageboy, Robert Kerr, who caught James's eye during a court tournament and was made a groom of the

Bedchamber.[38] Kerr dominated James's affections from 1607 until 1615, when he was implicated in a murder scandal at court for which he was tried and very nearly executed. He was quickly succeeded by another young gentleman – only this time English – George Villiers (1592–1628), whom the king created viscount and eventually (in 1623) duke of Buckingham. A legal student, Simonds D'Ewes, who got a close-up look at Buckingham, found 'everything in him full of delicacy and handsome features; yea, his hands and face seemed to me, especially effeminate and curious'.[39] James's extraordinary affection for Buckingham prompted his astonishing remark that 'as Christ had his John, so he [James] . . . had his George'.[40]

James's aversion to dealing with petitioners and court suitors meant that he was happy to allow Buckingham to take over and exercise royal patronage on his behalf. The young favourite had been groomed for his role by a court faction bent on using him to manipulate the king, but he quickly developed a political will of his own, and it was not long before he had eclipsed his court patrons in influence. With James's approval he set about packing the Bedchamber with his friends, and got so many of his kin and clients jobs or sinecures in Ireland that it became almost his private fiefdom. Inevitably, he was deeply resented by those who were unable or unwilling to ride his coat-tails. And as always with court upstarts, he was despised by members of the ancient nobility for usurping what they saw as their rightful place in the king's favour. As for James's fawning upon such a creature, that worried contemporaries more for what it supposedly said about his fitness to govern than as a sign of perceived sexual deviance. Effeminacy was equated with wilfulness, an inability to govern one's passions. In a political context it was associated with tyranny.

The sight of James heaping affection and rewards on his minions was a major reason his English Parliaments were so unwilling to vote him taxes. Why, asked MPs, should the king be granted public money to squander on 'private Favourites'?[41] It was only by exploiting the wave of loyalty that followed the discovery of the Gunpowder Plot in 1605 that the crown was able to secure a parliamentary grant that was even remotely equivalent to the scale of James's debts, and the effect was merely to fuel his spending. With Parliament reluctant to supply the king's needs, he was forced to experiment with prerogative taxation, which in turn made MPs distrust him even more. It was in the hope of breaking this vicious circle that Lord Treasurer Salisbury devised the 'Great Contract', whereby in return for a lump sum of £600,000 from

Parliament to settle James's debts, and an annual grant of £200,000 thereafter, the king would abolish some of his more grievous prerogative exactions. The Great Contract was extensively debated in the parliamentary sessions of 1610–11, but struck the same rock that had sunk James's union project. As much as they avoided saying so, the king and a powerful group at Westminster held fundamentally different philosophies about how the state should be governed. Parliament-men had no thought of grabbing power for themselves, but they did want James to govern in a 'parliamentary way' – that is, by counsel and consent – and some feared that if he had too large a regular income he would dispense with Parliament and 'the certaine rule of the law' and 'bring a new forme of arbytrary government upon the Realme' after the French fashion.[42] For the king, on the other hand, the Great Contract apparently came to represent the lurking dangers of 'popularity'. Privately, some of his ministers and Bedchamber men expressed the view that bargaining away 'the ancyent prerogatives of his Crowne' would diminish royal power, breed 'a generall contempt of the King', and offer 'a readie passage to a democracy, which is the deadliest enemie to a monarchy'.[43]

The collapse of the Great Contract seemed to James a good time to rid himself of a Parliament that had 'annoyed our health, wounded our reputation, emboldened an ill-natured people, encroched upon manie of our priviledges and plagued our purse with their delayes'.[44] He called another Parliament in 1614, in the hope that it would prove more cooperative, but it too began to dispute his prerogative, whereupon James dissolved it after a mere nine weeks, and imprisoned four MPs for seditious speeches. This 'Addled Parliament' aside, James deliberately avoided calling Parliament between 1611 and 1621, declaring that he would 'rather suffer any extremity than have another meeting with his people and take an affront'.[45] Instead, he and his advisers experimented with retrenchment and prerogative financial projects to make ends meet. Among the more controversial of these projects was the sale of hereditary titles – the rank of baronet, or hereditary knight, was invented in 1611 for precisely this purpose. The merchandising of rank in this way obviously made a mockery of Essexian ideals about the dignity of noble lineage. Likewise, the Bedchamber's gains under Kerr and then Buckingham, and James's appointment of – in the words of one Essexian nobleman – 'boys and base fellows' to the privy council, struck at Essex's legacy of aristocratic constitutionalism.[46] With no prospect of parliamentary supply, the virtue (as James saw it) of peace became a necessity, even though the rest of Europe was gearing up for all-out war. His pacifism and search for non-parliamentary sources of cash dovetailed neatly with plans to auction off one of the royal princes in return for a gigantic French or Spanish dowry.

James came to detest English Parliaments – as much perhaps for the contortions he had to go through to avoid calling them as the affronts he suffered when he did. As far as he and his successor Charles I were concerned, Parliament had a duty to relieve the king's necessities and support his honour, which was also the country's honour. James bluntly told MPs that Parliaments were but 'the shadow of a monarchy' and Parliament-men 'the kings men, called by him and for him'.[47] If Parliaments failed to act 'for him' by topping up the royal coffers then he could be forgiven for thinking that they were more trouble than they were worth. James confided to the Spanish ambassador in 1614 that English Parliaments were so disorderly that he was 'astonished that the kings his predecessors had consented to such a thing'.[48] Certainly the Commons, with its 'shouts and confusion', was a far cry from the brief and businesslike proceedings of the Scottish Parliament. Scottish Parliaments got things done; English Parliaments were often too busy wrangling with their king. MPs suspected that James and Charles would have liked to rule without Parliaments if they could, and they were probably right. They were also aware that other representative assemblies across Europe were fast disappearing or losing their powers, and that theirs might well be next. One MP famously declared: 'this is the crisis of Parliaments. By this we shall know whether Parliaments shall live or die.'[49]

Money problems made the crisis worse, even in those states, such as England, where the causes ran deeper. Representative assemblies tended to get in the way of cash-hungry rulers as they struggled to raise the revenue needed to offset inflation and to fuel their growing war machines. When the French equivalent of the English Parliament, the Estates-General, was summoned in 1614 and proposed tax cuts – this at a time when the monarchy needed more money, not less – it was swiftly dissolved, not to be called again until 1789. And before we dismiss the idea of such a long interval between *English* Parliaments, it is worth remembering that the Addled Parliament was axed in the very same year that the Estates-General was, and in even more acrimonious circumstances. More telling still is the fact that James and Charles got far more money from customs duties than they ever did from Parliament. 'My Customs are the best part of my Revenues, and in effect the

Substance of all I have to live on,' declared James in 1624, which simple truth alone was enough to raise a big question mark over Parliament's long-term usefulness to the crown.[50] It was doubly frustrating for James and Charles, therefore, when MPs refused to vote them taxes and then disputed their prerogative power to impose more customs duties.

The popular party in Parliament did not necessarily begrudge paying more money to their sovereign. Some of the crown's critics actually wanted to increase taxation and to make James and Charles more, not less, powerful. 'If this king [Charles I] will ioyne with us wee shall sett him upon as great groundes of honour and greatnesse in that all the worlde shall nott be able to moove him,' declared one veteran opponent of royal policies.[51] But 'greatnesse' here did not mean aping French and Spanish models of authoritarian monarchy, but rather the capacity to wage war in the Protestant cause. While the Stuart kings looked to the Catholic superpowers for patterns of strong kingship, their parliamentary critics found much to admire in the institutions and values of Europe's most formidable opponent of Habsburg tyranny, the Dutch republic. English Puritan writers praised the Dutch for their industry and ingenuity, by which 'they imploy a world of Shippes and men, and by this meanes are not only able to maintaine the warres [against Spain], but to helpe their neighbors also with Men and money'.[52] Dutch 'greatnesse' was built upon maritime commerce and a sophisticated and up-to-date taxation system centred upon a sales tax, the excise. Members of the earl of Warwick's circle, and probably also some of the more anti-Spanish figures at court, were so eager for the money to fight popery that they were prepared to contemplate the adoption of the excise in England – hugely unpopular though this new tax would be.[53] In the end it was perhaps fortunate for these would-be Protestant crusaders that neither James nor Charles showed much appetite for creating this kind of fiscal–military state.

What progress England made towards a Dutch model of greatness before 1640 owed more to market forces than to royal endeavour. The total tonnage of English shipping tripled between 1570 and 1640, with much of this expansion coming after the 1604 Anglo-Spanish peace and the reopening of trade with Spain and the Mediterranean. A fundamental reorientation in English commerce was taking place. The traditional cloth-export trade with northern Europe was declining, while luxury imports from southern Europe and Asia were on the rise. This so-called 'commercial revolution' was fuelled by the growing demand among the middling sort for foreign luxuries. Tobacco from the Atlantic colonies, spices from the Far East and currants from the Mediterranean were among a range of imported commodities that were beginning to find a mass market. The Venetian ambassador claimed that the English were so addicted to currants that they had been known to hang themselves when they could not afford to buy them.

In the race to satisfy these consumer cravings, England's merchants faced formidable competition from the Dutch. The republic had turned the necessity of attacking Spain's and Portugal's global empires into the virtue of founding profitable colonies and maritime trading companies. Even before their peace with Spain in 1609 the Dutch had emerged as Europe's greatest commercial power. Markets that English merchants and fishermen had long dominated were being overrun by the interloping Hollander. About the only place in European waters where the English penchant for heavily armed merchant ships gave them an edge over the Dutch was the pirate-infested Mediterranean. When Dutch trading fleets began rounding the Cape of Good Hope in the late 1590s to bring Asian commodities directly to the European consumer, it was the Mediterranean merchants who led the way in setting up a rival English enterprise, the East India Company (see chapter 7). The Dutch mercantile empire continued to grow rapidly during the 1610s, but then in 1621 the Spanish renewed their war against the republic. With Dutch trade hit by Spanish embargoes and privateering, English merchants gradually began to improve their market share. Cloth exports to northern Europe may have been in slow decline, but imports from the Mediterranean and the Far East were generally rising, and the transatlantic colonial trades were beginning to show a profit. Business was booming, and the kingdom prospering 'allmost to the extremity of wantonesse'.[54] The crown had finally found its El Dorado – not up the Orinoco River but in the customs revenues that now supplied over half of its annual income.

The crown's dependence on customs revenue had profound implications for foreign as well as domestic policy. The observation by the earl of Essex (of all people) in the late 1590s that the crown's wealth increased mostly through 'traffique and intercourse' and that 'almost all traffique is interrupted by . . . warres' was an unwitting admission that neither Parliaments nor an aggressive stance against European popery were necessarily permanent features of the British political landscape.[55] The longer James avoided war the better his chances of freeing himself from Parliaments altogether. But the monarchy's shift towards a systematic aversion to military engagement was sustainable only while Europe remained at peace. And unfortunately for James, by the late 1610s the Continent was about to erupt in the bloodiest war it had suffered for centuries.

The wars of Christendom

It says much about the spirit of the times that, in many quarters, James's love of peace was seen more as a vice than a virtue. His pacifism owed something to basic common sense. He knew that he lacked the money to cut a credible figure as a champion of European Protestantism. But there was more to it than mere expediency. Alongside his desire for Protestant acclaim was an equally deep-felt urge to heal the religious divisions within Christendom. This was a noble aspiration, and yet quixotic too, given that many Europeans were prepared, indeed eager, to kill in the name of their own particular brand of Christian orthodoxy. Dutch and French Calvinists wanted James to take a stand against the Spanish, not mollify them, and by 1615 were damning him for his 'resoleution not to assist the Churche of God nor the professors theirof'.[56] Far from encouraging moves towards peace and moderation, Europe's wars of religion had given more groups more cause, and stronger justifications, for taking up the sword.

Central to James's strategy as an international peacemaker was the forging of dynastic alliances with states on both sides of the confessional divide. Following dazzling (and staggeringly expensive) celebrations at court, James's daughter Princess Elizabeth was married in 1613 to Frederick V of the Palatinate, the leader of a coalition of Protestant German states known as the Evangelical Union. But James never felt comfortable at the sharp end of the Protestant cause, and his support for the Evangelical Union quickly faded. What he really yearned for was a prestigious Catholic bride for his heir. For several years he wavered between France – restored, under Henri IV, to its pre-civil war greatness – and Spain, uncertain which of them was prepared to offer the largest dowry. But by the late 1610s he had set his sights firmly on Philip III's daughter, the infanta María Anna (1606–46).

Although James was anxious to contain Habsburg power in Europe – covertly allowing the Dutch to recruit soldiers in England, and adroitly playing the Spanish off against their French rivals – he did not share the visceral Hispanophobia of many of his subjects. In fact, he rather admired the Spanish. Spain had never been Scotland's enemy as it had been England's. And to those of his courtiers who were not persuaded by an apocalyptic reading of European politics, the Spanish looked much less threatening to English interests than the French or Dutch did. On the contrary, this 'Spanish faction' at court saw Habsburg Spain as a means of containing the growing maritime power of the Dutch republic, and of halting the creeping 'disposition in some places to make popular estates [i.e. states] and leagues to the disadvantage of monarchies'.[57]

The desirability of a Spanish match was skilfully played up by Philip III's ambassador to Great Britain, Diego Sarmiento de Acuña, count of Gondomar. The witty and urbane Gondomar was able to tickle James's intellect and vanity in ways that few of his own courtiers could. Gondomar's influence in high places was supplemented by the cash he doled out among the Spanish faction – in strictest secrecy, of course.

A Spanish match might have made good financial and political sense to James, but to the majority of his Protestant subjects it was deeply sinister, not to say unpatriotic. Spain to them was the great engine of tyranny and popery, the power behind every major threat to Protestant lives and religion, from the Smithfield burnings through to the Gunpowder Plot. England's victories against Spain in the 1585–1604 war were proof in English eyes that God was on their side in this great struggle. But His blessings could not be counted on for the future unless they maintained the fight against popery both at home and abroad. Their dismay was understandable, therefore, when James seemed only too eager to climb into bed with the Whore of Rome – or have his son do so.

James could probably never have become king of England had he been a Catholic, and by the same reckoning he struggled to command his subjects' full allegiance while he pursued pro-Catholic policies. In print, in plays and in sermons his feeble showing in the fight against popery, and his indulgence of Gondomar, were the subject of highly unflattering comparisons with the glory days under Elizabeth. Gloriana had not flinched in the face of Catholic aggression. She had not fawned on presumptuous Spanish ambassadors. Nor had she lorded it over her people with talk of the high and mighty power of monarchs. These fond remembrances of Elizabeth were of course a gross distortion of reality. Elizabeth, like James, had distrusted popular Protestantism, resented parliamentary oversight, and baulked at the prospect of war. But then the myth of Gloriana was held up not as a mirror for her supposed merits but for James's failings. Yet what was he supposed to do? An aggressively Protestant foreign policy would damage trade and beggar the crown. James found himself in an impossible situation, therefore: damned financially if he went to war, damned politically if he didn't. To add to the irony of the situation, one of the focal points for criticism of his peace-loving policies was the court of his eldest son, Prince Henry. The young prince's martial zeal and devotion to the Protestant cause attracted many former Essexians to his entourage, including the earl's own son Robert Devereux, 3rd earl of Essex (1591–1646). Under their influence the prince began to revive Essex's plans for a patriotic alliance with France against Habsburg tyranny.

Despite Prince Henry's unexpectedly early and much-lamented death in 1612, the ghost of the 2nd earl of Essex continued to haunt James. Essex's political and, in some cases, lineal descendants were in the vanguard of the 'commonwealth interest' in James's Parliaments. Besides the troublemakers (as James saw them) in the Commons there was a group of 'popular lords' in the upper House 'that aimed at the publick Liberty more then their own interest . . . that supported the Old English Honour, and would not let it fall to the ground'.[58] To the Regians here was evidence of a 'Nobility tainted with . . . [the] desire of Oligarchy'.[59] But maintaining 'the Old English Honour' was not about over-mighty barons grabbing power for themselves. It was an expression of the Essexian concept of an aristocratic duty to preserve the commonwealth against arbitrary government, to wield the sword against popery that James refused to draw. Defending English liberties meant upholding aristocratic honour and the martial and patriotic values of Leicester, Essex and other Elizabethan heroes. This aristocratic constitutionalism was strongly influenced by Buchanan and Huguenot writers and their efforts to channel aristocratic violence for public ends by redefining the nobility's honour culture within a classical republican framework.

Aristocratic violence and the potential for honour rebellions were accepted features of early Stuart society. Chroniclers of James's reign would refer to 'those vigorous days of Duelling' when 'divers of the Nobility' nourished 'private quarrells . . . and from small beginnings to raise greater Rebellions and discontents'.[60] That peers and gentry fought duels in defiance of royal prohibitions was no light matter, for as Bacon observed: 'when Discords, and Quarrells . . . are carried openly, and audaciously; it is a Signe, the Reverence of Government is lost'.[61] According to one of London's leading fencing masters, the Italian

Vincentio Saviolo, no commandment whatsoever should deter a gentleman from seeking satisfaction when his honour had been impugned. Moreover, he and many other swordsmen thought that upper-class male violence – specifically, in the form of the duel fought with rapier and dagger – had a legitimate role in upholding 'vertue, and regard of the universall good and publique profite'.[62]

Frustrated either by James's passivity towards continental Catholicism or his aggression towards Irish Catholicism, significant numbers of English, Scottish and Irish gentlemen went abroad in the early Stuart period to serve in foreign armies – mostly those of the Dutch and Swedes in the case of the English and Scots, mostly those of Spain in the case of the Irish. Career opportunities for Jacobean swordsmen would increase dramatically from 1618 and the outbreak on the Continent of the Thirty Years War. The election of Ferdinand II, a fiercely Catholic Austrian Habsburg, as Holy Roman Emperor sparked a Protestant rebellion in Germany that then dragged in states across Europe after James's son-in-law Frederick V rashly accepted the rebels' offer of the crown of Bohemia (approximately the modern-day Czech Republic), to which Ferdinand had been elected two years before. What Frederick and Ferdinand started in 1618 was really just a flare-up in the long-running war for and against Habsburg hegemony that had troubled Europe since the early sixteenth century; and it would end, at least in the west, as a struggle for supremacy between the Continent's great Catholic rivals, Bourbon France and Habsburg Spain. But in its early stages, the Thirty Years War was fired by the religious enmity between Catholic and Calvinist, and looked to many in England like the much-anticipated crisis in history that would usher in the final apocalyptic struggle against Antichrist. They were naturally dismayed, therefore, when the early rounds went to the Catholics. Backed by money and troops from his Spanish relatives, Ferdinand and his allies in Germany quickly overran and recatholicised not only Bohemia but also Frederick's lands in the Palatinate on the west bank of the Rhine.

News of how the Protestant cause fared during the war had the English public in a ferment of anxiety, anger and anticipation. The people's hunger for news was fed by thousands of newspapers that poured into England from Holland and Germany during the 1620s, and which in turn became fodder for sermons, 'popular' verses and anti-Catholic pamphlets, many of them critical of James's soft line against popery. England's print culture had been growing steadily since the later sixteenth century, but the 1620s saw the emergence of a truly national public sphere as the life-and-death struggle of Europe's Protestants, and the crown's efforts (or generally failure) to come to their rescue, became the stuff of everyday conversation. 'I can come into no meetinges', wrote one pamphleteer, 'but I finde the predominant humor to be talking of the wars of Christendome and honour of theire country.'[63]

The resurrection of Parliament in 1621 played a vital role in public consciousness-raising, providing a national forum for 'licentious . . . discourse, and bold Censure in matters of state'.[64] Yet attacks upon James for his failure to help Frederick had only served to push him deeper into the clutches of Gondomar and the Spanish faction. James regarded the Bohemian rebellion much as Elizabeth had viewed the Dutch revolt – as an abhorrent act against a rightful ruler – and he suspected Frederick's actions were part of a plot by the Dutch to draw England into their rebellious war against Spain. James would consider playing the role of mediator, but he would not otherwise intervene in what he regarded as a purely German dispute. If he had to fight anyone, he would rather it was the Dutch than the Habsburgs. Yet such was the public pressure to act manfully in the Protestant cause that he was obliged to make warlike preparations, if nothing else. But war required money, and the only way to raise the necessary sums quickly was through Parliament. James had hoped to 'lay them [Parliaments] by for ever (as he often expressed) looking upon them as incroachers into his Prerogative . . . Yet now, finding the peoples desires high-mounted for regaining the Palatinate, he thought they would . . . liberally open their Purses, which he might make use of'.[65] The problem for James was that Parliament-men would not simply vote him cash and then go home. They wanted to vent the kingdom's grievances, to beat the drum for war, and generally to meddle in matters that James thought beyond their proper competence. When MPs began criticising his pursuit of a Spanish match for Prince Charles (heir to the throne after the death of Prince Henry) he angrily dissolved Parliament after it had voted a mere £140,000 or so in taxes, which was far too little to wage war effectively.

Lacking either the will or the money for a land war to regain the Palatinate, James pinned all his hopes on the Spanish match. It seemed to offer the perfect solution to his problems. The dowry would help pay off his debts, and as part of the marriage treaty the Spanish would withdraw from the Palatinate and persuade their Austrian relatives to pressure the Bavarians into doing likewise. This was James's reasoning, anyway, and it was by no means far-fetched, for one of the most frequently used maxims in Spanish foreign policy during the early seventeenth century was 'war with all of the world and peace with England'.[66] But Spain's leading politicians and churchmen were deeply divided over whether to surrender their country's conquests in the Rhineland, while Charles's sister Elizabeth and her husband, the dispossessed Frederick V, refused to condone any negotiations with their Spanish enemies.

Gondomar nonetheless assured the young prince that if he went to Spain in person his bride would be waiting for him – which was the cue for what, even in that chivalry-obsessed age, was as bizarre an act of knight-errantry as anything found in the pages of Cervantes' hugely popular novel *Don Quixote*. Determined to win his matrimonial spurs in person, Charles, accompanied by Buckingham, travelled incognito through France and into Spain, arriving in Madrid in March 1623. Not surprisingly, the Spanish were completely thrown by this démarche. They had hoped to string out the marriage treaty talks as long as possible to prevent James allying with the French or the Dutch, but with the suitor actually in Madrid it was only a matter of time before their ambivalence about restoring the Palatinate became obvious, even to so fanciful a pair as Charles and Buckingham. In October 1623, the two men – now inseparable friends after their humiliations in Spain – arrived back in England, infanta-less, to unprecedented national celebrations.

James's 'dear venturous knights', Charles and Buckingham, returned home determined to avenge the dishonour they had suffered in Madrid. They forced James to call a new Parliament, in 1624, in which they put themselves at the head of a 'patriot' coalition calling for war against Spain and harsher measures against Catholics at home. The obvious way to fight Spain was in alliance with her greatest enemy, and by now Europe's foremost maritime power, the Dutch. The patriots proposed an Anglo-Dutch diversionary strike against the Spanish Netherlands, as well as joint naval expeditions across the Atlantic. But James despised the Dutch, and knew that any return to the so-called 'blue-water' strategy of Drake and Hawkins – the belief that Spain could be defeated largely by attacking her trade and colonies – would cripple the crown's customs revenue. Only privateers and those involved in colonial–commercial ventures in the Americas, such as the earl of Warwick and his circle, stood to benefit from a maritime war, at least in the short term. If there must be war then James insisted it should be aimed specifically at regaining the Palatinate, and in alliance with the French, whom he regarded as marginally less duplicitous than the Dutch.

In the spring of 1625 James 'fell into a quartan ague, which, meeting many humours in a fat, unwieldy body . . . in four or five fits carried him out of the world'.[67] By the time of his death and Charles I's succession the crown was committed to a land campaign, and was duly criticised when the army raised for that purpose disintegrated through disease and poor planning long before it reached the Rhineland. Equally unpopular was Charles's decision to persist with the idea of allying with Catholic France. The result was Charles's marriage in 1625 to Louis XIII's sister (Henri IV's daughter), Henriette Marie,[68] and a promise to the French to relax the penal laws against English Catholics. Distrust of the monarchy ran so deep by now that the merest whiff of popery in royal counsels was enough to exhaust much of the 'popular' party's good will towards Charles – or more particularly, Buckingham, who was believed (conveniently, but wrongly) to be the evil genius behind the king's actions. Charles for his part probably believed the half-truth that 'this great opposition against the Duke, was stirred up and maintained by such as seek the destruction of this free Monarchy'.[69] Having called his first Parliament in 1625, Charles was forced to dissolve it precipitately when it became clear that Parliament-men were more intent on attacking Buckingham than on voting taxes to continue the war. The Parliaments of 1626 and 1628–9 foundered on this same basic lack of trust.

Buckingham came to symbolise the perceived incompetence and popish counsels blighting the war effort. It was Buckingham, as lord admiral, who was blamed after a naval expedition against Cadiz late in 1625 ended in farce when English troops advancing on the town refreshed themselves in nearby wine cellars and got horribly drunk. The many Parliament-men who saw the war as a Protestant crusade were right to be suspicious of Buckingham. The royal favourite, like Charles himself, was fighting to avenge his own and the nation's honour, not for Protestant victory in the great apocalyptic struggle against the popish Antichrist. The mismanagement of the war, however, together with Charles's marriage to a Catholic, aroused more general alarm, particularly about perceived popish influences at court. Much was made of the king's patronage of supposedly popish clerics (of which more below), and the fact that many of Buckingham's relations and friends were Catholics. Buckingham was more conscientious than his critics gave him credit for, but he never shook off his image as a Spanish stooge. Furthermore, it would have required almost superhuman abilities as a soldier and statesman to overcome the Spanish, his domestic opponents and the essentially medieval constraints upon royal finances. Yet not content with fighting Spain, Buckingham led a naval expedition against the French at La Rochelle in 1627 in an attempt to topple France's chief minister, Cardinal Richelieu, who was obstructing efforts to forge an anti-Habsburg alliance to recover the Palatinate. Albeit better funded than the Cadiz fiasco – a deeply unpopular 'forced loan' and other unparliamentary levies saw to that – this expedition too ended in shameful defeat, and 3,000 English dead. 'This only every Man knows,' wrote one 'patriot' of the fiasco, 'that since England was England it received not so dishonourable a Blow.'[70]

When Buckingham himself was killed – stabbed to death by a disgruntled soldier in August 1628 – the assassin was widely hailed as a patriotic hero. What had begun as a private grudge against Buckingham had turned lethal after the murderer had read a parliamentary declaration denouncing the duke as an enemy of the people. Charles was attending divine service when he received the news. He continued 'unmoved, and without the least change in his countenance, till the prayers were ended', and then suddenly departed to his chamber, where he broke down in tears; 'and he continued in this melancholic . . . discomposure of mind many days'.[71] His royal authority defied at home, his honour besmirched by defeats abroad, and now his best friend and chief minister murdered; it all amounted to one thing in Charles's mind – a deep-seated plot led by Puritan firebrands 'to erect an universal over-swaying power to themselves, which belongs only to us, and not to them'.[72]

The 'conjugall affections' that were supposed to bind king and people were wearing thin by the late 1620s.[73] Many in Britain were dismayed by the crown's ineffectual interventions on behalf of Europe's beleaguered Protestants, and by the trend begun under James towards 'popish' religious innovations. At Westminster, speeches by royal spokesmen in defence of free monarchy were denounced as 'damnable and desparate'.[74] Trust in royal government had reached so low an ebb in the months before Buckingham's assassination that some MPs believed that the duke was plotting to use the army he had assembled in southern England not for another crack at the French but to impose popery at home by military force. Meanwhile, Ireland's Catholics saw their religion prosper on the Continent while they remained outcasts in their own kingdom. True, the Stuart kingdoms were still at peace, unlike Germany and the

Low Countries, but the potential for insurrection was very real. Across the Narrow Seas some 20,000 English and Scottish troops were serving in the Dutch army fighting the Spanish. Here was a body of troops, sustained by money and volunteers from Britain's Calvinist networks, that was larger than any the crown mustered during the 1620s. Facing them in the Spanish forces were 4,000 or so Catholic exiles from Ireland who were busily imbibing the latest in military tactics and Counter-Reformation piety, eager for the day when they could return home and put an end to Protestant oppression. The armies of the Thirty Years War had become military academies for disaffected subjects, the nurseries of rebellion.

Courtier connoisseurs

The Jacobean peace might have left militant Protestants seething, but to those not obsessed with killing Spaniards it offered richer, more constructive ways of engaging with the Continent. The break with Rome and the triumph of the Word had turned Britain into something of a cultural backwater during the later sixteenth century, particularly in the visual arts. Peace with Spain in 1604, however, removed many of the travel restrictions with Catholic Europe and its rich store of art and architecture, creating the conditions in Britain for a visual renaissance. As the number of British peers and gentlemen visiting the Continent increased from the early seventeenth century there was a noticeable quickening of interest at the Stuart courts in classical and modern European artworks. A new aesthetic sensibility began to form towards dedicated 'works of art'. Prince Henry and several leading Jacobean courtiers, among them Buckingham, took up the Italian fashion of assembling collections of paintings by Renaissance and baroque masters, as opposed to simply commissioning or buying art for a specific purpose. And when he was not clambering over walls to catch a glimpse of the infanta, Prince Charles spent his time in Madrid being sketched by Velázquez and purchasing drawings by Raphael. During the early years of his reign, Charles would amass the finest art collection of any British monarch. The painter and diplomat Peter Paul Rubens claimed in 1628 that no European court could boast such a concentration of great masters as the galleries of King Charles and his courtier connoisseurs.

The greatest painter to emerge from Rubens's studio, and the man

who introduced the British to baroque portraiture in its full glory, was
the Flemish Catholic Anthony (or as he spelt his name, Antonis) Van
Dyck (1599–1641). Van Dyck moved to London in 1632 at the invita-
tion of Charles I and was installed at court as 'principalle Paynter in
Ordinary to their Majesties'.[75] Over the next nine years his studio turned
out nearly a painting a week, for a clientele that extended from the
monarch himself to country squires, and from the earl of Warwick and
other godly grandees to Hispanophile courtiers and their wives. His
success owed much to his ability to charm his demanding patrons, as
well as to his technical brilliance and imaginative powers to capture
their haughty characters. His paintings are full of movement and rich
colour, of a wit and eroticism that made the compositions of court
rivals such as the Dutchman Daniel Mytens look drab and lifeless by
comparison. Among Van Dyck's royal commissions are some of the
most iconic images of the British monarchy ever created, especially his
portraits of Charles – the king gazing serenely from the canvas in poses
and amid settings that manage to convey a sense both of imperial
majesty and aristocratic composure (see illus. 5). Queen Henriette Marie
also sat for Van Dyck, her youthful beauty as depicted in oils contrasting
sharply with the later reality of 'a little woman with long lean arms,
crooked shoulders, and teeth protruding from her mouth like guns
from a fort'.[76] At the painter's death in 1641 the king provided a monu-
ment for him in St Paul's Cathedral, inscribed with the words 'Anthony
Van Dyck, who while he lived gave immortality to many'.[77]

Such was Van Dyck's genius, the timeless quality of his portraits,
that he would inspire artists for generations to come. Awareness of his
work, and of fine art generally, was greatly enhanced in Britain as a
result of Parliament's fire-sale of the royal collection after the execution
of Charles I in 1649. This glut of paintings on the market made art
more accessible to gentry collectors and inspired native artists in a way
that Charles had never thought necessary or probably desirable. The
chief society portraitist of the Restoration era (1660–88), Peter Lely,
was heavily influenced by Van Dyck's work, as were the great Georgian
painters Sir Joshua Reynolds and Thomas Gainsborough.

The fashion in court circles for art collecting was one aspect of a
general shift in aristocratic values during the early seventeenth century.
Gentlemen acquired modern artworks to impress and entertain persons
of taste and refinement – namely, other gentlemen. They were not
acquired for the gaze of the rude multitude in the way of, for example,
a gentleman's rich court apparel. A few of the greater aristocracy kept

up the older forms of munificence and display. In 1635 the oleaginous gentleman-lawyer Bulstrode Whitelocke and his wife were overwhelmed by the medieval scale of hospitality that greeted them at Belvoir Castle as guests of the ageing earl of Rutland. Dining in the 'great chamber' was a particularly grand affair in which the earl and countess and their party were attended and waited upon by hundreds of servants, household officers, local 'gentlemen well fashioned and habited', and 'many strangers'. But after a week or so of this lavish and ostentatious socialising the Whitelockes grew 'weary of those great feastings & ceremonies, & often wished themselves att home, with their meaner fare & family'.[78]

The trend towards more genteel and private forms of sociability is clearly visible in the layout of gentry houses. The Stuart stately home was outwardly every bit as grand as its Tudor predecessor, and often displayed the same eclectic blend of classical and Gothic forms. But inside, the social space occupied by the gentleman's family contracted, becoming more intimate and exclusive, as the relationship between family members and their attendants grew more formal. Servants' quarters were relegated to the rear or basement of the house, away from the private suites above stairs, while the hall generally ceased to be used as a communal area, where the lord of the manor traditionally feasted his dependants and dispensed charity, but rather as a waiting room for persons of low rank. Gentry hospitality became focused more on other members of the gentry, while charity to the poor was doled out at the manorhouse gates. Good manners rather than good lordship became the essential mark of the gentleman.

This preference for paintings over pomp, for private viewings over public show, was driven partly by inflationary pressures. Van Dyck's portraits often cost no more than £50 or £60 – nothing compared with the splendid clothes and jewellery that adorned his sitters. At a time when peers and gentry were economising by abandoning some traditional forms of liberality and display, artworks represented a cheap yet fashionable way of keeping up aristocratic appearances. The monarchy, it is true, continued to keep state on the massive scale of the great medieval households, feeding and lodging hundreds of courtiers and royal servants – all at ruinous expense and in contrast to the trimmed-down establishments of the French and Spanish courts. Yet while royal proclamations urged the nobility and gentry to follow the traditional virtues of 'open' hospitality rather than 'a more private and delicate course of life, after the manner of foreine countreys', James and in particular Charles emulated foreign princes in reducing their contact with the public.[79] One of Charles's first royal proclamations advised those who wished to catch a glimpse of their new king not to bother: 'Hee is contented to dispence with those publike shews of their zeale, chearefulnes, and alacritie.'[80] The ultimate in courtly spectator sports, the chivalric tournament, went terminally out of fashion after Charles's accession, to be followed in the 1630s by most other forms of public royal display.

Besides saving money, this retreat from public ceremonies was of a piece with royal distaste for shouting plebeians and 'popularity'. Charles's love of order and his admiration for the formality of the Spanish court brought about a great change at Whitehall. 'King Charles was temperate and chast and serious,' observed the equally temperate and serious Lucy Hutchinson, 'so that the fooles and bawds, mimicks and Catamites of the former Court [James I's] grew out of fashion.'[81] Access to the king's person and private chambers was now strictly limited, and the niceties of rank and court ritual were minutely observed.

The early Stuarts' love of decorum found its fullest artistic expression in the court masque. Like the chivalric tournament, masques were a foreign import and owed much to French and Italian influences. They had been a part of courtly entertainments since Henry VIII's day, but they did not emerge in all their finery until after 1604. Usually staged at Whitehall as part of the court's Christmas festivities, masques were performed against a series of elaborate backdrops, and featured a mixture of dancing, music and poetry, all combining in a highly choreographed yet fluid spectacle. At some stage in the proceedings the masquers (costumed figures), who were often courtiers, would take out members of the audience to dance in the 'revels'. Buckingham excelled as a reveller, on one occasion executing 'a number of high and very tiny capers with such grace and lightness that he made everyone admire and love him'.[82] The audience for these caperings would have been the fashionable 'society' element at court. But the focus of the performance was always the monarch or some other royal figure, for masques featured at the courts of Queen Anne and Prince Henry. Although masques sometimes communicated subtly encoded, if mild, criticism of their patrons, they invariably emphasised the vision and ideals of the principal spectator. Caroline court masques often centred upon a platonic representation of the love between Charles and Henriette Marie, the harmony of their union epitomising the bridling of animal passions and hence the royal couple's fitness to impose order and peace upon the body politic. More than simply allegories of kingship, masques were designed to initiate participants and beholders in the mysteries of princely authority. How far they succeeded is open to question. Several of the court nobility who danced in the revels would end up confronting Charles on the battlefield.

Court masques reached a pinnacle of sophistication through the combined genius of the architect and designer Inigo Jones (1573–1652) and the dramatist and poet Ben Jonson (1572–1637). Jones designed not only the sets and costumes for many masques but also their most glamorous venue: the royal Banqueting House at Whitehall. Completed in 1622, the Banqueting House introduced a new style of architecture to Britain based upon the neoclassical ideals of the Italian Renaissance architect Andrea Palladio. Jones's principal collaborator at court, Jonson, was one of the main suppliers of the masques' literary content. It was hard to tell who was the more egotistical in this relationship, although Jonson probably edged it, 'especially after drink, which is one of the Elements in which he liveth'.[83] He too was a fervent classicist, although his life of drinking and duelling in London's demi-monde provided material for his richly vernacular 'city' comedies. The Jones–Jonson artistic partnership lasted from 1605 to 1631, when Charles's preference for music and visual forms over words enabled Jones to push Jonson from his courtly pedestal.

Jonson's partnership with Jones was typical of artistic productions of the time. *The Tempest* and Shakespeare's other late plays might never have been written – or at least not displayed the lightness of touch that distinguished them from his earlier work – but for his collaboration with another leading playwright, John Fletcher (1579–1625). Shakespeare may also have worked with Jonson; he certainly acted in several of Jonson's plays. Jonson was unusual, however, in his attempts to establish himself as an 'author' as we might understand the term – that is, as a lone creative genius rather than just another cog in an entertainment industry that included hacks, actors, craftsmen and publishers. He was one of the first writers who claimed intellectual property in his works – a notion that did not gain currency until the Restoration period (1660–88) – and to fix them in the public eye by having them printed in authorised editions. Most of his fellow poets preferred to publish their works via the more exclusive and unstable medium of the circulating manuscript miscellany. Despite his love of antiquity, Jonson wrote not in Latin, the lingua franca of literate culture, but in that marginal and generally despised (by continental Europeans) language, English.

Jonson was instrumental in establishing the Shakespearean canon as well as his own. In 1623, six years after Shakespeare's death, Jonson published the first folio edition of his friend's plays. He was a great admirer of Shakespeare; his bitchy remark in private that 'Shakesperr wanted Arte'[84] effaced by the praise he heaped on his old rival in the preface to the folio edition: 'He was not of an age, but for all time.'[85] Naturally, Jonson rated his own prodigious talents above those of Shakespeare, but then so too did most other people, at least until the eighteenth century.

By the time of Jonson's own death in 1637, the London theatre still had more friends – or more powerful friends – than it had enemies. But the gap between the two groups may have been narrowing. The godly had not relaxed their condemnation of stage drama as an incitement to the Almighty's wrath; and touring companies were increasingly coming up against municipal leaders who saw plays as fomentors of disorder and contempt for authority. When a troupe of travelling players visited Shakepeare's native Stratford-upon-Avon a few years after his death it was turned away by the town fathers. Plays could still speak truth to power, and none more audaciously than Thomas Middleton's 1624 box-office hit *A Game at Chess*, which satirised Gondomar (the Black Knight) and was implicitly critical of James's handling of Anglo-Spanish relations. But Charles I would be even less tolerant of such effrontery than his father was. Indeed, it was precisely this kind of 'popular' affront to the monarchy that the rigorous new style of government that he adopted from the late 1620s was designed to suppress.

New counsels

'The most gloomy, sad and dismal day for England that happened in five hundred years' was how Simonds D'Ewes remembered the 'tumultuary' events in the Commons on 2 March 1629.[86] Convinced that Charles was about to dissolve Parliament, a number of 'popular' Commons-men had pinned the Speaker in his chair and passed resolutions declaring that anyone who supported popish innovations in religion or the king's right to impose customs without parliamentary consent was an enemy of the kingdom and commonwealth. Charles's reaction to these unseemly goings-on was predictable: he dissolved Parliament and had the offending MPs imprisoned. On 27 March he announced in a royal proclamation: 'Wee shall account it presumption, for any to prescribe any time unto Us for Parliaments.'[87] At various points over the next two years or so Charles seems to have toyed with the idea of calling another Parliament, but he never did. Although it was not clear at the time, the calamitous conclusion to the 1628–9 Parliament marked the beginning of his Personal Rule: an eleven-year period of royal government without Parliaments.

With no immediate prospect of parliamentary taxes, the case for continuing the war became hopeless. Peace treaties were concluded with France in 1629, and with Spain in 1630. A further, secret, treaty was negotiated in Madrid for an Anglo-Spanish invasion of the Dutch republic. Charles failed to ratify this pact, but ennobled the diplomat responsible for it – further testament to his distaste for the Dutch and the Protestant cause.

Although the road to Personal Rule stretched back into James's reign, it had broadened and straightened after Charles became king. Barely a year into his reign and he began to consider 'new counsels': schemes put forward by the Regians at court for enabling him to subsist without Parliament. In private he talked of 'the means used by the kings of France to rid themselves of parliament'.[88] His desperate need for cash in the wars against Spain and France meant that he remained open to the persuasions of the pro-Parliament majority on the privy council, but appeals to necessity and reason of state became increasingly common at court during the later 1620s. The spectacle of Parliament-men holding the king to ransom – telling him, in effect, that until he abandoned Buckingham and other popish counsellors they would never vote enough taxes to fight the war – lent weight to the Regians' argument that Charles's duty to defend the realm justified prerogative taxation and extra-legal measures. What finally settled this debate in the Regians' favour were the violent scenes that D'Ewes had witnessed in the Commons on 2 March 1629. Parliament was dissolved; the will of the monarch had prevailed. Yet no one had really won. Parliament's turbulent life during the 1620s had left a bitter legacy of division. Charles's supporters referred darkly to 'the new coined distinction of subjects into royalists and patriots'.[89] The 'royalists', and there were many throughout the country, still believed in the sanctity, indeed the necessity, of free monarchy. They blamed Parliament-men, not Charles, for the disasters of the last few years, and looked forward to better days.

The loudest voices urging 'new counsels' and rapprochement with Catholic Europe emanated from a group of anti-Calvinists in the English

Church. These ultra-conformist churchmen had risen to prominence under Elizabeth as part of the general shift in the 1590s towards free monarchy. James too had tolerated their presence, seeing them as a counterweight to Puritan efforts to introduce greater 'parity' (or as James saw it, 'popularity') in the Church. He believed, no less than Elizabeth, that state and Church were interdependent, and that if order and hierarchy were threatened in the Church then anarchy must follow in the civil sphere. Whereas the more extreme Puritans associated episcopacy with spiritual and political tyranny, to James the crown-appointed bishops, with their power to suppress religious nonconformists, were the nearest thing the monarchy had to a politically dependent state administration, and were therefore a vital bulwark of royal authority – hence James's mantra 'No bishop, no king'.[90] His quarrel with the Puritans did not extend to doctrine, however, and for most of his reign as king of England he endorsed the moderate Calvinism that had prevailed among Puritans and conformists alike under Elizabeth.

This religious consensus quickly collapsed, however, following the outbreak of the Thirty Years War in 1618. Leading Calvinists, whether or not they were Puritans, still regarded the Church of England as part of the international Reformed community, and therefore they attacked James's precious Spanish match and were critical of his failure to champion the Protestant cause on the Continent. In response, James began to promote anti-Calvinist churchmen, who supported his Hispanophile diplomacy, while in Scotland he pushed for the adoption of English-style church ceremonies, to the horror of the Scottish Calvinist establishment.

Charles's enthusiasm for new religious counsels was not tempered as his father's had been by a rigorous Calvinist upbringing. If the more Puritan-minded among Prince Charles's chaplains had made an impression on their young master, it was evidently not a favourable one. On becoming king he allowed anti-Calvinist clerics to publish tracts and give sermons arguing that all Calvinists, whether conformists or Puritans, were the true enemies within, rather than the Catholics. Catholicism was a corrupt form of religion, to be sure, but it was not, as the Puritans thought, inherently Antichristian. Just as controversially, they declared that since the king was answerable to God alone he could raise taxes at will, without the consent of Parliament. 'All we had was the Kings,' one loyal cleric insisted. 'He might command all[,] wifes, children, estates and all.'[91] Such assertions scandalised Parliament-men (many of whom were themselves Calvinists), especially coming from those they regarded as popish wolves circling the Protestant fold. But rather than suppress the anti-Calvinists as some MPs demanded, Charles protected and promoted them. He shared their belief in the political factiousness inherent in evangelical Protestantism; he, too, tended to see conforming Calvinists as part of a 'popular' Puritan conspiracy against his authority.

The Puritans' zeal for reformation was in part at least a reaction to the impact of inflation and increasing social polarisation – most noticeably in the emergence of a large and permanent class of labouring poor. Charles and the anti-Calvinists were equally conscious of these social tensions. But to their eyes, Puritanism and 'popularity' were part of the problem, not the solution. For if the godly activism of the Puritans could be politically subversive then the Calvinist distinction they drew between the elect and the reprobate was socially divisive. Charles wanted to create an inclusive, vertically integrated society, and the best way to achieve this he thought was through obedience to divinely ordained hierarchy. To this end he encouraged his bishops to introduce greater ceremony and reverence in church worship, to restore that sensual and communal dimension to devotion that the anti-Calvinists felt had been lost at the Reformation. There was no better cure for the sickness of disobedience, Charles believed, than a sustained course of 'the beauty of holiness'. The churchman he put in charge of administering the necessary physic was Buckingham's chaplain and religious confidant William Laud (1573–1645), who had already begun the work of overturning decades of iconoclasm and Word-centred worship by the time he was appointed archbishop of Canterbury in 1633. From the late 1620s the considerable freedom of worship that James had allowed the godly at parish level was so far curtailed that some Puritans preferred to uproot their lives and start again in New England. 'God is going,' they lamented; 'England hath seene her best dayes, and now evill dayes are befalling us.'[92] They saw how the Spanish and their confederates had destroyed godly religion in many parts of Europe, and feared that England might be next.

Yet although Laud's insistence that religion should go richly dressed was not universally popular, it chimed with a strain of religious sensibility that had been growing in England since the early seventeenth century. At court, in the universities and in some parishes, particularly in London, there was a noticeable revival of interest in refurbishing churches and beautifying their interiors. Stained glass, religious images, elaborate wood carving and plasterwork, richly embroidered hangings – the adornments of the pre-Reformation church – gradually made a comeback after 1600. With them came a taste in some quarters for greater ritualism and reverence in church worship: for making the focus of piety the comely observance of the sacraments rather than (as evangelical Protestants did) the preaching of sermons. Organ and choral music began to be heard again in English parish churches (it had never ceased in the cathedrals and chapels royal). 'Cold statute Protestants' turned into prayer-book Protestants as the now familiar liturgy of the book of common prayer acquired the status of a cherished devotional guide to sacred time and space.

Laud and like-minded churchmen took these fashions further, sometimes into controversial territory, as in the policy of removing the communion table from the middle of the chancel and setting it up 'altarwise' at the east end of the church. To some, this smacked of Catholicism. But more and more people, including some doctrinal Calvinists, were beginning to value 'order and decency' in church worship, and to reject the old association of imagery with idolatry and altars with the Mass. A generation or two later and the Laudian emphasis on ceremony, the role of reason in faith, and on moral conduct over doctrine would be conventional. Much less appealing, in the short or long term, was Laud's and the king's determination to restore the clergy's medieval authority and sense of the ministry as a sacred calling. For the first time since the Reformation, clergymen were made ministers of state and appointed to the county magistracy. Many laypeople did not object to beautifying their parish church, but they deeply resented being ordered to do so by jumped-up clerics.

Laud's Protestant 'counter-reformation' carried much of the burden of Charles's hopes for his Personal Rule. It represented the ultimate expression of his love of order and ceremony, his desire to infuse kingship with mystical and sacramental meaning. This was why he put domestic church reform before the European military struggle – that, and the fact that reshaping his subjects' religious life, although an ambitious project, was a good deal cheaper than fighting wars. Charles would probably have made a good bishop. He certainly seems to have lacked the self-confidence and *savoir faire* to make a good king. His sense of personal inadequacy – a hangover from his days as understudy to his much-admired elder brother Prince Henry – was not mitigated by any obvious store of charm or empathy. Having little insight into other people's motives, he tended to interpret opposition to his will as an attack on him personally and therefore on monarchy itself. Emotionally inhibited, rigid of mind and unwilling to compromise, he was emphatically not a political animal.

These traits, along with his lack of physical presence – being of 'a low Stature' (he was about five feet tall) and with a tendency to stammer when 'warm in Discourse' – meant that Charles could not impose himself on his greatest subjects in the manner of a Henry VIII.[93] Nor could he command the respect of his 'fighting lords' as a Protestant champion. His evident admiration for the ancient nobility was undermined by his promotion of upstarts such as Buckingham and Laud – the latter described by D'Ewes as a 'little, low red-faced man of mean parentage'.[94] His willingness to employ bishops in the highest offices of state created 'Envy against them, and lessen'd the Love of the Nobility towards him'.[95] And his concern for the temporal wealth of the Church represented another potential threat to the power of the aristocracy, for one of his priorities was to restore the lands that the Church had lost to the laity – mostly the nobility and gentry – since the Reformation. He came closest to achieving this goal in Scotland, but at the cost of much resentment among the greater landowners there. Equally disturbing – at least to those convinced of a popish plot at court – was the close parallel between Charles's re-endowment programme and the policy that the Habsburg emperor Ferdinand II had imposed on Bohemia of forcing Protestants to hand back all the property they had seized from the Catholic Church since 1552.

In his style of kingship, however, Charles resembled no contemporary ruler so much as he did his predecessor, Henry VII. Both preferred to govern through cliques of yes-men; both were reluctant to delegate court patronage to their courtiers; and both had an obsessive concern with privacy. Charles was even more detemined than James had been to preserve the exclusivity of the Bedchamber. And although he made several royal tours of England and one of Scotland in the 1630s, he rarely displayed the common touch that had endeared Elizabeth to her people.

After the political ferment of the 1620s, Charles was determined to shut down debate in the public sphere. It was the king's command, wrote one of his ministers in 1629, that 'hereafter none do presume [without government approval] to print or publish any matter of news, relations, histories, or other things in prose or in verse that have reference to matters and affairs of state'.[96] Censorship was tightened, and theological debate forbidden, although on terms that favoured the anti-Calvinists. This narrowing of the political system worked against the interests of the earl of Warwick and other 'popular lords'. That they retained a foothold at court at all was thanks largely to the queen, whose Francophile, anti-Habsburg clique shared their eagerness to attack Spain's colonies in the Caribbean. They remained a force in the localities, though, where their belief that civil liberties should be earned through strenuous public service chimed with the urge towards active citizenship among the middling sort.

To the extent that Charles was interested in projecting an image to his people it was that of a bountiful, loving father – a role for which he drew inspiration from his personal life. After the death of Buckingham, Charles had fallen deeply in love with Henriette Marie, who became his soulmate and confidante. In 1630 their first child, the future Charles II, was born, to be followed in 1633 by another son, the future James II. In all they had nine children, with three sons and three daughters surviving infancy. Charles took immense pride in fulfilling his dynastic and husbandly duties. Moreover, the patter of tiny royal feet meant that his sister Elizabeth and brother-in-law Frederick were no longer his immediate successors, and therefore recovering the Palatinate was no longer a national priority. One of Charles's ministers assured the Spanish in 1636 that 'setting aside the bond of consanguinity, which seldom sways when reason of state or private interest intervene, the Palatinate itself is as remote from his interests as it is from his dominions'.[97] Charles's self-projection as *pater patriae* rather than Protestant warrior-king was in many ways commendable. But with the future of European Protestantism at stake it was hardly the most heroic pose to strike. And he was made to look even more ineffectual by a true Protestant paladin, the Swedish king Gustavus Adolphus, whose armies came near to destroying Habsburg power in Germany during the early 1630s. News of Gustavus Adolphus's death in battle in 1632 came as a great blow to many in England. The man who would one day preside over the court that tried Charles for high treason, John Bradshawe, believed that 'more sad or Heavie Tydings hath not in this Age bene brought since Prince Harrie's Death [in 1612] to the true Hearted English'.[98]

Abandoning the military struggle in 1629–30 made Charles even more prickly about his princely honour. The mantle of Protestant champion, which had never looked very comfortable about him, would clearly no longer fit. But this is where the likes of Inigo Jones and Ben Jonson came in useful, producing masques and poetry that redefined the cult of chivalry, at least at court, removing any awkward evocations of Elizabethan military triumphs or Gustavus Adolphus's heroics. The figure of the godly knight was now ridiculed as a quixotic has-been, tilting at windmills. Charles, by contrast, was represented as the epitome of a more refined form of chivalric honour in which moral virtue and peace were the central elements. Even so, he did not entirely forsake the quest for glory on the international stage.

In the absence of Parliament, the crown introduced or revived many prerogative levies during the 1630s, but none was more productive or controversial than ship money, whose proceeds went entirely on naval rearmament. Seapower represented an effective yet affordable way of giving Charles a military presence in the Thirty Years War. A few of his subjects openly complained that the tax was extraparliamentary and therefore illegal, but without a Parliament to give voice to this grievance or to protect protesters, most taxpayers stumped up and kept quiet. And besides, the argument for a stronger navy had become unanswerable by the early 1630s. Corruption and neglect during James's reign had so reduced the navy's operational effectiveness that Barbary corsairs were raiding the English and Irish coasts with impunity and seizing fishing and merchant ships. As many as 8,000 English and Irish people were carried off into slavery in north Africa between 1616 and 1642. At the same time a titanic struggle was taking place between the navies and privateer fleets of the Dutch and French on the one hand, and the Spanish on the other, for control of the sea lanes between Spain and its armies in the Low Countries, making the Channel unsafe for English shipping. The ship money fleets may have contained too many cumbersome, overgunned capital ships to protect English merchantmen from their nimble predators, but they briefly gave Charles what he most wanted: the power to keep the Channel open for his Spanish friends, and hence substance to his claim to sovereignty over the Narrow Seas.

Charles's favourite instruments of power-projection were not fleets or armies, however, but bishops. Consciously or not, he imitated a strand in Counter-Reformation Catholicism in hitching episcopacy to an authoritarian agenda for creating a more uniform society, whose members would be pliant to social and moral discipline. In Scotland, this involved extending James's policy of promoting compliant lawyers and other biddable men to high office. The inevitable result, of course, was that the Scots nobility started complaining that their privileges and influence were being usurped by a pack of grasping commoners. Unlike his father, Charles had no familiarity with his northern kingdom.

Indeed, when he came to the throne he knew less about Edinburgh than he did about Madrid. He visited his native land only once between 1603 and 1641, which was in 1633 for his coronation as king of Scotland. But the Scots knew enough about him by the mid-1630s to suspect (rightly) that he was preparing to use his prerogative to reform – and, from their perspective, to Anglicise – Scottish church life. The effect was to boost popular support for disaffected noblemen, and to push them into the arms of militant Presbyterian ministers – potential troublemakers who had been marginalised under James.

Charles's programme of authoritarian uniformity was extended to Ireland with the appointment of Thomas, Viscount Wentworth (1593–1641) as lord deputy in 1632. Wentworth was as keen to strengthen royal authority as Charles was, and in a kingdom like Ireland, in which the executive was less constrained by law and custom than it was in England, he found the perfect environment for his brusque, uncompromising style of government. Imposing 'civility' upon the Irish was part of his job description, but he had a larger project in mind. As a friend and court ally of Laud, he was determined to convert all of Ireland's peoples to the kind of worship favoured by Charles and his archbishop. In his eagerness to strengthen the episcopate – primarily, as in Scotland, by clawing back church lands lost to the laity – and to make Ireland pay its own way rather than leech on the English exchequer, Wentworth was just as liable to harass Protestants as Catholics. In fact, the wealthiest Protestants became his most high-profile targets, their very riches being evidence in his eyes that they had defrauded the crown and Church. Wentworth, more than any of Charles's ministers, and certainly more than Charles himself, was willing to use armed force, or the threat of it, to get his way. His success in ruling Ireland lent weight in Britain to one maxim of continental high politics in particular, that 'Majestie without force is unassured'.[99]

Charles's pro-Spanish neutrality and religious policies may have been offensive to some of his subjects, but in England – 'the Seat and Center of his Empire' – all seemed quiet in 1637.[100] For all his grand projects, Charles had merely to bide his time. His three kingdoms were beginning to show a surplus on their accounts; the 'beauty of holiness' was winning converts at the centres of power and learning; and – perhaps most importantly – the generation that had grown up in the shadow of the Armada, that had challenged the exercise of free monarchy so effectively since 1603, was beginning to die out, or had emigrated to New England. Even that arch-dissident the earl of Warwick seemed to be heading for the exit. In January 1637 he had confronted the king at court and begged him to call a new Parliament and to wage war against the Habsburgs, but the king, 'smiling and composed', had politely declined.[101] Despairing of Charles and all his works, the earl began preparing for a new life across the Atlantic. This same sad prospect – of bidding farewell to kin and country, of abandoning the godly in Europe to their fate – had recently confronted one of Warwick's distant acquaintances, an obscure East Anglian squire named Oliver Cromwell.

4

Behemoth and Leviathan, 1637–60

The wisest of Men saw it to be a great Evil, that Servants should ride on Horses, and Princes walk as Servants on the Earth . . . The meanest of Men, the basest and vilest of the Nation, the lowest of the People have got the Power into their Hands; trampled upon the Crown; baffled and misused the Parliament; violated the Laws; destroyed or supprest the Nobility and Gentry of the Kingdom; oppress'd the Liberties of the People in general; broke in sunder all Bands and Tyes of Religion, Conscience, Duty, Loyalty, Faith, common Honesty, and good Manners; cast off all fear of God and Man; and now lord it over the Persons and Estates of all sorts and ranks of Men from the King on his Throne, to the Beggar in his Cottage.

> Denzell Holles, *Memoirs of Denzil Lord Holles* (London, 1699 [written *c.*1647]), 1

By occasion of these unhappy differences, thus happening, most great and unusual Changes and Revolutions, like an irresistible Torrent, did break in upon us, not only to the disjoynting that Parliamentary Assembly among themselves . . . but to the creating such formed divisions among the people, and to the producing such a general state of Confusion and Disorder, that hardly any were able to know their duty, and with certainty to discern who were to command and who to obey. All things seemed to be reduced, and in a manner resolved into their first elements and principles.

> Sir Henry Vane, *The Tryal of Sir Henry Vane, Kt* (London, 1662), 40

Behemoth

On 23 October 1642 the first pitched battle of the English Civil War was fought to a bloody draw amid the gently rolling countryside of south Warwickshire. On a nearby ridge that the locals called Edgehill, Charles I looked on appalled as his subjects inexpertly killed each other in the name of all that was holy. The king had worn tournament dress armour for several of Van Dyck's portraits, but can hardly have imagined that he would ever play the soldier in earnest, much less on English soil. Yet this was not the first time that he had confronted armed rebellion. The Scots had reduced his power north of the border to that of a mere 'Duke [doge] of Venice', as he angrily put it, and had twice sent armies against him to make their point more forcibly.[1] In Ireland too his authority had been violently assaulted. A year before Edgehill, a Catholic coup d'état against the Dublin government had sparked an uprising across all of Ireland. The Stuart kingdoms' descent into bloodshed and confusion was already well under way by the time battle was joined in Warwickshire.

The first projectile in 'these fatall civil warres' was not a musket ball or roundshot but a piece of furniture. On 23 July 1637 the dean of the cathedral church of Edinburgh gave the first reading of a new prayer book that Charles and his bishops had devised for Scotland. Modelled on the 1549 English book of common prayer, it was part of Charles's 'pious designe . . . to settle an Uniformity of serving God in all his three Kingdomes', and to instil in the Scots the sense of reverence and decorum, of obedience to divinely constituted authority, that the king and his ministers had been striving for in England and Ireland.[2] The effect in Scotland, however, was precisely the opposite of that intended. Many Scots regarded the new liturgy as popish, and the high-handed manner of its imposition as a threat to Scottish autonomy. As soon as the dean began reading the book, a section of the congregation rose up and began hurling their stools at him, forcing him to take refuge in the church steeple. Although no one knew it at the time, this was the first sighting of what the English philosopher Thomas Hobbes (1588–1679) would refer to as Behemoth, the monster mentioned in the Old Testament that Hobbes used to symbolise rebellion and civil war. It was a fitting conceit. The disasters and convulsions that racked the three kingdoms during the 1640s and 1650s seemed almost biblical in proportion. Indeed, to some they presaged nothing less than the Apocalypse, the Second Coming of Christ.

The only force that could subdue Behemoth, thought Hobbes, was another biblical monster, Leviathan – in Hobbesian terms, an all-powerful state with cash and armies at its disposal. The problem of course, as Hobbes well knew, was that the Caroline monarchy was no such animal. The troubled Tudor borderlands had been integrated into the Stuart realm, but Charles's authority was weak in the Scottish Highlands, and, in so far as it was an expression of Protestant colonialism, resented by Ireland's Catholics. Even in England and Wales, the most tractable of the Stuart dominions, the king's will was mediated through thousands of unsalaried local officials, from county magistrates down to parish constables. Royal authority was mobilised through dialogue between and within governing bodies, and the state was the sum of these many parts – namely, the commonwealth – and not the person of the king as Hobbes and other 'royalists' would have it.

Charles's power was further constrained by the crown's medieval financial system. Customs revenues might be rising, but not rapidly enough to keep pace with the costs of modern warfare or to realise Charles's 'imperial' ambitions. Above all, Charles did not strike awe into his subjects in the manner of a Henry VIII or Elizabeth I. For all his authoritarian instincts he was too soft. Whereas the punishment for insulting the French crown could be gruesomely fatal, the worst that befell those who criticised Charles was to have their ears cropped. His domineering governor of Ireland, Viscount Wentworth, summed up the dangers of royal leniency: 'A Prince that loseth the Force and Example of his Punishments, loseth withal the greatest Part of his Dominion.'[3]

Charles's majesty was diminished still further by his failure to provide a charismatic and strenuously Protestant image of monarchy. Instead he seemed remote and, to some, popishly affected. His 'unseasonable Stiffness' and refusal to play the Protestant warrior-king also did little to inspire loyalty among his nobility.[4] Indeed, in Scotland he almost seemed to go out of his way to offend his most powerful subjects – threatening their property rights and promoting bishops and other royal 'creatures' at their expense.

By 1637 a group of dissident Scottish noblemen and militant Presbyterian ministers was ready to challenge Charles head-on, and the introduction of the new prayer book gave them the perfect opportunity to rally the people against his autocratic policies. In the wake of the July 1637 riots in Edinburgh, royal authority in much of Lowland Scotland effectively collapsed, and by early 1638 the protesters had set up what amounted to a provisional government. Their aim at this stage was to limit the exercise of the royal prerogative and replace the Scottish bishops and other 'evil counsellors' with members of the traditional ruling elite. Assuming that the king would be more likely to compromise if the entire nation was arrayed against him, the leading dissidents introduced the Covenant: an oath to be taken by every adult in Scotland in which loyalty was reserved to a 'covenanted king' – that is, a monarch who would agree to defend 'the true reformed religion' (in effect, Presbyterianism) and rule according to law.[5]

Naturally, Charles saw the Covenanter rebellion as part of a long-standing conspiracy 'to shake all monarchicall government and to vilifie our regall power justly descended [from God] on us over them'.[6] He refused to bow to the demands of 'traitors', and he knew too that if he gave in to the Covenanters then it would undermine his authority in his other two kingdoms. From the start, therefore, he showed little interest in a political solution. Instead, plans were drawn up for a coordinated offensive against the Covenanters using forces raised in England, Ireland and the western Highlands of Scotland. It was an ambitious plan. In fact, given the slender surplus in his coffers it was too ambitious, and once again exposed the glaring mismatch between Charles's imperial designs and the crown's medieval financial system. As it was, the only considerable force that the Covenanters had to face was the English army that Charles marched up to the border in the summer of 1639.

And the Covenanters were ready and waiting for him. In 1638–9 they had overhauled the Scottish state, creating what was in all but name a republic in which the king's prerogative powers were vested in the Edinburgh Parliament and his role reduced to that of a cipher. For experienced soldiers and arms, they looked to the Scottish diaspora in northern Europe. Veterans from the Swedish and other Protestant armies on the Continent flooded home, while Scottish merchants purchased munitions in Holland and the Baltic. Taxes were raised to levels that Charles could barely have dreamed of, and to sustain an instrument of political will that even his authoritarian instincts had baulked at: a professional standing army. It was the Scots, therefore, rather than the English, who took the first steps towards Leviathan in the three kingdoms.

The king's military preparations had been hampered by lack of cash and a general feeling in England that this was the wrong war. If Charles wanted a fight there were plenty of foreign Catholics to be killed without picking on his own Protestant subjects. But English national pride and anti-Scottish feeling were strong enough to provide him with an army of 15,000 men by June 1639, which at least equalled that of the Covenanters and was stronger in cavalry.

As it turned out, however, the so-called First Bishops' War (1639) ended with hardly a shot fired. Duped by the Scottish commanders into thinking that their army was larger and better supplied than his own, Charles lost his nerve and agreed to a treaty. The idea of a Puritan plot against him suddenly seemed all too real, and to some extent, as we shall see, he was right to be worried. But with an army at his command he at least had the chance to confront his demons. His decision to negotiate with the Covenanters rather than risk battle was one of the greatest mistakes of his life. The enormity of his error quickly became clear to him, which was why the treaty worked out in June that year was worthless. Within six months of its signing, both sides were preparing for a second campaign.

Charles put his most ruthless servant, Viscount Wentworth, in charge of defeating the Covenanters, and created him earl of Strafford as a mark of royal confidence. Strafford had quashed all opposition in Ireland, and was sure he could do the same in England and Scotland. He urged Charles to 'Goe on with a vigorous warr, as you first designed, loose[d] and absolved from all rules of government, beinge reduced to extreame necessitie, everything is to be done that power might admit'. One summer 'well employed' would settle the Scots. Roll the dice, he told Charles, the odds are in your favour. As for himself, 'I would carry it or lose all'.[7] But such a bold strategy required money, and the only way of raising the necessary amount quickly was on the back of parliamentary taxes. Strafford therefore advised the king to summon a Parliament in England – the first in eleven years.

The Short Parliament – so called because it sat for only three weeks – met in April 1640, and was a disaster. MPs refused to vote the king money until he agreed to end the 'abuses' of the Personal Rule. Charles angrily dissolved Parliament and put his trust instead in an alliance with Spain and a loan from Philip IV of £300,000. But unfortunately for Charles, a major revolt broke out in Catalonia in June 1640, dashing any hope of Spanish subsidies. And to add to his woes the failure of Parliament to endorse his Scottish war provoked a taxpayers' strike in England that retarded the war effort still further. The government imprisoned a few of the defaulters but it simply lacked the power to override popular resistance. Charles vented his frustration on his more gung-ho councillors, demanding what had become of their 'great promises of getting money' when they had advised him to dissolve Parliament.[8]

But there were more subversive forces working against Charles than disgruntled English taxpayers. The Covenanters would not have dared to rebel, claimed Charles's supporters, 'had they not been sure to have as good friends in England as they had in Scotland . . .'[9] 'If the flint and steele had not struck fire in England, the Tindar had never took Fire in Scotland; nor had the Flame ever gone over into Ireland . . .'[10] The rebellion, in other words, had roots in godly and aristocratic opposition to the Caroline regime not just in Scotland, but also in the most powerful of Charles's kingdoms: England.

Soon after the troubles in Scotland had started, the earl of Warwick and his circle had shelved their plans to emigrate and had begun – or, more likely, had begun in earnest – a secret correspondence with the Covenanters. As Charles's predicament worsened the conspirators were joined by Warwick's cousin the earl of Essex and several other veterans of the struggle against popery and Spanish power. By mid-1640 these men were actively encouraging the Scots to invade England. With a Covenanter army encamped in the North, they reasoned, Charles could be forced to call another Parliament, one that he could not peremptorily dissolve – for only Parliament could raise the money to pay off the English and Scottish armies – and that would reform Church and state according to 'commonwealth courses'. To make the Covenanters' task easier, the plotters suborned elements of the army that Charles had managed to assemble at York to resist the Scots, and staged a show of military strength in London that frightened the privy council out of the capital. And the plot succeeded. The Second Bishops' War ended late in August 1640 when the Scots routed a small and demoralised English force under Viscount Conway, at Newburn in Northumberland, and then occupied Newcastle. A few days later the dissident English peers presented a petition to the king at York, demanding that he summon Parliament. With Northumberland and County Durham in Scottish hands, his treasury empty and his enemies seemingly in control of London, Charles had no choice but to comply.

It was victory for the 'commonwealth lords', as they revealingly styled themselves, but it was bought at a high price. In helping a 'foreign' power – the Scots – invade England they had committed treason. They knew it, and so did Charles. For the moment he was powerless to act against them. But should he regain his lost sovereignty, he would make his enemies feel it. Having coerced the king, therefore, the commonwealth lords could no longer trust him with sufficient power to do them harm, which meant committing themselves to the destruction of free monarchy. More ominously, they had started a cycle of violence that would be very hard to reverse. Charles was now willing to consider military retaliation. And with his court and army full of angry and resentful swordsmen, eager to revenge the dishonour they had suffered in what to them was merely 'the first part of this action', he had the makings of an armed royalist party.[11] 'Warre', as Hobbes observed, 'consisteth not in Battell onely, or the act of fighting; but in a tract of time, wherein the Will to contend by Battell is sufficiently known.'[12] Such a state existed in England by the autumn of 1640. Open civil war was now less a question of if than when.

The junto

Viscount Conway was not one to take defeat lying down. 'I am comming to London to the battaile that is to be fought there,' he told a friend late in October 1640, 'I hope that you will stand to it better then we did at Newburne . . . arme your selfe with zeale; and with the sword of eloquence cut in two the Puritans, and chop of [sic] the heades of all Anti Monarchists.'[13]

The battle in London formally commenced with the meeting of Parliament early in November 1640. It would sit more or less continuously until 1653 – hence its name, the Long Parliament – but no one at the time anticipated such longevity. Parliament was still regarded as a temporary and largely non-executive institution. Power was located at court, and though the battle swirled around and within the Palace of Westminster, the ultimate objective of the leading combatants was supremacy at Whitehall. The commonwealth lords and their allies in the Commons – dubbed 'the junto' – used Parliament to try to pressure Charles into appointing them his ministers of state, and they were confident that with the privy council and the key offices at court in their control the king would have to do their bidding. Charles had other ideas, of course. At first he seems actually to have believed that Parliament would fund a renewal of hostilities against the Scots. When it became clear to him that the majority of Parliament-men were more concerned with the redress of English grievances, he made a few gestures towards a political settlement while allowing his Bedchamber men and courtiers close to the queen to devise plans for restoring free monarchy by force. The most ambitious of these plots involved bringing elements of the English army south to threaten Parliament. All were either foiled or were deliberately leaked to show that the king meant business, although their only effect was to hand the political initiative to his enemies.

Despite a general feeling at Westminster that Charles's innovative church policies and resort to unparliamentary taxation had been ill-advised (to say the least), by no means all Parliament-men were willing to go along with the junto. A sizeable contingent in both Houses loathed the Scots and distrusted the junto's intentions towards the king and the Church. However, by playing on fears of a king in thrall to his scheming Bedchamber men and 'popish' minions, the junto were able to have Strafford imprisoned and to build majorities at Westminster for new laws to curtail many of Charles's prerogative powers. The junto also effectively took over crown finances. The earl of Warwick's London residence became England's new exchequer, channelling parliamentary taxes to the junto's Scottish allies while leaving the king with barely a pittance.

The battle in London would turn on how the two sides deployed one weapon in particular: printed propaganda. The Covenanters had shown during the Bishops' Wars how much could depend on good public relations. Pamphlets pleading their cause had circulated widely in England and had probably won them many sympathisers. When censorship in England collapsed in 1640 the trickle of printed works turned into a flood. The extraordinary events of 1637–40 had created a huge demand for news, and the market for cheap print in London alone was massive, for the capital's population had swollen by 1640 to around 400,000, making it the largest city in northern Europe after Paris. Printed material of all kinds, from political reportage to bawdy verse, poured onto London's teeming streets and from there out into the provinces. Print and manuscript publications had been part of the political scene since Tudor times, but never before had they found such an eager readership – a reflection, in part, of the rise in grammar school numbers and literacy levels since the Reformation. This dramatic re-energising of the public sphere created a speculative free-for-all that drew in opinions from virtually all political and social groups, even women. Some of these opinions were highly subversive. Tracts appeared in 1640 denouncing the established Church as 'Diabollicall', and urging the godly to separate from 'polluted persons'.[14] Others suggested that it was 'high time for the whole State . . . to stand up as one man' to resist royal tyranny.[15]

London's print revolution played to the junto's strengths. Warwick and his circle had been cultivating allies among London's Puritan clerics and merchants – and through them with godly networks in Britain, Ireland and New England – for several decades. The junto and their propagandists were fluent in the 'popular' languages of commonwealth and anti-popery, and using print they could speak to thousands at a time. Print was vital in helping the junto mobilise popular support for the trial and execution of Strafford, the king's most dangerous minister, in the spring of 1641. Charles would probably never have signed Strafford's death warrant but for the large and menacing crowd that gathered outside Whitehall shouting 'Justice! Justice!'[16] Strafford made a courageous end upon the scaffold, the victim (so his friend and fellow prisoner Archbishop Laud believed) of an envious nobility, and of the faith he had placed in 'a mild and gracious prince, who knew not how to be, or be made, great'.[17] The king never forgave himself for what he called his 'basse unworthy' sacrifice of Strafford.[18] Yet despite his anger and shame he was reluctant to follow the junto's lead and raise a mob of his own. Loyalist gentry lamented the fact that 'the Parliament is far too nimble for the King in printing; the common people believe the first story which takes impression in their minds, and it cannot be beaten out'.[19] The marriage in May 1641 between Charles's eldest daughter Mary and the future William II, stadholder (de facto hereditary ruler) of the Dutch republic, was the perfect opportunity for the king to restore his Protestant credibility and appeal to the people. William was heir to the Calvinist House of Orange: the Dutch republic's leading family and renowned enemies of the Spanish Habsburgs. Instead, the king ordered that the ceremony should be performed with the utmost privacy, with the result that it barely registered in the press. Above all, the king was slow to strike at the junto's Achilles heel, its military reliance on the Covenanters.

Victory in the Bishops' Wars had strengthened the Covenanters' belief that the Apocalypse was close at hand. They were convinced that the Europe-wide war against Antichrist, no less than Scotland's future security, demanded the establishment of Presbyterianism in all three kingdoms. Charles's religious innovations had so offended some English Puritans that they too now endorsed Presbyterianism, and petitioned Parliament for 'root and branch' reform of the Church of England. Most English people, however, either wanted a return to the Church of King James's time or would settle for a 'reduced' episcopacy so long as it was under the ultimate control of Parliament rather than the king or the clergy. The majority of junto-men fell into this second category. They had no relish for a Scottish 'covenanted uniformity' in religion. Indeed, they wanted to keep the divisive issue of religion off the agenda altogether until they had gained power at court. But to do nothing towards godly reformation would alienate the Covenanters, and so the junto made noises about banning the book of common prayer, and allowed Puritan iconoclasts to smash altars and images in parish churches. Political necessity, therefore, forced the junto to endorse a programme of religious reform that was as controversial as anything that Charles and Laud had attempted during the 1630s.

The battle in London, and the fact that the Church looked like being one of the casualties, had implications well beyond Westminster. When the royalists belatedly joined the propaganda fray, they put church government at the centre of their message. Pamphlets and petitions began to appear in 1641 in which episcopacy was proclaimed as fundamental to law and order. Presbyterianism, sectarianism (setting up congregations outside of the Church of England), in fact anything that threatened the established Church, was equated with 'popularity', and 'must necessarily produce an extermination of Nobilitie, Gentry, and order, if not of Religion [itself]'.[20]

The sight of Puritans on the march in Britain was viewed with particular alarm by Ireland's Catholics. They may not have had fond memories of Caroline rule under Strafford, but they knew that things would be a whole lot worse if the junto and the Covenanters had their way. Fear among Irish Catholics of a Protestant plot to destroy their religion was possibly even more deep-rooted than Scottish and English fears of a popish plot against Protestantism. During 1641 a host of alarming rumours circulated in Ireland: that the 'Puritans' were planning to massacre all Catholics; even that the king had been executed. Aware that Charles was now powerless to shield Ireland from the hostile attentions of Britain's Protestants, a group of Ulster Catholics decided to get its retaliation in first, and on 23 October 1641 staged a military coup against the English administration in Dublin. But though the insurgents failed to capture their main target, Dublin Castle, their actions triggered a mass uprising that quickly spread from Ulster into the other three provinces as ordinary Catholics vented their fear and resentment on their Protestant overlords. It was only after savage reprisals by the Protestants, however, that both sides began to commit the atrocities for which the Irish Rising became infamous. In all, about 5,000 Protestants were killed in the first months of the Rising, and the number of Catholic dead was probably similar. Civilian bloodletting on this scale, though unparalleled in the Stuart kingdoms, was not uncommon in the Thirty Years War. In 1631 between 20,000 and 30,000 civilians had been killed in a single day after Habsburg troops had stormed the German city of Magdeburg.

The Palatinate had been recovered for Catholicism by the armies of the Counter-Reformation and it seemed to Britain's Protestants that Ireland would be next. Yet most Irish Catholic leaders couched their defiance in very conservative terms, as a struggle to 'vindicate the honor of our sovereigne, assure the liberty of our consciences, and preserve the freedom of this kingdom under the sole obedience of his sacred majesty'.[21] It was the intentions of Britain's 'anti-monarchists' that worried Irish Catholics, not those of the king. Tudor and Stuart policies towards Ireland had succeeded to the extent that the vast majority of Irish Catholics, despite their sufferings, regarded Charles as their rightful sovereign. And though they consciously imitated his British enemies in using force to wring concessions from him – notably freedom of worship – they hoped to improve their lot not by fettering the royal prerogative, as the Covenanters and the junto did, but by upholding it as the sole link between Ireland and England.

The Irish Rising brought England several steps closer to open civil war. When news of the Rising first broke in London, the press was awash with lurid tales of Irish Catholics raping, torturing and murdering defenceless Protestants. The reported number of Protestant dead eventually rose in most accounts to well over Ireland's entire Protestant population. The consensus in England was that the 'rebels' must be crushed before all Ireland was lost. Yet far from uniting Charles and the junto in this common cause, the Rising put them on a deadly collision course, for neither side would trust the other with an army. Although the king had grudgingly appointed Warwick, Essex and their circle to court office, he would have nothing to do with them, and their only safe course therefore was to follow the Covenanters' example and establish what amounted to an aristocratic commonwealth centred on Parliament, with Charles as a cipher-king. In the last months of 1641 they boldly signalled their intent by creating a parliamentary army under their own command to fight the Irish rebels. In addition, they used Parliament to approach the Covenanters for military assistance in Ireland. The Scots, anxious to protect their colonists in Ulster, were eager to oblige, and by the summer of 1642 had sent 10,000 troops to Ireland. The crown's Irish policy had been all but delegated to those set on turning Ireland into one vast Protestant plantation.

By encouraging his political and military emasculation in all three kingdoms the Irish Rising made Charles even more willing to strike at his enemies, for he preferred a fight to the death before life as a puppet monarch. Yet he still had political options in late 1641. In fact, in a full

House it is possible that a majority of Commons-men would have sided with him over the junto. Moreover, the Scottish army that had marched to the junto's assistance in 1640 had marched home by the end of 1641 upon the (mistaken) assumption that both king and Parliament were now committed to allowing the Scots a big say in the civil and religious government of all three kingdoms. Charles was still alarmed by the hostile crowds that filled London's public spaces, but he was also emboldened by the 'multitude of gentry and soldiers' that flocked to Whitehall in his support. 'I never saw the Court so full of gentlemen; every one comes thither with his sword,' reported one observer.[22]

If Charles had courted the London crowd and waited until the Commons filled up again after the Christmas festivities, he might have been able to regain control at Westminster. But goaded by the queen and several of his Scottish courtiers – who were accustomed to settling political quarrels by violence – he decided to force the issue. On 4 January 1642 he led an armed retinue of 'cavaliers' to Parliament to effect the arrest of six junto-men on charges of treason. Forewarned of his coming, the men fled Westminster, and Charles was left looking both tyrannical and incompetent. His perceived violation of parliamentary privilege offended people across the political spectrum, and he compounded his error a few days later when he allowed his fear of the mob to drive him out of London. He had surrendered his capital, with all its wealth and military resources, without so much as a fight.

Charles had lost the battle in London, but in circumstances that virtually guaranteed a further escalation of violence. Certainly the junto's violation of Church and monarchy had gone too far to leave him permanently friendless. Having arrived at York in March 'with a very mean Equipage and a slender Attendance of not above 30 or 40 Persons', Charles was soon surrounded by lords and gentlemen (including MPs) who had become alarmed by what they saw happening in London.[23] Royal propaganda that rebranded Charles as a law-abiding, Protestant monarch was beginning to find a receptive audience. The king now became a champion for all those who feared that the ancient constitution was in danger from a 'popular' puritanical faction led by the junto. Spurred on by the 'ambitious designs of rule in great men', the traditional Puritan killjoy had seemingly turned into something far more sinister: the 'sectary' or separatist, bent on sweeping away the Church and, with it, all moral restraints.[24] The 'prodigious tumults and disorders' that had driven the king from London were seen as proof of this sectarian menace, as was the junto's increasingly unbridled control of Parliament and central government.[25] With the king gone, and those Parliament-men who had defended free monarchy having left Westminster, or sensibly keeping quiet, the junto assumed the characteristics not just of a parliamentary faction but of a ruling party. Angry voters began fulminating against a 'dis-joyned part of Parliament' (the junto) that was manipulating the two Houses and London's 'mutinous rabble' in order to usurp the king's powers and intimidate his supporters.[26] We sent you 'to cleanse the Body Politique', voters complained, 'not with Authority to governe us or others' – that was properly the king's job.[27] In trying to prevent the king unseating them from power, as they had him, the junto-men had been forced to override established constitutional and legal norms to a greater extent than the king had ever done. So much so, in fact, that royalists could credibly claim that Charles was 'the first King that ever took up Armes for the Liberty of his Subjects'.[28]

While for royalists it was power-hungry politicians and sectaries who were to blame for the kingdom's turmoil, for Parliament's supporters it was the 'Jesuited papist' – the elusive but unrelenting enemy of English liberties and Protestantism since Elizabethan times. Anti-popery had grown monstrous by 1642 on a diet of scare stories and rumour, made all the more credible by Charles's various plots and, above all, by the Irish Rising. The junto-men even encouraged reports that the Rising had been instigated by the king in order to raise a popish army for himself. This was enough to convince some people, particularly Puritans, that Charles had forfeited all right of obedience, and that resistance to him – however violent – was not only lawful but necessary.

The coming war would divide the English people from top to bottom. A majority of the peers and gentry supported the king – although, interestingly, a number of the ancient nobility, particularly those personally familiar with the king, aligned with Parliament, as did perhaps a slight majority of the 'middling sort'. As in any war, most people tried to keep their heads down and avoid open commitment to either side. But though the spectacle of a king beset by over-mighty subjects was a grim reminder of England's medieval past, this would be no mere clash of baronial retinues, a rerun of the Wars of the Roses. A parliamentarian officer, writing in the 1650s, was right to insist that the 'lamented difficulties which have for some few Years past fallen out in these Nations . . . [were] so general that almost every Man was in Action or affection engag'd in them upon one part or other'.[29]

Nevertheless, many English people were slow to accept that the breach between king and Parliament was irreparable, and watched in dismay during the first half of 1642 as zealots on both sides battled to seize arms and places of strategic importance. Parliament raised an army under the earl of Essex, while command of the navy was given to the equally popular earl of Warwick. Parliament had replaced many of the gentlemen captains of Charles's warships with merchant mariners, privateers and other 'tarpaulins' close to Warwick; and most of the ordinary seamen preferred, like the buccaneering earl, to fight and plunder the Spanish, not make friends with them as Charles had done. The result was that almost the entire fleet revolted from the crown that summer. Charles too began raising forces, and relied for a war-chest on contributions from his leading supporters, in particular the fabulously wealthy Catholic peer the earl of Worcester. By the time Charles formally declared war on his English rebels – at Nottingham on 22 August 1642 – sporadic fighting had broken out in a number of counties, and two of the kingdom's major ports, Hull and Portsmouth, were under siege. Behemoth was devouring the three kingdoms.

The war of the three kingdoms

For mortality and material devastation the 1640s have no rival in British or Irish history. A higher proportion of the English population died in battle or (more commonly) from the diseases and misery that armies spread in their wake than was killed during the First World War. The 1640s witnessed the birth and demise of Catholic Ireland's first independent government before 1921, in a struggle for political and religious freedom that wiped out about a fifth of the island's entire population. Scotland too capitalised on the collapse of English power, exerting a greater influence across the three kingdoms than at any other time in her history, although again at a massive cost in lives and property, and, in the end, to national autonomy. The fighting in Ireland and Scotland was particularly savage because it often pitted Catholic against Protestant and Gael against *Gaill*. In England, where the combatants were mostly Protestant and from similar ethnic backgrounds, the defeated were usually given quarter. In Ireland and Scotland the combatants rarely took prisoners.

The outcome of the war in England was likely to be decisive in these struggles. England was the most powerful of Charles's kingdoms.

Whoever prevailed in England would likely decide the fate of Scotland and Ireland – and informed opinion, even at court, favoured Parliament. London, the south-east, East Anglia and most of the south and east Midlands – in other words, the richest and most populous parts of the Stuart realm – were broadly speaking under parliamentary control, leaving the king with most of Wales, northern England, the west Midlands and the south-west. Charles had to rely on the more despised sections of the population – Catholics and Welshmen – to form a respectable army. Nevertheless, by October 1642 he had raised about as many troops as Essex, or roughly 10,000 men, which was a remarkable achievement in the space of a few months, although compared with continental armies this was paltry. The longer the war went on the more London's huge population and financial resources would tell in Parliament's favour. And control of the navy was also a distinct advantage, if only because without it Charles could neither blockade London nor provide safe passage for any foreign troops that might come to his rescue. But the expectation on both sides was that one battle, Edgehill, would settle the whole sorry business.

In fact all that was decided at Edgehill was that neither side could destroy the other in one battle. The king's cavalry under his 23-year-old nephew, Prince Rupert (1619–82), drove the parliamentarian horse from the field, but then careered off in pursuit, or wasted time and energy plundering Essex's baggage train, rather than regrouping and attacking the enemy infantry. It was therefore left to the foot on both sides to fight it out 'at push of pike', and here the better-armed parliamentarians had the advantage, and would perhaps have won the infantry battle if nightfall and the returning royalist cavalry had not halted their advance. In terms of casualties, Edgehill was a draw, each side losing about 1,500 men. Strategically, though, the honours went to Charles, who marched his army down the Thames Valley to threaten London itself, before being checked at Turnham Green in mid-November by the massed ranks of the City militia. Both armies then retired to winter quarters, the king establishing his court and headquarters at Oxford.

Ten months on from Edgehill, and a war that had begun with some courtiers doubting whether Charles could even raise an army seemed likely to end in his total victory. The king's cavalry, though sometimes ill-disciplined, had ruled the battlefield, while Essex's army had withered through disease and desertion. Militarily the parliamentarians lacked a unified command structure; politically they had split into a faction that wanted a quick, negotiated end to the fighting (the peace party), and another, led at first by Essex and his supporters in both Houses, that wanted to keep fighting (the war party). By the summer of 1643 the cavaliers had overrun all of northern England, Wales and the West Country – save for a few isolated parliamentarian garrisons – and looked poised to advance upon London itself. 'The distractions of the rebels are such', wrote Charles, 'that so many fine designs are laid open to us, we know not which first to undertake.'[30] One design looked particularly promising: negotiating a truce with the Irish Catholics that would allow English troops in Ireland to be shipped home to fight against Parliament. The leading Scottish courtier James Duke of Hamilton (1606–49) assured Charles that he could prevent the Covenanters marching south again to help the beleaguered parliamentarians. But troops from Ireland would be a good insurance policy in case he failed.

Nowhere in the three kingdoms did rebellion lead to a more startling reversal of fortunes than it did in Ireland. By October 1642 the Irish Catholics had destroyed the old Protestant ascendancy and were in a strong enough position to set up an interim national government, the Confederate Association, based at Kilkenny in Munster. The Confederate leadership included many of the Old English and Gaelic aristocracy, as well as Catholic clergymen, and Irish officers who had returned home from the Spanish army in the Low Countries. Led by these veteran soldiers the Confederate forces penned the Protestants into three main areas: northern Ulster; a new Pale around Dublin under the command of the king's lord lieutenant the marquess of Ormond (1610–88); and an enclave in southern Munster. With the English miserably distracted by civil war, the Confederates might have been better off reviving Tyrone's plan to put Ireland under foreign Catholic protection than negotiating a truce; indeed, some Confederate officers flew the king of Spain's flag in order to encourage their men. But given most Irish Catholics' desire to remain subject to the Stuart monarchy, their long-term security depended upon a royalist victory in England, and therefore in September 1643 they concluded a 'cessation of arms' with Ormond that would release Protestant troops to fight for the king.

By courting Ireland's Catholics, Charles inevitably invited accusations by the parliamentarian press of popish plotting and betraying Protestantism. Nevertheless, the military positives of the Cessation just about outweighed the propaganda negatives. The same could not be said though of a court-sponsored design by Ulster's greatest Catholic nobleman Randal MacDonnell, earl of Antrim (1609–83), for a

Confederate–royalist offensive against the Covenanters in Scotland. Antrim's schemes, like the man himself, were audacious and self-interested, but not very practical. The so-called 'Antrim plot' never amounted to much. But its discovery and disclosure in the summer of 1643 was used by the parliamentarian war party to advance a fine design of their own: a military alliance with the Covenanters.

Yet even as the waters threatened to close over their heads, many parliamentarians hesitated to reach for a Scottish lifeline. Inviting in the Scots might well provoke the king to bring in Confederate troops or seek military aid from the French; indeed, in September 1643, Charles sent an ambassador to Paris for that very purpose. Had the king succeeded in obtaining a French army (never very likely given France's ongoing war with Spain), it would not only have tipped the military balance in England in his favour but also have brought all the attendant horrors of a foreign invasion and Catholic armies fighting Protestant. Englishmen killing Englishmen was bad enough without the atrocities and devastation of the Thirty Years War. Yet the Antrim plot suggested that the king was indeed prepared to deploy Irish Catholics against British Protestants. This revelation – which according to one parliamentarian MP 'did more work upon most men than anything that had happened during these miserable calamities' – enabled the war party at Westminster to arrange for a parliamentary delegation to be sent to Edinburgh to negotiate a military alliance.[31] In Scotland the Antrim plot had a similar effect. Under the leadership of Antrim's ancestral enemy the marquess of Argyll (1605/7–61) – chief of the Protestant clan Campbell – the hardline Covenanters were able to outmanoeuvre Hamilton. In September 1643 the Westminster and Edinburgh Parliaments agreed the Solemn League and Covenant, by which the Scots would send an army to fight against the king in return for what they took as a pledge by the parliamentarians, once victorious, to establish Presbyterianism in England and Ireland.

After Antrim and Hamilton had failed him, the king's only hope of preventing another Covenanter invasion was to win the English Civil War – and for a few weeks in August 1643 he had come close to doing just that. If his army had followed up its capture of Bristol (England's third-largest city) by marching on London, the mere news of its coming would probably have been enough to turn the trickle of high-level defections from Parliament into a torrent. Certainly Essex's few thousand, demoralised troops would not have offered much resistance. Instead, the king's forces became bogged down besieging Gloucester, and the moment passed. With his army reinforced by City militia regiments, Essex relieved Gloucester in September before fighting his way back to London and a hero's welcome.

The events of September 1643 suggested that there would be no quick end to the wars that had consumed the Stuart realm. Until that point the troubles in each kingdom had remained largely discrete, if causally interlinked. But under the impact of the Cessation and the Covenant, England became the main theatre in something not far short of a single conflict: the war of the three kingdoms. The king received his first shipment of Protestant troops from Ireland in October 1643; a large Covenanter army under the earl of Leven entered northern England in January 1644; and six months later a trimmed-down version of the Antrim plot saw a party of 'Redshanks' – Gaelic warriors from the Catholic clans of Ulster and the western Highlands – embark from Ireland for Scotland and a blood-soaked campaign that its leader, James Graham, marquess of Montrose (1612–50), hoped would end with the destruction of the Covenanter regime and a victorious march into England in support of the king.

As well as intensifying the wars within the Stuart realm, the Cessation and Covenant raised new fears and resentments at each kingdom's centres of power. This was particularly the case at Westminster, where they were midwives to the most aggressively anti-monarchist of the parliamentary factions: the Independents. The heads of this bicameral 'interest' were mostly former junto-men and members of the war party. But they also included several peace-party grandees: men so appalled by Charles's willingness to do deals with Irish Catholics that they regarded Scottish intervention as a necessary evil to secure his utter defeat and a dictated settlement that would strip him of power. Moving in the opposite political direction in the autumn of 1643 was the earl of Essex. An intensely proud man, Essex resented having to share military honours and Parliament's resources with the Scottish army. He now began to push for a swift, negotiated settlement that would restore the king to something like his former glory and Essex himself to his father's former role as Protestant Europe's greatest fighting lord. It was the Independents, however, who looked better prepared for the realities of life, and death, in the wake of the Cessation and Covenant. They had high hopes of the Scots, and were closely involved in the creation of a new parliamentary force to rival Essex's, the Eastern Association army.

The officer put in charge of the Eastern Association cavalry was the MP for Cambridge in the Long Parliament, Oliver Cromwell (1599–1658).

Both a gentleman and a Puritan, he spent most of his life trying to reconcile his attachment to the traditional propertied order with submission to God's overthrowing providence. He was not particularly easy on the eye or ear at the start of his political career, and yet was memorable for that very reason, as one courtier later recalled: 'I came one morning into the House [of Commons] . . . and perceived a Gentleman speaking . . . very ordinarily apparelled . . . his linen was plain, and not very clean . . . a speck or two of blood upon his little [neck] band . . . his countenance swolln and reddish, his voice sharp and untunable, and his eloquence full of fervour.'[32] But his boldness in the field, and obvious commitment to absolute victory, won him formidable allies at Westminster and among the London press. By 1644 he had matured into an unscrupulous politician, and was accounted even by his enemies as 'a very wise and active head'.[33] His genius as a commander was to instil in his men not only the courage and determination of Prince Rupert's Cavaliers but also the discipline to regroup after charging, rather than chasing off into the distance. His troopers, the famous Ironsides, became the elite cavalry of the English Civil War.

Cromwell won more admirers for his part in the largest battle of the war, Marston Moor. On 2 July 1644 one of the greatest-ever concentrations of troops on British soil prepared to do battle on heathland to the south-west of York. Facing the combined forces of the Eastern Association army, Leven's Scottish army and the northern parliamentarian army commanded by Ferdinando Lord Fairfax – in all, 28,000 men – were 20,000 royalist troops under Prince Rupert and the marquess of Newcastle. The royalists made up for their numerical inferiority by sweeping a large part of their opponents' horse and foot from the field. But the cavalry on the parliamentarian left under Cromwell and the Scottish commander David Leslie routed Rupert's horsemen, and then, with Lord Fairfax's son, Sir Thomas Fairfax, wheeled right and destroyed the unprotected royalist infantry. The marquess of Newcastle's famous regiment, the Whitecoats, refused to surrender and 'were killed in rank and file'.[34] The parliamentarians and Scots lost about 2,000 men, the royalists twice that number, and, more important, control of northern England.

The royalists' defeat in the North was partially offset by an unexpected victory over the earl of Essex in the south. Determined to regain the honour and influence that he had enjoyed before Parliament began looking elsewhere (most notably to the Covenanters) for military leadership, he disobeyed orders and attempted to reconquer the West

Country, only to end up by September with his army bottled up in Cornwall, the most royalist county in England. The earl himself escaped in a fishing boat: 'I thought it fit to look to myself, it being a greater Terror to me to be a Slave to their ['the royalists'] Contempts than a thousand Deaths.'[35] But his infantry were forced to surrender en masse, prompting one royalist hack to ask mockingly 'why the Rebels voted To live and die with the Earle of Essex, since the Earle of Essex hath declared he will not live and die with them'?[36] This and further military humiliations for Parliament that autumn convinced the Independents (and many others at Westminster) that the time had come for wholesale military reform, and in particular for removing Essex and other commanders who refused to fight for absolute victory.

In their eagerness to defeat the king the Independents had already jettisoned the Scots. Scottish intervention helped Parliament much more than the piecemeal importation of English troops from Ireland helped the king. But Montrose's campaign in Scotland – which would result in six straight victories against the Covenanters – prevented Leven's army from making a decisive thrust into southern England in case it should be needed at home. The Independents had gone along with Scottish plans for a covenanted uniformity in religion only on sufferance, as the purchase price of total victory. Once it became clear, as it had by September 1644, that Scottish intervention would not win the war, they switched their support from the Scots to the most resolute English fighters. Unfortunately for the cause of good relations between Westminster and Edinburgh, these men were often Puritans of Cromwell's stamp, who believed passionately that individual congregations should be free to govern themselves rather than be subject to the authority of a national Presbyterian Church as demanded by the Scots. This was the principle from which the Independents took their collective name.

The increase of these Congregationalists and more extreme sectarians, and their tacit protection by the Westminster Independents, persuaded Essex and his supporters to lay aside their hostility to the Scots. Both groups were becoming increasingly alarmed by the spread of radical ideas, particularly among Parliament's soldiers, and both believed that the introduction of a coercive, Scottish-style Presbyterianism would help preserve order – hence the name given to the Scots' new English allies, the Presbyterians. Politically this was a wise move by Essex and his friends. The Scots had an army in northern England, and strong support among London's Presbyterian leaders. In general, however, the

English people resented interference by the 'beggarly' Scots, and especially their insistence that the clergy should decide religious issues, not civil authorities such as Parliament. The Independents would prove very adept at exploiting this xenophobia and anticlericalism. Although just as keen on preserving order as the Presbyterians, they believed that the way to contain religious divisions was by allowing 'liberty of conscience' to godly nonconformists.

The Independent grandees were the architects of England's most celebrated fighting force, the New Model Army. Using their dominance of the Commons and of Parliament's main executive body, the Committee of Both Kingdoms, they welded the parliamentarian armies into a new, consolidated command under Sir Thomas Fairfax, with Cromwell as his lieutenant-general of cavalry. Essex resigned, pre-emptively, in the spring of 1645, and many other experienced officers were either laid aside or quit. This purge of military talent helped convince the king and his advisers that the 'New Noddle' would be no match for their veterans. Their complacency was such that when Fairfax caught up with them at Naseby, in Northamptonshire, on 14 June, they had only about 9,000 troops to his 17,000. Nevertheless, the battle began well for the royalists, with Rupert's cavalry routing their opponents on Fairfax's left. But though Rupert's troopers had long since learned not to disappear in pursuit of the enemy horsemen, as they had at Edgehill, they were daunted by the sheer number of parliamentarian troops protecting Fairfax's left. Rupert could do little, therefore, but regroup his men and return to the main battlefield, and by that time it was pretty much all up with the king's army. Fairfax's infantry, having repulsed a royalist advance in the centre, soon began to bear down on their outnumbered opponents, while Cromwell's Ironsides swept away the king's cavalry on the right and then wheeled left to deal with the royalist foot. In short order the king's infantry found itself beset on all sides and promptly surrendered.

Royalist casualties at Naseby were relatively light. It was the capture of 4,000 veteran royalist foot soldiers that made the victory decisive. Almost as damaging for Charles was the seizure after the battle of his private correspondence. These letters, which Parliament published, revealed the king's plans for using Irish and foreign troops in England. They seemed to vindicate the Independents' distrust of Charles and their insistence that there were 'noe hopes of peace but by the sword'.[37]

Naseby was the beginning of an almost unbroken run of victories for the New Model. Although the mopping-up operation against royalist resistance in the West Country, Wales and around Oxford would take another year, there would be no way back for the king after June 1645. Yet among parliamentarians too there were winners and losers. What Naseby really did was confirm the Independents and what was effectively their army, the New Model, as the most powerful force in the three kingdoms. The ascendancy of this anti-Scottish faction meant that the inevitable resurgence of English power after the war would threaten not just the Irish Confederates but also the Scottish Covenanters. A Presbyterian or a royalist victory would probably have preserved one, possibly both, of the other two kingdoms from English invasion. But in their determination to usurp the king's powers, and to pursue a general settlement with (in Cromwell's words) 'the English interest in the head of it', the Independents made conflict with the Covenanters probable, and the brutal reconquest of Ireland all but inevitable.[38] Of all the possible outcomes of the English Civil War, victory for the Independents was the most likely to prolong the war of the three kingdoms.

A military aristocracy

Charles and his courtiers spent the weeks after Naseby recuperating at Raglan Castle in south Wales, the fortress-cum-palace of the earl (now marquess) of Worcester. There they played bowls – and weighed up their options. Prince Rupert, like most professional soldiers, saw no virtue in fighting a lost cause, and urged his uncle to make peace with Parliament. But the king would not listen: 'God will not suffer rebels to prosper,' he insisted, 'or this cause to be overthrown.'[39] Charles hoped to press northwards to link up with Montrose, and got as far as Newark when he received news that Montrose's hitherto all-conquering army had been caught napping (almost literally) in the Lowlands by Leven's cavalry and annihilated. The Covenanters, though weakened, were back in control of Scotland.

Still the king would not surrender. His hopes now rested mainly on the Irish Confederates living up to their loyal protestations and sending him an army. The difficulty here was that the man charged with negotiating a royalist–Confederate alliance, the marquess of Ormond, was too conscientious a Protestant to make the necessary concessions on Catholic freedom of worship. Moreover, the Confederates' minimum terms expanded considerably following the arrival at Kilkenny late in 1645 of a papal nuncio (envoy), Giovanni Battista Rinuccini, with instructions to establish 'an unalterable right to the public exercise of the catholic religion' in Ireland.[40] Aware that the now defeated Charles was in no position to grant even the smallest of Catholic demands, Rinuccini urged the Confederates to conquer all of Ireland so that they could assist the king or resist Parliament from a position of maximum military strength. Events would prove that the Confederates lacked the resources and in some cases the political will to defeat Ormond's Irish royalists. But Rinuccini's influence ensured that no Confederate army would cross the Irish Sea to the king's rescue.

With succour from Ireland looking increasingly unlikely, some of the king's advisers began to consider an even more controversial course: a military alliance with their old enemies the Scottish Covenanters. The king's secretary of state, George Lord Digby, urged Leven's officers to consider the wisdom of remaining loyal to the English Parliament when it was dominated by men (the Independents) 'who make it evident to all the world that they both hate and contemne you and . . . meane nothing more then the subversion of monarchye it selfe'.[41] The royalists' furtive negotiations with the Covenanters were brokered by French agents as part of an attempt by Cardinal Mazarin's government to create an unlikely alliance between the royalists, the Covenanters, the English Presbyterians and pro-French elements at Dublin and Kilkenny to defeat the Independents. The French crown was too busy during the 1640s fighting either the Spanish or its own rebellious subjects to send Charles troops, but the last thing it wanted on its doorstep was an aggressive republican regime with a formidable army at its disposal. The French, with the help of their Scottish friends and the queen (who had left England for Paris in 1644), persuaded the king that the Covenanters were willing to defy the English Parliament on his behalf. So it was that in April 1646 a heavily disguised Charles, accompanied by just two servants, slipped through the parliamentarian forces besieging his head-quarters at Oxford and moved secretly and circuitously northwards to arrive at Leven's army in Nottinghamshire early in May.

Possession of the king was the ultimate prize in British politics. Without his consent no final settlement appeared possible. The Scots therefore, though they had anticipated Charles's arrival, could hardly believe their luck when he actually turned up in their midst. The Scots and the Presbyterians now apparently held the winning hand, for nobody doubted that they could persuade the king to abandon episcopacy for Presbyterianism, which was the minimum price at which Leven's army would support his restoration.

News of the king's flight to the Scots left some Independents angry, others 'drouping sorrowfull', but all generally in a 'great fright'.[42] Some royalists too found the idea of a restoration of monarchy at the hands of the Covenanters deeply troubling. The prominent courtier Sir Edward Hyde (1609–74) feared that it would spell the final ruin of the Church of England and other 'essential props and supports of the old Government'.[43] Only by keeping to 'known ways' could Charles revive the loyalty of the English people, which for Hyde was the only sure and legitimate foundation of royal authority. The queen and her circle, on the other hand, did not much care what the people thought. Like Strafford before them they believed that military force, not the people's affection, was what won and lost kingdoms, and they tried desperately to persuade Charles to accept Presbyterianism. But Charles, though browbeaten by Presbyterian preachers, just as his father had been, would not forsake the Church in order to gain Leven's army. This was partly a matter of conscience, partly a shrewd political calculation. Presbyterianism would destroy his royal supremacy in religion, and like Hyde (and Hobbes for that matter) he believed that the people were 'governed by pulpits more then the sword, in tymes of peace'.[44]

The longer Leven's army remained in England with the king in its midst the more likely it seemed that Anglo-Scottish relations would degenerate into an all-out war. At Westminster there were angry exchanges between the Independent grandees and Scottish representatives. 'Yow thinke yow walke in a mist,' the Scots told the grandees, 'but we p[er]ceave yow well ynoughe . . . we have reason to beleeve yow intend when opportunity is given to fall uppon us, but we neyther feare yow nor care for yow.'[45] But this was bluster. The Scots did not want war with the New Model over an 'uncovenanted' king. Besides which, even their closest English allies were now urging them to go home. While the Scots continued to occupy northern England a majority of MPs were unwilling to disband Fairfax's army – the Independents' main political prop – and the Independents could score easy propaganda points by portraying the Presbyterians as Scottish stooges.

Early in 1647, Leven's army handed over Charles to the English Parliament and marched back to Scotland. The Covenanters knew that surrendering the king 'would make them to be hissed at by all nations; yea the doggs in the streets would pisse uppon them'.[46] But they did not want an unregenerate Charles stirring up trouble in Scotland. Moreover, by withdrawing from England, the Scots handed the political initiative to their English allies. Even without their popular leader the earl of Essex – who had died in September 1646 after 'takeinge Could in huntinge the Stagg' – the Presbyterians were well placed to capitalise on the return of peace. Many parts of England, particularly the North and the valleys of the Thames, Severn and Trent, had endured years of warfare and plundering. And those regions that had escaped the fighting had been taxed at unprecedented levels. To add to the general misery the 1646 harvest had failed, driving up the price of basic foodstuffs and forcing tenants to default on their rents. By 1647 there was widespread longing for a return to 'known ways' – to the rule of king, law and Church – and the Presbyterians, as the enemies of the army and the sects, were seen as the party to deliver.

The Presbyterians' first mistake was to underestimate the New Model. Determined to destroy the army, they tried to disband the more radical units on the cheap, and pack the rest off to fight the Confederates in Ireland. Yet the fact that Fairfax's men had held together for many months without pay or plunder, when most soldiers would simply have deserted, is proof that the New Model was no ordinary army. The soldiers' incredible victories had convinced them that they were God's particular instruments for the restoration of England's honour and liberties. Having risked their lives in this cause they refused to stand tamely aside and let the Presbyterians take the spoils of victory. And they were incensed when, in March 1647, the Presbyterians branded them 'Enemies to the State, and Disturbers of the Public Peace'.[47] The army now mobilised for political action, publishing manifestos to win public support and moving menacingly close to London. In the thick of these events was Cromwell, who combined the roles of Independent grandee at Westminster and senior army officer to highly influential effect.

The Presbyterians' second mistake was to press for the return of Leven's army. This plan backfired spectacularly. Hamilton, the leader of the pro-intervention camp in Scotland, was contending with Argyll for control of the Scottish state, and in no position to send an army into England. Not only that, but when Cromwell and the Independent grandees discovered what the Presbyterians were up to they reacted by seizing the likely focus of any military action: the king. Early in June a force of New Model cavalry descended on Holdenby House in Northamptonshire, where Charles was being guarded by Presbyterian troops, and carried him off to army headquarters. When the Presbyterians took control of Parliament and London late in July in an attempt to overawe the army both politically and militarily, the New Model made them eat their defiant words by marching virtually unopposed into the capital.

The army and the Independents had now 'conquered' both king and kingdom, and all that remained was to make Charles acknowledge it. Late in July they presented him with peace proposals that they had drawn up in consultation with those royalists who wanted an exclusively English settlement, not one achieved by foreign intervention. These proposals were exceptionally generous to the king, and even left room for the establishment of a non-coercive episcopal Church. But Charles, unwilling to compromise his sovereignty or his conscience, had decided on a strategy of playing the various factions off against each other to see if he could reach an even better deal. His brinkmanship paid off late in 1647 when Hamilton's party in Scotland agreed to send down an army to restore him to power in return for a royal pledge to establish Presbyterianism in England for just three years. Hamilton had been able to get the better of Argyll by playing on Scottish fear of the Independents and their 'Sectarian army'. The Hamiltonians' agreement with the king, known as the Engagement, also stipulated that if they invaded England, Ormond would return to Ireland – which he had left early in 1647 after surrendering Dublin to the English Parliament – to lead a new royalist campaign. Whereas the Scots were threatened with military encirclement by the Independents, the peoples of Ireland – with the exception of the Independents' friends among the New English – faced ruthless subjugation. It was by harnessing this reaction in the three kingdoms against the rise of the Independents and New Model that Charles obtained the means to fight a second civil war.

In the event, the Second Civil War was a desultory and, from the king's point of view, calamitous conflict. Fought during the spring and summer of 1648, it consisted of a series of local insurrections in England and Wales, a bungled naval campaign by the English royalists, and an invasion by the Scottish Engagers. All these actions were inspired to varying degrees by a desire to restore the king, combined with resentment at the Independents' 'overrunning, disarming, and plundering [of England] . . . as if it were a conquered nation'.[48] The strategy of the royalists and Hamiltonians, in so far as they had one, was that the local risings would coincide with the Scottish invasion and thereby stretch Fairfax's army to breaking point. But when the Kirk and Argyll's party in Scotland discovered that the Engagement did not require Charles to establish a permanent Presbyterian Church in England, they did all they could to retard the war effort, which meant that it took Hamilton months to raise a mere 14,000 troops, and most of these were raw recruits. By the time he finally advanced southwards from his bridgehead in Cumberland in mid-August, the New Model and local parliamentarian units had either crushed or contained the most serious royalist risings, which were largely confined to Kent, Essex and south Wales. In consequence, Cromwell was left free to march north with a sizeable force of New Model troops.

The one major field engagement of the war was brutally decisive. What began as a battle at Preston, in Lancashire, on 17 August 1648 quickly turned into a rout as Hamilton's inept generalship and feeble army buckled under the onslaught of Cromwell's 10,000 veterans. When news of Hamilton's defeat reached Scotland, hardline Covenanters rose in the name of the Kirk and toppled the Engager regime that was held responsible for the defeat. And just to make sure that Scotland posed no further threat to England, Cromwell marched his army across the border in September and briefly occupied Edinburgh.

If the Second Civil War had been a popularity contest, the Independents would have lost comprehensively. The English and Welsh resented paying high taxes to maintain a pack of Puritan killjoys and an army full of sectaries. 'These Grandees', wrote one pamphleteer, 'govern by power, not by love, and . . . with military Aristocracy, or rather Oligarchy, rule this Nation with a rod of Iron.'[49] Had the Independents' enemies shown the same unity as Fairfax's army, the king would have been restored in 1648. But the First Civil War had created political and religious divisions that bit deep into local communities, preventing the kind of broad-based campaign of provincial unrest that had helped bring down Charles I's Personal Rule in 1640. Presbyterians distrusted royalists, royalists distrusted Presbyterians, and both distrusted the Scottish Engagers. One Cavalier allegedly declared that 'though they hated the Scots as bad as the Turkes, yet they would all joyne either with Scot or Turke to suppresse the Independ[en]ts & restore the King'.[50] But yet other royalists were reported as saying that they would prefer the king to perish than see him restored by Scottish hands. Infighting between pro- and anti-Engagement factions led the royalists to squander their greatest coup of the Second Civil War: the defection of eleven of Parliament's warships.

Back in April 1648, and facing the prospect of refighting a war they thought they had won, army officers had held a prayer meeting at Windsor at which they had vowed 'if ever the Lord brought us back again in peace, to call Charles Stuart, that man of bloud, to an account for the bloud he had shed'.[51] Yet far from punishing its royal prisoner for causing another war, Parliament – in defiance of the army – began negotiating with him in September. The public pressure on Parliament-men to reach a permanent agreement with the king had now become enormous. Even the Independent grandees regarded a royal restoration as better than the likely alternative: a settlement imposed by the army in which Charles was punished and the established political order radically overhauled.

Again, the ostensible sticking-point in negotiations was Charles's refusal to renounce episcopacy. But even after losing another civil war, he was still trying to scheme his way to a more advantageous deal. In fact, by November, he was simply playing for time, having received news that Ormond was engaged in talks with the Irish Confederates that appeared likely to bring all of Ireland under royalist control. Rinuccini's party, like Argyll's in Scotland, refused to accept any settlement with the king that did not meet its religious demands, although in the nuncio's case these related not of course to Presbyterianism but to Catholic worship. Even so, the majority of the Confederates were so desperate to see Charles restored, and so terrified of the New Model's intentions towards him, that they neutralised the nuncio's party by force and agreed a treaty that dissolved the Confederate Association and finally put its armies at Ormond's disposal.

Charles's power was hydra-like: cut off in England and Scotland, it had sprung up again in Ireland. Cromwell and many other soldiers had regarded Hamilton's invasion as a wicked design by the king 'to vassalise us to a foreign nation [i.e. Scotland]'.[52] By threatening to repeat this strategy using the Irish, Charles was risking not just his crown but his life.

The gauntlet that Charles had thrown down was taken up by the army. Early in December 1648 it broke decisively with the Independent grandees by purging the Commons of the 230 or so Members (or almost half the House's total number) who favoured negotiating with Charles – a group that included Independents as well as Presbyterians. About 100 more Commons-men boycotted the House in protest. With the army and its radical friends in control at Westminster, the way was now clear for a reckoning with the king. The grandees and their royalist allies of 1647 desperately tried to persuade Charles to appease the army by disavowing Ormond and resigning all claims to sovereignty. But with Ireland apparently his to command, and most of his subjects in England and Scotland vehemently opposed to the army's proceedings, Charles continued his old game of brinkmanship. Some soldiers reacted by baying for regicide. The king had defiled the land with innocent blood, and divine and natural law demanded his death. Yet it was only while he lived that Charles could call off Ormond and the royalist fleet, and prevent the Prince of Wales assuming the crown and instigating yet more foreign invasions from his base in the Dutch republic. It was therefore decided to put the king on trial as a last-ditch attempt at 'bargaining with menaces'. A 'high court of justice' was hastily convened on the apparent understanding that it would spare the king's life if he called off Ormond and his other dogs of war. But Charles, standing alone before his accusers in Westminster Hall, repeatedly refused to recognise the court's authority to try him. In effect, he was playing out the hand he had acquired in signing the Engagement, daring the court to do its worst in the knowledge that only his restoration could save Parliament from another, even bloodier, war. Charles was no would-be martyr, as he is often portrayed, but a king so convinced of his right and duty to rule that he was prepared to gamble with his life to regain his throne. And it was this determination to persist with his perceived design to 'vassalise' the English to the Celtic nations that removed any lingering doubts in the minds of Cromwell and other regicides that the providential moment for justice against 'that man of bloud' had finally arrived.

The 30th of January 1649 was a cold day; so cold in fact that the Thames had frozen over. Shortly after midday, Charles stepped onto a timber scaffold at Whitehall gate, within sight of the Banqueting House, that unsurpassed symbol of Stuart monarchy (see illus. 7). Wearing two shirts against the cold, in case a shiver might be mistaken for fear, he carried himself 'cheerfully' and spoke calmly and with dignity, forgiving the chief contrivers of his death, and maintaining his innocence except in one point: 'That an unjust Sentence that I suffered for to take effect [Strafford's execution in 1641], is punished now, by an unjust Sentence upon me.' Lying prostrate, his neck upon the block, Charles said his prayers, and then the executioner severed his head with one blow, held it up to the crowd, and uttered the traditional words: 'Behold the head of a traitor.'[53]

The world turned upside down

The astonishing events of January 1649 were the immediate consequence of royal miscalculation and the contingencies of battle. But Charles's fate, like that of his kingdoms, was tied to greater forces than

1. Henry VII by unknown
Flemish artist, 1505.

2. From *The Image
of Irelande* by John
Derrick, 1581. An
English army on
the march in Gaelic
Ireland, *c*.1580.

The 2ᵈ Fight betweene ỹ Engliſh
and Spaniſh Fleetes being the 23
of Iune 1588. wherein only Cock
an Engliſhman being wᵗʰ his litle
Veſſell in ỹ Midſt of ỹ Enemies died va-
liently. but ỹ Spaniards much worſted.

More then halſe ỹ Spaniſh
Fleet Taken and Sunck

Queene Eliz: Riding in Triumph through London in a:
Chariot drawn by two Hor-
ſes and all ỹ Companies
attonding her wᵗʰ their Baners

The Spaniards bewailing
ỹ misfortune of their friends

3. Armada playing cards, 1588.

4. From *Narratio regionum indicarum per Hispanos quosdam devastatarum verissima*, 1598. This engraving by the Flemish Protestant Théodore de Bry illustrates reports of Spanish atrocities in the New World. Images such as these contributed to the formation in England of the 'Black Legend'.

5. Equestrian portrait of Charles I by Anthony Van Dyck, 1633.

6. The *Tiger* by William Van de Velde the elder, *c*.1681. A drawing of the 46-gun *Tiger*, one of seven frigates that were built by order of the Long Parliament in 1646–7. Their design, with a few alterations, would be that used for royal navy frigates until the nineteenth century.

7. Opposite bottom: View of the beheading of Charles I by unknown artist.

8. East India Company Ships at Deptford by unknown artist, *c*.1660.

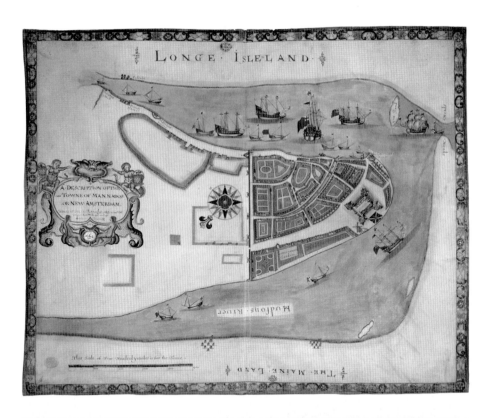

9. Opposite top: Duke's plan of New York, 1664. This is a copy of a Dutch map that the English made shortly after they had captured New Amsterdam.

10. Opposite bottom: London before the Great Fire, engraving by Pieter Hendricksz Schut, mid-17th century. London was described in 1661 by the diarist John Evelyn as 'this Glorious and Antient City … which commands the Proud Ocean to the Indies, and [yet is] … so full of Stink and Darknesse'.

11. *A Representation of the Popish Plot in 29 figures, c.1678.*

12. *The Common wealth ruleing with a standing Army*, 1683. This is a print illustrating the dangers of a return to republicanism. Leviathan is represented as a dragon that eats laws, church, and monarchy, and shits taxes. In the belly of the beast sits Parliament.

the movement of armies and the scheming of politicians. The collapse of royal authority since the late 1630s had provoked a more profound questioning of the established order, encouraging a revolution in ideas that would challenge received wisdom in everything from the use of fertilisers to biblical hermeneutics. Tensions within the Stuart realm, exacerbated by Charles's personal failings, had triggered this process of radical re-evaluation, but its form and content owed a great deal to the rich corpus of humanist scholarship and of religious works generated since the Reformation. And in the background there was the 'new science' of empirical observation and experimentation which, in the century or so before the 1640s, had weakened or destroyed many of the old assumptions about the relationship between humans, their social and political systems, and the natural world.

The most renowned exponent of the new science, whose publications were eagerly read by men of letters throughout Europe, was the Italian astronomer Galileo Galilei (1564–1642). Before his discoveries about the solar system gained currency in the seventeenth century, it was the traditional cosmography of Claudius Ptolemy (c.100–170) and other 'ancients' that prevailed. The Ptolemaic system posited a finite, geocentric universe in which the sun, stars and the planets (Mercury, Venus, Mars, Jupiter and Saturn) revolved around the Earth in a hierarchy of concentric crystalline spheres. For centuries man had stood at the centre of this little cosmos – a world designed for his use, sharing his fundamental nature, and ordered according to his laws and values. Beneath the celestial spheres there were the same hierarchical arrangements found in the heavens. Just as the human body was 'a little kingdom' in itself, so human society was understood in organic terms as the 'body politic', with the monarch as the head and his nobles and people as the organs, torso and members.[54]

But this fundamental identity between microcosm and macrocosm was systematically destroyed during the course of the sixteenth and seventeenth centuries. 'Moderns' such as Galileo – and later, Sir Isaac Newton (1643–1727) – would employ the new science to sweep the old celestial order from the sky, leaving humanity to stare out at an infinity governed by the impersonal laws of physics. The leaders of this revolution in natural philosophy began to distinguish more sharply between human subjects and natural objects, between the mind and inanimate matter, and to posit different laws governing each.

Yet in England at least, the political assumptions that went with the old cosmography lingered on well into the seventeenth century. Early Stuart politicians were virtually united in professing reverence for the 'ancient constitution' – a peculiarly English version of the body politic in which monarchy, Parliament, common law and the Church were thought to function in natural harmony. Where they disagreed was over how this system should operate in practice. As we have seen, there was a group of 'commonwealth' lords and gentlemen who favoured a restructuring of power within the ancient constitution, and in particular the abolition of free monarchy. In their ideal political world, the king would not be able to exercise his prerogative powers without the consent of his privy council and, ultimately, Parliament, 'upon any necessity, or pretended necessity whatsoever'.[55] Resort by royal ministers to reason of state arguments, which prioritised national interest over received moral principles, and talk in Warwick's circle of 'elective princes' and contractual monarchy, suggests movement in the decades before the Civil War towards a more pragmatic understanding of political power, such as prevailed on the Continent – most obviously in France under the unscrupulous Cardinal Richelieu.[56] Nevertheless, the consensus remained that the health of the state depended upon the monarch and the political classes performing their naturally allotted functions (however defined) and eschewing self-interest in virtuous regard for the common good. Indeed, in England it was precisely this attachment to the concept of an organic political community that hastened the outbreak of civil war, for both the king's party and Parliament found it very difficult to see the other as anything but a cankered member that needed lopping off before it infected the whole body.

In the event, of course, the attempted cure was worse than the disease. The old political order was broken, and all the king's horses and all the king's men could not put it back together again. Something could probably have been salvaged from the wreckage if Charles had followed Rupert's advice after Naseby. But, as we have seen, he refused to negotiate in good faith until he was denied all hope of military support; and, right to the end, Charles never quite relinquished his Micawberish hope that a military 'something' would turn up. Moreover, in a multiple monarchy in which sovereign power had fragmented among numerous competing camps, there was a good chance that he would not be disappointed. In the absence of a settlement, and with the structures of Church and state challenged and fought over, factional strife and unorthodox opinions flourished. Westminster became a battleground between the Independent and Presbyterian parties, and in 1646–7 a new political force had emerged, the Levellers.

Inspired by a group of radical pamphleteers, the Levellers had come together to defy attempts by the 'Scottified' interest in London and at Westminster to force everyone into the straitjacket of Presbyterian church discipline. They were mostly minor London gentry and tradesmen, and almost all radical Puritans of some kind. The Civil War had demonstrated to their satisfaction that God was no respecter of rank or learning, and that if He regarded all people as essentially equal, then humans should do likewise, although even their godly egalitarianism did not stretch to political rights for the destitute or women. In 1647 the Levellers supported Fairfax's army against the Presbyterians and in so doing made friends among the soldiers. But Cromwell and other senior officers, like most gentlemen, thought the Levellers' reliance on the power of the people was a threat to the propertied order. The Levellers' commitment to civil liberties and to keeping the executive small and accountable also put them at odds with the Independent grandees, who, as we shall see, were to breathe life into England's own version of Leviathan. Beyond London and the sectarian fringe, the Levellers' championing of the little man against big government seems to have alarmed rather than excited the common people. The English generally preferred 'known ways' to strange new constitutions; time-honoured hierarchy to God-ordained equality. It was in the fear they aroused, which spread to Scotland and probably Ireland too, rather than through anything they actually did, that the Levellers made their greatest impact.

Republican ideas came out of the gentleman's study and into the alehouse and military camp during the 1640s. Like the Leveller movement, the urge to pull down 'the Power of Monarchy . . . that Babilonishe rubbishe' fed upon resentment against the Scots' meddling in English affairs, and anger at the king for encouraging them.[57] It was Charles's flight to the Scottish army in 1646 that first provoked MPs to question openly whether 'his safety be not incompatible with the safety of the Commonwealth'.[58] But there were relatively few takers for a fully worked out republican system of government, even after the regicide. Republicanism, if it can be called that, consisted less in attention to constitutional detail, or even anti-monarchism, than an emphasis on virtue and active citizenship, expressed in godly and classical terms. The 'free state' rhetoric of government propagandists in the years after the regicide was largely a more self-conscious and determinedly anti-Stuart version of the godly aristocratic constitutionalism that had developed since Elizabeth's reign. Charles failed where Elizabeth had succeeded not because he was a king as such but because his vision of kingship allowed too little space for either citizen or commonwealth. His observation on the scaffold that his subjects' liberty was 'not for having share in Government . . . that is nothing pertaining to them' showed a fatal lack of political insight.[59]

Another casualty of the English Civil War was the principle that legitimate political action was defined by the ancient constitution. This idea, already contested, was overwhelmed during the 1640s by appeals from both sides to necessity and natural rights that were held to override particular codes of positive law. The parliamentarians turned with increasing confidence to the arguments that had been developed by the Huguenots and their allies in the late sixteenth century for resisting popish princes, while the king read histories of the French wars of religion for schooling in the dark arts of *raison d'état*. Confronted by the dissolution of the body politic into warring members, writers and politicians adapted another French intellectual import – interest theory – to grope towards a new, more realistic, understanding of the political process. One of the most sophisticated exponents of this new discourse was the journalist and serial turncoat Marchamont Nedham (1620–78). In his more considered pieces, he rejected the conventional wisdom that a well-grounded peace required the various parties to sacrifice their particular objectives for the public good. Instead, he argued that a settlement could be achieved through the successful manipulation of private interests to public ends. Used in this way, interest theory recognised and attempted to accommodate permanent ideological divisions within a single polity – an important step on the road to modern party politics.

So much for political theorists. In the real world of Civil War politics the protagonists were as likely to be guided by claims of conscience as by force of reason. In contrast to the rebellions that convulsed France in the late 1640s and early 1650s, the quarrel between the factions in Britain and Ireland was informed and inflamed by conflicting religious loyalties, and therefore cut much deeper, and was much harder to reconcile. In all three kingdoms the established churches had been destroyed by 1642, to be replaced in Covenanter Scotland by full-blown Presbyterianism, in Confederate Ireland by a Counter-Reformation episcopate, and in England – by nothing at all. Here, it seemed, was the Puritans' big moment, their long-awaited opportunity to complete the great work of reformation that had begun in the 1530s. Yet with power now in their hands they could not agree on whether salvation was best attained inside a compulsory national Church or by separating from the reprobate that such a Church inevitably included and forming 'gathered' congregations of the visibly godly. Nor did the Long Parliament help matters by passing legislation in 1645–6 for superimposing Presbyterianism onto the parish system, but then leaving the actual enforcement of this new church settlement to England's already fractured local communities.

Victory in the Civil War only deepened Puritan divisions, convincing some that outward forms of order and government were mere 'chaff' to be scattered in the gathering storm of the Apocalypse. The radical sects denounced the Reformation marriage between Church and state. God's spirit must be freed, they contended, from the contaminating influence of human institutions and ideas. This anti-formalist strain in Puritanism found its ultimate expression with the Quakers in the 1650s and their rejection of a trained ministry and fixed doctrine for a mystical reliance on the light of Christ within each individual. The Quakers were to be the most rigorously persecuted of all the radical groupings to have emerged from the turmoil of war and revolution.

Religious differences lay at the heart of the political divisions that afflicted local communities everywhere from the mid-1640s. The factional battle between 'royalists' and 'patriots' before the Civil War had largely been confined to the arenas of high politics – the court and (when sitting) the Parliament – and had drawn heavily on aristocratic ideas about counsel and honour. The Civil War served to popularise and sectarianise these political conflicts. Town corporations across England and Wales now contained entrenched and well-organised factions – royalist, parliamentarian, Presbyterian, Independent etc. – that purged their rivals from office as the vicissitudes of local and national politics allowed. There was no longer one or even two notions of the common good, but a cacophony of competing voices. None of these factions recognised the legitimacy of any other. But while the reality of a stable body politic had disappeared, its moral desirability remained as strong as ever, driving local factions to reunite their communities not through mediation – the method used before the Civil War, when local feuds had been rarer and more personal in nature – but by permanently excluding their rivals from government. Yet each purge by a triumphant local faction merely provoked the same measure in return as successive changes in national government gave different parties the upper hand in the localities. As early as 1649, the disease of partisan politics, and the religious hatreds that sustained it, had become incurable.

Religious pluralism might be a fact, but it was as repugnant to most Puritans as it was to the traditionalist majority that clung to the book of common prayer (which Parliament had outlawed in 1645). In worship even more than in politics there was a moral imperative on uniformity that made a general acceptance of religious diversity impossible. The army protected the self-styled 'saints' – the Congregationalists and the radical sects – from their would-be Presbyterian oppressors. But a toleration that embraced all of England's religious communities – and especially the Catholics – was unthinkable. One person's orthodoxy was another's impiety, the sufferance of which would bring down God's wrath upon the entire nation. The fall of the bishops in the early 1640s simply raised new conflicts as the Presbyterians and Congregationalists competed for political patronage and control of parish churches and ecclesiastical resources. Yet the ties between the two groups were always stronger than their differences, particularly given their similar social profiles, for most of the Puritan gentry either stuck with the Presbyterian parish system or joined the more respectable Congregationalists. Indeed, orthodox Puritans closed ranks in the 1650s against the Quakers and their public scorning of conventional religion and 'carnal' customs such as doffing one's hat to social superiors. The godly among the middling sort and the rank-and-file soldiers were as likely to end up in England's 250 or so Baptist congregations, or move from there into Quakerism. The sects probably accounted for less than 10 per cent of the English population by 1660, but, like the Levellers, made an impact upon the more conservative majority out of all proportion to their numbers.

For a brief interlude, England was a 'world turned upside down', a Bedlam of sects and millenarian visionaries, of 'king-cudgelling' republicans and utopian dreamers. 'God hath brought upon us a Confusion,' lamented the Presbyterian pamphleteer Clement Walker in 1649, 'a Babel not onely of Lips and Tongues, but of Heads, Hearts, Hands, etc. What Historian can find a method in so universal a Chaos?'[60] If there was an organising principle amid this maelstrom of radical ideas – and many then and since have struggled to find one – it lay in the still powerful impetus to build the New Jerusalem. Across virtually the entire spectrum of Puritan–parliamentarian opinion there was interest in educating individual consciences in pious self-control, in rendering them open to some form of godly reformation in preparation for Christ's imminent return, as foretold in the New Testament. Men must be educated to do good, and not simply for the fulfilment of God's great redemptive design, but also for the betterment of society in the interim. The writings and legislation of the 1640s and 1650s are full of schemes for eradicating poverty and vice through education and by disciplining the poor. A universal reformation seemed tantalisingly within reach. Christian humanism in Britain would never flourish again as it did in the mid-seventeenth century.

The most eloquent prophet to proclaim the coming of 'a new heaven and a new earth'[61] – indeed, perhaps the greatest Christian humanist since Sir Thomas More – emerged from this tumult: John Milton (1608–74). The son of a London scrivener, Milton received a gentleman's education at Cambridge before embarking on a career as a schoolmaster and man of letters. The collapse of censorship in 1640 gave him a chance to take up his pen in the Puritan (and later the republican) cause, and he soon emerged as one of London's most controversial polemicists. His impassioned pleas for easy divorce and freedom of expression – for Protestants, anyway – have won him an admiring modern audience. But his literary and political endeavours, certainly before 1660, looked back to the Christian humanist ideal of 'vertuous education, religious and civil nurture' as a way of realising the kingdom of God on Earth.[62] Though contemptuous of 'the common herd',[63] and adamant that government should be exercised not by tradesmen and merchants but by men 'bred up . . . in the knowledge of Antient and illustrious deeds', he believed strongly in the dignity of mankind, and his cosmography reflected his anthropocentrism.[64]

It is clear from the discussion between Adam and the 'sociable' angel Raphael in *Paradise Lost* that Milton knew all about the new Italian astronomy. Indeed, he was one of the few men in Britain who had actually met Galileo (during a sojourn in Italy in 1638–9). Nevertheless, it is the old and creaking Ptolemaic model of the universe that predominates in *Paradise Lost*. The new experimental science, with its open-ended interest in 'disinterested' facts, did not sit easily with Milton's humanist project in which knowledge served the explicitly moral purpose of building a godly commonwealth. To the extent that the new science threatened to displace humanity from the centre of the cosmos and purge the natural world of an inherent moral order, Milton preferred to ignore it. He kept his distance from England's emerging scientific establishment during the 1650s, and would doubtless have found its sceptical coffee-house talk and its leanings towards the rationalism and moderation of Anglicanism little to his relish. His work on *Paradise Lost* coincided with his own fall from grace – professional and political, if not religious – in 1660. He ended his public career as the butt of royalist pamphleteers, who ridiculed his old-fashioned humanist rhetoric and his quaint idea that republicanism was synonymous with the common good rather than, as his critics argued, just another political 'interest', and a fanatical one at that.

If Milton sought the cure for society's ills by reaffirming the values of Christian humanism, others denounced such remedies as quackery, and looked for answers in the scepticism and relativism made fashionable by Montaigne and taken up by the pioneers of the new science. Thomas Hobbes too had met Galileo, but unlike Milton he embraced the Italian's theory that secondary qualities such as colour and temperature were not inherent in nature but products of how the human mind processed sensory information. Having written powerfully in favour of royal absolutism during the Personal Rule, he fled to France in 1640 to avoid punishment by the Long Parliament. The outbreak of the English Civil War did not surprise him particularly – it was only to be expected, he believed, from a governing class grown disobedient on a diet of humanist ideas. Their enthusiasm for histories of what he dismissively termed 'the Greek, and Roman Anarchies',[65] Hobbes believed, encouraged the delusion that 'the Subjects in a Popular Common-wealth enjoy Liberty; but that in a Monarchy they are all Slaves'.[66] Classical philosophy was in Hobbes's opinion full of 'fraud and filth', and its ideal of a harmonious civil society a sham.[67] Faced with the world turned upside down, he rejected the humanist project outright. In keeping with his materialist science, he argued that humans – like nature itself – were just complicated mechanisms, their moral judgements merely passions based on the internal motions of attraction or aversion. In the absence of a pervasive moral order, the life of man in his natural condition was 'solitary, poore, nasty, brutish, and short'.[68]

The events of the 1640s offered ample proof, in Hobbes's view, that clinging to the notion of society as a natural community trusting to the politics of virtue was absurd. He suggested rebuilding it on the much lower but sturdier foundations of human self-interest. The one universal human impulse according to Hobbes was self-preservation, and the only security against a war of 'every man, against every man' lay in individuals surrendering their conflicting wills to the protection of an all-powerful ruler: Leviathan.[69] Hobbes's treatise of that name, which he began work on in the late 1640s, was probably aimed at Charles I's son and successor Charles II. It was a masterpiece – the first great work of English political philosophy. But to a world that still regarded politics as a moral exercise, Hobbes's pragmatism (like Machiavelli's before him) was deeply shocking. His enemies at the exiled royal court – notably Sir Edward Hyde – were outraged by his insistence on the need to subordinate law, religion, even conscience, to state power. Banned from court in 1651, Hobbes returned to England, where he found that the victorious parliamentarians had made more than enough progress towards Leviathan themselves to command his obedience.

Leviathan

'Cruel necessity', Cromwell's verdict on the regicide, sums up the spirit in which England's reluctant revolutionaries decapitated the ancient constitution during the early months of 1649.[70] It was only after the House of Lords had refused to pass legislation for trying Charles that 'the Rump' – the small group of radical Independents that had survived the army's December 1648 purge of the Commons – declared on 4 January that it alone possessed 'the supreme power in this nation'. Again, it was not until after Charles's execution on 30 January that the Rump passed laws abolishing the now defunct monarchy and the House of Lords. Most MPs were anxious to subdue any enthusiasm the regicide had stirred for a wider assault on the political and social order, and therefore they readmitted many of their colleagues who had quit the House in protest at the army's purge. England's legal system was left largely untouched by the events at Westminster, and the consolidation of the Independent interest in local government under the Rump largely represented a shift of power within the gentry rather than a dramatic widening of the governing class.

The regicide was such a momentous event that it obscured the one act of revolutionary change that truly reflected the long-term aspirations of many radical Parliament-men: the establishment of the Council of State. This new parliamentary executive, the most potent of any set up during the 1640s, represented the culmination of the drive among the Independents to appropriate the powers of king and crown for themselves.

But it was Charles's unprecedented and pitiful demise that inevitably captured the attention of people everywhere, and ensured that the Rump was hated at home and ringed by powerful enemies abroad. The regicide drew loud and windy protests from the European powers, although this was so much hot air. The treaty of Westphalia, concluded in 1648, may have resolved some of the conflicts of the Thirty Years War – the Spanish finally recognised Dutch independence; half the Palatinate was restored to its former Protestant rulers – but the two continental superpowers, France and Spain, now the only pugilists left in the ring, continued to slug it out. They were in no position to intervene in England.

The most immediate foreign threat to the Rump came in the form of a maritime treaty, concluded in December 1648, between the Irish Confederates and the Dutch. With Ormond's Irish royalists and the Confederates having joined forces by this time, the Rump faced the prospect of being blockaded into submission by an alliance of Irish, royalist and Dutch fleets. Moreover, once the royalist and Confederate armies had overrun the last remaining parliamentarian strongholds in Ireland, these fleets could be used to mount an invasion of England itself. And war threatened from another direction in February 1649, when the Covenanters proclaimed the Prince of Wales as Charles II, king of Great Britain – that is, of England and Ireland as well as of Scotland. The Kirk party feared for its own, and indeed Scotland's, survival without a covenanted monarchy in all three kingdoms.

England's 'first year of freedom' – the motto on the Rump's new great seal – looked likely to be its last. Yet four years on and this friendless state had conquered and incorporated Ireland and Scotland (for the first time in English history), trounced the mighty Dutch navy, and had the two European superpowers, France and Spain, vying for its alliance. By what arts did the 'frighted junto' of 1648–9 win such spectacular victories? How did war-torn England become, in Milton's words, 'another Rome in the west'?[71]

Although the new regime had many foreign enemies, it enjoyed a level of domestic security unrivalled by most of its neighbours. With the army's help, the Rump's leaders had become (as one of them was pleased to put it) 'absolute and compleat Conquerors' over their people and state, which was more than either the Covenanters or the Confederates could claim – or indeed the French crown, as the burdens of a royal minority and war against Spain sparked internal rebellion during the late 1640s.[72] Despite – or perhaps because of – the disorders of the 1640s, the English were knit together by shared reverence for national institutions, above all Parliament. There was no authority in England by 1649 to rival that of Parliament. The House of Commons embodied continuities of law and magistracy that spanned even regicide. Only the Levellers, with their ideas about natural rights, had developed a coherent appeal to supra-parliamentary authority, and it was their supporters in the army who mounted the only serious internal challenge to the fledgling republic – a challenge that troops loyal to Fairfax and Cromwell quickly suppressed. Control of Parliament and its army ensured the Rump's leaders a degree of compliance, or at least acquiescence, from the English people that the Kirk party, despite its dominance of the Scottish Parliament and army, could never hope to command from 'the Scots'.

But the Rump's conquest of England could not have happened without the monstrous birth of Leviathan. Until the 1640s the English state operated within a set of fiscal conventions and structures that were essentially unchanged since the Middle Ages. In peacetime the monarch was expected to 'live off his own' – that is, to run the government from the receipts of customs, traditional prerogative revenues and the profits from royal estates. In practice, the extensive sale of crown lands since the 1540s, and the unpopularity of prerogative taxation, meant that Charles struggled to meet his normal peacetime expenses, never mind the extraordinary costs of war. By and large the amount of cash the crown had available to it was not much greater than in Henry VII's time. In other words, Charles was having to muddle along on the salary and benefits of a medieval monarch. By 1640 he was in desperate need of a pay rise.

When the Long Parliament took over much of the crown's antiquated and inadequate financial system in 1641–2 it encountered the same problems that Charles had. In 1643, with its finances crumbling and its armies disintegrating, Parliament was forced to undertake a radical overhaul of state revenues, introducing two new forms of regular taxation, the assessment and the excise. The assessment, a direct tax on land, was adapted from Charles's ship money experiment. It was collected at first on a weekly, then a monthly, basis and quickly became the largest single source of parliamentary revenue. The second-largest source of parliamentary revenue, the excise, was perhaps copied from the Dutch and was an indirect tax on goods produced and consumed in England. Although the crown had collected a (narrow) range of inland duties before the 1640s, these had often been linked to royal monopolies and had generated a great deal of political ill-will.

Parliament's excise tax was far more swingeing, and allowed the state to tap the wealth of every adult, even those with no land, thereby breaking decisively with the traditional understanding that the propertied classes should bear the burden of taxation and the poor should be spared. The excise became a potent symbol for the oppressions of parliamentary rule. 'The exciser . . . is a word practically never knowen, till of late in England', wrote one embittered royalist in the late 1640s,

> & as it was invented by the lower house [of Commons] in hell, & first practised in the low-Countreys in Germ[any] so it was brought in by the sword of the Apocalypticall Beast . . . it grates upon all, high & low, rich & poore, & yeelds benefit to none, save only to the Cormorant, the Caterpiller, the Grasse-hopper, and the Palmer-worme [the larval stage of the locust], The Commons, the Committee-man, the Exciser, & the Souldier . . .[73]

The third major source of parliamentary revenue was the customs, which the two Houses, with their control of the navy and most of the major ports, appropriated in 1642.

These three taxes became the mainstay of English state finance until the introduction of income tax in the 1790s. It is one of the great ironies of the period that a civil war caused in part by resentment at Charles's fiscal exactions gave rise to a parliamentary state that taxed and spent at a vastly greater rate than any previous monarch. Moreover, Parliament sanctioned tax-collecting methods that were far more draconian than any the crown had employed. Tax-refusers could have troops billeted on them or their property forcibly confiscated and sold. London itself was allegedly 'awed by Red-coats'.[74] Even those who merely complained about high taxes might land in trouble – as in the case of one poor woman who had her tongue nailed to a tree for her temerity.

Fiscal reform paved the way for the English 'military revolution' associated with the creation of the New Model Army in 1645. Yet Parliament's financial initiatives would have proved useless, and the New Model itself would never have been created, had it not been for the political ambitions of certain leading Parliament-men. A small but ever-present group of peers and MPs was hungry for the power and resources not just to defeat Charles but to do what the first two Stuart kings had conspicuously failed to do: to restore English honour, and to make England the champion of the Protestant cause in Europe and master of an empire in the New World. The Independent grandees were prone to a particularly virulent strain of this English Protestant imperialism. The state must be strengthened to fight popery at home and abroad, and Leviathan was the monster that they were willing to let loose upon the English people to achieve that objective.

It was this same clique of Parliament-men that masterminded the New Model and the unified command structure and financial machinery that made Fairfax's army better led, better paid and better provisioned than any other force in the British Isles, and indeed in most of western Europe. Their names no longer resonate today,[75] but without their contribution neither Parliament's superiority in resources nor its financial innovations could have been exploited to decisive effect. Character was therefore vital to Parliament's success: not the Puritan character so often credited with defeating the king, but the aristocratic–civic mentality of the Independent grandees. By no means all of these peers and Commons-men were Puritans, but they were certainly more experienced at the top flight of government or more skilled in the political arts than their rivals. Even the royalists recognised as much. 'Is not their army [the New Model] (upon which they depend) regularly and strictly governed?' mused Sir Edward Hyde. 'Are not the Heads of the party the best Heads of the pack?'[76]

The financial and military innovations of the 1640s and 1650s laid the groundwork for England's transformation into a modern state. The New Model was designed according to best continental military practice, and by the mid-1650s had become England's first standing army in time of peace. The British army, that pillar of global empire, can trace its origins to the English royal army that was founded in 1661 and which in turn inherited its logistical structures, military traditions and – most famously – its red-coated uniform from its parliamentarian predecessors.

Sustaining and managing the war effort first against the king and then against the Irish, the Scots and the Dutch required Parliament to introduce a new kind of political structure, the bicameral executive committee. The privy council under James I and Charles I had set up standing committees to administer certain royal offices or policy initiatives. But these were largely advisory bodies, with limited authority to issue orders. The Long Parliament's standing committees, by contrast, had wide-ranging executive powers and in some cases their own revenue sources and national administrative networks. This 'State-Clockwork', as Nedham called it, provided a blueprint for the cabinet and the commission-based government departments that emerged during the later seventeenth century.[77] Modern parliamentary government is a descendant of the executive committee system developed at Westminster during the 1640s. The Independent grandees dominated most of these committees, and particularly those involved with 'fingring of the moneys of State'.[78] Their control of Parliament's purse-strings was rightly perceived as a design to 'draw a generall dependency after them, for he that commands the money, commands the men. These Committee-men are so powerfull that they over-awe and over-power their fellow members . . .'[79] Public affairs were managed not by Parliament, insisted Nedham, but by the grandees, who 'have gotten the Power in their hands, and swallow all matters of moment in . . . private committees of their Faction', or used their 'Vote-drivers' (the forerunners of today's Commons' Whips) to push their agenda on the floor of the House.[80] It was the grandees, therefore, who pioneered many of the unscrupulous methods of political management associated with ministerial government in the eighteenth century. The sharp political practice – or downright corruption, as many saw it – needed to make the State-Clockwork run smoothly would be the most distinctive feature, the heart, of the English, and later the British, Leviathan.

The 1640s had seen a massive and permanent increase not only in parliamentary taxation as a proportion of state income but also in the parliamentary management and oversight of the crown's financial affairs. Royal finances were gradually transformed into public finances, and taxes not voted for or administered by Parliament became a thing of the past. Indeed, Parliament was to assume responsibility for all state revenues after 1688, and paid the reigning monarch housekeeping money on the basis of the Civil List, an arrangement that persisted until the early twenty-first century. The large and reliable revenue streams established during the 1640s allowed for the development of new credit methods whereby the state could borrow the huge sums needed to meet spiralling military expenditure – a process that culminated in 1694 with the establishment of the Bank of England to administer a publicly funded line of government credit.

The birth of Leviathan was a far greater shock to the system, and a far more violent break with England's past, than the Civil War. The English had developed political and religious ideas that could accommodate fighting the king, even executing him and establishing a kingless government. But the new kind of state that emerged in the 1640s was unprecedented (in Britain, anyway) in its size and reach.

Leviathan created a new breed of politician and professional bureaucrat, and vastly increased the power of central government in relation to the localities, and of England in relation to Scotland and Ireland. For perhaps the first time in English history it began to dawn on the people that their precious Parliament could act just as tyrannically as any king. A great deal of the radical thought in Britain during the 1640s and 1650s was about trying to make sense of and contain the 'lawless unlimited power' of Leviathan. The Levellers, for example, directed most of their fire against what they saw as the tyranny of England's war-engorged state, and its over-mighty, unaccountable masters. 'Did you ever dream', asked the leading Leveller William Walwyn in 1648,

> that the oppressions of Committees would have exceeded those of the [Privy] Councel-table; or that in the place of Pattents and Projects, you should have seen an Excise established, ten fold surpassing all those, and Shipmoney together? . . . all the quarrell we have at this day in the Kingdome, is no other then a quarrel of Interests, and Partyes, a pulling down of one Tyrant, to set up another, and instead of Liberty, heaping upon our selves a greater slavery then that we fought against.[81]

The overwhelming feeling in the three kingdoms towards the political and financial practices that came in with Leviathan would remain one of alarm and distrust, mingled with incomprehension, until well into the eighteenth century.

Leviathan shrank in size after the restoration of the Stuart monarchy in 1660, but did not die, for some of the taxes and financial structures that had sustained it during the 1640s and 1650s were retained and developed by the crown. This was partly because they worked; partly also because of the administrative genius of a Harvard man – indeed, a member of the college's first graduating class after its foundation in 1636 – George Downing (1623–84). In common with hundreds of other New England Puritans, Downing had returned to England in the 1640s to fight the good fight against popery. He had joined the political retinue of one of the Independent grandees as a godly preacher, and like many of this crowd he was fired by hopes of restoring England as a major European power and building a colonial empire. But he was politically more supple than the grandees, adapting to the various regime changes of the 1650s before putting his expertise in Dutch financial methods – the most sophisticated in Europe – at the service of the restored monarchy. The diarist Samuel Pepys (1633–1703), who knew Downing well, and like him served both the Cromwellian regime and the restored monarchy, acknowledged his energy and industry, but damned him as a 'perfidious rogue' and 'a niggardly fellow' (Downing spent thousands on his estate while keeping his own mother living in near-penury).[82] Downing is best remembered today as the man who gave his name to Britain's most famous street, but his main achievement was the contribution his fiscal reforms made to sustaining England's great-power status – or as he put it, to showing the French that 'their is now alive, that brave old English blood and spirit that hath shewed itselfe on this side [of] the water [continental Europe] in former ages'.[83]

Prestige abroad demanded a new-modelled navy as well as army, and here again the Long Parliament delivered. Nourished by Leviathan, English seapower grew at a faster rate during the mid-seventeenth century than at any time since Henry VIII's reign. Charles I's fleet of forty-odd sail had been hampered by badly designed ships and royal meddling. It could patrol but not control the Narrow Seas, and it had been practically useless in protecting English fisheries and merchant shipping. This sorry state of affairs changed with the outbreak of the English Civil War, when the defection of most of the king's ships to Parliament brought together all the elements for a major shake-up in naval affairs – that is, ships, increased financial resources, and above all necessity. Annual spending on the navy nearly doubled under the Long Parliament; naval administration, shore establishments, and victualling arrangements were all improved; and the dockyards began producing ships that could actually fight, rather than the lumbering symbols of Caroline majesty launched during the 1630s[84] (see illus. 6). The squadrons that hounded the royalist fleet out of Irish waters in 1649, blockaded it in Lisbon in 1650, and destroyed it in the Mediterranean in 1651 were now capable of operating thousands of miles from home and for months on end.

The modern British navy had its baptism of fire in the Narrow Seas amid the cannonades and smoke of the first Anglo-Dutch war (1652–4). In 1651 the Rump had offered the Dutch a full-scale union with England in order to join their resources in the apocalyptic struggle against Antichrist. From an English perspective, a merger between the two states would end the threat of a Stuart–Orangist alliance and offer at least some protection to England's overseas commerce and markets from the massive expansion in Dutch trade that had followed the republic's peace with Spain in 1648. But the Dutch had been understandably reluctant to compromise their hard-won independence or their commercial superiority over the English, whereupon the Rump had denounced them as godless money-grubbers, in thrall to the monarchical House of Orange, and had turned the screw on their trade until war became inevitable. The fighting took place exclusively at sea, and, finally, it seems that the English adapted their tactics to exploit their superiority in firepower by deploying in a single straight line – the standard British battle formation until the Napoleonic wars and beyond. Advances in gunnery techniques and the development of specialist warships meant that the English could at long last win sea battles by standing off and outgunning the enemy.[85] Of the seven major fleet actions that occurred during the war, the English won five, prompting one Dutch admiral to inform his superiors that 'the English are now our masters and command the sea'.[86] This was true, perhaps, in the Narrow Seas, but elsewhere the Dutch had the better of the war. They chased the English from the Baltic and the Mediterranean, and generally inflicted huge damage on the most profitable sectors of England's overseas trade.

Peace in 1654 came as a blessed relief for both sides. The English had lost much in terms of trade and customs revenue, but had gained considerably in military reputation. By the end of the war the English navy had grown to over 200 state-owned warships (the practice of hiring commercial shipping to augment the fleet in time of war had ended), and by 1700 that figure had swelled to nearly 400, with some of the 'first-rates' mounting over 100 guns. Victories against the Dutch went some way towards erasing the memories of England's military humiliations before the Civil War. The French, Dutch and Spanish were left in no doubt that they had a new competitor in the race for mastery of the world's seas and trade. Two hundred years after the fall of the Plantagenet empire in France, England was back among the front rank of European powers.

King Oliver

The 'spaniel-fawning' English state of the 1630s had grown into a bull mastiff by 1649, when the Rump unleashed it on Ireland.[87] English naval superiority in the Irish Sea allowed Oliver Cromwell to embark for Ireland in August 1649 with 12,000 New Model veterans. A few days before he sailed, the newly reinforced parliamentarian garrison in Dublin inflicted a crushing defeat on Ormond's already fragile royalist coalition at the battle of Rathmines. Cromwell was now assured a secure landing-base near Dublin, while the royalist coalition was demoralised and divided beyond repair. Although they faced Protestant as well as Catholic troops, Cromwell's men fought with a savagery typical of a war of religion. In perhaps the most notorious of the Cromwellian 'atrocities' in Ireland, the taking of Drogheda, they killed 3,500 soldiers, civilians and clergy, and beat the garrison commander to death with his own wooden leg. But then warfare in Ireland had always been more brutal than in England. The New Model lost more soldiers to disease and combat in Ireland than it had in all its previous campaigns. Given the Rump's vast superiority in resources, however, and the steady disintegration of the Irish royalist coalition after Rathmines, the reconquest of Ireland was never in much doubt.

Ireland paid a terrible price for defying Puritan England. The reconquest – or as the Gaels called it 'the war that finished Ireland' – was followed by a Protestant land-grab of unprecedented proportions.[88] Thousands of Catholics were dispossessed of their property, and many were forcibly relocated in Connacht, the poorest part of Ireland, in what amounted to a policy of 'ethnic cleansing'. In addition, some 10,000 or so were shipped off to the Caribbean as slave labour. Ireland's population fell dramatically between 1641 and 1652, with most of these losses stemming from plague epidemics and economic collapse after 1649. Ireland by 1652 was as thoroughly devastated as parts of Germany after the Thirty Years War, and would take decades to recover. The cause of Catholic religious liberty and political equality with England under the crown was lost for ever.

National security and honour may have demanded that the Rump invade Ireland, but there was no such imperative with regard to Scotland. That is, until the Kirk party, fearing for its own survival without a covenanted monarchy in all three kingdoms, invited Charles II to Scotland in 1650. Faced with yet another Scottish invasion, the Rump decided that the best form of defence was attack, and as Sir Thomas (now Lord) Fairfax refused to act the aggressor against fellow Protestants, he was replaced as commander-in-chief by Cromwell. In July 1650, Cromwell crossed the Tweed at the head of 16,000 troops and attended by a supply fleet of 140 ships. Disease quickly took its toll of his army, however, and by August he was hemmed in at Dunbar, east of Edinburgh, by a Scottish force almost twice the size of his own. But while the English were united in adversity, the Kirk party's evident distrust of the king and its own army sapped Scottish morale. On 3 September,

Cromwell's veterans surprised and routed the ill-disciplined Scottish army, killing or taking prisoner 13,000 of them for the loss of just 20 men.

Defeat at Dunbar weakened the Covenanters sufficiently for Charles II and the Scottish royalist interest to take charge of the war effort. In August 1651 the king and about 12,000 Scottish troops crossed into England, hoping, as Hamilton had three years earlier, that the English would rally to their cause. But the will to resist Parliament and the army had been crushed during the Second Civil War. And in any case, nothing was more calculated to boost domestic support for the Rump than a Scottish invasion. Cromwell, who had hurried south from Scotland in the king's wake, caught up with the Scottish army at Worcester. On 3 September, the first anniversary of Dunbar, Cromwell's 31,000 troops made short work of the new king's army. Charles, after assorted adventures that ranged from hiding in oak trees to disguising himself as a woman, escaped to the Continent, but most of his soldiers were killed or captured.

The defeat at Worcester vindicated Sir Edward Hyde and other royalists opposed to seeking foreign help to restore the Stuart monarchy, and they dominated the exiled court thereafter until the Restoration. Back in Scotland, the majority of leading men quickly made their peace with the English. It would take the New Model several years to conquer the Highlands, but Lowland Scotland had been completely subdued by the end of 1651. The ironies were manifold. What had begun back in 1637 as a rebellion to prevent Scotland's reduction to the status of an English province had ended in precisely that fate.

The Covenanters' version of Leviathan had preceded and to some extent inspired the English one. But Scotland, like Ireland, never endured an all-out civil war as England did. Consequently, its unresolved internal divisions – political, religious and ethnic – left it vulnerable to the Cromwellian onslaught. Scotland did not suffer the same degree of material devastation that Ireland did during the 1640s. Nevertheless, the cost of financing and equipping countless military expeditions brought ruin to several sectors of the Scottish economy, while disease, famine and warfare literally decimated the population. It took many years for Scotland to regain the level of prosperity it had enjoyed in the 1630s.

Victory over the Irish and Scots produced paeans of praise for Cromwell from soldiers, saints and patronage-hungry poets. The military establishment grew too, to an unprecedented 50,000 troops.

Military intervention in English politics was an ever-present threat after 1648, but 'sword-law' never prevailed for very long.[89] The army's own divisions and basic political assumptions saw to that. Many leading officers were also gentleman politicians and, like Cromwell, were torn between the largely contradictory impulses of building the New Jerusalem and preserving the existing social order. Even those soldiers who were wholly committed to a fundamental transformation of society insisted that it must be accomplished by a legitimate civilian government. The problem was that most of the civilian politicians they relied on were as ideologically conflicted as Cromwell was. Yet if the army needed the politicians, the politicians needed the army even more. Knowing how deeply unpopular they were in the three kingdoms, they relied on the army to keep them in power until such time as the people had been educated in the ways of godliness and 'unkingship'.

The conflict in the Rump, and within individual Commons-men, between the forces of godly reformism and social conservatism could not be contained indefinitely. After their return in triumph from Worcester the soldiers were able to concentrate on pressuring the Rump for religious and legal reform. But they made little headway, and began to suspect that MPs were instead intent on purging the army and introducing electoral changes that would undermine its influence in future Parliaments. On 20 April 1653, Cromwell entered the Commons, pointing at various Members and saying: 'here sits a Drunkard to another there a Fornicator to a third [there a] cheater of the publick treasure to a fourth there a juggling or dissembling Hypocrite';[90] whereupon he called in 'five or six files of musqueteers' and preremptorily dissolved the Rump.[91] The doors of the House were locked and the 'junto' of parliamentary Independents 'quite dissolved'.[92] Charles I's irruption into the Commons in January 1642 had given life to the Long Parliament; Cromwell's in 1653 killed it. In its place the army installed an assembly of 140 hand-picked godly men that hostile pamphleteers referred to sneeringly as Barebone's Parliament after one of its 'fanatic' Members, the Baptist leather-seller Praise-God Barbon. Barebone's Parliament sat for just six months before the same kinds of internal conflict that had earlier stymied the Rump caused its conservative majority to surrender power back to the army. Not the least of the forces that undermined both the Rump and its short-lived successor was the huge financial pressures generated by England's naval war against the Dutch.

The army's next move recognised the need for the return to a form of government more acceptable to the political nation at large. Whereas the saints had hoped that the army would help establish the monarchy of Christ, what they got instead was the monarchy of Oliver Cromwell. In December 1653 a group of senior officers and their civilian friends appointed Cromwell lord protector and chief magistrate of England, Ireland and Scotland. But this was monarchy with a twist, for the Protectorate became the first – and to date, the only – British regime to have a written constitution, the Instrument of Government. The Instrument created an elective monarchy, a protectoral council and a new 'imperial' Parliament at Westminster in which Scotland and Ireland were each allowed 30 MPs. The Instrument's authors aimed to protect 'natural rights', notably liberty of conscience, by empowering the executive to restrain any tendency in future Parliaments towards oppressive government, and to this end the council enjoyed extensive powers. But it was Cromwell's role as protector that most worried the new regime's republican opponents. To these 'Commonwealthsmen' – still smarting at Cromwell's axing of the Rump – and even to some of the protector's own officers, 'government by a single person' seemed an affront to the ideal of parliamentary supremacy and a betrayal of everything that the army had fought for.

In many respects, the Protectorate resembled the monarchy that the Stuarts' critics had always yearned for. Cromwell's view of European politics remained that of a Jacobean Puritan gentleman, in which Spain was the great and predestined enemy – even though decades of fighting on innumerable fronts had left the Spanish exhausted by the 1650s and vulnerable to the growing power of France. The Protectorate consequently pursued an obsolete – indeed, almost Elizabethan – foreign policy, making peace with the Dutch, overtures to the French, and, in 1655, war on Spain. Finally the English were in a position to throw the resources of a powerful state into beating the Spanish, as they had dreamed of doing since the days of Drake and Hawkins. Indeed, Cromwell continued the Long Parliament's revival of English greatness to the point where (according to Hyde) it was impossible to tell which country feared him most, France, Spain or Holland, 'as they did all sacrifice their honour and interest to his pleasure'.[93] And in its ceremonial and architectural splendour the protectoral court – which made extensive use of former royal palaces and their furnishings – was careful to maintain the courtly majesty of the English state. Cromwell, in contrast to Charles, 'had a Manly stern Look' that commanded respect; and, though he dressed plainly, 'appear'd with Magnificence upon

Publick Occasions'.[94] He generally took counsel from an inner circle that included several of the Independent grandees and other men closely associated with the ancient nobility. Similarly, his vision of a godly commonwealth was not far removed from that of most early Stuart Puritan gentlemen. Even his appreciation of fine art, including 'popish' statues and paintings that scandalised lowbrow Puritans, was consistent with godly aristocratic tastes before the Civil War. Where he parted company with many godly gentlemen, however, was in the overriding commitment he shared with the army to liberty of conscience for those he deemed God's people – in practice, Presbyterians, Congregationalists and Baptists. This was what soured relations between him and his first Parliament (1654–5), for even after elections that had largely excluded royalists and other 'malignants' from voting or sitting, most MPs wanted less liberty of conscience and more suppression of sectaries.

Cromwell's willingness to impose godly reformation 'for the people's good not what pleases them' became abundantly clear with the rule of the major-generals.[95] Overreacting to a few half-hearted royalist upris-ings early in 1655, the protectoral council divided the country into twelve regions and put each under the government of a major-general with a remit to penalise the royalists and to suppress 'drunkennese, sweringe, profaininge the Lord's day [Sunday], and other wickednesses'.[96] The major-generals were generally hard-working and conscientious, but taken as a whole the initiative was a flop. Their allotted task proved too great and their support from the centre too little. All they really succeeded in doing was stirring up public resentment at rule by 'swordsmen'. Several months into Cromwell's second Parliament (1656–8), a group of Members led by the protectoral governor of Scotland, Lord Broghill, presented the Commons with a new constitutional blueprint, the Remonstrance, that proposed making Cromwell king, establishing a Cromwellian House of Lords, and narrowing the limits of religious toleration.

In rewriting the protectoral constitution in this way, Broghill and his friends had two chief objectives. They, and indeed most Parliament-men, were anxious to resolve what amounted to a succes-sion crisis – a situation that would have been instantly familiar to any Elizabethan politician – that is, the threat of civil strife and foreign invasion that loomed so long as Cromwell failed to confront his own mortality and name his successor. Making him king would effectively restore the principle of hereditary succession, and with it, clear and familiar rules for the transition of power after his death. Secondly, they were trying to reprise the strategy behind the 1647–8 Engagement, only this time using political instead of actual weapons to free central government from the thraldom of the English army and its allies. In essence, the plan was to cut the soldiery out of the political loop by uniting the army's opponents in Wales, Scotland and Ireland, together with the Cromwellian 'court party' and an assortment of Presbyterians and other conservative Parliament-men, in the cause of restoring 'known ways' in the three kingdoms under the hereditary rule of King Oliver I. After much soul-searching – and prudent calculation that the army would not stomach a return to rule by kings – Cromwell rejected the offer of the crown: 'I would not seek to set up that which Providence hath destroyed and laid in the dust . . . I would not build Jericho again.'[97] Instead, he settled for a watered-down and muddled version of the Remonstrance, the Humble Petition and Advice, which satisfied no one. Nevertheless, it did at least give the Protectorate a more civilian and monarchical character and broadened its support among the propertied classes.

If the new constitution had had longer to bed in, it is possible that the Stuart monarchy would never have been restored. As it was, Cromwell died on 3 September 1658, the anniversary of Dunbar and Worcester, barely a year after the Humble Petition's introduction. His passing was little lamented by the people, but there was a generally positive reaction to the succession of his eldest son Richard Cromwell (1626–1712). Richard's civilian background and outlook recommended him to virtually every group in society except the one that really counted: the army. Without military experience, he had no personal authority with the soldiers. Perhaps an exceptionally charismatic or ruthless politician could have won over enough of the army's leaders to sustain his rule, but 'Queen Dick' was neither. Besides, he faced difficulties as protector that would have tested Old Noll himself. The Protectorate's misguided and futile war with Spain had ruined the public finances and crippled English overseas trade. By late 1658 the state's debt had risen to a massive £2 million, mostly in arrears of army pay. Forced to call a Parliament to address the financial crisis, Richard was squeezed between the army and its pay demands on one side, and the civilian majority at Westminster that wanted tax cuts and drastic reductions in the military establishment on the other. Richard sided with the civilians – he could do little else – and sealed his fate. On 21 April 1659, those few senior officers who remained loyal to him were abandoned by their men as army units closed in around Whitehall. The next day, the army dissolved Parliament and scrapped the Protectorate. Richard went tamely into political retirement, into exile for several decades after 1659, and ended his days living in genteel obscurity in Hertfordshire with his former landlady. Such was the unprincely end of the 'protectoral House of Cromwell'.

The army had brought down the Protectorate with the help of the Commonwealthsmen, and in May 1659 these unlikely allies restored the Rump – only for the jealousies and distrust that had marked their relationship in 1651–3 to surface once again. In October 1659 the army forced the Rump to dissolve, citing its failure to settle the constitution, widen toleration and redress the soldiers' grievances over pay. By this point the kingless English state was altogether bankrupt. 'Never was their a pack of men seen', declared one leading politician, 'mor deserted of God and emptyed of witt, sense, reason, comon honesty and moral trustynesse . . .'[98]

This was also the conclusion of the commander of the English army in Scotland, General George Monck (1608–70), who was an ex-royalist and did not share the ardent sense of godly mission that animated most of the army grandees. He feared that the military regime in London would allow the Quakers and other 'fanaticall spirits' to destroy all civil and ecclesiastical authority and bring the three kingdoms under 'that intollerable slavery of a sword Government'.[99] In November 1659, he purged his army of radicals, and early in December he advanced to Coldstream on the border with England, and there he waited, pinning down the English army's best forces while the military regime in London disintegrated through lack of money to pay its soldiers. Sections of the army and most of the navy now revolted, and the political confusion and ongoing trading slump provoked uncontrollable protests in London and elsewhere in the country, with the result that late in December the Rump was restored for a second time. Army unity, the bedrock of the Independent and Cromwellian interest since the mid-1640s, was finally beginning to crumble.

Early in January 1660, Monck and his army crossed the Tweed unopposed. A month later he reached London. Monck's decision to allow the MPs purged in December 1648 to return to the Commons (in effect, restoring the Long Parliament), and to range his army behind the majority thus formed at Westminster for holding new and 'free' parliamentary elections, made the restoration of Stuart monarchy in some form virtually inevitable. Invasion from Scotland had ended England's eleven-year experiment in kingless government, just as it had Charles I's eleven-year experiment in personal rule.

The great Puritan endeavour to build a new Zion in the three king-doms was over. But the world 'Antipodis'd' during the 1640s and 1650s was to linger long and painfully in the public memory.[100] All that the revolution had touched seemed tainted. The mere word 'commonwealth' – appropriated so brazenly by the revolutionary regimes – fell quickly out of favour after 1660, although the concepts associated with it (the Protestant cause, active citizenship, resistance to free monarchy) lived on. Yet the state, in terms of taxing its people and fighting its enemies, had actually been turned the right way up during the Civil War period. The birth of Leviathan had not been quite as Hobbes had envisaged it, and had certainly not depended upon individuals surrendering their wills and consciences to a sovereign authority – far from it. Ireland and Scotland had been subjugated in true neo-Roman fashion, by a citizens' army. The 'democratical gentlemen' whom Hobbes so despised continued to have a strong voice in English government.[101] Moreover, prolonged warfare and political unrest, together with the state's increased reliance on credit, had allowed all sorts of groups, from financiers and merchants to soldiers, sectarians and other 'mean men', to intrude upon the aristocratic preserve of high politics.

Nevertheless, in one vital area of English national life the people did indeed subordinate their wills to state power, and that was taxation. Opposition to taxes, especially the indirect kind like excises, declined (though by no means disappeared) after 1640, even though the tax burden itself increased massively. Parliamentary oversight of public revenue, and a growing appreciation of the link between state finances and the national interest, undermined many of the traditional arguments for tax resistance. Only permanent taxation could sustain English greatness against foreign aggressors both military and commercial. If Behemoth and Leviathan had taught the people anything it was the dire conse-quences of not paying their taxes.

5

The French Connection, 1660–1714

The King of England [Charles II] will make a public profession of the Catholic faith, and will receive the sum of two millions of crowns, to aid him in this project, from the Most Christian King [Louis XIV] . . . The two Kings will declare war against the United Provinces [the Dutch republic]. The King of France will attack them by land, and will receive the help of 6,000 men from England. The King of England will send 50 men-of-war to sea, and the King of France 30; the combined fleets will be under the Duke of York's command.

Article of the Anglo-French treaty of Dover, 1670[1]

That there was at that time a Popish Plot, and that there always has been one since the Reformation, to support, if not restore the Romish Religion in England, scarce any body calls in question.

James Welwood, *Memoirs of the Most Material Transactions in England for the Last Hundred Years* (1700), 123

Restorations, 1660–73

One man dominated British history in the later Stuart period, and he was neither a Stuart nor a Briton. He was crowned six years before Charles II returned to the throne in 1660, and died in 1715, a year after Queen Anne, the last of the Stuart monarchs. He was head of Europe's most powerful state, creator of its most glamorous and fashionable royal court, and ruler of 21 million subjects, which was almost four times as many as those of his Stuart cousins. When he went to war it took the armies of half of Europe to deny him victory. He was Louis XIV of France.

No one so enthralled and appalled the Stuart nations as this man did, or so influenced the actions of the four British monarchs who ruled during his long reign. His style of government, his tastes and his wars defined the age. The first of the restored Stuart kings, Charles II, felt the pull of baroque France particularly strongly. He was half-French himself, of course, and having spent much of his exile in the orbit of the various royal courts in Paris, he returned to England in 1660 'altogether Frenchyfied'.[2]

The restoration of the Stuart monarchy in 1660 was greeted by an outpouring of some of the worst poetry in the history of the English language. Nowhere amid this deluge of doggerel was there much sense that the Restoration was anything but a marvellous event, a great and irreversible turning-point in the history of the three kingdoms. The object of this congratulatory verse, the so-called 'merry monarch' Charles II, was not so optimistic, however. To the end of his life he feared that rebellion would again topple the crown – an anxiety shared by his younger brother, James Duke of York (the future James II). With the advantage of hindsight it is clear that the Restoration restored not only Stuart kingship but also many of the problems that had plagued it before 1640. Nevertheless, to most of those caught up in the events of early 1660, the overwhelming feeling was one of amazement at the miraculous and inexplicable workings of providence. The army that had destroyed Charles I was bringing his son back in triumph.

Amazement quickly turned in most cases to joy. The Restoration was cue for the biggest street party in Stuart history. The navy, its ships newly emblazoned with the royal coat of arms, conveyed the king and his court from Holland to Dover, where they landed on 25 May 1660 to a rapturous welcome. Tens of thousands of people turned out to cheer the royal party as it made its triumphal progress through Kent. By the time Charles entered London on 29 May (his thirtieth birthday) his retinue included General Monck – the parliamentarian commander whose defection had precipitated the Stuart restoration – many of the nobility, the lord mayor and aldermen, and 'above 20000 horse & foote, brandishing their swords and shouting with unexpressible joy'.[3] More than one hundred thousand jubilant people lined the streets or watched from windows as the royal procession passed. Church bells pealed joyously; the fountains gushed wine; and cries of 'God save the King' resounded everywhere – doubtless to the dismay of the arch-republican John Milton as he lay low in a friend's house in London. 29 May would be a day of popular celebration for many years to come, and became known as 'sick sack' or 'zig zag' day, from the popular term of abuse for Puritans: 'shit sack'.[4]

After his wretched years in exile, moving from one foreign capital to another with his makeshift court, Charles was apparently home and dry. The majority of his subjects in the three kingdoms seemed only too eager to have him back, no questions asked – many, of course, had not wanted to be rid of the Stuart monarchy in the first place. The Long Parliament had dissolved itself in March 1660, and the interim 'Convention' elected in its place, having received assurances from Charles that he would govern in a constitutional way, had voted on 1 May to restore him without formal preconditions. Events in Ireland had moved even faster in the same direction. In mid-December 1659 a group of Protestant officers and gentry had seized Dublin Castle and other garrisons, purged the army in Ireland of radicals, and had called an Irish Convention which, when it met in February 1660, had declared for a restoration of monarchy, sparking unprecedented scenes of rejoicing. General Monck's intervention in England had triggered the Restoration in Scotland, and again there were elaborate public celebrations to mark 'this great deliverance'.[5] The 1650s union of commonwealths was dissolved. Scotland and Ireland became separate kingdoms once again, each with its own Parliament. Constitutional arrangements in Ireland reverted to their position prior to the 1641 rebellion. In Scotland the clock was turned back even further, to before the 1637 Covenanter rebellion. In England, too, the 'ancient constitution' was restored, and with it most of the monarch's prerogative powers. Charles could summon and dissolve Parliament virtually at will, veto legislation if he so wished, and had undisputed control over the county militia.

The one significant jewel in Charles I's crown that would not be restored was the monarch's right to use his prerogative powers to levy taxes. There would be no return to the financial 'projects' and unparliamentary taxation that had proved so unpopular since medieval times. Instead, the English Convention granted Charles II a financial package based largely upon customs and excise, which was expected to net him about £1.2 million a year, or roughly double his father's annual income in the 1630s. Indirect taxation was now expected to form the mainstay of royal revenues. Experiments in direct taxation based upon an *accurate* measurement of land or wealth – such as ship money – would henceforth be considered politically unacceptable. In practice, the yield from customs and excise depended upon buoyancy of trade, and it generally fell short of target, forcing Charles to seek large additional sums from Parliament. Yet though this arrangement left Parliament with considerable leverage over the crown and a regular interest in state finances, most

Parliament-men had no thought of taking over the reins of government. They saw their role in the traditional terms of drafting new laws and advising the king on matters of national importance.

With the old political order came much of the traditional festive culture that the Puritans had banned as popish. Maypoles featured prominently in the Restoration merry-making; Christmas was lavishly celebrated in 1660; and the theatres were reopened, this time with real women playing the female roles. The body of the arch-Puritan, Oliver Cromwell, was exhumed from Westminster Abbey and hung from a gibbet at Tyburn. His head was then removed and stuck on a spike atop Westminster Hall, where it would remain for almost twenty years, a grisly reminder of what royalists liked to call 'the Usurping times'.[6]

The euphoria surrounding Charles II's return proved far less enduring. After so many years in which so many people in Britain and Ireland had seen their hopes dashed and their worst fears confirmed, it was not surprising that expectations of the new king were so high or so widely shared. Yet the past twenty years or so had left such a legacy of political and religious division that any settlement would inevitably disappoint more people than it would satisfy. Simply restoring the old political structures and continuing as if the last two decades had never happened was not going to work.

In some ways the monarchy was in a stronger position than it had been before the Civil War. The financial and military reforms introduced in the 1640s and 1650s, and partially retained in 1660, meant that the government would be more powerful than it had been in 1640. By downsizing the New Model to a politically reliable and financially manageable few regiments, it had a small standing army. It kept much, though not all, of the formidable navy built up since 1642 – renamed the 'Royal Navy' by Charles. And it now had a professional bureaucracy for the collection of customs and excise. Retaining Leviathan in all its Cromwellian bulk would simply have been too expensive, and was, in any case, incompatible with Charles's overriding political need to bind up his kingdoms' wounds and move on. But the price of putting reconciliation before state-building would be that Charles's powers and revenues remained smaller than those of his European rivals – a source of resentment to him and his ministers, and therefore of political instability generally. In addition, the crown now had to contend with a whole spectrum of factional interests, from embittered royalists to unrepentant Commonwealthsmen. Conspiracies and insurrections against the restored monarchy – mostly by Puritan radicals – were worryingly frequent during the 1660s. Society had not merely cracked along religious lines, it had splintered. Episcopacy would return after 1660, but the near-monopoly on religious allegiance that the Church of England had enjoyed before 1640 was gone for good. Perhaps this would not have mattered so much had not most people (in all three kingdoms) clung tenaciously to the belief expressed by one royalist writer in 1661 that religious unity was 'the chiefest pillar that upholdeth human society, and obedience to supreme authority'.[7]

Political tension and contention in post-Restoration Ireland would centre upon land ownership. The victorious Puritans had left the Catholics holding under 10 per cent of profitable land in Ireland by 1660, a drop of more than 50 per cent from 1641. During the 1660s the Catholics would be restored to about 20 per cent of Irish land, but this still left plenty of disgruntled natives. As much as Charles may have wished to reward those Irish Catholics and Protestants who had fought for him, in practice he had little choice but to uphold the ascendancy of the Protestant settler interest. To do otherwise would be to undermine the monarchy in England, as his brother would find out in the 1680s.

In Scotland, the main losers as a result of the Restoration would be the Presbyterians. Charles decided to restore episcopacy in Scotland partly because bishops were his appointees and would do as they were told, and partly for the sake of congruity with England and Ireland. The Presbyterians had made this choice easy for him by their domineering and anti-aristocratic behaviour a decade earlier, which had lost them the support of most of the Scottish nobility. Without the patronage of the kingdom's most powerful men, the Presbyterians would not be able to defy the crown as effectively as they had twenty years earlier.

Charles, though not above settling old scores, was anxious during the early 1660s not to deepen the wounds of his long-suffering kingdoms by applying extreme remedies. Conscious of the lingering strength of Puritan feeling within the political nation and among the many thousands of soldiers who were disbanded in 1660–1, he tried to steer England away from a narrowly Anglican and intolerant church settlement. A few weeks before his return to England he had issued a declaration in favour of liberty of conscience, in the hope of reassuring those who preferred worshipping outside of the established Church. Politically, too, he was keen to build bridges – particularly with the powerful English Presbyterian interest – and this meant restraining the Cavalier desire for vengeance. Of his and his father's many former enemies, only the ringleaders of the Covenanting movement, and the fifty-nine men who had signed Charles I's death warrant in 1649, or who had been closely involved in the regicide, were exempted from pardon; and of these 'traitors', a mere sixteen – thirteen English and three Scots (including the marquess of Argyll) – were executed. The first of the regicides to be hanged, drawn and quartered was the Puritan firebrand Thomas Harrison, who looked – wrote Samuel Pepys – 'as cheerfully as any man could do in that condition. He was presently cut down and his head and his heart shown to the people, at which there was great shouts of joy.'[8]

As the reaction to Harrison's fate suggests, the mood in England was for smiting Puritanism and all its works, and this sentiment would override the king's desire for compromise. Although Charles, in his private devotions, dutifully observed the ceremonial form of Anglican worship associated with his father's senior churchman, Archbishop Laud, he had no desire to foist his religious preferences on his subjects, as Charles I had. Nor did Charles II share his father's exalted view of the Church of England. Many English people, on the other hand, having suffered the tyranny of the Word at first hand, longed for a return to the pre-war Church, and to the familiar rituals and undemanding piety of prayer-book worship. In time, the Laudian emphasis on ceremony, religious imagery and church music – if not the archbishop's clericalism – would gain widespread acceptance within the Anglican fold.

The first great blow against Puritanism was struck in the general election of 1661, which produced what a prominent republican would later describe as 'a parliament full of lewd young men chosen by a furious people in spite to the puritans, whose severity had disgusted them'.[9] This 'Cavalier Parliament' rejected the idea of liberty of conscience and Presbyterian schemes for a national Church that would accommodate orthodox Puritans (as opposed to Quakers and other sectaries), and instead passed a series of acts intended to reimpose Anglican uniformity. In came episcopacy and the book of common prayer, out went over 2,000 Puritan parish ministers. The 10 per cent or so of the laity, from Presbyterians to Quakers, who could not conform to this re-established Church of bishops, prayer book and ceremony, and who chose to worship in private 'conventicles', either as a supplement to or in complete separation from Anglican parish services, were labelled Dissenters.

Convinced of the dictum that 'it is impossible for a Dissenter not to be a REBEL', the Cavalier Parliament passed draconian legislation during the 1660s that threatened Dissenters with fines, imprisonment, transportation to the colonies, and even death.[10] Towns notorious for their godly defiance of Charles I during the 1640s had their walls demolished, and many Puritans, although by no means all, were purged from the county magistracy and borough corporations. The Corporation Act of 1662, which sought to exclude non-Anglicans from municipal office, gave legal form to – and therefore, inevitably, hardened and perpetuated – the 'divisions, contentions, factions, and parties' that had sprung up everywhere in England during the 1640s.[11] The 1662 Licensing Act represented another attempt to put the genie of factionalism back in the bottle. Newspaper publication for much of the Restoration period would be confined to the weekly journal the *London Gazette*, which was effectively the government's mouthpiece. Letters and sermons, rather than printed material, once again became the most important means of disseminating news.

The Edinburgh Parliament and authorities worked equally hard to quash Scottish Presbyterianism. But although their efforts proved unsuccessful, the Presbyterians – despite making up a far higher proportion of Lowland Scotland's population than did the Dissenters in England – had too few friends in high places to pose a major threat to the crown. The Dissenters, by contrast, were strongly represented among the overseas merchants and commercial sectors of London, Bristol and other towns. Moreover, a sizeable number of English Parliament-men, and even a few courtiers, were either Dissenters themselves or regarded the persecution of godly Protestants as a form of popery. The Dissenters' many friends sympathised with their plight and supported efforts for a more broad-based, less 'prelatical' national Church.

The Dissenters had one particularly well-placed ally, and that was the king himself. In 1662, and again in 1672, he attempted to introduce toleration by virtue of his prerogative power as supreme governor of the Church, but on both occasions he was forced to back down after loud protests in Parliament that he had acted unconstitutionally. Which is not to say that he had any great esteem for the Dissenters, although he sometimes found the Quakers rather amusing. Presbyterianism, for example, he thought incompatible with monarchy and 'not a religion for gentlemen'.[12] In fact, in trying to loosen the chains of Anglican uniformity he was more concerned to ease the lot of England's Catholics, who made up about 2 per cent of the population. His mother, sister and many of his relatives were Catholics; and Catholics had helped him escape to the Continent after his defeat at Worcester in 1651. On a more politic level, he was keen to encourage both Dissenters and Catholics to look to the crown for protection and leadership. By courting the Dissenters and Catholics, and by using his Bedchamber to circumvent his ministers of state and formal councils, he hoped to break the Anglican stranglehold on Church and Parliament that had been established, contrary to his wishes, in 1660–2. That he failed in this endeavour was partly because his love of life's pleasures exceeded his desire to assert royal power. 'The truth is,' wrote the Stuart memorialist James Welwood, 'King Charles was neither Bigot enough to any Religion, nor lov'd his Ease so little, as to embark in a Business that must at least have disturb'd his Quiet, if not hazarded his Crown.'[13]

Charles's religion was his pleasure. Which was a shame, because he had the makings of a great king. He had 'a softness of temper that charmed' and a common touch, and yet was of 'Noble Majestick Mien' (at six foot two inches he towered over most of his subjects) and highly intelligent.[14] He was also a master of the political arts: of reading men and of dissimulation; of playing court factions off against each other; and of using royal ceremonial to dazzle the people. But except when it came to naval affairs, in which he took a great interest, he suffered from an acute lack of application. One of his Bedchamber men joked about finding a job for 'one Charles Stuart – who now spends his time in imploying his lips and prick about the Court, and hath no other employ-ment'.[15] The king was famously well acquainted with what he called 'a little fantastical gentleman called Cupide', and famously well equipped to do him justice.[16] The courtier and rake John Wilmot, earl of Rochester, quipped that Charles's 'sceptre and his prick are of a length/ And she that plays with one may wield the other'.[17] Charles's childless marriage to the Portuguese infanta, Catherine of Braganza (1638–1705), seems merely to have whetted his carnal appetite. During the course of his lifetime he fathered fourteen offspring by various mistresses. Underlying all his behaviour was a profound cynicism, or as one observer put it, 'he had a bad opinion of all mankind'.[18]

Inevitably, the court took its moral tone from Charles, and was consequently among the most profligate and sleazy of any in Europe. No man cut any kind of figure there without whoring, gambling, swearing, drinking and fighting duels, preferably to excess. Some could handle the pace of court life better than others. The courtier Digby, Lord Gerard got into a drinking match at the Rose Tavern, Covent Garden, and died of the experience. He was just twenty-two. The earl of Middlesex gained notoriety not for wasting his wife's fortune in 'play and rioting' but for the ungentlemanly manner of his challenge to a fellow peer:

> I must forget your quality, since you have only a title, and no honour, therefore I must let you know you are the basest, and the most unworthiest person, that ever owned himself a gentleman, and as for the injury that you have done me, know that there is nothing but your sword shall ever give me a satisfaction for it, which if suddenly you refuse to give me, expect in print, on every post in the town to find yourself an infamous coward, this is all from him that scorns you, Middlesex[19]

Venereal disease was rife at court, and it was dirty in a more literal sense too, for Charles allowed his spaniels to whelp and wean in his Bedchamber, 'which rendred it very offensive, & indeed made the whole Court nasty & stinking'.[20] The courtiers themselves were no cleanlier. When the court decamped to Oxford in 1665 to escape the plague, they scandalised one academic by leaving 'their excrements in every corner, in chimneys, studies, colehouses, cellars. Rude, rough, whore-mongers; vaine, empty, carelesse.'[21]

It was not just what the king's brazen philandering said about his morals and piety, but also about his fitness to govern. If he could not control his passions, wondered contemporaries, then how could he restrain his princely will? And then there was the huge cost of so many mistresses and royal bastards – what Milton called 'the vast and lavish price of our subjection and their debausherie'.[22] It was not enough that Charles had halved the size of the royal household, or had drastically reduced the court's provision of free meals for its servants, thereby finally bringing royal court practice into line with the gentry's abandonment of traditional forms of 'open' hospitality. His and his court's moral incontinence negated such economies, both in terms of popular good will and money. As his principal minister Sir Edward Hyde (created earl of Clarendon in 1660) told him, 'the excess of pleasures which he indulged to himself . . . had already lost very much of the affection and reverence the nation had for him'.[23] Most damning of all perhaps was the perception that the king's mistresses commanded not just the royal member but also his ear. This would have been bad enough in the case of the self-proclaimed 'Protestant whore' Nell Gwyn,[24] but the king's other mistresses were almost all Catholics.

When it came to their monarch, the public still demanded a fighter, not a lover. For all the bad memories of 'Oliver's time' there was a recognition that Cromwell had at least stuck up for Europe's Protestants and restored England's martial reputation. His military triumphs loomed over Charles's reign just as Elizabeth's had over James I's. The people expected Protestant greatness. What they got instead was Catholic mistresses. Or as Rochester put it: 'He [Charles] Victory, and Honour refuses,/ And, rather then a Crowne, a Cunt he chooses'.[25]

The only foreign power that Charles could work up any martial zeal against was the Dutch republic, whose mere existence was an affront to his monarchical sensibilities. To Charles, as to Louis XIV, it was a political obscenity. Besides which, the Dutch were sheltering many of Charles's republican enemies who had fled abroad at the Restoration. To the English generally, or at least the non-Puritan majority, the Dutch republic represented the evils of unrestrained Protestantism. In a barrage of court-sponsored propaganda in the mid-1660s, the Dutch were demonised as ingrates – did they not owe their independence to English help? – and as enemies to the national interest for their supposed design to 'engross all the trade of the whole world unto themselves', and thereby achieve a 'Universal Dominion of the Seas'.[26] Certainly with their huge merchant fleet and outposts around the Atlantic and Indian Oceans the Dutch were easily Europe's most powerful trading nation. Fighting them would undoubtedly damage English commerce in the short term, but for Charles, as for the swordsmen at court, eager to show off their martial valour, this was a small price to pay. Victory would restore his flagging prestige and strengthen royal power at home. And surely England's formidable navy would swiftly teach the Dutch humility, as it had done in 1652–4? This was the thinking at court, anyway, where a powerful group of investors, headed by the lord high admiral the duke of York, stood to make a fortune if the Dutch could be plundered of their trade in West African slaves and gold.

In March 1665, Charles declared war on the Dutch republic; and in June the navy, commanded by York, showed that it was still top seadog by mauling the Dutch fleet in a battle off the East Anglian coast. But the war soon imposed huge strains on government finances. Military expenditure outstripped parliamentary supply, customs receipts plummeted, and the crown's credit – which depended on far less sophisticated and durable financial systems than that of the Dutch – effectively collapsed. Nature itself seemed to conspire against the English as bubonic plague ravaged London during the second half of 1665, killing a quarter of the city's population. Material devastation followed in 1666 when, in five terrifying days, fire consumed over 13,000 houses and the City's financial district, at an estimated cost of some £10 million. Preachers glossed the plague and fire as God's judgement upon the nation's sins; most people blamed the Catholics. The political strains of the war claimed Charles's chief minister, the earl of Clarendon, who was arrested early in 1667 and permanently exiled. And disaster turned to humiliation in June 1667, when the Dutch sailed up the River Medway to Chatham naval dockyard and burnt three of the navy's greatest warships and towed away the *Royal Charles*, the pride of the English fleet. Rumour had it that at the height of the Dutch attack Charles was sporting himself at his mistress's apartments 'in hunting of a poor moth'.[27] Once again the Stuarts were a byword for military bungling and impotence. Charles had had enough, and negotiated a quick end to the war.

Not the least of Charles's motives in fighting the Dutch was to catch the attention of his French cousin, Louis XIV (1638–1715). The 1659 treaty of the Pyrenees, which had ended the Franco-Spanish war begun in the 1630s, had confirmed what all of Europe already knew: that Bourbon France had overtaken Habsburg Spain as the Continent's greatest military power. The young Louis XIV's desire for dynastic glory and defensible borders would grow by the late 1660s into a nakedly expansionist policy towards France's northern neighbour the Spanish Netherlands (roughly modern-day Belgium). To some English observers, particularly radical Protestants, it seemed as if it was not simply more territory that Louis wanted, but to revive the supposed ambition of the Spanish Habsburgs for 'universal monarchy', supported on the twin pillars of absolutism (unfettered monarchical rule) and Counter-Reformation Catholicism. Yet Charles saw the situation rather differently. He was not blind to the recent growth of French naval power, or to Louis's designs on the Low Countries. Like his subjects, he did not want an area of such vital strategic importance to England, with deep-water ports ideal for harbouring invasion fleets, in the hands of a powerful enemy. But it all depended on whom one regarded as the enemy. In the end, Charles preferred to neutralise the threat from Louis by allying with him rather than with the Dutch; and he cared not a jot for the Protestant cause. One of the restored monarchy's first acts had been to end Cromwell's war with Spain. It was not the spread of Catholic power abroad that worried Charles, but rather the threat of republican agitation at home.

Charles's financial constraints and easygoing indolence meant that he never seriously considered adopting French methods for enforcing royal will in the localities, or emulating Louis XIV's incredibly grand and formal court arrangements. Charles certainly wanted to liberate the monarchy from some of its constitutional shackles, and to lessen its dependence on Parliament. But his efforts to strengthen the prerogative and build up a standing army were more in the way of insurance policies against being reduced, as his father had been, to a mere 'Duke of Venice'.

Charles's interest in obtaining French money and military support as security against his own potentially rebellious subjects was the background to perhaps the most astonishing diplomatic pact in English history: the 1670 treaty of Dover. In conditions of the greatest secrecy, Charles agreed to join with Louis in invading and dismembering France's traditional ally against Spain, the Dutch republic, which had angered Louis for its understandable reluctance to help him expand his dominions right to its southern border. In return, Louis would pay Charles an annual subsidy of £230,000. In an even more secret part of the treaty, Charles went so far as to promise to become a Catholic himself and to re-establish Catholicism in his three kingdoms, if necessary with the help of French troops. He had been dangling the prospect of his conversion in front of Louis for some time, though he was too shrewd to actually go through with it. But if playing up to Louis meant that he obtained the money to maintain his small standing army and pursue his pleasures without having to go cap in hand to the Cavalier Parliament, then so be it.

The treaty of Dover was reminiscent of the secret pact that Charles I had made with Spain back in 1630 for a joint attack upon the Dutch. But whereas nothing had come of that treaty, in 1672 Charles II honoured his military commitment to Louis by declaring war, with France, upon the Dutch republic. With an army raised to deal with the supposed Dutch threat, and – in the event of victory – his share of the spoils from an Anglo-French carve-up of the republic, Charles could rule much as he pleased, avoiding the need to cooperate with Parliament or the Anglican church establishment.

Despite growing anti-French feeling in England since the mid-1660s, many people trusted in the government's insistence that the Dutch were still England's natural enemy. As the war unfolded, however, it quickly became clear which side was the most serious aspirant to universal dominion. The success of the French land invasion was greater than anyone had anticipated, with Louis's armies advancing to within a few miles of Amsterdam itself. At sea, on the other hand, the French caused outrage in England by appearing reluctant to fight, which was seen as a perfidious design to let the Dutch and English fleets destroy each other and leave Louis the undisputed master of the oceans. In the event, the Dutch navy fought a series of brilliant defensive actions, while their privateers, hunting in packs, inflicted heavy losses on English shipping. The English benefited from the war only to the extent that it caused the Dutch people to rise up and murder their anti-Stuart republican leaders and reinstall as stadholder Charles's nephew William III (1650– 1702), prince of Orange, who was well disposed towards his uncle. Thanks to William's dogged leadership the French invaders were even- tually repulsed. But from this point onwards the struggle for and against a greater France took on elements of a personal feud between William and Louis.

The years 1667–74 would mark an important transition in British and European history. The French were clearly revealed as Europe's greatest troublemakers, and would remain such until the defeat of Napoleon in 1815. In England they were cast in the role they had played before the 1560s, as the principal objects of popular xenophobia and anti-popery. French absolutism now replaced Dutch republicanism as the English public's main international bugbear, even as French culture and fashions came to dominate the tastes of polite society (of which more later). Defying Louis's huge armies and fleets would stretch the British state almost to breaking point; resisting 'the Universal Monarchy for clothes' would be a lost cause altogether.[28]

'Forty-one is come again', 1673–81

The 1670s would be difficult years for a society still struggling to come to terms with its recent, rebellious past, for the political scenery looked disturbingly familiar. A decade that began with a secret treaty between the crown and Europe's greatest Catholic power would end with a Presbyterian uprising in Scotland, the Irish supposedly plotting new massacres, and London, in Charles's words, 'rotten ripe for rebellion'.[29] The king's alliance with France in 1670, and his attempt in 1672 to grant toleration by prerogative, took many people back to the 1630s, when Charles I had determined upon circumventing Parliament and aligning England with what had then been Europe's Catholic colossus, Spain. Yet if Charles II's actions seemed reminiscent of the 'creeping popery' of his father's Personal Rule, then the reappearance in the 1670s of large-scale, sometimes violent, agitation against royal policies would be evocative of the dark days of 1641, when Church and monarchy had been overwhelmed by power-hungry Parliament-men and enraged London mobs. In fact, so charged would be the political atmosphere by the late 1670s, so full of echoes of crises past, that many felt the three kingdoms were again on the brink of civil war.

The shadow of 1641 would loom even larger in the light of events on the Continent. The English were no less eager for foreign news than they had been during the Thirty Years War; and in the 1670s, as in the 1620s and 1630s, one issue would grip their attention like no other – the seemingly inexorable advance of Catholic power in mainland Europe. For it was clear by the early 1670s that Louis XIV's armies had taken up where those of Habsburg Spain and Austria had left off, accelerating a trend that would see the Protestant part of Europe shrink from about half the Continent in 1600 to less than a quarter by 1700.

To halt the seeming spread of popery at home, and in response to the king's attempt to grant toleration, the Cavalier Parliament passed the Test Act in 1673, which made receiving Anglican communion a requirement for holding public office. Unfortunately, the Act merely served to heighten fears of popery by 'outing' Charles's brother, James Duke of York (1633–1701), who resigned his post as lord high admiral. James had long admired the dignity of Catholic worship and the authoritarian strain within Counter-Reformation Catholicism. The Church of England he looked upon as corrupt and insincere. His conversion, thought one loyal Anglican, 'gave exceeding grief and scandal to the whole nation', not least because Charles had yet to father a legitimate heir, meaning there was now a real possibility that the throne would fall to a Catholic.[30] As if this was not bad enough, James, with a sublime lack of tact, decided to remarry in 1673 and chose as his bride the fifteen-year-old Mary of Modena, who was a Catholic princess and a French client to boot. If James should now have a son, his two Protestant daughters by his first wife would be superseded by their Catholic stepbrother.

James's 'apostasy' lent substance to Dutch propaganda about a cabal of popish grandees at court that had embroiled the English in a war against fellow Protestants in order to help Louis establish a universal monarchy 'and turn England into a French province'.[31] The clamour against the Dutch war became so great that early in 1674 Charles was forced to make peace, leaving Louis to fight on alone against William III and a coalition of European states.

Having flown too near *le roi soleil* and been burnt, Charles changed course in 1673–4. No longer would he try to protect the Dissenters, but would leave them to the mercy of local authorities; and, as a result, more of them died after 1672 as a result of confinement in England's overflowing and disease-ridden gaols than had suffered at the stake during Mary I's reign. He also dropped most of the cabal of unscrupulous courtiers that had replaced Clarendon in 1667 – a group that had included both Catholics and Presbyterians, all of whom were in receipt of pensions and secret handouts from the French crown. In its place, he promoted as de facto first minister the staunchly Anglican and anti-French Thomas Osborne (1632–1712), whom he created earl of Danby. Danby's mission was, as he put it, 'to settle the church and state; to defend the one against schismaticks and papists, and the other against commonwealthsmen and rebels'.[32] Using a mixture of bribery and good management he was able to strengthen the court party in the Cavalier Parliament. He was also instrumental in arranging the marriage in 1677 between James's eldest daughter by his first marriage, Mary (1662–94), and Louis's inveterate enemy, William III, who had been careful to cultivate powerful friends at Whitehall and Westminster. The match was intended to ease fears of a Catholic succession (Mary, a Protestant, was second in line to the throne after her father) and to improve Charles's Protestant credentials. But as a public relations exercise it was not much more successful than the marriage in 1641 between Charles's sister and William's father had been. What it did do was strengthen William's claim to the throne, both as a prince of the blood himself (he was Charles's nephew) and in right of his new wife.

Danby's efforts to put an Anglican and anti-French spin on royal policies were constantly undermined by Charles's Bedchamber intriguing for French cash and the political freedom that went with it. The king's lavish lifestyle was sustained in part by Louis's secret subsidies – and French influence did not stop there. 'A colony of French possess the court,' wrote one Restoration poet, 'pimps, priests, buffoons . . . Such slimey monsters ne'er approached a throne, Since Pharaoh's time.'[33] Charles and his leading courtiers were culturally in thrall to the French court. They wore French clothes, listened to French music, bought French artworks, even slept in French beds. Charles had his state rooms and private apartments at Whitehall rearranged according to the model he had seen at the French court during the 1650s. Moreover, as Charles's reign progressed, his devotional tastes would borrow more heavily from Catholic, and particularly French Counter-Reformation, worship. Early in the 1680s he would have the royal chapel at Windsor Castle, his summer residence, remodelled by a team of Catholic artists in the most sumptuous French and Italian baroque styles – a fitting venue for the music of England's greatest baroque composer, Henry Purcell, who was himself heavily influenced by French and Italian masters.

Yet Windsor was far enough from prying London eyes for the chapel not to cause a stir. The real scandal as far as the court's critics were concerned was a situation that would have been all too familiar to the 'patriots' of the 1610s and 1620s – that is, royal minions in the service of a Catholic power insinuating their own private counsels between the king and his loyal Parliament-men and privy councillors. The focus of suspicion before the Civil War had usually been the Bedchamber men and other 'unsworn' counsellors – after 1660 it would be the king's mistresses. One of Charles's privy councillors referred to the king's 'Female Ministry; for though he had Ministers of the [privy] Council, Ministers of the Cabinet [entourage], and Ministers of the Ruelle [mistress's bedroom]; the Ruelle was often the last Appeal'.[34]

The king's first long-term mistress, Barbara Palmer (1640–1709), countess of Castlemaine, was a serious power at court during the 1660s. A 'woman of great beauty', conceded one godly memorialist, 'but most enormously vicious and ravenous; foolish but imperious', she was also a Catholic convert, and, by the late 1660s, a court intelligencer for the French ambassador.[35] She certainly used her influence with Charles for political ends. The fall of Clarendon in 1667 owed much to the resentment his moralising and legal fastidiousness had aroused among the king's intimates, and in particular Castlemaine and the royal Bedchamber men. In the early 1670s, however, having borne the king five children, she was replaced in his affections by a woman who was not merely a friend to the French, she *was* French. Louise de Kéroualle (1649–1734) was the daughter of an impoverished Breton nobleman, and, like her predecessor as 'mistress of state', a Catholic. She was the love of Charles's life, and he showered her with gifts, including the title of duchess of Portsmouth.

Perhaps no other figure in Stuart court history, with the exception of the 1st duke of Buckingham, excited more gossip or attracted more criticism than 'the French bitch'.[36] At the centre of this writhing mass of speculation was one essential truth, which was that Portsmouth exercised an almost unrivalled influence over her royal lover. 'You govern every Councell meeting,' wrote one satirist, 'Make the fools do as you think fitting/Your royall Cully [dupe] has command/Only from you at second hand . . .' Her 'pocky bum/So powerful is of late', wrote another, 'It rules both Church and State.'[37] This was more than merely gutter-press hype. Portsmouth was a major patronage-broker at court, and on occasion she may even have swayed the king on matters of high policy. Her forty apartments at Whitehall – lavishly appointed in the finest French style, with 'ten times the richnesse & glory beyond the Queenes'[38] – usurped the king's own Bedchamber as the centre of unofficial power at court. Because Charles liked to conduct business informally, and was so often in Portsmouth's company, she could use her apartments to control access to him – and close proximity to the monarch was often the key to power. No wonder the French came to rely on her as their principal factotum at Charles's court, and rewarded her handsomely for her services.

For those without the distraction of French mistresses or French pensions, it was easy to assume that England had become a mere client-state of Louis XIV by the mid-1670s. The campaign to save the nation from its seeming slide into Catholic despotism bore many similarities to the 'patriot' opposition to royal policies before the Civil War. In the Cavalier Parliament a 'Country party' of disaffected peers and Commons-men emerged to cry up the Protestant cause and English liberties. Once again there was talk of a deep-laid design, driven on by popish courtiers and persecuting prelates, 'to change the Lawfull Government of England into an Absolute Tyranny, and to convert the established Protestant Religion into down-right Popery'.[39] The proposed remedies were equally familiar: frequent Parliaments; church reform that comprehended 'orthodox' Puritans; war against foreign Catholic aggressors; and the purging of 'evil counsellors' and their replacement by men who reverenced godly Protestantism. The patriotic and patrician rhetoric of the country party would have been instantly recognisable to any Jacobean politician. The leading country peer Anthony Ashley Cooper (1621–83) – created earl of Shaftesbury in 1672 – and his friend and secretary the philosopher John Locke (1632–1704), collaborated on an influential pamphlet in 1675 in which they referred to their allies in the Lords as 'stedfast in all good English Principles . . . [who] spoke plain like old English Lords'.[40]

The most explosive issue of the day was a throwback not to the 1620s and 1630s, however, but to the era of the last Catholic successor to the throne, Mary Queen of Scots. Shaftesbury and his friends had long suspected that the duke of York was a Catholic, and had tried, unsuccessfully, to have Charles's eldest bastard, the duke of Monmouth, declared legitimate so that he could inherit the crown. Talk of excluding James from the succession – which had been bruited in parliamentary circles since his 'outing' in 1673 – would become the stuff of everyday conversation late in 1678 as a result of the so-called 'Popish Plot'. This fraud upon the three kingdoms was perpetrated by perhaps the most despicable character in Restoration history: Titus Oates (1649–1705). To say that he was a con-artist, thief and perjurer is too complimentary. Unfortunately, his tall tales of a Jesuit plot for assassinating Charles and coordinating an Irish Catholic rebellion and a French invasion played to an audience so well primed by decades of Catholic conspiracy stories that he convinced many on the privy council and in Parliament. Accounts of the Plot spread throughout the three kingdoms, and were so well credited in some places that people feared they were about to be massacred by the plotters. The actual victims of the Plot, however, would be its supposed beneficiaries. Some thirty-five priests and alleged Jesuit fifth-columnists were judicially murdered on little more than Oates's word. When Danby tried to exploit the Plot to gain himself some much-needed credit at Westminster, his enemies revealed details of his (reluctant) involvement in Charles's secret negotiations with Louis for extra cash to suspend Parliament and thereby stifle calls for war against France. The two Houses now turned upon Danby and endeavoured to pull him down as they had Charles I's chief minister, the earl of Strafford, in 1640–1. With moves afoot to impeach Danby and to exclude James from the succession, the king dissolved the Cavalier Parliament in January 1679.

The Popish Plot would trigger the Exclusion Crisis. Just a few weeks after dissolving the Cavalier Parliament, Charles was forced to call another out of sheer financial desperation, for Louis XIV had cut his French subsidy in anger at the marriage in 1677 between William III and Princess Mary. Unfortunately for Charles, his need for parliamentary supply had come at what would be the worst moment in his reign for obtaining a compliant Parliament. Oates's revelations, and the disclosure that the crown was apparently in league with the French, had so alarmed the voters that most of the MPs elected to this and the two Parliaments that followed in rapid succession demanded legislation for excluding James from the succession before they would grant the crown supply. Shaftesbury and his allies saw their chance, and worked hard to secure the passage of the desired exclusion bill: 'If we do not do something relating to the Succession', insisted one of Shaftesbury's clients, 'we must resolve . . . to be Papists, or burn.'[41] Charles, however, was determined to resist what was effectively pressure to establish an elective monarchy, and he was far from alone in seeing the exclusion campaign as the thin end of a republican wedge.

Both sides in this stand-off feared that they stood on the edge of a familiar precipice. History seemed about to repeat itself, and the three kingdoms to be in danger of reliving the events of the late 1630s and early 1640s, when rebellion in Scotland and then in Ireland had helped turn a crisis in London into civil war. In the summer of 1679 the Scottish Presbyterians rose in arms against the rule of Charles's first minister in Scotland, the hard-headed and splenetic duke of Lauderdale, who had routinely deployed government troops – and, on one notorious occasion, Highlanders – to terrorise Presbyterian communities. Without significant support among the Scottish nobility the Presbyterians would be easily suppressed, and therefore the 1679 rebellion could not be used by disaffected elements elsewhere in the three kingdoms as had that of the late 1630s. Nevertheless, the crown's authoritarian proceedings in Scotland were regarded by Shaftesbury and his friends as the shape of things to come in England. Moreover, those alarmed by the persecution of godly Protestants in Scotland were equally worried by the toleration of Catholics in Ireland under Charles's lord lieutenant, the marquess (now duke) of Ormond. Rumours abounded in England during the late 1670s that the Irish, their confidence growing, were plotting another massacre of their Protestant governors, this time with the help of the French.

Were the three kingdoms really facing civil war? The signs in England certainly looked ominous. Nationwide petitioning campaigns in favour of exclusion, mass demonstrations in London, 'pope-burning' processions in towns across the country – this all smacked of the parliamentary junto's incitement of the people in the early 1640s, and everyone knew what the consequences of that had been. 'I desire you only to peruse the Records of 40 and 41,' wrote one loyalist pamphleteer, 'it is just as if the old Game was playing over again.' Like the junto, the gamesters in 1679 were adept at using 'seditious and factious Pamphlets . . . to render the present Government odious to the people'.[42] The lapsing of the 1662 Licensing Act in 1679 meant that the government temporarily lost control of press censorship, and the result was another huge outpouring of propaganda and all manner of printed material, on a scale not seen since the 1640s.[43]

The glut of 'Pamphlets seditious, profane scandalous rebellious, Atheisticall, and Blasphemous' made the earl of Rochester begin to question the value of liberty itself: 'Since the meere shaddow of Lyberty, I meane this of the Press had allready introduced the most abject slavery subjecting us to the Tyranny one of another, by allowing our Insolent equalls or envious Inferiors the ridiculous prerogative of defameing and Vilifying our persons, Lives; Laws, and Religion and all that is nearest and dearest to us without Lett or Controule.'[44] Other loyalists took a more practical approach, recognising the need to use print to mobilise popular support. As the loyalist journalist Roger L'Estrange put it: ''Tis the press that has made 'em mad and the press must set 'em right again' – though he believed that once it had done its job, and quieted the giddy multitude, the press should be all but silenced again.[45] L'Estrange's racy style made his pamphlets a big hit with the public, while John Dryden, Aphra Behn and other loyalist writers, with their biting satires on Shaftesbury and his allies, generally had the best of the literary contest.

The struggle between exclusionists and loyalists grew so heated it generated two new political labels: Whigs and Tories. These names originated as terms of abuse. Whig referred originally to a radical Scottish Presbyterian; Tory was the name for an Irish Catholic bandit. Leaving aside the issue of exclusion, the loosely organised national parties that gathered under these banners were divided along roughly the same lines as the Civil War parliamentarians and royalists. The Whigs' view of the monarchy was implicitly contractual. They thought that kings were beneath the law and accountable to the people's representatives in Parliament, and that if they forfeited the people's consent by acting illegally they could be resisted and even dethroned. The Whigs regarded elements of the Anglican Church, particularly the lordly pretensions of the bishops, as popish and a betrayal of European Protestantism. They sympathised with godly nonconformists and wanted either a more inclusive national Church or some form of toleration.

The Tories, on the other hand, subscribed to what was essentially James I's theory of divine right kingship. Though kings were obliged by custom and conscience to rule according to law, this obligation was ultimately moral in nature and there were no enforceable limitations upon their authority, which was unaccountable and could not be actively resisted. The Tories revered the established Church as the acme of European Protestantism; the Dissenters they regarded as dangerous individualists who must be forced for their own and society's good back into the Anglican fold, for as L'Estrange warned: 'The State that allowes the People a Freedom to choose their Religion, is reasonably to Expect that they will Take a Freedom likewise to choose their Government.'[46] They abhorred popery as much as the Whigs, and like them feared for the fate of Europe's Protestants under the shadow of Louis XIV. But they believed that royal counsels were fundamentally sound, and that the greatest weapons in the war on popery were a strong monarchy and Protestant unity, both of which they thought were imperilled by Whiggery and Dissent. Unlike the Whigs, they did not regard Protestantism as doomed under a Catholic king. James was doing a good job defending the episcopal establishment in Scotland – where Charles had packed him off as de facto viceroy in the autumn of 1679 – and they saw no reason to think he would not do the same in England when he became king. They even had hopes that, once crowned, he would lead the fight against French tyranny. They were convinced that the Whigs were using the issue of his exclusion merely as a stalking horse for re-establishing a Puritan commonwealth.

A few leading Whigs were indeed outright republicans, but most would have been happy simply to divert the succession to a Protestant (ideally, James's eldest child Mary, wife of the Dutch stadholder William III), and perhaps clip the monarchy's wings a little. Yet as we have seen in the 1640s, the line between aristocratic constitutionalism and support for a commonwealth in which the king was merely a figurehead was very thin, and whether politicians crossed that line depended upon political circumstances as much as ideological conviction.

The reason that relatively few Whigs made that short journey during the Exclusion Crisis was because, put simply, the king won. When the third of the so-called 'Exclusion Parliaments' met in March 1681 and proved as troublesome as its two predecessors, Charles dissolved it after just one week. His only reason for calling Parliament in the first place had been for money, and this the Commons had withheld until he would agree to James's exclusion. But the king was now back in his French cousin's good books after Louis had realised that cutting the subsidy was simply weakening Charles at the expense of their common enemies. With Louis's gold, and rising revenues from customs, Charles would not need to call another Parliament for the rest of his reign, and without Parliament the Whigs lacked any real political leverage against the government. Nor was there any possibility in 1681 of a timely intervention by the Scottish Presbyterians of the kind that had helped bring down the Personal Rule in 1640 and prevented Charles I from dissolving the Long Parliament. For by the 1680s the Scottish Presbyterians were too weak to control even the Edinburgh Parliament, which needed little prompting from Scotland's royal governor, James, to declare roundly against exclusion. Another Irish Catholic uprising might have destabilised England to the point of rebellion. But Ireland was quiet under the lenient oversight of the duke of Ormond.

The royal grip on London was also secure. Although the Whigs dominated London's municipal government, its military resources – the militia and those units of the standing army guarding Whitehall and Westminster – were firmly under royal control. There would be no question of Charles having to flee the capital as his father had in 1642. Besides which, he was a more forceful character than Charles I had been. His presence in the House of Lords during 1680–1 was enough to daunt all but the staunchest of Whig peers. He was also more politically astute. Although he shared the Stuart instinct for keeping people and press as far apart as possible, he recognised the importance of winning the propaganda war. His government would be much quicker and better at putting its case to the public than Charles I's had been.

Charles II may have been a stronger king than his father, but equally his opponents lacked the fame and popularity of Charles I's grandee adversaries. It is striking how many of the leading Whigs were either close relatives of the men who had plotted treason against Charles I in 1639–42 or were themselves former parliamentarian leaders. None of them, however, enjoyed anything like the popular admiration of the early Stuart 'commonwealth lords' the earls of Essex and Warwick. These men had stood in the same Protestant military tradition as the heroes who had defeated the Armada. Most of the leading Whigs, by contrast, had less military experience than their Stuart opponents. They had political influence – enough to make Charles and James offer them concessions at various times. But when it came to the crunch, a large majority of the peers and all of the bishops voted against exclusion. Anxiety about renewed civil war made for caution and compromise at all social levels, but particularly among those with the heaviest invest-ment in the established order. The duke of Ormond was speaking for the great majority of the ruling elite in the three kingdoms when he assured the king in 1681 that 'the Wrack of the Crown in the King your Father's time is fresh in the memory of many of us; and the rocks and shelves he was lost upon (tho' they were hid to him) are so very visible to us, that if we avoid them not, we shall perish rather derided than pitied'.[47]

Monarchy rowz'd, 1681–8

> When, from the filthy Dunghil-faction bred,
> New-form'd Rebellion durst rear up its head,
> Answer me all: who struck the Monster dead?
> See, see, the injur'd PRINCE, and bless his Name,
> Think on the Martyr from whose Loynes he came:
> Think on the Blood was shed for you before,
> And Curse the Paricides that thirst for more . . .
> Let Royal Pardon be by him implor'd,
> Th'Attoning Brother of your Anger'd Lord:
> He only brings a Medicine fit to aswage
> A peoples folly, and rowz'd Monarch's rage.[48]

In the spring of 1682, the duke of York returned to England after his brief but effective stint governing Scotland. Before leaving London, in 1679, he had been jeered at in the streets as a 'popish dog'.[49] Now he was feted by Tory crowds as the saviour of the three kingdoms. His warm welcome home in 1682 registered the gradual turnaround in the monarchy's fortunes since 1679. Charles had kept his throne during the Exclusion Crisis, but he had lost control of the Commons, and had found the basic task of ruling very difficult. This humiliating challenge to his authority brought about what the memorialist James Welwood thought was 'a sensible Change in his Temper; for from an Easiness and Debonairness that was natural to him, he came at length to treat men with Hard Names, and upon some occasions to express a Severity in his Disposition, that he had been ever averse to before'.[50]

With Parliament now dissolved, and public opinion turning his way, Charles was determined to ensure nothing like the Exclusion Crisis would occur again. While maintaining a highly effective media campaign to rally the common people behind hereditary monarchy, the government acted in 1682 to ban all but two newspapers, of which one was L'Estrange's Tory tabloid *The Observator*. In 1682–3 the crown effectively forced a Tory lord mayor upon London and then confiscated its municipal charter, leading one peer to declare admiringly that 'now the King has master'd this greate beaste the Cittye'.[51] Several half-baked Whig conspiracies to raise rebellion or assassinate the royal brothers then gave the government an excuse to undertake a thoroughgoing purge of Whigs and Dissenters from borough corporations and the county magistracy. Many leading Whigs either fled abroad – as Monmouth, Shaftesbury and Locke did – or suffered show trials and execution, while the Dissenters endured the most intense bout of persecution in their history.

The Tory reaction of the early 1680s rendered Charles more powerful than any English monarch since Henry VIII. His 'personal rule' of 1681–5 was based, as Charles I's had been, on a neutralist foreign policy and financial independence. French subsidies helped, but Charles II's new-found solvency was thanks largely to the rapid expansion in England's overseas commerce after the third Anglo-Dutch war of 1672–4. Increased trade meant increased customs revenue. By 1684–5 the king was receiving almost £1.5 million a year from customs alone, and on that kind of money he had no need for parliamentary supply. He was even wealthy enough to commission Sir Christopher Wren – the architect who had overseen the rebuilding of London after the Great Fire – to build a vast new royal residence at Winchester that would imitate and rival the great baroque palace at Versailles, where Louis had recently moved his court from the bustle and unrest of Paris. The new palace at Winchester would be at a similar remove from London and its unruly mob, and may have been intended to replace Whitehall as the main seat of royal government, although as it was never finished we will never know.

Charles made the monarchy appear so formidable during the early 1680s by placing himself at the head of his realm's most powerful political constituency: the English Tory–Anglican interest. Rather than binding all aristocratic groupings to royal service, as Louis XIV had done in France, Charles had made himself the prisoner of one. He had strengthened the monarchy by agreeing to rule as loyalist gentry had always wanted him to – that is, by respecting the law, defending the established Church, and helping them oust the 'factious party' (namely, the Whigs) from local government. The result was not a French-style absolutist regime, therefore, but a more broadly based version of the Caroline Church-state of the 1630s.

Charles fell unexpectedly and seriously ill on 2 February 1685, and died four days later. The thirteen attending physicians, armed with all the latest medical treatments, were more than usually efficient in killing off their patient. Poisonous 'tonics' were administered to make him vomit; enemas and clysters were inserted up his anus; pungent powder was pushed up his nose; and red-hot cupping glasses applied to his skin. But even more remarkable than these physical ministrations was the attention paid to his spiritual well-being. A few hours before the king died, James arranged a secret religious service in which the king was received into the Catholic Church. Whether this unexpected denouement to Charles's life reflected a sincere attachment to Catholicism, or was merely a case of him surrendering *in extremis* to the wishes of James and the duchess of Portsmouth is impossible to say. His great achievement was to die of natural causes (with a little help from his doctors), having not just kept his crown but strengthened the monarchy to the point where it could withstand even a popish successor.

The 51-year-old James II of England and VII of Scotland was one of the most experienced men ever to succeed to the crown of either kingdom. He had served in both the French and Spanish armies during exile in the 1650s, as England's lord high admiral in the 1660s, and as viceroy in all but name of Scotland in the early 1680s. If he had a talent for anything it was soldiering. An 'extream lover of Soldiery and Military Exercises', he was brave, and had made a capable naval commander.[52] He was also, in marked contrast to Charles II, hard-working. What he conspicuously lacked, however, were his brother's nimble intelligence and people skills. His understanding of human nature was simplistic, his belief in the personal loyalty he thought was owed him almost childlike. Haughty, hot-tempered and bullishly self-confident, he made an even poorer politician than his father had. And like Charles I, he took his religion – in his case, Catholicism – very seriously. His one great moral weakness, as he saw it, was women, for he had a number of mistresses, all of whom were 'ugly trollops' in Charles II's opinion.[53] On the other hand, he did not gamble and was never drunk. His court was similarly restrained. The extravagance and debauchery of court life under Charles II gave way under James to 'seriousness and businesse'.[54] Duellists, drunkards and womanisers were banned, ceremony and etiquette restored.

King James came to the throne on a huge wave of popular good will. A Catholic he might be, but most of his Protestant subjects were desperate to believe his assurances that he would uphold their religion and liberties. Congratulatory addresses poured into Whitehall, even from Puritan New England, and there were public celebrations in the three kingdoms that almost rivalled those of 1660. Eager to capitalise on his popularity, James called general elections in England and Scotland in 1685, and the result was solidly loyalist majorities in both Parliaments. In the House of Commons a mere 57 of the 513 MPs elected were Whigs. The English Parliament voted James the same annual revenue of £1,200,000 that Charles II had enjoyed, although improvements in financial administration, a reduction in court expenditure, and increasing foreign trade, and therefore customs receipts, meant that he would pocket nearer £2 million a year. The public mood was such that when the once-feted Titus Oates was put in the pillory in May 1685, large crowds of Londoners turned out to pelt him with eggs.

Yet not everyone was convinced by James's pledge to 'preserve this government both in Church and state as it is now by law established'.[55] In the late spring and early summer of 1685, the dissident Scottish nobleman the earl of Argyll (the son of the marquess executed at the Restoration) and the Whig leader the duke of Monmouth embarked from Holland for the western Highlands and the English West Country respectively in a badly coordinated attempt to raise rebellion in both kingdoms. But neither man proved capable of reaching out to the Protestant mainstream. From what little the public could make of their actions, the two men seemed like religious fanatics, intent on plunging the three kingdoms into the civil war that had loomed in 1679–81. Their ragtag armies were routed, and both men were executed.

The defeat of the 1685 rebellions was for James nothing less than a sign of God's will, a divine mandate to fulfil his long-term ambition of re-establishing the Catholic Church in the three kingdoms. Brimming with renewed confidence, he told English Parliament-men that they must not object if he employed Catholic officers in his army in contravention of the Test Act. Yet object they did, Tories as well as Whigs, angered that James was altering the law at will. James dismissed such opposition as the work of a factious minority, and prorogued Parliament. It would never meet again during his reign.

James's missionary zeal in the cause of Catholic restoration led him into highly controversial territory for a British monarch. At court, he converted the royal chapels to Catholic worship; he encouraged the setting up of Catholic churches and chapels throughout his realm, and a stronger Catholic presence in the universities; and he surrounded himself with Catholic advisers, particularly those such as the Jesuits who looked to Louis XIV rather than Pope Innocent XI as the standard-bearer of Counter-Reformation Catholicism. Although James opened full relations with the papacy, receiving a papal nuncio at court and sending an embassy to Rome, he was determined to retain the exclusive authority over the Catholic churches in his three kingdoms that he enjoyed over the established Protestant churches. His rejection of papal sovereignty followed Louis XIV's example, and was consistent with his reliance on the advice of French, anti-papalist Catholics, and the close correspondence he kept up with Louis's Jesuit confessor.

This French context to James's transformation into a 'popish' king would heighten fears among his Protestant subjects of a design at court 'to model us after the sad example of our neighbour country', meaning France.[56] Louis XIV, like James, was a committed Catholic, but with far more draconian methods for propagating the faith. In 1685, the year that James became king, Louis offered France's Protestants, the Huguenots, a simple choice: conversion or annihilation – and over the next few years thousands of them fled to the Dutch republic, England and other Protestant countries. The persecution of the Huguenots was seen in Britain as further evidence of Louis's intention to destroy European Protestantism – an objective that James's admiration for Bourbon Catholicism suggested he shared.

It was the power that Louis wielded as much as his intolerant Catholicism that so alarmed Britain's Protestants. Since the end of France's wars of religion in the late sixteenth century the French monarchy had restructured the state in order to bring the nobility and the army under royal control. The growth of princely power had stalled during Louis XIV's minority in the mid-seventeenth century, but had then accelerated again once he took the reins of government in 1661. Louis, even more than previous French kings, identified the good of his realm with his own personal and dynastic interests. Similarly, in international affairs he put the glory of the House of Bourbon before the prevailing desire in Europe by 1700 for peaceful equilibrium. To make himself all-powerful in France, however, meant cultivating the good will of his noblemen, for he relied heavily upon their support to govern the localities. The aristocracy were therefore co-opted into royal service through the granting of offices – most notably in the army and amid the elaborate court flummery at Versailles – and the conferral or confirmation of aristocratic privileges. That other potential source of opposition to the crown, the Parlement of Paris, was also brought to heel during the 1660s and 1670s. Even the arts were bent to Louis's will. Painters, pamphleteers, musicians and architects were employed to create and project an image of French regal majesty, French culture and French manners that held all of Europe spellbound.

More than any of his royal predecessors, Louis succeeded in creating a system in which the monarch could raise taxes, promulgate legislation and wage war without serious hindrance from the nobility, the legal establishment or the Church. By mulcting France's huge population, he was able to maintain the largest armies seen in Europe since Roman times. He also channelled resources into the construction, virtually from scratch, of a powerful battle fleet that could vie with those of the Dutch and English. The French model of government would be imitated by the Tsar and Scandinavian rulers, and some of the German states were already moving in a similar direction by the later seventeenth century. Would the three Stuart kingdoms follow?

Although James did not introduce recognisably French forms of government, he certainly set about building the bureaucratic apparatus of an efficient, centralised state. He introduced new institutions and surveillance methods in an attempt to stifle all criticism of the regime or Catholicism, and he employed L'Estrange and other loyalist writers to create a sophisticated propaganda machine. Determined to make the judiciary and local government more subservient to royal authority, he employed professional bureaucrats, answerable to Whitehall, to enforce his will, rather than depending on the tiresome old ways of negotiating consent with local governors and communities. Where he clearly differed from Louis was in his apparent lack of interest in trying to co-opt the nobility to his project, which was understandable, perhaps, given the weakness of the Catholic aristocracy in Britain. But he did emulate the French king in creating a standing peacetime army that would answer to the monarch rather than to the landed elite. He doubled the size of the English army to about 20,000 troops, had it drilled according to French military regulations, and officered it where possible with Catholics. This was a relatively small force compared with Louis's massive army, and retained the same basic role that it had under Charles II: to secure the kingdom against republican rebellion. But James used it in a more politically aggressive fashion, quartering troops on towns, even taverns and coffee houses, where the 'factious' questioned his princely intentions. One of his most influential advisers would urge him to go further, and to ground his authority upon a large and intimidating Catholic army, thereby 'to reduce the government of the countys nearer to that of the provinces in France'.[57] This drive under James to increase the government's power and reach was intended partly to serve the pious work of Catholic emancipation. But it also reflected his authoritarian mindset; his wish to be obeyed 'without reserve'.[58]

Rights for Catholics and strengthening the arm of government were laudable, or at least understandable, objectives. But attempting both was overambitious, and proved impossible without eroding the bedrock of royal support: the Tory–Anglican interest. Tories were furious that James appeared to have betrayed his public pledges to uphold the rule of law and the Protestant establishment. Like most Protestants they could accept the idea of Catholics worshipping in private, but to empower Catholics – a group supposedly guided not by law, conscience or patriotism but by their 'foreign' Church – was seen as a foundation for tyranny. Amazingly for a king whose British subjects were over-whelmingly anti-Catholic, James was, and would remain, genuinely baffled as to how he had offended them so much. Nor could he grasp that the Tories' much-vaunted loyalty to the monarchy was implicitly conditional on him respecting the laws that maintained the Restoration Anglican ascendancy in Church and state.

With many Tories and Anglican churchmen having fallen out of love with James by 1686, he decided to woo the Dissenters instead. The crown made sweeping purges of the county magistracy and town corpo-rations from late 1686, only this time removing Tories and replacing them with Dissenters and Catholics. In 1687, James used his prerogative power to override parliamentary law by granting Catholics and Dissenters the freedom to worship and hold public office without having to take the required oaths and tests of loyalty to the established Church. Yet James tolerated toleration only as a means to an end – that is, the conversion of his subjects to Catholicism – not as a virtue in itself. He believed that all sensible people, given a free choice about their faith, would choose as he had. Some Dissenters were willing to separate religious from civil liberty, as James did, but most were alarmed by the idea of toleration based upon the monarch's arbitrary will. They also suspected (rightly) that James despised their religion. As one leading Anglican assured them, they were being 'hugged now, onely that you may be the better squeezed at another time'.[59]

One group that certainly felt the squeeze was Scotland's episcopalian elite. Like his father during the 1630s, James used his northern kingdom as a political laboratory. The prerogative offensive against the episco-palian establishment would begin in Scotland, where Catholics were given the plum jobs in government, toleration was granted by royal fiat, and the Mass was celebrated openly in Edinburgh. The king's will was now invested with the force of parliamentary law – a principle that most leading Scots could stomach when it came to keeping themselves in power, but not to promote Catholicism. By breaking the Restoration alliance between the crown and the episcopalian elite, James was destroying the very foundations of royal authority in Scotland. The Edinburgh crowd, the ultra-loyalist Parliament elected in 1685, even some of the Scottish bishops all made it clear to him that he was courting disaster. But he refused to listen. The irony here is that Scotland's Catholics, like their English co-religionists, were too few in number to derive much benefit from the king's policies. The real winners, as in the 1630s, were the Presbyterians, who took advantage of James's assault on the established order to gather their political strength for the struggles to come.

As if James had not alarmed British Protestants enough, his programme of Catholic emancipation was extended to Ireland. Following the duke of Ormond's retirement in 1685, royal policy in Ireland had fallen under the control of James's long-time political fixer and procurer of mistresses, Richard Talbot, earl of Tyrconnell (1630–91). His goal was to return power in Ireland to his fellow Catholics, and ultimately to reclaim much of the land seized by the Protestant New English and Scottish settlers. Within a year or so of James appointing him lord deputy of Ireland, early in 1687, Catholics had replaced the New English at almost every level of government, and the Irish army had been transformed from an overwhelmingly Protestant force into an overwhelmingly Catholic one. Fearing the worst, Protestants began to leave Ireland for England and the Continent. Some cashiered Protestant officers, eager to rejoin the struggle against popery, took service under Louis XIV's great enemy, the Dutch stadholder William III.

James's final mistake was to perform the first duty of all monarchs: provide an heir. In December 1687 it was announced from Whitehall that the queen was pregnant. Convinced more than ever that God was on his side, James decided to use his supposedly loyal Anglican clergy to confirm his right to grant toleration by royal prerogative. But to no one's great surprise, except James's, the vast majority of clergy refused to sanction his power to dispense with parliamentary laws. 'Cholerick upon Provocations',[60] the king then committed the public relations disaster of having seven recalcitrant bishops put on trial for allegedly attempting 'to diminish the regal authority'.[61] When, late in June 1688, the jury delivered a verdict of not guilty, Dissenters as well as Anglicans went into paroxysms of joy. Bonfires, 'pope-burnings' and fireworks lit the night sky.

A few weeks earlier, however, on 10 June, an equally momentous event had occurred: the queen had given birth to a son, James Francis Edward. The king might have lost the trial of the seven bishops, but with an heir to the throne he could now afford to play the long game. For the Protestant establishment, on the other hand, the waiting patiently for better days – for James to die and for his daughter Mary, wife of William III, to succeed him – was over. Time had run out.

The Glorious Revolution, 1688–9

On the very day that the seven bishops were acquitted, seven prominent Englishmen – four Whigs and three Tories – sent a letter to William III. They assured him that if he invaded England with even a small army, the aristocracy and the people were 'so generally dissatisfied with the present conduct of the government' that they would rebel.[62] Writing this letter was of course high treason – as one of the seven, Edward Russell, would have been acutely aware, for his grandfather had been one of the 'commonwealth lords' who signed a very similar letter to the Scottish Covenanters in 1640, all but inviting them to invade England against Charles I. In fact, the parallels between the conspiracy against James in 1688 and that against his father in 1640 were numerous. William and his agents had been plotting with members of the Protestant establishment for months. Secret plans were afoot to suborn elements of the royal army and navy. Dissident noblemen had promised to organise risings to divide the king's forces. And leading English and Scottish opponents of free monarchy, many in exile at William's court in Holland, were concerting measures to bring about a radical transformation of the Stuart state.

The letter to William in June 1688 would be only one small element in a complex and evolving invasion plan that owed as much to Dutch as to English circumstances. The three kingdoms occupied a vital position on Europe's strategic map, and one that William had assumed would fall to him, via his wife (James's eldest daughter Princess Mary), when James died. It was becoming clear to William by early 1688, however, that he would have to take pre-emptive action if he were to enlist or at least neutralise British military resources in his highly personal struggle to contain the power of Louis XIV. Not only was James's queen pregnant, but it also looked as if Louis was preparing to resume hostilities against the Dutch, and that James would join him.

James certainly had plenty of reasons for wanting to finish the job that his brother and Louis had started in the 1670s. The Dutch sheltered his bitterest enemies, they fostered anti-monarchical political ideas, and above all they were England's main trading rivals. It was to help Louis destroy the Dutch and to parcel the spoils – commercial and colonial – between them that James and his 'Secretary of the Marine', Samuel Pepys, had initiated a programme for refurbishing the royal navy.

William shrewdly exploited this threat of Anglo-French aggression against the Dutch republic, although Louis played right into his hands by launching a trade war against the Dutch and then, in September 1688, a brutal attack upon the Rhineland. By the end of that month, William could count on the support of Carlos II of Spain, the Holy Roman Emperor and, crucially, Amsterdam's civic leaders, who were the paymasters and powerbrokers of the Dutch republic. William's aim at this stage was apparently not to supplant James as king of England, but rather to force him to cooperate with a 'free Parliament' for bringing the Stuart kingdoms into the emerging 'Grand Alliance' against Louis. William and the Dutch were largely indifferent as to the fate of England's ancient constitution, although they carefully concealed this fact from their English friends. Their objective was to invade England before James could help Louis to invade them.

At four times the size of the Armada of 1588, the Dutch invasion fleet of 1688 would represent one of the greatest feats of organisation in European history. With a speed and efficiency that astonished observers, 500 transports and warships were assembled to carry an invasion force of 20,000 men – mostly Dutch regulars, and mercenaries and volunteers from across Protestant Europe. Almost half of these troops were British professionals in Dutch service or volunteers from Britain and Protestant Ireland. Thousands more British people, from noblemen and London's merchant grandees right down to commoners, sent over money for William's war chest. But powerful and well funded though it was, the expedition was a huge gamble. It virtually guaranteed that Louis would declare war on the Dutch republic, which he duly did, although having committed most of his troops to plundering the Rhineland he could do nothing to hinder William's invasion preparations. Moreover, launching a seaborne invasion so late in the year was to risk rough seas in the Channel and harsh campaigning conditions once ashore. But on this occasion, fortune favoured the brave. Early in November, line upon line of Dutch ships, their colours flying and their guns thundering out salutes to the English and French garrisons at

Dover and Calais, sailed down the Channel. The 'Protestant wind' that carried the Dutch fleet southwards would keep the royal navy penned in port, unable to intercept it; and two days of unseasonable calm then allowed William to disembark his army at Torbay on the south coast of Devon. On 9 November he rode into Exeter (the capital of the West Country) on a white horse, with forty-two footmen running alongside him, and fifty gentlemen bearing a banner that read 'God and the Protestant religion'.

William had succeeded where Philip II had not: he had landed a foreign army on English soil. Nevertheless, the advantage still lay with James, at least on paper. He had been slow to grasp that Dutch military preparations were aimed at himself rather than Louis – partly because he could scarcely credit that his own daughter and son-in-law could be so disloyal. But when in September he had finally awoken to the danger he was in, he had hastily begun to backtrack on his Catholicising policies, and at the same time to make military preparations of his own. His main field army, bolstered by units from Scotland and Ireland, numbered some 30,000 men by November – perhaps 10,000 more than William disposed of – and although they were not as experienced as their opponents, they were well paid and well fed and they had home advantage. On 19 November, James arrived at Salisbury to take command in person, and the stage seemed set for Britain's largest and bloodiest battle since Marston Moor. Yet at precisely the point where kings were expected to show their mettle, James lost his nerve, just as Charles I had in June 1639. After ordering his army to retreat towards London, he returned to Whitehall, where he hastily packed his family off to France and made preparations to join them.

James, 'a man naturally Martial to the highest degree', had retreated ignominiously in the face of battle.[63] Clearly he had suffered a huge loss of confidence, but why? The answer would seem to lie not in irresolution or cowardice on his part, but a realisation that he had already failed the most crucial test of all, that of retaining his subjects' allegiance. His moral authority as king – his 'Strength to aw[e]' as one of his advisers put it – had been crumbling since the summer.[64] The acquittal of the seven bishops, and the refusal of many local governors, even those expressly appointed by James, to cooperate with Whitehall, were signs of his waning majesty. Naturally, most people were unwilling to defy him openly until they were certain that William's invasion had succeeded. But a series of large, aristocrat-led insurrections across England and Wales during November, attacks by the London mob on

Catholic chapels and property, and a growing number of high-profile defections to William's camp soon made it clear which way the tide was turning. Even James's own daughter, Princess Anne (1665–1714), joined the rebels.

What finally convinced James that the rot was unstoppable was the questionable loyalty of his army. The huge popularity among the soldiers of the Whig satirical ballad 'Lilliburlero', which tarred the king with the brush of Irish popery, was ominous; and disaffection was not confined to the ranks. The lieutenant general of James's army, John Churchill (the future duke of Marlborough), and other senior officers were secret Orangists and would desert to William during the second half of November. William, as one pamphleteer later put it, 'had the Hands, the Hearts, and the Prayers of all honest men in the Nation: Every one thought the long wish'd for time of their Deliverance was com. King James was deserted by his own Family, his Court, and his Army. The Ground he stood upon mouldred under him.'[65] The Dutch invasion succeeded not through overwhelming military force, therefore, but by exploiting and completing a British conspiracy and an English rebellion, although it did so in the service of a European cause: the defeat of France.

James's escape to France late in December 1688 was fraught with even greater consequences than William's invasion. With London and many other places subject to riots and plundering by the 'tumultuous rabble', James had feared for his safety while he remained in England.[66] Equally, he was too proud and pious to defer to William and to make the kind of concessions to Protestant loyalists that had gained his father a political and military following in 1642. He preferred to go abroad to regroup, with his Catholic conscience unsullied. His flight averted a possible civil war, at least in England, and the radicalisation of politics that had occurred in the 1640s. Republicans and swordsmen would not be allowed another headlong tilt at the ancient constitution. Instead, James's exit turned a rebellion and foreign invasion into a dynastic revolution. It was decisive in persuading William that he could go one better than invading – that he could be king of England himself. Since arriving in London to cheering crowds on 18 December, he had consulted with an 'assembly of peers' and the surviving Commons-men from Charles II's last Parliament about how best to settle the kingdom's affairs. Both bodies were divided on the issue, but James's self-exile effectively made their decision for them. They invited William to issue orders for electing a Convention Parliament and to take the reins of government until it met on 22 January 1689.

The general election produced a House of Commons in which Tories and Whigs were fairly evenly balanced, although the Tories had a majority in the Lords. Everyone agreed that a quick settlement of the kingdom's problems was essential. But James's flight and William's desire to take the throne for himself had destroyed the bipartisanship that had marked the autumn rebellion. The Tories had supported a Dutch invasion in order to bring James to his senses – to make him subordinate his conscience to the requirements of Protestant kingship – not to remove him altogether.

The debate over how to fill the vacuum at the heart of government was played out in the Convention and in another massive outpouring of pamphlet literature. Tories were anxious to uphold the principle of hereditary monarchy and to deny the legitimacy of violent political resistance. James, they argued, had jumped rather than been pushed (deposed), and therefore the throne was not vacant. Ideally, they wanted him restored on suitable terms, or a regency of some kind, but failing that, then the settling of the crown on his eldest daughter Princess Mary (William's wife), and on her alone. The Whigs, and much Williamite propaganda, appealed to the equally well-established idea of contractual monarchy. Having violated the 'fundamental laws' and then deserted the kingdom, James had broken his contract with the people and could legitimately be deposed. In other words, the throne was vacant and the position of monarch effectively elective – and the obvious candidate for the office was William. William agreed, and let it be known that if he was not offered the crown he would return to Holland and leave England's ungrateful leaders to the mercies of the rabble, and of Louis XIV.

The dreadful prospect of being kingless, and of the kingdom plunging into anarchy, concentrated the minds of both Whigs and Tories wonderfully, as did the presence in London of thousands of Dutch and German troops, almost 20,000 by mid-1689. Dutch soldiers would occupy London until 1690. The more radical Whigs also resorted to the by now familiar pressure tactics of mass demonstrations and 'popular petitioning' in support of William's claim. The Tories, especially in the Lords, put up a strong rearguard action, but defending James's title in his absence proved impossible. Besides, very few Tories could argue hand-on-heart that James was the man to save Europe and its Protestants from the torrent of destruction that Louis seemed ready to pour on them. Early in February the Convention endorsed a qualified version of the Whigs' reading of the constitutional situation, and offered the crown to William and Mary. They were proclaimed William III and Mary II, joint monarchs of England and Ireland, on 13 February 1689.

William exploited his position as England's military protector to secure the crown on relatively generous terms. Although he and his wife were crowned jointly, the monarchy's executive power was vested in him alone. Like his royal predecessors he would enjoy the power to decide domestic and foreign policy; appoint ministers of state; call and dissolve Parliament; and veto parliamentary legislation. But before being proclaimed king he had to listen (nothing more) to a Declaration of Rights that outlined the limits of the royal prerogative. This was essentially a statement of what its framers thought was existing law, and was tame in comparison with the terms that the parliamentary junto had tried to impose upon Charles I in 1641–2. Nevertheless, by clarifying a number of contentious issues between the Restoration monarchy and the English political establishment, Whig and Tory alike, the Declaration could be said to have broken new constitutional ground, particularly in stating that 'the pretended power' of the crown to dispense with or suspend parliamentary laws, and to maintain a standing army contrary to the will of Parliament, were illegal.[67] The Declaration further stipulated that if William and Mary had no children then the throne would pass to Mary's younger sister Princess Anne and her heirs rather than to any offspring of William's by a new wife. In their coronation service at Westminster Abbey in April 1689, William and Mary became the first English monarchs who swore specifically to rule according to the 'Protestant reformed religion', after which they were each handed a Bible, 'To put you in mind of this rule and that you may follow it'.[68] That December, their first Parliament passed the Bill of Rights, which gave the Declaration statutory force. It would now be very difficult for the monarch to claim to be above the law or to govern without Parliament. And the Bill included the important proviso that whoever occupied the throne could neither be, nor be married to, a Catholic. The Whigs had belatedly won the Exclusion Crisis.

Popery had been defeated by this 'Glorious Revolution', or so it was hoped, but the problem of Protestant Dissent and its relationship with the Anglican establishment had yet to be resolved. It was generally agreed that the Dissenters deserved some form of relief for having generally stood firm with the established Church against James. William favoured toleration for Dissenters, and though a sincere Calvinist he wanted the same for Catholics (with the Spanish and Austrian Habsburgs for allies he could hardly do otherwise). Equally, most leading Anglicans had come round to the view that persecution was counterproductive, and that liberty of conscience was acceptable so long as it did not weaken the Church's privileged status. Some Anglicans went even further, and considered schemes for 'comprehension' – that is, a more generously defined national Church that would accommodate Presbyterians and other 'sober' Dissenters. But church reform was opposed by most Tories and members of the clergy, and consequently, in the spring of 1689, Parliament passed a Toleration Act that merely exempted Dissenters from punishment for holding their own religious services. A great opportunity to bring the majority of Puritans back into the Anglican fold had been missed, and now all Dissenters would remain for ever outside of the Church of England. Furthermore, the Anglican majority at Westminster insisted on the retention of the Test Acts that barred all non-Anglicans from public office and the universities. There would be no official toleration of Catholicism, although Catholics would not be troubled so long as they worshipped in private. Nor were people allowed simply to opt out of religious observance if they wished. The only legal way to avoid parish church services on a Sunday was by attending a Dissenters' service instead.

Yet even the qualified legal recognition of religious difference that was achieved in 1689 was important. The state now acknowledged that God alone ruled an individual's conscience; the long, slow and often painful separation between established Church and civil society had begun. Limited though its provisions were, the Toleration Act would gradually help to reduce the religious tensions that had contributed so powerfully to political conflict since the Reformation.

Anglican leaders would probably have reached out further to the Dissenters in 1689 but for the markedly anti-episcopal direction taken by the revolution in Scotland. In attempting to foist toleration – an essentially English policy – on a people as proud of their independence and as anti-Catholic as the Scots, James had succeeded in temporarily uniting most of Scotland's Protestants against his rule. Just as disastrously, his policies had revived support for the Presbyterians among a small but powerful section of the nobility. By the summer of 1688 the crown's authority had begun to crumble, as it had in England, and when news of his capitulation reached Scotland that autumn there was virtually a rerun of the events of July 1637, with anti-Catholic rioting in Edinburgh and a takeover of royal government by leading opponents of James's policies. It is possible that Jacobite loyalists might have contained the unrest had not most of the Scottish army been ordered down to England to help resist William – futilely, as it turned out. In its absence, the Presbyterians in the south-west of Scotland were able to mobilise for political action unopposed. A widening of the franchise in the elections to the Scottish Convention that met in Edinburgh in March 1689 meant that the Presbyterians achieved a parliamentary majority, and the result was a revolutionary settlement that was more radical and divisive than anything seen in England.

The Scottish Convention deposed James for, in effect, breaking his contract with the people. Like its English counterpart it then offered the crown to William and Mary, who became William II (not III, as in England) and Mary II of Scotland. But the Scottish Convention's constitutional manifesto, the Claim of Right, did not merely reassert what was taken to be existing law, but aimed at replacing the vigorously personal monarchy that had emerged in Scotland since the Restoration with a legally limited one similar to that established under the Covenanters in the mid-seventeenth century, although again the changes demanded in 1689 were not as far-reaching as those that had been achieved in the 1640s. The general thrust of the Claim was to elevate the power of the Scottish Parliament at the expense of the royal prerogative. As for church reform, it called for the abolition of episcopacy as 'a great and insupportable grievance . . . and contrary to the Inclinationes of the generality of the people' – which was a disingenuous way of demanding the re-establishment of Presbyterianism.[69] William was not happy about relinquishing his royal supremacy in religion to a clericalist Kirk, nor about allowing the Scottish Parliament to encroach on the powers of the monarchy. But with no Dutch troops in Edinburgh to 'guard' it as they had done London, and desperate as he was to secure Scotland quickly and with minimal fuss, he had little choice but to compromise.

In solving the problem of the rebellious Scottish Presbyterians, the revolutionary settlement in Scotland created another: the rebellious Highland Jacobite. By no means all Scots welcomed the revolutionary settlement, or the return of an intolerant Presbyterian Church. Episcopalian sympathies remained strong among the aristocracy and the people of north-eastern Scotland, who were soon likening their treatment under the triumphant Presbyterians to that of the Huguenots under Louis XIV. But hostility to Presbyterianism rarely translated into active Jacobitism. Few Protestants trusted James not to revert to his old popish ways if he was restored as king. The 2,000-strong Jacobite army that defied the revolutionary settlement in Scotland consisted largely of enemies of the Williamite clan Campbell. They were commanded by John Graham, Viscount Dundee, the scourge of the Presbyterians during the Restoration period, who would demonstrate a skill in Highland warfare reminiscent of his illustrious kinsman the marquess of Montrose. At the battle of Killiekrankie in July 1689, the viscount's army inflicted a crushing defeat on the government's forces. Yet even as the Highlanders made their usual mincemeat of the Lowland infantry, Dundee was hit by a musket ball and died. Even had he lived it is unlikely that his makeshift army would have troubled the government for long. The new Williamite regime in Scotland was soon firmly in control of the kingdom, and would take its revenge on the Highlanders in 1692 by having thirty-eight members of the Jacobite clan Macdonald massacred at Glencoe.

James's overthrow would be felt no less keenly in the transatlantic colonies. Once reports of the regime change in Britain were confirmed in the spring of 1689, many of the colonies staged largely bloodless coups against their royal governors and set up pro-Williamite govern-ments in their place. The only one of James's former dominions where Jacobites outnumbered Williamites was Ireland. The revolutionary struggle there would take a different course than it did in Britain and the colonies, and would be more closely enmeshed in the wider conflict between Louis and his enemies on the Continent. It was the long-term consequences of being drawn into this European war that made the Glorious Revolution so profound an event in British history. William's dynastic coup would lead to a radical shift in foreign policy, which in turn would require the construction of a fiscal–military state that would outrival even the Cromwellian Leviathan. In much the same way that the war of the three kingdoms had restored England to the front rank of European powers, so 'King Billy's War' against France would help transform Britain into a global superpower.

King Billy's War, 1689–1702

On 27 February 1689 the Commons-men at Westminster declared unanimously that they would 'stand by and assist the King [William] with their Lives and Fortunes, in supporting his Alliances abroad . . . and in Defence of the Protestant Religion'.[70] Few in the House were under any illusions that England would have to pay dearly in blood and treasure to honour this commitment. Nevertheless, Whigs, Tories and, in Scotland, the Presbyterians were resolved to support William 'against that great Monster the French king', for they regarded it as not merely his cause but their own.[71]

Since the 1560s a growing number of British Protestants had been convinced that the only real safety for their religion and liberties lay in military alliance with those on the Continent trying to resist popish tyranny, be they fellow Protestants like the Dutch or Catholic rulers such as Henri IV of France. Indeed, the English did not merely want to join such an alliance, they wished to lead it.

The Austrian Habsburg emperors and kings of Spain had been perceived as the first great popish aggressors, but their strength had waned since the 1630s, and by the 1670s a new 'generall enemie to the libertie of Christendome' had emerged: Louis XIV.[72] With the French annexing Habsburg territory along the Rhine and in the Netherlands, the Spanish and Austrians had made common cause with Louis's – and formerly their – enemies, the Dutch, to build a coalition that British people of all persuasions were eager for Britain to join. Their quarrel was not with Catholicism as such – erroneous though it was thought to be – but with international popery: that fearsome combination of Counter-Reformation zealotry and expansionist absolutism. By drawing this distinction between Catholicism and popery, the cause of resisting Louis could be conceptualised as a war to defend both Christendom, in the sense of the moral community of all Christian nations, and Europe's Protestant interest. To Charles II and James, however, Anglo-Dutch republicanism had seemed the greater menace. They had been content to take Louis's money and stand aside while he had terrorised his neighbours. It was only with the warrior-prince William III, whose engagement with continental politics exceeded that of any English monarch since the Plantagenets, that the British finally obtained a king fit for purpose. War against France for what the House of Commons termed in April 1689 the 'liberties of Europe' was a, perhaps the, key objective of the Glorious Revolution.[73]

In the 1680s, as in the 1580s, this struggle against continental popery was often perceived in a strongly apocalyptic light. It was not uncommon for British Protestants to identify Louis XIV with the Beast referred to in the Book of Revelation, and to regard William's invasion in 1688 as heralding the final destruction of the popish Antichrist. Inevitably, this euphoric reaction to the Glorious Revolution was not shared by Irish Catholics, and even as William's grip on England and Scotland tightened during the winter of 1688–9, James's lord deputy of Ireland, the earl of Tyrconnell, began assembling a large army of Catholic resistance. Although there were no massacres in Ireland on the scale of 1641, large numbers of Protestants fled to England, and by the spring of 1689 they held just a few beleaguered towns in Ulster. The rest of the kingdom, Dublin included, was in Catholic hands. Fear of the popish threat from Ireland fuelled mob violence in England and Scotland in which Catholics were attacked, sometimes killed, and their chapels destroyed; and this 'Irish Fright' would do much to strengthen support for William and Mary among Britain's Protestants.

James landed in Ireland in March 1689, hoping to use it as a spring-board for invading Britain, much as his father and brother had done during the war of the three kingdoms. But as in that earlier conflict, the monarch's priorities were not always those of most Irish Catholics. The Parliament that James called at Dublin in the spring of 1689 passed legislation that, in the event of a Jacobite military victory, would restore political power, land and ecclesiastical authority to the Catholics, thereby destroying not only the Protestant ascendancy but also much of the English crown's authority over Ireland. James, however, was prepared to accept this Catholic revolution as the price of Irish support, leaving William with the same challenge that had faced Cromwell in 1649, although unlike Cromwell he had little appetite for invading Ireland. He wanted to be fighting Louis on mainland Europe, not wasting time and troops campaigning on its periphery. But he could not afford to leave Ireland to the French, so fight there he must. His problem was that the English army he had inherited from James, unlike the New Model, was next to useless. Divided, demoralised and unprofessional, it needed thoroughly modernising. In the summer of 1689, William sent several patched-together expeditionary forces to Ulster to hold the fort while the core of the English army underwent on-the-job retraining with the veteran Dutch infantry on the Continent. Dutch officials were also put in charge of rearmament and logistics. The English army's emergence by 1700 as one of the finest fighting forces in Europe would owe a great deal to Dutch military expertise.

The revolution in Ireland was long, hard-fought, and not the least bit glorious – a far cry from William's relatively bloodless victory in England. It was partly a war of religion – although William deployed many Catholic troops, just as James did Protestant ones – and partly a struggle for greater national autonomy. Either way there was enough combustible material in Ireland to feed the flames of war from mainland Europe, just as there had been with Tyrone's rebellion at the end of

Elizabeth's reign. It was Louis who effectively masterminded James's Irish expedition. Indeed, it had taken considerable pressure from the French to persuade James to go to Ireland at all. His overthrow in England had completely unmanned him. Left to himself he would have passed his time hunting and praying at the château that he and his court in exile had been assigned near Paris. Louis, on the other hand, was determined to make both James and William fight for their Irish kingdom. Besides dispatching James to Ireland he sent money, arms and some 7,000 French, Walloon and German troops, including high-ranking officers. William's army in Ireland, which he led in person in 1690, was even more cosmopolitan in character. It contained veteran troops from all over Europe, while most of its leading officers were Dutch, German or Huguenot.

The 'war of the two kings' in Ireland is best remembered today for the Ulster Protestants' successful defence of Derry – commemorated annually by the town's Unionists – and for its greatest battle, fought along the River Boyne, about thirty miles north of Dublin, on 1 July 1690. On this occasion James did not shirk the fight, although he might as well have done, for he proved a pale shadow of the 'martial man' he had once been. Predictably, his 25,000 troops, who were mostly Irish volunteers, proved no match for William's 36,000 professionals. William captured Dublin shortly after the battle, while James hastily decamped back to France, earning himself the Gaelic sobriquet *Séamus an chaca*: James the shit. The Jacobites fought on valiantly under French leadership only to suffer an even bloodier, and this time terminal, defeat at the battle of Aughrim in Galway in July 1691. Afterwards, William approved a lenient treaty with the Catholics, for he had never been the Protestant tribal leader of Unionist mythologising; and besides, he wanted the war in Ireland over quickly in order to free up troops for the Low Countries. The 12,000 or so Irish Jacobites who left Ireland for the Continent under the terms of this treaty were the original Wild Geese. Their defeat and departure all but ended Irish Jacobitism as an organised force.

Ireland's traumatised Protestants would use their influence at Westminster, and William's desperate need for parliamentary supply, to override the terms of the 1691 treaty. But it would be the English Parliament that profited most from the war of the two kings, taking advantage of William's lack of interest in Ireland to make itself the ultimate arbiter in Irish affairs. The undoubted losers, as usual, were Ireland's Catholics. The Catholic aristocracy was driven into quiescence, or abroad, and Catholic land ownership suffered yet more Protestant erosion. About a fifth of Irish land had been owned by Catholics in 1688; by 1702 that figure stood at 15 per cent and falling.

Yet because the Jacobite cause was tied to Louis's war plans it had a staying power far beyond its domestic strength or indeed James's own military inclinations, such as they were. The struggle between Louis and the Grand Alliance, usually known as the Nine Years War (1688–97), would hinge upon naval supremacy in the Channel and the campaigning in the Low Countries. Had the French deployed their formidable battle fleet to cut the supply lines between Britain and Ireland in 1689–90, then the Irish Jacobites would have defeated William's forces 'without striking a stroke', or so Tyrconnell believed, 'for he [William] could have sent hither neither forces nor provisions'.[74] A French naval victory over the now combined English and Dutch fleets in the Channel in July 1690, just before the battle of the Boyne, left England exposed to French invasion, but none had been prepared. The French did assemble invasion forces against England in 1692, and again in 1696, only to be foiled on the first occasion by allied naval victories in the Channel, and on the second by the failure of a Jacobite assassination plot against William. But they never fully committed themselves to invading England, just as they never threw their full military weight behind James's Irish campaign, for their main objective in both cases was to force the allies to divert troops from the main theatre of operations: the Spanish Netherlands.

The military struggle on the Continent was a particularly dismal war of attrition, fought with vast means for limited ends. Louis wanted to consolidate the territorial gains he had made in the 1680s; the allies wanted to peg him back to the borders agreed on in earlier peace treaties. On the battlefield itself, advances in weaponry – the replacement of the cumbersome matchlock musket and pike by the flintlock and socket bayonet – were largely nullified by a massive increase in the size of armies. Allied and French armies of sixty thousand troops or more lumbered across the largely flat, often waterlogged region between Dunkirk and Liège in a brutish war of siege, plunder and devastation. The logistical and tactical challenges presented by such huge masses of men and horses often overwhelmed their commanders, including William, who was the first English king to lead an army on the Continent since Henry VIII. Although he was frequently outgeneralled by the best of the French commanders, strategy and resources were devoted less to winning battles than to defending and capturing frontier fortresses for trading at future peace talks. The contribution made by Parliament and the crown to this land war was considerable. By the mid-1690s, the English state was maintaining about 45,000 British and 20,000 Dutch, Danish and German troops, or something like half of the allies' 'Confederate Army'. British troops and cash were therefore vital to the allied war effort, although it was Dutch military professionalism and William's leadership that kept the Confederate army in the field.

The Nine Years War was the first world war between Europe's main colonial powers. In Europe, the French more than held their own, and their privateers, operating from the Channel ports, seized thousands of allied ships. But outside of Europe they were hard pressed on several fronts. The Dutch captured French bases in India, the Spanish and the English raided their colonies in the Caribbean, and the English tried, though without success, to conqueror Canada (see chapter 7). If any of the powers could be said to have profited from the war outside of Europe then it was probably the English, although more at the expense of their Dutch allies than of the French. With the Dutch focused largely on defending the Spanish Netherlands, the English gained commercial ground on them in India, the Caribbean and West Africa. New markets overseas could not compensate for the crippling costs of the European land war, however. The French economy was in serious difficulties by 1693; Dutch trade slumped; and England's monetary system went into meltdown in 1695–6 – literally, as confidence in sterling collapsed and the coinage had to be reminted.

The exhausted combatants downed weapons in 1697 and concluded a treaty, the Peace of Ryswick, in which Louis agreed to recognise William as king of England, and to hand back most of the territories France had seized between 1678 and 1684. Louis could afford to be conciliatory because he held the dynastic ace in the pack, inasmuch as his grandson had the strongest claim to the soon-to-be-vacant Spanish throne (of which more below). The treaty therefore represented a quali-fied victory for William. But he had succeeded only in containing Louis for the time being, no more.

Despite early military setbacks in the Low Countries, the mounting death toll, and expenditure on the army and navy of almost fifty million pounds, the British ruling classes had stuck with William and the war to the bitter end, for the only alternative had seemed to be a restoration of James II at the point of a French bayonet. This was why the Calvinist William could win national, parliamentary consent for a huge standing army (admittedly, deployed abroad) and the massive tax hikes needed to pay for it in a way that the 'popish' Charles and James never could. In the 1690s, as in the 1640s, fear of popery became a force *for* building a powerful state, not against it, as had been the case before the revolution. The link between political consent and state expenditure, broken under Charles and James, had been restored. In the words of one contemporary, 'nothing but Liberty, our Interest in the Laws, and Property, could have made us willing to endure such a heavy War, and able to bear its Expence'.[75]

Prolonged warfare in defence of liberty and property would breathe new life into Leviathan: the fiscal–military state that had emerged in England since the 1640s. With Dutch help, England would be transformed during William's reign from a satellite of the Sun King into the centre of an international coalition that fought Europe's most powerful nation to a standstill. To sustain the massive military expenditure that went with this new role would require the new-modelling of state finances. In the face of vehement opposition from leading Tories, Parliament approved a proposal in 1694 for setting up the Bank of England, which was something that Whig merchants and writers had been advocating for years. A public fund was created, administered by the Bank, to extend a reliable line of credit to the government. Investors bought shares in the Bank, raising capital that it then lent to the government at interest, secured against future tax revenue. Short-term loans on the word of the monarch were gradually replaced by a long-term national debt that was serviced by parliamentary taxes and underwritten by the wealth of the nation – at first, principally from direct taxation on property, but from the early eighteenth century, increasingly from indirect taxation upon trade and consumption. Using the Bank of England, the crown could borrow and spend out of all proportion to the size of its taxable population. The establishment of the Bank would also have major constitutional implications, for it institutionalised William's dependence on parliamentary supply, at once reducing the monarch's fiscal autonomy while ensuring that Parliament became a permanent feature of government. No year has passed since 1689 without a Parliament in session.

The financial revolution of the 1690s created a whole new *rentier* class. In 1688 the London stock exchange opened – eighty-six years after its Amsterdam equivalent – and quickly became a major part of national life. The thousands of people, among them Dutch investors, who bought government securities, stock in the Bank of England or shares in the multitude of private joint-stock companies that sprang up in the 1690s (for which, see chapter 6) were effectively buying into the Glorious Revolution and the success of the war. It was no accident that most leading members of this new 'monied interest' were Whigs. Investment became a political act.

Parliament followed the Dutch model again by introducing many more excises during the 1690s: on salt, leather, carriages, even the registering of births, marriages and burials. Sex and death would now be taxed. Customs duties were increased and imposed on a whole new range of imports. Direct taxes were also raised to unprecedented levels. The Land Tax, based upon the Civil War assessment, would be the most productive form of taxation between 1689 and 1714. Overall, the tax yield rose from two million pounds a year in the late 1680s to over five million in the 1690s, which was more than twice the sum obtained annually under Oliver Cromwell's military dictatorship. From being relatively undertaxed, the English had become one of the most highly taxed people in Europe. Yet this burden was to some extent self-imposed inasmuch as it was sanctioned and overseen by Parliament. The public accepted paying higher taxes because, fundamentally, it shared the government's determination to defend the national interest against foreign rivals, above all the French.

Turning higher taxes into larger armies demanded a larger, more sophisticated executive. The Treasury and other government departments in all three kingdoms had been expanded and modernised during the 1670s and 1680s (particularly under James II), and this process accelerated after 1688 as new ministries were created and 'put in commission' – that is, run by committees, as in the 1640s. The business of government would shift from the privy council to a range of these institutions, whose heads – the ministers of state – met regularly as a 'cabinet' or ministry to coordinate their activities and to manage Parliament.

Bigger government meant, in turn, a larger, more professional bureaucracy. The number of full-time state employees would treble between 1689 and 1714, from 4,000 to 12,000 – a proportionately greater increase than in any other period in British history. Most of these new administrators were customs and excise officials. Career bureaucrats and technical experts began to fill government jobs at the expense of courtiers, or their clients. Among this new breed of civil servant was the greatest scientist of the age, Isaac Newton, who was appointed Warden of the Mint in order to supervise the great recoinage of 1696. But employing disinterested servants of the state, supposing there were such creatures, did not necessarily make for stronger or more efficient government. As in the 1640s and 1650s, the machinery of state tended to work best where it was aligned with, and could therefore harness, the networks of trust, friendship and financial credit to be found within political parties. The spread of party politics in Britain and Ireland, and the political corruption that went with it, far from weakening the state as was generally supposed, may actually have helped in the long run to render it more powerful than its European rivals.

As departments mushroomed, and the number of state employees grew, so concern over misuse of the royal prerogative began to give way to worries about political corruption, and particularly the insidious influence of government patronage at Westminster. William's reversal of James's court reforms and the consequent expansion in the size of the royal household would put yet more men on the Whitehall payroll. What price English liberties, asked Leviathan's critics, if the Commons were full of MPs rendered supine by government offices and pensions?

The 1690s were not, of course, the first time such fears had been raised. The same concerns about 'placemen' and corruption at Westminster had been voiced in the 1640s and under very similar circumstances – i.e. prolonged warfare and Parliament in continuous session. In fact, most of the structural changes (and the political vices associated with them) that occurred after the Glorious Revolution were built on ideological and institutional foundations that had been laid down since the 1640s. For example, the cabinet system of government that stood in for William while he was away soldiering had been road-tested by the Long Parliament's main executive bodies, the Committee of Both Kingdoms, the Derby House Committee and the Council of State. If the English state had not already undergone a financial and military revolution in mid-century it is unlikely that it could have sustained the war against Louis forty years later. In the 1640s it had been the Independent grandees who had led the way in constructing and managing the parliamentary war-state. In the 1690s, Leviathan was nurtured by the so-called 'junto' or ministerial Whigs – a faction composed of the Independents' political and, in one or two cases, literal heirs. Like several of the Whig grandees of 1679–81, the junto Whig leaders Charles Montagu, Edward Russell and Thomas Wharton were descendants of the junto-men who had defied Charles I in the 1640s.

The junto Whigs were at the centre of a major role reversal in English party politics after 1688. In their eagerness to defend the revolution settlement the Whigs, or most of them, began to shake off the ways of opposition and become the party of government and the court. The Glorious Revolution also tamed the republican fringe of the anti-court interest. The commonwealthsmen of the Restoration period had been distinguished by their defiance of monarchy and prerogative power. The republicans of the 1690s were keener on moralising about the corrupting influence of Leviathan. For their part, the Tories appropriated the Whigs' old mantle of the champions of English liberties against an over-powerful executive. It was the same in the localities. The Whigs colonised the upper reaches of local government, while the Tories became the party of populist resistance to oligarchy. It was now the Tories rather than the Whigs who were more likely to adopt a 'Country' position and refer reverentially to the values of 'old England'.

This Country interest was more of an outlook than an actual party; a backbench reaction to corruption in government, waste of public money, and executive encroachment upon the people's liberties. Under this broad political canopy would gather all those who were fearful of or disillusioned with Leviathan, from Jacobites and dyspeptic Tory squires to sanctimonious republicans. The common political language among this heterogeneous grouping was derived from the deep familiarity of many gentlemen with Tacitus and other classical writers and their depiction of Roman history as a great struggle between civic virtue and imperial tyranny.

The rise of the junto Whigs was for William just another consequence of the many unseemly trade-offs he was compelled to make between obtaining parliamentary taxes and preserving his kingly authority. The House of Orange was one of Europe's great ruling families, and William took much the same exalted view of kingship that the Stuarts had. He even shared their taste for French court art and architecture. He had initially preferred the Tories to the Whigs because Tory grandees were more respectful of free monarchy. Mary, too, favoured the Tories. But her soothing influence upon royal counsels ended when she died of smallpox in 1694. In truth, William despised party politics and the shifts and compromises it involved. War with France demanded, to his mind, a strong and united executive and a powerful king to lead it. Not until 1694 did the Whigs finally persuade him that their programme of financial reform – of which establishing the Bank of England was the centrepiece – and the checks upon personal monarchy that came with it, offered the best chance of victory in Europe. Yet such was his desire to humble Louis that he was willing to purchase the necessary political and material resources with his own prerogatives – a quid pro quo that no Stuart monarch would ever have accepted. He might have preserved more of his sovereignty but for his aloof, almost contemptuous, manner and his preference for policy-making and socialising with his Dutch Bedchamber men, which fuelled rumours that he was a homosexual.

William's reign saw the beginning of a process whereby the monarchy itself was put in commission. The crown would retain all its powers, but they were increasingly taken over and managed by the cabinet. William all but lost his capacity to summon and dissolve Parliaments and to veto legislation, and he was effectively limited in his choice of cabinet ministers to those who could command a working majority in the two Houses – a job so important that its leading practitioners became England's first prime ministers. Even the king's precious army was taken from him as Tories and 'Country' (i.e. backbench) Whigs used the advent of peace in 1697 to cut the military establishment to just 7,000 troops. Moreover, with war against France looming again by 1701, he had to accept further limitations on the prerogative in the form of the Act of Settlement. This stated that if his successor, Princess Anne, died childless (which looked likely) the English crown would pass to her nearest Protestant relation in line of succession – namely, Princess Sophia, dowager duchess of Hanover (James's I granddaughter by Frederick V of the Palatinate) – further evidence, if it were needed after 1689, that the monarchy was essentially elective. William heartily approved of the Hanoverian succession, but the Act did not stop there. It also stipulated that all future monarchs must be conforming Anglicans, and that Parliament had the last word when it came to waging foreign wars and approving the judiciary.

William's willingness to trade the prospect of an absolutist monarchy for a militarily competent state did not mean that the eighteenth-century British crown would be any less powerful or intrusive than its French counterpart. Leviathan, as Hobbes had argued – and as the Long Parliament had amply demonstrated in the 1640s – could flourish just as easily under a sovereign assembly as an absolute monarch. What the Glorious Revolution and its aftermath confirmed was that Britain and France would possess different political cultures. Parliamentary monarchy in Britain would allow heterodoxy in a variety of forms to survive, and encourage the growth of a libertarian, commercially oriented society. The hegemony of the old order, of the established Church and the aristocracy, of ideas of God-ordained hierarchy and subordination, would remain. But free monarchy as Henry VII or James II had understood it was history. Not everyone welcomed its demise. 'Our Monarchs', complained one Jacobite, who 'were ever Sovereign and Imperial', were now little more than 'Dukes of Venice', forced 'to dance after the Pipe of a Common-wealth'.[76] Initiating this shift from personal to parliamentary monarchy was what made the Glorious Revolution truly revolutionary.

'When will this bloodshed ever cease?': 1702–14

In 1711 the Tory propagandist Jonathan Swift (1667–1745) marvelled at the folly of the British people. Posterity, he thought, would be at a loss to explain how

> after ten years Sufferings . . . and during a short Peace, while they were looking back with Horrour on the heavy Load of Debts they had contracted . . . racking their Invention for some Remedies or Expedients to mend their shattered Condition: That these very People, without giving themselves time to breath, would again enter into a more dangerous, chargeable, and expensive War, for the same, or perhaps a greater Period of Time . . .[77]

The first war he was referring to was the Nine Years War; the second would become known as the War of the Spanish Succession (1702–13). The stresses and strains these two conflicts imposed upon the three kingdoms were indeed immense, rending and reshaping the political and economic order, the relationship between England and Scotland, even the dynamics of everyday social interaction. Most remarkably of all, the wars of 1689–1713 would witness a conscious and sustained attempt – the first since the Hundred Years War – to remodel the state not in order to fight a civil war or strengthen the monarchy but to intervene decisively on mainland Europe.

The War of the Spanish Succession was all about unfinished business. It was fought because the man destined to be the last Habsburg monarch of Spain, Carlos II, was an inbred, senile valetudinarian, incapable of siring a successor. Of the several possible heirs to the Spanish throne the two with the strongest claims were Carlos's relation on his Habsburg side, Archduke Charles of Austria, son of the Holy Roman Emperor Leopold I; and Carlos's great-nephew, Philip de Bourbon, duke of

Anjou, who was none other than Louis XIV's grandson. Anxious that Spain's empire should not fall entirely into Bourbon hands upon Carlos's death, William III secretly negotiated 'partition treaties' with Louis in 1698 and 1700 for dividing Carlos's vast inheritance between the principal claimants, but ensuring that Spain, Spanish colonies and the Spanish Netherlands – in other words, those territories of greatest strategic and commercial interest to the English and Dutch – should be placed in Austrian Habsburg hands. William was particularly concerned to keep the French out of the Spanish Netherlands, for as one pamphleteer put it, 'if Flanders be an accession to France, Holland must soon follow, and England next. They are like Nine-pins, the throwing down one carries the rest.'[78] Similarly, William was convinced, as most Whigs now were, that a strong Austrian empire was vital in preserving 'the balance of Europe' against France.

Unfortunately for William, neither the Spanish government nor the emperor accepted these treaties, and when Carlos finally died in October 1700, having declared Philip his heir, nor did Louis. One of Louis's main reasons for rejecting the treaties was his appreciation of William's progressive military and political enfeeblement since 1697. Parliament's dismantling of William's army in 1698–9 had convinced Louis that the English and Dutch were too divided and weak either to uphold the partition treaties or to offer serious resistance to Franco-Spanish union.

When Parliament learnt about the partition treaties it was outraged that William had presumed to speak for England behind its back, which strengthened Louis's conviction that William had lost the support of his English subjects. The treaties certainly added to William's considerable unpopularity. Daniel Defoe, a Whig, lamented in 1701 that London was 'full of Lampoons and Invectives against Dutchmen, Only because they are Foreigners, and the King Reproached and Insulted by Insolent Pedants, and Ballad-making Poets, for employing Foreigners, and for being a Foreigner himself'.[79] The 1701 Act of Settlement pointedly included a clause that no monarch could lead the nation into foreign war without parliamentary consent.

The Tories headed the opposition to continuing military engagement on the Continent. But they were forced to rethink after French troops invaded the Spanish Netherlands and Louis began diverting the wealth of Spain's transatlantic colonies to France. Their reluctant support for war was sealed in September 1701, when the stroke-afflicted James II was hastened to his grave by the attentions of his doctors, and Louis promptly recognised James's Catholic son, the so-called 'Old Pretender', as rightful king of England. In 1701–2 the Grand Alliance against France (now minus Spain) re-formed in the cause of preserving the balance of Europe against the overweening power of France. Keeping the French and Spanish crowns separate was the allies' main objective. The English and Dutch were also keen to stifle French trade in the Mediterranean and the Spanish Americas. But it was Louis's renewed support for a Stuart restoration that probably weighed most heavily with the English, persuading them that the war was fundamentally a fight to preserve the Protestant succession.

The main architect of the Grand Alliance would not live to see it tested a second time. In March 1702, William III died of a pulmonary fever. Largely unmourned, he would come to be regarded by Tories as one of the greatest scoundrels in English history – the inevitable fate of a foreigner who had usurped the throne merely to fight his European battles. His successor in Britain and Ireland, James II's rebellious younger daughter Anne, was much more popular, at least in England. 'I know my heart to be entirely English,' she announced in Elizabethan tones to her first Parliament.[80] Like Elizabeth, she recognised the importance of public displays of royalty. She was also a loyal daughter of the Church of England, and to that extent a Tory. She detested the sordid business of party politics, just as William had. But unlike him she was willing to work through rather than around her cabinet. Her closest friend was Sarah Churchill, the devoted wife of James's and then William's courtier and general John Churchill (1650–1722), created duke of Marlborough in 1702. Within a few weeks of her succession, Anne had appointed Marlborough captain-general of the army and ambassador-extraordinary to the Dutch republic. It would be Anne and Marlborough, with the backing of the Whigs and most of the Tories, who would steer England into renewed war against France.

The War of the Spanish Succession began promisingly for Louis. His grandson Philip, though a Bourbon, was well received by his new Spanish subjects, and the French won a series of victories against the Austrian Habsburgs in northern Italy and the German Rhineland. It was the prospect of the French and their Bavarian allies knocking the Empire out of the war at an early stage that produced one of the greatest feats in English military history: Marlborough's Blenheim campaign. During May and June 1704 the duke led an army of some 21,000 allied troops on a 300-mile march around the north-eastern flank of France, down the Rhine, and then across country to rendezvous with the main Imperial army, north of Bavaria. Only minute planning by Marlborough, backed up by Dutch logistical know-how and the cooperation of the German Rhineland principalities, could have carried off this bold stroke. No English army had marched so far from its base since the Black Prince's expedition to Spain in 1367 during the Hundred Years War.

On 13 August, Marlborough and the Imperial general Prince Eugene of Savoy threw 52,000 allied troops – 10,000 or so British, the rest mostly Dutchmen, Hanoverians, Hessians, Danes and Prussians – against a strong Franco-Bavarian position held by 56,000 men in and around the Bavarian village of Blindheim (rendered Blenheim in English), on the upper Danube. While Eugene pinned down a superior enemy force on the allies' right, Marlborough on the left skilfully exploited poor – or, more often, no – decision-making by the Franco-Bavarian high command to win a famous victory. The allies suffered roughly 12,000 casualties; the French about twice that, with 14,000 taken prisoner, including their commander-in-chief. In an age when decisive battles were rare, the allies had destroyed an entire French army. Back in England a grateful queen and Parliament granted funds to build a new family residence for the Marlboroughs – and the result, some three decades and several hundred thousand pounds later, was Blenheim Palace.

Tory critics of the land war, who demanded instead a naval campaign with colonial objectives, sneered that French losses at Blenheim had been 'no more than to take a bucket of water out of a river'. To which Marlborough replied that 'if they [the French] allow us to draw one or two such buckets more, I should think we might then let the river run quietly and not much apprehend its overflowing and destroying its neighbours'.[81] During the next seven years in the Spanish Netherlands he would try his best to draw more bucketfuls from the river, and at the battles of Ramillies (1706) and Oudenarde (1708) he largely succeeded. The allies' grand strategy was to surround France and Spain with military threats such that Louis could not concentrate his massive army on any one front, and thereby to defeat him piecemeal. This meant deploying armies in the Low Countries, the Rhineland, northern Italy and the Iberian peninsula. As in the previous war, neither side was prepared to invest heavily in military operations beyond Europe. They both sent sizeable task forces across the Atlantic at various times during the war, but the usual difficulties when it came to power-projection thousands of miles from home – poor planning, bad weather, disease and logistical overstretch – ensured they had little effect on the overall balance of colonial power either in the Caribbean or in North America.

At the war's centre, however, in western Europe, the French slowly began to buckle under the allies' onslaught. Marlborough reconquered the Spanish Netherlands; Eugene drove the French from northern Italy; Anglo-Dutch naval forces virtually took over the Mediterranean; and allied armies from Portugal and Catalonia seized Madrid on two occasions, although popular support for Philip ultimately made Spain too hot to hold. Above all, Marlborough demonstrated that with just a little more risk-taking by the allies, his army could break through the ring of fortresses defending north-eastern France and descend on Paris itself.

Marlborough was prevented from striking into the heart of France more by his own government than by the French themselves. In his last great field battle, at Malplaquet in 1709, he suffered over 20,000 killed or wounded, which was more than twice the number of French casualties. 'When will this bloodshed ever cease?' was reportedly Anne's reaction to this 'victory'.[82] Almost as unnerving as the loss of life was the sheer scale of British involvement. Britain was paying for 170,000 troops by 1709, over half of them foreign. In the 1710 general election, the war-weary British voted in the Tories, whose leaders opened unilateral talks with Louis, who had been desperately putting out peace feelers since 1706. They also exploited anti-war feeling and the collapse of the friendship between the queen and the duchess of Marlborough to have the duke dismissed as captain-general and vilified in Parliament and the press as a war profiteer. To cries of 'perfidious Albion' from her allies, Britain withdrew its troops from the land war in 1712, thereby forcing the Dutch and the emperor to sue for peace as well.

By the terms of the treaty of Utrecht in 1713, Philip was recognised as king of Spain and its overseas empire, provided that the two Bourbon crowns of France and Spain were never united and that the Spanish Netherlands were handed over to the Austrian Habsburgs. In return for having a Bourbon installed on the Spanish throne, and territorial gains in Europe that rounded out France's borders, the French ceded Acadia (just south of the Gulf of St Lawrence, and renamed Nova Scotia) and their half of St Kitts, in the West Indies, to Britain, and confirmed British possession of contested territory in Newfoundland and Hudson Bay. The Spanish did the same for Gibraltar and Minorca, and granted Britain the lucrative *asiento*: the monopoly of selling African slaves to the Spanish colonies. The Dutch, who were still regarded by the Tories as Britain's greatest trading rivals, were denied any colonial prizes of their own, but they were given 'barrier fortresses' in the Spanish (now Austrian) Netherlands. Finally, Louis agreed to recognise the Protestant succession in Britain.

The treaty of Utrecht announced to all Europe that Britain was now France's greatest rival in the Old World and perhaps her master in the New. The British ended the war with 131 ships of the line, including 20 formidable three-deckers, each carrying 96–100 guns. By contrast, the French navy had atrophied since 1707, while the Dutch republic's huge commitment to the land war had weakened it economically and as a maritime power. With vital strategic bases in the Mediterranean, dominance of the transatlantic trade, and its colonial rivals faltering, Britain was poised to take the lead in the race for empire.

Imperial greatness would have proved much more elusive, however, were it not for another vital legacy of the French wars: the 1707 Anglo-Scottish union. Schemes for various types of closer union had regularly been discussed by the English and the Scots during the seventeenth century, and all had either been rejected or short-lived. Stuart Britain's most ardent proponents of closer union had been the mid-century Scottish Covenanters. Fifty years on, however, and many Scots wanted fewer rather than more ties with England. Anti-English feeling was stoked up by William's insensitive handling of Scottish affairs, and the justifiable perception that his foreign policy was concerned with advancing Dutch and English interests rather than those of Scotland. Certainly the Nine Years War had created a massive trade slump in Scotland, made worse by dreadful harvests during the 1690s that had caused a devastating four-year famine. The Scots particularly resented the fact that they, like other 'foreigners', were banned by the English from trading with England's colonies. The Scots retained the option of asserting their commercial as well as political independence from the English by founding colonies of their own, as they had tried to do, though without notable success, since the 1620s. But when they had launched a new colonial venture in the late 1690s – to establish a trading settlement on the Darien peninsula in Panama – William had deliberately starved it of cash and naval protection in order to protect English commercial and strategic interests. The result had been the loss of some 2,000 Scottish colonists and investments totalling perhaps a quarter of Scotland's liquid assets. As hostility to the English had mounted during William's last years so too had support for radical constitutional reform and Jacobitism. Scotland was fast becoming ungovernable.

In focusing on the danger from France the London government took an already lazy eye completely off Scottish interests. The 1701 Act of Settlement – designed to secure the Protestant succession against the

French–Jacobite threat – was passed without consulting the Scots and was seen by them as just another example of English arrogance. Then in 1702 the English effectively dragged the Scots into war with France by ministerial sleight of hand, without thought for what another prolonged conflict would do to Scotland's already battered economy. The Scottish Parliament was having none of this, and in 1703 retaliated with two highly provocative pieces of legislation. The first stated that if Anne died without an heir then the Scottish Parliament would not follow Westminster in recognising the Hanoverian succession unless Whitehall agreed to relinquish some of its ministerial powers over Scotland and allow the Scots free trade with England and her colonies. The second piece of legislation stipulated that when Anne died the Scottish Parliament would assume the power to conclude peace with France even if England itself was still at war. In effect, the Scots were threatening not only to break the regnal union but also to make Scotland once again a back door through which the French could invade England.

There seemed only one way out of the hole that the English had dug for themselves over Scotland, and that was Anglo-Scottish union. In 1705, Westminster responded with an act for treating all Scots in England as foreign nationals and banning Scottish imports unless Scotland recognised the Hanoverian succession or agreed to open negotiations towards union. It was now dawning on leading Scots that the only likely winners in a stand-off with England would be the Jacobites, and thus negotiations for a union began in earnest in 1706. Many Scots, probably a majority, were vehemently against the whole idea. The Jacobites because it tied Scotland to England and the Protestant succession, the Presbyterians because they feared spiritual contamination from the 'prelatical' English. Likewise the English Tories opposed union because it meant endorsing the Presbyterian Kirk's triumph over Scottish episcopacy. The strongest selling point for union was the supposed economic benefits that Scotland would reap – notably, untrammelled access to English markets and the chance for Scots to fulfil their imperial destiny in partnership rather than competition with the English.

On the English side the key consideration was securing the Protestant succession and keeping the door to French and Jacobite encroachment firmly shut. Only by uniting, argued England's pro-union propagandist-in-chief, Daniel Defoe, could the two countries resist the popish threat of France. Privately, the English calculated that by merging Scotland into a single British system they could better control its volatile politics.

They could also put a stop to the vigorous illegal trade that Scotland's merchants were conducting with English colonies in the Americas. This Scottish interloping was damaging colonial revenues at precisely the time when England needed all its resources to fight the French. Through a mixture of good management, bribery and concessions to Scottish Presbyterian and nationalist feeling, the government persuaded the Edinburgh Parliament to agree to a treaty of union, which the Westminster Parliament then endorsed and which came into force on 1 May 1707.

The 1707 Act of Union created 'the United Kingdom of Great Britain' – a title that disguises the fact that this new state was more the product of European geopolitics than of genuine British sentiment. As in 1607, so in 1707, the English would accept nothing less than a thoroughgoing incorporating union, and thus what they opted for was a version of the Cromwellian parliamentary merger of the 1650s – another instance of the Glorious Revolution building upon mid-century foundations. The Scottish Parliament was abolished (as was the Scottish privy council in 1708) and replaced with a nominally British, but in fact just a greater English, Parliament at Westminster. The Scots were allocated a mere 45 seats in the Commons – one more than Cornwall – and 16 places in the Lords. Scottish MPs were initially courted, then sidelined. They had been accustomed to the learned and rather formal debates of the Scottish Parliament, and did not adapt easily to the raucous arena of the Commons, where the din was sometimes such that MPs could hardly hear a word that was being said. Once represented at Westminster, Scottish parties would slowly align with the English Whig–Tory division.

The Scots gained free trade with England and her colonies as a result of the union, and compensation for their losses in the Darien debacle. The union established one official flag – the Union Flag – and one currency: England's. However, each country retained its own legal system and established churches. A shared Protestantism could not overcome the mutual enmity of Kirk and Church of England. The two countries would also retain their separate national identities. The union would create not a new nation but a London-centred British state and British imperial interest.

As well as raising the temperature of Anglo-Scottish relations, the French wars injected much of the heat into what Swift called 'this damned business of party'.[83] Since the Exclusion Crisis of 1679–81 the feuding between Whigs and Tories had spread throughout English society like a plague, reaching epidemic proportions during the War of the Spanish Succession. Parliament-men, town governors, the voters out in the constituencies, and the general public right down, if we can believe Swift, to chambermaids, apprentices and schoolboys were all split along party lines. The Whig–Tory rivalry infected Scotland and Ireland too during Anne's reign, partly eclipsing the older divisions between Presbyterians, episcopalians and Catholics. In London and other cities the parties formed their own political-cum-dining clubs, usually based in coffee houses and taverns, where the faithful socialised, shouted the odds, and planned their next move. A Tory who wandered by mistake into a Whig coffee house in 1705 soon realised he was on enemy territory when he 'heard the Tories censured with as much violence and malice as Whiggish principles could furnish 'em with'.[84] Party politics permeated almost every area of social activity. It could even affect a person's love life. When one Whig gentlewoman was informed by an acquaintance that her political views would deter potential suitors, she replied: 'I despise all Tories . . . were their estates never so large; and yet don't despair, for I am sure the Whigs like me better for being true to my party.'[85] Swift claimed that 'when a Man changeth his party, he must infallibly count upon the Loss of his Mistress'.[86]

The rage of party was inflamed by frequent general elections: twelve between 1689 and 1716, or roughly one every two and a half years. Political participation, at least at election time, was also increasing. The electorate in England comprised a larger proportion of the English population during the later Stuart period than at any time before the electoral reforms of the nineteenth century. Perhaps as many as one in four men had the right to vote. Party strife was stoked up still further by an increase in print warfare from the mid-1690s. After failing to reach agreement about a new licensing (censorship) act, Parliament had allowed the old act to lapse in 1695, and once again London became awash with pamphlets and newspapers debating current affairs and criticising the nation's political leaders. Inevitably, there was a great deal of hand-wringing by politicians and their supporters about the evils of an unrestrained press, and repeated calls for the reintroduction of censorship. All were ignored, however. Politicians after 1695 would generally deal with bad publicity by trying to manipulate the print media, not by attacking the public sphere itself.

Yet although parties had become a normal part of politics, indeed an inescapable feature of everyday life, the idea of party itself was still reviled. Parties in Swift's view 'not only split a Nation, but every Individual among them, leaving each but half their Strength, and Wit, and Honesty, and good Nature'.[87] Tories and Whigs preferred to see their rivals not as legitimate opponents, but as a 'factious', corrupt minority, while they themselves constituted the 'loyal', public-spirited and non-partisan majority.

The battle between the parties raged most fiercely over one question above all: how best to maintain British security and prosperity against French aggression. The Whigs embraced the fundamental consequences of the Glorious Revolution – that is, an essentially contractual monarchy; a commitment to defending the Protestant succession at home and the Protestant interest abroad; and the extension of state power in order to safeguard all three. Along with ministerial Tories such as Marlborough, they believed that the only way to defeat France and preserve the balance of Europe was at the heart of a European alliance and at the head of the allied armies fighting the French. Unless Louis XIV was stopped on his own doorstep, they believed, neither Britain nor other Protestant states could enjoy any security.

The Tories, on the other hand, were deeply uneasy about the challenge the Glorious Revolution had posed to their ideals of non-resistance and hereditary monarchy. Although the Whigs constantly smeared them as crypto-Jacobites, few Tories, certainly in England, really wanted James or his son back. But then few, too, could muster much enthusiasm for William III or the Hanoverian succession. As the Nine Years War dragged on they grew sceptical about the wisdom of a land war whose main beneficiaries seemed to be a pack of grasping foreigners. The Land Tax and similar financial innovations were seen by Tories as devices to wrest money from England's 'landed-men' and dole it out to her self-serving continental allies and London's 'moneyed men'. Swift and other Tory propagandists depicted politics as a conflict between the 'honest' and overtaxed 'Gentlemen of Estates' and a 'set of Upstarts' – namely, Whig junto-men and merchants and other war profiteers, interested only in 'the Advancement of private Wealth and Power'.[88] Rather than squander British lives and money merely to aggrandise the Dutch and Austrians, the Tories favoured the time-honoured 'blue water' strategy for channelling resources into a maritime war that would divert French and Spanish trade and colonial wealth to Britain and thereby compel Louis to the negotiating table. What these Tory and other 'navalists' could not, or would not, grasp was that France was primarily a land power, not a maritime one, and could lose all of its overseas trade and still smash its rivals to pieces, as Napoleon would demonstrate all too clearly.

More than a century of infighting over the nation's religious identity would reach its climax during the era of the French wars. The Whigs, and that small but influential group of 'low' churchmen (including most of the bishops appointed after 1688) which had accepted toleration with good grace, did their best to protect the Dissenters' interests. The Tories and a majority of Anglican clergymen, on the other hand, cried up the idea of 'the Church in danger', which became a semi-official Tory party slogan. The increasingly high profile of the Dissenters in London and other cities, and the spread of unorthodox religious ideas after 1689, aroused fears that the Anglican establishment and traditional Christian doctrine were being undermined. Tub-thumping Anglican clerics exploited such concerns, as well as discontent at the progress of the war, to stir up the mob to attack Dissenters' chapels. During the Tory ascendancy of 1710–14 it seemed that Protestant freedom of worship was in real jeopardy. But conflict between Whigs and Tories over religious issues, as also over the conduct of the war, would be contained by their shared commitment to defending international Protestantism against popery.

Party strife was tempered, too, by a queen whose watchword was 'moderation'. For most of her reign, Anne presided over a mixed ministry and an uneasy alliance of moderate Tories, under the able leadership of Britain's first prime minister worthy of the name, Robert Harley (supported by his cousin Abigail Masham in the queen's Bedchamber), and the junto Whigs. War fatigue and anxiety about 'the Church in danger' gave the Tories landslide election wins in 1710 and 1713, which would leave them well placed when the last of the Stuart monarchs died on 1 August 1714 – a little over two months after the death of her designated successor, Princess Sophia. The 49-year-old Anne had been in poor health for many years, and was so fat and gout-ridden by the end that she was no longer able to walk. Some Tory Parliament-men, perhaps a majority, would have accepted James II's son, the Old Pretender, as king if he had agreed to renounce his Catholicism. But this he refused to do, leaving the Tory party divided and in disarray. A commission of regency, dominated by Whigs and pro-Hanoverian Tories, would thus preside over the peaceful succession of Princess Sophia's eldest son, Georg Ludwig of Hanover (1660–1727), who was duly crowned George I of Great Britain and Ireland in October 1714.

Politeness

The many years of warfare that the three kingdoms endured between 1637 and 1713, either with each other or the continental powers, contributed to a remarkable transformation in their social and economic conditions. Whereas the seat of the Stuart empire, England, had still been an overwhelmingly agrarian society in 1603, by 1700 less than 60 per cent of English people lived primarily off the land. Fully a third of the kingdom's wealth was now being generated by merchants, clothiers, shopkeepers, artisans, metalworkers, miners and other non-agricultural sectors of the economy. This shift in the means of production reflected the boom in English trade and manufacturing during the second half of the seventeenth century. The cloth industry, still the bedrock of England's manufacturing sector, was thriving as never before – the development of light, good-quality fabrics having created a mass market for English cloth in southern Europe and the North American colonies. Output in the coal and shipbuilding industries was also breaking all records, while demand from the metalworking industry was so great that it could only be met by importing iron from the Baltic. Across a wide range of indicators England was outpacing the rest of Europe by 1700. Its road network, navigable waterways and travel infrastructure (stagecoach services, inns etc.) were all expanding; the number of shops across the country probably exceeded 100,000; its postal service was delivering over a million letters and parcels a year; and per capita incomes were rising dramatically. In 1500, lowland England had been no more than moderately wealthy by contemporary European standards. Two centuries later and Britain was set to overhaul the Dutch republic as the Continent's most advanced economic power.

One major source of economic stimulus was the improvement in farming productivity from the late sixteenth century that we noted in chapter 2. Increasing agricultural output would supply the food surpluses needed to fuel urban manufacturing. Another boost to the economy came from the massive military build-up in England from the 1640s. Wartime contracts for the supply of England's armies and battle fleets would turn the West Midlands into the country's main centre for metalwares, and the naval dockyards at Chatham, Harwich, Portsmouth and Plymouth into some of the largest industrial complexes in Europe. Britain's wars nourished huge business empires, such as that of the Tyneside forgemaster Sir Ambrose Crowley (1658–1713), who built a company that employed tens of thousands in making nails and other iron products for the navy and colonial markets. A third cause of the late seventeenth-century boom was England's burgeoning foreign and colonial trade. The New World colonies not only provided additional (and exclusive) markets for English manufactures but also cushioned domestic producers from the worst effects of continental trade tariffs and enemy privateering (see chapter 7).

What made England's commercial revolution after 1640 all the more remarkable was that it occurred in the context of a static population. The number of people in England and Wales roughly doubled in the century before 1640 to about 5.3 million and 330,000 respectively. Then, for the remainder of the century it either stabilised or went into slight decline. There was, it is true, an influx of Dutch, Huguenot and Venetian migrants to England during the later seventeenth century, who brought with them vital technical know-how, particularly to the cloth, paper and glass-making industries. But this 'abundance of Foreigners', which elicited the usual complaints from the English – 'they eat the bread out of our mouths, they sell their goods when we can't, they work cheaper than we, live in holes, pay neither scot nor lot [taxes]' – did little to alter the basic demographic trend.[89] Scotland's population rose from about 750,000 in 1600 to about 1.2 million in 1700, but again with most of that increase occurring in the first half of the century. Ireland, as usual, was the exception to this pattern. Its population stood at about 1.5 million in 1640; dropped to 1.3 million or less as a result of the Cromwellian invasion; and rose again to around 2 million by 1690. The population of Ulster grew particularly dramatically during the 1690s as Scots crossed the North Channel to escape famine in their homeland. A war-ravaged wasteland in 1650, Ulster by 1700 was perhaps the most heavily populated and economically advanced region in Ireland.

The communities that most emphatically bucked the general demographic trend were, significantly, Britain's towns and cities. While the urban population in most European countries stagnated after 1660, in England it rose dramatically during the seventeenth century to about 25 to 30 per cent – a level of urbanisation exceeded only by the Dutch.[90] The percentages of town-dwellers in Scotland and Ireland were lower, but the upward curve was the same. Dublin had 60,000 inhabitants by 1700, and Edinburgh approximately 40,000. Yet significant though their growth was it was dwarfed by London's. In contrast to the majority of European cities, which generally did little more than maintain their population size during the seventeenth century, London grew from about 200,000 inhabitants to around 575,000, making it the biggest city in western Europe by 1700. A century later and it had reached the one million mark and, with Beijing and Tokyo, was the largest city in the world. One in every dozen people in England by 1750 was a Londoner, while one in every six probably had some experience of London life, there being (in Defoe's words) a 'general Dependence of the whole Country upon the City of London, as well for the Consumption of its Produce, as the Circulation of its Trade'.[91] For London was not just more populous than almost every other European city, it was also reckoned 'the Largest, Richest, and Chiefest City in the World, for Trade'.[92] 'The number of shops both in the City and suburbs . . . is so great, and indeed so far beyond that of any foreign city,' thought one observer, 'that it is to strangers a just matter of amazement.'[93] And it was not just their number but also their luxuriousness that was eye-catching. The drapers' shops on Ludgate Hill, for example, were described in 1709 as 'perfect gilded theatres', and their male shop assistants 'the greatest fops in the kingdom'.[94] A young Frenchman visiting London in the 1720s thought its four main shopping streets – the Strand, Fleet Street, Cheapside and Cornhill – 'the finest in Europe'.[95] But perhaps nothing spoke more eloquently of the city's commercial vitality than the 'Forest of Ships of all Nations' that filled the Thames downstream of London Bridge.[96]

London's growth was exceptional only in scale. The capital's rocketing population turned Newcastle, the supplier of its coal, into the largest and most prosperous town in northern England. The international commerce on which much of London's expansion in size and wealth after 1660 depended would thus fuel the growth of the coal industry, which was a major contributor (as we shall see in chapter 8) to Britain's astonishing economic progress in the eighteenth century. Manchester and Birmingham, having ranked outside the thirty largest English provincial towns in 1660, both grew rapidly in the century that followed to join the top five or so with populations of 20,000 or more by 1750. Along with Leeds and Sheffield they were fast emerging by the early eighteenth century as the nation's leading manufacturing centres. Similarly, England's increasing orientation towards the Atlantic and colonial trades was transforming Liverpool and Bristol into major ports, just as it was Boston, New York and Philadelphia across the Atlantic.

Growing prosperity led to a shift in urban economies towards the leisure industry, while new towns arose to cater specifically for the recreational and consumer demands of the well-to-do. Tunbridge Wells, little more than a hamlet in 1660, had developed by 1700 into one of the country's most fashionable resorts and spa towns. The rise of Bath as provincial England's pre-eminent social watering hole dates from the early 1700s. The distinctive features of the Georgian townscape – large squares, broad thoroughfares (with pavements), classical terraces, assembly rooms etc. – were beginning to replace the late medieval and Tudor legacy of higgledy-piggledy, timber-framed housing and narrow streets, several decades before George I succeeded to the throne. A major source of inspiration in civic improvement schemes throughout Britain would be the English form of urban classicism that had marked the rebuilding of London after the Great Fire of 1666 – although the very first town houses in the 'Georgian' fashion had been built to Inigo Jones's design for the Covent Garden piazza development in the 1630s.

Urban society had become a magnet by 1700 for the landed aristocracy, the leisured classes, indeed for anyone with pretensions to gentility. The popularity of London's West End and other fashionable urban locales was paralleled by the elite's abandonment of the universities and a decline in the royal court and the Church of England as centres of cultural production. The court's failure after 1660 to revive or retain many of its traditional ceremonial functions and forms of hospitality had made it more dependent on the London social scene, and the character of the monarch, for its popularity – which was a viable arrangement so long as the monarch was outgoing and fun-loving like Charles II. But his royal successors were cut from drabber cloth. 'Dutch William' seemed to resent even the smallest concession to joviality or the social graces, while Queen Anne's drawing rooms reportedly had 'more the air of sollemn places of worship, than the gayety of a Court'.[97] Why go to Kensington Palace (the court's main location after much of Whitehall was destroyed by fire in 1698) and be confronted with Anne's gouty foot in 'nasty bandages', when before you lay all of London, with its pleasure gardens, assembly rooms, concert halls, masquerades and clubs?[98]

Fashionable town life provided the main backdrop for the emergence of a new form of sociability in the late seventeenth century: politeness. In a society increasingly dominated by commercial relations and their benefits, and at the same time riven by party rivalries, politeness represented an attempt to reconcile virtue with the values of a modern, consumerist age. Politeness would divert the mainstream of English sociability away from active citizenship and godly patriotism, with their Miltonic overtones of austere self-denial and political engagement, into less partisan, more consumer-friendly channels. Politeness was all about the cultivation of good manners, of civility without affectation, and of genteel taste and attention to the latest fashions and luxury goods. In women, it was associated with gracefulness and sexual passivity. Politeness set the ground rules for social interaction in the new and largely urban settings of the club, the assembly room, and above all the coffee house.

The first coffee house in England (and probably western Europe) had opened in Oxford in about 1650, and by 1700 there were thousands throughout the three kingdoms. Unlike today's equally ubiquitous coffee shop, the coffee house was believed by its devotees to 'civilise our manners, enlarge our understandings, refine our language, [and] teach us a generous confidence and handsome mode of address'.[99] Coffee houses were important discursive spaces, where men and women of all ranks and parties could exchange news, debate current affairs and conduct business. Lloyd's, the insurers and bankers, began life as a coffee house. To compete in a crowded market, coffee-house keepers provided free newspapers for their clientele, which put coffee houses at the centre of news distribution networks. Another reason for their popularity was the invigorating effects of coffee itself. This 'wakeful and civil drink' certainly made for clearer heads than the traditional English morning tipple of beer or wine, although there were those in government who disliked coffee-drinking for precisely that reason.[100] 'Every carman [carter] and porter is now a statesman,' complained one London patrician in 1673, 'and indeed the coffeehouses are good for nothing else. It was not thus when we drank nothing but sack [fortified white wine] and claret, or English beer and ale. These sober clubs produce nothing but scandalous and censorious discourses.'[101] Coffee, chocolate and (later) tea introduced the British to another morning novelty besides sobriety – namely, breakfast.

The free and (ideally) friendly conversation that defined and refined politeness was regarded by the more liberal-minded as the very corner-stone of political liberty. A leading trendsetter in polite society, Joseph Addison – a writer for *The Tatler* (established in 1709) and co-founder of *The Spectator* in 1711 – famously declared that his intention was to bring speculation and free inquiry 'out of [gentlemen's] Closets and Libraries, schools and Colleges, to dwell in Clubs and Assemblies, at Tea-Tables and in Coffee-Houses'.[102] But the 'amicable collisions' of polite discourse could operate only within certain limits. It was accept-able to talk politics and even religion so long as the conversation was decorous and disciplined by good manners. The 'one great general Rule' in conversation, observed Addison's literary collaborator Sir Richard Steele, was 'That Men should not talk to please themselves, but those that hear them'.[103] What was not acceptable, therefore, were fervent expressions of personal piety. Such outbursts were 'apt to end in Disgusts, if not in quarrels'.[104]

This squeamishness about baring one's soul in company was part of a larger trend in late seventeenth-century society: the repudiation of religious 'enthusiasm', or the claim to special revelations. Reacting to the Puritan excesses of the 1640s and 1650s, many writers and churchmen began to privilege reason and self-control in religion over faith and spiritual inspiration. The theological disputes and doctrinal issues that had so vexed early Stuart Protestants began to seem increasingly irrelevant after 1660. The showy yet angst-ridden piety of the godly was denounced as tartuffery, morbid self-indulgence, or simply madness. Religion, it was now argued, was not all about suffering and affliction, but could also embrace earthly happiness and material comfort. Enthusiasm, especially the sectarian variety, was the enemy not only of true religion but also of politeness. It was, declared one Anglican cleric in 1670, 'Godliness without Religion, Zeal without Humanity, and Grace without good Nature, or good Manners'.[105] Enthusiasm would take over some of the negative connotations of 'popularity'. Godly 'enthusiasts' like Milton were accused of deluding and stirring up the masses. The drift among Restoration writers away from the sometimes flowery verbiage of the Puritans and humanists – or what one royalist cleric called 'a Romantick showre of words . . . stuffed with Bombast, & confusion . . . the meer Excrements of Language' – towards a plainer prose style was just one aspect of the general rejection of enthusiasm.[106] Similarly, the rhetorical (and often uncritical) use of classical texts that had been a central feature of humanism was rubbished in the early 1700s by self-consciously 'modern' scholars, who denigrated the cult of antiquity.

As Protestantism shifted during the later seventeenth century from a religion of faith and the Word towards one of morality and manners, it shed much of its theological load, particularly from its Puritan side. The political defeat of Puritanism in the early 1660s cooled the fires of apocalyptic zeal among the godly. It did not look likely that Christ would return in triumph 'to dissolve Satan with his perverted world' (in Milton's words) any time soon.[107] Calvinist doctrines on faith and salvation would have many subscribers among both Dissenters and Anglicans far into the eighteenth century. But after 1660, Calvinism lost the (admittedly, often contested) status of orthodoxy that it had enjoyed for much of the preceding century. The emphasis in learned circles after 1660 would not be on the inherent sinfulness of human nature but on man's natural sociability. This optimistic view of humanity was championed by the philosopher John Locke, notably in his controversial *An Essay Concerning Human Understanding* (1690). Rejecting the concept of innate ideas, he argued that all knowledge derived from reason or revelation, and that though capable of enlargement through education it could not encompass much of what passed for received wisdom. Locke's message was that there were few things people could be certain about, including religious tenets. His work would lend impetus to that vast epistemological effort that gradually moved religion from the realm of truth to that of opinion.

The years after 1660 would be hard ones for the godly, and not simply because the political and theological tide had turned against them. As they adjusted to life outside of the established Church, the Dissenters suffered a gradual loss of spiritual vitality. The Presbyterians became more inward-looking and, after 1688, drifted towards Unitarianism. The Baptists complained in 1689 that 'much of the former, strength, life and vigour, which attended us is . . . gone'.[108] The Quakers ceased quaking and became respectable. Yet the Church of England struggled too, particularly after 1688 as the clergy divided between a pro-toleration 'low church' minority and a 'high church' majority that longed for the old days of Anglican uniformity. Levels of church attendance among the laity began to drop after 1688, but so too did the number of Dissenters. Anticlericalism, on the other hand, seems to have hit new heights. 'Priestcraft', or prelacy and clerical obfuscation, was widely excoriated, while the talk on all sides was of the 'visible decay of Religion', and the 'monstrous increase of Deism, Prophaneness, and Vice'.[109] Orthodox Christians were convinced by the early eighteenth century that scepticism and atheism were rife. Certainly the doctrine of the Trinity, and belief in the power of the devil and witchcraft, were being increasingly questioned in educated circles.

The perceived spread of vice and irreligion after the Glorious Revolution led to the establishment of societies in London and other towns during the 1690s for the reformation of manners. Concerned Anglicans and Dissenters would roam the streets making citizen's arrests of anyone breaking the laws against 'debauched incontinency, and bastard-getting' – mostly drunkards, swearers, prostitutes and sabbath-breakers.[110] These moral vigilantes tended to justify their actions on law-and-order grounds rather than, as early reformers would have done, with reference to saving people's souls and averting God's wrath. The Christian humanism of Milton's stamp, which had harnessed classical knowledge and apocalyptic belief in the cause of creating a godly commonwealth, was changing into concern for social improvement; godly reformation was giving way to politeness. Although the movement for reformation of manners would last well into the eighteenth century, it faced considerable opposition almost from day one. The societies were particularly vulnerable to the criticism that many of the vices they tried to suppress, such as drinking, served to boost trade and prosperity and were thus themselves of considerable public benefit.

For all the lamentations of the faithful, there was probably no great falling away from Christianity in the late seventeenth century, much less the onset of secularisation. Rather, there was a move among the laity towards a more informal, more tolerant and more companionable kind of religion. 'What is Religion good for,' asked one Anglican churchman, 'but to reform the Manners and Dispositions of Men?'[111] True piety would express itself in 'courtesy, gentleness, and affability'.[112]

Advances in the 'new science' after the Restoration reinforced this polite conception of religion. The Royal Society was set up in 1660 to promote 'sober' scientific knowledge so that 'the next Age' might be inured against 'all the inchantments of Enthusiasm'.[113] The Society was dominated in its early years by moderate Anglican divines and men of sincere piety such as Isaac Newton and Robert Boyle. Boyle claimed that his main aim in studying nature was 'to raise in himself and others, vaster thoughts of the greatness and glory, and of the wisdom and goodness of God'.[114] Newton, who spent years studying biblical prophecy and dabbling in alchemy, declared: 'A continual miracle [by God] is needed to prevent the Sun and fixed stars from rushing together through gravity.'[115] Both he and Boyle saw their scientific work as a powerful testament to the existence of God and the fundamentals of Christianity. Yet if the new science did not necessarily lead to atheism or even to scepticism about such things as witchcraft and the spirit-world, it certainly tended to weaken belief in an interventionist, wrathful deity. God was increasingly regarded by the intellectual elite as a benevolent yet distant being, the regulator of an ordered, mathematically defined universe.

Contesting the values and meaning of politeness became something of a literary obsession after 1660. Poetry, plays, what today would be called literature, were conscripted in the war of words between the Restoration parties, with writers such as John Dryden (for the Tories) and Andrew Marvell (for the Whigs) smearing their opponents' works as fanatical, while proclaiming their own as exemplars of true civility. Politeness struggled to contain the passion of party feeling, which spilled over in satirical plays, scurrilous verse, and what one Whig (referring specifically to the Tory polemicist Swift) termed an 'inexhaustible fund of malice and calumny'.[116] Under the competing demands of politeness and party zeal, the frequently conflated genre of poetry and political polemic began to separate during the later Stuart period – a process that would end with poetry, its reading and composition, becoming the generally private affair that it is today.

The royal court, like the political parties, occupied an ambiguous position in the contested space between enthusiasm and politeness. Charles II and his courtiers were great patrons of the theatre – or rather of London's two public playhouses allowed by royal charter – and as such supported plays that in tone and content were generally hostile to Puritan fanaticism. The theatre was more courtly, socially exclusive and fashionable after 1660 than it had been before the Civil War. Equally, Dryden and other Restoration dramatists believed that their productions were far more refined than those of Shakespeare and Jonson, in spite of the lurid scenes of sex and violence that often played across the overlapping worlds of court and stage.

The gold standard in matters of cultural refinement was set by the French. Paris was the fashion capital of Europe by the late seventeenth century, and Louis XIV's court at Versailles its shop window. Louis's finance minister Jean-Baptiste Colbert wrote: 'Fashion is to France what the gold mines of Peru are to the Spaniard.'[117] An important outpost of the far-flung French fashion empire was the Stuart court, which took a lead in showcasing French manners, French baroque architecture and painting, French clothes and, of course, the wearing of periwigs, which would spread from Versailles to become de rigueur for European gentle-folk everywhere until the late eighteenth century. In 1673 an English pamphleteer lamented that the French 'look upon us as a nation to whom they give the laws of mode . . . this is a great pride to them, whilst they see themselves to preside over our genius, and to guide it into all the fashions which their rambling fancies take'.[118]

The rise of the 'Town' and the West End during the Restoration period, however, saw a corresponding decline in the court as the cyno-sure of polite society. Indeed, 'true politeness' as formulated by Addison and his Whig friends in the early eighteenth century was defined explicitly in antithesis to the toadying and empty civilities of the royal court. Politeness caught on precisely because it rejected court cliquishness. With its stress on style over substance, it set the bar of social respectability quite low, enabling people who lacked court connections, good breeding or landed estates to socialise with their betters on something like equal terms. The Tatler insisted that: 'The Appelation of Gentleman is never to be affixed to a Man's Circumstances, but to his Behaviour in them.'[119] Gentility could be appropriated by anyone who had the money and time to look and sound the part; and in the rapidly expanding world of the late Stuart bon ton that included professional men, merchants, manufacturers, well-to-do tradesmen and so on. But politeness was more than just socially inclusive, for by allowing interaction on the basis of a shared set of manners and cultural tastes it had the effect of flattening out social distinctions among the leisured classes. This levelling process can be seen in the simplification and homogenisation of genteel dress during the later seventeenth century. The court costumes of the aristocracy remained as opulent and, from the 1660s, as ostentatiously French as ever. But for everyday wear, the gentleman's coat, waistcoat and breeches (the forerunner of today's three-piece suit) and the lady's 'mantua' gown became the standard attire among the aristocracy and urban middling sort, making it increasingly difficult to distinguish rank by mere appearance. The same cultural uniformity can be seen in the popularity of classical forms in polite architecture, from the terraced town house to the Palladian country pile.

Politeness challenged some of the social conventions of the aristocracy, to be sure, but it did so without altering the basic facts of aristocratic life. Despite the confiscation, sale and restitution of estates among the winners and losers of the civil wars and the Restoration, there would be no fundamental change in the distribution of land or political power during the seventeenth century. England, Scotland and Ireland remained profoundly hierarchical societies in which a close connection still existed between land ownership and the exercise of government. There were perhaps as many as 20,000 gentlemen – from dukes down to parish squires – in England and Wales by 1700, a fourfold increase since the early 1500s. The number of peers by 1700 had climbed to 173, up by over 100 from a century earlier, and their average income would double during the course of the eighteenth century to about £10,000 a year. The House of Lords and the peers as a class, though divided along party lines, enjoyed at least as much political influence as London's

mercantile elite and monied interest. Moreover, as high wartime taxes
and the cost of polite living forced many lesser gentry landowners to
the wall, the nobility were well placed to snap up their estates. The
duke of Marlborough did particularly well out of this buyers' market,
and would die, in 1722, one of the wealthiest men in all of Europe,
with property and investments reckoned to be worth one million
pounds. The expanding size and wealth of the aristocracy helped fuel
the mania for mansion-building that gripped the elite between the
1680s and the 1740s. In 1708, the great architect Sir John Vanbrugh
– the designer of Blenheim Palace and Castle Howard – remarked that:
'All the World [by which he meant the English aristocracy] are running
mad after Building, as far as they can reach.'[120]

The later Stuart nobility proved equally adept at responding to the
commercial opportunities offered by the French wars. Whig peers in
particular invested heavily in the stock market, in effect becoming
monied men themselves. Some of the country's most profitable coal
and lead mines were owned by noblemen, who made a fortune from
the increased demand for raw materials after 1688. 'Gentlemanly
capitalism' was not the oxymoron in Britain that it was in some
continental countries. On the contrary, the great and the good repeatedly
extolled the virtues of commerce, while taking care, of course, to
preserve a due distinction of rank between themselves and the trading
classes.

Yet despite the proliferation of grand country houses during the later
Stuart period, there was a growing tendency among the aristocracy to
disengage from rural society. Some noblemen abandoned their country
estates and the burdens of traditional hospitality for the company and
gaiety of the town, while the growth of parliamentary government after
1688 obliged the more conscientious peers to reside close to Westminster.
Virtually all great landowners, whether they enjoyed country life or
not, were losing their sense of obligation to and connection with their
tenantry. From the late seventeenth century they began to have walls
built, hedges and trees planted, public footpaths closed, and in some
cases entire villages moved, in an effort to put greater distance between
themselves and the rural hoi polloi. The gap left by this withdrawal of
the elite from county affairs would be filled during the eighteenth
century by the lesser gentry and the urban bourgeoisie. The county
magistracy, once the preserve of the gentry, began to be colonised by
clergymen and 'trading' justices.

Sensitised by the civil wars to the dangers of popularity and enthusiasm, the middling sort would establish an iron grip on parish government after 1660, and looked to join their betters in the ranks of polite society. As for the common people, the aristocracy's retreat from rural life was more likely to encourage insolence and insubordination. Villagers would doff their hats and tug their forelocks by day, and poach game, maim livestock and pull down fences by night. Overall, the period 1660–1714 was not the worst of times for the labouring poor. A static population meant low inflation and a modest rise in real wages. The French wars and the growth in manufacturing offered good job opportunities for the working man; and for those who could not find gainful employment there was always the promise of a new life in the colonies. At least the poor did not starve en masse as they would do with depressing regularity in France and the Scandinavian countries until the early nineteenth century.

Politeness was a powerful ameliorating force in later Stuart Britain. Amid the incessant chatter of polite society it was possible if not to forget party quarrels, then at least to reach a gentlemanly modus vivendi. Religious divisions were narrowing, too, as the Toleration Act and the trend towards a less doctrinaire, more polite, style of Christianity gradually blurred the lines separating Anglicans and Dissenters. But the strongest force for political unity among British Protestants was a desire to contain the power of Catholic France – a desire that the Glorious Revolution and the accession of the Calvinist, warlike William III would finally allow the governing classes to indulge. They might differ as to the means, but the end – maintaining the 'balance of Christendom' in order to preserve Protestant liberties at home – was generally agreed. The treaty of Utrecht in 1713 and the succession of George I the following year represented no more than qualified victories in the struggle against French popery. Perhaps a greater cause for optimism would be the news that reached Britain in September 1715 of the death, after seventy-two years on the French throne, of His Most Christian Majesty, Louis XIV.

6

The Balance of Europe, 1714–54

Tho' the malcontents in Britain warmly declaimed against a land war, and urged, that as an Island, we should vigorously carry on the war by sea, and take no share in the affairs of the Continent; Yet 'tis certainly the interest of Britain to maintain the power of the House of Austria as the only proper Rival to the House of Bourbon [France]; for whoever conquers and gives law on the Continent, will soon do so likewise in the Islands; and if once the Netherlands and united Provinces are subdued by France, the Religion, the liberties, the trade of Britain cannot long subsist.

Anon., 'A Concise Account of the War begun with
Spain in 1739' (c.1748)[1]

Germans and Jacobites

> When George in Pudding time came o'er,
> And Moderate Men looked big, Sir,
> My Principles I chang'd once more,
> And so became a Whig, Sir.
> And thus Preferment I procur'd,
> From our Faith's great Defender
> And almost every day abjur'd
> The Pope, and the Pretender.[2]

It is hard to imagine a more dismissive label for the reign of a monarch – or two in this case, George I and George II – than 'Pudding time'. Although very unfair to the early Georgian period, the phrase, with its associations of easy, unexciting indulgence, has stuck. Admittedly, the first two Georges, who reigned from 1714 until 1760, were not the most glamorous of monarchs. Plodding and boorish, they lacked the imagination to blunder on the magnificent scale of some of their

predecessors. Their lives and times have typically been thought of as
an age of oligarchy and, after the convulsions of previous reigns, stability
– a world made safe at last for the propertied elite. The images the
early Georgian era tends to evoke are those of bewigged, red-faced
gentlemen drinking, hunting and otherwise indulging themselves. And
it is true that after the 1710s there is little of the high drama of the
Stuart period – the great constitutional crises, the revolutions, the armed
stand-offs in London.

Yet if we shift the perspective slightly, away from Westminster and
Whitehall to the Jacobite heartlands in Scotland and Ireland, or to the
gin-fuelled London crowd so scathingly detailed by William Hogarth
(1697–1764), there is still plenty of hurly-burly to be found. Borough
corporations were still riven by party rivalries, as they had been since
the mid-seventeenth century. Henry Fielding (1707–54), the novelist and
social reformer, insisted that even parish vestries were the scene of 'plots
and circumventions, parties and factions, equal to those ... found in
the courts'.[3] Perhaps a quarter of the English aristocracy would flirt with
Jacobitism at one point or other during the period 1714–45, which was
many more than had done so under William III and Queen Anne. And
when not at each other's throats, the better sort of Whig and Tory glanced
nervously at the common people, particularly London's vast and unruly
populace. Egged on by a growing and largely unfettered press, the honest
householders of southern England worked themselves into a moral frenzy
during the late 1710s and early 1720s, as criminal gangs robbed people
in the streets, held up coaches and poached game seemingly at will. Not
since the 1590s had men of property been so worried about the threat
of crime and the breakdown of law and order. Many blamed this scourge
of lawlessness on the nation's favourite new tipple, gin. But more insidious still, thought critics of the government, was the ill example of a
ruling elite rotten with vice and political corruption.

Crime and disorder were often the cue for good Hanoverians like
Daniel Defoe to smell a Jacobite rat. In 1715 he took it for a 'solid
Maxim' that 'whoever is for this MOBBING and RABBLING must be
a Friend to the Pretender'.[4] He was wrong to see Jacobitism under so
many beds, but right to be worried about the Jacobite military threat.
Scottish Jacobites mounted two invasions of England during the first
half of the eighteenth century, in 1715 and 1745; and they were involved
in one way or another with invasion plans by either France or Spain in
1708, 1719, 1744, 1746 and 1759. Britain had been drawn into the
mainstream of European affairs by the Glorious Revolution, and for

the next twenty-five years or so her role had seemed clear: defeat Bourbon France and all its works (under which heading came Jacobitism). But the death of Louis XIV in 1715 and the accession of his five-year-old great-grandson, Louis XV, under a regency government, threw all the old certainties in doubt. The French were now all for a quiet life while they repaired their war-torn economy and waited for their king to come of age.

In these altered circumstances, was the national interest still best served by playing a full and active part in Europe? Or should Britain concentrate instead on building her maritime empire? This foreign policy dilemma was made all the harder to resolve by the rise during the first half of the century of two new powers in the east, Prussia and Russia, and the decline of Britain's old allies the Austrian Habsburg empire and the Dutch republic. The old order was gone, and Britain's statesmen would now struggle to find solid ground amid the shifting sands of continental politics. When war with France resumed in the mid-1740s the British would find themselves dangerously isolated in Europe and facing the prospect of military encirclement by the French. If this was stability then most Britons would happily have swapped it for the glorious instability of Marlborough's day.

The 54-year-old Georg Ludwig, elector of Hanover (1660–1727), was proclaimed George I, king of Great Britain and Ireland, on 1 August 1714. He boasted two attributes that recommended him to most of his new subjects. First, he was the eldest surviving Protestant of Stuart royal descent (he was James I's great-grandson). And second, he hated French popery. One Whig declared him 'not to be exceeded in his Zeal against the intended universal Monarchy of France, and so is most hearty for the common Cause of Europe'.[5] And George had indeed contributed manfully to the German war effort in the Grand Alliance against Louis XIV. His greatest virtue as a ruler was prudent self-interest. Although Hanover, with its robust form of monarchy, remained his first love, and he spent many contented months there while king of Great Britain, he did a decent job of sticking within the accepted limits of the British constitution and the royal prerogative. This said a lot for his good sense as king. But only his considerable girth might justify calling him a well-rounded human being. To the cultivated and witty courtier Philip Stanhope, earl of Chesterfield, who knew him well, he was nothing but 'an honest, dull German gentleman'.[6] In company he was stiff and withdrawn, and much preferred socialising in private with 'waggs and buffoons'.[7] He shrank away from crowds and any form of public display. It was probably his reserved nature as much as his liking for an 'enlightened', Germanic style of kingship that led him to reject court rituals that made the monarch an object of veneration. The cult of sacred kingship that the Tudors and early Stuarts had so carefully nurtured had largely vanished by the end of George I's reign. His diversions were of the usual variety for early modern monarchs – namely, hunting and sex – but unlike Henry VIII and James I, who had also been devotees of the chase, he did not possess an interesting intellectual hinterland. His pleasures, like his mind, were 'lowly sensuall . . . No woman came amiss to him, if she was but very willing, very fat, and had great breasts'.[8] Too unimaginative to deviate from the religion he had been raised in, he was a practising Lutheran – a creed alien to Britain, though influential in the formation of the Church of England – but had little difficulty conforming to Anglican worship while he was in England (he never went to Scotland or Ireland). His preferred language was French, which was the language of his British court. His command of English improved, but remained rudimentary.

George's very obvious foreignness met with a predictable reaction from a section of the British people. Pamphlets and broadsides attacked the new king and his German entourage as greedy interlopers, and their 'Germanised' Whig supporters as sectaries, atheists and enemies of the Church of England.[9] Tory writers eagerly recycled their old anti-Williamite rhetoric, accusing the court of putting foreign – in this case, Hanoverian – interests before those of Britain. More damningly, they alleged that there was a Whig and court-backed plot to use instability on the Continent as an excuse for maintaining a standing army at home – for there remained, insisted Tories, 'an old English spirit in the People' that could not be subdued except with 'Red-Coats, the usual Instruments of Bondage'.[10] This talk of England in thrall to despotical Germans would be a staple of Tory and Jacobite propaganda for decades to come. At George's coronation in October 1714, Church-in-danger mobs rioted in many English towns, smashing up the loyalists' celebrations and shouting 'Down with Roundheads', 'Down with foreigners', 'A new Restoration' and other Tory slogans.[11] The violence flared up again in the spring and summer of 1715, and it was even worse this time. Dissenters' churches were attacked or demolished, Whig-owned windows broken, and in London there were street battles between the rioters and the militia. The capital would continue to be rocked by anti-Hanoverian riots until late 1716.

George was not entirely the innocent victim in all this Tory mud-slinging and rioting. Like the Whigs, he regarded the 1713 treaty of Utrecht as a Tory betrayal of Hanover and the rest of Britain's allies. George arrived in England, therefore, with a deep dislike and distrust of the Tories. He snubbed their leaders in public, stripped them of high office, and selected his first cabinet almost exclusively from men of proven commitment to the Hanoverian succession and a Eurocentric foreign policy – namely, Whigs. It was not long before Tory grandees stopped coming to court altogether, or bowed to the times and turned Whig themselves. The political proscription of the Tories was not confined to central government. Many were purged from county magistrates benches and other local offices in 1714–15 and replaced by Whigs. The coronation riots were the Tory crowd's way of showing its disgust at what seemed George's rejection of the Church of England's most loyal defenders.

Appeals to high church feeling and popular xenophobia were about the Tories' only option in the face of the crown's support for the Whig party in the 1715 general election. Not that it did them much good. The Whigs mounted a skilful propaganda campaign, portraying them-selves as patriotic upholders of the Protestant succession and the Tories as Jacobite and French stooges – and the boroughs, if not the counties, bought it. The Whigs won a majority of 341 to 217 in the Commons, which they then used to bear down even harder on the Tories. The Riot Act introduced in July 1715, which empowered troops to fire on rioters if they refused to disperse, was just one of several measures that the Whigs used to stamp out Tory protests. Indeed, the use of the military to overawe the people would be widespread and sometimes brutal during the early years of George's reign. The Whigs had replaced the Tories as Britain's party of authoritarian government. At Westminster, prosecutions were begun against Harley and other Tories who had 'set on foot a private, separate, dishonourable, and destructive negotiation of peace' – in other words, the treaty of Utrecht.[12] Tory leaders were imprisoned or forced into exile. Leading this parliamentary witch-hunt was the Whig party's rising star and most formidable debater, the Member for King's Lynn, Robert Walpole (1676–1745).

The sight of English Tories routed and rioting in England contributed powerfully to the Jacobite rising in Scotland of 1715–16. The 1707 union had been deeply unpopular with a great many Scots, and had a Franco-Jacobite invasion fleet managed to sail in the right direction in 1708 and make landfall it would almost certainly have triggered a major rebellion in Scotland. Seven years on and Scottish grievances had not subsided – quite the reverse. New taxes had been imposed on Scotland by the English-dominated Westminster Parliament, while the supposed economic benefits of union had largely failed to materialise. Nationalist resentment, and xenophobic dislike of George I, translated readily into Jacobitism, especially among Scotland's long-suffering episcopalian and Catholic communities. A Jacobite rebellion in Scotland was unlikely to succeed, however, without French backing, and that was not on the cards after Utrecht and the death of Louis XIV.

Yet if the French could not help the Jacobites then it seemed that the English might – or at least that was how the Pretender and his court in France interpreted the 1714–15 riots in England. Some of the rioters genuinely wanted James instead of George. But though dislike of the new Hanoverian–Whig regime was running high, this did not mean that large numbers would rise to put a popish one in its place, especially without significant foreign intervention. The majority of rioters were probably aggrieved Tory–Anglicans, or just plain aggrieved, but not Jacobites. The only community in England that might be counted on in a fight was the Catholics, and they made up a tiny fraction of the population. Most leading Jacobites recognised that success was impossible without powerful foreign backing. One of the few who did not was the embittered Scottish Tory John Erskine, 6th earl of Mar. He agreed with the Pretender – 'now more than ever Now or Never!'[13]

In September 1715, Mar raised the standard of 'James the 8th and 3rd' at Braemar, in Aberdeenshire. Within a few weeks he had attracted a massive 20,000 followers, including eighteen peers, and Lowlanders as well as clansmen. Yet when the Scottish Jacobites most needed a Montrose or a Dundee to lead the charge, none was to hand. Mar knew nothing about soldiering, and dithered when he should have attacked, even though he had all of Scotland at his mercy. After almost overpowering a government army at the battle of Sheriffmuir, in November, he failed to press home his advantage, and instead retreated northwards. A 2,000-strong Jacobite invasion force penetrated as far as Preston, to link up with a small rising by the Lancashire Catholics, but as soon as the rebels encountered government troops they surrendered. By the time the Pretender landed in Scotland in December, Mar's army was melting away while government forces were being strengthened by English and Dutch regiments. The Pretender himself did little to inspire confidence in his men. On the contrary, they came to despise him for his lack of spirit and vigour. After little over a month in Scotland he beat a hasty and humiliating retreat back to France, just as his father had done after the battle of the Boyne. Perhaps under strong leadership the Jacobites might have held Scotland for a season. But without support from France or the English people to prevent the full weight of Leviathan bearing down on it, the 'Fifteen was only ever going to end one way.

Ireland in 1715 was not so much the dog that failed to bark as one that had already had the fight beaten out of it. The voters – Ireland's Protestant minority – had handed the Tories an even greater drubbing at the polls in 1715 than they had suffered in the English general election, leaving the Whigs firmly in control of the Dublin Parliament for years to come. Ireland's Catholics, meanwhile, though overwhelmingly Jacobite in sympathy, still lay prostrate under the burdens of defeat in 1691. They would not risk another rebellion unless it was backed by the Catholic powers. Moreover, those that might have led such a rebellion generally went abroad to join the Irish brigades fighting for the French, and so were lost to the Jacobite cause at home. The main troublemakers in Ireland after 1715 were its Protestant Whig elite and the Dublin Parliament, which was the most powerful legislature in the Georgian realm after Westminster. Resentful of the way Britain's Whig oligarchs exploited Ireland for power and profit, they adopted the familiar Catholic strategy of trying to assert Ireland's sole dependence upon the English crown, not upon the British Parliament at Westminster. It would take some aggressive legislating by Westminster, and political finessing by politicians at Whitehall, to re-establish stable relations between the two Parliaments and their respective leaders.

The 'Fifteen came as manna to the Whigs as they progressed towards the promised land of one-party rule. Besides giving added force to their claims that the Tories were crypto-Jacobites, it handed the government a good excuse to cull yet more Tory officeholders in the localities. The final blasting of Tory hopes came with the passing of the Septennial Act in 1716, which lengthened the interval between British general elections from three to seven years. Frequent elections, claimed the Whigs, had made the voters the tools of factious and dishonest politicians (i.e. the Tories), and so destabilised domestic politics that Britain was seen as a liability in the eyes of its continental allies. Behind these high-sounding motives for electoral reform was the grubby reality that the Act gave the Whig grandees plenty of time to fine-tune their methods of political patronage – indispensable in nurturing Leviathan – and generally to secure a good tight grip on the levers of power. Unless the Whigs fell out among themselves the Tories were looking at a long time – six years at least – in opposition.

Among the big fish in the stagnating pond of British politics there were three that particularly caught the eye: James, Earl Stanhope (1673–1721), Charles, Viscount Townshend (1674–1738), and Townshend's brother-in-law Robert Walpole. The king had made Stanhope and Townshend his secretaries of state for southern and northern Europe respectively, which were positions of even greater importance now that Britain was conjoined with a continental state. Both men were hard-working, intelligent, and well versed in European affairs. Neither was agreeable company, however. Stanhope had a 'vehemency and fervidness of speech, that always hurt his hearers';[14] while Townshend's inelegant and vulgar conversation annoyed everyone subjected to it. Walpole, on the other hand, was an artful speaker with great skill at winning friends and influencing people. Appointed first lord of the Treasury, he had an unrivalled grasp of the workings of government, particularly state finances. With a supportive king, majorities in both Houses, and the Tories in retreat, this new Whig junto looked impregnable. Nevertheless, there was one highly sensitive area of policy it had yet to master, and that was how to balance British and Hanoverian interests in a European state system without the familiar, ultimately stabilising, presence of an aggressive French monarchy.

Balance and Bubble, 1714–22

George I and his Whig ministers were keen to re-engage with 'the general system of Europe' (Townshend's phrase) that the Tories had tried to opt out of during the last years of Queen Anne's reign.[15] Their thinking on Britain's relations with the Continent was shaped by one concept in particular: the balance of Europe.

Balance-of-power language was slowly replacing the older and often more stridently Protestant rhetoric used in condemnation of universal monarchy. It focused less on the need to destroy 'popish' states such as Bourbon France and more simply on containing them by means of a system of alliances. France, so the theory ran, should be allowed, like other great European powers, to remain strong in order to form one side of the balance. An under-mighty France was potentially as great a danger to the balance as an over-mighty one. As Defoe succinctly put it, 'a just Ballance of Power is the Life of Peace'.[16] Europe's Protestant states – the so-called 'Protestant interest' – were thought to constitute a vital weight on one side of the scales, but as in former times, they could only act effectively in alliance with non-popish Catholic states. Britain and Hanover might therefore have to make periodic shifts between the continental powers in order to preserve the balance of Europe and (as one British foreign minister put it) to 'prevent any one from aggrandising itself in such a Manner, as to become formidable to the rest'.[17] For the Whigs this meant maintaining a professional army, if only a small one, ready to intervene against continental aggressors. They saw this 'continentalist' strategy as vital to the maintenance of British interests overseas. If France, for example, was allowed to grow too powerful in Europe then it was feared she would have a free hand to challenge more effectively for colonial supremacy. The Tories, as ever, tended to favour a 'blue-water' or navalist strategy, insisting that maritime power would generally suffice to hold the balance between the contending powers. A standing army, they argued, might well be used to destroy the domestic liberties it was intended to preserve.

Although the handiwork of Eurosceptical Tories, the 1713 treaty of Utrecht actually committed Britain to remaining very much involved in continental affairs. By its terms, Britain became a guarantor of an ambitious blueprint for preserving the future peace and stability of Europe. The Whigs may have thought the treaty a sell-out at the time, but once back in power they were keen to defend and build upon it. This meant a new treaty with the Dutch in 1715, and with the Austrian Habsburg emperor Charles VI (1685–1740) in 1716. These alliances looked to future security, as well as appeasing the Dutch and the Austrians after the Tories had abandoned them in 1713. Much more remarkable was the treaty signed in November 1716 with the grand old adversary, France – now, of course, sans Louis XIV. The Dutch signed up too in 1717 and the Austrians in 1718, to form the Quadruple Alliance. The four allies did not trust each other very much, but they were all keen to avoid another war, and, in the case of Britain and France, to gain time for their new ruling regimes – those of George I and the regency of the boy-king Louis XV – to establish themselves. As Britain's allies, the French were obliged to recognise the Hanoverian succession and to expel the Pretender and his court, which took up residence in Rome on a small papal pension.

The alliance with France quickly proved its worth against southern Europe's new rogue state, Spain. Although Britain signed commercial treaties with Spain in 1715 and 1716, she remained a major trading rival. More to the point, she was the only power unwilling to accept the terms of the treaty of Utrecht – mainly because the forceful Italian princess Elizabeth Farnese, second wife of the Spanish king Philip V, was determined to regain Spain's ancient territories in Italy (forfeited at Utrecht to Austria) as inheritances for her children. In 1717–18 the Spanish retook Sardinia and Sicily, and as the Austrians had no navy to speak of there was little they could do to stop them. In joining the Quadruple Alliance in 1718, however, they became allies of Britain and France, who *did* have navies, and who were both determined, for commercial and dynastic reasons, that Spain should stick to the script agreed at Utrecht. Without bothering with the tiresome formality of actually declaring war, a royal navy fleet under Admiral John Byng engaged a smaller Spanish force off Cape Passaro, Sicily, in August 1718. The Spanish ships proved no match for the more heavily armed British first- and second-raters and most were captured. Yet crushing though the victory at Cape Passaro was, it did little to dislodge the Spanish from their conquests in Italy, or to convince them that the allies meant business. With an audacity equal to Byng's own, they sponsored a Jacobite invasion of the Scottish Highlands in 1719, although spring gales prevented them landing enough troops to trouble the government's forces for very long. In the end it took concerted pressure by the allies, culminating in a French invasion of northern Spain, to really drive the message home. Early in 1720 the Spanish admitted defeat and themselves joined the Quadruple Alliance.

If chastising the Spanish in the Mediterranean worked to the advantage of both George I and Britain, the same could not be said of British involvement in trying to calm the equally troubled waters of Europe's northern sea, the Baltic. The problem for Whitehall here was Hanover. Neither the defence of the Electorate against Peter the Great's Russia and other expansionist states in the region, nor George's own designs on the territory of his neighbours, notably the Swedish outposts in northern Germany, related in any obvious way to British national interests. Whereas George was naturally worried by Swedish and, increasingly, Russian aggression on the borders of the Electorate, all the British really cared about was ensuring an uninterrupted supply of essential commodities from the Baltic, especially the timber, tar, hemp and cordage that was needed for building warships. George's ministers had to perform a delicate balancing act, therefore – between, on the one hand, their need to retain the king's trust, and on the other to preserve their credit with a public and Parliament which resented anything that smacked of the subordination of British to Hanoverian interests. The deployment of a British fleet in the Baltic in the later

1710s made walking this political tightrope particularly difficult. George was pleased, of course, but it diverted ships from homeland defence and risked dragging Britain into the war between Sweden and her imperial rivals. It also raised major constitutional issues, for loaning out the navy to a 'foreign' monarch (George in his capacity as elector) was a clear breach of the 1701 Act of Settlement.

A split now emerged in the Whig ministry between Stanhope and his friends, who were prepared to indulge George on the question of Hanover, and Townshend, Walpole and their supporters, who were not. Townshend's difficulties with the king's Baltic policy saw him removed from office in mid-1717, at which Walpole resigned from the cabinet in support. This was a major blow for George, and even more for the Whig party. At a stroke, the government had lost one of its leading foreign policy experts, along with indisputably the best man at the Treasury. The money markets got the jitters – Walpole had been seen as a safe pair of hands by the City – and the government was left dangerously exposed to its critics in Parliament and the press. Nor were the ousted Whigs prepared to suffer in silence. Walpole, in particular, made a nuisance of himself in the Commons, where he and other anti-ministerial Whigs joined with the Tories to attack the government. He became so worked up lambasting his former colleagues that on one occasion he suffered 'a violent bleeding at the nose', and had to leave the House.[18] In an attempt to reunite the Whig party behind the ministry, Stanhope and allies launched an attack on the Church of England, and succeeded in removing some of the obstructions on the Dissenters holding public office. They also played up the Jacobite menace, revealing details of a Swedish plot in support of the Pretender. As far as foreign policy was concerned, George, aided by Stanhope, continued to have his way. But by 1719 the government's majority in the Commons was beginning to crumble under repeated assault from secessionist Whigs, Tories, and Walpole's impassioned oratory.

Besides shooting itself in the foot, the Whig party was caught in the cross-fire between the socially dysfunctional royals. Divorcing and then imprisoning his wife in 1694 had not been the ideal way for George to earn the affections of their son – from 1714 the Prince of Wales – who grew up disliking his father intensely and determined to cross him wherever he could. Predictably, he lent his support to the ousted Whigs, and they reciprocated. The king hit back by banning the prince from all royal palaces, and taking over the upbringing of his children. The quarrel between the two royals grew so bitter that one government minister actually urged George to send the prince to the colonies unless he showed more filial respect.

The madness of King George and the feuding Whigs ceased as quickly as it had arisen. During the winter of 1719–20 it became clear to the disputants that their continued quarrelling was self-defeating. The only winners would be Tories and Jacobites. Walpole used his considerable influence with Princess Caroline (1683–1737), the wife of the Prince of Wales, 'whom she governed absolutely', to persuade her husband to act (if nothing else) the dutiful son.[19] In April 1720 the prince made his formal submission to the king. Relations between them would always be strained, but they managed at least an icy civility towards each other. The Whig grandees also decided to make their peace with one another, and were observed walking 'with their Arms round each other to show they are now all one'.[20] Townshend and Walpole were brought back into the ministry – though in less powerful positions than when they had left it – and there seems to have been a tacit agreement by George to maintain a proper distance between his British and Hanoverian affairs, and by all the Whig grandees to support his interests in Germany.

The grandees had barely time to repowder their wigs and reapply their maquillage (in a fixed smile of party unity) before the South Sea Bubble burst in their faces. The South Sea Company had been founded in 1711 as a rival to the Whig-dominated Bank of England, but by 1720 had attracted investors from all political quarters, among them the king himself. The sea involved was the south Atlantic, and the company's most prized asset was the *asiento*: the contract obtained from the Spanish crown at the treaty of Utrecht to supply slaves to its American colonies. War with Spain in 1718–20 had obviously been bad for business, and hence the company had pitched upon an ambitious flotation scheme, recently pioneered in France, to take over the national debt. By offering the Treasury £7.5 million, together with over half a million in cash and share options (bribes) to politicians, courtiers and probably the king himself, the company secured an Act of Parliament allowing public creditors to exchange their government annuities for SSC shares – an attempt, in effect, to privatise the national debt. Not content with letting the scheme stand on its own merits, however, the company's directors tried to lure in investors by resorting to what the House of Lords termed 'the fraudulent and pernicious practice of Stock-jobbing' – that is, driving up share prices by ramping the market.[21]

Fraudulent it may have been, but stock-jobbing was like a red rag to the rampant bull market of 1720. Since the 1690s there had been a huge upsurge of interest in financial speculation among those with spare capital to invest. And to a consumerist society that had been primed for generations on stories of the fortunes to be made from colonial trade, the SSC share offer seemed too good an opportunity to pass up. Even before the company secured its Act, in April 1720, it was reported that London was 'quite mad about the South Sea . . . one can hear nothing else talked of'.[22] In the first half of 1720 there was a frenzy of share-buying in the City, and between the markets of London, Paris and Amsterdam. Investors crowded Exchange Alley from dawn till dusk – 'all go thither as to the mines of Potosi. Nobility, Ladys, Brokers, & footmen all upon a level'.[23] The price of SSC shares shot up dramatically, from £120 in January 1720 to £1,000 by June, and there were increases in the stock value of other companies too, though nothing on the scale of the SSC. The effect, as some at the time predicted, was to push the price of SSC shares well above the company's actual worth; and the result was equally predictable. Parliamentary moves to regulate the stock market, and a withdrawal of foreign investment, triggered a rapid deflation of the Bubble that autumn, and the SSC share price fell back to below £200.

Canny investors who had sold before the crash were richly rewarded for their foresight. But they were a minority. Although Walpole made a small fortune playing the market in 1720, he lost money on SSC shares. Other losers by SSC shares included Sir Isaac Newton and King George, who said goodbye to £56,000. But those who suffered most in the crash were those investors who had borrowed heavily against rising share prices and then failed to cash in in time. They went to the wall, sometimes taking their creditors with them. Suicides in London in 1720 rose well above the normal yearly average. The general belief was that the Bubble had ruined thousands of innocent people, and reduced a multitude of families to poverty. In fact, the bulk of SSC shares had been purchased not by the general public but by the great and the good, and consequently most investors were not immiserated when the Bubble burst. But this did not stop the press fulminating against the company directors, stock-jobbers and corrupt politicians who had 'bubbled' the people. A new weekly journal, *Cato's Letters*, appeared in November 1720 with the express purpose of bringing the guilty parties to justice: 'Let us pursue to Disgrace, Destruction, and even Death those who have brought this Ruin upon us, let them be ever so great, or ever so many.'[24]

The Bubble was the first great international stock-market crash, and in terms of the value wiped off share prices one of the worst in world history. Yet what made it such an emotive issue at the time was not so much its financial consequences as its political and social implications. It had exposed what many believed was the corruption and cronyism at the heart of government. Bought with dirty money by greedy private speculators, the politicians had in turn sold the public down the river (there was, of course, no thought for the West Africans sold into slavery as a result of the company's activities). Critics, moralists and satirists all had great sport with the Bubble. Perhaps nothing better captures contemporary outrage over the scandal than Hogarth's famous work of 1721, *Emblematical Print on the South Sea Scheme*, in which a winged devil with a scythe throws chunks of Fortune's body to the greedy London crowd (see illus. 13). The Bubble repelled and fascinated because it was seen as symptomatic of a society consumed by self-interest and luxury. As one hack put it: 'Our prevailing Passions in England, of late, have been Hope, Avarice, and Ambition; which have had such a headlong Force upon the People, that they are become wretched and poor, by a ravenous Appetite to grow great and rich.'[25]

For all the froth and splutter in the press about ruined families and blighted lives, the Bubble had little effect on the wider British economy. What it did leave was public finances in disarray and a nasty political mess. But cometh the hour, cometh the man. Walpole, with the help of his banker, conjured up various schemes to restructure the national debt and force the South Sea Company to disgorge some of its ill-gotten gains. His grasp of financial policy, indeed his mere presence in the ministry, went a long way to reassuring the markets and to restoring confidence in the government's handling of the nation's finances. Parliament's hunt for the perpetrators of what had been very largely a scandal of its own making resulted in many of the South Sea directors being stripped of their assets to compensate the sufferers. The backlash at Westminster claimed the chancellor of the Exchequer – deemed guilty of 'most notorious, dangerous and infamous corruption' and sent to the Tower – and the first lord of the Treasury, both of which offices were given to Walpole.[26] Stanhope died of a stroke early in 1721 after retiring ill from a heated exchange in the Lords with the duke of Wharton, who had lost £120,000 in the Bubble. Clearly parliamentary debates could be injurious to one's health in the eighteenth century. Townshend replaced Stanhope as secretary of state for northern Europe.

Walpole emerged from the crisis with not only money in the bank but also great political credit. He was now powerful enough to obstruct

investigation of the Bubble – much to the relief of a highly compro-
mised court and cabinet. His adroit management helped the Whig party
shrug off the effects of the 1720 crash and win another big Commons
majority in the 1722 general election. The Whigs had probably not won
the popular vote, but that did not matter, for the electoral system was
rigged in their favour (as we shall see). Walpole followed up his party's
electoral victory by exploiting revelations of a crack-brained Jacobite
plot for Russian-sponsored invasions of Scotland and Ireland, to create
the (largely false) impression that only prompt government action had
averted a major rebellion. His seeming vigilance in defence of the
Hanoverian succession did much to banish memories within his party
and at court of his disloyalty during the Whig schism. Whig MPs now
united behind him, and the king showed him more trust than he had
previously. As usual when the Jacobite card was played, the losers were
the Tories, some of whom had foolishly, if only briefly, dabbled in the
plot. Now they were left utterly discredited, and seemingly in terminal
decline. The Whigs, on the other hand, looked a sound investment for
the future, and the bubble of political expectation was growing around
one man in particular: Walpole.

The old system, 1722–39

The markets had stabilised and the Whigs seemed closer than ever to
one-party rule, yet there was still an unsettled feeling to British affairs
in the early 1720s – a case of more questions than answers. How, for
example, would the ministry's parliamentary supremo, Robert Walpole,
keep his position? Surely so corrupt a figure would attract too much
criticism from press and public to retain his Commons majority or the
king's favour for very long? And in foreign affairs, could Britain and
its exposed continental appendage, Hanover, rely on their former enemy
France to contain the rising powers of central and eastern Europe? The
Continent was full of enemies, warned one government minister, just
waiting to 'throw off the mask';[27] and although the navy was strong
enough to intervene effectively in the Mediterranean and Baltic, it would
require troops on the ground to preserve the balance of Europe, and
yet neither Britain nor Hanover was a land power.

Walpole mostly left the king and his secretaries of state to worry about
the balance of Europe; his sphere was domestic policy. His rise to

greatness was akin in some ways to that of another East Anglian squire made good: Oliver Cromwell. Besides their similar backgrounds they both scaled the summit of power at a relatively late stage in their careers and via routes pioneered by more radical politicians. But there the similarities ended. Walpole was florid and fat of belly, coarse-featured and often coarse-minded, fond of bawdy stories (of which he had an immense store), and shameless in lining his pockets from the public purse. He was also a political prodigy in a way that Cromwell had never been. No politician of the time possessed his tact or persuasive skills, his intuitive grasp of human weakness and motive, and none was better at managing men and, consequently, Parliament. This is what Chesterfield had to say about him:

> An artfull rather than eloquent Speaker, he saw as by intuition, the disposition of the house [of Commons], and pressed or receeded accordingly. So clear in stating the most intricate matters, especially in the Finnances, that while he was speaking the most ignorant thought that they understood what they really did not. Money, not Prerogative, was the chief Engine of his administration, and he employed it with a success that in a manner disgraced humanity.[28]

But Walpole's administration was exceptional – or disgraceful, depending on one's point of view – only in performance, not in its basic design. In essence, it was a souped-up version of the prototype developed by the Independent grandees back in the 1640s. It used much the same instruments – talented politicians in both Houses, and control of key committees – and ran on the same fuel: money in the form of bribes and patronage. If Walpole had an easier ride than the grandees it was largely thanks to the finely tuned machinery of party government. The Hanoverian Whigs were far more organised both at Westminster and nationally than any Civil War faction had ever been. In addition, the idea of party allegiance was much more deeply ingrained by the 1720s, if still tainted. Another important difference was that the smooth running of the machine became for Walpole almost an end in itself. Securing the Hanoverian succession was his only big political principle. Otherwise he liked to travel light, unencumbered by ideals or scruples. In his own words he was 'no Saint, no Spartan, no reformer'.[29]

The real innovation in Walpole's ministry was the very direct and personal link he provided between king and Commons. He was the first political grandee to reject a peerage so that he could remain in, and help manage, the lower House. It was his ability to get the crown's business through the Commons that guaranteed him the frequent and easy access to the king that was still vital to ministerial power. Control of the Treasury, and with it the secret service money – effectively a party-political slush fund used to create what one critic of Leviathan termed 'a criminal Dependency' in Parliament – made him even more valuable to George, who nonetheless considered him a vulgar upstart.[30] Walpole's real admirer at court was the influential Princess Caroline, the future queen consort. His success with the royals, which saw him made a knight of the Garter in 1726, was all the more remarkable in that he did not speak their customary language, French.

Walpole's increasingly assured command of domestic affairs contrasted with the state of near-constant jitters among his Whig colleagues handling foreign policy. Townshend and his fellow secretary of state John Lord Carteret (1690–1763) shared George's sense of foreboding at the growing might of Russia in the Baltic and along the eastern borders of Germany. Townshend referred to 'the manifest dangers and irritations which a neighbour [of Hanover] so formidable so restless and so enterprising must inevitably give rise to'.[31] Fearing the worst in the Baltic, Walpole began looking to the American colonies as an alternative source of essential naval supplies. Not until the death of Tsar Peter the Great in 1725, and the consequent likelihood of domestic turmoil in Russia, could Britain and Hanover afford to relax their guard against the Russian bear. By then, however, George and his ministers were getting worked up about a threat to European stability from a new and unexpected quarter, Emperor Charles VI. Although George was keen to assure Vienna that he wanted nothing more than to continue the 'old system' of friendship between Austria, Hanover and Britain, he was beginning to see the Austrians as something of a liability. They could offer little help to him in the Baltic or the Mediterranean, and they had proved useless in standing up to Russian aggression. In fact, Austria seemed just as land-hungry as Russia did, having recently seized considerable blocks of territory in Hungary and the Balkans from the Ottoman empire. Moreover, it had territorial ambitions in Italy and the Mediterranean. Even more worryingly, Charles's determination to strengthen his authority within the empire was widely seen as part of yet another Counter-Reformation surge against European Protestantism – what the British had no hesitation in labelling popery. Protestants everywhere once again spoke of defending the Protestant cause and the liberties of Europe in the same breath. For their part, the Austrians had not forgotten how 'perfidious Albion' had abandoned them towards the end of the War of the Spanish Succession. Nor did Charles react well to George trying to position himself at the head of Europe's Protestant interest, seeing it as a thinly veiled challenge to imperial authority.

The old system broke down dramatically in 1725 with the signing of the treaty of Vienna: an alliance of convenience between Austria and Spain (hitherto, apparently bitter enemies) to promote their various claims and grievances. Austrian diplomacy also drew the Russians into the fold. The treaty left Hanover vulnerable to imperial and Russian attack; Britain exposed to invasion from the Austrian Netherlands; and much of the Continent alarmed by what Townshend called 'the vast projects the Imperial and Spanish courts seemed to have formed together to awe and confound the rest of Europe'.[32] One of the treaty's clauses committed Austria to backing, or at least not obstructing, Spanish demands for the restitution of Gibraltar and Minorca from Britain. In response, Townshend quickly cobbled together an alliance between Britain, France, Hanover and Prussia – the treaty of Hanover – aimed at preserving the balance of power established at Utrecht. The Dutch republic, Denmark, Sweden, a host of smaller German states (mostly Protestant) and even the Ottoman empire would subsequently sign up to this alliance. Europe was now divided into two armed camps.

Although Britain's forward base in what looked like an impending European war would be Hanover, the Electorate was not a military power. Prussia could not be relied on to stand against Russia and the Empire; indeed, it would switch sides in 1726. The mainstay of British hopes, therefore, was France. As a Rhineland power the French were expert at fishing in troubled German waters, and had increased their army to 160,000 men by way of precaution. British ministers wrote of France as the 'Kingdom it is now so necessary to support in order to preserve the balance of Europe'.[33] Britain's reliance on France led to the unusual spectacle of her ministers trying to persuade the French to think seriously about military intervention in Germany. At this point, however, with Europe steeling itself for another major war, the Austrians came to their senses. On reflection, they realised that taking on Britain, France and the Ottoman empire together would not be prudent, particularly given the unreliabilty of their own allies Russia and Prussia, and the fact that Spain and its American treasure – the Austrians' war-chest – were vulnerable to British naval power. The Spanish could not even take Gibraltar, though they laid siege to it for most of 1727.

Tensions in Europe would remain high for the rest of the decade, but except for a brief period of Anglo-Spanish hostilities, in 1727–8, peace would prevail.

Britain and Spain were still unofficially at war when George I died of a stroke on his way to Hanover in June 1727. His passing was little lamented, at least in Britain, where all eyes turned to his estranged eldest son the Prince of Wales, who became, at the age of forty-three, George II (1683–1760), king of Great Britain and Ireland, and elector of Hanover.

The new king was a chip off the old blockhead. Chesterfield, who spent more than thirty years in close attendance upon him, thought his royal master mean-spirited and incapable of forming a strong attachment to anything except money. This was harsh, perhaps, but George certainly had a very bureaucratic cast of mind. He liked lists and routine. Everything in his court and personal life was highly regimented. He even fornicated by numbers, arriving at his mistress's boudoir at the same hour every day, and staying for precisely the same length of time. Though fond of music, and of opera in particular, he was not a conspicuous patron of the arts. His lack of interest in people or ideas, however, did have the saving grace of making him a conscientious king, for the business of governing would be one of his chief diversions. His others included hunting and his evening card game (his court was, if anything, even more boring and unglamorous than his father's had been). He would exert considerable influence over foreign policy – still a major area of government business – and his judgement in diplomatic matters was usually sound. Like his father he loved to play the soldier. There was nothing the first two Georges enjoyed more than a military review or fussing over regimental insignia. Again like his father, George II remained emotionally attached to Hanover, and would spend many summers there. On ticklish domestic issues he was generally guided by his ministers and above all, it seems, by his politically astute wife Queen Caroline. 'No prince', it was said at his death in 1760, 'ever kept more strictly within the bounds of power prescribed by law.'[34] And he spoke English fluently, though with a strong German accent. Overall, there was not much here to warm the hearts of his new subjects, but at least they did not riot or rebel as they had in 1714–15. The tranquillity of George's succession was perhaps his father's greatest legacy.

A change of monarch naturally raised expectations of a major cabinet reshuffle. Perhaps the Tories' travails in the political wilderness would finally be over? Queen Caroline was known to favour some degree of rapprochement with them. And surely Walpole was finished? After all, the new king had denounced him as 'a great rogue', and Townshend as 'a choleric blockhead'.[35] What saved Walpole, and with him the ministry, was the obvious fact that when it came to the all-important job of managing Parliament, he was unsurpassed. His court patron Queen Caroline probably had little trouble convincing George that Walpole was indispensable, and Walpole did himself no harm by offering to secure parliamentary approval for a larger civil list than any monarch had previously enjoyed. In the general election that by law must follow a new royal accession, the Whigs claimed 424 seats in the Commons while the Tories slipped from 180 to a mere 130.

The early years of George II's reign were the heyday of 'the Robinocracy', which was the press nickname for Walpole's insidious and apparently all-powerful administration. The coils of this serpentine system wrapped around Parliament, penetrated the court and the City, and even extended into Scotland and Ireland. Walpole's political managers in Scotland were the imperious duke of Argyll and his brother, the earl of Ilay, who were to dominate Scottish politics until the late 1730s. Walpole relied on a similar arrangement in Ireland, contracting out government business to local Whig managers. He himself concentrated on managing Parliament and the king's most intimate counsels. This was a daunting task, but he made life easier for himself by the studied moderation of his policies. He tried to steer clear of anything that might annoy the high church interest, or stir up the Whigs' old, though now rather moribund, friends the Dissenters. At the same time he worked hard to keep taxes low, well aware that high taxation during the French wars had boosted country Toryism. For most of his administration the land tax was kept down to just 2 shillings in the pound.

Walpole's first serious political blunder was his attempt in 1733 to extend the range of excise duties to tobacco and wine as part of the government's continuing effort to shift the tax burden away from land and on to trade and consumption. The scheme met with fierce opposition from powerful commercial interests in London, and was none too popular with Britain's huge retail sector either. More worrying still for Walpole was the reaction of the general public. People and press had come to regard any expansion in the tax system, particularly one that gave yet more power to the hated excise men, as an attack upon civil liberties by an intrusive and corrupt state (see illus. 14). Faced with backbench revolts in both Houses, and a well-orchestrated spoiler campaign involving riots in London and other cities, Walpole prudently dropped the whole idea. The Robinocracy had been weakened, but not fatally. The Whigs would pay for their leader's mistake with a reduced Commons majority in the 1734 general election. Once again they lost the popular vote, but did enough in the smaller, more easily corruptible boroughs to confine the Tories to a mere 149 seats. The death of Queen Caroline in 1737 devastated George, and left Walpole anxious about his position at court. But in the event it did not diminish George's loyalty to him.

The success of the Robinocracy was not all down to Walpole's considerable talents as a politician. He was also the beneficiary of a peculiarly benign political climate – for the Whig party, at least – in which the Protestant succession was secure; the monarchy was content to abide by the Williamite constitutional settlement; the Tories had been frozen out at court; Jacobitism was receding in Scotland, and prostrate in Ireland; Dissent was in the doldrums; the Church was more or less satisfied; and crown and ministerial patronage had virtually fused into one comprehensive and irresistible system.

The one front on which the Robinocracy looked vulnerable was foreign affairs. In the uncertain, post-Louis XIV world there was no knowing what foreign powers might do, or whether a politically damaging conflict of interest might arise between the British and Hanoverian strands of royal policy. Walpole did not need to have the Tory leadership's mail opened (though he did anyway) to tell him that they 'build great hopes upon the difficultys they promise themselves will arise from the foreign affairs'.[36] Foreign policy and its impact on taxation, overseas trade and the delicate balance between state power and civil liberties were easily the most divisive issues at Westminster under the first two Georges. Walpole tried to minimise the damage and expense that foreign affairs might inflict on the administration by pursuing an essentially Tory policy of limited engagement with continental Europe – in other words, avoiding a major land war, and looking to France or some other powerful ally to take the strain in preserving a peaceful equilibrium. He found this strategy easier to pursue after the retirement in 1730 of his old patron, turned enemy, Townshend, who could no longer endure playing second fiddle to his upstart protégé. He was replaced as secretary of state for southern Europe by a firm Walpolean, Thomas Pelham-Holles, duke of Newcastle (1693–1768).

A cheap and non-committal foreign policy was all very well, but by the late 1720s it meant ignoring the elephant in the room: a resurgent, expansionist France. The ambitions of Emperor Charles VI still worried London, and hence Britain and her allies moved to split the axis between

Vienna and Madrid by negotiating peace treaties with the Spanish in 1728–9 that (among other things) ended the siege of Gibraltar and restored the *asiento* to the South Sea Company. Breaking apart the treaty of Vienna enabled Walpole to reduce the number of troops in British pay, thereby easing the financial pressures at home. However, it did little to address the main cause of tension in Anglo-Spanish relations – that is, Spain's constant harassment of British merchant ships entering what the Spanish continued to regard as their exclusive territorial waters in the Americas. More to the point, a tough stance against the Austrians played into the hands of the French, who now wanted not just to clip the emperor's wings (as the British did) but to tear them off completely.

This new French assertiveness owed much to the birth of the Dauphin – young Louis XV's first male child – in 1729, which secured the French royal succession. Whig radicals (for whom the Robinocracy was a betrayal of the Glorious Revolution) and the Tories laid the blame for the re-emergence of a strong and aggressive France squarely at the feet of the government. By relying on Versailles to protect the vulnerable Hanover from its enemies further east, the ministry had aggrandised the French 'at the Expence of the Emperor [Charles VI], against Treaties, against Justice, and against all Policy'.[37] The chorus to this complaint was a familiar one: that the good of Britain and the liberties of Europe had been sacrificed to the interests of Hanover. Rather than this policy of 'Subserviency' to Versailles, the ministry's critics demanded a renewal of the 'old system', the Grand Alliance between Britain, Austria, Prussia, the Dutch republic, 'and all the antient Confederates'.[38]

The resurgent power of France was so obvious by 1730 that even the ministry could no longer ignore it. Versailles, it was clear, wanted to dismantle the emperor's power in Germany and to extend its own borders at the Habsburgs' expense, beginning with the imperial duchy of Lorraine in what is today north-eastern France. Once containing French ambitions had resumed its place at the head of Whitehall's foreign policy agenda, there was nothing else for it but to bolster the Austrian–imperial position in Germany. In short, to do a foreign policy U-turn. The recognition in London of the need to restore the old system was one of the reasons behind the resignation of the staunchly anti-imperial Townshend, the architect of the treaty of Hanover. In 1731, Britain and Austria signed the second treaty of Vienna, by which London recognised the so-called Pragmatic Sanction: Charles VI's right to leave the Austrian throne and Habsburg lands to his eldest daughter. The emperor had been pushing this proposal since 1713, when it had already looked very unlikely that he would be succeeded by a male heir.

To the French, who were busily building up an anti-Austrian and anti-Pragmatic Sanction interest among the German princes, the treaty represented a great act of betrayal by London. Though the ministry tried its best to appease and reassure Versailles, the treaty effectively killed the Anglo-French alliance that had preserved the balance of Europe since 1716. Worse still, it pushed the French into the open arms of the Spanish. In 1733 the first 'Family Compact' was concluded, uniting Bourbon France and Spain against British interests in Europe and the New World.

The upside of Britain forfeiting French good will should have been a strengthening of relations withVienna, but this largely failed to materialise. First, because the quarrel between the two had been too recent and too bitter (in the case of Britain it meant reversing nearly a decade of anti-Austrian diplomacy). Second, because the parsimonious Walpole was so determined to avoid a costly land war that he wanted to have his cake and eat it – that is, to rebuild the Grand Alliance whilst at the same time making 'pacifick Overtures' to the French.[39] The effect was to make Britain despised and distrusted by both Versailles and Vienna.

Britain's isolation in Europe deepened during the war of the Polish Succession (1733–8). Ostensibly a conflict over who should occupy the Polish throne, in reality it was another struggle between the Austrian Habsburg empire and France, the latter supported by Spain. Britain was obliged by the second treaty of Vienna to come to Austria's aid, but Walpole chose to stay neutral and save money, and British lives. He boasted to Queen Caroline in 1734: 'Madam, there are fifty thousand men slain in Europe this year, and not one Englishman.'[40] Yet while Walpole congratulated himself on his prudent policy of non-intervention, the Austrian – and, by extension, the British – position in Europe was crumbling. By the time most of the fighting was over, in 1736, the French and Spanish had chased the Austrians out of southern Italy, and France had all but annexed the imperial duchy of Lorraine. As well as smarting at their losses, the Austrians were outraged that Britain had abandoned them in their hour of need yet again. With their continental enemies beaten or, in the case of the Dutch, terrified, the French were now free either to strike into Germany (including, of course, at Hanover) and the Austrian Netherlands, or to commit more resources to building up their navy to challenge Britain's maritime empire and trade. Walpole's younger brother and political collaborator, Horatio

Walpole, was forced to concede late in 1736 that: 'Our affairs abroad are in a most loose and shattered situation.'[41] Britain and Hanover would finish the decade with not a single European ally of any substance. In fact, British diplomats thought it possible that 'the greatest part of Europe would unite against us'.[42]

Anger and frustration at the ministry's pusillanimous foreign policy welled up in the late 1730s in one mighty cry in press and Parliament for war. Not war with France, however, at least not directly, but with its ally, Spain. Much as they feared French efforts to wreck the balance of Europe, and deplored what they saw as the government's shameful treatment of the emperor, the ministry's opponents had no more wish to commit large numbers of British troops to a European land war than Walpole had. Standing armies, they insisted, were the instruments of absolutism and popery. And besides, they argued, it was pointless trying to rebuild the Grand Alliance around Austria and the Dutch republic – the ministry's craven foreign policy had left them too weak and scared to be useful allies. Rather than send armies across the Channel or hire foreign troops to prop up the tottering pillars of the old system, Britain should use the royal navy to seize its enemies' trade and colonies. Trade and empire were seen as a zero-sum game (see chapter 7); war was good for business. A noisy and self-styled 'patriot' coalition of Tories and opposition Whigs, eager to climb into power upon the ruins of the Robinocracy, demanded a vigorous maritime war. If French trade was hit then so much the better. But the navy should begin by pounding Spain.

The Spanish had been asking for trouble since their thrashing off Cape Passaro in 1718. As if menacing Gibraltar and sponsoring Jacobite invasions were not bad enough, they had waged an undeclared war on British commerce in the Americas, their coastguards boarding and searching ships in a vain but often brutal attempt to prevent illicit foreign trade (i.e. smuggling) with Spanish colonies. Walpole and the ministry had been reluctant to retaliate over such incidents, however, provoking 'great outcries' in Parliament, the press and the merchant community.[43] Eager to put himself at the head of this protest campaign was no less a figure than Frederick Lewis, Prince of Wales (1707–51), who hated his father as cordially as George had his. Dramatists, poets and artists likewise took up the warlike refrain. One satirical print of the time depicts Walpole standing idly by, his hand resting on the head of the British lion, while a Spaniard pares the beast's claws (see illus. 16). An indignant public demanded the government defend the nation's

honour and commerce, legal or otherwise, and raised a great clamour
at the plight of captured British sailors held in Spanish gaols and forced
to live on 'bug food'.[44] The public's appetite for war was whetted by the
conviction that Spain was weak and decayed, hated by its downtrodden
colonial subjects. 'Millions of miserable People wou'd bless their
Deliverers [i.e. Britain]; their Hearts and their Mines wou'd be open to
us.'[45] Spanish colonies and treasure fleets were simply there for the
taking. All it required was firm action by the government. Walpole
feared that a naval war with Spain, itself a risky and expensive undertaking, would end in a land war against France. But he was losing
ground in the cabinet to the duke of Newcastle and other bellicose
counsellors. Under intense public pressure the ministry finally gave
way, and in October 1739 war was declared.

In an ominous repeat of events in the 1580s, the crown had been
bounced into open hostilities against Spain without an ally worthy
the name. Not that this bothered the opposition. 'Protestant, free,
virtuous, united, Christian England' could withstand 'the whole force
of slavish, bigoted, unchristian popery, risen up against her', announced
the *London Daily Post* in 1739.[46] 'Under Queen Elizabeth, Sir,' exclaimed
one 'Patriotical' Whig, 'we neither had, nor did we stand in need of
Allies . . . Let us for once change our sneaking Conduct, and all will
be well.'[47]

Patriot games

The face of popular patriotism and xenophobia was immortalised in
Hogarth's painting *The Gate of Calais*, published as a print in 1749 (see
illus. 17). Most of the figures in the painting, as its title suggests, were
French: a fat monk salivating over a joint of English beef; strutting,
emaciated French soldiers; an impoverished, garlic-eating Jacobite
Highlander; bowed and cringing servants; tattered nuns, grinning foolishly at what they take to be a likeness of Christ's face in the underside
of a flatfish.[48] One of Hogarth's friends wrote a poem to accompany
the painting – a paean of praise to roast beef, that noble fare 'Unknown
to Frenchman's palate' and his diet of 'Soup-meagre, frogs, and salad!'[49]
The French more than ever, more than even the Spanish or the Irish
Catholics, were the detestable 'other' against which Protestants in Britain
(and probably Ireland too) measured their own liberties and greatness.
Popish, superstitious, decadent yet wretched, reduced to eating frogs

– the French made a satisfying and instructive comparison with freeborn and Protestant Britons, grown strong on beer and beef, resistant to the mental and physical shackles of their tyrannical neighbours. Imagining and repeatedly fighting the French became a powerful bond between Britain's various and varied Protestant communities, the key element in an emerging sense of Britishness that complemented rather than supplanted older, more localised loyalties among the English, Scottish and Welsh. Resisting popery, particularly the French variety, encouraged people everywhere in Britain to define themselves collectively in opposition to this hostile and alien force.

War with France would be equally powerful in shaping the material conditions of Hanoverian Britain. The British were effectively in open hostilities with the French or Spanish for over two decades during the first half of the eighteenth century. Only France among the European powers was so war-prone. The number of troops mobilised in Britain itself was typically less than 100,000, as against France's wartime establishment of 350,000, although France, of course, had a much larger population than Britain. On the other hand, Britain's navy and its infrastructure (dry docks, roperies, stores etc.) were more formidable, and more expensive to maintain, than those of its rivals. Between 1688 and 1815 more than 80 per cent of public money would be pumped into military expenditure – a figure exceeded only by the tiresomely bellicose Prussians. Inevitably, the British would also be more heavily taxed than almost any other European nation, including absolutist France.

The pain of all this taxing and spending would have been unbearable but for Britain's sophisticated system of deficit-financing, which in turn depended upon the creditworthiness engendered by its relatively transparent and broad-based political system. No other representative assembly in Europe commanded anything like the moral and political authority within the polity that the British Parliament did. Nor did any other state rely so heavily for its governance on the active participation of its citizens.

But how was all this wealth and strength to weigh in the balance of Europe? By intervening on the Continent, or a 'blue-water' strategy? This was the one issue that could still send sparks flying at Westminster. A London lawyer who witnessed the furious parliamentary debates of 1739 over whether to go to war against Spain was convinced that only the seventeenth century could show 'more melancholy instances of party rage than the present'.[50]

Yet once the debate moved away from contentious questions about foreign policy and the projection of British power abroad, there is evidence of a cooling of political passions after 1714, at least at Westminster. Now that they were in power and had the king on their side, the Whigs abandoned the subversive ideas they had inherited from the Essexians and the Civil War parliamentarians. Whig adherence to the 'revolution principles' of contractual monarchy and the people's right of resistance had been dwindling since the 1690s, and after 1714 the Whig leadership would drop them completely, and develop instead a narrow and conservative understanding of the Glorious Revolution. 'The principle, the great, the only end of the Revolution,' claimed one loyal Walpolean, 'was then to settle the government upon its ancient and proper basis, which the measures of a mad bigot [James II] had almost destroyed.'[51] William III and George I had gained the throne because God had placed them there – a theory of providential divine right that was applied to government as a whole. God had sanctioned and ordained the parliamentary monarchy established after 1688 and it must be obeyed accordingly.

Across the narrowing ideological divide in British politics, the Tories too found ways of discarding or at least lightening their more embarrassing ideological baggage, in particular hereditary divine-right kingship. Many were apparently willing by the 1720s to acknowledge the Hanoverian succession, if only with recourse to Hobbes's idea in *Leviathan* that allegiance should be given to whatever power or ruler could provide protection against a return to the state of nature. And just as royal prerogative powers had largely been transferred to crown-in-Parliament, so the Tories would transfer their doctrines of the subject's duty of passive obedience and non-resistance from the monarch to the government. Both parties now embraced notions of parliamentary sovereignty and the divine right of governors. Gone were the gaping divisions among the political elite that the people had exploited in the 1640s and very nearly again in the 1670s and 1680s. There was a similar convergence between Whigs and Tories over religious issues. Most Whig leaders grudgingly defended the authority and privileges of the Church (largely because they controlled who got the plum jobs in it); most Tories grudgingly accepted the toleration of Protestant Dissenters established in 1689. All were united in rejecting religious 'enthusiasm' and persecution. And even on foreign policy issues the Whigs and Tories disagreed not on whether but simply by what methods to resist French popery and preserve the Protestant interest and the balance of Europe. In short, the principles established in 1688–9 and 1714 became sacrosanct for both parties.

Politeness, as we saw in the last chapter, also brought greater cultural cohesion to the ruling classes. Elite manners in Scotland and Ireland had been converging with those in England since Tudor times, and politeness quickened this process. In prizing the social graces above learning and the humanist 'politic arts', the conventions of polite society were able to create consensus, or at least mutual toleration, among different and potentially hostile groups. As politeness gained ground it helped to weaken provincial identities and loyalties, creating a national culture, centred upon London, to which all could subscribe: the middling orders and the aristocracy; the Irish, Welsh, and Scots; and the transatlantic colonists.

The relative calm of political life after 1714 can be deceptive, however. Pudding time might well have ended messily if George I and George II had not been such well-behaved monarchs. There was, after all, no guarantee that they would remain good little constitutional kings and not get greedy for the more extensive prerogative powers they enjoyed as electors of Hanover. Perhaps the lack of revolutionary upheavals under the first two Georges was due to nothing more than their imperviousness to the charms of French court culture or, worse, Catholicism. As it was, their unswerving loyalty to the Whigs, and the consequent emasculation of the Tories, helped to lower the temperature of party politics. Similarly, because both Georges were so obviously committed to defending the Protestant interest in Europe, the government's opponents were denied use of the most powerful propaganda weapon of any in post-Reformation Britain: the claim that a popish clique at court was in league with foreign Catholics to introduce absolutism. The government's critics would be forced instead to fight on the narrower front of 'country' issues, deploying the rhetoric developed in the 1640s and 1690s of a corrupt ministry drunk on the power from taxes and a standing army.

Fears that Leviathan would swallow up civil liberties tended to cut across and blur party divisions. Given Walpole's commanding majority in the Commons, ambitious opposition leaders needed to build a coalition of Tories and dissident (often radical) Whigs if they were to put the ministry under any real pressure and thereby claw their way into office. The pro-war movement of the late 1730s described in the previous section is a good example of an opposition joint operation to storm the Walpolean citadel. Holding together this unstable alliance necessarily meant seeking out the patriotic common ground: promoting Britain's maritime power; fighting French popery; and standing up for landed gentlemen and 'honest' merchants, for free and frequent Parliaments and the rule of law. For the Tories it meant sidelining their small but vocal Jacobite contingent; for the Whigs, downplaying their disregard for the Church. The aim was to use political languages and reference points that appealed to both parties, and hence the opposition's exaltation of England's mythical ancient constitution, or the ideals of public-spiritedness found in classical republican writings. The Tories grew so used to talking in this classical republican strain that, as the philosopher and political analyst David Hume (1711–76) put it: 'they seem to have made converts of themselves by their hypocrisy, and to have embraced the sentiments [i.e. in favour of liberty], as well as language of their adversaries'.[52] Opposition leaders and polemicists would even try to persuade people that 'the distinction between Whigs and Tories is now in effect abolished'.[53] The influential opposition journals *Cato's Letters* (1720–2) and *The Craftsman* (1726–44) peddled the line that the old party labels were invidious and redundant. Politics was now a matter not of Whigs versus Tories but of country patriots against a corrupt ministry. Little of which was true. 'Party consists of all' remained the general verdict.[54] But the mere attempt to smooth over partisan differences had the effect of flattening out the political landscape at Westminster.

The Whig ascendancy, however, although a stabilising force inside Parliament, provoked a high degree of political volatility 'out of doors'. The opposition could outflank Walpole's parliamentary phalanx only by mobilising public opinion through impassioned appeals to the causes of patriotism and civil liberties; these tactics, as we have seen in the 1640s, created a political platform for all kinds of groups, including non-electors and the 'giddy multitude'. The opposition was playing with fire, therefore, appealing to and invoking a political constituency that it could not fully control and that, in decades to come, would nurture challenges not just to the government but to the patrician state itself. For the extremists were still out there: radical writers who demanded a widening of the parliamentary franchise; libertarian Tories and Jacobites; Whigs who celebrated the anniversary of Charles I's execution, and who thought the Glorious Revolution had not merely restored England's ancient constitution but ushered in a new era of popular sovereignty. All these groups were united in their determination to liberate Parliament and the nation from the trammels of Leviathan.

If the old parties and the enemies of Leviathan were still alive and kicking under the stifling blanket of Whig oligarchy, then so too were the old assumptions about party as a factious, self-interested minority. It is worth noting that the phrase 'His Majesty's Opposition' was not coined until the 1820s, and then only as a joke.[55] 'A form'd general Opposition', hostile not just to specific policies but to the government generally, was still seen as one of 'the most wicked combinations that men can enter into'.[56] The enemies of the Robinocracy were careful to portray themselves as honest, patriotic politicians, dedicated to the public good, while they denigrated Walpole and his cronies as a corrupt court faction, masquerading as a legitimate government. The Walpoleans hit back, denouncing the ministry's critics as a 'criminal faction' and 'popular Patriots', who played upon the wayward and unruly passions of the mob.[57] Ordinary people had no legitimate place in politics, they argued. Their duties were to pay their taxes; to honour and pray for their rulers; and, above all, to obey them. Churchmen loyal to the Robinocracy preached sermons, warning that

> the Voice of Faction and Discontent is still heard in the Land: private Piques, and personal Animosities are work'd up into national Grievances; disappointed Ambition has assumed the Robe of Patriotism, and under the popular Masque of Love for the Community licentiously asperses that Power, which is the only Stay and Support of it.[58]

'Popularity' still retained much of its old meaning of a subversive appeal to the mob. But although the terms of political abuse had not changed much, the argument on the ministerial Whigs' side was moving into new territory. With the help of their friends in the London press they set about challenging the opposition's appeals to the ancient constitution or classical republican virtues as touchstones of good government. Reference to antiquity, classical or English, was rubbished in good Hobbesian fashion as 'romantic notion, and mere visionary virtue', with no relevance for modern times.[59] Big and powerful government – Leviathan – was needed in order to guard against human depravity and foreign popery, and to achieve that in a system where the power of the Commons had become so great required expert management and the harnessing of natural self-interest – in short, corruption.

Away from Westminster, and the rage of party still burned with much of its old intensity. Although defeated at court and in Parliament, the Tories continued to do battle with the Whigs in many urban corporations, sometimes with violent consequences. The struggle between the parties in Norwich, England's second-largest city, was attended by 'seditious' publications, riots, running battles in the streets, and lengthy disruptions to civic government. So strong was popular Toryism in the city that Townshend set up an artillery company there to keep down the 'high church' party. As the Hanoverian period wore on, the religious content of local party rivalries would begin to fade. Legislation and a string of court decisions after 1714 gradually made the presence of Dissenters in local government less contentious. But in place of the old quarrels over prelacy and Dissent came new points at issue: Walpolean corruption, oligarchy, the excise, trade, Jacobitism etc. The content of local partisan politics might have changed, but the fact of party strife did not.

Parliamentary elections after 1714 also lost none of their capacity to divide and enrage the people, even those not qualified to vote. Elections in most constituencies did not involve a contest or a poll. A contest occurred only when the leading county landowners or municipal governors could not reach an agreement over who should be elected, or when the voters rejected the candidates on offer and tried to have their own nominees returned. Yet in the six general elections after 1715 more seats would be contested than in the six preceding elections. In the relatively open county constituencies, where the middling sort had a chance to exercise a choice, almost half of the elections would be contested (though this figure had dropped to just 16 per cent by 1800). Clearly the people still wanted to make their voice heard – the trouble was the electoral system would not let them. This fact was acknowledged even by MPs themselves. 'It is well known', declared one Tory in the Commons, 'how unequally the nation is represented in this House . . . which shewes, that we ought not to judge of the sentiments of the better sort of people, from what appears to be the sentiments of the majority of this House.'[60]

Despite winning the popular vote in the 1727, 1734 and 1741 general elections, the Tories lost all three. Their thousands of votes in the county constituencies yielded just fifty or sixty MPs, whereas the far more numerous urban constituencies, sometimes with highly restricted electorates of just a few dozen, returned hundreds of Whigs. The Whigs had systematically built up proprietorial interests in many of these towns – the infamous rotten boroughs – and where their grip was less sure they resorted, or so their opponents alleged, to 'prodigious bribery'.[61] Voters in some boroughs actually formed clubs to extract higher electoral bribes. At the very least they expected plenty of free food and drink, and generally to be buttered up, even when no contest was expected. The 'disgustful' and licentious scenes that often attended parliamentary elections, particularly in boroughs, led some people in places without representation – which included Manchester, Birmingham, Leeds and Sheffield – to regard their unenfranchised condition as a blessing.

The rising cost of fighting elections during the early eighteenth century stacked the deck even more heavily in the Whigs' favour, for they had the spoils of office and government slush funds at their disposal. The Tories responded by forming constituency clubs to mobilise their grass-roots support and orchestrate resistance to the Whig electoral oligarchy. Losing elections that they had so obviously won brought out the more populist and radical elements in Toryism. Tories had a vested interest in championing electoral reform and wider franchises. Walpole and his fellow Whig oligarchs, on the other hand, now turned their back on the middling tradesmen who had once formed the core of urban Whiggery.

Because standing for Parliament was often very expensive, most MPs during the eighteenth century were wealthy landowners. Only about 15 per cent were merchants and lawyers, and some of these were clients of the aristocracy. Very few MPs were men of 'new' wealth, such as manufacturers, and none came from the labouring classes. At the same time, the electorate itself was becoming more exclusive, falling from about 23 per cent of the adult male population at the start of the eighteenth century to about 17 per cent by the end of it. Throughout the century there would always be more officeholders – constables, churchwardens etc. – than there were voters. This was especially true of Scotland, where the entire electorate numbered a mere 3,000.

The 'vile Corruptions' of the electoral system encouraged the people to participate more directly in the political process.[62] A great deal of the legislation that came before Parliament during the eighteenth century would be drafted not by the government but by private interest groups – merchants, manufacturers, tradesmen, farmers etc. – and would be pushed through the Houses with the help of the press, petitioning, and lobbying campaigns. The fact that certain people were denied the vote did not make them politically impotent. In 1721, for example, England's weavers employed a variety of pressure tactics, including lobbying, petitioning and violent demonstrations, to persuade Parliament to ban the import of cheap Indian calicoes that was threatening to destroy their livelihoods. Opposition to Walpole's excise proposals of 1733 became 'the theme of Coffee-Houses, Taverns, and Gin-Shops, the Discourse of Artificiers, the Cry of the Streets, the Entertainment of Lacquies, the Prate of Wenches, and the Bugbear of Children'.[63] Anti-government demonstrations played a major part in persuading Walpole to back down. Similarly, in 1753 the government was forced to repeal the recently introduced Jewish Naturalisation Act after a vicious and shamelessly populist campaign, orchestrated by the *London Evening-Post*, against 'those ravening Wolves, the devouring blaspheming Jews'.[64]

The power of the press, for good or ill, prevented early Georgian society falling under the enervating spell of one-party rule. 'The people of Great Britain are governed by a power that never was heard of as a supreme authority in any age or country before,' lamented one Whig MP in 1738, 'it is the government of the press.'

> The stuff which our weekly news-papers are filled with, is received with greater reverence than acts of parliament; and the sentiments of one of these scribblers have more weight with the multitude than the opinion of the best politician in the country.[65]

London acquired its first daily newspaper in 1702 (eighty or so years before the French did), and by the 1730s there were half a dozen dailies and several thrice-weeklies and weeklies serving the capital and the south-east. Across England as a whole there were about fifty newspapers by the 1780s, most of which borrowed heavily from the London and international press. Scotland had nine newspapers by then, as well as numerous periodicals. A Welsh newspaper did not appear until the early 1800s. The most influential newspapers under the first two Georges were the weekly *The Craftsman* and the daily *London Evening-Post*. Both were aligned with the opposition; indeed, *The Craftsman* carried editorials by leading 'Patriotical' politicians. At the height of its popularity in the early 1730s *The Craftsman* had a circulation of perhaps 12,000, and was reprinted in several provincial towns, as well as in Amsterdam and New York. The *Post* gradually proved more popular because, as its sister publication the *Universal Spectator* put it, 'this Journal . . . contains about six Times more Domestick News than the Common Journals; with several material Paragraphs of fresh News, not in any other Paper'.[66]

The London press was merely in the vanguard of a vast army of writers and artists eager to attack Walpole, the politician everyone loved to hate. 'Sir Bob', 'the Great Man', 'Bob of Lynn' was the subject of satirical squibs, popular ballads, poems, plays, and the nation's latest publishing phenomenon, printed political cartoons.[67] One such print, called *Idol-Worship or The Way to Preferment*, shows Walpole, his breeches down, his backside bare and ready to be kissed, astride a corridor leading to the halls of office and power (see illus. 15). Inevitably, he was likened to Cardinal Wolsey, the 1st duke of Buckingham and other power-hungry upstarts from the pages of history. Henry Fielding was far from being the only writer to invite comparisons between Walpole and London's criminal mastermind Jonathan Wild, who was hanged, to popular jubilation, in 1725. The playwright John Gay facetiously professed amazement that the 'Talents requisite for a great Statesman are so scarce in the world since so many of those who possess them are every month cut off in the prime of their Age at the Old-Bailey'.[68]

Swift, Fielding, Alexander Pope (1688–1744), Samuel Johnson (1709–84) and a host of lesser writers put their pens at the service of the Tories and the patriot alliance during Walpole's ascendancy. The most popular of their works was Swift's *Gulliver's Travels*, first published in 1726, which, according to Gay, was read by everyone 'From the highest to the lowest . . . from the Cabinet-council to the Nursery'.[69] The book was at its savagely satirical best attacking the political and moral legacy of Leviathan. Walpole is caricatured as the weaselly Flimnap, the shrewdest political trickster in the emperor of Lilliput's cabinet.

Walpole and the ministry did not submit tamely to this beating, however. They brought libel cases against newspaper editors; introduced a law for censoring new stage productions; set up a formidable surveillance network to report on suspicious journalism; and bought up several London rags and turned them into government mouthpieces. Swift was outraged at Walpole's readiness to hire 'Scoundrels . . . Beasts and Blockheads for his Pen-men, whom he pays in ready Guineas very liberally' – doubly so as he would have taken the government's guineas too if they had been offered.[70]

The people were as politically restive as they had ever been; the will to fight the Robinocracy was clearly there. But the inequities of the electoral system and the growth of ministerial authority combined to concentrate power in ever fewer hands. The Bedchamber, for example, which had still contained major political players under William, had lost any independent influence by the time George II came to the throne. George concerted policy not through his entourage but the royal 'closet' at court – that is, a favoured inner circle of cabinet ministers. The king could admit whom he liked to the closet, but his range of choice was limited by his ministers' standing in relation to their party and Parliament. If enough Parliament-men wanted a minister gone, he generally went – the king had little say in the matter. Influence with the king depended ultimately on influence in Parliament, and that in turn was managed largely by the ministry. The first two Georges might have resisted this trend a little more effectively if they had not spent quite so much time in Hanover, for their absence inevitably encouraged the ministry to assume greater responsibility over royal policy. At least the emergence of the closet system ended once and for all the old grievance of 'unsworn counsellors'. Party politicians, not royal minions, now ran the show.

The Grumbling Hive

> Vast Numbers throng'd the fruitful Hive;
> Yet those vast Numbers made 'em thrive;
> Millions endeavouring to supply
> Each other's Lust and Vanity . . .
> Then leave Complaints: Fools only strive
> To make a Great an honest Hive.
> T'enjoy the World's Conveniencies,
> Be famed in War, yet live in Ease
> Without great Vices, is a vain
> Eutopia seated in the Brain.
> Fraud, Luxury, and Pride must live,
> Whilst we the Benefits receive.[71]

In an age that was more than commonly fond of the sound of its own voice there was one issue that people never tired of discussing, and that was luxury. Hacks, politicians and churchmen all insisted that luxury was an unmitigated evil, a major cause of social breakdown and moral decay. Wherever the champions of moral improvement and patriotic values looked, they saw virtue – usually thought of as the subordination or harnessing of self-interest to the public good – succumbing to the corrupting influence of luxury.

This was the prevailing view, anyway. But not everyone thought of luxury or indeed virtue in these black and white terms. In fashionable intellectual circles it was conceded that luxury would destroy virtue, and therefore that virtue, if there was such a thing, could never be fully attained and that it was ridiculous to pretend otherwise. An alternative social model must be found, and it is here that we encounter the most original thinker in early eighteenth-century Britain: Bernard Mandeville (1670–1733). After Mandeville, luxury and consumption would increasingly be seen not as moral problems but as economic issues.

Born in Rotterdam of Dutch parents, Mandeville had emigrated in his twenties to London, where he had set up as a physician and journalist and married an Englishwoman. In 1705 he had published *The Grumbling Hive*, a verse fable mocking the moral anxiety and censoriousness of the English, a publication he incorporated into another in 1714, *The Fable of the Bees*. Building upon the scepticism of Montaigne and Hobbes, Mandeville concluded that self-denying virtue was a sham. It was society's appetites and vices, its very 'Plagues and Monsters' – 'the sensual Courtier that sets no Limits to his Luxury; the Fickle Strumpet that invents new Fashions every Week' – that conduced to the general good.[72] Forget virtue, he said, pride was the key to human happiness. 'We are possess'd of no other Quality so beneficial to Society, and so necessary to render it wealthy and flourishing.'[73] Without pride and self-liking there would be no chasing after the latest fashions and the pleasures of life, and hence no demand for new products, no capitalism, no economic growth. Whereas traditional theory held that the common good could only be achieved by the moderation of personal desires, Mandeville held precisely the opposite. The common good was grounded in commerce and consumption, and these relied upon some of humanity's vilest qualities: envy, emulation, lust and greed. Politeness, for Mandeville, bore no relation to inward virtue. It was merely a necessary hypocrisy: 'a Fashionable Habit . . . of flattering the Pride and Selfishness of others, and concealing our own' in order to get what we want.[74] 'It is impossible we could be socialised creatures', he argued, 'without hypocrisy.'[75] Mandeville was one of the first thinkers to accept unflinchingly the ugly side of the consumerist society that Leviathan had spawned. His influential, if highly controversial, ideas would have a major impact upon many of the great philosophers of the Enlightenment, in particular David Hume and Adam Smith (1723–90).

Each level in the grumbling hive of Georgian society was partial to its own particular vices, its own brands of luxury. The nobility and gentry, almost by definition, were freer to indulge their hedonistic inclinations and leisured interests than the mass of humanity toiling away beneath them. In fact, excessive expenditure and lavish consumption were de rigueur for men in the public eye, as most gentlemen were. That prudent Treasury man Sir Robert Walpole could easily devote £20,000 (an absolute fortune) to his pleasures each year. His accounts for 1733 show that he and his guests spent £3,000 on white wine and chocolates alone. Needless to say, he died as he had lived, heavily in debt, which was the fate of many a Georgian grandee. In 1779 his heirs would be forced to sell his fabulous art collection to Catherine the Great of Russia for the knockdown price of £40,000.

Huge debts aside, these were exceptionally good times for the aristocracy, and for the nobility in particular. As Britain entered the age of the Enlightenment and the industrial revolution, the peerage was growing more powerful than at any time since the Wars of the Roses. Half of England's 400 or so *grands seigneurs* by 1780 – those with estates of 10,000 acres or more – were peers, and as a whole this group owned 20 to 25 per cent of English land, or about 5 per cent more than it had in 1700. As this statistic might suggest, their influence at Westminster and at county level remained enormous. True, the institutional power of the House of Lords vis-à-vis the Commons would decline over the course of the eighteenth century, and there was a feeling, certainly in the 1730s and 1740s, that Walpole's practice of securing peerages for his cronies had diluted the ancient nobility with 'mean, contemptible persons'. But the peers' hold on the lower House through electoral patronage or simply through their sons or relations occupying seats was nonetheless increasing. They held most of the top jobs in county government, and they continued to expect (if not necessarily to receive) high command in the armed forces.

The key to advancement into the nobility was, more than ever, land ownership. The bigger and wealthier your estate the better your chances of receiving a peerage. New peers would be drawn overwhelmingly from the ranks of the 5,000 or so greater gentry who between them owned perhaps as much as two thirds of the land in Britain and Ireland. Wealthy families from trade and industry who wanted to swap the hustle and bustle of town life for a more leisurely existence among the landed gentry – and by no means all did – usually took two or three generations to become fully integrated into their new social surroundings. Money and land by themselves were not enough; it required subtler distinctions – to begin with, a public school education, preferably at somewhere very exclusive like Harrow or Westminster.

Nothing prepared a boy for the gambling, duelling and general vicious-ness of aristocratic life better than public school. Henry Fielding, thinking back fondly to his own alma mater, Eton, branded public schools the 'Nurseries of all Vice and Immorality. All the wicked Fellows I remember at the University were bred at them.'[76] After public schooling would sometimes come a spell at one of the better Oxford or Cambridge colleges, though the universities were notorious at this time for drinking and whoring – or worse in the case of Oxford, Jacobitism. The scions of good families were often kept away. In 1700 only 35 per cent of English peers attended university.

The pinnacle of elite education was the Grand Tour, which was perhaps the true formative ritual of the eighteenth-century landed class. British aristocrats had been accustomed to touring the Continent since the sixteenth century, but the experience became more formalised after 1660. The grand tourist would usually take in Paris, the south of France, Switzerland, and finally the Italian cities – all the while mixing with fashionable continental society; refining his manners and his French (the preferred language of the European aristocracy); studying art and architecture; buying paintings and sculpture; and above all soaking himself in the culture of classical antiquity, the defining feature of a gentlemanly education. Typically, the tour would last two or three years and cost upwards of £5,000. Once our expensively polished young aristocrat was back from the tour then a good marriage had to be arranged. The often tawdry side of aristocratic match-making was captured brilliantly by Hogarth in his series of paintings *Marriage à la Mode*, which follows the spendthrift earl of Squanderfield as he arranges the sale of his dissolute heir in marriage to the daughter of a wealthy merchant. Finally, no arriviste could truly be said to have arrived without at least a seat in Parliament, where Walpole and his friends would happily divest the nouveau aristocrat of whatever scruples he had left.[77]

For those parvenus really desperate to impress there was only one option: build a large country house and fill it with old masters and French and Italian furnishings. Across Britain and throughout the century, stately homes were built or redesigned according to a variety of continental styles, from austere neoclassicism to baroque and Gothic, and invariably at vast expense. This was the first age of landscape gardening, of William Kent and Lancelot Brown – better known as 'Capability' Brown for his habit of referring to the capabilities of the country estates he transformed into the 'natural' gardens that would become so much the vogue in the second half of the century. The box hedges and symmetrical parterres of the parks fashionable during the later Stuart period (think Versailles) began to give way from the 1710s to rolling meadows, ha-has, glades, and classical temples and grottoes.

Walpole's gentry friend Thomas Coke (created earl of Leicester in 1744) employed Kent and other fashionable architects and designers in building a grand Palladian mansion, Holkham Hall, in Norfolk, complete with a statue gallery running the entire length of the house to show off the collection of classical sculpture (mostly Roman copies) that he had acquired on the Grand Tour. But he was outdone by Sir Robert himself, who rebuilt the family home at nearby Houghton, creating what one contemporary called 'the greatest house in the world for its size, capable of the greatest reception for company'.[78] The guest lists for Walpole's sumptuous gatherings at Houghton included local nobs and friends, political grandees, courtiers, bishops, ambassadors, even European royalty; and Houghton was designed to cater for the lot, with the ground floor 'dedicated to fox-hunters, hospitality, noise, dirt and business', while the first floor was one of 'taste, expense, state and parade'.[79] One guest recalled that dinner parties of thirty or more would wallow 'up to the chin in beef, venison, geese, turkeys, etc., and generally over the chin in claret, strong beer and punch'.[80]

The 'gross Luxury' of Walpole and his like was attracting considerable criticism by the mid-eighteenth century. In print and in sermons a veritable army of moralisers traced Britain's ills, and above all its military failings during the 1740s and 1750s (for which, see below), to what Defoe, in *Robinson Crusoe*, had called the 'vicious living, luxury, and extravagences' of the elite.[81] The apparent rot at the top of society was supposedly leading to national degeneration. Hogarth's portrayal of the earl of Squanderfield as diseased and emasculated, riddled with the 'French pox' (syphilis), was meant to be emblematic of the corrupting spread of foreign fashions in British society. Another symbol for Hogarth of the earl's degeneracy was his taste for paintings in the 'grand style' of the Italian old masters. Hogarth had a particular reason for resenting this penchant for baroque and rococo art – he lacked the skill to match it. But then that was true of most Georgian artists before Joshua Reynolds (1723–92). Britain remained a backwater as far as the latest trends in European art were concerned. Foreign musicians, painters and sculptors poured across the Channel during the first half of the eighteenth century to satisfy the market for continental refinement that the home-grown talent could not. What little interest

George I and II took in the arts was largely confined to attending and subsidising the opera. Their one great legacy to the nation's artistic life was the music of Georg Friedrich Händel (1685–1759), the kappelmeister of the court of Hanover, who by dint of royal patronage became something of a national institution. But the court had long ceased to be a major centre of artistic fashion – in fact not since the days of Charles II. George I spent far more on the upkeep of his stables than he ever did on the arts.

The craving for luxuries and the aping of French manners were not confined to the elite. The middling orders were equally addicted to consumer fripperies, and collectively their spending power was huge. 'Their well-faring', wrote Defoe, 'gives Occasion to the vast Consumption of the foreign, as well as home Produce, the like of which is not to be equalled by any Nation in the World.'[82] By the 1750s the number of people between the upper bourgeoisie (yeoman farmers, lawyers, doctors etc.) and the tenant farmers and poor tradesmen on £40 or £50 a year – the point at which parishioners became liable to pay rates for the poor – had risen to perhaps a million, or about 20 per cent of the British population. Within this group were the hundreds of thousands of ratepayers who elected and, by turns, served as parish officers. Again, not all of them wanted to emulate the tastes and manners of the gentry, but many did, particularly the town-dwellers. Economic improvement, urban growth and a fall in the cost of living – largely because of a static population during the early 1700s – swelled the middling orders and gave them more cash to indulge their pretensions to gentility. There would thus be a widening and deepening of consumer demand during the eighteenth century. Clocks, mirrors, glass and chinaware, bed and window curtains, began to feature significantly in middling-class homes from the early 1700s. Wallpaper grew rapidly in popularity during the early eighteenth century, as did the French penchant for using forks (to keep hands from food) at meal times. Where householders, more often housewives, could not afford foreign fabrics and ceramics they bought cheaper British imitations.

One little luxury that no bourgeois consumer would happily forgo was polite reading matter. High literacy rates among town-dwellers created a voracious reading public that gorged itself on an increasingly wide range of printed material, much of it aimed deliberately at 'the middling Rank of People'. Newspapers, periodicals, trade journals and digests appeared all over Britain during the first half of the eighteenth century. One of the most popular of the periodicals was Edward Cave's

Gentleman's Magazine, a monthly compendium of news items, articles, reviews and advertisements, with a circulation by the 1740s of 15,000. It began life in 1731 as the *Gentleman's Magazine or Trader's Monthly Intelligencer*, but the shortened form was quickly adopted as 'giving the whole a more genteel and elegant Turn'.[83] After all, tradesmen now liked to think of themselves as gentlemen as well.

It was in the decades after the publication of Defoe's *Robinson Crusoe* in 1719 that a new literary form, the novel, made its first appearance. Samuel Richardson's moralistic potboiler *Pamela* (1740) – satirised by Fielding under the title *Shamela* – and Fielding's comic masterpiece *Tom Jones* (1748) were instant commercial successes. Novels, one churchman claimed in the 1780s, 'for half a century have made the chief entertainment of that middle class which subsists between the court and the spade'.[84] And harmless entertainment too, by and large, though again the moralisers scorned the public's reading habits: 'weekly Essays, amatory Plays and Novels, political Pamphlets, and Books that revile Religion; together with a general Hash of these, served up in some monthly Mess of Dulness, are the meagre literary Diet of Town and Country'.[85]

It was luxury not poverty that the governing classes pilloried for the crimes of the labouring poor. 'Is it not notorious,' asked the Reverend Thomas Wilson in 1736, 'that Luxury and Extravagence were never at a greater height than at present, amongst the laborious and even the meanest part of Mankind?'[86] The particular luxury that he and other moral reformers had in mind was gin. For several centuries it had been noted that the English exceeded any other nation in their 'beastly drinking and quaffing'.[87] The evil brew in the age of the Puritans had been beer – a drink introduced from the Low Countries that had largely replaced the lower-strength ale over the course of the fifteenth and sixteenth centuries. Then in the late 1600s, British soldiers returning from the wars on the Continent had introduced the drinking public to a new Dutch spirit, 'Genievie', or gin for short. Gin had several major advantages for both producer and consumer: it was easy to make, packed a lot more punch than beer, and was as cheap as you like. So cheap in fact that drunkenness could be enjoyed even by the very poorest, 'who were formerly so far happy in their Poverty', insisted the bishop of Salisbury, 'that their Want secured them from many Vices'.[88] The rich too were enamoured of 'Mother gin' – so called because many poor women were involved in selling and buying spirits. Walpole was partial to her, having taken to alcohol at an early age because his father had thought it improper to get drunk himself while his son remained sober. But it was 'dram drinking' among the common people that worried the governing classes. Popular consumerism, it was feared, would produce a drunken, disinhibited and ungovernable people, with no respect for their superiors or the law. The 1729 act for imposing a duty upon distilled liquor was just one of numerous attempts to curb gin consumption by the masses, and to make money for the government in the process. Its preamble would have struck Mandeville as the very height of hypocrisy:

> the drinking of Spirits and Strong Waters, is become very common amongst the People of inferior Rank, and the constant and excessive use thereof tends greatly to the destruction of their Healths, and enervating them, and rendering them unfit for useful Labour and Service, intoxicating them, and debauching their Morals, and driving them into all manner of Vices and Wickedness.[89]

In truth, the gin craze was largely confined to London, and even there its ill-effects were greatly exaggerated by the moralists. That much of respectable London was united in trying to stop the poor enjoying themselves 'in their own way' was in part because 'their own way' was not unlike that of respectable society.[90] Mother gin's detractors included Hogarth and his friend Fielding, who besides being a novelist was a Middlesex magistrate and the founder of the Bow Street runners, the first modern metropolitan police force. In 1751 he published a detailed analysis of the link between luxury and social disorder, while Hogarth produced his famous engravings *Beer Street* and *Gin Lane*, showing the wholesome effects of good honest English beer as opposed to the evils of drinking nasty 'foreign' gin (see illus.18 and 19). Both men timed their productions to support what would become the Gin or Tippling Act of 1751, which imposed tough new restrictions on gin sellers. With this legislation, and a rise during the 1750s in the cost of grain (the distillers' raw material), Mother gin would fade back into the Georgian crowd.

The gin craze, Britain's first major drug scare, was much like today's moral panics, in that it said more about the anxieties of society's managers than about 'wickedness' among the managed. Mother gin epitomised the fear of London's elite that out-of-control consumerism was breaking down customary patterns of deference and obedience among the city's large and growing population of labouring poor. Interestingly, the most sophisticated arguments against plebeian gin-drinking were conducted not in the language of moral reform but within an essentially Mandevillian framework. Anti-gin writers argued that the wealth generated by the spirits trade benefited society less than having a healthy and productive workforce, or soldiers and sailors who were not too stupefied by drink to defend the realm.

It was just as well that plebeian binge-drinking was neither as common nor invariably as fatal as was often painted, for the numbers involved would have been frightening. Perhaps a quarter of the people in England – and probably an even greater proportion in Scotland and Ireland – depended at one time or other on parish poor-relief and other forms of charity to make ends meet. The number of poor obviously grew when times were hard. Fortunately, aside from a few years scarred by dearth and national epidemics of smallpox, typhus and 'putrid fever' (the plague had vanished from Britain after the 1660s), the reigns of the first two Georges were not too bad for the ordinary working man and woman. Abundant harvests, slow population growth and an increase in manufacturing meant a rise in real wages and plenty of cheap food. Defoe was more or less correct in claiming that 'the working manufacturing people of England eat the fat, and drink the sweet, live better, and fare better, than the working people of any other nation in Europe' – and, had he known it, the rest of the world also, with the possible exception of the Dutch republic and New England. 'They make better wages of their work,' he continued, 'and spend more of the money upon their Backs [clothes] and Bellies, than in any other country.'[91] Foreigners were amazed by the amount of meat the common people consumed compared with the poor on the Continent. The popular hit 'The Roast Beef of Old England' was more than just patriotic swagger.

Popular culture, drink-related or otherwise, came under growing attack from polite society during the course of the eighteenth century. The attitude of educated people to what seemed to them the increasingly alien world of plebeian values and customs is captured perfectly in Defoe's comments on Horn Fair, at Charlton in Kent:

> a Village famous, or rather infamous for the yearly collected Rabble of Mad-people . . . the Rudeness of which I cannot but think, is such as ought to be suppress'd, and indeed in a civiliz'd well govern'd Nation, it may well be said to be unsufferable. The Mob indeed at that time take all kinds of Liberties, and the Women are especially impudent for that Day; as if it was a Day that justify'd the giving themselves a Loose

to all manner of Indecency and Immodesty, without any Reproach, or without suffering the Censure which such Behaviour would deserve at another time.[92]

By distancing themselves from this world of plebeian 'rudeness' the polite classes were able to define their own aspirations and values in terms of genteel socialising and the consumption of luxury goods.

The people continued to take all kinds of liberties regardless of what Defoe and his kind had to say. Whether it was jeering at foreigners on the London streets or pelting homosexuals to death in the stocks, the crowd was more than ever a powerful arbiter and enforcer of customary values. It was no respecter of rank either. When George II's German mistress Amalie Wallmoden was installed in London in 1738, the crowd greeted her coach with cries of 'Hanover Whore';[93] and it mocked the young George III for his filial devotion by asking, 'as the King passed in his [sedan] chair to visit his mother . . . if he was going to suck?'[94] Collective bargaining for higher wages, and food riots to remind the authorities of their duty to the poor, were other ways in which the ordinary people made their wishes known to their betters – who ignored them at their peril, for there was no police force to hide behind in this period.

The crowd often had the tacit approval of sections of the elite when it attacked Catholics or Dissenters, but much less so when persecuting another supposed enemy of society: witches. Although the laws against witchcraft were repealed in 1736, popular belief in witches and ghosts seems to have remained as strong as ever. In 1751 the mob threatened to burn down the Hertfordshire town of Tring unless its workhouse governors handed over a destitute old woman who was commonly accounted a witch. The governors capitulated and the mob ducked her in a nearby river and then beat her to death. The organiser of this murderously popular event, who was handsomely rewarded by the crowd for his pains, was later tried and hanged while 'many thousands' looked on, grumbling that 'it was a hard case to hang a man for destroying an old wicked woman who had done so much mischief by her witchcraft'.[95]

Superstition was seen in polite society as akin to that other deplorable tendency among the common people: religious enthusiasm. Certainly the great evangelical revival in the 1730s made most headway among the lower orders, and especially those touched by the charismatic preaching of John Wesley (1703–91), George Whitefield (1714–70) and other leaders of the Methodist movement (Wesley defined a Methodist as 'one that lives according to the method laid down in the bible').[96] Although Wesley and most of his colleagues began their ministries as sincere, indeed intensely dedicated, Anglicans, and would never formally separate themselves from the Church, their missionary zeal would far exceed that of the average clergyman. Like the first Quakers, the apostles of Methodism went out into the streets and fields to evangelise among those who had been neglected by the Church of England – indeed, in many cases had never heard the Christian message before. And rather than discourse learnedly on the reasonableness of Christianity and its compatibility with the established order, Methodist preachers delivered impassioned sermons on the rewards of heaven and the terrors of hell, on the saving grace of Christ as revealed in the Scriptures. In some places the Methodist message was greeted with scenes of ecstatic frenzy; in others, the mob attacked Methodists as Puritan troublemakers or, perversely, Jacobites. Yet though Wesley and other evangelicals utterly rejected the gaming and revelry that featured so heavily in popular culture, just as they did the vanity and consumerism of the polite classes, they shared the common people's belief in the power of the supernatural. 'The giving up of witchcraft', Wesley declared angrily, 'is in effect, giving up the Bible.'[97]

The evangelical revival was in part a reaction against the liberal and intellectualised piety that spread within the Church of England during Pudding time. The Church would continue to play a major role in the provision of education and charity during the eighteenth century. Anglicans still dominated the political, military and academic establishments, and the parish remained the basic unit of local government. But to evangelicals such as Wesley the Church under the Robinocracy had lost its way. In trying to defend orthodox Anglicanism against popery and enthusiasm, too many leading churchmen had adopted a reasoned approach to religion that downplayed or questioned biblical revelation and the fundamentals of Christianity. Among a few of the more free-thinking clergy and laity this scepticism shaded into deism: the belief that the existence of God and other basic religious truths were accessible through reason and observation from nature rather than through the Bible or church doctrine, both of which were seen as merely human inventions. Little wonder then that the Church had found it relatively easy to adapt to advances in scientific understanding. In fact, a neat division of labour had emerged, with scientists (many of whom, like Newton, were devout Anglicans) providing evidence of

God's works in nature, while churchmen acclaimed their findings as the uncovering of divine majesty.

The Church's accommodation with the world was felt at a more mundane level too. Under the Whig supremacy of the first two Georges the clergy were subordinated more than ever to the state, and lost much of their remaining power to discipline the morals of the laity. The Church's political divisions compounded its weakness. The bishops and other senior clerics were mostly government-appointed Whigs, whereas a large (though declining) proportion of the parish clergy were Tories. Yet despite dire warnings from churchmen that luxury and 'refinement' were breeding atheism, the religious impulse in England – and in Scotland and Ireland for that matter – remained as strong as ever. It was simply that the Whig-dominated administrations post-1714 cared too little about the Church for it to regain the authority and reverence it had commanded before the Glorious Revolution.

The old system in crisis, 1740–54

Never has the British public welcomed the outbreak of war with as much relish as it did in 1739. The insulting Spaniards, with their depredations against British merchants, had been spoiling for a fight, and now, at long last, they would have one. The press and the opposition rubbed their hands at the prospect of 'making incursions, and plundering the coasts of their dominions, even in Europe. Can they prevent this as long as we are masters at sea? No, sir.'[98] Walpole and his friends were less sanguine, however, and with good reason. Although the fighting in the Caribbean went well at first (as we shall see in the next chapter), it was assumed at Whitehall that Louis XV would come to the assistance of his Bourbon cousins in Spain, and that Britain would again face a French invasion. 'I think all is at stake,' wrote Horatio Walpole in 1740, 'the whole power of France employed jointly with that of Spain against England without a special Providence will prevail; nothing but a diversion upon the Continent can save us.'[99]

Providence, in the end, played a vital part in staving off disaster for Britain. The French, as predicted, sent a powerful naval force across the Atlantic, where it would almost certainly have clashed with British squadrons had it not been devastated by hurricanes and disease. Then in 1740 came the diversion upon the Continent that Horatio Walpole had prayed for, although it quickly confirmed the old saying that one should be careful what one wishes for. Firstly, in May 1740, the Prussian king Frederick William I died and was succeeded by his glory-hunting son, Frederick II; then, in October, Emperor Charles VI also died, leaving his Habsburg inheritance to his eldest daughter Maria Theresa, but no son to succeed him on the imperial throne. The Austrian empire, Britain's main bulwark against the might of France, looked more vulnerable than ever. If France was going to dismember the Habsburg territories and have a French puppet elected emperor, here was its opportunity.

But the first power to sink its teeth into the vulnerable Austrian empire would not be France but Prussia. Late in 1740, the new Prussian king unexpectedly invaded the rich Austrian province of Silesia (mostly in present-day southern Poland). From that moment onwards the war with Spain across the Atlantic became an expensive distraction, for France as well as Britain. Preserving the balance of Europe, and with it the security of Hanover and of Britain itself, now hung upon the twists and turns, the ever-shifting military configurations, of the War of the Austrian Succession.

Frederick II (1712–86) embodied the vainglory and volatility that permeated the European state system. He had many of the qualities, and not a few of the defects, of the man whose epithet he came to share, Alexander the Great. Like the ancient Macedonian king he inherited a large and superb army (of about 80,000 men), a state geared for war, and a bulging treasury. He too was full of boundless ambition. He spoke of himself as having 'a rendezvous with Fame'.[100] And like his ancient namesake, he would make his army the most feared and imitated of his age.

Military tactics and technology had not changed much since the late seventeenth century – except in the increasing use of light horse and infantry, often irregulars, to raid and disrupt enemy supply lines. Pitched battles were relatively rare, and decisive ones even rarer. Large armies and artillery-resistant fortifications generally prevented swift advances and aggressive strategies. If casualty rates remained high, it was largely because battles were still dominated by close-range musketry exchanges between massed infantry formations. Although low on accuracy and muzzle velocity, muskets fired soft lead bullets that spread on impact, inflicting terrible wounds. Frederick's military genius lay in his daring, his attention to organisation, and above all in mercilessly drilling his army so that it could outfire and outmanoeuvre all opposition.

The Austrians proved largely powerless to prevent Frederick seizing and retaining Silesia. Their army was poor, their statesmen mediocrities, and their finances shambolic. The empire's evident weakness and distress excited the other circling sharks – Saxony, Bavaria, Spain and the Ottoman empire – raising fears in Britain that 'the Austrian Dominions must be infallibly torn in pieces'. But the big worry for Britain was Versailles's determination to finish off the Habsburgs once and for all. For if Austria succumbed, then Germany and the Dutch republic would probably follow, leaving Britain isolated and, as the ministry's foreign policy expert the duke of Newcastle put it, 'exposed to the whole resentment of France'.[101]

In the summer of 1741 the French allied with the Prussians and then marched a Franco-Bavarian army into Austria, bound for Vienna itself. Not until its final collapse in 1918 would the Habsburg empire again face such a perilous situation. George II was beginning to fear the worst for Hanover too. French and Prussian troops now threatened his beloved Electorate, and as much he felt for the plight of his Austrian allies, and resented Frederick – hailed as Europe's new 'Protestant' champion, despite being a deist – he was not about to jeopardise Hanover in order to rescue Maria Theresa. In September 1741, therefore, he negotiated a treaty of neutrality with France. In return for French assurances that Hanover would not be attacked, George promised to withhold all assistance from Maria Theresa and to support the French candidate – the Bavarian ruler Charles Albert – in the election for emperor. George made this treaty in his capacity as elector rather than as king of Britain, for a policy of effectively surrendering Austria to France ran a coach and horses through Newcastle's and the British government's stated commitment to maintaining the 'old system' and the balance of Europe. But though shamelessly abandoned by their allies (yet again), the Austrians roused themselves and managed to avert what had seemed like inevitable disaster. By exploiting the many divisions and jealousies among their enemies they were able to win a series of victories late in 1741 that ended not only with the French and Bavarians being driven out of Austria but also the capture of Bavaria itself. Yet Frederick still held Silesia, and by December the French, Saxons and Bavarians had bitten off another chunk of Habsburg territory, namely Bohemia (in the modern-day Czech Republic). More humiliation would follow in January 1742 with the election of Charles Albert as the new Holy Roman Emperor. The French appeared to be winning the war of the Austrian Succession.

The British public's anger at its government's supine response to French aggression against Austria would be directed mainly at Walpole. The fall or defection of key ministerial allies in Scotland and the City during the late 1730s took their toll in the May 1741 general election, leaving the government with a Commons majority of under twenty. Defeats in the Caribbean during the spring and summer, and then the crown's apparent betrayal of British security to the interests of Hanover, were added to the lengthening charge sheet against the ministry. Sensing their hour had finally come, opposition politicians pressed home their attacks, accusing Walpole and his colleagues of what amounted to treason. The crisis came in February 1742. With his Commons majority reduced to wafer-thinness, and his friends telling him that his resignation had become 'absolutely necessary, as the only means to carry on the public business' – i.e. to keep themselves and the Whig party in power – Walpole stepped down from office.[102] His fall was greeted with celebrations and mock funerals all over the country. The opposition was all for stringing up 'the grand Corrupter'.[103] But the king, who had stuck by his prime minister to the end, had him elevated instead to the House of Lords as the earl of Orford. And those who had hoped for great things once Walpole had gone – an end, no less, to the ills and abuses of Leviathan – were to be disappointed, for all that happened was a Whig reshuffle. The ministry, supported by the king, bought off and co-opted leading Whigs among the patriot opposition, leaving their Tory allies in the lurch and out of office. In Scotland and Ireland too it was business as usual. The 'great betrayal' of 1742 would confirm and deepen the public's cynicism about parliamentary politics.

The fall of Walpole cleared the way for a more dynamic policy against the French, and a new chief minister to lead the fightback: John Lord Carteret. Unlike Walpole, Carteret had an intimate knowledge of continental affairs and was determined to make British power felt in Europe. As the newly appointed secretary of state for northern Europe he began a concerted diplomatic and military offensive to bolster Austria and prevent further French incursion into Germany and Italy. British troops and cash were sent to help secure the Austrian Netherlands; Maria Theresa and Frederick were persuaded to declare a truce so that the Austrians could concentrate on fighting France; and naval resources were transferred from the Caribbean to the Mediterranean, where British warships resumed their aggressive strategy of the late 1710s. In 1742 a British fleet sailed into the bay of Naples and informed the Neapolitan king that unless he withdrew from the anti-Austrian coalition it would pound his palace to rubble. He withdrew immediately.

At the heart of Carteret's plan was the creation of a British-funded army in the Rhineland made up of about 16,000 British troops, 14,000 Austrians and some 22,000 Hanoverians in British pay. In June 1743 this so-called 'Pragmatic Army', with George II himself nominally in command, would be lured into a trap laid for it at Dettingen, on the River Main in Bavaria, by the experienced French general the Marshal de Noailles. Noailles's 45,000 troops had the Pragmatic Army at their mercy, pinned down against the north bank of the Main, until his cavalry commander attacked, against orders, exposing the French lines to an allied counter-attack that drove them across and into the river with heavy losses, mostly by drowning.

The stakes at Dettingen had been enormous. Had Noailles won, as really he should have, and George been captured, then the French could have invaded not only Austria (again) but also Hanover and perhaps the Low Countries, with all the dire threat that posed to British security. Victory at Dettingen was greeted therefore with wild celebrations in Austria and Britain. For a brief moment, George II, who would be the last British monarch to lead his troops in battle, became a popular hero. But Dettingen would prove even less decisive than Blenheim had been. Ever mindful of his precious Hanover, George refused to risk the Pragmatic Army either in pursuit of the defeated French or in invading France, with which Britain was still not officially at war. Moreover, allegations that he had shown undue favour to his Hanoverian troops and mistreated the British contingent provoked another eruption of anti-Hanoverianism at Westminster and in the press. 'It is now apparent,' thundered the MP (and future prime minister) William Pitt (1708–78), 'that this great, this powerful, this formidable kingdom, is considered only as a province to a despicable Electorate.'[104]

Dettingen was the high point of Carteret's European policy. Over the course of 1744 the British position on the Continent steadily worsened, and as it did so Carteret and the ministry suffered ever more criticism in Parliament, press, and at the bar of public opinion. It was not so bad that France formally declared war in March 1744, for this merely regularised the existing situation. Much more inflammatory was Carteret's perceived pandering to George's Hanoverian concerns. This was blamed for a series of diplomatic blunders that led Frederick to believe that Prussia was threatened by Britain and her German allies. In mid-1744, therefore, he joined the French in a new anti-Austrian alliance, while at the same time building up his already formidable army.

Frederick's military preparations went largely unnoticed at Whitehall, however, for by this point the scene of war had shifted to the Low Countries. In May a large French army under Marshal de Saxe invaded the Austrian Netherlands, where it found the allied defence force weak and hopelessly divided. The British and Hanoverian contingents distrusted each other; the Austrians could barely field more than a few thousand troops; and the Dutch were in a state of complete funk. The Dutch republic was falling into economic and cultural decay, and neither its governors nor soldiers had any appetite for war with France. In the space of a few weeks the French took half a dozen or so fortresses in the Austrian Netherlands with no concerted resistance from the allies. An Austrian invasion of eastern France looked likely to halt the French advance in the north, but then in August, Frederick invaded Bohemia, which of course forced the Austrians back onto the defensive. Although Frederick's invasion was eventually repulsed by the Austrians, the calamities that befell Britain and her allies during 1744 demanded a scapegoat at Whitehall, and in November Carteret resigned under pressure from his ministerial colleagues. An irate George II assured his ministers that Carteret was 'a man of the greatest abilities this country ever bred: you have forced him from me; and I am weary of you all'.[105]

British fortunes in this most unpredictable of wars would plummet still further in 1745. The year began well for their Austrian allies, with news reaching Vienna that Emperor Charles Albert had died, and that his successor as ruler of Bavaria was willing to sue for peace and to support the candidacy of Maria Theresa's husband, Francis Stephen of Lorraine, in the election for the next emperor. Even the French acknowledged that Francis Stephen was the only viable candidate, and he would duly be elected emperor in December. The imperial title, and the prestige that went with it, was back in Austrian–Habsburg hands. But having lost one battle after another to the Prussians in central Europe, Maria Theresa was compelled that same month to make peace with Frederick at the treaty of Dresden, and – bitterly though she resented it – to recognise his conquest of Silesia. The Austrians would be free once again to fight the French, which was good news for Whitehall, to be sure. But heartening though the treaty of Dresden was for the British, it was overshadowed by disasters closer to home.

From the spring of 1745 the French had left Frederick to fend for himself in Germany and concentrated instead on their offensive in Flanders. In May the Pragmatic Army, under the nominal command of George II's younger son the duke of Cumberland, confronted Saxe's French army at Fontenoy in the southern Austrian Netherlands. An heroic advance by British and Hanoverian infantry, under heavy fire from three sides, succeeded in penetrating the French centre and would probably have overwhelmed a less resolute and resourceful general than Saxe. But his skilful reorganising of his lines, and Cumberland's failure to pin down the left and right wings of the French army before advancing, resulted in an allied defeat. The two sides suffered roughly the same number of casualties – about 7,500 – making Fontenoy the bloodiest battle in western Europe since Malplaquet. After the battle the British complained bitterly, and with reason, about the 'inexpressible cowardice' of the Dutch troops.[106] The one consolation the British could take from Fontenoy was the knowledge that the best of their infantry were better than the best of the French. In most other respects, however – quality of leadership, unity of command, and troop numbers – the French had the advantage, and by the end of 1745 they had overrun much of the Austrian Netherlands.

The resumption of open warfare between Britain and France lent a new and sharper edge to the Jacobite cause. The French had made serious preparations over the winter of 1743–4 for an invasion of England, urged on by some Tory leaders who were still smarting at their betrayal by the patriot opposition after Walpole's fall. When Versailles had then dropped its designs on England as impractical, they were taken up by the Old Pretender's son Charles Edward Stuart (1720–88) – known to his enemies as 'The Young Pretender', to his well-wishers as 'Bonnie Prince Charlie'. Charles Edward hoped to force the hand of the French government by staging an invasion of his own; and in the aftermath of Fontenoy, with the British compelled to send more troops to the Low Countries, the Hanoverian regime had never looked more vulnerable. In unconscious imitation of Henry Tudor, the prince begged a few favours from the French (including the loan of a warship) and borrowed money from sympathetic financiers to fit out a small expeditionary force. In July 1745 he and his companions landed in the western Highlands of Scotland, and within a few weeks several thousand clansmen had rallied to the cause of a Stuart restoration and an end to 'German despotism'.[107] But though Catholic and episcopalian Scots, in particular, still had little love for the Hanoverians or the 1707 union, recruiting would prove much harder for the Jacobites in 1745 than it had in 1715. People remembered how the 'Fifteen had ended. Nevertheless, with the attention and resources of the British state focused elsewhere, a Jacobite army of just a few thousand Highlanders represented a formidable war-host. It certainly proved adequate to deal with the main government army in Scotland, which although larger than Charles Edward's force, consisted mostly of raw Lowland recruits. Fifteen minutes of Highland charging and brisk work with the broadsword would be enough to break loyalist resistance at Prestonpans, near Edinburgh, in September, and leave the battlefield 'a spectacle of horror, being covered with heads, legs, arms, and mutilated bodies'.[108] Scotland was once again a Jacobite kingdom, leaving the ministry no choice but to bring home a sizeable number of British troops from the Austrian Netherlands.

In 1745, the War of the Austrian Succession would penetrate to the heart of England. A Jacobite force of about 5,000 Highlanders crossed the border in November, and marched as far as Derby with little or no opposition. London seemed tantalisingly within reach. But two insurmountable obstacles now confronted the invaders: the thousands of enemy troops massing between them and the capital; and the fact that Charles Edward simply had too little support in England to make a Stuart restoration practicable. For all the Jacobites' bravery, and the complacency and frequent bungling of the ministry, they could not prevail against the overwhelming strength of anti-popery in the heartlands of the British state. English Tories had assured the prince otherwise, but only if he invaded at the head of a powerful French army. In the absence of French intervention, the 'Forty-five, like the 'Fifteen, would be doomed. Ignoring Charles Edward's protests, the Jacobites retreated to Scotland, where their temerity in assailing Leviathan without serious foreign backing was savagely punished at the battle of Culloden in April 1746. A series of uncoordinated charges by some 5,000 Highlanders and troops from the Scottish and Irish brigades in the French army were repulsed with heavy loss by the disciplined musketry, cannon-fire and serried bayonets of 9,000 government regulars – mostly Scottish and English, but a few Ulstermen, Austrians and Hessians – commanded by the duke of Cumberland. Charles Edward fled into the western Highlands and islands, hotly pursued by government ships and troops, and had to rely on the kind of escapades that had saved his great-uncle Charles II in 1651 in order to make it back to France. And that was the end of the 'Forty-five.

Yet the mere fact that the Jacobites had invaded England was a major victory for the French. For little more than it cost to give (mostly) empty promises of support to Charles Edward they had succeeded in distracting the British government and tying up troops and ships that might otherwise have been deployed against them in the Low Countries or in the colonies. The Pragmatic Army and the morale of Britain's allies both suffered accordingly. The French, on the other hand, were so heartened by Prestonpans that they revived their own invasion plans, only to abandon them again early in 1746. The British government's lingering fear of a French invasion helps to explain the savagery with which it set about dismembering the Highland clans and their culture (even down to banning the wearing of kilts) in the years after Culloden. 'If this power of the Highlands is not absolutely reduced,' thought the duke of Newcastle, 'France may play the Pretender upon us whenever she pleases.'[109] Defeat in 1745–6 and Charles Edward's subsequent lapse into alcoholism would gradually finish Jacobitism as a political force, and what military potential it retained in Scotland and Ireland would depend entirely upon the possibility of French invasion.

Much more worrying for the British government than the Jacobite advance into England was the crumbling of the allies' position in the Low Countries. Victories over the Pragmatic Army at the battles of Rocoux (1746) and Lauffeldt (1747) brought the French to the very borders of the Dutch republic. In both battles the Austrians had largely stood by as Saxe's forces overwhelmed Cumberland's British and Hanoverian infantry. The Dutch had no heart for the fight, while the Austrians were now willing to surrender their interest in the Netherlands to anyone, even Versailles, if it allowed them to concentrate on recovering Silesia. Lauffeldt left the Dutch republic at the mercy of Saxe's army, and once the Dutch had succumbed then surely the British would be next. Whitehall now had no choice but to sue for peace, for as Chesterfield confided to Newcastle: 'When you are beaten and can't carry on the war any longer unless to be beaten still more (which is our present case), all I know is that you must make the best peace you can, and that will be a bad one, which is always the case of the vanquished.'[110]

In fact, the treaty that ended the War of the Austrian Succession would not be nearly so bad as the British had feared. Their capture in June 1745 of the French fortress of Louisbourg (for which, see the next chapter) on the Gulf of St Lawrence, and two resounding naval victories in the Bay of Biscay in 1747 that all but destroyed the French navy and gave Britain effective control of the north Atlantic, meant that they would not come to the negotiating table empty-handed. French power relied not on overseas trade, however, but on European territories and population. What disposed Versailles towards peace was not the ravaging of France's merchant marine by the British, but, as one of Louis XV's ministers told him, 'the shortage of food [the French harvest had failed in 1747], the depopulation of the state and the disorder of the finances'.[111] On the brink of outright victory in the Low Countries, France was on the brink of economic disaster at home. By the terms of the treaty of Aix-la-Chapelle, concluded in October 1748, the French agreed to return all their conquests in the Low Countries, while the British handed back Louisbourg and a few other captured French colonies. The main losers by the peace, as they had been for much of the war, were the Austrians. Besides Silesia, they ceded territory in Italy to the Spanish (who were angry nonetheless that Britain was allowed to retain Gibraltar, Minorca and the *asiento*). All that Maria Theresa received for her losses in Germany and Italy was the restoration of the Austrian Netherlands, which she would gladly have exchanged for territory nearer home – ideally, of course, Silesia.

There was, inevitably, a public outcry in Britain at having to hand back Louisbourg, just as there was, and with greater reason, in France at returning the territory conquered by Saxe's army ('*Bête comme la paix*' – 'idiotic as the peace' – became a Parisian saying).[112] But British ministers were adamant that denying the French access to the deepwater ports of the Low Countries, and maintaining a reasonably intact Austrian Habsburg empire, were far more important for national security than retaining far-off Louisbourg. To the extent that the balance of Europe had been preserved, just about, then Britain had something to show for eight years of warfare. Nevertheless, Aix-la-Chapelle was seen by almost all parties to it as little more than a glorified truce. 'We are entering a house made of cardboard,' was the verdict of the Austrian foreign minister Kaunitz.[113] The inability of the Dutch and the Austrians to stop the French from simply marching back into Flanders, should they so choose, was just one of several issues that the treaty left up in the air. Another was the ill-feeling between Austria and its enemies – and indeed between Austria and its allies. Maria Theresa could not accept the permanent loss of Silesia and Austrian territories in Italy, and she was very bitter that Britain had used its financial and military dominance within the alliance to negotiate what amounted to a separate peace with France (Aix-la-Chapelle) by which Austria had been forced to make precisely these concessions. To her this seemed like deliberate treachery on Britain's part. Above all, the struggle for strategic supremacy between Britain and France, both in Europe and across the globe, had not been resolved.

The treaty of Aix-la-Chapelle guaranteed nothing except the resumption of war. 'Never have the European powers kept such large forces in being as since the peace,' wrote a Prussian officer in the late 1740s: 'We keep our weapons sharp, and follow the principle that a large and well-schooled army is the best rampart of the state.'[114] An anxious British commentator agreed: 'It is the concern of every Power, while Peace continues, to be watchful and prepared, for a small spark in any one corner, may set the whole Political frame of Europe in a flame.'[115] The French, for their part, began to build up their navy from the late 1740s with the deliberate aim of challenging British commerce and colonial expansion. Versailles was now convinced that dominion in America and the Atlantic held the key to power in Europe. Deny Britain the fruits of her transatlantic empire, divert her naval and military strength to protecting her American colonies, 'and she would no longer be in a position to bear the expenses of all the quarrels that she or her allies are always disposed to pick with France'.[116] British foreign policy in the late 1740s and early 1750s concentrated on trying to reinvigorate the 'old system' – that is, the Grand Alliance that had preserved the balance of Europe and contained French power since the 1670s. With the Dutch now a spent force, a strong Austria was more than ever vital to British interests in this respect, and Newcastle and William Pitt – the ministry's main parliamentary manager by 1750 – would do their best to revive Habsburg power in Germany and to end Austria's debilitating quarrel with Spain over their various dynastic claims in Italy. But while Britain valued Austria as a bulwark against the French, the Austrians themselves no longer regarded France but Prussia as their main enemy.

In France too there was a feeling that the old rivalry with the Habsburgs was so much wasted effort if it diverted resources from challenging Britain. The idea of an enduring rapprochement between Austria and France was beginning to take shape in both Vienna and Versailles – accelerated on the Austrian side by their deep distrust of British intentions, and a well-founded suspicion that Britain would like to add Prussia (as well as Russia) to the Grand Alliance against France. Prussia's rise to military greatness under Frederick, and the loathing his conquest of Silesia had generated between Vienna and Berlin, would soon prove too much for the creaking 'old system' to endure.

The fragile peace established at Aix-la-Chapelle was bound to fail. The old system could simply no longer contain the hatreds and rivalries among Europe's great powers. Another major war was expected; indeed, for some it could not come soon enough. And yet despite Versailles's eagerness to weaken Britain's power across the Atlantic, few could have anticipated how and where the fighting would begin: with a skirmish between British and French forces in a remote American valley in 1754. And no one would have dreamt that the British colonial officer whose soldiers fired the fateful shots – a youthful George Washington (1732–99) – would one day become the first elected leader of a transatlantic republic forged in this crucible of global war. The remainder of this book will tell how the weak and divided Britain of the early 1600s came to possess an empire that was the envy of all Europe, only to lose half of it after her greatest imperial triumph.

7

Greatness of Empire

Your well-built Ships, companions of the Sunn,
As they were Chariots to his fiery beams,
Which oft the Earths circumference have runn,
And now lie moar'd in Severn, Trent, and Tems,
Shall plough the Ocean with their gilded Stems,
And in their hollow bottoms you convay
To Lands inrich'd with gold, with pearls and gems,
But above all, where many thousands stay
Of wronged Indians, whom you shall set free
From Spanish yoke, and Romes Idolatry.

Thomas Gage, *The English-American, His Travail by Sea and Land*
(1648), prefatory poem by Thomas Chaloner

. . . a Spirit of Commerce, and strength at Sea to protect it, are the most certain marks of the Greatness of Empire . . . whoever Commands the Ocean, Commands the Trade of the World, and whoever Commands the Trade of the World, Commands the Riches of the World, and whoever is Master of That, Commands the World it self.

John Evelyn, *Navigation and Commerce* (1674), 15 (paraphrasing
Sir Walter Ralegh, paraphrasing the Athenian general Themistocles
[*c.*524–459 BC])

Western designs, 1600–60

On 29 September 1665 the Great Plague of London claimed its most famous victim. 'I hear for certain this night', wrote Samuel Pepys, 'that Sir Martin Noell is this day dead of the plague in London, where he hath lain sick of it these eight days.'[1] Noell's name has long since slipped from the national memory, but by the time of the Restoration in 1660 he was probably the best-known entrepreneur and financier in all of England. The younger son of a Stafford tradesman, he had served his apprenticeship in London, and by capitalising on his marriage to the daughter of a wealthy citizen, and the business opportunities afforded by the English Civil War, he had broken into the City's lucrative mercantile sector. Thereafter he had made his fortune as a pioneer in new lines of merchandise – notably slaves and sugar (the two went together, as we shall see) – and from the influence he had enjoyed as an adviser and moneylender to Lord Protector Oliver Cromwell.

Noell's will and the inventory of his personal estate give some idea of the amazing range of commercial and public ventures in which he had dabbled. His London mansion house was a veritable Aladdin's Cave of luxury foreign wares and exotic bric-a-brac. On the walls were Dutch paintings; Delftware complemented rich Spanish tables; and Japanese cabinets, trunks and assorted lacquerware vied for attention with curtains of 'India silk', 'Callicoe sheets' and an 'East India Hamocke'. There were silver-rimmed ewers from China and many other pieces of Chinese porcelain; furniture decorated with 'East india beasts and birds'; '5 Jappan figures of wood'; '2 peeces of Currall'; '2 China Jarrs & snakes skinn'; '1 Estridge Egg'; and the 'Jaw of a Tyger'.[2] It was just as the great social commentator Joseph Addison would observe: 'Our Rooms are filled with Pyramids of China, and adorned with the Workmanship of Japan' – except that he was writing over forty years after Noell's death.[3] Among Noell's other assets were an extensive estate in Ireland, the part-ownership of several merchant ships, and a half-share of a sugar plantation on Barbados, complete with 'negroes'. His debts amounted to a staggering £30,106 (millions in today's money), and his principal creditor was the crown, to which he owed large sums as a farmer and receiver of public revenues. So complicated were his business affairs that according to Pepys no one could work out how much he had been worth, 'he having dealt in so many things, public and private, as nobody can understand whereabouts his estate is, which is the fate of these great dealers at everything'.[4]

A man of such vast and varied financial interests as Noell, and yet with no background among London's merchant princes, would have been impossible to find in England just forty years earlier. Outsiders like him had been largely excluded from the most lucrative overseas markets by the big London trading companies. His rise to wealth and political influence is the story of the major changes that had occurred in the nation's overseas trade and colonial enterprises since the early 1600s.

*

As we have seen, England's foreign trade had diversified considerably since the mid-sixteenth century and the interruptions to the Antwerp market. The bulk of English overseas commerce was still with continental Europe, and would remain so far into the eighteenth century. However, some of the London merchants had abandoned the centuries-old cloth export trade with the Low Countries and Germany in favour of importing luxury goods from the Mediterranean and the Far East. It was the lure of rich new markets that brought the first English ship to Japan in 1613, and to China in 1635 – a century or so after the Portuguese had made 'first contact'. These intrepid English voyagers and the trading interests they represented had barely considered founding colonies in the sense of communities of settlers who would work the land – what contemporaries called plantations – for reasons we shall return to later.

The first faltering steps of the British and Irish to plant colonies were taken not in the Far East but in the Americas in the late sixteenth and early seventeenth centuries, and these too were focused more on trade and plunder than on territorial conquest. The only transatlantic colonising venture that James I showed any interest in, and then not much, was Virginia, which began life in 1607 as the tiny settlement of Jamestown. The king's indifference was entirely understandable. Built on swampy ground, at a tidewater location where the settlers' own excrement ebbed and flowed around them, Jamestown was a pestilential death trap. London's merchant grandees were similarly short on enthusiasm for the new venture. Some invested in the Virginia Company in its early years, but once it became clear that there were no easy profits in the transatlantic trade – no precious metals, no north-west passage to the East Indies – they got out, leaving outsiders like Martin Noell to colonise the uncertain commercial world of Virginian tobacco.

The American dream was sustained by a variety of seemingly contradictory motives. Fantasies of carving out a golden empire in imitation of the Conquistadores sat uneasily alongside the desire to bring true religion and civility to the Indians. Humanism offered no easy answers as to the rights or wrongs of planting colonies. Traditional humanists like John Milton believed that political power sprang from self-sacrificing virtue and the defence of civil liberties, and were therefore suspicious of the commercial and imperialist aspects of colonisation. On the other hand, the increasingly influential Tacitean strain of humanism that had emerged in the late sixteenth century laid stress on commerce and overseas expansion as the surest foundations of national greatness. Yet whatever agenda inspired the early European colonisers it usually referred at some level to the play of religious and political forces back in Europe. The French monarchy, for example, set up colonies in North America as a bulwark against Spanish power and the spread of Protestantism. Likewise, English colonisers often saw themselves as agents in the great struggle to advance the Protestant cause against European popery.

The first wave of English adventurers to cross the Atlantic were generally too busy hunting for El Dorado or plundering the Spanish to bother with founding colonies. They tended to stay in one place no longer than it took them to loot it dry. A trickle of English settlers set up tiny colonies on the coast of 'Guiana', on the southern shores of the Caribbean, in the early 1600s. They too searched greedily for Indian gold mines, and if they grew tobacco it was merely to make a little cash on the side. Good business sense began to prevail in the 1610s, however, when small groups of English and Irish settlers set up dedicated tobacco-growing colonies around the mouth of the Amazon. But their daring and initiative did not impress the Spanish and Portuguese, and they rarely prospered before being evicted or killed. The threat of Iberian aggression almost certainly deterred would-be South American adventurers. Equally off-putting, however, would have been James I's appeasement of the Spanish, for while he did not accept Iberian claims to exclusive dominion in the Americas, he decreed that any of his subjects who chose to colonise lands claimed by Philip III should be 'left unto the peril which they should incur thereby'.[5] Leading Puritans would later complain that 'through the prevalency of the . . . Spanish faction [at court]', neither James nor Charles I had afforded would-be colonisers 'that publick Protection which was due unto them, and which was suitable to the Honour and Interest of this Nation'.[6] In 1607, James even toyed with the idea of sacrificing the Virginia venture in return for an alliance with Spain; and in 1619, eager to secure a Spanish bride for Prince Charles, he obliged Gondomar and Philip III by pulling the plug on the recently established Amazon Company.

James's pandering to Spanish interests had a major bearing on the most famous group of English colonisers – now, if not then – the Pilgrim Fathers. Catholic victories at the start of the Thirty Years War, and the seeming spread of popery at home, convinced some Puritans that they must build a new Ark across the Atlantic before the deluge came. The Pilgrims had originally planned to settle in the tropical climes of Guiana, but in terminating the Amazon Company, James made it clear that he was washing his hands of colonial intrusion on Spanish territory. Consequently, they decided to sail for the 'howling wilderness' of North America, well beyond the horizons of even Philip III's territorial ambitions. The timing of their departure was also intimately bound up with European geopolitics. They left the Old World in 1620 because the imminent renewal of war between Spain and the Dutch republic (where they had moved from England to set up independent congregations) threatened their freedom of worship.

For those in England unwilling or unable to retreat before the threat of popish inundation there was always the option of agitating for a naval campaign against the Spanish empire in the Americas. This 'blue-water' strategy was aimed ultimately at making the Protestant powers 'master of all that treasure [in the New World], which . . . is the great support of Popery in all parts of Christendome'.[7] In the 1620s and 1630s a group of leading English Hispanophobes tried (unsuccessfully) to interest Charles I in establishing a West India Company to wrest control of the Caribbean from the Spanish. 'Cutting the Liver veyne that supplies the Bodie of Spaine wth such immence sum[m]es of money', the company's proponents claimed, 'will humble them and give a generall Peace and security soe much longed for to all Christendome.' Central to this project was the establishment of colonies-cum-privateering bases that would 'like a Gangraine eate into the heart of the Silver Indies'.[8] The English urge to colonise, like their desire to fight popery on the Continent, was born of the anger and fear generated by Europe's wars of religion.

Ousted by the Spanish and abandoned by their own government, disgruntled Amazon settlers were involved in establishing England's first island colonies in the Americas. Between 1612 and 1632, while Spain was largely preoccupied fighting the Dutch, the English grabbed Bermuda, off the coast of North America; Nevis, Montserrat, Antigua, Barbados, and half of St Kitts (with the French) and St Croix (with the Dutch), in the West Indies; and Providence Island in the Caribbean. These islands were not prime colonial real estate, however. Most had been too small and – inasmuch as some of them were inhabited by warlike Carib Indians – forbidding to prove attractive to earlier European colonisers. Daniel Defoe, a century later, would call them 'the Dregs of the Spaniards first Extraction, the Refuse Part of their Conquests, their meer Leavings'.[9] Their main advantage as far as English settlers were concerned was their relatively secure location, for the clockwise wind patterns in the Caribbean meant that the Spanish, whose colonies were mostly to the west, would have to beat back to windward to deal with them. Tropical diseases, hurricanes, and attack by European rivals and Carib Indians combined to make life hazardous for the early English settlers in the Caribbean. High mortality rates and a lack of women colonists meant that down to 1700 the islands required some 220,000 migrants from Britain and Ireland to maintain a white population of about an eighth of that number.

Tobacco was their first successful export. But then in the early 1640s it was discovered that most of these islands, and especially Barbados, were better suited to a much more profitable crop: sugar cane. The macro-economics for English sugar production were promising. Brazil, Europe's main source of sugar, became a war zone in the mid-1640s as the Portuguese settlers there – emboldened by Portugal's regaining of its independence from Spain in 1640 – rebelled against their Dutch conquerors. In England, meanwhile, the outbreak of civil war had rid the Caribbean colonies of the stultifying oversight of their royally appointed proprietors, whose authority had collapsed with that of the king. Most importantly, perhaps, the Dutch were ready to supply the technology and know-how to refine the raw cane into sugar, anticipating healthy profits by selling slave labour to the English planters and shipping the refined sugar to Europe. With European demand for sugar seemingly inexhaustible, exports from Barbados alone would be worth over 3 million pounds a year by the 1650s, making it the wealthiest place in the English-speaking world.

Martin Noell was involved in the sugar boom both as slave-trader and planter. He was one of the 'new merchants': men from outside of London's mercantile elite who had come to dominate the import of West Indian sugar, Virginian tobacco and other colonial products. Some of the leading new merchants were strong Puritans. Indeed, this probably explains why they were drawn into transatlantic trade in the first place. Making money and challenging Spanish power had run together for decades in the Atlantic, and the new merchants frequently collaborated with England's greatest privateer the earl of Warwick and other godly grandees in promoting English colonisation in the Americas.

Colonies preceded empire by many decades. Neither James I nor Charles I had the military resources or the appetite for war and colonisation across the Atlantic, and therefore the crown generally handed over responsibility for settling new lands to private companies or aristocratic proprietors. The royal charters granted to these groups and individuals asserted the crown's sovereign and imperial authority over

13. *Emblematical Print on the South Sea Scheme* by William Hogarth, 1721.

14. *Excise in Triumph*, c.1733. This is a satire on the Excise Bill:
Robert Walpole is depicted as an excise man, sitting astride a barrel.
The British lion, yoked and bridled by Walpole and a standing army,
wears wooden shoes, a symbol of French-style oppression.

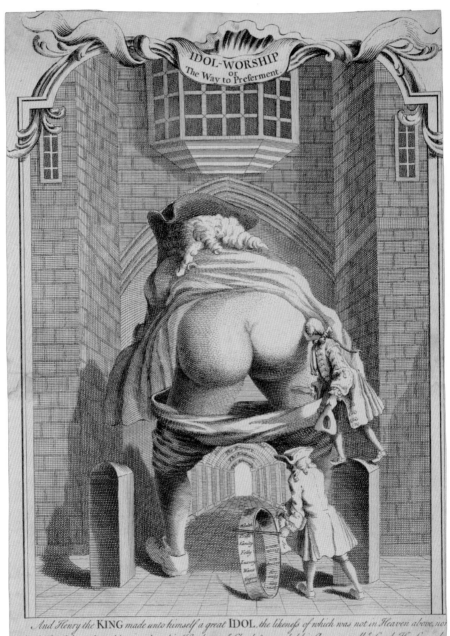

And Henry the KING made unto himself a great IDOL, the likeness of which was not in Heaven above, nor in the Earth beneath; and he reared up his Head unto ẏ Clouds, & extended his Arm over all ẏ Land; His Legs also were as ẏ Posts of a Gate, or as an Arch stretched forth over ẏ Doors of all ẏ Publick Offices in ẏ Land, & whosoever went out or whosoever came in, passed beneath, & with Idolatrous Reverence lift up their Eyes, & kissed ẏ Cheeks of ẏ Postern.

15. *Idol-Worship or The Way to Preferment*, 1740.

16. *The Lyon in Love*, 1738.

17. *O the Roast Beef of Old England (The Gate of Calais)* by William Hogarth, 1748, engraved by C. Mosley.

18. *Beer Street* by William Hogarth, 1751.

19. *Gin Lane* by William Hogarth, 1751.

20. *The Abolition of the Slave Trade* by Isaac Cruikshank, 1792. This print illustrates the evils of the slave trade. Such images are rare before the 1790s.

21. Slaves processing sugar cane, *c.*1667–71.

22. *Fort St George on the Coromandel Coast* by Jan van Ryne, 1754.

23. *The Ballance, or The American's Triumphant*, 1766. The figure on the left of the balance represents Britain; the figure on the right, the American colonies. Behind the five 'Stampmen' (tax collectors) on the broomstick is the devil, exclaiming, 'I shall have you all soon.'

24. *The Mob destroying & Setting Fire to the Kings Bench Prison & House of Correction in St Georges Fields*, 1780. This print illustrates the Gordon Riots in London, 1780.

25. *The Free-born Briton or A Perspective of Taxation*, 1786. An enraged John Bull labours under the intolerable burden of taxes.

the colonisers' activities, but this meant little on the ground. Even the aims of the charter-holders themselves were often frustrated as the colonists quickly took charge of their colony's government and econo- mies. In contrast to their French and Spanish counterparts, English colonies underlined their political autonomy by setting up their own representative assemblies (in effect, mini-Parliaments) and asserting their native right not to be taxed without consent. When, in the mid-1630s, Charles I tried to assume control over the production and sale of Virginian tobacco as part of his ill-fated design to impose 'one uniforme Course of Government' throughout his dominions, the council of Virginia threw out the king's governor.[10] It was Virginia, therefore, not Scotland, that first rebelled against Charles's imperial project.

The war of the three kingdoms in the 1640s threw England's overseas commerce open to all-comers. The collapse of royal power, and Parliament's opposition to state-licensed monopolies, stripped London merchant princes of most of their trading privileges. Noell and other new merchants were able to muscle in on the East India trade during the 1640s, and to promote schemes for setting up colonies around the Indian Ocean. They were quick, too, to grasp the profit-making and colonising opportunities in the 1641 Irish rebellion, investing heavily in Parliament's efforts to reconquer Ireland and turn it into one vast English plantation. Given their vested interest in an aggressive Protestant state it is also not surprising that they supported the 1640–2 junto and the Independent grandees in defeating the king and creating the parlia- mentary Leviathan of the 1640s. By the time Charles I was executed, in 1649, they were an important political force in both the Rump Parliament and in London's municipal government.

Backed by the Rump and its formidable navy, the new merchants succeeded in destroying the last vestiges of royal authority across the Atlantic, and began clawing back the shipping trade to and from English colonies that the Dutch had grabbed following their peace with Spain in 1648. The refusal of the Dutch to bow to English pressure for a political and economic merger of the two republics led to the first Anglo-Dutch war of 1652–4. When peace was declared in April 1654, the way was finally clear for Oliver Cromwell, now lord protector, to pursue the policies of war and colonisation in the Caribbean that Warwick's circle and the new merchants had been pushing for since well before the Civil War. The protector himself had long-standing ties to Warwick and other members of the Providence Island Company: the most militantly anti-Spanish of the English colonial ventures.

Cromwell's 'Western Design' against the Spanish island of Hispaniola (modern-day Haiti and the Dominican Republic) in 1655 was the first and only time the English state threw its full weight behind a colonial expedition to the New World. Before the design was launched there was a debate in government circles as to whether attacking Spain was a wise move. Within a very few years it would become clear that it was France, not Spain, that posed the greatest threat to English security. But Louis XIV's time had not yet come. France was still a country where Protestants (the Huguenots) enjoyed liberty of conscience. And while the Spanish had the riches of the Americas to draw upon, they remained a danger to Europe's Protestants, or so Cromwell reasoned. The simple fact was that, like many Puritans of his generation, he could not see past Spain as (in the words of one of his councillors) 'the greatest enemye to the Protestant cause in the world; an old enemie to this nation when it prospered best [i.e. under Elizabeth]'.[11] To defeat the Spanish in the New World seemed like the next step along that providential path which God had laid before the English nation since the Reformation.[12] Besides, as Cromwell's advisers – such as Noell – assured him, the Spanish were militarily overstretched in the Caribbean. Seizing Hispaniola would be relatively easy, and would give England an ideal base from which to intercept their treasure fleets. Cromwell trusted in providence to bring about victory – much as Philip II had with the Armada of 1588 – and, like Philip, he was to be bitterly disappointed.

It did not help that the expeditionary force consisted mostly of raw recruits and pressed men; that profiteering by Noell and other contractors deprived it of vital supplies and equipment; or that the Spanish knew precisely where it was headed. Add to that poor planning and leadership by the English, and skilful use of the jungly terrain on Hispaniola by the Spanish, and the result was one of the biggest humiliations in England's military history. An invading army of 9,000 troops was seen off by a mere 500 or so defenders. In all the English lost about 1,000 men to disease and enemy ambush, and were so spooked by the end of their ordeal that they mistook fireflies in the Caribbean night for the burning matches of Spanish musketeers come to kill them. To salvage something from this fiasco, the English landed on Jamaica, where the Spanish had no advance warning and mounted little resistance on the mistaken assumption that this was simply a particularly large raiding party, not an invasion force. As it turned out, Jamaica was perfectly adequate for English purposes. It had plenty of fertile land and was just as well placed as Hispaniola to annoy the Spanish. Noell certainly had no reason to complain. He had played a leading role in organising and financing the Western Design – receiving lucrative government contracts for war supplies which he then failed to honour – and was granted 20,000 acres on Jamaica for his trouble. Yet the defeat on Hispaniola was regarded by most in England as a national disaster. Cromwell was haunted by it to the end of his life. As one royalist glee-fully reported, it 'strikes him in point of reputacion with the vulgar in England, who beleeved him invincible, and the souldiery in regard of former successe thought themselves soe too'.[13] The only reason Cromwell could find for God's sudden abandonment of the English was their sins and pride. The rule of the major-generals was part of Cromwell's response to this divine admonition, as was his refusal to accept the crown when it was offered to him in 1657.

The Western Design would be the last colonial venture inspired by an apocalyptic and essentially Elizabethan world-view in which Spain was the great Satan, and New World treasure the key to supremacy in Europe. The new gods of colonial enterprise would be the riches and international power to be derived from the trade in sugar and other consumer products. The competition for marketable resources would drive the next generation of transatlantic adventurers and would-be empire-builders, not Puritan zeal or the lure of Spanish gold.

An empire of goods

The first Anglo-Dutch war of 1652–4 was evidence of a new approach among the architects of the English parliamentary Leviathan to the related issues of foreign policy, international trade and the colonies. While Oliver Cromwell and his godly circle remained committed to an alliance with the Dutch republic against the Spanish empire – even as English and Dutch warships pounded each other in the Channel – other politicians in the Rump Parliament of 1648–53 sought to redefine the national interest in more commercial and worldly terms. With the support of leading figures among the new merchants, they promoted policies for establishing a system of government control over the nation's commerce that would better enable it to compete, militarily as well as economically, with its European rivals. This 'mercantilist' philosophy was articulated in particularly influential form by the political lobbyist Benjamin Worsley, who argued: 'It is by Trade, and the due ordering and governing of it, and by no other means, that Wealth and Shipping can either bee encreased, or upheld; and consequently by no other, that the power of any Nation can bee susteined by Land, or by Sea.'[14] For some years now, insisted Worsley, the main challenge to the national interest had come not from the Catholic powers but the Protestant Dutch, who had striven 'to laie a foundation to themselvs for ingrossing the Universal Trade, not onely of Christendom, but indeed, of the greater part of the known world'.[15] He would doubtless have been even more alarmed had he known that the combined tonnage of the Dutch navy and merchant marine by the mid-seventeenth century (about 500,000 tonnes) was over twice that of the English.

The Rump Parliament's response to Dutch commercial dominance was the 1651 Navigation Act, by which all imports from outside of Europe either to England or its colonies had to be carried exclusively in English (but not Scottish or Irish) ships. The Act's immediate purpose was to shift the significant proportion of English overseas trade that was carried in the holds of foreign (mainly Dutch) merchantmen to those of English vessels. Leviathan must swim in shark-free waters. But the Act's promoters also had a more ambitious objective, which was to build the maritime and financial resources that would enable England to go head to head with its more powerful European neighbours. The Navigation Act, and its successors, established the framework for an imperial system that was based not simply on exploiting foreign territory and its resources (the Spanish model) but upon nurturing overseas commerce in order to strengthen the sinews of state power.

Like many other parliamentarian fiscal reforms, the Rump's mercantilist system was retained at the restoration of Charles II. In fact, more than retained, it was considerably augmented. George Downing masterminded the passing of further navigation acts by Parliament in 1660 and 1663, making it illegal for the colonies to export products such as tobacco or sugar to anywhere besides England or other English colonies, or for foreign goods to be shipped to the colonies without going via England first. The navigation acts accounted in large part for the boom in imports, and in the re-export of overseas products to the Continent, that began in the late 1660s and would last, on and off, until the 1690s. It seemed that the commerce and wealth of England had never increased so fast as during the Restoration period. 'We have most part of the trade of the World,' claimed one particularly upbeat hack in 1677, 'many of our poor Cotagers children be turn'd Merchants and substantial Traders [and] . . . our houses be built like Palaces, over what they were in the last Age.'[16]

The Restoration government was too weak to enforce full compliance with the acts, particularly across the Atlantic, but English and American merchants and shipowners responded to the challenge of fierce competition within their protected market to improve efficiency and increase investment. The roaring transatlantic trade in particular served to drive down carrying costs to a price that matched the Dutch, and to boost England's manufacture of long-haul shipping. England's ocean-going commercial fleet was the largest in Europe by the 1680s, and consisted predominantly of English-built ships. The mercantilist system created by the navigation acts probably did more to hasten London's eclipse of Amsterdam – in the early eighteenth century – as Europe's greatest entrepôt for colonial commerce than all three of England's wars against the Dutch put together.

The post-Restoration boom in overseas trade also owed much to the British people's insatiable appetite for imported commodities. Consumer demand for currants, fruit and spices had been rising since the late sixteenth century, and these old favourites were joined in the seventeenth century by the much more addictive tobacco and coffee. Well before the Civil War, the anti-smoking brigade had lamented the fact that 'every tinker, rogue, scavenger, or hangman is a Tobacconist [pipe-smoker]'.[17] Thirty years on, and a visitor to Cornwall in 1662 found that 'everyone, men and women, young and old' were 'puffing tobacco, which is here so common that the young children get it in the morning instead of breakfast'.[18] Coffee, as we have seen, was all the rage in polite society. But the real force to be reckoned with in the mass consumer market was the British sweet tooth. Annual imports of sugar more than doubled in the period 1660–1700, while prices halved accordingly, and what the British could not consume themselves was sold to the continentals. It was a commonplace by the late seventeenth century that there was 'no one commodity that doth so much encourage navigation, advance the King's customs and our land and is at the same time of so great a universal use, virtue and advantage as this king of sweets'.[19] Sugar was used in all sorts of ways: as a sweetener in wine, coffee and drinking chocolate, or on fresh and dried fruit; as a spice in savoury dishes; and as an essential ingredient in the cakes and pies for which England was becoming famous.

Another must-have for the British consumer – at first the aspiring and fashionable, but by 1700 just about everybody – was Asian textiles. The East India Company had been re-founded in the late 1650s (see below), and the bulk of its imports consisted of calicoes and chintzes (plain and printed cotton textiles), and silks and white cotton muslins, from India. About the time that Noell was buying his 'India silk' and 'Callicoe sheets', Pepys was acquiring an 'Indian gown' for himself, 'a very noble parti-coloured Indian gown' for his wife, and 'a painted Indian Calico for to line her new Study, which is very pretty'.[20]

The potential benefits of harnessing consumer demand to the crown's financial needs were apparently appreciated by Pepys's political masters at court. Certainly mercantilist ideas became well established at Whitehall after the Restoration. Charles II's privy councillor, George Villiers, 2nd duke of Buckingham, opined that: 'The undoubted Interest of England is Trade, since it is that only which can make us either Rich or Safe; for without a powerful Navy, we should be a Prey to our Neighbours, and without Trade, we could neither have Sea-Men nor Ships.'[21] A new, trade-centred imperialism surfaced at court in the early 1660s in the circle of the king's brother, James Duke of York, the future James II. James was the driving force behind the capture of the Dutch colony of New Netherland in 1664 – renamed New York in the duke's honour – which Charles then granted to him as his own private property (see illus. 9). James was clearly attracted by the idea of establishing a quasi-military fiefdom in North America, but his empire-building was also part of a larger design to promote English overseas trade (ideally at the expense of the Dutch) as a way of boosting the crown's customs revenue and thereby giving it greater freedom from Parliament and other irksome constitutional restraints. In the twenty or so years after the Restoration the English founded or acquired, besides New York, the colonies of Carolina (which split into North and South Carolina in 1719), New Jersey and Delaware, and Pennsylvania. Existing colonies along the Atlantic seaboard also experienced rapid territorial and economic expansion, so that by the early eighteenth century nearly the entire North American coast from Maine to Florida had been settled. The English Americas' white population had grown dramatically too, numbering about a quarter of a million people by the 1680s.

Colonial expansion, in turn, would help boost domestic manufacturing. The colonists in the English Americas demanded (and received) all sorts of products from home – everything from four-wheeled carriages to parrot-cages to tombstones. In 1700 less than a fifth of British manufacturing exports were shipped across the Atlantic; the remainder went almost entirely to Europe. A century later, and nearly half would go to North America and the West Indies. 'How great a Consumption of the British Manufacture has the Encrease of these Colonies been to this Nation?' Defoe would ask in the 1720s. 'Let the yearly Export of all

Kinds of Goods from hence to New-England, Virginia, Barbadoes, and Jamaica, besides all the lesser Colonies, be a Proof of it.'[22]

Colonial imports were of more immediate benefit to the Restoration government, however, for they contributed to the customs duties that during the 1670s and 1680s made up 30 to 40 per cent of crown revenue. Besides generating customs revenue and boosting domestic manufacturing, colonial and international commerce helped to build the merchant marine that supplied most of the navy's sailors in times of war. Maritime trade was no less important in stimulating the growth of financial services and credit systems that were necessary for managing the massive costs of fighting the Dutch or whoever else seemed to threaten English security and prosperity.

Charles II and his ministers were too busy indulging themselves, or dealing with domestic crises, to make a sustained effort at erecting a strong system of imperial government upon the commercial foundations established by the navigation acts. Nevertheless, the Restoration regime did attempt, by fits and starts, to play a more direct role in the running of the colonies. On hand to offer his expert opinion to the government was its flexible friend Martin Noell. He advised Charles II that it was of the 'highest Consequence' that he establish a council 'solely dedicated to the Inspection, Care, and Regulation of all forreigne Plantations belonging to the Crowne of England ... to which Government they ought to bee accountable'.[23] Someone at Whitehall seems to have been listening to this or similar advice, for during the 1660s and 1670s a plethora of executive councils, of varying competence, was set up to administer colonial policy and to enforce the navigation acts. The duke of York in particular was keen to bring the colonies more firmly under royal authority – ideally through the appointment of quasi-military governors with a permanent revenue that would free them from dependence on colonial legislative assemblies. The drive towards direct rule grew stronger from the mid-1670s after the North American frontier was convulsed by war and political unrest.

Had the Restoration government worked harder and faster to impose itself on the Puritan colonies of New England it might have prevented what, relative to the population sizes involved, was the bloodiest and most destructive war in American history. The fault was not all the crown's. The New England colonists had emigrated precisely to put as much distance between themselves and the Stuart monarchy as possible. In effect, they had been thumbing their noses at Whitehall almost from the moment they had left England. As their numbers had increased they had cheated and chivvied the coastal Indian tribes – first the Pequots, then mainly the Wampanoags – out of ever more land, and neither the parliamentarian regimes of the 1640s and 1650s nor the restored monarchy had shown much interest in stopping them. Largely unchecked by the English government, the colonists' pressure on the Wampanoags' farmland and hunting grounds had begun to cause serious tension between the two communities by the late 1660s. And while the colonists pressed from the east, the Wampanoags were menaced from the west by their Iroquois enemies, the Mohawk.

War eventually broke out in the summer of 1675, when the Wampanoag chief, Metacom – known to the English as King Philip – and his warriors began attacking English farms and towns in the Plymouth Colony. Soon, virtually all the coastal tribes had joined the fighting in a desperate bid to drive the English out of New England. Indiscriminate retaliation by the colonists against any 'savages' they could find persuaded those Indians disposed to remain neutral that if they did not hang together then assuredly they would hang separately. Unable to defend themselves against their highly mobile and well-armed enemy (the Indians were deadly with both flintlock and tomahawk), the English retreated to their coastal strongholds for safety. Even so, the Indians penetrated as far as Plymouth – on the Massachusetts coast – in March 1676, and a few weeks later burned Providence (the capital of Rhode Island) to the ground. The colonists were able to fight back effectively only after forming alliances with the Wampanoags' tribal enemies, who trained them in the Indians' 'skulking way' of forest warfare. Metacom was assailed from the east by colonial columns which destroyed vast quantities of his forces' corn and military provisions, and from the west by Mohawk war parties – the first fruits of treaty negotiations begun in 1675 between the governor of New York, Edmund Andros, and the Iroquois Confederacy.

In August 1676, his forces depleted by hunger, disease and desertion, Metacom was tracked down to a swamp – a native word that first entered the English language in 1676 – and shot by a Christian Indian. His body was quartered and hung in trees, the colonists decreeing that having 'caused many an Englishman's body to be unburied, and to rot above ground, not one of his bones should be buried'.[24] His head was stuck on a spike at the entrance to Fort Plymouth, and one of his hands was given to his killer as a keepsake.

The costs to both sides in King Philip's War were enormous. Some 3,000 coastal Indians were killed in the fighting, and many of those who survived either fled New England, were executed, or were sold into slavery in the West Indies. Of the region's 20,000 or so Indians before the war, only about half remained when the dust had settled. By 1750 the Indian population of New England had dropped to just a few thousand. The English suffered fewer casualties – that is, about 600 out of a population of around 50,000. But it would take many years to recover from the material devastation of the war. Almost half the English towns from Maine to Connecticut had been attacked, and a dozen laid waste, along with countless farms and plantations – the richest acres in New England.

The colonists' land-hunger and Iroquois aggression sparked another war in 1676, this time in the volatile marcher territories along the Virginian and Maryland frontiers. Under pressure from the Iroquois, the Susquehannock Indians of what is today eastern Pennsylvania moved southwards in the mid-1670s, and in the process clashed with English settlers spreading into the Chesapeake backcountry. In 1676 the Virginian planter Nathaniel Bacon led an irregular army of enraged frontiersmen against the Susquehannock, who then retaliated in force, killing at least 300 colonists. When Virginia's governor refused to back this unwarranted and needless war, Bacon and his men seized control of Jamestown and destroyed it – a fitting response, so they thought, to the governor's 'unjust taxes' and his failure to prevent the Indians' 'many invasions, robberies, and murders committed upon us'.[25] Bacon's Rebellion, as it became known, collapsed soon after the death of its leader, probably from dysentery, in October 1676, but not before the crown had dispatched six warships, eight transports and over 1,000 redcoats from England to reimpose royal authority. This was much the most powerful military force that an English monarch had yet sent to North America.

The wars along England's North American frontier encouraged Whitehall to mount what would be its only sustained attempt at shattering colonial autonomy before the 1760s. In Virginia and some of the West Indian plantations the crown appointed new, more powerful governors – often army or navy officers, who acted aggressively to emasculate colonial assemblies and undermine the planter elites. The duke of York's appointees as governor of New York – Andros and his successor, Thomas Dongan – largely ignored their colonies' legislative assemblies. Instead, they imposed taxes as they saw fit, and used the alliance with the Iroquois – known as the Covenant Chain – as a military buffer against the French Canadians. Charles and James blundered in 1681 by granting a block of territory in North America that was considerably larger than Ireland to the Quaker leader William Penn (1644–1718), who used it to mount his 'Holy Experiment' of Pennsylvania. But this was altogether exceptional. Penn was well connected at court, and Charles owed his father £16,000. The Puritan colonists of New England were shown no such indulgence. Indeed, in 1684 the Massachusetts Bay Colony had its charter liquidated and came under direct royal rule.

When James succeeded to the throne in 1685 he was resolved to reduce all the colonies 'to an Immediate Dependence upon the Crown'.[26] His most ambitious plan involved merging eight of the north-eastern colonies into the Dominion of New England, under a de facto viceroy with the power to dispense with colonial assemblies. The no-nonsense Andros was chosen for the job, and proceeded to promote Catholics and toleration, enforce the navigation acts (the New Englanders were notorious smugglers), and to levy taxes at will. There was no room for negotiation or equivocation as far as Andros was concerned. 'Either you are Subjects,' he told his opponents, 'or you are Rebels.'[27]

'Those Plantations which heretofore were looked upon as desperate adventures', wrote one colonial administrator in 1685, 'are now become necessary and important members of the main body.'[28] Yet for all the talk at Whitehall of making the colonies part of the main, the Stuart crown fell well short of integrating its overseas territories into a greater British state. If the transatlantic colonies comprised more than the sum of their parts before the mid-eighteenth century it was as a seaborne trading network. Loyalty to the crown was probably less important in creating a sense of interdependency and common community in the transatlantic colonies than the growing trade among themselves and with Britain. The Caribbean sugar boom and the slave trade were particularly important in building the kind of economic links that would turn Britain's scattered colonies in the Americas into an inter-connected system that bore at least some of the marks of empire (more on these commercial networks later).

The 'first' British empire – that is, the empire before the American Revolution in the 1770s – as seen through the eyes of the settlers, certainly, was little more than a loose federation of largely self-governing colonies. The lack of any strong sense of Britishness, much less of a common identity that encompassed all the Stuart nations, was duly exported to the colonies. The majority of colonists before 1700 were English, but there were growing populations of Scots, Irish, and West African slaves in many of the New World colonies by the late seventeenth century. The law here was English common law, and virtually all settlers, whatever their nationality, claimed for themselves the legal and constitutional liberties of Englishmen. Religious diversity had very quickly become a fact of colonial life, and therefore freedom of worship was adopted (formally or informally) in most colonies well before the 1689 Act of Toleration in Britain. Just about the only creed that united Catholic settlers in Maryland, Puritans in Massachusetts, Jews and assorted sectaries in Rhode Island, Quakers in Pennsylvania and Anglican planters in Virginia and the West Indies was their supposed rights under English law to travel, worship and make money as they pleased with minimal interference from London. Life, liberty and the pursuit of happiness in embryo.

The phrase 'the British empire' meant little before the 1660s except in relation to the territory within the three Stuart kingdoms. By the late seventeenth century people were beginning to refer to a British or an English empire of, or in, America. The trading settlements in the Far East were either left out of the imperial reckoning altogether, or were seen as a separate empire in their own right. What contemporaries usually meant when they referred to these various British empires was simply those regions where British naval power and commerce held sway – rather than the idea that gradually emerged from the mid-eighteenth century of a single empire governing a diverse assemblage of subjugated territories and races. Moreover, to most people in Stuart Britain the colonies and colonial expansion were not seen as good things in themselves, but as a source of enrichment for the mother country in its struggle to contain popery and generally compete with its European rivals. The European state system was the focus; victory – usually against Spain or France – was the end; and trade and colonies the means.

Far-flung battle lines, 1660–1720

Christopher Columbus (bef. 1452–1506) had been convinced that his discoveries in the New World heralded the Apocalypse, and in a way he had been right. Two centuries of European colonial expansion since his arrival in the Caribbean had destroyed whole peoples and consigned their cultures to an irrecoverable past. The Europeans had introduced new weapons, and a new type of warfare aimed not at balancing relations between communities – the native way of fighting – but at eradicating them altogether. Even more lethal were the diseases they had brought from the Old World, to which the peoples of the New had no immunity. Well over three quarters of the native population of New England, for example, were wiped out by smallpox, measles, typhus etc. in the decade or so after English settlers had arrived in the 1620s. Most culpably of all, perhaps, the invaders had carried across the Atlantic the murderous rivalries of the European state system. From Brazil to Florida there had been intermittent warfare since the mid-sixteenth century as the Portuguese and Spanish struggled to hold back successive waves of French, Dutch and English interlopers, while from the 1630s to the 1760s, the French and English and their Indian allies would vie for strategic and commercial supremacy over a vast area of the North American interior.

Although European colonisation had itself been colonised by the religious and political forces unleashed at the Reformation, by the mid-seventeenth century, as we have seen, the rivalry among the maritime powers was becoming more of a straightforward competition based upon national interest. England's main overseas competitors were the Dutch and the French. In the early 1660s the crown set up the Royal African Company to challenge Dutch dominance in the Atlantic slave trade, and in 1670 the Hudson's Bay Company to challenge French dominance in the North American fur trade. This struggle for overseas resources often turned into open fighting when the powers went to war in Europe. During the second Anglo-Dutch war of 1665–7, the English overran Dutch colonies in the West Indies, only to see the French – in their last military undertaking as the Dutch republic's allies – drive the English from Antigua, Montserrat and St Kitts. The English made good these losses either through counterstrikes in the Caribbean or at the negotiating table afterwards. But they were very fortunate that Louis XIV did not support Dutch demands for the restitution of their captured colony of New Netherland, for the war-ravaged English would have been much too weak to hold on to it otherwise.

The French king's hunger for *la gloire* found plenty to feed on in Europe without unduly troubling the rest of the world. He was keen at the start of his reign to strengthen French power in the Americas, but fortunately again for the English, his ambition and aggression were directed mainly towards the Spanish and, from the late 1660s, the Dutch. With Spain a spent force in Europe, Louis was determined to build a greater France upon its vulnerable outliers, and in particular the Spanish Netherlands. His problem with the Dutch, by contrast, was that they were altogether too vigorous, and he imposed stiff customs tariffs in order to stop their manufactures and colonial products flooding France, although at the cost of provoking counter-tariffs from other European states. The English were spared the worst effects of this tit-for-tat protectionism because of the growing demand for their manufactures across the Atlantic, without which some domestic industries would have struggled to survive. Louis's wars against his neighbours tied up the continental powers to such an extent during the 1670s and 1680s that the English were given the time to spread themselves in North America and the West Indies, and to strengthen their foothold in Asia.

The Anglo-Dutch partnership created by the Glorious Revolution of 1688–9 was sustained by common dread of French ambitions in Europe. Yet the English were also uncomfortably aware that France was now their main rival in the struggle for imperial dominion in the Americas. That the Dutch were still Europe's dominant commercial power rankled with many English people, especially Tories, and put England's alliance with the republic under severe strain. But more worrying still was Louis's supposed desire for universal monarchy, and France's rapidly expanding overseas trade. Given the vastness of the potential markets and territories that the Europeans had their eyes on, it might seem as if there was enough to go round without the need for belligerence. But the mercantilist ideas that prevailed in England, and indeed across Europe, encouraged the view that a nation's commerce could grow only at the expense of its trading rivals. Trade could not add to the nation's wealth, a parliamentary report would state in 1697, 'but what is gained from foreigners and foreign countries'.[29] The problem with regarding trade as a form of undeclared warfare was that in England's case it tended to assume an alarming circularity. To protect and increase the colonial and international trade that was beginning to generate a sizeable part of the taxation revenue and maritime resources needed to fight the French meant – fighting the French. Belief in static markets, in international commerce as a zero-sum game, demanded an aggressive foreign policy, together with high tariff walls to raise revenue while hitting French trade and protecting British manufacturing from foreign imports. War with France was good because, as one colonial planter put it, 'our trade will improve by the total extinction of theirs'.[30] This is why English merchants accepted the outbreak of war, indeed sometimes welcomed it, even though they often suffered heavy losses as a consequence.

It was the Tories who bayed loudest for war on the high seas. They wanted the navy to sweep the trade of foreign nations from the oceans and to sack their colonies. They rarely had their way, however. Charles II and James II had shown a lively interest in maritime affairs, but not much in an aggressive foreign policy. William III, on the other hand, though clearly up for a fight, was obsessed with the Low Countries and the balance of Christendom. He had only the sketchiest notion of or interest in the world beyond Europe. He used the royal navy in the 1690s largely to attack and contain France in European waters. Similarly, if the people were 'proud and fond of their Empire in the sea' – meaning English maritime power – it was because it promised protection for seaborne trade and (occasionally) glorious naval battles against the French, not more colonies.[31]

With fear of popish plots and French attacks sweeping the English Americas in the late 1680s, most colonists welcomed the Glorious Revolution. In New England they threw Andros and his henchmen in prison, and reverted to their pre-Dominion governments. But the revolution also had a decidedly inconvenient aspect for the colonists: war with France in Europe. The pressing need to reconquer Ireland and defend the Netherlands against Louis's armies meant that William would have little time or resources to spare for the colonies. Once the war inevitably brought New England and New France (French Canada) to blows, the colonists would largely have to fend for themselves. Moreover, William's wish to defend England's far-flung frontiers without actually committing troops and money there persuaded him that enterprising soldier–administrators such as James II's former colonial governors might have their advantages. In 1691, William effectively imposed a royal governor on the colonists of Massachusetts, and in 1692 he appointed Andros as governor of Virginia. Overall, though, he was not vitally concerned about the fate of the colonies – except England's lucrative sugar plantations in the Caribbean – and in consequence the imperialist and centralising drive begun under Charles II was gradually drained of all momentum. Whitehall's wish to preserve the American colonies in 'due dependence' upon the crown would retreat during the first half of the eighteenth century in the face of the colonists' claims to English-style freedoms, above all the right to be governed by their own elected assemblies.

If the Nine Years War in North America had been decided simply on the basis of the available manpower on each side it would barely have been a contest. At fewer than 20,000 people by the 1690s, the colonial population of French Canada was over ten times smaller than New England's. But while the English certainly had the numbers to defeat the French, they did not have the necessary unity. John Locke, a member of Whitehall's council of trade and plantations, described the colonies in 1696 as 'so crumbled into little Governments, and So disunited in those distinct Intrests [sic], that they ... do and always will refuse one another Mutual Assistance, minding more their present profit than Common Defence'.[32] The French enjoyed another major advantage over the English, and that was better relations with the Indians, who were vital to successful military operations in the interior. The Indians were well aware that the English wanted to seize their land if they could, whereas the French, besides posing less of a threat in terms of sheer numbers, were more interested in trading with the Indians for furs. French diplomacy among the Indians during the later seventeenth century would allow them to extend their influence down the St Lawrence and into the country around the Great Lakes.

Hard pressed by the growth of French power in the region were the English crown's Indian allies the Iroquois, who lived mostly in what is now upstate New York. Determined to take revenge on the French for their 'unjust attacks', the Iroquois raided New France in 1689, massacring the inhabitants of a village near Montreal.[33] The governor of New France, the comte de Frontenac, responded with a plan for wiping New England off the map, only to come up against a situation familiar to all colonial governors: the unwillingness of the mother country to spare the ships or troops needed to see the job done. Instead, Frontenac had to settle for several large raids into New England in the hope that by inflicting his own Indian allies and the horrors of frontier warfare on his more numerous enemy he might crush their will to fight. In fact, all his raids succeeded in doing was to unite the ever-bickering colonists behind a plan for wiping New France off the map. They managed to scrape together the men and ships for a sea and land assault, but disease, bad weather and even worse planning meant that both expeditions fizzled out before reaching their targets. Thereafter, the New England colonies returned to squabbling among themselves and trying to avoid as much responsibility and expense as possible, while outsourcing most of the hard fighting to the increasingly disillusioned Iroquois. Their enemies in disarray, the French and their Abenaki Indian allies were able to strike at the smaller English frontier settlements more or less at will, although they lacked the strength to threaten the existence of New England itself in the way that Metacom's warriors had twenty years earlier. By the end of the Nine Years War in 1697, the French were the points victors in North America, but after eight years of fighting, neither side had very much to show for its efforts.

William supplied considerably more military aid to the Caribbean colonies in the 1690s than he did to New England. Thanks to naval support and regular troops, the West Indian colonists generally had the better of the French without ever landing a decisive blow. Their greatest achievement was in enabling Britain's Spanish allies to maintain their trade in the New World, and above all their *flotas*: the regular bullion fleets whose cargoes of Peruvian silver helped to pay the allied armies in Europe. Once the scourge of the Spanish Main, the English had become Spain's chief protectors in the Caribbean.

The New World assumed even greater strategic significance in the War of the Spanish Succession (1701–14). The installation of Louis's grandson as king of Spain in 1700 raised the prospect of the French taking over the Spanish empire from within and employing its vast wealth to tip the balance of power in Europe decisively in their favour. This war, like its predecessor the Nine Years War, would be decided in Europe. But now France had a major new stake in the Americas, while the English were reduced once again to having to hunt for and attack Spain's treasure fleets. The French and the English both sent squadrons to the Caribbean at the start of the war to lay claim to the *flota*, but when the two forces met off the coast of what is now Colombia, about half the English warships were unable or unwilling to close for action and the French escaped. Two of the English ships' captains were later court-martialled for cowardice and shot. Commodore Charles Wager redeemed the royal navy's reputation in the Caribbean when his flag-ship took on the *flota* single-handedly in 1707, sinking the warship carrying most of the official bullion shipment and capturing another full of 'unregistered' treasure. But it was the colonists on either side who bore the brunt of the fighting in the Caribbean. The English invaded the French half of St Kitts and spent two months plundering France's main Caribbean colony, Guadeloupe. The French retaliated by sacking Nevis, Antigua and Montserrat. Neither side was interested in making conquests, for that would simply have added to the commercial competition within their respective economic systems. Colonial war here was all about wrecking the enemy's plantations and stealing their slaves. It was often devastating in terms of lives and property, but rarely decisive.

The distinction between plundering the enemy and outright piracy had never been very marked in the Caribbean, and during the 1710s it all but disappeared. England's first imperial adventurers such as Sir Walter Ralegh had been little more than pirates, for all their fine talk about serving the Protestant cause. Some of the second and third generation of these transatlantic buccaneers had managed to parlay their ill-gotten gains into more respectable forms of colonial wealth. The Welsh seaman Henry Morgan, for example, had opened his account in the Caribbean with a piratical attack on a Spanish settlement in 1663, and had closed it in 1688 with a knighthood to his credit, several stints as acting governor of Jamaica, and a fortune in sugar plantations and slaves. At least he had always sailed under letters of marque. The pirates who congregated in their thousands in the Bahamas at the end of the War of the Spanish Succession, when maritime order in the eastern Caribbean had all but disappeared, were freebooters pure and simple.

Of all the buccaneers who sailed the Caribbean during the early eighteenth century, there was one who in many ways has defined the modern stereotype of the pirate: Edward Teach (c.1680–1718), aka Blackbeard. Teach performed such extravagant feats of wickedness – including an attempt to recreate Hell, complete with fire and brimstone, in the hold of his own ship – that he was 'looked upon with a kind of Envy' by his piratical peers.[34] In little over a year after joining a pirate crew in 1716, Teach had command of his own flotilla that took and plundered any merchant vessel that crossed his path. Often the mere sight of the black flag being hoisted on his ship was enough to make his victims strike sail and take to their boats. His boldest stroke was to blockade the busy port of Charleston, in South Carolina, seizing and ransoming all incoming and outgoing vessels. His brazenness and fearsome reputation were such that even while his ships ranged offshore, he and some of his crew could swagger through Charleston's streets unmolested.

The pirates of the Caribbean flourished in all their glory for only a few years. The royal navy and the British colonial authorities in the Americas had hunted them almost to extinction by the mid-1720s. The French did the same with their own pirates. As a result of this clean-up, merchant ships crossing the Atlantic could at long last dispense with deck guns. Those pirates who did not opt for early retirement often had their careers terminated on the gallows. Teach, however, after briefly trying life on shore with what was reputedly his fourteenth wife, could not resist returning to piracy – and he would go down fighting. Late in 1718, his famous beard, which he had sometimes decorated with slow-burning fuses to heighten his fearsomeness, would finish up with the rest of his head – hanging from the bowsprit of one of the two navy sloops that had waylaid his ship off North Carolina.

The agony and seeming futility of the struggle between New France and New England continued during the War of the Spanish Succession, except that the English appear to have learnt from some of their mistakes in the Nine Years War. Now when the French and Abenakis raided into New England the force of their attacks was largely blunted by a screen of fortified settlements with permanent garrisons. Occasionally the English defences failed, as they did in 1704, when the frontier town of Deerfield, Massachusetts – a regular target of French–Indian aggression – was pounced upon and destroyed. Over fifty of its inhabitants were cut down on the spot, and another 100 or so marched 300 miles through the ice and snow of a North American winter to Quebec, where those that survived this gruelling ordeal were ransomed. The colonists mounted reprisal raids using flying columns of rangers: colonial guerrilla units that had mastered the Indian tactics of ambush and hit-and-run. But these attacks did no more than even the score. The only long-term solution was for the New Englanders to use their massive superiority in numbers to destroy the New French menace at source. A major land and sea offensive against Quebec was organised in 1709, but had to be called off after vital military support from Britain was diverted to protect the allies' gold shipments from Portuguese Brazil.

In 1710, however, there emerged the potentially winning combination of a Tory government eager to reverse the Eurocentric priorities of the Whigs and a genuine will among New Englanders to work together to crush the serpent's head. The following year a major force of 54 ships and 5,000 troops was sent over from England to join up with the colonial militia for another crack at Quebec. But yet again the winning combination proved to be one of farce and tragedy. Bad weather and even worse piloting resulted in the loss of seven transport ships on the north shore of the St Lawrence, miles from the target. Eight hundred men drowned in the breakers. The pieces of New France that Britain gained by the treaty of Utrecht in 1713 were more a reflection of her victories in Europe than across the Atlantic.

War with France, or the threat of it, became one of the few unifying features of the empire in the decades after 1689. Crown authority in the colonies operated much as it did in England's counties – which is

to say it was mediated through local authorities and subject to negotiation and evasion. Armies, fleets and even parliamentary statutes rarely
played any direct role in governing the colonies. That task was left
mostly to crown-appointed governors and elected colonial assemblies.
Governors had the power to call and dissolve their colony's assembly
and veto its legislation. Assemblies were mainly responsible for voting
taxation and passing local laws; although many, especially in the North
American colonies, would extend their powers during the eighteenth
century to cover such matters as public accounts and expenditure and
the salaries of royal officials. The official position was that assemblies
were a privilege granted by the crown, but the colonists increasingly
saw them as their constitutional right. Whitehall was repeatedly warned
that some of the crown's supposed subjects in the Americas were determined to vest all power in their assemblies and 'to make themselves an
independent people'.[35] But no one in London seemed very interested
in reversing this trend. As ever, the government was too focused on
domestic affairs and the European state system to worry about a few
upstart colonists.

Europe first, the colonies a distant second, was very much the order
of business at the centre of imperial government during the first half
of the eighteenth century. Royal officials in the colonies answered to
the Board of Trade – the main clearing house of imperial business –
and to the secretary of state for the southern department, which was
not a very satisfactory arrangement for anyone concerned. In the first
place, the Board lacked political authority, and was very much in the
shadow of the Treasury and the Admiralty, both of which had numerous
other duties and concerns besides colonial affairs. And secondly, the
secretary's main brief was not the colonies at all but foreign policy in
relation to southern Europe. He reported to the cabinet and to the
privy council. In other words, imperial government was handled as it
had always been – except during the 1640s and 1650s – by the king's
ministers, not by Parliament. Parliament, it is true, passed a series of
laws in the 1690s and 1700s that strengthened royal authority and
revenues in the colonies. Indeed, there was a moment in the early
eighteenth century when it looked as if imperial rule would assume a
more parliamentary form, and the colonists perhaps be persuaded to
accept the sovereignty of king-in-Parliament that had emerged in Britain
after the Glorious Revolution. Most Parliament-men, however, were no
keener than ministers on the hard work of challenging colonial interests
in the name of efficiency and imperial integration. Nor did they want

to legislate too closely for the colonies for fear that it would reinvigorate free monarchy. After all, the colonies belonged to the crown, not to Parliament. The Whig ministries that dominated British politics after 1689 were all for keeping colonial administration quietly ticking over and trade revenues coming in while they worried about what the French would do next. Not until the 1760s would the ministry and Parliament combine to bring the full weight of Leviathan to bear against the colonies, and by then the moment for incorporating the Americans into the British parliamentary state had long since passed.

Eastern promise

The peoples of Britain and Ireland knew more about Asia by the end of the eighteenth century than they had three hundred years earlier, but that was not saying a great deal. As late as the 1760s they tended to use a blanket term for the lands that lay east and south of Persia (modern-day Iran) – sometimes 'The East Indies', often simply 'the East'. As for 'India', they associated the name at first with the mighty Muslim empire of 'the Great Mogoll': the heirs of Genghis Khan and Timur who had swept down from Afghanistan in the sixteenth century to conquer much, though not all, of the subcontinent. It was only in the eighteenth century, as the Mughal empire crumbled, that the British began to think of the area to the south of the Hindu Kush and the Himalayas as one land, Hindustan. Much of their knowledge about India before the mid-eighteenth century came not from any history of British empire-building on the subcontinent, of which there was little, but from the flow of exotic goods that passed across the Indian Ocean, round the Cape of Good Hope, and back to Britain and its Atlantic colonies. One institution dominated this trade, from its founding in 1600 to its nationalisation in 1858, and that was the East India Company. Service in 'John Company' would shape the careers of national heroes such as Robert Clive (1725–74), Warren Hastings (1732–1818) and the victor of Waterloo, Arthur Wellesley, duke of Wellington. The exploits of this new breed of soldier–administrator would extend the reach of European rule to the far corners of the subcontinent – part of a process that saw the British empire's centre of gravity shift from the Americas to India. But the Company's heyday came earlier, when Britain's 'empire of the seas' was at its height, and thoughts of territorial expansion in Asia were largely subordinate to the business of making money.

The English had dreamed of gaining direct access to the fabled riches of the East since the late Middle Ages. For over a century after John Cabot's expeditions to the New World in the 1490s, they had ranged the north Atlantic in search of 'a Passage by seas into the . . . East Indies by the Northwest thorough some p[ar]te of America'.[36] There was, of course, no north-west passage at that time, and lacking the kind of maritime expertise and government support that had opened the world's oceans to their Iberian competitors, English merchants had instead traded in the Levant (the eastern Mediterranean) for spices, pepper, silk and other Asian goods that had been brought overland through Persia and Arabia – an arrangement that involved foreign middlemen and was both expensive and unreliable. By the time war with Spain broke out in 1585, Drake and other English mariners had acquired the skills needed for oceanic voyaging. But what finally persuaded Elizabeth I to bow to merchant pressure for a state-sponsored sea venture to the East was the prospect of the Dutch monopolising the import trade from the Indies by bringing large quantities of Asian luxuries round the Cape and directly to Europe at a much lower price than even the Portuguese could manage, never mind the English who relied on the traditional overland routes. The return of Dutch ships from the Indies in 1599, laden with spices and other Asian commodities, sparked near-panic among the London merchants trading with the Levant. If the Dutch made such voyages a regular thing, as they were evidently determined to do, it would destroy English trade in Asian goods altogether. Late in 1600, therefore, the queen granted a royal charter establishing 'The Governor and Company of Merchants of London, Trading into the East-Indies', or the East India Company (EIC) for short.

Forming a company to trade with Asia was one thing – actually getting to and from the Indies and establishing viable markets there, quite another. Voyages to the Indian Ocean were long and fraught with danger. Typhoons, pirates, capricious local rulers, and attacks by the Portuguese, who claimed exclusive rights to sail beyond the Cape, were among the potential hazards. Because trading to the East Indies was so risky and expensive, the Company was set up as a joint-stock enterprise, which was an idea borrowed from the Venetians and the Dutch whereby the costs, the risks and of course the profits were spread among a group of merchant-investors. To give the Company added security it was granted a monopoly on English trade between the Cape of Good Hope and Cape Horn, although on the understanding that it would provide loans and gifts to the crown in return for this great privilege.

Then there was the problem of what to trade in exchange for eastern goods, for there was very little demand in Asia for England's traditional export products of woollen cloth, lead, tin etc. The cargo that most interested Asian merchants was silver, which certainly enjoyed a higher value in the East than it did in Europe, but it was feared that exporting large quantities of it would denude England of specie and damage the economy. Besides the huge sums required to buy silver bullion, there was the expense of fitting out the large, well-armed galleons needed to carry it to the Indies. The ships themselves, and the experience of trading in dangerous waters, were provided by London's Levant merchants, who also supplied much of the Company's early leadership and capital. Further costs were incurred in creating the infrastructure to support a commercial operation spanning two oceans. Here the Company copied the Portuguese and the Dutch in obtaining permission from local potentates to set up 'factories', or permanent trading stations-cum-warehouses, at strategic points around the Indian Ocean. Little or no thought was given at this stage to founding plantations. There was no need, at least from a commercial standpoint; and anyway the locals were usually more than capable of seeing off uninvited guests.

For the first twenty years or so of its existence the EIC did a roaring trade and delivered handsome returns for its investors. Profits approaching £1 million were made re-exporting pepper to the European markets, making the EIC one of the wealthiest trading companies in England. The Asian end of the Company's operation also seemed to be thriving. Naval victories against the Portuguese in Surat, on the north-west coast of India, in the mid-1610s persuaded the Mughal emperor Jahangir to grant the EIC official permission to set up factories on his territory. Having no regular navy of his own, Jahangir had relied on the Portuguese to police maritime affairs in the empire. Now, with Portuguese power in the Indian Ocean visibly on the wane, he switched his patronage to the English. By the early 1620s the Company had established factories at Muscat in the Red Sea; Surat; Masulipatam on the east coast of India; on many of the spice islands in the Indonesian archipelago; and even at Hirado in Japan.

But the good times did not last long. The various wars between England, France, Spain and the Dutch republic during the 1620s led to a trade recession in western Europe; and with Dutch as well as English ships bringing back large quantities of pepper from the Indies, the market had become saturated by 1630 and the price collapsed.

Investor confidence and the Company's finances took a further buffeting as a result of Stuart royal projects. Although both James I and Charles I appreciated the contribution the EIC's trade made to their customs revenues, their eagerness to tap new sources of wealth was such that they authorised what were effectively rival trading companies to the EIC, breaking its monopoly. One of these ventures, the Courten Association of the late 1630s, degenerated into little more than piracy, and cost the EIC a great deal in lost trade and good will in the Indies, where the locals often found it hard to distinguish between the Company's ships and the Courten interlopers.

But the greatest challenge facing the fledgling East India Company was competition from the Dutch. In 1602 the Dutch had consolidated their various ventures to the east in one united company, the Vereenigde Oost-Indische Compagnie (VOC). The VOC was much better funded and organised than its London counterpart, and, unlike the EIC, the VOC set out to build forts as well as factories in the Indies, and to use violence against anyone who stood in its way. EIC captains were not above extracting trade concessions at gun-point. Like the Portuguese before them, they had discovered that Indian ships were lightly built and could neither withstand European gunnery nor mount cannon of their own. But the English sent far fewer galleons and men to the Indies than the VOC did, and lacked the audacity of the Dutch in, for example, hiring Japanese *ronin* – masterless Samurai warriors – as colonial auxiliaries. With the will and weaponry to destroy shipping and blockade ports, the Dutch were able to change entire trading patterns in the Indies – something that the EIC could never do during its early years.

The rivalry between the EIC and the VOC turned particularly ugly in 1623, when the Dutch authorities on Ambon in the Indonesian archipelago beheaded ten EIC employees for supposedly plotting to seize control of the island's spice trade. The victims' confessions were extracted under 'extreme torment' – mostly water-boarding, although there was also some 'splitting of . . . toes' and imaginative use of gunpowder.[37] The 'Amboina massacre' caused uproar in England, but neither James nor Charles was willing to make a big issue of it with the Dutch. Partly in response to Dutch aggression, partly by way of financial retrenchment, the EIC abandoned most of its factories on the spice islands and at Hirado and concentrated instead on trade with India, where it had managed to secure a few years' head start on the VOC. This shift in the EIC's centre of operations resulted in more cargo space being given to Indian goods, and particularly to calicoes and brightly printed chintzes – products that English consumers found irresistibly exotic. The hunt for marketable textiles led the EIC to set up new factories at Madras, on the Coromandel coast of south-east India, in 1639–40, and at Hugli, in Bengal, in 1651.

The EIC was already struggling when it was very nearly dragged under with the wreckage of royal authority during the early 1640s. Hostility among leading parliamentarians to crown-sponsored monopolies like the EIC – which were regarded as instruments of Stuart despotism – cleared the way by the mid-1640s for a variety of merchant interlopers and would-be colonisers to try their own luck beyond the Cape of Good Hope. Although none of these ventures was successful, and a few – particularly involving attempts to set up colonies – were downright disasters, they nevertheless damaged the EIC's operations and reputation. Inevitably, too, the war of the three kingdoms diverted money and ships that might otherwise have been put to good use by the Company. The English free-for-all in the East had done so much damage to the Company's trade by the mid-1650s that it threatened to sell its Indian assets unless Lord Protector Cromwell granted it a new monopoly charter. It was now recognised in England that the EIC represented the most efficient way of conducting a profitable trade with the Indies, and when the company was refloated late in 1657, therefore, the massive sum of £740,000 was subscribed for a new joint-stock venture.

With fresh investment and its monopoly reaffirmed first by Cromwell and then Charles II, the EIC flourished again during the Restoration period. Pepper and spices remained among its stock-in-trades, but what the consumers wanted above all was calicoes and other Indian textiles – and the Company obliged. The main threat to its profit margins post-1660 was not unrest at home but war in India between the Marathas – the Hindu peoples of western India – and the Mughal emperor Aurangzeb. After the Marathas plundered Surat in 1664 and again in 1670 the Company set about fortifying the island of Bombay, 100 or so miles down the coast. The Portuguese had handed over Bombay to Charles II as part of his marriage treaty with Catherine of Braganza in 1661, and after it proved too expensive for him to run he had leased it to the Company for a peppercorn rent. Caught between the warring Mughals and Marathas, Bombay too was often attacked and besieged, but the English managed to hold on behind their fortifications. Yet even the minimal protection offered by the English at Bombay proved attractive to the region's inhabitants, so that by the

1680s the town had a mixed European and Indian population of about 60,000, which was five times what it had been in 1660. In 1687 the EIC transferred its headquarters on the west coast from Surat to Bombay.

Madras, on India's south-east coast, was even more susceptible to the violent attentions of the locals, who tried repeatedly to wipe out the town's Europeans. At times, only Fort St George, built by the Company in the 1640s, stood between Madras's few hundred English inhabitants (mostly merchants and soldiers) and annihilation. Yet the trade and protection that the Company offered at Madras enabled it not only to survive but to flourish. The combined population of the 'white town' of English and Portuguese settlers, and of the 'black town' of Asian and Eurasian traders surrounding it, numbered anywhere between 80,000 and 400,000 by the early eighteenth century, making Madras the largest 'British' city after London.

Bombay and Madras formed two of the Company's three main trading centres in India by the late seventeenth century – the third was Calcutta, in Bengal, where the English had settled in 1690. Bengal sustained a rich and thriving textile industry, turning out calicoes, taffetas or silk cloth and cotton muslins, and as demand for these fabrics grew in Europe, the region became the EIC's main cash-cow and the centre of its commercial operation in the Indies. Sixty per cent of Asian imports to Britain by the early 1700s came from Bengal. The construction of Fort William at Calcutta in the late 1690s and the growing English trade there drew huge numbers of Indian merchants and workers to settle in the town, as had happened at Bombay and Madras.

The three 'presidencies', as they were known, of Calcutta, Bombay and Madras were unusual among the EIC's factories not only in attracting large Indian populations but also for being guarded by forts with small garrisons of regular troops. The force that had always backed the EIC's trade was moving on shore, and as it did so the Company leadership began to think more ambitiously about how to govern and tax the growing communities its guns protected. Revenue from taxes and *farman* – grants provided by Indian rulers for providing services, usually military – were 'no less the subject of our [concern]', insisted the EIC's leaders in the 1680s, 'as our trade'. Tentatively at first, the Company worked to build (in its own words) 'a Politie of civill & military power and [to] create and secure Such a large Revenue . . . as may be the foundation of a large well grounded sure English Dominion in India for all time to come'.[38]

Nevertheless, the EIC's settlements in India had not changed that much since the early seventeenth century. They were still microscopic enclaves, a scattering of trading posts containing just a few thousand Europeans, perched precariously on the edge of a vast and politically unstable subcontinent with a population twenty times that of Great Britain.

Dutch aggression in the Indies and their superiority in ships and bases continued to shape the EIC's trading patterns. In general, the Company tried to keep out of the VOC's way in the spice islands and further east, and to concentrate instead on India. What was good for business, however, did not necessarily fit with the determination of Louis XIV and the Stuart royal brothers to destroy the Dutch wherever their forces could find them. When France sent its first battle fleet into the Indian Ocean in 1670–1 it was to help establish a French trading company in the Indies to compete with the VOC, although if this venture succeeded then the EIC's profits would likely suffer as well. The Company was thrust even further into harm's way in 1672 with the outbreak of the third Anglo-Dutch war and a combined Anglo-French attack on the republic and its trading empire. Louis's armies might sweep all before them in the Low Countries, but threatening the Dutch in Asia was like grabbing the tail of a tiger. The VOC duly mauled the French in India and Ceylon (Sri Lanka), and an English naval squadron in the Bay of Bengal. All the French gained from the war was a trading station at Pondicherry, about fifty miles down the coast from Madras.

Yet at least the French had stood up to the Dutch, and that was bound to win them friends in Asia. When King Narai of Siam (Thailand) finally ran out of patience with the VOC, he turned in 1680 to France for military support – a strategy that he entrusted to one of a growing band of EIC employees-turned-freebooters, Samuel White. White's only loyalty, as it turned out, was to himself, and he used the king's ships to wage a piratical war in the Bay of Bengal, seizing Indian and Burmese vessels, including several belonging to EIC officials, and selling their cargoes for private profit. He also embezzled the king's money by claiming wages for a non-existent garrison of soldiers at the royal fort of Mergui. His drunken carousings with an EIC captain who had been sent to Mergui to arrest him angered the town's inhabitants so much that they massacred every European they could find – White being among the fortunate few who escaped. After further adventures he made his way back to England, where he brought a lawsuit against the EIC in 1689, claiming damages of £40,000 for what amounted to defamation of character. But before he could add perjury to his list of crimes he died, and was buried within the respectable confines of Bath Abbey. His main legacy was to close Siam to business opportunities for the EIC and open the region to French intervention.

If the EIC was to deal with the likes of White and the far larger problem of the VOC it needed more power – and where better to find it in the 1680s than at the court of the arch-imperialist James II? Taking advantage of the war between Emperor Aurangzeb and the Marathas, the Company's governor Sir Josiah Child – James's economic adviser – and his accomplices launched a joint land–sea offensive against the Mughal empire in the late 1680s. This wildly overambitious project – sheer madness given the disparity in size and wealth of the combatants – was designed to forge an English empire in India that would serve as a springboard for an all-out assault upon the VOC. Yet just as the English were outgunned by the VOC at sea, so their pikemen and slow-firing musketeers were no match for the Mughal cavalry on land. After suffering several defeats the Company had to go begging Aurangzeb for forgiveness. Fortunately for the English, the emperor regarded them as no more than a minor irritant, and fined the Company a mere £15,000 for its temerity, while reaffirming its trading privileges.

Defeat in India and the fall of James II at the Glorious Revolution in 1688–9 put the EIC once again in a difficult position. The Company spent lavishly on bribes to William III, his courtiers and Parliament-men in an attempt to stave off its mostly Whig enemies, who were determined to crush this monopolistic bastion of Tory power once and for all. But bribery only succeeded in buying the Company time. In 1698 a cash-strapped William took out a loan of £2 million from a group of Whig magnates and their City backers, and in return he granted them a charter for a new and more open company to trade with the Indies in competition with the EIC.

The new company had money and political influence to spare. What it lacked, however, was experience of trading in the East. The game was not yet over, and the old company played its remaining cards to perfection. Using its factories and contacts in Asia to stifle competition, and by acquiring a £315,000 stake in the new company, it was able to take over its rival from within. After lengthy negotiations between the two companies they merged in 1709 to form the United Company of Merchants of England Trading to the East Indies, or the Honourable East India Company. The merger meant the EIC was obliged to bring in new blood, but it was still dominated by London's mercantile elite, and it was better financed than ever before. The fact that the EIC had survived the rage of party under William III and Queen Anne, when most other monopoly trading companies had been abolished, highlights just how important its huge lending power, and the revenue streams sustained by its trade, had become for the British state.

In the long run the Glorious Revolution would also solve the Company's persistent Dutch problem. The VOC's preferred method of dealing with the EIC – hard pounding – obviously became unacceptable once the Dutch and English had the same ruler and were joined in alliance against France. After 1688, therefore, the VOC could do little to slow the EIC's penetration of the Indian textiles trade, which put the English at a distinct commercial advantage. For while consumer demand for calicoes, chintzes, silks etc. was growing, and would continue to do so well into the eighteenth century, demand for pepper and spices – the Dutch specialities – was static at best. Dutch aggression had inadvertently pushed the English into what turned out to be the most profitable sector of the Asian market. The VOC could always appeal to William III if it felt hard done by, but he could scarcely afford to make himself even more unpopular in England by appearing to favour Dutch trading interests over English ones. Concentrating on the spice trade would doom the VOC to slow but inexorable decline during the eighteenth century, and by the 1720s the EIC was clearly the more dynamic and profitable of the two companies, sending up to thirty large ships to the Indies each year, and recording annual sales of anywhere between £1,250,000 and £2 million.

The EIC had discovered an even richer source of profit than Asian textiles by the 1750s: tea. 'Tcha . . . alias Tee' was being served in some London coffee houses by the late 1650s. Pepys had his first brew in the autumn of 1660, when he wrote of taking 'a Cup of Tee (a China drink) of which I never had drunk before'.[39] It was not until the 1690s that tea-drinking really caught on in fashionable circles. Once it did so, however, the dynamics of politeness quickly turned tea into an item of mass consumption. Tea-drinkers in Britain were downing stupefying quantities of the stuff by the mid-eighteenth century. As much or more tea was consumed by the colonists in North America, rich or poor, whatever their nationality. Aficionados might drink up to fifty cups a day, for tea was touted by its purveyors as a cure for anything from flatulence to scurvy. Demand outstripped supply – at least at the legal, duty-paid price – hence tea smuggling in defiance of Company and crown was big business on both sides of the Atlantic. Tea stimulated more than just the human body. The polite rituals of tea-drinking required the use of fine chinaware, tongs, caddies, silver spoons perhaps, maybe a tea table. And as tea caught on, so the sugar used to sweeten it became even more of a household staple. Tea is a particularly good example of how one new consumer product heightened demand for a whole host of others – many either manufactured in Britain or imported from Britain's colonies. The raw material itself, along with profitable lines in silk and ceramics (including teaware), came from China – or, more specifically, Canton, which was the only port where the Chinese authorities would allow the EIC and other European buyers to do business.

The opportunity to become extremely rich in Company service would help draw it ever deeper into Asian affairs. The EIC paid its officials modest salaries on the understanding that they would make money by going into business for themselves as shipowners and merchants in the trade between ports in the Indian Ocean and China Seas. The profits from this so-called 'country trade' could be spectacular. 'We have seen several Persons return from those Employments [in the Indies], after a Stay of three or four Years only', reported *The Craftsman* in 1727, 'laden with immense Wealth; affecting the Port and Grandeur of British Noblemen; and cultivating Alliance with the most powerful Families in the Kingdom.'[40] These 'Persons' were, of course, the 'nabobs', which was a corruption of the Mughal word for governor: *nawab*. Eager to acquire an influential position in British society, some nabobs used their money to buy themselves a seat in Parliament – most notoriously in the case of Thomas 'Diamond' Pitt (William Pitt's grandfather), who was MP for the rottenest of rotten boroughs, Old Sarum (number of voters: ten). No wonder the nabob became synonymous with the corrupting influence of Leviathan and abuses of ministerial power. But in order to make their fortunes in the first place, nabobs would often bankroll or borrow from native merchants, take native business partners, and generally embroil themselves in Indian affairs. The breakup of the Mughal empire during the early eighteenth century into a patchwork of warring states sucked in these Company entrepreneurs even further as bankers, administrators and military advisers to the newly independent nawabs.

British entanglement in Indian politics reached a point of no return in the mid-eighteenth century. The French East India Company had been trading in the Indian textile market in a big way since the 1720s, but without causing too much friction with the EIC. It was the

extension of the global rivalry between France and Britain to India
during the War of the Austrian Succession that brought the two companies to blows. With the fitful and always inadequate backing of their
respective governments, they waged a complex series of wars across
the subcontinent from the mid-1740s until the mid-1760s. Most of the
fighting before the 1750s was done through native proxies. Company
officials helped to finance and manage the armies of friendly nawabs
against their French-backed rivals. Their main goal was to grab plunder
and concessions for themselves and their presidencies, not to pursue
some imperialist agenda devised in London. Company bosses, for their
part, tended to favour the continuance of prudent government and
revenue collection within the EIC's existing enclaves. From their headquarters in Leadenhall Street, London, they warned their distant subor-
dinates against behaving like 'a military colony [rather] than the factors
and agents of a body of merchants'.[41] But India was half a world away,
and there was little they could do if their people on the ground favoured
a more aggressive approach to business – their own as well as the
Company's.

It was the French who had the best of the fighting in India before
the 1750s. Through an innovative combination of modern, quick-firing
field guns and well-drilled sepoys (who came considerably cheaper than
European soldiers) with flintlocks and bayonets, they destroyed much
larger native armies. In 1746 the French captured a poorly defended
Madras, but were obliged to return it to the British after the treaty of
Aix-la-Chapelle in 1748. The Company raised its own sepoy armies
under energetic young commanders like Robert Clive, and the fact that
it enjoyed far healthier profit margins and credit ratings than the French
in India was bound to tell in its favour the longer the fighting continued.

The size of the British and French armies in India was tiny by
European standards. Clive had just a few thousand sepoys and only
900 European troops when he defeated the nawab of Bengal at Plassey
in June 1757, which was not so much a battle as a brisk skirmish that
was decided by the defection of the nawab's commanders rather than
Clive's generalship. More decisive and certainly bloodier was the
Company's victory at Buxar in 1764 over a native alliance involving
the Mughal emperor himself. All of the troops who fought at Buxar
were Indians.

Plassey and then Buxar allowed the British to take over Bengal –
India's wealthiest kingdom – destroying French and Dutch outposts as
they did so. Once again, Clive and other Company leaders had not

been out to win territory as such, but to regain their commercial footing in the region and to punish the nawab of Bengal for foolishly imagining that Calcutta still belonged to him. In 1756, the nawab's troops had ransacked the town and crammed seventy or so British prisoners into the tiny dungeon of Fort William – the 'black hole of Calcutta' – where about forty of them had suffocated. Clive's recapture of Calcutta and the Plassey campaign had been bankrolled by the nawab's Indian enemies – one among countless examples of Indian rivalries playing into European hands. The EIC's new puppet nawab lavished over £1 million in gifts on his allies, Clive alone receiving £170,000. His total share of Indian spoils and plunder was about £300,000 by the time he returned to England in 1760.

The mid-century wars in India marked the painful and unexpected birth of the British Raj. Whether the Company's directors liked it or not, the EIC had become a major political player in India by the 1760s. As a territorial power, notably in Bengal, it was obliged to defend its borders, its trade and its allies from hostile nawabs and the French. That meant keeping up a large and very expensive army. The Company had 23,000 sepoys under arms by 1761, and that figure would rise over the next forty years to nearer 200,000. To maintain this massive war machine the British would have to become directly, and sometimes violently, involved in local government. Taxation, above all from Bengal, paid for the soldiers that protected the trade and collected the revenues that kept the machine running. Profit, military power and the hunt for taxable resources to service war-debts – the interplay of European and Indian rivalries from the 1740s had set in motion an imperial chain reaction that would consume the entire subcontinent.

That eventuality was not the government's concern. What worried Whitehall by the 1760s was whether the EIC was fit to handle its new role as an Indian power, for if not, it was a liability to itself and to the British state. Since the 1690s the EIC had been an integral part of Leviathan. The customs revenue from its trade had proved vital in sustaining the public credit that underwrote the fiscal–military state, while the Company itself had lent huge sums to the government, and had allowed the ministry to barter EIC jobs for political influence in Britain. The government was not particularly keen on interfering in the Company's affairs, but as events would show, the EIC could not continue to make a profit *and* fight wars and rule millions of people in India. Apart from anything else it lacked the expertise in governing on this scale, as the Bengalis would discover to their cost in the 1770s, when the Company's extortionate taxes contributed to a famine that killed millions. Yet if the Company failed or its Indian provinces fell to the French, then the effect on Britain's economy and military power would be devastating. From the mid-1760s the ministry moved slowly but surely to bring the EIC directorate and its wayward Conquistadores under closer parliamentary control.

The British Atlantic

In the spring of 1750 the music teacher Gottlieb Mittelberger left the Rhineland in a ship crammed full of German immigrants bound for England, and from there for Philadelphia, the largest city in British America. Although the long and perilous journey to the New World was for him a giant leap into the unknown, it had become but one small step for mankind. Hundreds of ships now crossed the Atlantic each year. The voyage, give or take the odd storm, had become routine. Migration as well as trade sustained this traffic, and yet the ships that plied the seas between Europe and America were built to carry cargo, not passengers. The poor immigrants 'packed densely, like herrings' in the hold were merely profitable ballast.[42] Herr Mittelberger doubtless expected an arduous passage, but nothing had prepared him for the conditions he encountered on board:

> When the ships have for the last time weighed their anchors near the city of Kaupp [Cowes] in Old England, the real misery begins . . . For from there the ships, unless they have good wind, must often sail 8, 9, 10 to 12 weeks before they reach Philadelphia . . . during the voyage there is on board these ships terrible misery, stench, fumes, horror, vomiting, many kinds of sea-sickness, fever, dysentery, headache, heat, constipation, boils, scurvy, cancer, mouth-rot, and the like . . . Many hundred people necessarily die and perish in such misery, and must be cast into the sea . . . Children from 1 to 7 years rarely survive the voyage. I witnessed misery in no less than 32 children in our ship, all of whom were thrown into the sea. The parents grieve all the more since their children find no resting-place in the earth, but are devoured by the monsters of the sea . . . The water which is served out on the ships is often very black, thick and full of worms, so that one cannot drink it without loathing, even with the greatest thirst. Toward the end we were compelled to eat the ship's biscuit . . . [although] there was

scarcely a piece the size of a dollar that had not been full of red worms and spiders nests.[43]

It is sobering to think of the number of people who must have endured similar voyages in the early modern period, and of the countless thousands who perished at sea.

No Europeans felt the pull of the New World more strongly than the British and Irish. Roughly 350,000 people from England and Wales, along with 30,000 Irish and 7,000 Scots, traversed the Atlantic in the seventeenth century. The great majority of these migrants went either to Jamaica and Britain's other sugar plantations in the Caribbean or to the Chesapeake: the tobacco-growing colonies of Virginia and Maryland. The pattern changed in the eighteenth century as transatlantic emigration became less of an English and more of a British and European phenomenon. Of the 300,000 or so who left the British Isles for the Americas in the period 1700–80, over a third were from Ireland – mostly Presbyterian 'Scots-Irish' from Ulster – and about 75,000 from Scotland. Joining this exodus were 100,000 people from Germany and central Europe, with the traumatised Mittelberger in their midst. The Caribbean was no longer the prime destination of choice. Instead, the majority of European immigrants flooded through Philadelphia into the American backcountry; some pushing out westwards towards and even across the Appalachian mountains; others taking the Great Wagon Road south to the Shenandoah Valley, or on to the Carolinas.

The horrors of the Atlantic crossing, and the numbers involved, were of a different order of magnitude for the West Africans shipped to the Americas as slaves. About the time that Mittelberger was crossing the Atlantic, so too was the newly enslaved Olaudah Equiano (c.1745–97).[44] This is how he remembered the voyage:

The stench of the hold while we were on the coast was so intolerably loathsome, that it was dangerous to remain there for any time, and some of us had been permitted to stay on the deck for the fresh air; but now that the whole ship's cargo were confined together, it became absolutely pestilential. The closeness of the place, and the heat of the climate, added to the number in the ship, which was so crowded that each had scarcely room to turn himself, almost suffocated us. This produced copious perspirations, so that the air soon became unfit for respiration, from a variety of loathsome smells, and brought on a sickness among the slaves, of which many died ... This wretched situation was again aggravated by the galling of the chains, now become insupportable; and the filth of the necessary tubs, into which the children often fell, and were almost suffocated. The shrieks of the women, and the groans of the dying, rendered the whole a scene of horror almost inconceivable.[45]

The English had joined the slave trade later than the Portuguese and the Dutch had, but helped by the navigation acts and the growing demand for labour in their Caribbean colonies they had emerged by the 1670s as Europe's leading slavers – a position they maintained until 1807, when Parliament abolished the slave trade (though it did not outlaw slavery itself until the 1830s). The British alone transported over 3 million Africans to the New World between 1660 and 1807, or close to a third of all those trafficked across the Atlantic. The numbers were so huge because the majority of British-owned slaves lived and worked in grinding, disease-ridden misery on the Caribbean sugar plantations, where death-rates for the white minority, let alone slaves, exceeded birth-rates until the nineteenth century. Sugar production was hot, back-breaking work. It meant clearing the ground; sowing, tending and harvesting the cane; crushing it in a sugar mill; and then boiling the juice to prevent it fermenting (see illus. 21). Popular opposition to slavery was beginning to emerge in Britain and the northern colonies in America by the mid-eighteenth century. Before then, though, the loudest denunciations of slavery were usually heard from relatively marginal members of the relatively marginalised Quakers. Rather than condemn slavery outright, the Quaker leader George Fox (1624–91) urged slaves to 'be Sober, and to Fear God, and to love their Masters and Mistresses, and . . . then their Masters and Overseers will Love them, and deal Kindly and Gently with them'.[46]

Racism in its modern form – that is, attributing social and intellectual qualities on the basis of inherited traits such as skin colour – is intimately bound up with the Atlantic slave trade. That said, full-blown racialist arguments for slavery were not common in the Atlantic world before the mid-eighteenth century. In seventeenth-century England it was accepted that slavery could be imposed upon 'either Blacks or any other Foreigners, not being Christians'.[47] And by the same reckoning it was widely believed that slaves could gain their freedom by being baptised. Colonial slave-owners saw matters somewhat differently. Black Africans in their view were of 'brutish and barbarous nature'[48] – in other words, natural slaves, or at least the only people who were 'constitutionally qualified to sustain the Toil of Planting in the [tropical] Climates of our Island Colonies'.[49]

Nevertheless, the English made slaves of white Christians too. One reason why the rate of emigration relative to population was at its highest in the British Isles in the mid-seventeenth century was the thousands of Scottish, Irish and royalist prisoners that the parliamentarians shipped in chains to the Caribbean. In 1659, Martin Noell had to defend himself in Parliament against accusations that he had been profiteering from the transportation of political prisoners to Barbados, where they had allegedly suffered 'most unchristian and barbarous usage . . . being bought and sold . . . from one planter to another' like cattle.[50] A century later, Gottlieb Mittelberger would be shocked at how poor immigrants, on reaching Philadelphia, were forced to sell themselves or their children to pay for their passage money – and at how eagerly Pennsylvanians flocked to buy them.

The great majority of people shipped across the Atlantic in the early modern period had no say in the matter. But why did so many British and Irish people more or less freely decide to risk all for a new life in the New World? The short answer in a great many cases was desperation. Over two thirds of English immigrants to the Americas in the early modern period were destitute and largely unskilled young men for whom signing up to years of drudgery as, for example, an indentured servant on a tobacco plantation in the Chesapeake seemed better than trudging the roads of England in a futile search for work. Starting over in the colonies was their last throw of the dice. Disastrous harvests, unemployment, and 'want of Tillage' were powerful driving forces behind Scottish and Irish emigration across the period. Persecution and revolution, and a brisk market in kidnapping young men and women for servitude in the colonies, pushed a great wave of migrants out to the Americas in the mid-1600s. A rise in Britain's population, and hence greater pressure on jobs and food prices, contributed to another in the 1760s and 1770s.

But there were 'pull' factors too, and these became stronger during the eighteenth century. The tens of thousands of Scottish Highlanders and Ulster Presbyterians who left for America in the 1760s and 1770s included not only the poverty-stricken, fleeing recession and rising rents, but also skilled workers and yeomen farmers who hoped to better themselves still further in the colonies. The Highlanders who crossed to North America in the 1770s were reportedly 'far from being the most indigent, or the least capable of subsisting in their own Country. No;

it was not Poverty or Necessity which compelled but Ambition which enticed them to forsake their native Soil.'[51]

The Anglo-Scottish union of 1707 threw England's empire wide open to ambitious Scottish and Ulster businessmen and professionals. The exploits of these commercial pioneers were vital in preparing business communities in Scotland and Ireland to respond more vigorously to expanding colonial markets, as they began to do in the mid-eighteenth century. Where there was money to be made in the colonies there were usually Scottish planters, merchants, doctors, clergymen, lawyers etc. in close attendance. They had invaded the trade of the Chesapeake to such an extent by 1760 that Glasgow's 'tobacco lords' were doing more business than their London rivals. Of Virginia in the 1770s it was observed that 'all the Merchants and shop-keepers . . . through the Province, are young Scotch-men'.[52] Almost every medical professional practising in the colonies had been trained in Scotland. The East India Company too was overrun with Scots by the mid-eighteenth century – a consequence in part of Whitehall buying votes and political influence in Scotland with Company offices. Hundreds of Scots had entered Company service in India by the 1770s. Their number was so great that even some Scots began to grumble about it. In the Chesapeake, and probably in most places where Scots moved in strength into commerce or administration, they were cordially detested – as thrusting, successful people usually are. But the colonies and the EIC would have been much the poorer, literally, without their drive and eye for the main chance. The empire was thriving by the 1760s largely because it had become emphatically more British than Britain was itself.

Trade held the British Atlantic together more securely than the makeshift chassis of imperial government. The navigation acts channelled a huge stream of colonial merchandise back to Britain. Sugar and coffee from the Caribbean, tobacco from the Chesapeake and rice from the Carolinas were the most valuable colonial imports. Far more was shipped over than the British could possibly consume themselves, and about three quarters of these products, like most of the calicoes brought from India, were re-exported to the Continent. The economies of the Chesapeake and the Carolinas, not to mention that of Britain itself, depended heavily on the success of British merchants in selling colonial produce to mainland Europeans. Moving the other way across the Atlantic were all manner of manufactured goods. The rapidly expanding population of colonial America was spending about a third of its income on imported products by the 1770s. British ceramics, metalware and the like complemented Caribbean sugar, Indian calicoes and tea from China. Another growing market for British manufactures was Portuguese Brazil, for since the early 1700s, when Britain had taken Portugal under its protection, the Portuguese empire had become virtually a British subsidiary. British exports to Brazil and Portugal's other colonies were worth £1 million a year by 1750, and were paid for in Brazilian gold that then helped finance the EIC's bullion shipments to the East Indies. There was in fact a wide and varied range of commercial links between the Atlantic and Asian spheres of the British empire, producing a far more integrated system than existed at the political level.

Britain was merely the main anchor point for a complex web of commercial networks that criss-crossed the British Atlantic. Because New England had much the same climate as northern Europe it produced little that the consumer markets there could not source more locally, and therefore the vast bulk of its exports – mainly grain, meat and livestock, timber, rum, and fish and whale products – went either to the West Indies or directly to southern Europe and Africa. In return the New Englanders imported sugar from the West Indian slave plantations that they distilled into rum and then exported back around the Atlantic. There was also a large and highly profitable trade between the North American colonies and the French sugar islands in the Caribbean, which was maintained regardless of the navigation acts or whether Britain and France happened to be at war. The British government would pay dearly in American loyalty in the 1760s by trying to crack down on this smuggling free-for-all.

The best-known, or rather most infamous commercial network in the British Atlantic was the triangular trade between Britain, Africa and the Americas. Ships would leave British ports (mainly London, Bristol, and Liverpool) with cargoes of East Indian textiles, manufactured goods, alcohol etc. and sail south to equatorial West Africa. These goods would then be sold for slaves, who would be shipped across the Atlantic on the second leg of the journey, the so-called 'middle passage'. The slaves that survived this hellish ordeal, and most of them did, would be sold in the Caribbean or the American colonies, where the ships' holds would be cleaned and filled with colonial produce or, more often, simply ballast, for the journey back across the Atlantic. The entire trip could take upwards of eighteen months.

Without the slave trade the British Atlantic could not have functioned as a single economic system; indeed, it would hardly have existed at all. Slave-trading not only joined Britain, its African trading stations and its colonies in the Americas in profitable exchange, but also supplied the continual stream of African labour that made the mass production of sugar and other Atlantic staples possible. The 'African trade' was 'of such essential and allowed Concernment to the Wealth and Naval Power of Great Britain', the economist Malachy Postlethwayt assured his readers in 1745, 'that it would be as impertinent to take up your Time in expatiating on that Subject as in declaiming on the common Benefits of Air and Sun-shine . . .'[53] Yet expatiate on it he did, pleading eloquently not for the welfare of the slaves, but the plight of the British economy without them:

> Is it not notorious to the whole World that the Business of Planting in our British Colonies, as well as in the French, is carried on by the Labour of Negroes, imported thither from Africa? . . . If we have no Negroes, we can have no Sugars, Tobaccoes, Rice, Rum, etc. nor further Improvements in Plantation Commodities; consequently, the Publick Revenue, arising from the Importation of Plantation-Produce, must be annihilated: And will not this turn many hundred Thousands of British Manufacturers a Begging, as well as Numbers of our Publick Creditors, whose Securities depend upon the Appropriation of those very Revenues, if our African and American Trades are undone?[54]

The slave trade was vital even for those North American colonies without slave-based economies. New England, for example, relied for much of its prosperity on the foodstuffs and timber that it traded to the slave plantations in the Carolinas and the Caribbean. The entire British Atlantic rested upon African foundations.

Trade dulled or transmuted the Protestant idealism of the early colonisers, and slavery corrupted trade. The New Jerusalem of Massachusetts and its neighbours was the last to fall to the forces of commerce, but fall it did. Praising God, raising families and honest toil had marked New England at its beginning. 'It is not trade that God will set up in these parts,' the governor of Massachusetts had declared in 1636, 'but the p[ro]fession of His trueth; and therefore if Gods ends bee not followed, Mens ends will never bee blessed, nor attayned.'[55] The 'ill successe of other Plantations', thought Boston's godly founder John Winthrop, came about because 'thir mayne end was Carnall and not Religious'.[56] Yet baser motives prevailed among some of the first New Englanders as well. One minister, preaching to a congregation in Maine, 'urged them to approve themselves a Religious People from this consideration; That otherwise they would contradict the main end of Planting this Wilderness', whereupon one of the local worthies cried out: 'Sir, You are mistaken . . . our main End was to catch Fish.'[57]

There was a visible waning of godly zeal in New England after 1660, just as there was in Britain. Massachusetts' Puritan patriarchs bemoaned their fellow colonists' 'Inordinate affection unto the world', and especially their 'insatiable desire after Land'.[58] By 1700 the link between church membership and political power had been broken. Older and distinctively Puritan ideas about God's design for New England were giving way among its leading ministers and merchants to an understanding of providence that focused on the power of Britain's commerce and empire to defeat popery and promote prosperity, politeness and civil liberties throughout the Atlantic world. This re-evaluation of the workings of God's will naturally appealed to merchants and landowners grown rich on the proceeds of New England's thriving commerce throughout the British Atlantic. At the other end of the social scale there was a corresponding increase after 1660 in white poverty and black slavery. Despite some colonists' efforts to protect the rights of 'black mankind', there were about 15,000 Africans or African-Americans in New England by 1770, mostly employed as sailors, dockworkers and household servants. The New Jerusalem had become like most other places in North America: consumerist and market-oriented.

Slave-holding was more common in the 'middle colonies' of New York, New Jersey and Pennsylvania. Between 6 and 9 per cent of the population here during the eighteenth century were African slaves. The proportion may have been even higher in the late seventeenth century, before the Quakers developed a more thoroughgoing aversion to slavery. The largest slave-holder in New York and New Jersey in the 1670s was the Quaker and former Barbadian planter Lewis Morris. Quaker leader and slave-owner William Penn, the founder of Pennsylvania, made no bones about combining the free worship of God and 'Busy Commerce' using African 'servants' as he primly called them.[59] In fact, he preferred slaves to indentured whites, 'for then a man has them while they live'.[60] The Quakers used slaves shipped to the colony in 1684 by a Bristol merchant's company to clear the ground for the construction of Philadelphia, the city of brotherly love. Most Philadelphians came to prefer buying German or Scots–Irish indentured servants rather than Africans to do their dirty work, as Mittelberger would discover. Nevertheless, the Swedish scientist and travel-diarist Pehr Kalm observed on his visit to the city in 1750 that African slaves had been bought 'by almost everyone who could afford it', and that the Quakers owned 'as many negroes as other people'.[61] For middle-class Philadelphians with limited capital to invest, buying a slave took priority over buying a house.

Slavery would leave an equally ugly mark on eighteenth-century New York. Up to 30 per cent of the population in some rural parts of the colony and in eastern New Jersey were slaves. Slaves made up a fifth of New York city's 11,000 population by the 1740s, and a third of its workers. The first slave revolt in northern America occurred in New York in 1712, for which nineteen Africans were burned, hanged or broken on the wheel. Tales of this revolt would inspire a plot in 1741 by a motley group of Afro-Hispanic slaves and Irish soldiers in the New York garrison – what the authorities called 'the outcasts of the nations of the earth' – to seize the city and end the oppressions of its slave-owning mercantile elite.[62] Some of the ringleaders were slaves who had been sold by their West Indian masters to unwary Yankees precisely because they were troublemakers and fomenters of slave rebellions. The plot was discovered and four whites and thirty-one slaves were executed.

New York and the other middle colonies had economies with slaves; the plantations of the Chesapeake and Carolinas, on the other hand, became slave economies. The Chesapeake's unfettered, tobaccocentric commercialism produced a deeply divided society – not at first between blacks and whites, but between the poor indentured servants who worked the plantations and the ruling elite of wealthy planters. The servants were not true slaves in that they could work off their bondage, if they lived long enough. But they called themselves 'bond slaves'. They felt as if they were enslaved. And indeed for much of the seventeenth century, white servants and black slaves worked together, and sometimes ran off together as well. One such 'white negger'[63] recalled in verse that 'We and the Negroes both alike did fare, Of work and food we had an equal share'.[64] But that commonality of the oppressed began to change in the 1670s as the wealthier planters bought African slaves in large numbers and imposed a brutal sunup–sundown gang-labour regime. Harsh new laws were introduced governing every aspect of the slaves' lives, and whites and blacks were effectively segregated. Free people who married slaves were banished. Slaves would comprise up to 40 per cent of the Chesapeake's population by the mid-eighteenth century.

Massive imports of slaves to work the paddy fields of South Carolina helped turn the colony into the wealthiest and most unequal society in North America. An incredible 97 per cent of whites in the Charleston district owned slaves by 1770. South Carolina seemed to some European immigrants 'more like a negro country than like a country settled by white people'.[65] Yet though slavery widened the economic divide between rich and poor whites in the Chesapeake and Carolinas, it actually narrowed the gap between them socially and culturally. However poorly off a white man was, he was not a black slave, and he cherished all the more the English liberties common to those of European blood.

The Carolinas, like the rest of mainland America, were chained economically to the sugar plantations of the West Indies, the hub of empire in the British Atlantic. The islands imported more slaves and generated more wealth than any other part of the British Americas. White indentured servants had at first outnumbered black slaves in the English Caribbean, but both alike had generally been treated abysmally by the planters. When a Spanish fleet attacked the island of Nevis in 1629, some English servants greeted them with cries of 'Liberty, joyfull Liberty'.[66] Planters had to build their houses like forts to protect themselves from their own employees.

The switch in the English Caribbean from white indentured to black slave labour began in the 1640s with the onset of the sugar boom. Sugar production was so gruelling, and the numbers needed to make it pay so large, that even a nominally free workforce would not stand for it. Barbadian planters were buying hundreds of slaves from the Dutch by 1645, 'and the more they buy', George Downing observed, 'the more they are able to buy, for in a year and a half they will earn as much as they [the slaves] cost'.[67] The number of slaves on Barbados rose from 5,680 in 1645 to about 70,000 by 1700, while the white population fell from 30,000 to 15,000. By 1780, fewer than 50,000 whites controlled a slave population in the British West Indies of nearly 500,000 blacks. Only the vilest and most systematic form of repression could sustain this disparity between free and enslaved. White militias, government troops and the harshest penal codes in the British Atlantic were all part of the planters' arsenal. A starving slave who stole bread would be executed, but a white man who wilfully killed a slave merely fined.

Fear was a weapon that cut both ways, however, for slaves fought the system as ferociously as the planters tried to impose it. There were more than seventy planned or actual slave revolts in the British West Indies between the early seventeenth and early nineteenth centuries. Most were ruthlessly suppressed and those involved were hanged, or sometimes gibbeted and slowly burned to death. But the British met their match in the case of the Maroons: the community of runaway slaves turned guerrilla fighters in the hills of Jamaica (Britain's richest colony by the eighteenth century). Their night-time raids on plantations had reduced the island by 1733 to what one colonial official described as 'a tottering state'.[68] The Maroons' heroic defiance of the mighty British empire helped inspire major slave conspiracies and revolts throughout the Atlantic colonial world during the 1730s and 1740s. The 'contagion of rebellion', as the governor of Jamaica called it, was particularly strong among the Akan people, or Coromantees, who were enslaved Africans from the warlike tribes of the Gold Coast.[69] Unable to beat the Maroons, the British had to resort to the old imperial trick of buying them off. The Caribbean planters' reliance on government troops whenever their slaves decided to make a stand largely explains why they would remain loyal to Britain during the American War of Independence.

The extremes of wealth and brutality in 'the hot country' encouraged a culture of incredible self-indulgence among the planters. For 'Sumptuous Houses, Cloaths and Liberal Entertainment', observed the writer of *Great Newes from the Barbadoes*, in 1676, the Jamaican planters 'cannot be Exceeded by . . . their Mother Kingdome it self'.[70] One visitor to the island in 1688, though put off by the vulgarity of what he saw, admitted that the planter elite lived in 'the Hight of Splendor, in full ease and plenty, being sumptuously arrayed, and attended on, and served by their Negroe slaves'.[71] With huge profits and plenty of free manpower to hand, planters could afford to entertain on a lavish scale. One plantation host had punch made for his guests using 2,400 bottles of wine and rum, and the juice of 2,600 lemons, poured into a marble pond built specially for the occasion in his garden.

The web of empire in the Atlantic was, or became, as much a cultural as a commercial construct. Society in many places in the British Americas long remained an unstable amalgam of different ethnic groups, religions, and ideas about civilised life. Colonists and Indians alike struggled, sometimes violently, to come to terms with outlandish new folk and their barbarous customs. Amid this chaos of clashing cultures and social dislocation there was an increasing turn towards English – and especially London – mores and fashions as a way of lending civility to fractured colonial communities.

Genteel society in the Americas embraced politeness very quickly after the English did themselves – that is, in the late seventeenth century – and it was soon spreading among the middling sort of colonial people, English or otherwise. English political rights were demanded in the

British Americas by virtually all colonists, whatever their ethnic origin. Equally in demand were tea and other British imports, and these, as we have seen, helped to infuse in consumers the tastes and manners – and, according to American moralists, the luxurious vices – of polite metropolitan society.

Although English politeness contained cultural DNA from several countries, notably France and Italy, it made relatively few concessions to the local environment. West Indian planters insisted on living in their stiflingly hot and humid Georgian mansions rather than build in the airier and cooler style of Spanish colonial. Even so, polite performances varied according to the audience being played to. The extravagance of planter politeness would not have worked in the drawing room of a Boston merchant. Some shows of gentility did not work in any social setting. Passing through Maryland in the 1740s, the peripatetic Scottish physician Alexander Hamilton ridiculed one of his travel companions – 'a very rough spun, forward, clownish blade, much addicted to swearing, [and] at the same time desirous to pass for a gentleman' – for proclaiming that he had 'good linnen in his bags, a pair of silver buckles . . . [and] that his little woman att home drank tea twice a day'.[72]

The burgeoning consumer society of the British Atlantic offered rich pickings not just for manufacturers and merchants. The Church of England shrewdly exploited the growing prosperity among the American colonists to increase its transatlantic flock in the early eighteenth century. Stylish new churches were built in the main coastal towns, and thousands of converts made among the upwardly mobile, who were drawn to the Anglican tradition of order and hierarchy. The SPCK (Society for Promoting Christian Knowledge: est. 1698) and SPG (Society for the Propagation of the Gospel in Foreign Parts: est. 1701) helped the Church to establish Anglican outposts in Pennsylvania and New Jersey, and even in the Puritan citadel of New England. But the sheer number and variety of Dissenters in most colonies made it hard for the Church to flourish outside of its strongholds in Virginia, Maryland and the West Indies. Religious pluralism was greatest in ultra-tolerant Pennsylvania, where Mittelberger encountered in the 1750s a bewildering kaleidoscope of Protestants, Catholics, 'Freemasons . . . Freethinkers, Jews, Mohammedans, [and] Pagans'. In a single household, he claimed, '4, 5, and even 6 sects, may be found'.[73]

Religious life in the northern American colonies would be turned upside down in 1739 with the arrival from England of the Anglican clergyman and proto-Methodist George Whitefield. This smallish, somewhat cross-eyed man was the British Atlantic's most charismatic preacher. A master of oratory and dramatic timing, he could work an audience like no other minister. His exhortations, and exertions, were legendary. Olaudah Equiano remarked that Whitefield sweated during a sermon 'as much as I ever did while in slavery'.[74] Of himself and his transatlantic mission, Whitefield wrote: 'Great and visible effects followed his preaching, almost wheresoever he went . . . There was never such a general awakening, and concern for things of God known in America before.'[75] Up and down the eastern seaboard his sermons drew huge crowds that devoured his impassioned call for born-again Christianity and his terrifying descriptions of the fate that awaited unrepentant sinners. Although himself an Anglican, Whitefield was well aware that the majority of American colonists – three quarters by 1775 – were Dissenters from the Church of England, and he pitched his message accordingly. To his fellow Anglicans in America his preaching was 'monstrous enthusiasm', but they were powerless to prevent it.

In England, where his sermons were equally popular, Whitefield would become a leading figure in the emergence of Methodism. In America it was his preaching tours that more than anything else sparked the Great Awakening: the fundamentalist revival that swept the colonies in the early 1740s and exerted a profound influence upon evangelicals back in Britain. The Awakening recast and revitalised the colonies' Dissenting communities, particularly the Presbyterians and Baptists. To reach and engage with their audience the Awakeners borrowed the commercial jargon and the aggressive marketing techniques of the British Atlantic's pervasive consumerist culture. Whitefield, it was said, made sermons 'a vendible Commodity'.[76]

More vendible still were other human beings. Whitefield defended the institution of slavery as a commercial necessity, and well he might. Sugar had become Britain's most valuable import by the 1750s; and sugar was the product of slavery. It was little use Benjamin Franklin (1706–90) – Whitefield's American publisher – trying to excuse slave-holding as the privilege of a wealthy few, a luxury foisted on the colonists by the British. The lifeblood of the British Atlantic was slavery. Slavers supplied the plantations with cheap labour, and North American farmers and merchants supplied the plantations with food. Between them they produced the sugar and other colonial products that flowed back to Britain – just as textiles and tea did from Asia – to generate the taxation revenue that oiled the wheels of imperial commerce and public credit. Slavery helped pay for the navy that kept the sea lanes open for British manufactures and colonial imports. Slavery bought political power. The West Indian planters were the most influential lobby at Westminster by the 1730s. Leviathan was borne in stately progress upon the backs of African slaves.

Salutary neglect, 1713–54

The growth of British power and commerce in the Americas and the Indian subcontinent during the first half of the eighteenth century would be shaped by the administrative and conceptual frameworks established the previous century by the monopoly trading privileges of the EIC and the navigation acts. Despite the burgeoning economies and populations of the Atlantic colonies, and the expanding commercial horizons of the EIC in the Far East, there was little interest at Whitehall in stronger imperial rule or closer integration. Affairs in Europe continued to preoccupy the government and public, and understandably so, for Britain's main enemies and allies were in Europe, and the bulk of its overseas trade in the early 1700s was still with Europe. Similarly, the Continent supplied most of Britain's imports and took at least two thirds of its domestic and colonial exports. National interest aside, however, the British focus on Europe reflected a certain degree of complacent satisfaction about how well the empire was apparently performing. As far as Whitehall was concerned, certainly, the imperial system established under the navigation acts did not need strengthening or replacing, for by the early eighteenth century it had helped to transform the beleaguered English republic of the early 1650s into the world's greatest maritime power.

It was probably during the 1720s that the British overhauled their old trading rivals the Dutch as the dominant force in global commerce. Untroubled by a major war between 1713 and 1739, Britain's merchant marine expanded considerably – so much so that by the 1740s fully half of the western world's cargoes were being carried in British merchant ships. Leviathan had swallowed up not just the British state but also a large slice of the world's trade. Who now was intent upon 'ingrossing' the commerce of 'the greater part of the known world'? – the accusation that the English had flung at the Dutch in the 1650s.[77] Meanwhile, as if to bear out those who argued for trade as a zero-sum game, the Dutch economy had gone into reverse. Defending its vulnerable borders in the French wars of 1689–1713 had imposed a massive strain on the republic, but it was the rise of trading and manufacturing rivals across northern Europe during the early eighteenth century that was the root cause of the slump in Dutch overseas commerce and shipbuilding after 1720. The Dutch themselves had contributed to their decline by investing heavily in the London stock market, where interest rates were higher and business opportunities more plentiful than in Amsterdam. In effect, they had starved their own business sector of investment in order to feed that of their nearest rivals, and one of the results of this reversal in economic fortunes – London's emergence as the financial capital of Europe – is still evident today.

Yet having seen off one commercial superpower by the early eighteenth century the British were promptly confronted by another. For the prize to the country with the fastest-growing overseas commerce in the eighteenth century would go not to Britain but to France. Between the 1710s and 1780s the value of French colonial trade increased tenfold. Moreover, the relative cheapness of French products, particularly sugar, coffee and dyestuffs, gave France the edge over Britain in the European re-export market. By the mid-eighteenth century the French sugar island of Saint Domingue (present-day Haiti) was the richest colony in the world. The French were now pushing the British hard in the Caribbean and off West Africa, and had supplanted them in the eastern Mediterranean, one of Britain's oldest commercial outlets. The popular newspaper *The Craftsman* devoted its editorials of 9 and 16 December 1738 to the 'Rise and Progress of the Commerce of France; and by what means They are now become so considerable a Trading Nation as to rival Great Britain'. France's commercial success, thought the editor, should give 'greater cause of Jealousy and Uneasiness to the other Powers of Europe, than all the Conquests and military Projects of Louis the 14th, who in all Probability had gained his Point, had He . . . made the Care of Trade precede all Thoughts of War'.[78] French trade and maritime power were growing so fast, argued the Whig politician Horatio Walpole in 1740, that 'if France has a mind to be the formidable power by sea, without pushing conquests by land, I do not see how we can hinder it'.[79]

Walpole was one of the first Englishmen to register the revival of French and Spanish seapower in the 1720s and 1730s. The Spanish embarked on a major programme of shipbuilding in the 1720s, making large, durable but lightly armed ships for convoy duty and swift

patrolling between their far-flung colonies. The French built for range
and speed too, but also with an eye to naval combat. Most of the men-
of-war they launched in the 1720s and 1730s were lightly built but
heavily armed two-deckers. These were the ships of the future, the
workhorses of a modern battle fleet, as opposed to the cumbrous three-
deckers among the royal navy, some of which could not use their lowest
tier of gun ports in anything but the lightest seas. Building ships was
one thing, however; keeping them afloat for more than a dozen years
(the average life expectancy of a French ship of the line), and crewing
them with experienced seamen, quite another. Here Britain still enjoyed
a major advantage over its Catholic rivals, having invested much more
money and over a far longer period in dry docks and all the other
facilities needed to keep warships in fighting trim. Thanks to Britain's
huge merchant marine she also had a much bigger pool of experienced
sailors to draw from than did the French and Spanish. The royal navy
would remain the biggest and the best for most of the eighteenth
century. The trouble for Britain's politicians, particularly the notoriously
war-shy Robert Walpole, was that the British people knew it. What,
they asked, was the point of paying the high taxes needed to sustain
Britain's naval superiority if it was never put to use?

For few people doubted by the early 1730s that war with France or
Spain was on the horizon. The Anglo-French entente established in
1716 had held for some fifteen fretful years, during which London and
Versailles had tried their best to maintain at least the pretence of friendship. But relations between the two nations out on the high seas and
in North America and India had often been marked by tension, shading
into open violence. The settlements that the French had begun to
establish around the Great Lakes and in the lower Mississippi valley
– which included, in 1718, the city of New Orleans – were of particular
concern to the British. The French government liked to think of these
colonies as an 'advance guard' against any British attempt to push south
and westwards from the eastern seaboard, but British colonists in the
1720s thought they detected the beginnings of a French design aimed
at 'surrounding us with their settlements'.[80] In 1732 the chief justice of
the Pennsylvania supreme court, James Logan, penned a memorandum
to Whitehall in which he warned: 'It is manifest that if France could
possess itself of those [British] dominions [in North America] and
thereby become masters of all their trade, their sugars, tobacco, rice,
timber and naval stores, they would soon be an overmatch in naval
strength to the rest of Europe, and then be in a position to prescribe

laws to the whole.'[81] To meet the French threat, argued Logan, would require a thorough overhaul of imperial government and finances in the colonies. Logan's report is known to have reached the hands of prime minister Robert Walpole himself, though to no observable effect. Governing Britain was a tricky enough business without opening a colonial can of worms as well. When a former governor of Pennsylvania advised Walpole in 1739 to introduce new taxation in the American colonies, the prime minister was incredulous: 'I have old England set against me, and do you think I will have new England likewise?'[82] Privately, Walpole and his circle opined: 'It would be better for England if all the Plantations were at the Bottom of the Sea.'[83]

Walpole's dismissive attitude towards the colonies was not typical. He was interested in them largely in so far as customs revenue from colonial trade helped him to keep domestic taxes within reasonable limits. The majority of British people were proud of their colonies, although less as territorial assets in themselves than as commercial prizes and as markers and bulwarks of Britain's great-power status in Europe. The Americans never tired of telling their fellow Britons how much colonial trade and resources, particularly of the transatlantic variety, contributed to Britain's formidable weight in the European balance. Coverage of colonial affairs in the press was usually linked to Britain's strategic interests in Europe. But though the colonies were seen as vital to sustaining Britain's status as a great power, only a few newspapers called for the acquisition of more territory 'to Enlarge Dominion and Power'.[84] Interest in imperial expansion was limited before 1750. That was the kind of thing the Bourbon powers went in for, striving to extend their despotic rule over weaker peoples. Regardless of their deep involvement in the slave trade, the British still saw their empire as an enterprise based upon the benefits of commercial prosperity and shared liberties among free peoples, not on brute force and tyranny.

Public enthusiasm for an 'empire of the seas' – that is, an empire built on naval power and focused primarily on trade and the accumulation of wealth – largely dictated how Britain would respond to the Franco-Spanish maritime resurgence after 1713. The most serious threat to the empire was probably French infiltration of the American interior, as events in the 1750s would show. Few people in Britain, however, were interested in forging a stronger and larger land empire in North America. The foundation of the last of the original Thirteen Colonies, Georgia, in 1732 was partly a philanthropic exercise – to provide a productive haven for Britain's 'worthy poor' and foreign Protestant refugees – but also deeply reactive: to create a much-needed buffer between the Carolinas and the Spanish in Florida. Colonial expansion was of little advantage, it was thought, unless it advanced Britain's trade at the direct expense of her rivals – and how could pushing further into the wilderness of America achieve that? No, the way to make British greatness felt was to vie for supremacy at the source of French and Spanish colonial wealth: the Caribbean. Justice as well as national interest seemed to demand just such a campaign, for, as we have seen, the Spanish authorities in the West Indies had excited the public's wrath in the 1730s by continually stopping and searching, sometimes imprisoning and torturing, British merchants whom they suspected (often correctly) of illicit trading with Spanish colonies. It was 'too plain' (to British hacks, at least) that 'we had been treated by Spain with the utmost Injustice, the utmost Barbarity, and the utmost Contempt'.[85]

The incident of Spanish 'Barbarity' that caused the greatest uproar was perpetrated against master mariner Robert Jenkins. In 1731 he had been beaten up by the *guarda-costa* after they had boarded his merchant vessel off Havana, and a Spanish officer had sliced off part of his ear, 'bidding him to carry it to his Master King George'.[86] It was not until 1738, however, when the press raked up the story to feed the public Hispanophobia, that it became a *cause célèbre*. In February 1739 there was a 'splendid Appearance' at a masquerade performed in London

> where, among many humourous and whimsical Characters, what seemed most to engage the Attention of the Company, was a Spaniard, very richly dressed, who called himself Knight of the Ear . . . and across his Shoulder hung . . . a large Halter, which he held up to several Persons disguised like English Sailors, who seemed to pay him great Reverence; and, falling on their Knees before him . . . suffered him very tamely to rummage their Pockets . . .[87]

The main target of this burlesque, as is clear from the sailors' role, was not the Spanish but the Walpole government's perceived cowardliness in failing to stand up to popish aggression.

Harassment of merchants was not the stuff of which wars were usually made in the eighteenth century. The British and Spanish governments were both anxious to avoid hostilities. But the war against Spain that the public, press and 'patriot' opposition in Parliament forced upon the Walpole government in October 1739 was not really about trade and empire as such. Fundamentally, it was a war against Leviathan. Between September 1739 and October 1740, thirty-two constituencies wrote to their MPs demanding action on ministerial corruption, the lack of free and frequent Parliaments, excessive indirect taxation (the excise etc.), and other political grievances that, if truth be told, actually allowed for the efficient running of the fiscal–military state, and had been an essential feature of any powerful government since the 1640s. To Britain's self-styled patriots, however, war with Spain had become necessary to cleanse the Augean stable of national politics. War, particularly maritime war, fraught with its Elizabethan associations of defying Catholic despotism, would sweep away the state of popish servility that, due to Leviathan, was sapping British moral fibre and patriotism. War held out the prospect of new political leaders, indeed a new kind of politics: one that put empire and colonial trade before Eurocentric pandering to the London monied interest; that replaced the effeminate and Frenchified tastes of the aristocracy with manly British values; and that depended not upon a corrupted ministry but the public-spirited counsel of a patriotic Parliament. James Thomson's ode 'Rule Britannia', composed in 1740, would become the patriots' battle hymn.

The icon of the war movement was one of Walpole's sternest parliamentary critics, Admiral Edward Vernon (1684–1757). Even before the War of Jenkins' Ear had officially begun, Vernon had sailed to the West Indies with a small squadron of warships, and on 20 November 1739 had captured Porto Bello, on the Isthmus of Panama, the main base for the dreaded *guarda-costa*. When news of this victory finally reached Britain the following March it caused a sensation. British seapower had triumphed again, just as patriotic 'navalists' had boasted it would. Vernon instantly became a national hero. There were celebrations in London and across the country; the Lords and Commons voted him their thanks; taverns and streets were named after him (most famously, London's Portobello Road); and he was feted in the press as a latter-day Drake or Ralegh. Vernon mania also gripped the colonies. George Washington's father named his Virginian residence Mount Vernon in honour of the admiral. Vernon became a powerful public symbol for everything that Leviathan and its instruments were thought not to be – incorruptible, patriotic, a champion of trade and English liberties, an empire-builder.

Sadly for Vernon's devoted public, the rest of the war did not pan out quite as expected. The British people, if not their government, were almost as persuaded as Cromwell and his advisers had been in the

1650s that Spain's empire was weak, its treasure ships and colonies ripe for the plucking. In fact, Spanish defences in the Caribbean were strong, well maintained, and guarded not by beggarly poltroons, as the press and public fondly imagined, but by hardened colonials, men acclimatised to the heat and diseases of the tropics that killed soldiers fresh out from Europe in their thousands. Vernon and other experienced naval officers were well aware of the difficulties in fighting such a long way from home and in such pestilential conditions, but were trapped under the weight of public expectation, which in Vernon's case was of his own making. A fleet carrying 8,000 troops that sailed from Britain in 1740 to capture Cuba or some other major Spanish colony suffered almost an identical fate to that of Cromwell's Western Design of 1655. Just as in that earlier fiasco, the naval and infantry components could not combine effectively – partly because of Vernon's tendency to play to the public gallery – with the result that an assault on the Spanish port of Cartagena in March–April 1741 was repulsed with heavy losses. The British tried again in July, attacking Santiago de Cuba, and suffered another humiliating defeat. This was not the worst of it, however, for the 600 or so troops lost in combat were as nothing to the thousands of men carried off by yellow fever and other tropical diseases. Back home the Walpole government was accused of deliberately starving Vernon of ships and troops, and certainly the ministry was afraid that if Britain was too successful in the Caribbean it would bring in the French on the side of Spain. But what really killed the War of Jenkins' Ear, as we have seen, was Frederick the Great's invasion of Silesia late in 1740. From that point onwards the government turned its attention and most of Britain's military resources to the unfolding War of the Austrian Succession on the Continent. The only good to come from the war in the Caribbean, from the patriots' perspective anyway, was its contribution to bringing down Walpole in 1742.

France's formal entry into the war, early in 1744, gave the navalists and patriots one last, unlikely, hurrah during the 1740s, and that was the capture of the great French fortress of Louisbourg on Cape Breton Island (Nova Scotia), at the mouth of the St Lawrence River. The fortress had little strategic value, as the French never stationed enough ships there for it to serve as anything but a privateering base. Its role was primarily economic, in guarding France's rich cod fishery on the Grand Banks, and it was this prize that attracted the attentions of the colonists in Massachusetts, although only after they had been provoked by French raids against New England. The colonists had the men to mount an expedition against Louisbourg, but not the warships, and for these they appealed to Peter Warren, commander of a naval squadron in the Caribbean, who had long been convinced that the fortress held the key to a successful conquest of Canada. In the spring and summer of 1745 he and the colonists proved that combined operations could work – where there were no political agendas and clashing egos to get in the way – by blockading Louisbourg and forcing its surrender. A French expeditionary force to recover their lost fortress and honour was so hopelessly ill-equipped and badly organised that the crew of one ship, limping back across the Atlantic, was reduced to cannibalism.

The taking of Louisbourg produced the same hysterical tub-thumping by press and public that had greeted Vernon's capture of Porto Bello five years earlier. British seapower had been reaffirmed, and – in light of the string of allied defeats in the Low Countries during the mid-1740s – the navalists seemingly vindicated in their insistence that Britain should wash its hands of unwinnable and expensive land wars that benefited only foreigners, and instead devote itself to its empire of the seas. And to some extent the capture of Louisbourg was indeed a game-changer. Colonial expansion as an end in itself still had few advocates, but after 1745 the government and public began to attach more weight to the idea that enlarging the empire would (as one colonial governor put it) 'lay a foundation for a superiority of British power upon the continent of Europe'.[88] More colonies would mean more maritime trade and resources, reinforcing Britain's naval superiority and its power to maintain the balance of Europe. So compelling did this line of reasoning now seem that the government gave serious consideration to an expedition for conquering all of New France, although the War of the Austrian Succession ended before anything could come of it.

It would be the doctrine of preserving the balance of Europe directly, rather than indirectly through colonial acquisitions, that prevailed at the treaty of Aix-la-Chapelle in 1748, in which Britain handed back Louisbourg in return for France relinquishing its conquests in the Low Countries. Nevertheless, the whole Louisbourg saga – its capture and its opportune trade-off to preserve the European balance – had encouraged a new appreciation among Britain's political leaders of the importance of the colonies as territorial as well as commercial assets. Moreover, the treaty's failure to resolve the power struggle between Britain and France did little to calm the government's nerves regarding French intentions, especially now towards Britain's colonies. Some British politicians and journalists were convinced that the French had accepted peace in Europe in order to challenge more effectively for imperial supremacy around the globe.

The empire's increasing importance in the government's strategic calculations lent greater prominence at Whitehall to issues of colonial administration, or the lack of it. The politician and philosopher Edmund Burke would describe imperial rule under the first two Georgian kings as a matter of 'wise and salutary neglect'.[89] He was looking at the issue from the centre of power, of course. From the perspective of royal officials across the Atlantic, the government's handling of imperial affairs smacked less of salutary neglect than of complete indifference. Colonial governors frequently complained that their colony's assembly showed 'little or no defference to any opinion or orders . . . from the Ministry at Home', and they pleaded for help from the Board of Trade, ministers and Parliament – and much good it did them.[90] By the 1740s, the American colonies had been allowed to become what one government official called 'Independent Common Wealths', with representative assemblies that were 'absolute within their respective Dominions', and largely unaccountable to Whitehall for their laws and actions.[91]

The lethargy that characterised imperial government was yet another consequence of the growth of Leviathan. Like other government departments, the Board of Trade – the body charged with supervising the colonies – had become clogged with ministerial clients by the 1740s, and its responsiveness to colonial problems had suffered accordingly. Appointment to imperial offices at Whitehall and out in the colonies had been used by Walpole and other ministers not to promote efficiency but as a reward for services at Westminster. In building this system of patronage management, moreover, ministers had deprived colonial governors of the offices and perquisites to create their own political followings to assist them against their assemblies. The expansion of Leviathan at the centre, therefore, had stunted its growth at the periphery. It had also saddled the Board with placemen who lacked either the interest or ability to make reforms, or indeed to attempt anything that might embarrass their patrons. The result was a culture of complacency in which more and more of the initiative and power in the colonies passed from royal officials to colonial assemblies.

With salutary neglect looking more like culpable negligence by the late 1740s, the government began to take a more assertive approach to colonial administration. The new president of the Board of Trade, George Dunk, earl of Halifax, worked hard to increase the Board's authority by reclaiming where possible its lost powers and patronage, and he encouraged colonial governors to stand no nonsense from their assemblies. Parliament, too, took a new interest in colonial affairs during the late 1740s and early 1750s – most notably in drawing up legislation for overriding Jamaica's notoriously fractious colonial assembly. Yet none of these initiatives produced much in the way of effective action. Parliament contented itself with a general assertion of its authority in colonial matters, and shied away from intervening in Jamaican affairs. Similarly, although the Board reported that New Jersey and New York were in a 'state of entire disobedience to all authority' by the late 1740s, rocked by riots, and their assemblies out of control, the ministry, after a lot of bold talk about reform and punishment, did nothing.[92]

Halifax's work as president of the Board would earn him the unofficial title of 'the Father of the Colonies', but some of the colonists developed a very low opinion of his parenting skills.[93] The deputy governor of Pennsylvania, after being effectively forced out of office by his colony's assembly in the mid-1750s, dismissed the earl as one

> who deals out American facts upon very slight foundations, without the necessary enquiry; and was he not join'd in the ministry by men more ignorant than himself, he would soon be found out. His weight in parliament is very little; and nothing keeps him high in administration, but the opinion that he has knowledge in American affairs, and is diligent in the management of them, the first arises from the superlative ignorance of his fellow ministers, and the latter from a deal of bustle and stir about things of little consequence, made without judgement, without any plan or system and without understanding enough to form one.[94]

No knowledge, no plan, no system. That about summed up the drift and incoherence in Whitehall's administration of the colonies since the early seventeenth century. To be fair, the crown had never shown much interest in conquering and ruling new lands and peoples overseas. The navigation acts had been designed not to create a large territorial empire but to nurture maritime and commercial resources for use at home. With the rare exception of men like Noell and James II, politicians and princes had avoided the challenge of empire-building. It had often been the haphazard pursuit of profit, glory and the Protestant cause by thousands of daring and sometimes deluded individuals that had forced the pace of colonial expansion. Britain's empire, although a massive force-multiplier in the otherwise unequal struggle against France, had been acquired piecemeal, and with little thought for how it should best be governed. Yet if the British were to continue relying on the Louisbourg scenario to get them out of trouble in Europe, the ministry would have to grasp the nettle of imperial rule. The prospect, by the late 1740s, of a maritime war with France, a war for empire, left politicians considerably less squeamish about using the power of the British state to bring order to the colonies. Whether the colonies were similarly ready to embrace Leviathan was another question entirely.

8

New World Order, 1754–83

... these Colonies of the English [have] increas'd and improv'd, even to such a Degree, that some have suggested, tho' not for Want of Ignorance, a Danger of their revolting from the English Government, and setting up an Independency of Power for themselves ... the Notion is absurd, and without Foundation ...

> Daniel Defoe, *A Plan of the English Commerce*
> (London, 1728), 143

Let not the people of England imagine that the Colonists have a wish but for their welfare, and to partake of it as fellow-subjects. For the people of the colonies would sacrifice their dearest interests for the honour and prosperity of their mother country; and the last wish of their hearts will be for ever to belong to it.

> Thomas Pownall, *The Administration of the Colonies*
> (2nd edn London, 1765), sig. A3v

It is in vain, it is delerium, it is frenzy to think of dragooning three millions of English people out of their liberties, at the distance of 3000 miles.

> *The Remembrancer, or Impartial Repository of Public Events*
> (London, 1775), 10

The Seven Years War

A gulf had emerged by the mid-eighteenth century between how the British public and its leaders thought their empire was governed, and the reality of imperial power at the colonial periphery. The prevailing assumption at the empire's metropolitan core was that it functioned – or at least, that it ought to function – as a single political and institutional entity under the ultimate authority of king-in-Parliament. That was the theory, so to speak. In practice, as we have seen, the empire's political structure was far less hierarchical, with effective power dispersed among its constituent parts, particularly in the transatlantic colonies. Common interests generated by trade and the threat of French aggression had tied the colonies more closely to each other, and to the mother country, than the fitful projection of imperial authority from the centre. This gap between metropolitan assumption and colonial reality had largely been obscured during the first half of the eighteenth century by the preoccupation of Britain's statesmen with containing French ambitions in Europe. But a policy (if such it can be called) of 'salutary neglect' towards the colonies would appear increasingly untenable from the late 1740s as the French began to look beyond Europe for the means to achieve hegemony within it. War with France for imperial dominion would bring the colonies to the centre of the British public's attention for the first time. 'The whole nation has been very neglectful of them [the colonies],' observed one pamphleteer in 1757. 'We seem to have paid no regard to them, 'till the French opened our eyes about them, and made us take notice of them, whether we would or not.'[1] French aggression would convince British politicians in the 1760s of the need for closer imperial integration and the due subordination of colonial interests to those of the crown. Different parts of the empire would react in different ways to this new imperial agenda, but in America, certainly, it would prove profoundly destabilising; for the nearer the British state drew to the colonists, the less they liked what they saw.

The 1748 treaty of Aix-la-Chapelle had brought an end to the fighting in Europe, but it did not bring peace of mind. British ministers were soon referring darkly to Versailles's intentions of continuing the war by other means – that is, of encircling or attacking Britain's colonies as part of France's supposedly inveterate bid for 'universal monarchy'. Their suspicions were shared by the press and the public. Every Briton should be aware of France's 'eternal thirst after universal dominion', wrote one journalist in the mid-1750s,

> her continual incroachments on the properties of her neighbours . . . of her perfidious policy, and perfidious practices, with regard to Europe in general, and the welfare and commerce of this island in particular, for upwards of a hundred years past . . . [T]ill a proper reduction of

her exorbitant power be accomplished . . . it is most certain, that our trade, our liberties, our country, nay all the rest of Europe, will be in continual danger of falling a prey to the common enemy, the universal cormorant, that would, if possible, swallow up the whole globe itself.[2]

This was preaching to the converted. The possibility that Britain and its empire might appear equally threatening to the French was barely considered. Yet the French naval build-up from the late 1740s (their biggest since Louis XIV's day), and efforts to push their various colonial claims around the world, were apparently part of a strategy to contain what they in turn regarded as Britain's own pretensions to global supremacy. If Britain could be forced to divert more resources towards defending its empire, or, better still, be denied the fruits of its colonial commerce, then it would be all the easier to neutralise in Europe. For France was still determined to have its wishes deferred to by the rest of Europe, and to that extent the British were right to be worried. But by the 1740s it generally preferred to pursue this objective by coaxing or bullying other states, not by expanding its own borders.

Fear outweighed ambition in Versailles as well as London. But whichever motive prevailed, the result on the ground would be much the same: another huge build-up of tension, sometimes spilling over into violence, wherever Britain and France faced each other around the world. In North America the French feared that the British were determined to break out across the Appalachians, while the British detected a French design to confine them to a vulnerable coastal strip. In the Caribbean the two powers jealously eyed each other's sugar plantations. And in India they continued to fight regardless of the peace back in Europe.

The two powers' fears and aspirations for their respective empires would eventually collide with greatest impact in the North American interior. From the mid-1740s the French began to increase their infiltration of the Ohio country, south of the Great Lakes, as part of their long-term plan to create a chain of settlements from Canada down to the mouth of the Mississippi, and thereby keep the British penned in east of the Appalachians. In the short term they wanted to stake their claim to the strategically vital Ohio valley, and that meant stopping colonial traders peddling British goods (which were often better and cheaper than French wares) – and, in effect, British influence – among the Ohio Indians. A policy of calculated terror had served the French well in the past, and it did so again. In one notorious attack upon a

British trading post in 1752, Chippewa and Ottawa warriors, allied with the French, cut out the heart of one trader and ate it, and then boiled and ate the settlement's Indian headman as a lesson to other British sympathisers. This scared away the traders, to be sure, but by advertising French intentions in the Ohio country it also galvanised the various groups of land-hungry colonial speculators that had had their eyes on this vast and fertile wilderness for decades. Alarmed by French penetration into what they saw as their own territorial limits – remote at the moment, but ripe for future colonisation – they too began to push settlements out towards the Ohio valley. One of the frontier surveyors for the most aggressive of these syndicates was the ambitious Virginian gentleman George Washington.

The British prime minister, the duke of Newcastle, was fully convinced of Versailles's imperialist intentions. If French aggression in the Ohio valley was tolerated, he believed, 'All North America will be lost . . . no War can be worse to this Country than the suffering such Insults as these.'[3] But though keen to halt what he saw as French encirclement of British North America, he was at the same time anxious to prevent hostilities there escalating into another war in Europe. He and the cabinet proceeded cautiously, therefore, by encouraging a Virginian expedition to dislodge the French from the Ohio valley without (it was hoped) causing major ructions with Versailles. The sharp end of this vital mission was entrusted, in true penny-pinching colonial fashion, to a mere 160 volunteers led by Washington, and predictably it turned into a shambles. Washington, a greenhorn when it came to frontier fighting, could not prevent his Indian allies massacring French prisoners, nor the French from killing or wounding over 100 of his own soldiers.

Washington's defeat allowed the duke of Cumberland – Britain's most powerful military figure – to override Newcastle's softly, softly approach. The professional (though hardly battle-hardened) soldier Major-General Edward Braddock was sent out from Britain with two regiments of foot as part of a wholly unrealistic plan to attack the French in America on four fronts simultaneously. Undeterred by a general lack of colonial cooperation and the huge logistical problems of dragging an army over several hundred miles of mountainous and forested terrain, he had managed, by July 1755, to cut his way to the Monongahela River, close to the French fort at what is now Pittsburgh. Yet though this in itself was a remarkable achievement, he should have put at least as much energy and thought into narrowing the gulf in military experience between his own troops and the French. Like Washington (his aide-de-camp), however, he thought purely in terms of a 'civilised' fight between British and French regulars. He took little account of the help offered him by friendly Indians or of the highly irregular battle tactics of the Canadian militiamen and Indian warriors who attacked his advance guard. Standing out in the open, in close formation, firing in platoon order, as they had been trained, his redcoats were mown down in their hundreds by enemy musketry from the surrounding trees, and by friendly fire from their own terrified comrades. Braddock himself was shot in the back – possibly by one of his own men – and died a few days later. Had he been victorious, and had the navy managed to prevent a convoy of French troop ships slipping through to Louisbourg, then it is just possible that Versailles would have backed down. As it was, a general war was now unavoidable. For perhaps the first time in history, the tide of blood would flow from the colonies to Europe rather than the other way round.

Impending war with France meant that Britain must look to her defences in Europe, and there too the signs were worrying. The Grand Alliance for containing French power in Europe – the so-called 'old system' – was close to collapse. The Dutch had sunk into impotence, and too late did Newcastle realise that the Austrians, traditionally Britain's main ally against the French, had finally had enough of seeing their interests (and specifically the recovery of Silesia) sacrificed to those of British security. Worse still – though Newcastle did not know this – the French and Austrians had secretly been working towards a rapprochement for several years. It would not be until late 1754, however, when Britain was already committed to war in America, that Newcastle discovered that 'the great System is on the point of being dissolved . . . The conduct of Vienna is astonishing. They act as if they had no occasion for Us.'[4] In desperation, the British concluded a treaty with Russia in September 1755 in order to deter France's ally Prussia from attacking the now exposed Hanover. Frederick the Great had always feared the looming Russian threat on his eastern flank, but instead of strengthening his ties with France he concluded a treaty of his own with Britain, early in 1756, by which he received British money to protect Hanover, and a guarantee that Russia's British-subsidised troops would leave Prussia alone.

Given the narrow focus of this alliance, neither the British nor the Prussians expected it to disturb their broader alignments: Prussia with France, and Britain with Austria. They could not have been more wrong.

The Anglo-Prussian treaty was seen as an act of betrayal at Versailles and Vienna, not to mention Moscow, and finally persuaded the French and Austrians to settle their differences and sign a mutual defence pact (which Russia soon joined) that repudiated their old alliances.

A diplomatic revolution had occurred. Two centuries of Habsburg–Bourbon rivalry, and with it the balance of Europe, had been swept away, stripping Britain and Prussia of their strategic cover. Britain now had just one effective ally on the Continent, Prussia, and that was being sized up for attack by both the Austrians and Russians. Meanwhile, France was free to focus all her military energies on challenging Britain's empire of the seas, and indeed to invade Britain itself.

As in 1740, it would be Frederick the Great who struck first and brought war to mainland Europe. Rather than await the inevitable onslaught, he invaded Austria's German ally, Saxony, in August 1756, thereby exposing all of the Habsburg empire's northern border to Prussian attack. Austria and Russia now prepared for full-scale retaliation, and France mobilised in support of its Austrian allies. A general war in Europe was just what Newcastle and his ministry had been most desperate to avoid. Britain was committed to subsidising a heavily outnumbered ally, Prussia, while Hanover was in danger not only from the French but now the Austrians as well. Such incompetence in the conduct of foreign policy could not go unpunished. Yet the main scapegoat would not be Newcastle but Admiral John Byng, whose feeble attempt to prevent the French seizing Britain's naval base on Minorca in 1756 led to his execution by firing squad the following March, prompting Voltaire's famous observation in *Candide* that the British occasionally found it beneficial to shoot an admiral '*pour encourager les autres*'. Nevertheless, Newcastle was forced to admit to George II that he had lost the public's confidence and that only one man had the political stature to do the crown's business, and that was William Pitt.

Pitt had been a fierce critic of Newcastle's blundering efforts to protect Hanover. In fact, he had made his reputation by lambasting the ministry for supposedly overindulging the king's devotion to the Electorate. Not surprisingly, George detested him. However, with a national crisis looming he bowed to necessity and appointed Pitt secretary of state.

What Pitt lacked in royal good will he made up for in self-confidence. 'I am sure I can save this country,' he declared, 'and nobody else can.'[5] But what he also had, or would develop, was a subtler version of Newcastle's classic Whig strategy of continental engagement as a prerequisite of colonial and maritime success. Rather than focus exclusively on victory across the Atlantic – a policy he had cried up in opposition – Pitt would work tirelessly to entangle France in a European war: a task made easier by the pro-Austrian faction at Versailles, led by Louis XV's chief mistress, Madame de Pompadour, which was determined to commit France decisively to a land war. With their resources devoted largely to attacking Prussia and Hanover the French would be hard-pushed to challenge Britain's empire of the seas, on which much of its military power depended. Pitt's 'divine plan' (as one of his supporters termed it) envisioned continental intervention and colonial expansion as two sides of the same coin.[6] His formidable skills as an organiser and parliamentary manager would be vital to this endeavour. Equally important were a favourable press and the backing of Newcastle, who controlled the Treasury and was a major patronage-broker at Westminster. If Pitt was successful in managing the king's 'German business' then he would be guaranteed what was still the greatest asset in British politics: the assurance of royal favour. And so it was that Westminster's most robust critic of continental engagement would channel vast sums to Frederick the Great and dispatch more troops to mainland Europe than he would ever send to defend the colonies.

If British taxpayers craved blood and glory in a great European land war they certainly got their money's worth. Backed by British subsidies and whatever men and money he could pillage from Saxony and other conquered territory, Frederick waged a relentless war against the immense confederacy that had formed against him. Beset though he was from every quarter, he won some spectacular victories – notably at Rossbach and Leuthen in 1757, when he defeated much larger French and Austrian armies – sealing for ever his reputation as a master tactician. To British and Irish Protestants he was a hero, resisting the forces of Catholic tyranny. Women donated food for his troops; pubs were named after him; and his face adorned all manner of consumer goods. But he lost battles too – or won Pyrrhic victories – sometimes through his own sheer arrogance and pigheadedness. After the Austrians and Russians had destroyed almost half his army at the battle of Kunersdorf in 1759 – the worst defeat of his military career – a self-pitying Frederick briefly contemplated first suicide and then abdication. Simply by staying in the war he kept Pitt's continental strategy alive. But he could not fight on indefinitely. Prussia might have begun the war with the army of a front-rank power, but it did not have the territory or population to match. Frederick needed, but failed, to land knockout blows, and the longer the war dragged on the less willing the British became to pour millions of pounds into sustaining it, the more his army shrank in size and quality, and the closer his enemies came to destroying Prussia entirely. Relief from this immense pressure, at least on Frederick's western flank, was provided by the German–British Army of Observation under his brother-in-law Ferdinand, duke of Brunswick – a humane and cultured man, and a virtuoso on the violin (Frederick was no more than an accomplished flautist). His army of Hanoverians and Hessians, reinforced by six British regiments, scored a decisive victory over the French at the battle of Minden, in north-west Germany, in 1759, that at the time saved Frederick from complete ruin.

Meanwhile, the French and Indian War – as the Seven Years War was known in North America – continued as disastrously as it had begun. Despite enjoying vastly superior numbers and resources, the British suffered a virtually uninterrupted run of defeats in the three years following Braddock's debacle in July 1755. French and Indian war parties once again murdered and looted all along the frontier. 'All our colonies in north America', lamented one pamphleteer, 'are not able to resist a handfull of French, but are likely to be overrun by a few ragamuffins in Canada.'[7] At the root of the problem was the lack of trust between colonial leaders and the man sent out as commander-in-chief of the crown's forces in America, the proud and irascible Scot, John Campbell, earl of Loudoun. His commission required, and he expected, unstinting cooperation from the colonists. What he met with instead, as he saw it, was foot-dragging, obstruction, and self-interested appeals to 'Rights and Privileges'. On encountering such opposition his response was invariably to threaten the use of force, persuading some colonists that he posed almost as much of a danger to their liberties as the French did. To cap it all, he had to deal with the military incompetence of the colonial militia, who were, of course, civilian part-timers.

Far from being the crack shots and wily woodsmen of legend, most colonial soldiers were complete novices in frontier warfare – unlike the French Canadians, who were a match even for the Indians. General James Wolfe (1727–59), Loudoun's most famous successor, confided to a colleague that: 'The Americans are in general the dirtiest, most contemptible cowardly dogs that you can conceive . . . They . . . desert by battalions, officers and all. Such rascals . . . are rather an encumbrance than any real strength to an army.'[8] Loudoun, like Wolfe, failed to grasp that American volunteers were generally young men of good family and prospects. To expect them to accept the same harsh military discipline imposed on British redcoats – who were mostly riff-raff, the sweepings of the gaol – was unrealistic. Loudoun was further hampered by a lack of cash, having been sent to America on the wholly mistaken assumption that the colonies would pay for the war.

Not until Pitt took American affairs by the scruff of the neck, late in 1757, did the British ever look like winning. Riding a wave of popular approval – thanks partly to Frederick the Great's victories that year – Pitt had the public support (and certainly the drive and determination) to do whatever it took to extinguish the threat of New France for ever. He had Loudoun recalled and cut the powers of his successor; he sent out 14,000 more troops, under talented commanders with orders to treat colonial soldiers respectfully; and he negotiated directly with colonial assemblies, as partners, rather than trying to bully them. Above all, he threw huge amounts of British taxpayers' money at the war effort. The result was an improvement in relations between the army and colonial authorities, and a great upsurge in patriotic endeavour among the colonists. Never again would they enlist so readily and fight so heartily for king and empire as they did in the late 1750s. Moreover, as the British began to look more formidable so the Indians grew more willing to help them or to quit the French. Fear of being tortured and eaten by 'savages' was a powerful force-multiplier for the French. The Indians' dreaded war whoop alone could turn British troops into a panic-stricken mob. The French commander-in-chief, the marquis de Montcalm, certainly valued the Indians as irregular auxiliaries. Yet like his British counterparts he believed that the war would be decided ultimately by civilised battles between well-drilled European regulars. He deplored what he saw as the Indians' ungovernable barbarity, particularly when it besmirched his and France's honour. Discouraged from scalping prisoners or taking captives for ransom (or ritual eating), his Indian allies grew increasingly reluctant to take up the hatchet, or else died in the great smallpox epidemic and famine winter of 1757–8.

The most famous battle for North America would be fought in September 1759 on the Plains of Abraham, a plateau just outside the walls of French Canada's main city, Quebec. The fall of Louisbourg to the British the previous year had allowed a fleet to proceed up the St Lawrence River in the summer of 1759 to lay siege to the city. Commanding this expedition was the young and talented, but sickly and neurotic, Wolfe. Unable to penetrate Quebec's defences or to goad the French into giving battle, Wolfe mounted a highly risky amphibious operation that succeeded through daring and good planning in deploying 4,500 of his redcoats on the city's more vulnerable landward side. Better still, it threw the normally cool-headed Montcalm into a panic, and instead of just waiting a few hours to catch the British between his own army in Quebec and a French column approaching from the west, he ordered an immediate attack.

Wolfe's troops were all experienced regulars with the discipline to hold their fire on the raggedly advancing French until the last moment. At about forty yards the redcoats, their muskets double-shotted, loosed a massive volley that did terrible slaughter. Stepping through the smoke of this first volley, the redcoats fired again, and those Frenchmen who were still standing fled, with the British in hot pursuit. Wolfe's regiment of Scottish Highlanders 'made dreadful havoc with their broad-swords', taking revenge no doubt for the nickname the French had given them – 'the English [!] savages'.[9] At the height of the battle, Wolfe was hit in the stomach and chest by musket balls. Plagued by illness for many months, he had longed for an honourable death in combat, and now he had his wish. Montcalm too was fatally shot and would die the next morning. Five days after the battle, Quebec surrendered.

The celebrations and grief in Britain over Wolfe's heroic victory and death marked an important change in the public's attitude towards the army. The navy had been lionised since Elizabethan times as the nation's front-line defence against Catholic tyranny, but the professional soldiery had acquired an invidious reputation as the instruments of government oppression. The tributes paid to Wolfe, however, reflected a growing respect for the army and a sense that it was a necessary, if not always welcome, feature of British society. His death came to symbolise the sacrifices made by British soldiers throughout the empire.

Yet dearly bought though Quebec was, it did not hold the key to victory in North America – that lay in the contest between the French and British navies in European waters. With the war in America and Germany going badly for the French by 1759, they decided to win it at a single stroke, by invading Britain. 'In every port they were building im[m]ense numbers of flat-bottomed boats; their coasts were lined with troops, which were daily practiced in the exercise of embarking and disembarking . . . & even a time was fixed for the departure of the fleet.'[10] But if time and tide did not wait for the French then nor did the royal navy. In September 1759 a British fleet defied tempestuous weather and treacherous reefs to sink, run aground or otherwise put out of action at least fifteen French warships at the battle of Quiberon, off the Brittany coast. This great victory – the Trafalgar of its day – saved Britain from possible invasion and destroyed France as a naval power.[11] The Irish Jacobites had planned an insurrection in Dublin to coincide with the invasion, but 'upon the news of that defeat [at Quiberon], like a compressed bubble, [it] was instantaneously quashed'.[12] British naval dominance prevented the French from retaking Quebec in 1760 – which they would otherwise have done – and any supplies or reinforcements from reaching the beleaguered defenders of Montreal, who succumbed to a massive, three-pronged British offensive in September 1760. New France was no more, absorbed into Britain's fast-expanding empire. Pitt's boast 'that America had been conquered in Germany' was fully justified.[13]

Britain's command of the seas was vital to victory not just in America but all round the world. Naval superiority in the Indian Ocean opened the way for Robert Clive's recapture of Calcutta in 1756 and the subsequent expansion of British power throughout Bengal. A French fightback during the late 1750s was doomed once bad weather and British warships had knocked their Indian fleet out of the war. Defeat at the battle of Wandiwash in 1760 – the largest battle ever fought between Europeans on Indian soil – and the British capture of the French headquarters at Pondicherry would all but destroy France as a power in India. While the royal navy ferried the East India Company's cohorts to and from battle, and pounded French settlements in India, a British squadron descended upon France's trading stations on the west coast of Africa and took every one, along with their rich trade in slaves, gold and ivory. And in 1759 the British defied a French fleet to capture the incredibly lucrative sugar island of Guadeloupe, to which they added Martinique and France's other Caribbean colonies in 1762.

But it was the victories at Quebec and Quiberon that appeared most marvellous in the public's eyes. After years of military humiliation in North America, 1759 was Britain's 'annus mirabilis' – 'this wonderful year' in the royal navy's official marching song 'Heart of Oak' – when Parliament voted and the public paid 'immense sums' in taxation 'without murmuring because they saw their treasure in earnest used, as the sinews of war'.[14] 'Such were the events of that prodigious year!', gushed one chronicler of the war, in which Great Britain displayed her power and influence beyond what she had ever done, in the most shining periods of history. In Europe, in Asia, in Africa, & in America, her greatness had conspicuously shone out. Her fleets rode triumphant in all seas; her armies conquered, wherever they appeared. Her open enemies severely felt her vengeance; & her secret ones durst only brood in private over their malice.[15]

The tools of despotism

The cup of patriotic fervour overflowed in 1759–62. On both sides of the now Britannicised north Atlantic the public greeted each new imperial success with wild celebrations. In Philadelphia, New York and Boston there were bonfires and illuminations, gun salutes and loyal toasts. In Britain, victory parades and other military spectacles were staged in many cities and towns to cheering crowds. 'Our bells are worn threadbare with ringing for victories,' remarked Horace Walpole (Sir Robert's son; 1717–97) facetiously.[16] In countless sermons in New and Old England the essential moral was drawn: that having chastised His people for their immoral, luxurious ways by humbling them in defeat, God had reaffirmed, through the workings of providence, the special place of the Protestant British in His great apocalyptic design. The government too, and its chief minister, Pitt, were now to be counted among His blessings. Never had the ministry been more popular either in Britain or America. More remarkably still, imperial conquests and victories on such a scale went some way towards justifying Leviathan – the fiscal–military state – to many people who for several decades had associated big government with ministerial tyranny and corruption. During this brief softening in the relationship between libertarian, 'patriot' sentiment and Leviathan would be laid the cultural foundations of the populist but conservative patriotism that would flourish in Britain during the American and Napoleonic wars. But from its break-down would also emerge a more radical, indeed revolutionary resistance to Leviathan on both sides of the Atlantic.

The first step back towards unremitting conflict between the self-styled patriots and a supposedly self-interested and corrupt ministry came with the death of George II in October 1760. The old king had suffered a heart attack early one morning while straining on the lavatory. He was succeeded by his 22-year-old grandson George III (1738–1820), who was the first home-grown Hanoverian monarch, and the first never to visit Hanover. Although not the most talented man ever to become king, he had some good qualities nonetheless. Contemporaries found him an intelligent young man, frugal and regular in his habits, 'of a temper rather reserved', and if inclined to be judgemental yet also 'steady in his attachments' to those he trusted and to ideas he held true.[17] In later life he learnt French and German, became a good musician, developed a passion for book collecting, and was a patron of the arts and sciences. It was largely thanks to George that the Royal Academy of Arts was founded in 1768 for the training and promotion of British artistic talent. He was also a loyal supporter of the British Museum, which had been established in 1753 to the profound indifference of George II.

But the trait that would define George III's early years as king was a tendency to play up his Britishness. He had inherited from his father Prince Frederick – who had died in 1751 – not only a resolve to lessen the crown's dependence on the Whig party but also a keen desire to present himself as a patriotic Briton. In George's accession speech to Parliament – for which he was coached by the famous actor James Quin – he declared, 'to great applause',[18] that having been 'Born and educated in this country, I glory in the name of Britain'.[19]

George's patriotic posturing translated in political terms into support for a Tory navalist and colonial strategy. He wanted out of the German war as quickly as possible. There should be no more subsidising that 'too ambitious monarch' Frederick the Great,[20] and no more indulging that 'snake in the grass', that 'blackest of hearts', Pitt.[21] George's hatred of his chief minister was stiffened by his Bedchamber man, mentor and 'dearest friend', John Stuart, earl of Bute (1713–92). Neither of them could forgive Pitt for having forsaken the patriot cause and then dragged Britain into Frederick's German nightmare. Yet though Pitt remained hugely popular, more and more people came to share George's dislike of the German war: 'Many mouths were at that time [1760] open in England upon the ruinous consequences of a German war; & some popular, & sensible pamphlets were dispersed among the people, on this subject, which contributed not a little to inflame them.'[22] In March 1761 the king made Bute a secretary of state alongside Pitt, who oblig-ingly resigned in October when the cabinet refused to support his demand for a pre-emptive strike, à la Prussienne, against Spain, which was moving closer to France in alarm at Britain's imperial expansion.

For all Pitt's arrogance and financial myopia he had made a superb war minister. Under his administration the British military had attained a level of efficiency and capability, particularly in mounting land–sea operations, unrivalled by any other power. 'With all his faults', declared the duke of Newcastle, 'we shall want Mr Pitt . . . I know nobody, who can plan, or push the execution of any plan agreed upon, in the manner Mr Pitt did.'[23] As the doyen of the Whig continentalist tradition – the last of the great Whig ministers who had dominated British government since 1714 – the duke too was vulnerable; and sure enough in June 1762 the king and Bute forced him out of office, seemingly oblivious to the dangers of dismantling the most popular and effective ministry in living memory. He was replaced as prime minister by Bute.

Pitt had been right, of course. The Spanish were clearly preparing to join the war in support of France and must be dealt with. In January 1762, Britain declared war on Spain, and won fresh laurels, with naval expeditions seizing the valuable prizes of Havana in the Caribbean and Manila in the far-off Philippines. At home, however, the advocates of Britain's alliance with Prussia and involvement in the German war were losing their particular battle. Defeat came in mid-1762, when the subsidies to Frederick were stopped and Britain bailed out of the war in Germany, prompting Whig accusations that Bute and his friends were reprising the greatest of all Tory betrayals of Europe's liberties, the 1713 treaty of Utrecht. And indeed so eager was Bute to conciliate the French that he actually encouraged them, in secret of course, to make a strong stand against British troops on the Continent. Frederick by this stage was facing annihilation, and was only saved by what to him seemed like a miracle – that is, the succession in Russia of the passionate Prussophile Tsar Peter II, who provided him with enough soldiers to mount a successful reinvasion of Silesia. With France on its knees, Austria bereft of Russian support, and Spain digesting the painful loss of Havana, the way was clear for the cessation of hostilities worldwide.

The Seven Years War, in so far as it involved Britain, France and Spain, was put to bed at the 1763 treaty of Paris. In Britain there had been much debate as to what among its huge haul of conquests it should insist on keeping and what it should relinquish. On one side were those who wanted to keep the lucrative gains made in the Caribbean in return for handing back cold and 'barren' Canada. New France, argued some astute commentators, had kept the British colonists in North America in a state of fear, and therefore dependent on British power. Without this French threat the colonies might rebel and go their own way (a prediction that was usually rubbished). On the other it was argued that while keeping Canada would provide lasting security for Britain's colonies in North America, returning most of the conquests made elsewhere would prevent France and Spain becoming too bitter and vengeful.

It was this latter view that generally prevailed in the peace negotiations. Britain returned France's most lucrative colonies in the Caribbean and most of its trading posts in Africa and India, although the French recognised Britain as the dominant European power on the Indian subcontinent. France ceded Minorca, Canada, the Ohio territory, some of its smaller colonies in the Caribbean, and the eastern half of Louisiana. Spain handed over Florida to Britain in return for Havana and Manila. Prussia and Austria signed a separate treaty that, in effect, turned the clock back to 1756. In other words, Frederick kept Silesia, but not Saxony. Prussia, Austria and France had bled themselves dry for next to nothing.

The Seven Years War would accelerate the shift of power eastwards within the European state system. Spain and the Dutch republic, though they still had large or wealthy colonies, were fallen giants. The five great powers were now Britain, France, Austria, Prussia and Russia – a configuration that would last until the First World War. Moreover, the great tectonic rift in continental geopolitics would no longer run between France and her neighbours in the Grand Alliance, as it had before 1748, but along the borders in central and eastern Europe between Prussia, Russia, Austria and the Ottoman empire. If any state now threatened the balance of power in western Europe it was not France, but Britain. George III ruled the most powerful maritime empire the world had ever seen. The war had been exceptionally good for British commerce, partly because the navy had swept the oceans clean of French merchant ships. Even French privateers had hardly dared peep out of port. Conquests in North America and in India confirmed and enhanced Britain's dominance of the Atlantic trade in slaves, sugar and tobacco, and the Asian trade in Indian textiles and China tea. And while Britain's credit and economy had held up well during the war, despite a massive increase in the national debt, France had effectively gone bankrupt.

Yet significant though Britain's conquests were, they actually left her feeling less not more secure. The British empire in North America was now a vast and sprawling entity whose vulnerable borders contained some 70,000 resentful French Canadians – all Catholics of course – who were not expected to take kindly to their new Protestant overlords. As for the Iroquois and other troublesome frontier tribes, they could no longer hold the line against European encroachment by playing France and Britain off against each other, and they reacted in 1763 by joining in their thousands to attack British settlements and forts south of the Great Lakes.

At home too there was growing unrest. The war had left a legacy of high taxes, high prices and rising unemployment. 'We hear of insurrections and tumults in every part of the country,' observed George III gloomily in October 1763, 'there is no government, no law.'[24] Ireland had remained quiet for most of the war, but then in the early 1760s it was hit by a wave of rural disturbances led by gangs of Jacobite sympathisers known as the 'Whiteboys'. These secret paramilitary groups targeted the property of those farmers and landlords who were driving the commercialisation of Irish agriculture, but to English eyes the Whiteboys looked less like agrarian protesters than a French-backed fifth column.

Although the British probably overestimated the extent of French infiltration in Ireland, they were correct in assuming that the main threat to Britain's post-war imperial ascendancy came from a familiar direction. The generous terms that Versailles had been given at the treaty of Paris did wonders for France's post-war recovery. On the one hand she had been relieved of New France and other expensive and unprofitable burdens in North America; on the other, she had been left with vital strategic and commercial footholds in India (notably her trading station and naval base at Pondicherry on the south-western rim of the Bay of Bengal), the Caribbean and in the Newfoundland fisheries. Moreover, British concessions at Paris did absolutely nothing to weaken French determination to be revenged against that 'arrogant power [which] relished the pleasure of having humiliated us'.[25] Although they kept up their alliance with Austria after 1763 they were determined not to get sidetracked into another German bloodbath. Success in any future war would mean hitting Britain where it hurt most, on the high seas, and to this end both France and Spain began rebuilding their navies, and would soon be launching new warships at double the rate that Britain was. By the early 1770s the combined tonnage of the Franco-Spanish fleets had outstripped that of the royal navy.

More worrying still for Whitehall was Britain's isolation in post-war Europe. Every one of the other great powers either held some kind of grudge against her or simply saw no point allying with a state whose interests were fixed so firmly on its overseas empire. If Britain was to divert France and Spain from a naval arms race she needed to re-engage with Europe, and yet the breakdown of the old system and the rise of the eastern powers had severely reduced her diplomatic options on the Continent.

The search for allies in post-war Europe would be made all the harder by George III's preference for Tory navalists over Whig continentalists. Few of his ministers had a sensitive appreciation of European affairs. Faced with tricky foreign policy issues they were far too inclined to send in the navy, which was a blunt diplomatic instrument that was effective only in convincing other nations of Britain's arrogance. And arrogant is what the British were now becoming, for victory in the Seven Years War had finally convinced them that they indeed ruled the waves and should not be afraid to show it.

British ministers might have tried harder to make friends on the Continent if they had not been too busy simply trying to keep their jobs. The king's attachment to Bute and to the idea of making the crown independent of any one party made the task of forming a stable ministry all but impossible. Bute was blamed (unjustly) for the resignation of the people's great hero Pitt, and by Whig continentalists and radicals for forsaking Frederick the Great in return for a sell-out peace with the French. But perhaps Bute's greatest crime was simply being a Scot, for the English people and press found it very difficult to accept a non-Englishman as their prime minister. By the spring of 1763 he was the most hated man in England, and the target of a vicious smear campaign by John Wilkes (1725–97) and other 'patriot' polemicists, who accused the 'Northern Machiavel' of urging George to revive free monarchy.[26] It was too much for Bute to bear, and he resigned from office. For the next seven years or so the king went through a succession of prime ministers and cabinets, but nothing seemed to work.

Ministries may have come and gone during the 1760s, yet one issue stayed firmly put: reform of the empire. The colonies, as we have seen, had rarely made headline news before the Seven Years War, and had been relatively lightly governed. But that was changing. The war and its conquests had generated huge public interest in the empire, with greater focus on the colonies as territorial prizes rather than mere generators of wealth and trade back in Europe. At the same time, of course, they now posed even greater administrative challenges for the government. Britain's gains in the Seven Years War had been almost too great, too varied. Before the war the empire had been mostly Anglophone, mostly Protestant, and therefore mostly consistent with the British people's sense of themselves and their values. After 1763 the empire was, as Edmund Burke observed, 'vast, disconnected, infinitely diversified'.[27]

Looking westwards the problem was fundamentally one of coherence. How was the crown to govern its newly distended empire in the

Americas, where it had added French Catholics and their former Indian allies to an already unwieldy mix of peoples, religions and local jurisdictions? Ireland too was a security headache that demanded reforms to bring 'our principal colony' more firmly under government control.[28]

Looking eastwards it was more a question of distance and numbers. The acquisition of Bengal, for example, had extended British rule to perhaps 20 million new 'subjects'. 'We don't want conquest and power,' the East India Company had insisted, somewhat disingenuously, only larger profits.[29] Self-enrichment and quelling their French rivals had indeed motivated the Company's officers more than grandiose notions of territorial conquest. Yet as we have seen, in dealing with Mughal rivalries and French intervention, Clive and his like had been forced to tap native manpower and money with ever greater ruthlessness, dragging the Company ever further into Indian affairs and turning it into a landed power. Moreover, this growing British presence in the subcontinent was of considerable strategic and commercial importance to the government. The Company and its trade were vital sources of tax revenue and investor confidence. There could be no retreat from empire in India.

With the Company struggling to manage its liabilities as a quasi-nation state, and running up massive debts in the process, the government gradually recognised that it must assume ultimate control over the running of British India, and by the mid-1780s it had done precisely that. What it did not recognise, however, was any duty to extend British liberties to the Indian peoples. The natives were not interested in political freedom – or so it was claimed – merely benevolent rule and impartial justice. This authoritarian creed, and the general bloodshed and plunder that accompanied conquest in India, were repugnant to many Britons on both sides of the Atlantic. Absolute dominion ran counter to the traditional idea of Britain's empire as one of shared liberties and free trade. Nabobs like Clive were denounced as 'fiends who have fattened on the famine and butchery of the inoffensive Asiatics'.[30] A wide range of people in Britain and America, from Nonconformist ministers to patrician grandees, regarded the emergence of an exploitative, militaristic empire in India, as indeed in Canada, as a sure sign of national degeneration.

But the rapid post-war recovery of France and Spain made imperial reform all the more urgent. A stronger, more unified empire seemed to be essential if the British state was to reap maximum military and financial advantage from its victories. At its most basic, the empire must be protected, and that meant deploying troops where necessary, above all in North America. With Indian war parties again on the rampage, and fears that the French Canadians would join the mayhem, the government stationed 7,500 regulars in North America in the mid-1760s at a cost of more than £250,000 a year. In truth, there was no long-term rationale for stationing such a large force in America. The very last place the French were interested in was Canada, and so long as the navy controlled the St Lawrence there was no chance of a revival of French power in the American interior. And besides, where was the money to come from? Fighting the Seven Years War had left Britain in hock to the tune of £133 million,[31] and over half the government's peacetime revenue went simply on servicing the national debt.

With money at home so tight, both the government and public were adamant that the colonists should bear more of the financial burdens that had been shouldered on their behalf. British taxpayers had helped them defeat New France; it was time they helped British taxpayers. Many colonists recognised that imperial government and finances needed reforming if the British empire was to continue growing, but they saw themselves not simply as loyal subjects but as partners with Britain in a common imperial enterprise. They were proud of their role in forging a new and mightier empire, and anticipated working with Britain to extend imperial rule and English liberties westwards across the entire continent. At the very least they believed themselves worthy of greater respect and encouragement from the mother country. Unfortunately, this was not the prevailing view back in Britain. No matter that Benjamin Franklin and other colonial spokesmen, seconded by the few MPs who actually knew something about America, informed the Commons that the colonists had more than pulled their weight in the war, and that Britain derived millions from its transatlantic commerce. MPs would have none of it. The 'Americans' – as the British increasingly referred to the colonists – must do as they were told and contribute more to the empire's defence, as must the Irish and Britain's new subjects in India.

Just how little the government respected the colonists' hopes of partnership in a common imperial endeavour was made clear in the royal proclamation of October 1763. Worried that the French Canadians would rebel, and anxious therefore to appease the frontier Indians, the government forbade the colonists from expanding westwards much beyond their existing settlements. All lands beyond the Appalachians were reserved for the Indians as their hunting grounds. Exactly how the crown's isolated military governors in trans-Appalachia would stop European settlers crossing the mountains, or turn them back once they had, was left unclear. But besides being utterly unworkable, the proclamation seemed to renege on the promises of land and profit that had encouraged colonists such as Washington to fight for the empire in the first place.

While the colonists digested the fact that their own government now wanted to corral them east of the Appalachians just as the French once had, Parliament imposed a series of taxes upon the American colonies in order to defray the huge costs of guarding Canada and the frontier. 'If America looks to Great Britain for protection,' pronounced one MP, 'she must enable [us] to protect her. If she expects our fleets, she must assist our revenue.'[32] Although it had long been assumed in London that Parliament's authority over the colonies was unlimited, this was the first time that the two Houses had levied taxation on the colonists' internal activities (as opposed to maritime trade, for example). Nevertheless, there was near-consensus at Westminster that: 'In an Empire, extended and diversified as that of Great-Britain, there must be a supreme Legislature, to which all other Powers must be subordinate.'[33] Parliament, according to the renowned jurist William Blackstone (1723–80), was 'the place where that absolute despotic power, which must in all governments reside somewhere, is entrusted by the constitution of these kingdoms'.[34] All British people, wherever they were, were supposedly represented 'virtually' in Parliament. To leave imperial government to the crown, it was now thought, would be to break up the amalgam of king-in-Parliament formed after 1688 and to revive free monarchy, and not even George III wanted that. Ministers were adamant that to defy the will of Parliament was 'the highest species of treason', and, in the case of the Americans, tantamount to a declaration of independence.[35]

The reaction in the colonies to Parliament's new taxes was abrupt and violent. 'Don't imagine that your acts of parliament have no power here,' wrote one colonist, sarcastically. 'They have the power of working miracles; of turning . . . as good, faithful, and affectionate subjects, as any government ever had, into little less than downright rebels.'[36] From New Hampshire to South Carolina, mobs took to the streets – often at the instigation or with the blessing of leading men in the community – destroying and looting the houses of tax collectors, and threatening them with a new weapon in the American arsenal of vigilante justice:

tarring and feathering. The protesters reserved their greatest contempt for the ministry: 'They loaded their names with most opprobrious invectives, and in nine several provinces burnt them in effigy.'[37] In Boston and elsewhere patriotic clubs calling themselves Sons of Liberty formed to resist the government's demands and to hound crown officials in the colonies.

The ministry could hardly have picked a worse moment to begin asserting its power across the Atlantic. A severe recession had hit the Thirteen Colonies after the Seven Years War, exacerbated by the massive debts that some of them had run up fighting it. The last thing that the colonies, or those in Britain who traded with them, needed was new laws and taxes that restricted the flow of money. When the economic and political unrest in North America began to hit British manufacturing, Parliament hastily repealed the most unpopular of the new taxation laws: the Stamp Act. But having apparently learnt nothing from the Stamp Act protests, a new ministry imposed further taxes on the Americans in 1767, partly in a conscious effort to strengthen imperial government in the colonies at the expense of the provincial assemblies. Once again there were mass demonstrations. Regiments were sent from Canada and Ireland to quell the unrest, and from 1768 Boston was effectively placed under military rule.

Americans objected to paying for the upkeep of troops that threatened their liberty or were stationed in frontier areas where they themselves were forbidden to venture. But their resistance to parliamentary taxes went much deeper than that. Just as the ministry insisted that defying the will of Parliament was unconstitutional, so the colonists appealed to that most sacred of English liberties, the right not to be taxed without consent. Westminster could legislate for matters that affected the empire as a whole, such as intercolonial trade, they agreed, but only their own provincial assemblies had the right to levy internal taxes and legislate on domestic affairs. The colonists' argument was encapsulated in a slogan first voiced by Barbadian planters (and slave-owners) in the seventeenth century: 'No taxation without representation'.[38]

Fear and anger were only to be expected when confronted by what America's second president John Adams called 'That enormous Engine, fabricated by the british Parliament, for battering down all the Rights and Liberties of America'.[39] To tax the colonies and integrate them into a greater Great Britain required the ministry to begin the process of extending Leviathan to the colonies. Assertions of parliamentary (in effect, ministerial) authority were followed by swarms of new tax officials, tougher enforcement of the navigation acts (smuggling was rife in the colonies), measures to increase the authority of imperial governors, and (eventually) the use of troops to compel obedience. To effect this 'horrid Policy', claimed one colonial newspaper in 1765, the British had sent over 'Men of War, Cutters, Marines with their Bayonets fixed, Judges of Admiralty, Collectors, Comptrollers, Searchers, Tide-Waiters, Land-Waiters [customs officers], with a whole Catalogue of Pimps'.[40]

Ministries might have been unstable and transitory during the 1760s, but the power of the British fiscal–military state remained formidable. The British people themselves still saw Leviathan as a threat to their liberties and customs, and, as we shall see, would require thousands of troops and militiamen to keep them in order. So it was no surprise that the first encounter with Leviathan came as a shock to the colonists, just as it had to the English in the 1640s. In fact, the colonies would be subject to even more aggressive state intervention than was normally used in British home affairs. Yet until the 1760s they had been lightly governed and even more lightly taxed compared with Britain. An American taxpayer paid roughly a shilling a year, whereas the average British taxpayer paid twenty-five times that amount. The most powerful institution in American life was not a ministerial executive, as it was in Britain, but the provincial assembly. Colonial government was essentially Parliament without Leviathan.

Different experiences of government would encourage fundamentally different views of the empire on either side of the Atlantic. The British increasingly saw it as a single realm under a sovereign Parliament. The colonists, on the other hand, had begun to think of the empire as a federation of more or less equal states, some with their own sovereign assemblies, and united only as the three kingdoms under the early Stuarts had been: in common allegiance to a protector-king. The colonies, they insisted, were properly subject not to Parliament, far less to its ministerial managers, but to the crown alone.

The majority of the colonists were still fervently loyal to the House of Hanover. Since the Glorious Revolution a cult of Protestant monarchy had taken root in the colonies even as such king worship was assuming more moderate and nuanced forms back in Britain. The absence of powerful imperial government in the American colonies had encouraged an intense personal loyalty to the king, particularly in his supposed role as the defender of Protestant liberties against French popery. Some Americans had even begun to sound like English Civil War royalists with their talk about the sacredness of kings. In Britain, by contrast, there was a more tempered attachment to the king; and in England, especially, loyalty to the monarchy had partly been subsumed in reverence for Parliament and the constitution.

The roots of American independence lay not in hostility to George III, therefore, or to the British people, but to Leviathan and its instruments. Colonial leaders would still look to the king to save them from Leviathan even as their fellow 'rebels' were killing his soldiers at Concord, Lexington and Bunker Hill. The colonists reserved their bitterest condemnations for the ministry and its 'system': the machinery of political patronage by which (as they saw it) cabinet ministers had turned the crown against the very English liberties it was supposed to protect. When Washington, John Adams and other American patriots lambasted London's 'tools of despotism' and 'corrupt and designing Ministry' they were protesting not only against evil counsellors but also the whole style of British parliamentary government.[41] And where Protestant Britons, American or British, perceived the exercise of a corrupt and arbitrary power they tended to associate it with popery, and hence many colonists came to regard the ministry's efforts to extend Leviathan to America as part of a transatlantic quasi-Jacobite conspiracy. Which was ironic, for in exalting the crown as the sole link between the constituent parts of the empire, and as a shield against a corrupted and tyrannical Westminster, the colonists actually resembled no political groups so much as the Catholic Irish of the 1640s and the Jacobites.

If colonial government was Parliament without Leviathan, then the London government was denounced by patriots on both sides of the Atlantic as Leviathan without Parliament. The colonists had many sympathisers among England's religious Dissenters, as also among the London radicals who had found new and even more vitriolic voice in the attack on Bute. The colonists hailed that populist firebrand and scourge of the ministry John Wilkes as a hero of liberty in what they perceived as a common struggle against government tyranny. Patriots in Britain and the colonies alike drew heavily on the legacy of anti-Leviathan ideas developed by the Levellers in the 1640s, and framed in the neoclassical language of civic virtue by the opponents of the junto Whigs in the 1690s and of the Robinocracy in the 1720s and 1730s. Only a manly and virtuous public, they insisted, could resist the torrent of consumerist luxury and the swelling power of the ministry. Parliament, the once faithful guardian of English liberties, had been 'degenerated' by ministerial patronage 'into a body of sycophants, dependent and venal, always ready to confirm any measures' right down to the most despotic of them all – the use of troops against a free citizenry.[42]

This improving age

As the British contemplated the prospect of war with their own colonies they began to observe the Americans' rapid rate of multiplication – once a source of pride and satisfaction – in a new and ominous light. The population of the Thirteen Colonies had increased more than tenfold in the century preceding 1770 to about 2.5 million, at rates of growth that in New England, for example, were over fifteen times higher than in Britain. An abundance of cheap land in the colonies had generally allowed couples to set up home earlier, and have more children, than was practicable in Europe. Ireland had around 2 to 3 million people by the 1770s, and England, Wales and Scotland about 7.5 million (of whom almost 800,000 lived in London), but this represented a rise of only about a million since 1670. Moreover, this shallow upward curve had been punctuated by periods when the population had actually fallen, as in Charles II's reign and the 1720s. Not until the 1740s had numbers begun to rise steadily and (as it proved) unstoppably, before rocketing in the late eighteenth century as never before. Most of this upsurge was due to the interrelated benefits of a growth in manufacturing and export markets, increasing consumer spending and the long-term rise in agricultural productivity as a result of improvements in the way land was worked (new crops, more efficient farming methods etc.). A lowering in the age at which couples might respectably get married may also have helped.

Britain and its American colonies were very different societies top to bottom, of course. And it was at the social extremes that these differences were most starkly revealed. Monarch, nobility and bishops – the supposed pillars of British society everywhere – remained very much the products of their European environment. George III had begun his reign as the perceived friend of 'patriot' policies for colonial expansion, although until the 1770s he showed little interest in America. His increasingly forceful and assured performance as royal politician from the late 1760s – uninterrupted by the long holidays in Hanover that the first two Georges had taken – and his willingness to make and break ministries in accordance with his strong sense of duty and the national interest, convinced some disgruntled politicians, wrongly, that he wanted to revive Stuart-style absolutism. Their error owed much to the understandable difficulty contemporaries had in separating the power of the monarchy from that of Leviathan. In fact, George, like his predecessors since James II, continued to lose ground to Parliament and the ministry over control of foreign policy, public finances and political patronage. He enjoyed nothing like the personal authority even of William III, let alone of Frederick the Great and most other continental monarchs.

Where George made up ground on his royal predecessors, albeit slowly, was in the affections of his British subjects. His image gradually improved once he had distanced himself from his youthful dependence on the much-reviled Lord Bute; and the king's stubborn defence of parliamentary sovereignty in the face of insolent colonials would win him, in time, considerable popular approval throughout Britain. The abstemious, domestic nature of his private life also went down increasingly well with the public. For the first time in British history the king and queen would become the embodiment of middle-class family values – 'the head of our morality' as Walter Bagehot would later put it[43] – their patriotic appeal heightened by the king's patronage of home-grown artists and the queen's attempts to promote English fashions over French fripperies. The royal couple's partial retreat into proto-Victorian domesticity at Windsor Castle and Buckingham House (later rebuilt and renamed Buckingham Palace) from the late 1770s would lead to a further shrinking of the court's political and social functions.

The British aristocracy would respond rather less successfully to trouble in the colonies than would their sovereign. None of the nobility or gentry lived or had much property in North America, so in a sense they had little to lose, and any crisis of empire gave them plenty of opportunity to play the patriotic hero. In practice, they did not travel well across the Atlantic. Those who made the journey were mostly soldiers and bureaucrats, out to further their careers at home, and they usually met with a colonial response ranging from disregard to utter contempt. Wolfe was one of the few British gentlemen – and a low-born one at that – who covered himself in glory in America, and he paid dearly for his fame. Nor did his example or that of Clive in India suffice to quell the growing criticism of the patrician class in Britain itself.

Yet in terms of affluence and influence the top tier of the aristocracy, certainly, was doing exceptionally well during the later eighteenth century. George III's determination to eradicate party rivalries in common service to crown and Parliament helped kill off the already moribund Whig and Tory parties during the early 1760s. Now that Jacobitism was also defunct, Tories were admitted to royal favour alongside Whigs, and into county government en masse. In place of the old two-party structure there emerged a series of competing aristocratic factions, most of whose members saw nothing much wrong with the established Church and constitution, or in trying to restrict political involvement to 'gentlemen of large property and hereditary interest'.[44] This reintegration of Whigs and Tories into a more cohesive ruling class would inject new vigour into the aristocracy, and strengthen its domination of Britain's political and professional establishments. Economically too, the aristocracy was more than holding its own, helped by a huge rise in rental values, and the energy with which many of the *grands seigneurs* exploited the mineral resources as well as the agricultural and proprietorial potential of their estates.

Fresh blue blood would enter the system from the mid-eighteenth century as the Celtic elites used their growing prosperity to buy or marry their way into large landed estates in England. Scottish peers and gentlemen came south of the border in growing numbers to procure parliamentary seats and to take up fashionable residence in London. The hitherto largely separate aristocracies of England, Wales, Scotland and Protestant Ireland were merging politically and socially into a unitary ruling class.

A standardised upbringing would help forge a common sense of identity among this Anglicised yet 'British' aristocracy; and no institutions did, or still do, esprit de corps better than England's public schools. By 1800 just four of these elite nurseries – Eton, Harrow, Westminster and Winchester – were educating, and by turns civilising and brutalising, the majority of young gentlemen who would one day govern Britain and its empire.

Complacency in the enjoyment of all this privilege was the aristocracy's worst enemy. Stories of rich young men squandering fortunes at London's gaming tables were standard merchandise for Georgian society's pedlars in moral outrage. This kind of extravagance, particularly when juxtaposed with the sometimes poor quality of aristocratic leadership in Britain's wars under George II and George III, encouraged the view that 'luxurious' persons of rank were mere drones. Mounting public interest in the moral failings of the great and not-so-good was gratified from the 1750s by a series of sex scandals involving members of the nobility that issued in a stream of sordid revelations in the courts and newspapers about their personal lives. Politically too, the landed elite was regarded with suspicion. Pamphleteers drew attention to the aristocracy's intimate and lucrative relationship with Leviathan, in which ownership of a high proportion of the overall value of public stock was heavily concentrated among a clique of peers, government officeholders, London monied men and senior army and naval officers, many of whom also held government contracts.

Sensing that they had to work harder to justify their exalted position, the more thoughtful among the ruling class began putting greater effort from the mid-eighteenth century into displaying their public-spiritedness. Peers deigned in growing numbers to become patrons of learned and philanthropic societies. Enterprising landowners paraded the social benefits of their commercial interest in canal-building and agrarian improvement. And high-society women began venturing into philanthropy in an organised way, led by a group of London's ladies who formed the Bluestocking circle in the early 1750s for the promotion of learning and social reform.

An unwitting ally in the cause of improving the aristocracy's image was the humble fox. Fox-hunting became more organised during George II's reign with the breeding of faster horses and dogs with a more acute sense of smell. Here was a gentlemanly sport that allowed unprepossessing squires to dress up like soldiers and ride around flaunting their courage and vigour, while at the same time making themselves useful to their tenants by ridding the countryside of vermin. That 'glorious, manly, British [in fact, English]' sport, cricket – which was also acquiring new rules and devotees at this time – similarly helped to showcase aristocratic virtues, for even the grandest noblemen were prepared to join commoners to play up and play the game, setting aside their rank in selfless commitment to the team.[45]

The main audience for the pamphlet and press assault on aristocratic luxury was the middling orders, or approximately those who earned between £40 and £400 a year. These 'polite and commercial people' would grow in number and spending power over the course of the eighteenth century, particularly in the towns. By the late 1700s they were well on the way to acquiring a strong sense of collective identity. But they were not quite yet a distinct and self-conscious class like the aristocracy and gentry. They generally supported the existing social and political order – or at least a somewhat idealised version of it that left little room for the necessary evils of Leviathan – and favoured reform rather than revolution, the sovereignty of a public-spirited and more accountable Parliament rather than individual natural rights. They had long defined themselves in opposition to what they regarded as the moral incapacity of the undeserving poor. But from the mid-eighteenth century they grew more and more critical of certain aspects of elite culture, especially the aristocracy's taste for French fashions, Italian opera and other supposedly corrupting influences on manly British patriotism.

By indulging 'every Foreign Folly . . . or Vice', declared the Reverend John Brown in his influential tract *An Estimate of the Manners and Principles of the Times* (1757), 'the higher Ranks' had created an enervating miasma of 'vain, luxurious, and selfish EFFEMINACY'. Avarice was only natural in a wealthy trading nation like Britain, he conceded. But 'a rich Nobility or Gentry', living idly off their rents, would be wholly given over to 'Expence and Luxury', and talk of nothing but 'Dress [clothes] and Wagers, Cards and Borough-jobbing [buying up rotten boroughs], Horses, Women, and Dice'.[46] 'Estimate' Brown and other moralists damned that quintessentially aristocratic experience, the Grand Tour, as merely an education in foreign degeneracy. An aristocracy exposed to such influences, they argued, would be incapable of providing leadership in time of war, leaving Britain 'Prey to the Insults and Invasions of our most powerful Enemy [i.e. France]'.[47]

Britain's empire of the seas was held up by patriotic writers as an antidote to the rot at the top of society. Propaganda during the Seven Years War depicted the American colonies as home to a hardy and industrious people that was still capable of resisting luxury. In fact, as we have seen, the market for consumer goods in North America was growing almost as fast as merchants and manufacturers in the British Atlantic system could supply it. Where the colonies looked more plausibly like a bourgeois paradise was in the opportunities they offered for self-betterment. Because land was relatively cheap in North America compared with Britain it meant that more families could buy their own farms and improve their lot. Moreover, there was generally plenty of work to be had at good wages – except where owning slaves had taken root. The labouring poor comprised a much smaller fraction of the population in the colonies, particularly in New England and Pennsylvania, than they did in Britain, and on average the colonists enjoyed a higher standard of living. The result, in the northern colonies anyway, was a large and literate middling sort. That such prosperous and populous communities should have fewer spokesmen at Westminster than, say, Cornwall's pilchard fishery was a political disaster waiting to happen.

Fears in the mid-eighteenth century that British power was succumbing to foreign effeminacy would lead to the establishment – primarily by well-to-do tradesmen – of so-called patriotic societies. The first of these, the Laudable Association of Anti-Gallicans, was set up in London in 1745 to persuade retailers and artisans to buy British rather than French products. This and similar associations soon spread to most of the major cities in Britain and to New England, and gave new and more powerful expression to the feeling that society's traditional leaders and institutions were failing in their duty to resist Frenchified corruption.

Political clubs and a variety of antiquarian, natural history and philosophical associations had begun to flourish in England during the later seventeenth century – and throughout Britain during the eighteenth – in a way not seen on the Continent. Many of these early clubs, particularly the political variety, had been dominated or led by the aristocracy, and had provided a social bridge between the governing elite and the trading classes. Freemasonry – which spread into the provinces after the first Grand Lodge was founded in London in 1717 – drew men from the upper as well as the middling ranks. The Prince of Wales, no less, became a Mason in 1737. But the patriotic and philanthropic societies that sprang up in their thousands from the 1740s to reclaim public life from the pernicious effects of French influence would recruit the vast majority of their (mostly male) members from the urban bourgeoisie, and would undoubtedly do much to strengthen the middling order's collective identity and assertiveness. There also emerged from the 1760s a new breed of clubs that catered specifically to the political aspirations of the middling sort. Some rode the familiar hobby horses of empire and English liberties; others, though, espoused more radical causes, including constitutional reform and an end to Leviathan. These societies sometimes rejected not only the hedonism associated with aristocratic sociability but also aristocratic patronage.

Radical agitation during the later eighteenth century was largely orchestrated by educated men from the urban middling sort, and above all by the controversial figure of John Wilkes, the son of a London distiller. Journalist, MP and libertine, Wilkes succeeded, through sheer eloquence and showmanship, in turning vice and attention-seeking into political virtues. Liberty was not just his watchword, it was his personal creed. He was, as one plebeian admirer put it, 'free from cock to wig'.[48] His flamboyant immorality, though frowned upon in polite circles, helped him appeal to the not-so-genteel labouring classes, many thousands of whom turned out in London and other larger towns during the 1760s and 1770s to celebrate (often riotously) his political triumphs and to protest his harassment by the government. In the colonies too he was hailed as a great patriot. South Carolina's assembly even sent him £1,500 (a fortune) as a token of its esteem.

Since the late seventeenth century there had been relatively few calls for a major overhaul of the constitution. Franchise reform, for example, had often been couched in terms of taking votes from the 'poor, sordid, unthinking wretches' in rotten boroughs, who sold their allegiance to the highest bidder (usually the Whig ministry), and redistributing them among independent men of property.[49] But as the old party rivalries faded during the 1750s and 1760s, and aristocratic politicians shied away from enlisting popular support in libertarian causes, the banner of parliamentary reform was, of necessity, taken up by men of more humble and radical stamp. Wilkes and his like took the attack upon Leviathan to a whole new level. For them, it was not merely a case of corrupt politicians abusing a system that was otherwise sound; it was the system itself that was flawed. Parliament must be made more accountable, they argued, and not merely to a narrow propertied oligarchy but to everyone whose taxes fed Leviathan's ever-growing maw. In other words, even relatively poor men should have the vote. There should also be frequent general elections, and a 'more equal representation' in which rotten boroughs were abolished and their parliamentary seats given to Birmingham, Manchester and other manufacturing giants.[50]

This new generation of reformers might well have adopted the campaign slogan 'no taxation without representation', but they never did. Nor would a broad-based protest movement emerge in Britain during the 1760s and 1770s to rival that in the Thirteen Colonies. The government was too powerful, and too adept at exploiting the habitual deference of that large swathe of society which preferred the established order, or feared a populist revolution. The radicals themselves never developed an agreed programme or an effective means of implementing change besides petitioning and press campaigns. Practical ideas, consensus-building, were lost in a welter of threats and high language. Radical journalists likened George III to Charles I or James II, and hinted that it would be no bad thing if he suffered similar fates to theirs. Others eulogised the revolutionary heroes of the 1640s and 1680s, and revived seventeenth-century resistance theories and arguments for contractual government. King, upper classes and the patrician state were all subject to vicious criticism and mockery. Before the 1790s, however, relatively few even among the more radical reformers wanted to ditch hereditary monarchy and the established social order in favour of democratic republicanism. A more representative Parliament would suffice to end arbitrary power, they believed, and to destroy Leviathan. Only a tiny minority went further, abandoning the appeal to the historic liberties of Englishmen for truly revolutionary ideas like inalienable natural rights – for men, anyway. Barely anyone, even among the enlightened literati, gave thought to empowering women. 'Let woman share the rights and she will emulate the virtues of man' – Mary Wollstonecraft (1759–97) – was a notion that would require a far greater rupture with the old order to give it ideological purchase.[51]

Men of middling rank who wanted to showcase their public-spiritedness without taint of political radicalism could seek appointment to improvement commissions. These local statutory bodies mushroomed over the course of the eighteenth century – between 1760 and 1799 alone there were 427 new commissions established – and the property qualifications for participation on them were increasingly relaxed. Groups of concerned citizens would come together to obtain 'private' (i.e. not drafted or sponsored by the government) acts of Parliament that empowered them to perform one of any number of functions – to maintain harbours and markets, for example, to establish workhouses and town watches, or to supply communities with fresh water and better sewerage. London's often foul and congested thoroughfares were improved almost out of recognition during the 1760s by commissions for installing paving, lighting and street drainage. It was the improvement commissions that were largely responsible for overseeing the construction of Georgian Britain's dense network of turnpike (toll-funded) roads and canals. In many cases, the setting up of commissions reflected either dissatisfaction with the oligarchic rule and self-serving practices of the old municipal corporations, or a recognition by civic elites that they needed to secure a broader measure of consent and cooperation from ordinary ratepayers if they were to govern effectively.

Improvement would proceed hand in hand with the unabating war on popular immorality. Recession and demobilisation in the aftermath of the Seven Years War pushed up the unemployment and crime rates, and with them the apprehension and indignation of respectable folk. Stories in the press about the depredations of highwaymen were not entirely fanciful, for 'gentlemen of the road' were operating by 1760 on most of the major routes into London, and indeed much further afield. One Scottish gang boasted that 'more could be made on the highway in one night than by sneaking about the country for twelve months'.[52] Crime was naturally associated in Georgian minds with plebeian licentiousness, and during the 1750s and 1760s there were renewed attempts by public authorities and voluntary associations, particularly in London, to clamp down on bawdy houses, illicit gambling and street fairs. Alongside repression and tighter regulation, however, were philanthropic initiatives to rehabilitate destitute unfortunates through a blend of medical treatment, hard work and religious instruction. Hospitals for the poor, 'lying-in' infirmaries (maternity units) for 'distressed' women, orphanages, lunatic asylums, workhouses, refuges for repentant prostitutes, and other such charitable foundations – mostly funded and run by private subscribers from the upper and middling classes – proliferated from the mid-1700s.

Grist to these mills of improvement were the poor commoners, or so it was hoped. But they would doggedly resist refining, and had their own rough-and-ready ways of setting the world to rights. Britain's rising population and prices during the later eighteenth century brought an end to the relatively benign conditions that the labouring masses had enjoyed since the late seventeenth century. A series of wet summers and freezing winters, a run of bad harvests, sky-rocketing inflation – the worst since the 1590s – and plummeting real wages made the 1750s, 1760s and 1770s a time of acute hardship for the poor. The result, all over England, was some of the most violent food riots and strikes of the entire century. It is no wonder that the rhetoric of workers' 'combinations' – the forerunners of trade unions – in the mid-eighteenth century often harked back to 'better days'.[53]

But the Georgian poor were not simply the victims of circumstance. The shift in the tax burden under Leviathan from land to consumption, via excise duties on common necessities like beer, tea and soap, bore hardest on the poorest consumers. The excise appeared all the more oppressive because it was enforced by a veritable army of revenue officers – some fourteen thousand strong by 1783 – with statutory powers of search, and assisted by networks of informers. The tax was not just burdensome, therefore, it was seen as a violation of English liberties, an affront to the traditional order. Public demonstrations against the excise – in which symbols associated with the tax, such as Lord Bute's emblem the jackboot, were ritually hanged or burned – were shot through with this sense of moral indignation. It was also present, perhaps, in the extraordinary savagery sometimes meted out to excisemen who fell into the clutches of smugglers: 'They began with poor Galley [William Galley, an exciseman], cut off his nose and privities, broke every joint of him and after several hours' torture dispatched him.'[54] In open confrontation between state and people, the power lay with Leviathan – as the Northumberland colliers would learn to their cost in 1761, when troops opened fire on them for protesting against compulsory service in the wartime militia, killing at least fifty. With the government stationing tens of thousands of army regulars around the country by the 1760s to help quell popular disturbances, it was a wonder there were not more tragedies like this.

Anti-popery remained as virulent as ever among Britain's lower orders, even as the demise of Jacobitism and the emergence of fashionably enlightened attitudes towards religious diversity persuaded the polite classes to take a more relaxed view of Catholicism. It was in the 1760s that Britain's two-centuries-old links and sense of solidarity with Protestants on the Continent began to fade. An important test case of public opinion on the legitimacy of allowing Catholics and other outsiders to serve the crown – and merit state concessions in return – was recruitment to the British army. At the height of the Seven Years War the government gave the go-ahead to raise troops among Highland clans once notorious for Jacobitism. Scottish regiments would do 'excellent service' in North America, as the English readily acknowledged, and fought with notable distinction thereafter 'in all the . . . expeditions in which they were engaged'.[55] Pitt later boasted to Parliament that he had been the first British minister to bring that 'hardy and intrepid race of men . . . to combat on your side . . . and [they] conquered for you in every part of the world'.[56] At the same time and for the same reason – military necessity – the army began recruiting on the quiet among Ireland's Catholic majority, and by the 1770s thousands of Irish Catholics were openly enlisting. Ordinary British Protestants again reacted violently to this transgression of hallowed boundaries (see the Gordon riots, below). But a troop-hungry Leviathan would brook no opposition. And from the 1750s the descendants of the Gaelic warriors who had terrorised the Tudor and Stuart state would play an heroic part in preserving and extending the Hanoverians' British empire.

Resistance, revolt, revolution

On a cold March evening in 1770 a crowd of angry Bostonians gathered to hurl insults at the sentry guarding the town's customs house. Defying customs regulations had become the townspeople's way of facing down Leviathan. Indeed, it was the reason that British troops had been sent to Boston in the first place. The sentry knew he was guarding a hated symbol of government oppression, and should therefore have thought twice before striking an apprentice with his musket in what had started as a petty dispute over a wigmaker's bill. The crowd grew bigger and angrier as night fell. The officer in charge of the relief column had his men load and fix bayonets. Knowing that the soldiers needed permission from a local magistrate to open fire, the crowd taunted them and threw snowballs. When a redcoat was knocked down by one of the protesters, the soldiers' discipline snapped and they loosed an uneven volley that hit eleven men, killing three on the spot. Two more would later die of their wounds.

The 'Boston massacre' was one of a series of flashpoints by which American resistance to Leviathan turned, in 1775, into open revolt. Boston was the scene of another, even more celebrated (or outrageous, as most British people saw it), act of American defiance – namely, the Boston tea party of December 1773, when 100 or so Bostonians boarded three East India Company ships and dumped 90,000 lb of tea (worth about $1.7 million today) into the harbour. The government had given the financially stricken Company a monopoly on the sale of tea in America, but had refused to remove the parliamentary duty on it, stoking further colonial outrage at being taxed without consent.

A still greater provocation to the colonists would be the 1774 Quebec Act. As war with France and Spain loomed again in the early 1770s, the government tried to appease the French Canadians and the frontier Indians by granting toleration of Catholicism in Canada and extending imperial authority in Quebec – which was authoritarian in leaving no room for elected assemblies, but liberal in allowing French legal customs – throughout the so-called 'Indian Reserve', thereby putting an area roughly corresponding with present-day Illinois, Indiana, Michigan, Ohio, Wisconsin and eastern Minnesota effectively out of bounds to American settlers. At the stroke of a pen the Protestant supremacy in North America was weakened, and the threat to the Thirteen Colonies of French Canadian encirclement revived – only this time, apparently, with the British government's blessing. Here, it seemed to patriots in

Britain and America, was conclusive evidence of the popery and despotism at the heart of the British state. 'Every tie of allegiance is broken by the Quebec Act,' declared a leading colonist, 'the compact between the King and the people is done away with.'[57]

In the event, the territorial provisions in the Quebec Act would prove as unenforceable as those of the 1763 proclamation had been. Colonial population was doubling every twenty years by the mid-eighteenth century, pushing thousands of white settlers out towards – and in many cases across – the Appalachians. Freed since the 1760s of the French threat to the west, syndicates of land speculators in Pennsylvania, Virginia and adjacent colonies vied for concessions from the colonial authorities and the Indians. This unstoppable westward surge added to the government's American problems, but it also held a possible solution. For wise politicians would have ceased trying to extend Leviathan across the Atlantic, opened the frontier to American settlers (Britain could not protect the Indians anyway), and played divide and rule between the colonies and commercial interests scrambling for a stake in history's greatest-ever land bonanza. By choosing instead to put imperial defence and consolidation before American expansionism the ministry thought it was acting prudently and far-sightedly, whereas in fact it was provoking civil war.

The Quebec Act was part of a legislative package dubbed in America the 'intolerable acts'. Passed to widespread approval in Britain, the acts put Massachusetts – regarded by the government as the epicentre of colonial resistance – under the cosh. Troops were quartered upon civilians, Boston port was closed until compensation had been paid for the tea party, and the elective elements in the colony's government were replaced by a new imperial executive and what amounted to martial law. The ministry responsible for what the colonists and their friends at Westminster damned as 'a wanton exercise of power' was led by Lord North (1732–92).[58]

North's unstatesmanlike appearance – his protuberant eyes and 'thick lips and inflated visage', which Horace Walpole thought 'gave him the air of a blind trumpeter' – belied a ready wit and a skill unmatched since Sir Robert Walpole at managing the Commons.[59] North's ministry, which had begun in 1770, would last until 1782. George III had finally found a prime minister who could stay the course. But the king would need more than a good parliamentary manager, he would need a war leader – and the panic-prone and easygoing North was not that. Above all, he could not impose his will upon the clashing egos and agendas among his cabinet colleagues. His ministry might be durable, but it was weak. Unfortunately, too, North lacked insight into American affairs. At best he could steady the ship of state. What he could not do was chart a course away from impending danger.

Far from isolating Massachusetts and cowing the rest of the colonies, the intolerable acts brought them together in a common resolve to take power in America until the government came to its senses. After all, what Britain could do to Massachusetts it could do to any of them. The ministry had achieved almost the impossible, for even the Americans themselves had assumed that nothing could unite the colonies – each with its different constitution and strong economic ties across the Atlantic – in common purpose against the mother country. From the summer and autumn of 1774 the colonies placed embargoes on British goods, while at local level the people began 'modelling a new Form of Government, by Committees and Associations . . . The wild Fire ran through all the Colonies.'[60] In September the first Continental Congress convened at Philadelphia to approve and coordinate the committees' activities and to deny that Parliament had any power to legislate for the domestic affairs of the Thirteen Colonies. That right, Congress asserted, lay with the provincial assemblies – soon to be transformed into elected state legislatures that, in some cases, would adopt highly democratic constitutions by contemporary standards.

Colonial elites continued to profess loyalty to the person of George III, but reverence for the king among ordinary colonists had been declining since 1773 – particularly after the passing of the intolerable acts – to be replaced in many cases by a virulent hatred of George and any who remained devoted to him. Those who had once looked to the king for protection against Leviathan now cursed him as a despot. His rule, they claimed, was like that of any European tyrant. The only difference was that he employed a 'venal parliament' to do his bidding rather than a standing army.[61] Patriot mobs no longer targeted just imperial officials for tarring and feathering, but anyone suspected of remaining loyal to the king. Anglican ministers and indeed any clergymen who continued to conduct prayers for the royal family were high on their hit list. Popular hostility even extended to the material objects of imperial allegiance. Anything from royal statues and portraits to tavern signs bearing the king's arms would be violently expunged from colonial communities.

By late 1774, relations between Britain and the colonies had reached an impasse. Parliament, declared Lord North, 'would not – could not

– concede'.[62] To admit that parliamentary authority was not sovereign was unthinkable, a betrayal of the principles enshrined at the Glorious Revolution. Besides which, giving in to the colonies would make Britain 'the scorn of Europe'.[63] Neither George III nor his prime minister was yet ready for all-out war in America. They both hoped that by applying more pressure to Massachusetts and prohibiting colonial trade with Britain the colonies might yet be brought to submission. But long before such a strategy had any chance of succeeding, it would be obliterated in a hail of musketry.

In mid-April 1775 the governor of Massachusetts, General Thomas Gage, received secret orders from London to use force against the leaders of 'open Rebellion' in the colony. On the night of the 18th he sent 900 redcoats from the Boston garrison to destroy stocks of weaponry that loyalist spies reported were hidden at Concord, a town about twenty miles to the north-west, and to arrest the leading 'rebels' Samuel Adams and John Hancock. Whether or not Gage and his men fully grasped it, theirs was a daunting task. Massachusetts was already foreign, indeed hostile, territory; and, thanks to Paul Revere and other patriot dispatch riders, the enemy knew they were coming. After skirmishing with rebel militiamen at Lexington, the redcoats moved on to Concord, where they exchanged volleys with a large militia force, before running a deadly gauntlet on the road back to Boston. Militiamen 'fired from Houses, & from behind Hedges, Trees & Stone Walls' at the retreating redcoats.[64] The British lost 65 dead and 207 wounded or missing; American losses were about 50 dead and 44 wounded or missing. Perhaps as many as five thousand militiamen had gathered along 'Battle Road' that afternoon, and more would soon arrive from neighbouring colonies to pen in Gage and his 3,500 troops on the Boston peninsula. The French and Indian War had honed the 'Martial spirit' that John Adams now detected among the people.[65] New England was a society ready for war.

The 'Will to contend by Battell', and therefore a state of war as Hobbes defined it, had been present among ordinary colonists well before April 1775. But the British government took time to be convinced that only force would decide the fate of the Thirteen Colonies. When Whitehall had dispatched reinforcements and three junior generals – William Howe, Henry Clinton and John Burgoyne – to Boston in January there was a lingering hope among senior politicians and soldiers that reconciliation might still be possible. They could not credit that the colonists were really set on going to war – largely because they assumed that

America's citizen-soldiers were the same amateurish rabble that had lost the first half of the French and Indian War, and hence no match for British professionals. Franklin had overheard one officer boasting that 'with a Thousand British grenadiers, he would . . . go from one end of America to the other, and geld all the Males'.[66] Once the colonists had encountered real soldiers, reasoned the ministry, they would surely realise what they were up against and sue for peace.

That notion, already weakened by Concord and Lexington, would be blown to shreds in June 1775 after Gage ordered a frontal assault on entrenched rebel positions on Breed's Hill across the Charles River from Boston. The attack was led by General Howe, who refused to believe what his own eyes told him – that even militiamen, if firing en masse from cover, could mow down exposed redcoats rank upon bloody rank. It was only after the Americans had run out of ammunition and been reduced to throwing stones at their attackers that the British clawed their way to the redoubt. Once there, however, their bayonets and swords made short work of the defenders, who fled towards Bunker Hill (which gave the battle its name). Almost a third of the 1,500 Americans on Breed's Hill were killed or wounded, but that was nothing compared with the butcher's bill run up by Howe. Of his 2,300 troops, 226 were killed and 928 were wounded. Although technically a defeat for the Americans, Bunker Hill had shown that they could inflict crippling casualties on their enemy. Another 'victory' like that, thought Howe's colleague General Clinton, would spell ruin.

The American War of Independence began as more than just a contest between redcoats and militiamen however – it was also a civil war. About a fifth of white Americans in the Thirteen Colonies, and an even higher proportion in places like New York and Pennsylvania with large numbers of recent immigrants, would remain loyal to the king. The loyalists were a mixed bunch: Anglican clergymen; customs officials and other imperial bureaucrats; merchants with close commercial ties to the rest of the empire; Indians who looked to Britain to stem the tide of American settlers; black slaves hoping to win their freedom by fighting for the crown; and Scottish Highlanders, Germans and other minorities that rejected the Puritanism or the English culture of the majority of patriots. Some of these groups were of doubtful military value, but the Highlanders, the Indians and the slaves all made fine irregular troops, although the British, in their disregard for mere colonials, generally disdained to use them.

Although the loyalists were dubbed 'Tories' by the rebels, this was not a struggle for or against free monarchy as the English Civil War had been, but a falling out among Whigs, a clash between rival interpretations of the Glorious Revolution. The majority of British people were satisfied that the Revolution had confirmed the fusion and sovereignty of the executive and legislative branches of government (king-in-Parliament), and that there could be no appeal to individual rights against the authority of Parliament. British and American patriots, on the other hand, still thought in terms of a separation and tension between executive (the monarch and his ministers) and legislature (Parliament). They were like the radical Whigs of the seventeenth century in arguing for the contractual nature of government and the legitimacy of resisting even Parliament itself when it violated the fundamental laws of the constitution. British politicians might admire this 'language of liberty' in theory, but when it was directed against king-in-Parliament they thought it 'destructive of all government'.[67]

Shortly before Howe 'murdered' his own men at Bunker Hill, Congress voted on 14 June 1775 to raise troops for the 'American Continental army'.[68] The officer it chose to command this new force was the Virginian congressman and veteran of the French and Indian War, George Washington. At six foot three inches tall and a svelte 209 pounds, the 43-year-old Washington cut an imposing figure. In public he was all gentlemanly gravitas, although he could turn on the charm too, when there were ladies present. But lurking behind his reserved and dignified manner was a volcanic temper and a sense of inferiority towards his often better-educated and more cultivated peers. Acutely image-conscious, he reacted badly to criticism, and nursed grievances against congressional officials, tenants, business partners, even his poor slaves. With the help of a Prussian drillmaster and congressional orders for long-term enlistment and conscription, he fulfilled his ambition of turning a makeshift and constantly fluctuating body of citizen-soldiers into something like a professional European army. In the field too, after the inevitable early setbacks, he became a wily and occasionally audacious opponent. But his real talent as a general was his ability to inspire devotion in his men. Through sheer grit and unswerving dedication to what he called this 'glorious Cause', he would preserve the nucleus of a fighting force even after defeat and the innumerable hardships of war had taken their toll.[69] Simply holding the army together would be his greatest accomplishment, his most decisive contribution to the American war effort.

Congress's stated aims in creating Washington's army were limited.

Not many colonial leaders were yet committed to American independence. Instead they wanted relations with the mother country restored to what they had been in 1763, with an implicit commitment from Britain to allow westward expansion in America while keeping Parliament and the ministry firmly out of the colonies' internal affairs. Britain's war aims were equally limited – that is, scotch the rebellion in New England and then reach some arrangement with the cowed and chastened rump of supposedly more tractable colonies to the south. Retaining the Thirteen Colonies was thought (wrongly) to be absolutely essential to Britain's prosperity. Even so, a protracted, debilitating war would be almost as bad as defeat. Either way, as one MP warned, Britain would 'lose her power and consequence in the system of Europe, and be exposed almost a defenceless prey to the first neighbour who shall choose to invade her'.[70]

In March 1776, General Howe, who had succeeded Gage as British commander-in-chief, evacuated Boston. The port had become untenable, and New York – dubbed 'Torytown' for its strong loyalist sympathies – would make a much better base for blockading the American coast and driving inland against the rebels. The ministry too had finally realised what a numerous and resolute enemy it faced, and was now scrabbling around for all the troops it could find, including Hanoverians, Hessians, American Indians and Gaelic Scots and Irish. After refitting in Nova Scotia, Howe sailed south at the head of 130 ships, dropping anchor off Staten Island in June. His expeditionary force was already one of the largest that Britain had ever mounted, and every week would bring more men and supplies from across the Atlantic until he had almost 30,000 troops, including 12,000 crack German mercenaries.

Between August and December 1776, Howe slowly but systematically drove Washington's outnumbered and, at times, poorly led army from Long Island, New York city, Manhattan and much of New Jersey. Meanwhile, American efforts to invade Canada and take Quebec had met with stiff opposition from British regulars, and indifference from the French Canadian population, and had ended with the loss of much precious equipment and 1,000 men killed or captured. The momentum was with the British, and had Howe acted more aggressively at certain key moments, then he might have crushed Washington's retreating army and perhaps forced Congress to the negotiating table. 'The fact is their army is broken all to pieces,' gloated one British officer late in 1776, 'it is well nigh over with them.'[71] Washington thought so too: 'I think the game is pretty near up,' he confided to his brother.[72] But Howe was reluctant to go for the rebels' jugular. Hard soldiering was much less fun than dallying with the lovely Elizabeth Loring, who was married but entirely amenable. Howe, wrote one of his officers, 'shut his eyes, fought his battles, had his little whore'.[73]

In truth, Howe disliked the war. He had taken command in America largely to explore the possibilities of a reconciliation, not to batter the colonists into submission. Moreover, his resolution had never fully recovered from the carnage he had witnessed at Bunker Hill. Unnerved by the thought of yet greater bloodshed, he unwittingly repeated the mistake of Parliament's commander in the English Civil War, the earl of Essex, in continuing to pursue a negotiated settlement long after it had become clear on both sides that the sword must settle the issue. But Howe was too far away for the ministry to keep a close eye on him, and it would have to leave a great deal to his initiative and discretion – a trust that he repeatedly abused.

In the year between Bunker Hill and Howe's descent on New York the Thirteen Colonies moved from rebellion to revolution. The English republican turned American patriot Thomas Paine raised popular support for independence to new heights with his bestseller *Common Sense* (1776), and its witty exposure of the absurdity in remaining subject to a distant and apparently uncaring regime. An independent America would be a beacon of hope and liberty, argued Paine, an egalitarian paradise in a world full of tyranny. Congress, however, dominated as it was by gentlemen with strong economic and cultural ties to Britain, would be slower to embrace the cause of independence, and when it did so it would be largely for pragmatic reasons. Its hand would be forced to some extent by the intransigent attitude of George III, who had turned a deaf ear to colonial pleas that he intercede against Parliament. 'I am fighting the battle of the legislature,' he had roundly declared.[74] Then came news of the disaster in Canada, and that the British were preparing to deploy Germans, Scottish Highlanders and other 'foreign mercenaries' against the colonies. If the mightiest empire on the planet was going to such lengths then Congress too must take bold action, or face defeat. It was this calculation that persuaded congressmen to put aside their distaste at having to approach the European powers for help. The French had been secretly supplying the colonists with arms for some months in the hope of weakening Britain to the point where it would be safe for France and Spain to join the attack. The problem for the Americans was that no European power would enter into a formal alliance with mere rebels or men who might yet patch up their quarrel with Britain and leave their allies in the lurch. Foreign policy considerations therefore demanded independence. 'It is not choice then,' confessed one congressman, 'but necessity that calls for Independence, as the only means by which foreign Alliance can be obtained.'[75]

On 4 July 1776 the Thirteen Colonies adopted a formal Declaration of Independence and had it printed beneath large capitals that christened the new republic 'The United States of America'. Penned for the most part by Thomas Jefferson (1743–1826), the Declaration was largely taken up with a somewhat exaggerated list of George III's misdeeds that was reminiscent of the 1689 Bill of Rights' denunciation of James II for having subverted the constitution. Jefferson had been quicker than most colonial leaders to shift the ultimate blame for the war from the ministry and Parliament to the king. He was in the vanguard of the revolution, too, in recognising that, by declaring themselves independent, his compatriots could no longer appeal to the historic liberties of Englishmen, as he himself had been wont to do just a few years earlier. They must now follow the parliamentarian and Whig radicals of the seventeenth century in asserting the natural rights of all mankind, hence the Declaration's most famous words: 'We hold these truths to be self-evident, that all men are created equal, that they are endowed by their Creator with certain unalienable Rights, that among these are Life, Liberty and the pursuit of Happiness.' Few English radicals would have bypassed the ancient constitution in this audacious manner. And by invoking universal principles the Americans themselves ran into an immediate problem: slavery. Jefferson, like many other American revolutionaries, kept slaves. Did they too not have an unalienable right of liberty? 'How is it,' asked Samuel Johnson, 'that we hear the loudest yelps for liberty among the drivers of negroes?'[76] Finding answers to these questions would vex American politics until well into the twentieth century.

Sensibility

Had Samuel Johnson and Thomas Jefferson ever met it would surely have proved a memorable encounter. On the face of it the two men had little in common. Jefferson, who set much store by outward appearance, and was himself a man of very fine features, would have been not a little put off by the huge and badly dressed figure of Johnson, with his alarming repertoire of twitches and gesticulations, his one good eye continually blinking in a face scarred by scrofula and smallpox. Hogarth was astonished that a man he took at first glance for an 'ideot' could speak as if touched by God. Johnson, for his part, was suspicious of self-styled patriots – especially American ones – distrusted politicians, and reverenced the Church of England. No wonder his friend James Boswell was advised against introducing him to the notorious radical and libertine John Wilkes. As it turned out, Johnson and Wilkes got on famously on the one occasion they dined together in company, although Wilkes worked extra hard to get on Johnson's good side. 'Pray give me leave, Sir. It is better here – A little of the brown [meat] – some fat, Sir – A little of the stuffing – Some gravy – Let me have the pleasure of giving you some butter . . .'[77] Boswell had recognised that besides good food and conversation they 'had so many things in common – classical learning, modern literature, wit, and humour, and ready repartee'.[78] And in affecting to despise the Scots as a 'crafty, designing people, eagerly attentive to their own interest', the two men could 'perfectly assimilate'.[79]

Jefferson too might have had a few choice words to say on that subject, and on others equally close to Johnson's heart. For all that he defended the sovereignty of king-in-Parliament against 'American usurpation', Johnson scorned the political corruption that nourished Leviathan.[80] In his *A Dictionary of the English Language* (1755) he had defined a pension as 'pay given to a state hireling for treason to his country'.[81] Jefferson would have appreciated that, as he would Johnson's fascination with new and useful inventions and scientific discoveries – for it was still possible, just, for learned gentlemen to spread themselves across the fast-diverging worlds of literature, philosophy and science. Neither man had much time for the metaphysical, and Johnson in particular was furiously intolerant of humbug. 'My dear friend,' Johnson advised Boswell, 'clear your mind of cant . . . it is a mode of talking in Society; but don't *think* foolishly.'[82]

It seems almost sacrilege to place Johnson alongside Jefferson in the pantheon of luminaries associated with that most liberal of early modern movements, the Enlightenment. Johnson's hatred of Whigs and Dissenters, his legendary prejudices, partook far more of John Bull than of the French *philosophes*. Yet his universalist mode of thought and his desire to influence and engage with public opinion were integral to many of the intellectual currents that characterised the Age of Reason.

The old idea of the Enlightenment as an essentially French endeavour that was republican in its political sympathies and hostile to religion has been exploded. But defining what the Enlightenment *was*, as opposed to what it was not, is very difficult. In essence, it relates to the preoccupation among eighteenth-century thinkers with human progress and betterment as worthy ends in themselves, without regard for divine approval in this world or the next. By this reckoning the Enlightenment flourished most fully between 1740 and 1790, although it had deep intellectual roots in the work of Thomas Hobbes, John Locke and other seventeenth-century philosophers and scientists.[83]

The Enlightenment in England is hard to pin down precisely. It is not even clear that there was such a thing. Progressive thinkers in England were notably less anti-establishment than they were in France – a combination, perhaps, of the presence of liberal Anglican clergymen among their ranks, and the fact that the British had already secured many of the rights for which the *philosophes* campaigned, such as trial by jury and religious toleration. Jefferson may have ended up rejecting the ancient constitution, but Voltaire and his like generally shared Johnson's admiration for the liberties and mixed system of government that the British people had won for themselves.

But it was Johnson's response to those things he found objectionable in English life that reveals him in true Enlightenment colours. Rather than play the stoic or address himself solely to men of power and education, he poured his energy as a journalist, novelist, poet and critic into nurturing public opinion as a force for good in society. He was committed to the idea of the public as the ultimate arbiter of truth and good taste, and saw his task as that of educating ordinary readers in this noble role. His willingness to cultivate meaner intellects than his own was consistent with his belief in the uniformity of human nature. He could see no virtue peculiar to the British that justified their greed for empire, particularly at the expense of non-European races. He abhorred slavery. The racial stereotyping in Jefferson's *Notes on the State of Virginia* (1787) would have disgusted him.

Johnson's many gibes against the Scots – most famously, that the noblest prospect a Scotsman could ever see was the road that led to England – reflected not contempt for the Scottish people but for their Presbyterianism, which he associated with cultural debasement and mob rule. It must have galled him considerably, therefore, that for those seeking the noblest prospects of the mind the road actually led north, to Scotland. Edinburgh and other Lowland cities were remarkable by the mid-eighteenth century for their concentration of academic and cultural resources. Thanks to an excellent parish school system, literacy rates in Lowland Scotland were among the highest in Europe. Add to that a plethora of scientific and philosophical societies; a lively market in printed works; a group of Presbyterian churchmen well disposed towards polite learning; plenty of urban wealth (largely from the colonial trade); and above all, five universities with more innovative courses than the rather tired curricula at England's two (Oxford and Cambridge), and the result was a vibrant republic of letters that produced some of the world's greatest and most influential thinkers.

Johnson was familiar with these men either personally or by reputation, and usually found reason to dislike them. Adam Smith, the father of modern economics, he thought a most disagreeable fellow – partly because he 'bubbled' wine in his mouth at dinner. And though he never met David Hume (so far as we know), or read his work, he had no hesitation in branding him and his sceptical, empiricist philosophy as immoral and 'Hobbist'. Hume hit back at Johnson via Boswell, and avoided his company when in London. Had they ever conversed, and had Johnson laid aside his distaste for Hume's irreligion and Scottishness, they would have discovered they had a surprising amount in common. Both men decried 'enthusiasm', had deep misgivings as to the benefits of empire, and shared a conviction that the passions, not reason, were the mainspring of civil society. But Johnson, unlike Hume, never reconciled himself to the reality or necessity of Leviathan. Hume built on the ideas of Mandeville, Hobbes and other proto-Enlightenment philosophers to develop a sophisticated account of political institutions in which the historical interplay of national culture and human self-interest created the necessary artifices of government. And he deviated even more from the neoclassical 'patriot' line in treating luxury and consumerism not as solvents of civic virtue but as progressive social forces. Hume's perspective on Leviathan was, in consequence, far more penetrating and dispassionate than the usual spluttering invective on the subject. Compare, for example, Johnson's definition of 'pension' with Hume's verdict on ministerial manipulation of Parliament:

We may, therefore, give to this Influence what Name we please; we may call it by the invidious Appellations of *Corruption* and *Dependence*; but some Degree and some Kind of it are inseparable from the very Nature of the Constitution, and necessary to the Preservation of our mixt Government.[84]

Hume's death in 1776 boosted confidence among respectable believers that the tide of atheism and deism that had seemed about to engulf England earlier in the century was receding. The Anglican Church was certainly regaining some of its vigour under George III – a king devoted to its rites and well-being – after years of ministerial neglect and political division. A group of Oxford-educated clergy emerged after 1760 to lead the defence of core doctrines such as the Trinity against the sceptics. The Methodist challenge had been contained; indeed, although the Methodists were developing their own distinct organis- ation they had not yet formally left the Church. Their numbers, too, were relatively modest – a mere 72,000 or so by the time John Wesley died in 1791 – and mostly drawn from the English lower orders. Moreover, the movement was deeply divided between those for and against a Calvinist doctrine of salvation. Anglican 'church evangelicals', on the other hand, were recruiting outstanding parish ministers in the 1770s and 1780s, and winning highly placed followers.

The view of that astute commentator Horace Walpole that 'there were no religious combustibles in the temper of the times' did not mean that religious feeling itself was declining.[85] Not for nothing did one of Johnson's friends refer in 1771 to 'these, our moral and religious days'.[86] It is interesting that though Hume had died in great composure, sticking 'indecently and impolitely' to his scepticism about an afterlife and the immortality of the soul, good Christians felt moved to invent stories about how the 'great infidel' had recanted on his deathbed, with a prayerbook tucked discreetly beneath his pillow, out of sight of his atheistical philosopher friends.[87]

This heightened moral sensitivity in genteel society was intimately linked from the mid-eighteenth century with a new phase in the devel- opment of politeness – namely, sensibility, or the sentimental. Hume had laid the intellectual foundations for this trend with his theory that human sociability and morality were grounded not in reason (Locke) or narrow self-interest (Mandeville) but in our innate capacity to observe and enter into the feelings of others and to communicate our own sentiments via the 'agreeable movements' of 'social sympathy'.[88] Another source of fashionable theories for the novelists and hacks who helped popularise the cult of sensibility was the medical profession. By the mid-eighteenth century the notion of the body as a complex hydraulic mechanism for regulating the four humours (blood, phlegm, black bile and yellow bile) had largely been replaced by an understanding of human physiology based on a wire-like system of 'nervose fibres'.[89]

In the sentimental literature of the period the body was often likened
to a finely tuned instrument that responded movingly to even the most
delicate of stimuli. Persons of sensibility were capable of finer feelings
and greater sympathy than others, but for that very reason were susceptible to 'the English Malady' (depression) and similar 'Disorders which
have been commonly call'd Nervous, Hypochondriac, or Hysteric'.[90]

Sensibility attempted to revive what was supposedly the true essence
of politeness by reconnecting inward virtue and outward manners.
Mere external elegance would no longer suffice; indeed, it might serve
as a mask for immorality. The rake, that stock figure of sentimental
literature, used exterior politeness to hunt his standard prey, the innocent young heiress. Politeness might not simply mask deceit but hinder
spontaneous feeling and genuine sociability. 'True politeness', insisted
one literary reviewer in 1775, 'consists, not in modes and ceremonies,
but in entering with delicacy into the feelings of our companions.'[91]
This imperative to convey sympathy with others encouraged the adoption of more natural and affective forms of expression such as weeping,
sighing, blushing and trembling. Where formerly such behaviour might
have aroused suspicions of 'enthusiasm', by the 1770s and 1780s it was
regarded as a token for both men and women of that delicacy of inner
feeling and moral capacity that polite society so prized. By downplaying
mere etiquette in this way, sensibility could be made to accommodate
even rude and abrasive characters like Johnson: 'To be sure', wrote his
friend, the poet and playwright Oliver Goldsmith, 'Johnson has a rough-
ness in his manner, but no man alive has a more tender heart.'[92] The
religious impulse itself was located by some writers within the expanding
realm of sensibility: 'Its seat [religious feeling] is in the imagination
and the passions, and it has its source in that relish for the sublime,
the vast and the beautiful, by which we taste the charms of poetry and
other compositions.'[93]

The cult of sensibility would be fostered by the book clubs and
circulating and town libraries that were set up in increasing numbers
from the middle of the century. For a modest subscription, those with
too little money to buy books in any number could now indulge their
appetite for improving literature – from the sentimental morality tales
of most novels to the latest scientific and theological works. Greater
access to books – and to at least a basic education – explains why
literacy levels by 1760 were approaching 60 per cent for men and 40
per cent for women. And it is women who seem to have made the most
of the proliferation of libraries to expand their emotional as well as

mental horizons. A particular favourite with female readers were the novels of the doyen of sentimental fiction, Samuel Richardson. His writing exerted enormous power over some of his devotees, as the most eminent of them, Lady Dorothy Bradshaigh, confessed in one of her letters to him:

> I verily believe I have shed a pint of tears, and my heart is still bursting, tho' they cease not to flow at this moment, nor will, I fear, for some time . . . in agonies would I lay down the book, take it up again, walk about the room, let fall a flood of tears, wipe my eyes, read again, perhaps not three lines, throw away the book, crying out, excuse me, good Mr. Richardson, I cannot go on.[94]

Sentimental feeling abounded in the literature of the later eighteenth century. The political satires and picaresque novels favoured by Defoe, Swift and Fielding had given way to more intimate and pathetical musings. Common subjects of sentimental writing were the plight and rescue of the neglected and vulnerable – repentant prostitutes, poor prisoners, children, animals etc. – and the melancholic contemplation of some desolate scene. In the hands of great writers such as Goldsmith (?1728–74) the effect could be sublime. His elegiac poem *The Deserted Village* (1770) was rightly praised for the tenderness of its sentiments even by those who disputed its theme of luxury and commerce driving virtue from the countryside. As for the comic and ironic potential within sentimentalism, no writer could compare with Laurence Sterne (1713–68), whose book *A Sentimental Journey through France and Italy by Mr. Yorick* (1768) started the trend of novels declaring themselves to be 'sentimental'.

But the strivings of lesser writers for sentimental effect often descended into mawkishness and prudery. The moral didacticism that ran through the cult of sensibility gave rise to an artistic squeamishness about treating of anything bawdy or otherwise indelicate. Of course, to the *Sentimental Magazine* (1773–7) and similar publications this was a source of satisfaction rather than regret: 'As we have increased in Politeness, we have likewise increased in the Chastity of our literary Productions . . . Our Ancestors placed their Amusement in Laughter, we place our's on Chastity of Sentiment.'[95]

The rise of sentimentalism coincided with the era of the greatest actor and theatre manager of the eighteenth century: David Garrick (1717–79). Garrick was a lifelong friend of Johnson. Indeed, the two of them had left their Staffordshire home town together, arriving in London to seek their fortunes with just one horse and a few pennies between them. Starting as a humble player in one of London's illicit playhouses, Garrick built up the Drury Lane theatre – one of only two in the city that were licensed to perform plays for paying customers – into the most profitable entertainment business that Britain had ever seen. His success owed a lot to his business acumen, but rested ultimately on his genius as an actor. The traditional style of acting, before Garrick, had involved the players coming to the front of the stage and declaiming to the audience in stentorian tones, adopting artificial, rhetorical postures, and ignoring any dialogue with the other characters. Garrick changed all that with his emphasis on ensemble acting and using observation and sympathetic imagination to invest his characters with more natural mannerisms and poses. His performances were so powerful that they stunned the audience. It took the society painter Sir Joshua Reynolds three days to recover from Garrick's portrayal of King Lear, which was generally considered his finest tragic role.

Garrick developed an almost proprietorial interest in Shakespeare, who was now widely regarded as England's greatest-ever playwright. He referred to Drury Lane as 'the house of William Shakespeare'.[96] Twenty per cent of the theatre's 'mainpieces' – the principal production in a typical four- or five-hour evening performance of plays, songs and comedy 'drolls' – were works by Shakespeare. Garrick presented versions of the plays that were more faithful to the originals, but he also adapted them (excising and adding material) himself, in keeping with the sentimental expectations of the audience. His *Romeo and Juliet*, for example, omitted Romeo's relationship with Rosaline, and had Juliet awaken before Romeo's death so that he could expire in her arms. And though he restored much of the original version of *King Lear*, he retained the play's by now obligatory happy ending in which love and reconciliation triumphed. Even the unromantic Johnson preferred this maudlin denouement to Shakespeare's own bleak conclusion to the play. With Johnson's help, Garrick more or less invented the modern cult of Shakespeare as England's national poet. His Shakespeare Jubilee at Stratford-upon-Avon in 1769, though a rain-soaked washout, inaugurated the Shakespeare souvenir and tourist industry that we know today.

The more adventurous seekers after the sublime and pathetic found their sentimental thrills communing with nature. Denied easy access to the Continent by war with France, the landed elite under George III looked increasingly for diversion in exploring Britain. Their new-found passion for touring upcountry was now relatively easy to indulge thanks to the great improvement in the road network since the seventeenth century. Daniel Defoe on his tour of Britain in the 1720s had shuddered in horror at what we now call the Lake District, thinking it 'a Country eminent only for being the wildest, most barren and frightful of any that I have passed over in England, or even in Wales'.[97] Fifty years on, however, regions like the Lake District and the Scottish Highlands that previous generations had dismissed as remote and uncivilised were revered by patrician tourists for the wild beauty of their scenery and the unaffected simplicity of their inhabitants. Similarly, the ruined abbeys and monasteries that witnessed to the greatest act of cultural desecration in British history were languished over as sites of special emotional interest – a variety of romantic indulgence that was inspired in part by the Gothic revivalism of Horace Walpole and his antiquarian friends. Probably the most famous of the period's sentimental journeys was that of Johnson and Boswell to Scotland in 1773. Boswell's account of their travels was avidly consumed by the reading public, but Johnson, true to form, refused to glamorise the Highlands or to affirm the romantic myth of the Highlanders as people of 'savage virtues and barbarous grandeur'.[98]

The remoter parts of Britain appealed to the aristocracy precisely because they were more inaccessible, and therefore exclusive, than the usual holiday destinations. The bourgeoisie had to make do with Bath and other watering places, or with upland scenery in easy reach of the turnpike, such as the Peak District. The variety of pleasure resorts for the polite classes increased from the 1750s, however, as the public swallowed the latest medical advice that seawater taken both internally and externally was good for the health. The great seaside towns of Aberystwyth, Blackpool, Brighton, Margate and Scarborough were first developed during the later eighteenth century. About the furthest George III and his family ever ventured from London was to take a restorative dip at Weymouth on the Dorset coast.

Sensibility and commerce existed in close and generally harmonious partnership. There was money in sentiment, and not just from writing and publishing. Tasteful objects, whether beautiful in themselves or by association with people of delicate feeling, could move the susceptible to tears almost as effectively as melancholy poetry, Gothic ruins, or the plight of a distressed heroine in one of Richardson's novels. An increasing range of manufactured wares – particularly the fashion items and home furnishings purchased by or for women – were marketed and consumed during the later eighteenth century as objects of emotional attachment. Manufacturers deliberately appealed to this sentimentalism. The pottery magnate Josiah Wedgwood (1730–95) was a master at producing objects that tugged at the heartstrings – most notably, his anti-slavery medallion of 1787 depicting a slave kneeling in chains above the motto 'Am I Not A Man And A Brother?'[99] Refined consumerism became part of the sentimental style.

True, there was a growing sense by the early 1800s that sensibility had sold out, and had succumbed to the greed and insincerity it was supposed to stand against – a perception implicit in its change of meaning during George III's reign: from 'exhibiting refined and elevated feelings' to 'addicted to indulgence in superficial emotion'.[100] But sensibility, like politeness, generally adapted to the consumerist reality of Georgian Britain in which manufactured goods were transforming the domestic lives of the middling orders out of all recognition. The carpets, wall-hangings, mirrors and fine china that adorned the houses of many tradespeople by the 1770s would have been rarities even in aristocratic mansions a few generations earlier.

Bourgeois consumerism, and high import duties on foreign luxuries, would stimulate innovation, artful design and astute marketing throughout British manufacturing, but nowhere more so than in the pottery industry. Demand was growing by the mid-eighteenth century for fine majolica and, above all, for porcelain substitutes (the real thing was, as Johnson complained, too expensive for ordinary pockets). Supplying and shaping this taste for affordable yet luxurious tableware were the new potteries at Chelsea, Bow, Worcester, Derby, and later in Staffordshire, all copying and adapting Chinese, French and classical patterns. Undisputed king of the Staffordshire potteries was Wedgwood, the 'Vase Maker General to the Universe', who would be worth £500,000 by the time he died.[101] Not bad for the thirteenth son of a working potter. His endless ingenuity in the art and manufacture of ceramics created new types of high-quality earthenware that brought aristocratic fashions in classical vases and porcelain within the price range of middle-class incomes. His 'creamware' – a light and lustrous porcelain substitute – was in turn imitated in France and elsewhere on the Continent. It was so good, he joked, that even the Chinese might come to England to discover its secret.

The Staffordshire potteries were among the first businesses in Britain to undergo a process of something like modern industrialisation. Ceramics production by the late eighteenth century had shifted from people's homes to factories, and was characterised by division of labour, a focus on national and export markets, and the emergence of highly urbanised communities that were largely independent of their rural surroundings. It is still too early to talk of an industrial revolution. The potteries, for example, or the Lancashire cotton industry – where a series of ground-breaking inventions had accelerated mechanised production – were precocious. Most sectors of the economy would not experience an industrial 'take-off' until several decades into the nineteenth century when manufacturers began switching en masse from horse or water power to coal-fired steam technology that dramatically increased productivity. It would only be by harnessing the energy contained within its abundant coal deposits that Britain would become the first country in the world to escape the straitjacket of the traditional 'organic' economy powered by agriculture and the elements.

Yet something extraordinary was happening in Britain during the eighteenth century, providing the critical impetus for its emergence as the workshop of the world in the nineteenth. Urban growth and rising consumer demand – driven largely by Britain's dynamic overseas trade, its low energy costs (from coal), and its ever more efficient and productive farming sector – had pushed up wages to well above European averages. The high price of labour, in turn, incentivised manufacturers to develop new technologies for replacing people with machinery, thereby increasing output while driving down production costs. Foreign know-how obtained through industrial espionage or, more commonly, from the immigrants who had come to Britain since the late seventeenth century made a vital contribution in the textile and glass-making industries in particular. But it was Britain's highly educated commercial and professional classes that supplied most of the talent to meet the technological challenges and reap the business opportunities presented by its burgeoning economy. From this coming together of expertise and investment emerged a myriad of technical innovations for imitating and customising expensive imports, creating affordable consumer products that by 1800 were the envy of all Europe. Two of the leading innovators in the field of textile machinery were part of Johnson's circle – namely John Wyatt and Lewis Paul, the son of a Huguenot. Wyatt was also linked with perhaps the age's most celebrated association of inventors and philosophers, the Lunar Society of Birmingham (c.1765–c.1800), whose leading members were Wedgwood and his fellow manufacturing pioneer Matthew Boulton. Boulton and his business partner, the Scottish engineer James Watt, developed the steam engines that would help power British manufacturing towards the industrial revolution.

The effect of all this getting and spending (and inventing) was to create an exceptionally prosperous country by the late 1700s with an economy that was following a trajectory not seen anywhere else in Europe, or indeed in Britain's own past. British businesses and households, for example, were burning around 15 million tons of coal a year by 1800 – five times more than the rest of Europe combined. Well before steam power transformed British industry, industrialisation was transforming Britain's human geography. The age-old superiority in wealth and population of the southern lowlands was disappearing as improvements in agricultural productivity allowed hundreds of thousands of rural job-seekers to head for the 'regions of smoke' – the manufacturing towns of Lancashire, Yorkshire, the Midlands and the Central Belt between Edinburgh and Glasgow, or the coalfields of south Wales.[102] Sentimental writers generally had little to say about the miseries of life in Britain's early industrial slums. Goldsmith, in *The Deserted Village*, portrayed the evils that befell those 'to city sped' using the familiar sentimental trope of the 'poor houseless shivering female' seduced by some heedless urban sophisticate.[103]

Britain's march towards industrial supremacy was accelerated by the economic impact of its fiscal–military state. Massive and sustained investment in naval power (to resist the commercial and armed might of popery) kept the sea lanes open for British business, boosting urban growth and manufacturing. The royal navy was so powerful by the mid-eighteenth century that British exports increased even in wartime. Burgeoning international trade, particularly with Asia and the Americas, turned London into the financial centre of an expanding global economy. At home and on the high seas, Leviathan supplied the military muscle to protect property and assets, provide long-term security for businessmen and investors, and stimulate the industries – coal, shipping, manufacturing and financial services – necessary for the development of Britain's high-wage, cheap-energy, economy. The British war on popery would create, if unwittingly, the preconditions for the industrial revolution.

The road back to Paris

Five months on from all the fanfare that had surrounded the Declaration of Independence, and talk of 'the most memorable Epocha in the History of America', it looked as if the world's newest nation would also be its shortest-lived.[104] Of the men who had signed the Declaration at Philadelphia in August 1776, none had felt the republic's subsequent humiliation, as Howe and his army chased the 'Continentals' from Long Island and Manhattan, more painfully than Washington had. He agonised over his failures, and fumed at the absurdity of trying to fight a war with half of his men either falling in or falling out again to look after their farms and families. Part-time militiamen were better than nothing, but he needed more 'Continentals' – that is, regular soldiers – if he was to make a proper fight of it. What he also needed, and quick, were victories to boost his army's flagging morale and give New Jersey and the surrounding states good reason not to surrender to Howe at the first convenient opportunity. On Christmas night, therefore, he launched a daring attack on Trenton that ended with the capture of three German regiments. Ten days later he outmanoeuvred the British and drove their garrison from Princeton. Fearful of further surprise attacks on his overextended lines, Howe abandoned most of New Jersey to the rebels.

The ministry should have sacked Howe at the end of the 1776 campaign and replaced him with someone who would obey orders and push for absolute victory. In New York the loyalists fulminated that: 'Gen[eral] H's Conduct ever since he has had the Command of the Army has been a heap of blunders, & rediculous delays, that have rather tended to encourage the Rebels . . . than to extinguish the Rebellion by spirited exertions, or following up the many Opportunities he has had of utterly destroying the whole Rebel Army.'[105] Yet even supposing the ministry could find a 'spirited' and able commander – for few high-ranking officers relished being sent to a military backwater like America – it was too weak and divided to bring down Howe, and the 1777 campaign would suffer accordingly.

Howe revised his strategy in light of Washington's winter victories. The only way to end the rebellion, he now reasoned, was by defeating Washington in a single decisive battle, and the only way to make him stand and fight would be to march upon the home of Congress: Philadelphia. At the same time, he had not completely given up hope of achieving a reconciliation. Caught between the two stools of war to the death and a negotiated settlement (assuming that Congress would negotiate, which it showed little interest in doing), he would merely succeed in adding to his heap of blunders. For despite defeating Washington at the battle of Brandywine in September 1777, he then abandoned his plan of trying to destroy the Continental Army. In addition, he ignored the ministry's expectation that he would at some point during the 1777 campaigning season march northwards to join with a British army from Canada under General John Burgoyne in an attempt to sever New England from the bleeding stump of rebellion further south. Howe's neglect of orders followed inevitably from his failure to get his army in the field until July; for by the time he took Philadelphia two months later it was too late for him to help Burgoyne, whose army was being cut to pieces in the Hudson valley. Admittedly Burgoyne's predicament was largely of his own making. 'Gentleman Johnny' was a blusterer and glory-hunter, and all in all another poor choice by the ministry. Although he knew by August that his army was heavily outnumbered and that Howe would not come to his rescue, he also knew that to retreat would ruin his career as surely as defeat. And so – being the compulsive gambler that he was – he pressed ahead anyway, hoping that boldness might carry the day. It did not. His 6,000 or so British and German troops were mauled twice in battle and then surrounded and forced to surrender, at Saratoga, on 17 October. In November 1777 Howe tendered his resignation, which the ministry accepted, replacing him as commander-in-chief with General Henry Clinton.

Britain and France had been heading for war months before Burgoyne's surrender at Saratoga. French arms-smuggling to the Americans (which the British were fully aware of) and the machinations of Benjamin Franklin at Versailles had already put the two powers on collision course. The American victory at Saratoga would merely strengthen the case of the French war lobby that the time was now ripe for France to avenge its losses in the Seven Years War and to cut an over-mighty Britain down to size. In February 1778 the French and Americans signed an alliance at Paris by which they agreed to fight on together until Britain had formally acknowledged the independence of the United States. For Franklin, one of the signatories to the treaty, it was a case of if the British would not help their transatlantic cousins build an American empire, then independence and French support surely would. The British desperately tried to conciliate the Americans by repealing all the 'intolerable' legislation passed since 1763 and by relinquishing Parliament's claim to tax the colonies. But all this succeeded in doing was to encourage the French to rally the Americans with promises of great victories ahead, which Congress lapped up eagerly. It was at this point that Britain's isolationism under George III would come back to haunt her. Unimpeded by having to fight Britain's allies on the Continent (of which there were none), France was now free to concentrate her resources on taking the offensive at sea, with potentially disastrous consequences for British security on both sides of the Atlantic. Sending more warships to America, warned the first lord of the Admiralty, would leave Britain dangerously exposed to French invasion.

War with France forced the British into a major strategy rethink. From 1778 the ministry's priority would not be defeating the Americans but preventing the French taking possession of Britain's lucrative colonies in the Caribbean. Jamaica and Britain's other sugar islands were nowhere near as big a market for British manufactured goods as the mainland colonies, but the import and slave-related trades they sustained were thought to be more valuable to the British economy. In 1778, therefore, many British warships in the North American theatre, as well as 10,000 of Clinton's troops, were switched to the Caribbean. The percentage of British land forces deployed in America fell from 65 per cent at the start of 1778 to a mere 29 per cent in September 1780.

With fewer military resources to go round, the ministry effectively gave up on the northern colonies – at least until France could be defeated – and focused, in the American theatre, on reclaiming those in the South, particularly Georgia and the Carolinas. The southern colonies were closely tied in economically with the sugar islands in the Caribbean, and partly for that reason contained a higher proportion of loyalists than the northern colonies. The weakness of the loyalist presence in the north made it impossible for the British to hold any territory there beyond the range of their field guns and the navy's supply lines. Where the patriots' hold was weaker or contested there often raged a vicious civil war of terror and retaliation between loyalists and patriots, in which the two sides fought with 'the most relent[less] Fury killing and destroying each other wherever they meet'. But it was usually the patriots who had the numbers, the organisation and the more able commanders to carry the day. It was the poor loyalist showing in Pennsylvania that forced Clinton to abandon Philadelphia in June 1778 and march back to New York.

The Franco-American alliance turned the war over independence into a struggle for European and global hegemony. Isolated in Europe, bloodied and overstretched in America, and with France determined to fight it out on the high seas rather than in Germany, Britain entered this new phase of the war in much the most vulnerable position she had been in since as far back as the 1580s. And the likelihood of her emerging victorious would decrease even further in April 1779 when the Spanish made common cause with the French to 'avenge', as their alliance treaty was pleased to put it, 'their respective injuries, and to put an end to the tyrannical empire which England has usurped, and claims to maintain upon the ocean'.[106] More specifically, the Spanish wanted Gibraltar back, along with Minorca and some of the territory in Florida that they had ceded to the British at the treaty of Paris in 1763. In that last war the royal navy had been larger than the combined Franco-Spanish fleet, but British naval spending had declined in the decade or so after 1763 in an effort to save money. Indeed, in 1775–8 the fleet had been completely neglected as Britain concentrated on the land war in America. France and Spain, meanwhile, had been busily building state-of-the-art warships, and by 1779 the tables had been well and truly turned. The British now had 95 ships of the line as against the allies' 121, which was a big enough gap to compensate, at least temporarily, for the royal navy's superiority in the basic logistics of seapower such as skilled seamen, victualling, and dockyard facilities.

Between 1778 and 1782 the French captured the British sugar islands of Dominica, St Vincent, Grenada, Tobago, St Kitts, Nevis and Montserrat, while the Spanish seized New Providence in the Bahamas and drove the British out of West Florida. The British also lost their naval superiority in the Mediterranean. There was even a danger that they would lose control of the Channel itself. In the summer of 1779 the French and Spanish fleets were poised to sail northwards and pulverise the heavily outnumbered British Channel squadron, clearing the way for a French invasion force of almost 40,000 men. 'I believe this country was never in so perilous a situation as it is at present,' announced the undersecretary of war, and he was right.[107] It was only the usual, if fortuitous, combination of poor planning, unfavourable winds and a lack of French resolve that doomed the enterprise.

Britain's list of enemies would lengthen still further in 1780. In an attempt to deny the Americans vital war supplies the British had taken to stopping neutral ships and confiscating any cargoes they suspected were bound for rebel ports. This did not go down well with other European nations, and in March 1780 the Russians launched what became the League of Armed Neutrality to protect neutral shipping against Britain's stop-and-search policy. Eventually the League would include Austria, Denmark, the Dutch republic, Prussia, Russia and Sweden. The most flagrant carriers of French supplies to the Americans were the Dutch, who never missed a commercial opportunity. Their shipping suffered so much harassment by the royal navy that, late in 1780, they threw off the last shreds of friendship with their oldest allies and declared open war on Britain. The coast of western Europe from north Germany to Portugal was now hostile territory. 'Can it be possible,' asked the Austrian foreign minister Kaunitz, 'that Great Britain has determined to quarrel with the whole world?'[108]

Yet even as Britain foundered amid a sea of enemies in Europe, its fortunes seemed to improve in America. Franco-American naval expeditions to capture the British base at Rhode Island in 1778, and to seize the port of Savannah in 1779 – the British having invaded Georgia late in 1778 as part of their new southern strategy – had both failed miserably. In 1778–9, it is true, patriot armies had defeated small British forces in present-day Indiana and Illinois, and ravaged the territory of the Iroquois tribes that had remained loyal to Britain. This is perhaps when Washington, who had ordered the devastation of Iroquois territory, acquired the Indian nickname of 'town destroyer', which is how some Iroquois still refer to a US president. But though many Indian refugees froze or starved to death in the winter of 1779–80, this did not stop Iroquois warriors and loyalists from raiding and killing along the northern frontier.

But Britain's most effective ally, by far, was extreme war fatigue among the Americans. Three years on from the Declaration of Independence, and rampant inflation was hammering the United States much harder than the British ever could. Congress's new currency, the continental dollar, was insufficiently backed by specie or bullion, and by late 1779 was barely worth the paper it was printed on. It was, as one Connecticut Yankee put it, 'Bum Fodder' (toilet paper).[109] A hat now cost $400, a horse $20,000. Washington's soldiers in their customary winter quarters at Valley Forge, Pennsylvania, were reduced to eating dogs and shoe leather.

While Washington struggled to prevent mutinies in the Continental Army, Clinton acted with uncharacteristic vigour. Late in 1779 an expeditionary force of some 9,000 redcoats and loyalist regulars marched through the streets of New York to board an armada of transport ships. Howe had disdained to use loyalist fighters in any formal capacity; Clinton could not afford to be so choosy. The expedition's target was Charleston, on the coast of South Carolina, which it took, along with 6,700 enemy troops, in May 1780, after a four-month siege and a display of exemplary incompetence by the garrison commanders. American fortunes would hit a new low in August, when an army sent to drive the British from South Carolina was itself routed at the battle of Camden, with the loss of 1,900 killed or captured.

Charleston and Camden provided a much-needed tonic back in Britain. The public had had precious few victories to crow about since 1775 – certainly compared with the glory years of 1759–62. Yet any triumph in a war that pitted Protestant Britons against each other was bound to raise conflicting emotions at home. Although many addresses and petitions to Parliament in the mid-1770s had expressed support for coercive measures against the colonists, many also, particularly from those towns and cities with large Dissenter communities, had urged concessions and accommodation. In fact, the war had divided the public as no other overseas conflict had ever done before. What seems to have been a majority of the common people had rallied behind George III and the government in stressing obedience to parliamentary authority, while many (though by no means all) of the middling sort had put more emphasis on defending English liberties throughout the empire. A powerful strand in anti-war thinking had followed the colonists in tracing the root of all evil to Leviathan: 'the Americans have been forced into the present unhappy contest by the new and arbitrary system of government which your Majesty's Ministers have of late years adopted'.[110] The stresses and strains of war stirred all kinds of people, from urban radicals to country gentlemen, to demand reform of Parliament and an end to the ministry's 'system' of corruption and high taxes. There were calls for universal manhood suffrage, even the curtailment of parliamentary sovereignty in line with the Americans' radical interpretation of the Glorious Revolution. Loyalists, of course, branded such talk at a time of national crisis as unpatriotic, even traitorous.

British victories in America in 1780 dampened the public's enthusiasm for bridling Leviathan. Moreover, the widening of hostilities to include France, Spain and the Dutch republic, although disastrous from a military standpoint, broadened the war's appeal in Britain and strengthened the ministry's hand in resisting reform. The Americans' alliance with the French and Spanish, 'our ancient, inveterate and perfidious foes', persuaded a growing number of British people to see the conflict as a patriotic struggle against the forces of popery and universal monarchy.[111]

Scotland was seen as the heartland of British opposition to 'American principles'.[112] The British drew so many recruits either from Scotland or among Scots (particularly Highlanders) who had emigrated to North America that Jefferson, in an early draft of the Declaration of

Independence, had felt moved to include a denunciation of the British for sending over 'not only soldiers of our own blood [Englishmen], but Scotch and other foreign mercenaries'.[113] Ireland too had provided recruits for the war, although many among the Catholic majority still hoped for a French or Spanish invasion and a Jacobite restoration. Ireland's Protestant political leaders generally deplored the war, and sympathised with the Americans' struggle to assert their independence if not necessarily from Britain then certainly from the British Parliament and ministry. By skilfully exploiting anti-war and 'patriot' sentiment on both sides of the Irish Sea they would compel the ministry to allow Ireland free trade with Britain's colonies and, more importantly, legislative independence for the Dublin Parliament.

Britain's desperate need to recruit Scottish and Irish troops to fight in America would spark the worst bout of mob frenzy in eighteenth-century Britain. Anti-Catholic feeling, heightened by war with France and Spain, was given a domestic focus in opposition to the 1778 Papists Act, which removed some of the discrimination against Catholics, including the need to take a religious oath when joining the army. In scenes reminiscent of the mob intimidation at Westminster in 1640–1, a huge crowd descended on the Houses of Parliament in June 1780 to heckle and manhandle MPs and to raise the old cry of 'No Popery'. Heading the protesters was the charismatic (possibly borderline insane) anti-popish campaigner Lord George Gordon. Deputed by a frightened Commons to placate the crowd, he as good as told it to do its worst, whereupon a drunken mob rampaged for several days through the capital, destroying Catholic chapels and private houses, looting distilleries and breaking open prisons (see illus. 24). 'Figure to yourself every man, woman and child in the streets, panic-struck,' wrote one observer, 'the atmosphere red as blood with the ascending fires, muskets firing in every part, and consequently women and children lying sprawling in the streets; all the lower order of people stark mad with liquor, huzzaing and parading with flags.'[114] That the Excise Office and the Bank of England were also attacked is highly revealing – underlining the close connection in people's minds between Leviathan and popish tyranny. The rioters were venting their hatred against an authoritarian state that they believed was subverting traditional Protestant liberties. Order was restored only after the army was called in and opened fire on the rioters, killing 285 and wounding another 200. There were battles in America less bloody than this.

Washington might well have envied North's ministry even as it temporarily lost control of London, for it always had the resources to keep a tight grip on the army. Washington's own army began to mutiny in the winter of 1780–1 over lack of pay and the deplorable conditions at Valley Forge. 'We have no Magazines, nor money,' warned Washington, 'and in a little time we shall have no men.'[115] To the frustration of Jefferson and other American leaders he was, and had long been, obsessed with retaking New York (which is why his army did nothing for three years after 1777), leaving the officer Clinton had put in charge of Britain's southern strategy, General Charles Cornwallis, free to consolidate the British bridgehead in South Carolina and recruit thousands of the colony's slaves and white loyalists. A British advance into North Carolina stalled after two of their armies, one composed entirely of loyalist irregulars, were wiped out in the backcountry at the exceptionally vicious battles of King's Mountain and Cowpens. Soldiers on both sides in these engagements had continued to fire and hack at each other even after quarter had been pleaded for. But aside from worrying signs that the backcountry patriots were more numerous and better led than the coastal loyalists, Clinton and the ministry were confident that the 'rebellion in America [was] . . . at its last gasp'.[116] Crucially, by early 1781 the French were spiralling into bankruptcy almost as rapidly as the Americans were, and were gambling on one last push to win a decisive allied victory. If that failed then the French intended to sue for peace, leaving a truncated United States at the mercy of a victorious Britain. The best course for the British, therefore, would be to sit tight in New York, Georgia and South Carolina, wage a war of attrition against the Americans, and let the republic's plummeting economy and the withdrawal of French support do their work for them. But while General Clinton lacked the confidence to deviate very much from this strategy, Cornwallis was tired of following a 'defensive [plan], mixed with desultory expeditions'.[117] He preferred a bold strike northwards into the heart of the rebellion, to finish it off, once and for all.

In May 1781, Cornwallis took the fateful step of disobeying orders and marching his army north into Virginia. Though his intention had been to force a decisive battle, the enemy would prove too wily and elusive for him, and Virginia loyalists too few or too scared, to justify advancing northwards and effectively abandoning South Carolina to the Americans. By mid-1781, Clinton was expecting a major Franco-American attack on New York, and at first ordered Cornwallis to send him nearly half of his 7,500 troops. Cornwallis refused – and then in July he received a truly bizarre order from Clinton: to deploy his army in fortifying the small tobacco port of Yorktown on the western side of the Chesapeake bay. This time Cornwallis obeyed, even though he realised that could not have 'the smallest influence on the war' and would leave his army 'forever liable to become a prey to a foreign enemy with a temporary superiority at sea'.[118] For once he was prescient.

Clinton's inexplicable decision to leave Cornwallis mouldering in Yorktown was pounced on by Washington and the comte de Rochambeau, general of the French expeditionary army in America. Instead of attacking New York as they had planned, they decided to march their forces towards Virginia. There was still time for Clinton to have Cornwallis's army shipped back to New York, but he never gave the order, and soon it was too late, for on 29 August the entire French Caribbean fleet of almost thirty ships of the line arrived at the entrance to Chesapeake Bay. With a boldness that was more characteristic of the royal navy, the French had achieved naval superiority at exactly the right time and place. The commander of the British squadron in North America, Admiral Thomas Graves, attempted to break the French blockade, but with only nineteen ships of the line he was outmatched. The French fleet was soon joined by a further eight battleships, and all Graves could do was to return to New York and await reinforcements. At this point too, Cornwallis's attacking instincts deserted him, and instead of trying to break out of Yorktown before the net closed around him, he simply stayed put, praying for a miracle that never came. Besieged by 19,000 allied troops, his army subject to merciless bombardment, he was a beaten man, and on 19 October 1781 he surrendered to Washington and Rochambeau. As Cornwallis's dejected troops filed out of Yorktown (or what was left of it) between long rows of French and American soldiers a redcoat band played mournfully in the background, sounding the requiem for British dominion in the Thirteen Colonies.

The French gamble had paid off. It was the allies who had won what would turn out to be the decisive battle of the war over American independence. All Lord North could say when he heard about Yorktown was 'Oh God! It is all over', although from a purely military perspective that was not necessarily true.[119] Britain was still in better shape than its enemies. Financially, the French and Americans were on their knees. And the British still had garrisons in New York, South Carolina and Georgia. All they had done was lose a small army in a secondary theatre of a larger war. But politically, North was right, for Yorktown killed the public's remaining appetite for fighting the Americans. In February

1782 the Commons voted to suspend offensive operations in America, and the following month it authorised the ministry to open peace talks. On 20 March, North resigned.

The war at sea against France and Spain was not over, however, and on it depended the balance of power where it still mattered most: in Europe. An outright British victory in North America had always been unlikely, particularly after the French had joined the fray. The difficulties in waging a land war at thousands of miles' remove, across huge tracts of mountainous and wooded terrain and against a seemingly inexhaustible supply of enemy troops, would have taxed even the great Pitt himself – and Lord North was no Pitt. But the ministry had fewer excuses for losing the naval war as well. Indeed, had the British concentrated their ships in home waters in 1778 they might have inflicted enough damage on the French navy to have all but knocked France out of the war, or at least discouraged the Spanish from joining in as well. Instead, the ministry had sent squadrons off on wild goose chases around the globe and left Britain dangerously open to invasion. Of all the disasters that the ministry had courted by this wayward strategy, Yorktown was actually something of a let-off.

It was only after the war in America was effectively over that the British began to claw back their lost naval superiority. In April 1782, Admiral Rodney, with thirty-six ships of the line, defeated a French fleet of thirty-three ships at the battle of Saintes, off Dominica, thereby averting a massive Franco-Spanish invasion of Jamaica. In October 1782 a British fleet commanded by Admiral Richard Howe (General Howe's younger brother) faced down a superior Spanish force and relieved the besieged Gibraltar. And in the Indian Ocean a British squadron, though often outnumbered by enemy warships, did enough to help the governor-general of Bengal, Warren Hastings, repel the French and the Marathas (though the British suffered several heavy defeats on land, notably at the hands of the formidable Haidar Ali, ruler of the kingdom of Mysore in southern India). These naval actions ensured that Britain would enter peace talks with the allies in a stronger position than she had enjoyed after the debacle at Yorktown.

Britain's overriding objective in the negotiations was to separate the Americans from the French as quickly as possible. An independent America was a major blow to British power and prestige; an independent America aligned permanently with France would tip the European balance of power decisively in Versailles's favour. This was certainly the view of Britain's new prime minister, the earl of Shelburne, who assumed charge of the negotiations on the British side. After protracted talks the combatants hammered out a peace deal, which they signed in Paris on 23 September 1783 – twenty years after the first treaty of Paris that had ended the Seven Years War. By the terms of the 1783 treaty, the British ceded every one of the Thirteen Colonies to the United States, which they now recognised as an independent sovereign nation. They also handed back Minorca and East Florida to the Spanish, and returned to the French a few of their former settlements in India, although without undermining Britain's status as the dominant European power on the subcontinent. However, the British kept Canada and Gibraltar, and were handed back most of their sugar islands in the Caribbean. The last British troops in America sailed from Long Island and Staten Island on 4 December 1783. Washington delivered up his commission to Congress on 23 December amid scenes of high emotion, and returned home, to Mount Vernon, in time for Christmas.

The British fixation on the balance of power in Europe explains, if it does not excuse, why they abandoned many of their Indian allies by ceding to the United States all the territory from the Appalachians out to the Mississippi River. Over the next fifty years the States would subjugate or eradicate all the Indians living in this vast new American interior. The British government would at least make some effort towards compensating the 60,000 or so white loyalists who had fled the United States, mostly for a much less comfortable life in Canada and the West Indies.

The treaty of Paris was a colossal humiliation for Britain. Like France in 1763, Britain had lost more than half of its empire. France, of course, regained much of the prestige she had forfeited in 1763. Even so, Britain's position in the West Indies and India was little affected by the treaty, and American independence would do no permanent damage to British trade with the United States. Moreover, thanks to Shelburne's success during the treaty negotiations in prising apart the French and Americans there was no great alteration in the European balance of power. The international repercussions of losing the war would do less harm to the national interest than the several years of chronic political instability that followed Lord North's resignation. Defeat to the Americans was widely blamed upon the insidious influence of Leviathan – briefly opening a window for measures to reduce the number of public offices and pensions at the government's disposal. George tried to hold firm against peacemakers and reformers alike, but as Lord North had warned him: 'The torrent is too strong to be resisted.'[120] As it turned out, the king need not have worried. Within a few years the political establishment had rallied and stifled moves for further reform, and the British people would recover from the loss of the Thirteen Colonies with similar alacrity. Indeed, there was almost a sense of relief at offloading this heavy imperial burden. Even George quickly came to terms with American independence, consoling himself with the thought that 'knavery seems to be so much the striking feature of the inhabitants [of America], that it may not in the end be an evil that they will become aliens to this kingdom'.[121]

EPILOGUE

On 28 August 1782 the *Royal George* was anchored off Portsmouth for routine repairs before she sailed with Admiral Howe's fleet to relieve Gibraltar. As she was being heeled over to work on her hull something went wrong – either her officers were negligent or some of her timbers broke – and water flooded through her gun ports and she quickly sank. Down with her went most of the crew, their visiting relatives, and the tradesmen and prostitutes who were on board at the time selling their wares. Over 800 people were drowned, making the sinking of the *Royal George* one of the most serious maritime disasters in British waters.

The loss of the *Royal George* added to the mood of national despondency that had settled on Britain after Yorktown. Yet if any moralists were tempted to draw parallels between the ship's fate and that of the empire she had helped to create, they wisely refrained. The British lion was not dead yet. Indeed, rarely has a country fared so well in the wake of catastrophe as Britain did after 1781. Even in defeat she remained Europe's greatest, certainly its most resilient, maritime and economic power. Neither the American war, nor the much more gruelling ones to follow against revolutionary and Napoleonic France, would deflect her progress towards the industrial revolution. By the time peace was restored to Europe after the battle of Waterloo in 1815, Britain's allies and rivals were too exhausted to challenge her dominance of the world economy.

It had not always been so, of course. No judicious observer of European affairs in 1485 would have predicted a glittering imperial future for the British and Irish peoples. Ireland at that time was ruled by warlords who either held the English crown in contempt or used its authority to beat down their rivals. Fifteenth-century Scotland may have been a paragon of monarchical stability compared with its southern neighbour, but the Renaissance sophistication of its court culture belied the kingdom's political and economic backwardness. England was a fallen realm, with seemingly further still to drop. The days when an

Edward III or Henry V could conquer French dukedoms and humble the flower of European chivalry were over. Bosworth was a victory for the French as much as for Henry VII. It put a king on England's throne who knew that invading France was a dangerous diversion from the unfinished business of winning the Wars of the Roses for the House of Tudor. His eventual triumph would allow Henry VIII to think and, occasionally, act like his Plantagenet heroes, but all the plundered wealth of England's magnificent medieval Church could not sustain that dream. His main legacy would not be a new continental empire but the English Reformation, and the strong navy needed to defend it.

The Reformation sprang from Henry VIII's desperate desire for a male heir, and it survived by the mere dynastic chance of Mary I's untimely death (which also helped to secure the Scottish Reformation) and Elizabeth I's longevity. Had Elizabeth died before the 1580s then England would surely have been torn apart by religious strife just as France had been. With precious time to grow, Protestantism fused with English and Scottish national identity, and in so doing sundered Britain from Ireland and from Europe's new Catholic superpower: Habsburg Spain. The Dutch revolt brought Spanish *tercios* into the Low Countries – too close for comfort across the Narrow Seas. England could not sit out Europe's wars of religion – or so argued some Elizabethan politicians and adventurers – not while the Protestant cause hung in the balance. The English must return to the Continent with fire and sword, but this time not for conquest or glory but to lead the crusade against Antichrist and save Christendom from Habsburg tyranny. They must use their naval superiority to build a transatlantic English empire that would cut off Spanish power at source. But Elizabeth was not convinced. She expended just enough on sustaining Dutch and French Protestantism to defend England – no more. Ireland was finally conquered only because it had become another front in the war with Spain. One violent Tudor frontier had nonetheless been eradicated, or so it was hoped. And another dynastic accident – Elizabeth's refusal to produce an heir – would lead to the succession in 1603 of James VI of Scotland and the union of the Tudor and Stuart crowns.

That James succeeded to a kingdom which was still not a front-rank power did not trouble him unduly. The problem was that his English subjects expected it to act like one. Defeating the Armada had persuaded them that the national interest meant more than simply defending the realm. What the public wanted, particularly after the outbreak of the Thirty Years War in 1618, was vigorous action in the Protestant cause.

James, on the other hand, wanted peace and a Spanish match. The quarrel between him and his critics over these issues was complicated by the ideological divide that Europe's wars of religion had opened up in British politics between 'patriots' and 'royalists' – or as they preferred to see each other, 'popular' pro-Dutch dissidents and popish pro-Spanish stooges. James distrusted Parliament, the focus for popular questioning of his policies. Parliament-men doubted his commitment to fighting popery and upholding English liberties, the most cherished of which was the medieval convention that the crown could not impose taxes without parliamentary consent.

Until the monarchy bowed to 'popularity', England would remain incapable of effective intervention on the Continent. After several years of military humiliation at the hands of the Spanish and French, Charles I reached the same conclusion, and made peace. There were some in Britain who looked enviously at the small yet mighty Dutch republic and offered to make Charles similarly formidable, but only in the service of the Protestant cause. This bargain – military glory abroad in return for a popular state at home – was not one that he was willing to make. His own experiment in strong government would end disastrously with the setting up of a Scottish republic in the late 1630s. But the champions of a Protestant commonwealth in England would have their chance only when it was too late, when fighting popery demanded not a continental crusade but defending Parliament in a war against their own king. Their political and financial revolution would transform England in a matter of just a few years from an underpowered monarchy into an all-conquering war machine.

The birth of 'this monster of the STATE' had traumatic consequences for anyone who got in its way.[1] Leviathan crushed its English, Irish and Scottish enemies, and then defeated the Dutch, England's great trading rivals. The Navigation Act of 1651 – a major cause of the Anglo-Dutch war – represented the extension of this aggressive state-building to maritime policy, and would help to drive England's rapid colonial and commercial expansion thereafter. Only belatedly, under Cromwell, was Leviathan turned against Spain, and by that time it was the French who posed the greater threat to Europe's Protestants.

Charles II kept as much of the parliamentary state as was politically and financially practical. He did not need its ruinously high taxes and large standing army because, like his father and grandfather, he had no interest in combating popery. Quite the reverse, for he was a client of the French king Louis XIV, who was the very epitome in Protestant eyes of popish tyranny. James II found the idea of French-style government even more alluring, and paid for it with his crown. The Glorious Revolution that replaced James with the Dutch stadholder William of Orange in 1688–9 was swift and relatively bloodless, at least in England and its colonies. Defending the revolution was anything but. Ireland had to be reconquered, and Scottish nationalism neutralised through an incorporating union in 1707.

What made the revolution truly glorious in the eyes of many English people, however, was their new king's readiness to lead the realm against continental popery. William was already committed to this struggle, and the price he was willing to pay for the resources to resist Louis was the revival and extension of the 'popular', parliamentary state of the mid-seventeenth century. Parliament reaffirmed its control over all forms of taxation, while its grandee managers again encroached inexorably upon the crown's powers. Once the English had finally gained a monarch fit for purpose, and had grafted Dutch financial methods onto the root-stock of their own revolution in government since the 1640s, war and money would do the rest.

The cost to the public of permanent parliamentary government and the massive bureaucracy needed to administer the fiscal–military state was measured not only in high taxes. The alarming spectacle of court popery gave way, as it had in the 1640s, to one of political corruption and partisanship. Making the new system work would require British statesmen to encourage and exploit these insidious forces. But though the public revelled in the superpower status and the 'empire of the seas' that Leviathan conferred, they never accepted the political arts needed to maintain it.

The new-modelled state that emerged in Britain between 1637 and 1707 became the chief component in a series of European alliances that succeeded first in checking the power of France and then, in the Seven Years War (1757–63), comprehensively defeating it. Given the disparity in population between the two leading combatants it is little wonder that many Britons saw this victory as the work of divine providence. But it was the combination of their own desire to defeat popery, and the legitimacy that Parliament possessed to impose the necessary taxes, that proved decisive. With compliant taxpayers and a comparatively accountable political system, the government was able to raise huge public loans, both in real terms and relative to the British population. A ratio of military expenditure to income that no developed state today would dare even contemplate produced a navy so powerful that it eventually allowed the British to dominate global commerce and acquire the greatest empire ever seen. Trade and colonies, in turn, generated resources vital for sustaining government spending and nourishing urban and manufacturing growth. By the 1760s the British were the most prosperous people in the world, and their unflinching war on popery was helping to create many of the economic and social preconditions for the industrial revolution.

The timing of England's reimmersion in European power politics was also crucial to the long-term success of the British state. Protected by the Channel and their navy, the English largely escaped the crushing military and financial pressures imposed by Europe's wars of religion. When they finally joined the race for colonial empire in earnest (in the 1650s), and returned in force to the Continent (in the 1690s), they had experienced a Reformation and civil wars that had weakened or toppled many of the internal barriers to a powerful Protestant state. Moreover, by arriving fortuitously late upon the scene they had avoided the debts, the bloated, self-serving bureaucracies and the entrenched aristocratic interests that incessant warfare had bred in their rivals. They entered the wars against France, therefore, with a relatively underexploited tax base and a strong, centralised and publicly approved government, eager for the fight. The kingdom that the French had regularly humbled since the mid-fifteenth century was all set to return the compliment.

Britain's 'first' empire of 1600–1775 had been created by the forces of the European state system, and it would be destroyed by them. British ministers, their eyes fixed firmly on the balance of power in Europe, had paid little attention to the colonies before the 1750s, but the unstable mix of peoples and territories acquired in the Seven Years War convinced them that a more integrated empire was vital to Britain's strategic interests. Thus the fateful decision was taken to transport Leviathan across the Atlantic to bring greater order and financial accountability to the Thirteen Colonies. Nothing had prepared the colonists for this close encounter with the British state. Their inability to accept its sudden intrusion upon their lives, and the ministry's inability to imagine exerting British authority in any other way, made war inevitable. French intervention clinched victory for the Americans at the last gasp, and Britain lost half its empire. Yet far from destroying Anglo-American trade, as was feared, Independence actually led to an increase in the flow of goods across the Atlantic. It was France that suffered most by the British defeat at Yorktown. Fighting the American War of Independence had further weakened its stricken economy, leaving the

Bourbon monarchy discredited politically as well as financially. The *ancien régime* was already tottering when the French Revolution struck in 1789.

Whitehall's drive for imperial integration failed ignominiously in America, to be sure. But this same basic strategy gave rise to an even greater 'second' empire in India, Africa and Australasia. Ireland too was tied more firmly to the British state with the 1800 acts of union – essentially an Anglo-Irish version of the 1707 incorporating union with Scotland – to create the United Kingdom of Great Britain and Ireland. Losing the American colonies convinced the British that they had, if anything, been too indulgent of colonial freedoms. They would run a tighter imperial ship in future, and take a more hierarchical and racialised view of those they governed. Never again would Britons think of colonial subjects as equals, or regard any part of the empire as an extension of their own Protestant homeland.

Having won and now lost America in Europe, George III's ministers were anxious to renew old friendships on the Continent. Before the French Revolution set Europe ablaze in the early 1790s they had managed to rebuild Britain's alliances with Prussia, Austria and the Dutch republic. The revolutionaries' violent renunciation of Catholicism would make it impossible to persist with the old assumption of a French-led popish plot against European Protestantism. In fact, the British ruling classes increasingly came to regard the Catholic religion as a conservative bulwark against the rising tide of atheism and revolution (although this change of outlook was less evident in Ireland, where the old religious hatreds still smouldered). For the first time in over two centuries, anti-popery ceased to have a major bearing on the public's perception of Britain's international relations.

In the 1760s and 1770s, another established feature of British political life disappeared: the substantial overlap between radical reformism and support for the imperial project. Authoritarian rule in Canada and India, and war against Protestant patriots in America, persuaded middle-class radicals that the empire was a corrupt and oppressive enterprise, a tool of Leviathan. Some now espoused enlightened internationalism, or supported rights for Catholics. All of them washed their hands of the plebeian mobs that they had once incited in the name of empire, Protestant liberties and 'No popery'. In the aftermath of defeat in America the polite classes would take refuge in renewed campaigns of moral and social reform – most notably, the movement to abolish slavery. Abolitionism afforded pious Britons the luxury of believing that their empire could, after all, be an enlightened and beneficent project.

The fight against slavery found influential support among a new breed of upper-class evangelicals. William Pitt the younger (1759–1806), the prime minister for much of Britain's struggle against revolutionary and Napoleonic France, had friends among this priggish and puritanical set. His moral integrity and innocence of character helped make him the hero of the respectable middle classes, and contrasted sharply with the vulgarity and extravagance of his early Georgian predecessor, Walpole.

Britain's ruling elite cleaned up its act in the late eighteenth century. The need to appease middle-class opinion inspired a retreat from the aristocratic excesses of an earlier age into a world of domestic felicity and attention to stern duty. Gentlemen now dressed more soberly than ever, and stopped wearing swords in civilian life. They thought less about exhibiting refined sentiment and good manners and more about appearing scrupulously religious and public-spirited. Drained of its remaining moral content, politeness would give way in the nineteenth century to the narrower ideal of 'etiquette', mere outward civility.

The French Revolution provoked a more searching and broad-based critique of Leviathan, as well as a stronger resolve to defend the old order. It was only with the final defeat of France in 1815 that the British set about the wholesale modernisation of the fiscal–military state. And even then it was not until the 1830s and 1840s, and above all with the Reform Act of 1832, that the campaign against 'old corruption' would dismantle what remained of Britain's early modern war machine. The result, by the mid-nineteenth century, would be a minimalist state and a commitment among the patrician class to cheap and responsible government in the service of the public. Leviathan had breathed its last.

BIBLIOGRAPHY

Principal secondary works consulted

General

Asch, Ronald G., Adolf M. Birke (eds), *Princes, Patronage, and the Nobility: The Court at the Beginning of the Modern Age c.1450–1650* (Oxford: Oxford University Press, 1991)

Ashworth, William J., *Customs and Excise: Trade, Production, and Consumption in England 1640–1845* (Oxford: Oxford University Press, 2003)

Berg, Maxine, 'French Fancy and Cool Britannia: the Fashion Markets of Early Modern Europe', *Proceedings of the Istituto Internazionale di Storia Economica*, 32 (2001)

Borsay, Peter, *The English Urban Renaissance: Culture and Society in the Provincial Town 1660–1770* (Oxford: Oxford University Press, 1991)

Braddick, Michael J., *State Formation in Early Modern England c.1550–1700* (Cambridge: Cambridge University Press, 2000)

Brenner, Robert, *Merchants and Revolution: Commercial Change, Political Conflict, and London's Overseas Traders, 1550–1653* (Cambridge: Cambridge University Press, 1993)

Burgess, Glenn, *British Political Thought, 1500–1660: The Politics of the Post-Reformation* (Basingstoke: Palgrave Macmillan, 2009)

Claydon, Tony, *Europe and the Making of England, 1660–1760* (Cambridge: Cambridge University Press, 2007)

Collins, James B., *The State in Early Modern France* (Cambridge: Cambridge University Press, 1995)

Corfield, P. J., *The Impact of English Towns 1700–1800* (Oxford: Oxford University Press, 1982)

Cromartie, Allan, *The Constitutionalist Revolution: An Essay on the History of England, 1450–1642* (Cambridge: Cambridge University Press, 2006)

Donoghue, Joseph (ed.), *The Cambridge History of the British Theatre*, vol. 2, *1660 to 1895* (Cambridge: Cambridge University Press, 2004)

Ellis, Steven G., 'The Collapse of the Gaelic World, 1450–1650', *Irish Historical Studies*, 31 (1999)

Erskine, Caroline, Roger A. Mason (eds), *George Buchanan: Political Thought in Early Modern Britain and Europe* (Farnham: Ashgate, 2012)

Escosura, Leandro Prado de la (ed.), *Exceptionalism and Industrialisation: Britain and its European Rivals, 1688–1815* (Cambridge: Cambridge University Press, 2004)

Ferguson, Niall (ed.), *Virtual History: Alternatives and Counterfactuals* (London: Picador, 1997)

Fincham, Kenneth, Nicholas Tyacke, *Altars Restored: The Changing Face of English Religious Worship, 1547–c.1700* (Oxford: Oxford University Press, 2007)

Floud, Roderick, Paul Johnson (eds), *The Cambridge Economic History of Modern Britain*, vol. 1, *Industrialisation, 1700–1860* (Cambridge: Cambridge University Press, 2004)

Gunn, Steven, David Grummitt and Hans Cools, *War, State, and Society in England and the Netherlands 1477–1559* (Oxford: Oxford University Press, 2007)

Halliday, Paul D., *Dismembering the Body Politic: Partisan Politics in England's Towns 1650–1730* (Cambridge: Cambridge University Press, 1998)

Harris, Tim (ed.), *The Politics of the Excluded, c.1500–1850* (Basingstoke: Palgrave Macmillan, 2001)

Heal, Felicity, Clive Holmes, *The Gentry in England and Wales 1500–1700* (London: Macmillan, 1994)

Hindle, Steve, *The State and Social Change in Early Modern England, 1550–1640* (Basingstoke: Palgrave Macmillan, 2002)

Hutton, Ronald, *The Rise and Fall of Merry England: The Ritual Year 1400–1700* (Oxford: Oxford University Press, 1994)

Israel, Jonathan, *The Dutch Republic: its Rise, Greatness, and Fall 1477–1806* (Oxford: Oxford University Press, 1998)

Kearney, Hugh, *The British Isles: A History of Four Nations* (Cambridge: Cambridge University Press, 2nd edn 2006)

Lake, Peter, Steven Pincus (eds), *The Politics of the Public Sphere in Early Modern England* (Manchester: Manchester University Press, 2007)

MacCulloch, Diarmaid, *Reformation: Europe's House Divided 1490–1700* (London: Allen Lane, Penguin, 2004)

Manning, Roger B., *An Apprenticeship in Arms: The Origins of the British Army 1585–1702* (Oxford: Oxford University Press, 2006)

Marshall, Peter, Alec Ryrie (eds), *The Beginnings of English Protestantism* (Cambridge: Cambridge University Press, 2002)

Mason, Roger (ed.), *Scotland and England 1286–1815* (Edinburgh: John Donald, 1987)

Milling, Jane, Peter Thomson (eds), *The Cambridge History of the British Theatre,* vol. 1, *Origins to 1660* (Cambridge: Cambridge University Press, 2004)

Morrill, John (ed.), *The Oxford Illustrated History of Tudor and Stuart Britain* (Oxford: Oxford University Press, 1996)

Munck, Thomas, *Seventeenth-Century Europe: State, Conflict and Social Order in Europe 1598–1700* (London: Palgrave Macmillan, 2nd edn 2005)

O'Brien, Patrick K., Philip A. Hunt, 'The Rise of a Fiscal State in England, 1485–1815', *Historical Research,* 66 (1993)

O'Brien, Patrick, 'Political preconditions for the Industrial Revolution', in O'Brien, Roland Quinault (eds), *The Industrial Revolution and British Society* (Cambridge: Cambridge University Press, 1993)

——, Philip Hunt, 'Excises and the rise of a fiscal state in England, 1586–1688', in W. M. Ormrod, Margaret Bonney and Richard Bonney (eds), *Crises, Revolutions and Self-sustained Growth: Essays in European Fiscal History, 1130–1830* (Stamford: Shaun Tyas, 1999)

——, 'Mercantilism and Imperialism in the Rise and Decline of the Dutch and British Economies 1585–1815', *De Economist,* 148 (2000)

——, 'The nature and historical evolution of an exceptional fiscal state and its possible significance for the precocious commercialization and industrialization of the British economy from Cromwell to Nelson', *Economic History Review,* 64 (2011)

Parker, Geoffrey (ed.), *The Cambridge History of Warfare* (Cambridge: Cambridge University Press, 2005)

Pocock, J. G. A. (ed.), *The Varieties of British Political Thought 1500–1800* (Cambridge: Cambridge University Press, 1993)

Pryce, Huw, John Watts (eds), *Power and Identity in the Middle Ages: Essays in Memory of Rees Davies* (Oxford: Oxford University Press, 2007)

Robertson, John, *The Case for the Enlightenment: Scotland and Naples, 1680–1760* (Cambridge: Cambridge University Press, 2005)

Rodger, N. A. M., *The Safeguard of the Seas: A Naval History of Britain 660–1649* (London: HarperCollins, 1997)

——, *The Command of the Ocean: A Naval History of Britain 1649–1815* (London: Allen Lane, Penguin, 2005)

Rowlands, Guy, *The Dynastic State and the Army under Louis XIV: Royal Service and Private Interest, 1661 to 1701* (Cambridge: Cambridge University Press, 2002)

Scott, Jonathan, *When the Waves Ruled Britannia: Geography and Political Identities, 1500–1800* (Cambridge: Cambridge University Press, 2011)

Shagan, Ethan H., *The Rule of Moderation: Violence, Religion and the Politics of Restraint in Early Modern England* (Cambridge: Cambridge University Press, 2011)

Shapin, Steven, *The Scientific Revolution* (Chicago: University of Chicago Press, 1996)

Sheehan, M., 'The Development of British Theory and Practice of the Balance of Power before 1714', *History*, 73 (1988)

Slack, Paul, *From Reformation to Improvement: Public Welfare in Early Modern England* (Oxford: Oxford University Press, 1999)

Starkey, David (ed.), *The English Court from the Wars of the Roses to the Civil War* (Harlow: Longman, 1987)

Stone, Lawrence (ed.), *An Imperial State at War: Britain from 1689 to 1815* (London: Routledge, 1994)

Sutherland, N. M., 'The Origins of the Thirty Years War and the Structure of European Politics', *English Historical Review*, 107 (1992)

Todd, Margo, *Christian Humanism and the Puritan Social Order* (Cambridge: Cambridge University Press, 1987)

Warner, Jessica, 'The naturalisation of beer and gin in early modern England', *Contemporary Drug Problems*, 24 (1997)

Whyte, Ian D., *Scotland's Society and Economy in Transition, c.1500–c.1760* (Basingstoke: Macmillan, 1997)

Withington, Phil, *The Politics of the Commonwealth: Citizens and Freemen in Early Modern England* (Cambridge: Cambridge University Press, 2005)

——, *Society in Early Modern England: The Vernacular Origins of Some Powerful Ideas* (Cambridge: Polity Press, 2010)

Wrigley, E. Anthony, 'Urban Growth and Agricultural Change: England and the Continent in the Early Modern Period', *Journal of Interdisciplinary History*, 15 (1985)

Britain and Ireland, 1485–1603

Barron, Caroline M., 'Church music in English towns 1450–1550: an interim report', *Urban History*, 29 (2002)

Beer, Barrett L., 'Seymour, Edward, duke of Somerset [known as Protector Somerset]', *Oxford Dictionary of National Biography*

Bernard, G. W., *Power and Politics in Tudor England* (Aldershot: Ashgate, 2000)

——, *The King's Reformation: Henry VIII and the Remaking of the English Church* (New Haven, Conn.: Yale University Press, 2005)

Bowler, Gerald, '"An axe or an acte": the Parliament of 1572 and resistance theory in early Elizabethan England', *Canadian Journal of History*, 19 (1984)

Brigden, Susan, *New Worlds, Lost Worlds: The Rule of the Tudors 1485–1603* (London: Allen Lane, Penguin, 2000)

Burgess, Clive, Andrew Wathey, 'Mapping the Soundscape: Church Music in English Towns, 1450–1550', *Early Music History*, 19 (2000)

Canny, Nicholas, 'O'Neill, Hugh [Aodh Ó Néill], second earl of Tyrone', *Oxford Dictionary of National Biography*

Collinson, Patrick, *The Elizabethan Puritan Movement* (London: Jonathan Cape, 1967)

——, *The Birthpangs of Protestant England: Religious and Cultural Change in the Sixteenth and Seventeenth Centuries* (Basingstoke: Macmillan, 1988)

—— (ed.), *The Sixteenth Century 1485–1603* (Oxford: Oxford University Press, 2002)

——, 'Elizabeth I', *Oxford Dictionary of National Biography*

Croft, Pauline, 'Trading with the Enemy 1585–1604', *Historical Journal*, 32 (1989)

Cunningham, Sean, 'Loyalty and the usurper: recognizances, the council and allegiance under Henry VII', *Historical Research*, 82 (2009)

Currin, John M., '"The King's Army into the Partes of Bretaigne": Henry VII and the Breton Wars, 1489–1491', *War in History*, 7 (2000)

Daniell, David, 'Tyndale, William', *Oxford Dictionary of National Biography*

Davies, C. S. L., John Edwards, 'Katherine [Catalina, Catherine, Katherine of Aragon]', *Oxford Dictionary of National Biography*

Doran, Susan, Glenn Richardson (eds), *Tudor England and its Neighbours* (Basingstoke: Palgrave Macmillan, 2005)

Duffy, Eamon, *The Stripping of the Altars: Traditional Religion in England 1400–1580* (New Haven, Conn.: Yale University Press, 2005)

Ellis, Steven G., *Ireland in the Age of the Tudors 1447–1603* (Harlow: Longman, 1998)

——, 'Fitzgerald, Gerald, eighth earl of Kildare', *Oxford Dictionary of National Biography*

——, 'Fitzgerald, Gerald, ninth earl of Kildare', *Oxford Dictionary of National Biography*

Gajda, Alexandra, 'The State of Christendom: history, political thought and the Essex circle', *Historical Research*, 81 (2008)

——, 'Debating War and Peace in Late Elizabethan England', *Historical Journal*, 52 (2009)

——, *The Earl of Essex and Late Elizabethan Political Culture* (Oxford: Oxford University Press, 2012)

Graves, Michael A. R., *Henry VIII: A Study in Kingship* (Harlow: Pearson, Longman, 2003)

Grummitt, David, 'Henry VII, Chamber Finance, and the "New Monarchy": some new Evidence', *Historical Research*, 72 (1999)

——, 'The Defence of Calais and the Development of Gunpowder Weaponry in England in the Late Fifteenth Century', *War in History*, 7 (2000)

—— (ed.), *The English Experience in France c.1450–1558: War, Diplomacy and Cultural Exchange* (Aldershot: Ashgate, 2002)

——, 'Household, politics and political morality in the reign of Henry VII', *Historical Research*, 82 (2009)

Gunn, S. J., 'The Duke of Suffolk's March on Paris in 1523', *English Historical Review*, 101 (1986)

——, 'The Courtiers of Henry VII', *English Historical Review*, 108 (1993)

——, 'Henry VII', *Oxford Dictionary of National Biography*

——, 'Lovell, Sir Thomas', *Oxford Dictionary of National Biography*

——, 'Warbeck, Perkin', *Oxford Dictionary of National Biography*

Gunn, Steven, 'Henry VII in Context: Problems and Possibilities', *History*, 92 (2007)

Guy, John, *Tudor England* (Oxford: Oxford University Press, 1988)

Haigh, Christopher, *Elizabeth I* (3rd edn, Harlow: Pearson, Longman, 2001)

Hammer, Paul E. J., 'The Use of Scholarship: the Secretariat of Robert Devereux, Second Earl of Essex, c.1585–1601', *English Historical Review*, 109 (1994)

——, *The Polarisation of Elizabethan Politics: The Political Career of*

Robert Devereux, 2nd Earl of Essex, 1585–1597 (Cambridge: Cambridge University Press, 1999)

——, *Elizabeth's Wars: War, Government and Society in Tudor England, 1544–1604* (Basingstoke: Palgrave Macmillan, 2003)

——, 'Devereux, Robert, second earl of Essex', *Oxford Dictionary of National Biography*

Hanson, Neil, *The Confident Hope of a Miracle: The True History of the Spanish Armada* (London: Doubleday, 2004)

Harriss, Gerald, 'Political Society and the Growth of Government in Late Medieval England', *Past and Present*, 138 (1993)

Hicks, Michael, *The Wars of the Roses* (New Haven, Conn.: Yale University Press, 2012)

Hoak, Dale, 'Edward VI', *Oxford Dictionary of National Biography*

Horowitz, Mark R., 'Henry Tudor's treasure', *Historical Research*, 82 (2009)

——, 'Policy and prosecution in the reign of Henry VII', *Historical Research*, 82 (2009)

Horrox, Rosemary, 'Richard III', *Oxford Dictionary of National Biography*

Ives, E. W., 'Anne [Anne Boleyn]', *Oxford Dictionary of National Biography*

——, 'Henry VIII', *Oxford Dictionary of National Biography*

Jack, Sybil M., 'Wolsey, Thomas', *Oxford Dictionary of National Biography*

Jones, Evan T., 'Alwyn Ruddock: "John Cabot and the Discovery of America"', *Historical Research*, 81 (2008)

Keay, Anna, *The Magnificent Monarch: Charles II and the Ceremonies of Power* (London: Continuum, 2008)

Kelsey, Harry, 'Drake, Sir Francis', *Oxford Dictionary of National Biography*

Leithead, Howard, 'Cromwell, Thomas, earl of Essex', *Oxford Dictionary of National Biography*

Lock, Julian, 'Grey, Arthur, fourteenth Baron Grey of Wilton', *Oxford Dictionary of National Biography*

Macdougall, Norman, *An Antidote to the English: The Auld Alliance, 1295–1560* (East Linton: The Tuckwell Press, 2001)

Matusiak, John, 'Puissance and Poverty: Henry VIII and the Conquest of France', *History Review*, 64 (2009)

McDermott, James, *England & the Spanish Armada: The Necessary Quarrel* (New Haven, Conn.: Yale University Press, 2005)

McDiarmid, John F. (ed.), *The Monarchical Republic of Early*

Modern England: Essays in Response to Patrick Collinson (Aldershot: Ashgate, 2007)

McSheffrey, Shannon, 'Heresy, Orthodoxy and English Vernacular Religion 1480–1525', *Past and Present*, 186 (2005)

Morgan, Basil, 'Hawkins, Sir John', *Oxford Dictionary of National Biography*

Morgan, Hiram, '"Never any realm worse governed": Queen Elizabeth and Ireland', *Transactions of the Royal Historical Society*, sixth series, 14 (2004)

——, 'Essex and Ireland before 1599' (paper given at the Tudor–Stuart midsummer seminar at the Institute of Historical Research, London, 16 Aug. 2010)

Nicholls, Mark, Penry Williams, 'Ralegh, Sir Walter', *Oxford Dictionary of National Biography*

Parker, Geoffrey, *The Grand Strategy of Philip II* (New Haven, Conn.: Yale University Press, 2000)

Penn, Thomas, *Winter King: The Dawn of Tudor England* (London: Allen Lane, Penguin, 2012)

Pollard, A. J., *The Wars of the Roses* (Basingstoke: Palgrave Macmillan, 2001)

Potter, David, 'Anglo-French Relations 1500: the Aftermath of the Hundred Years War', *Journal of Franco-British Studies*, 28 (1999)

Quinn, David B., 'Columbus and the North: England, Iceland, and Ireland', *William and Mary Quarterly*, third series, 49 (1992)

Richardson, Glenn (ed.), *'The Contending Kingdoms': England and France 1420–1700* (Aldershot: Ashgate, 2008)

Rigby, S. H. (ed.), *Blackwell Companion to Britain in the Later Middle Ages* (Oxford: Blackwell, 2003)

Riordan, Michael, 'Henry VIII, privy chamber of', *Oxford Dictionary of National Biography*

Roberts, Peter R., 'Henry VIII, Francis I and the Reformation Parliament', *Parliaments, Estates and Representation*, 27 (2007)

Rodger, N. A. M., 'Queen Elizabeth and the Myth of Sea-power in English History', *Transactions of the Royal Historical Society*, sixth series, 14 (2004)

Ryrie, Alec, *The Age of Reformation: The Tudor and Stewart Realms 1485–1603* (Harlow: Pearson, Longman, 2009)

Salmon, J. H. M., *The French Religious Wars in English Political Thought* (Oxford: Oxford University Press, 1959)

Shagan, Ethan H., 'Protector Somerset and the 1549 Rebellions:

New Sources and New Perspectives', *English Historical Review*, 114 (1999)

Smuts, Malcolm, "'Patriot Essex" and his concept of the state' (paper given at the Tudor–Stuart midsummer seminar at the Institute of Historical Research, London, 16 Aug. 2010)

Sutton, Anne F., *The Mercery of London: Trade, Goods and People, 1130–1578* (Aldershot: Ashgate, 2005)

Tittler, Robert, Norman Jones (eds), *Blackwell Companion to Tudor Britain* (Oxford: Blackwell, 2004)

Trim, David, 'Calvinist Internationalism and the English Officer Corps, 1562–1642', *History Compass*, 4 (2006)

Tucker, Penny, 'Reaction to Henry VII's style of kingship and its contribution to the emergence of constitutional monarchy in England', *Historical Research*, 82 (2009)

Watts, John L. (ed.), *The End of the Middle Ages? England in the Fifteenth and Sixteenth Centuries* (Stroud: Sutton, 1998)

Weikel, Anne, 'Mary I', *Oxford Dictionary of National Biography*

Wells, Stanley, *Shakespeare and Co.: Christopher Marlowe, Thomas Dekker, Ben Jonson, Thomas Middleton, John Fletcher, and the Other Players in His Story* (London: Allen Lane, Penguin, 2006)

Worden, Blair, *The Sound of Virtue: Philip Sidney's Arcadia and Elizabethan Politics* (New Haven, Conn.: Yale University Press, 1996)

Britain and Ireland, 1603–1714

Adams, Simon Lester, 'The Protestant Cause: Religious Alliance with the West European Calvinist Communities as a Political Issue in England, 1585–1630' (Oxford D.Phil. thesis 1973)

Adamson, John, *The Noble Revolt: The Overthrow of Charles I* (London: Phoenix, 2009)

—— (ed.), *The English Civil War: Conflict and Contexts, 1640–49* (London: Palgrave Macmillan, 2009)

Andrews, Kenneth R., *Ships, Money & Politics: Seafaring and Naval Enterprise in the Reign of Charles I* (Cambridge: Cambridge University Press, 1991)

Baron, Sabrina Alcorn, "'The Board did not Think Fit and Order": the structure and function of the Privy Council of Charles I, c.1625–41, with Special Reference to the Personal Rule' (University of Chicago Ph.D. thesis 1995)

Bosher, J. F., 'The Franco-Catholic Danger, 1660–1715', *History*, 79 (1994)

Braddick, M. J., *Parliamentary Taxation in 17th-Century England: Local Administration and Response* (Woodbridge: Boydell, 1994)

Brown, Keith M., *Kingdom or Province?: Scotland and the Regal Union, 1603–1715* (London: Macmillan, 1992)

Burgess, Glenn, Rowland Wymer and Jason Lawrence (eds), *Accession of James I: Historical and Cultural Consequences* (London: Palgrave Macmillan, 2006)

Burtt, Shelley, 'The Societies for the Reformation of Manners: between John Locke and the devil in Augustan England', in Roger D. Lund (ed.), *The Margins of Orthodoxy: Heterodox Writing and Cultural Response, 1660–1750* (Cambridge: Cambridge University Press, 1995)

Campbell, Gordon, 'Milton, John', *Oxford Dictionary of National Biography*

Childs, John, *The Nine Years' War and the British Army 1688–97: The Operations in the Low Countries* (Manchester: Manchester University Press, 1991)

Claydon, Tony, 'William III and II', *Oxford Dictionary of National Biography*

Coward, Barry (ed.), *Blackwell Companion to Stuart Britain* (Oxford: Blackwell, 2003)

Cramsie, John, *Kingship and Crown Finance under James VI and I 1603–1625* (Woodbridge: Boydell, 2002)

Croft, Pauline, *King James* (London: Palgrave Macmillan, 2003)

Cross, Robert Stuart Davis, 'To Counterbalance the World: England, Spain, & Peace in the Early 17th Century' (Princeton Ph.D. thesis 2012)

Cruickshanks, Eveline (ed.), *The Stuart Courts* (Stroud: The History Press, 2009)

Cuddy, Neil, 'The Conflicting Loyalties of a "vulger counselor": the Third Earl of Southampton, 1597–1624', in John Morrill, Paul Slack and Daniel Woolf (eds), *Public Duty and Private Conscience in Seventeenth-Century England* (Oxford: Oxford University Press, 1993)

——, 'The Real, Attempted "Tudor Revolution in Government": Salisbury's 1610 Great Contract', in G. W. Bernard, S. J. Gunn (eds), *Authority and Consent in Tudor England: Essays Presented to C.S.L. Davies* (Aldershot: Ashgate, 2002)

Cust, Richard, Ann Hughes (eds), *Conflict in Early Stuart England: Studies in Religion and Politics 1603–1642* (Harlow: Longman, 1989)

Cust, Richard, Peter Lake (eds), *Politics, Religion and Popularity in Early*

Stuart Britain: Early Stuart Essays in Honour of Conrad Russell (Cambridge: Cambridge University Press, 2002)

Cuttica, Cesare, 'Thomas Scott of Canterbury (1566–1635): Patriot, civic radical, puritan', *History of European Ideas*, 34 (2008)

Daly, James, 'Cosmic Harmony and Political Thinking in Early Stuart England', *Transactions of the American Philosophical Society*, 69 (1979)

Donaldson, Ian, 'Jonson, Benjamin', *Oxford Dictionary of National Biography*

Fitzgibbons, J., 'Why Was Oliver Cromwell Offered the Crown?' (paper given at 'Revolutionary England: Politics, Religion, and Government: a Conference in Honour of Clive Holmes', at Lady Margaret Hall, Oxford, 10 Sept. 2011)

Glassey, Lionel K. J. (ed.), *The Reigns of Charles II and James VII & II* (Basingstoke: Palgrave Macmillan, 1997)

Graham, Aaron, 'Partisan Politics and the British Fiscal–Military State, 1689–1713' (Oxford D.Phil. thesis 2011)

Gregg, Edward, 'Anne (1665–1714), queen of Great Britain and Ireland', *Oxford Dictionary of National Biography*

Guibbory, Achsah, *Ceremony and Community: Literature, Religion and Cultural Conflict in Seventeenth-Century England* (Cambridge: Cambridge University Press, 1998)

Harris, Tim, 'The Legacy of the English Civil War: Rethinking the Revolution', *The European Legacy*, 5 (2000)

——, *Restoration: Charles II and His Kingdoms* (London: Penguin, 2006)

——, *Revolution: The Great Crisis of the British Monarchy, 1685–1720* (London: Penguin, 2007)

Hattendorf, John B., 'Churchill, John, first duke of Marlborough', *Oxford Dictionary of National Biography*

Heinemann, Margot, 'Rebel Lords, Popular Playwrights, and Political Culture: Notes on the Jacobean Patronage of the Earl of Southampton', *Yearbook of English Studies*, 21 (1991)

Hesketh, Christian, 'The Political Opposition to the Government of Charles I in Scotland' (King's College London Ph.D. thesis 1999)

Hexter, J. H. (ed.), *Parliament and Liberty: from the Reign of Elizabeth to the English Civil War* (Stanford, CA: Stanford University Press, 1992)

Heyd, Michael, 'The Reaction to Enthusiasm in the Seventeenth Century: Towards an Integrative Approach', *Journal of Modern History*, 53 (1981)

Holmes, Geoffrey, *The Making of a Great Power: Late Stuart and Early Georgian Britain 1660–1722* (Harlow: Longman, 1993)

Hoppit, Julian, *A Land of Liberty?: England 1689–1727* (Oxford: Oxford University Press, 2000)

Houston, Alan, Steve Pincus (eds), *A Nation Transformed: England after the Restoration* (Cambridge: Cambridge University Press, 2001)

Israel, Jonathan, 'Competing Cousins: Anglo-Dutch Rivalry', *History Today*, 38 (1988)

—— (ed.), *The Anglo-Dutch Moment: Essays on the Glorious Revolution and its World Impact* (Cambridge: Cambridge University Press, 1991)

Johnston, Warren, *Revelation Restored: The Apocalypse in Later Seventeenth-Century England* (Woodbridge: Boydell, 2011)

Keeble, N. H., *The Restoration: England in the 1660s* (Oxford: Blackwell, 2002)

Kelsey, Sean, 'Rich, Robert, second earl of Warwick', *Oxford Dictionary of National Biography*

Kishlansky, Mark A., John Morrill, 'Charles I', *Oxford Dictionary of National Biography*

Klein, Lawrence E., 'Liberty, Manners, and Politeness in Early Eighteenth-Century England', *Historical Journal*, 32 (1989)

——, 'The Political Significance of "Politeness" in Early Eighteenth-Century Britain', in N. T. Phillipson (ed.), *Cicero, Scotland, and 'Politeness'* (The Proceedings of the Center for the History of British Political Thought, vol. 5), The Folger Shakespeare Library, Washington, 1993

——, *Shaftesbury and the Culture of Politeness: Moral Discourse and Cultural Politics in early Eighteenth-Century England* (Cambridge: Cambridge University Press, 1994)

——, 'Coffeehouse Civility, 1660–1714: an Aspect of Post-Courtly Culture in England', *Huntington Library Quarterly*, 59 (1996)

——, 'Sociability, Solitude, and Enthusiasm', *Huntington Library Quarterly*, 60 (1997)

Knafla, Louis A., *Law and Politics in Jacobean England: The Tracts of Lord Chancellor Ellesmere* (Cambridge: Cambridge University Press, 1977)

Levillain, Charles-Edouard, 'William III's Military and Political Career in Neo-Roman Context, 1672–1702', *Historical Journal*, 48 (2005)

Little, Patrick, *Lord Broghill and the Cromwellian Union with Ireland and Scotland* (Woodbridge: Boydell, 2004)

—— (ed.), *The Cromwellian Protectorate* (Woodbridge: Boydell, 2007)

Lockyer, Roger, *Buckingham: The Life and Political Career of George Villiers, First Duke of Buckingham 1592–1628* (London: Longman, 1981)

Malcolm, Noel, 'Hobbes, Thomas', *Oxford Dictionary of National Biography*

Marshall, Alan, 'Oates, Titus', *Oxford Dictionary of National Biography*

McCullough, P. E., 'Andrewes, Lancelot', *Oxford Dictionary of National Biography*

McDonald, Russ, *Shakespeare's Late Style* (Cambridge: Cambridge University Press, 2006)

McElligott, Jason (ed.), *Fear, Exclusion and Revolution: Roger Morrice and Britain in the 1680s* (Aldershot: Ashgate, 2006)

Mijers, Esther, David Onnekink (eds), *Redefining William III: The Impact of the King-Stadholder in International Context* (Aldershot: Ashgate, 2007)

Morrill, John, 'Cromwell, Oliver', *Oxford Dictionary of National Biography*

Newman, John, 'Jones, Inigo', *Oxford Dictionary of National Biography*

Ohlmeyer, Jane (ed.), *Ireland from Independence to Occupation 1641–1660* (Cambridge: Cambridge University Press, 1995)

Parry, Graham, *The Arts of the Anglican Counter-Reformation: Glory, Laud and Honour* (Woodbridge: Boydell, 2006)

Peacey, Jason (ed.), *The Regicides and the Execution of Charles I* (Basingstoke: Palgrave Macmillan, 2001)

Pincus, Steve, 'Popery, Trade and Universal Monarchy: the Ideological Context of the Outbreak of the Second Anglo-Dutch War', *English Historical Review*, 107 (1992)

——, '"Coffee Politicians Does Create": Coffeehouses and Restoration Political Culture', *Journal of Modern History*, 67 (1995)

——, 'From Butterboxes to Wooden Shoes: the Shift in English Popular Sentiment from Anti-Dutch to Anti-French in the 1670s', *Historical Journal*, 38 (1995)

——, 'The Making of a Great Power? Universal Monarchy, Political Economy, and the Transformation of English Political Culture', *The European Legacy*, 5 (2000)

——, 'The European Catholic Context of the Revolution of 1688–89: Gallicanism, Innocent XI and the Catholic Opposition', in A. I. Macinnes, A. H. Williamson (eds), *Shaping the Stuart World 1603–1714: The Atlantic Connection* (Leiden: Brill, 2006)

——, *1688: The First Modern Revolution* (New Haven, Conn.: Yale University Press, 2009)

Pursell, Brennan C., 'James I, Gondomar and the Dissolution of the Parliament of 1621', *History*, 85 (2000)

Richards, Judith, '"His Nowe Majestie" and the English Monarchy: The Kingship of Charles I before 1640', *Past and Present*, 113 (1986)

——, 'The English Accession of James VI: "National" Identity, Gender and the Personal Monarchy of England', *English Historical Review*, 117 (2002)

Scott, David, *Politics and War in the Three Stuart Kingdoms, 1637–49* (London: Palgrave Macmillan, 2004)

Scott, Jonathan, *England's Troubles: Seventeenth-Century English Political Instability in European Context* (Cambridge: Cambridge University Press, 2002)

——, '"Good Night Amsterdam". Sir George Downing and Anglo-Dutch Statebuilding', *English Historical Review*, 118 (2003)

Seaward, Paul, 'Charles II', *Oxford Dictionary of National Biography*

Slack, Paul, 'Material progress and the challenge of affluence in seventeenth-century England', *Economic History Review*, 62 (2009)

Smuts, R. Malcolm, *Court Culture and the Origins of a Royalist Tradition in Early Stuart England* (Philadelphia: University of Pennsylvania Press, 1987)

—— (ed.), *The Stuart Court and Europe: Essays in Politics and Political Culture* (Cambridge: Cambridge University Press, 1996)

——, *Culture and Power in England 1585–1685* (London: Macmillan, 1999)

Sommerville, J. P., *Royalists & Patriots: Politics and Ideology in England 1603–1640* (Harlow: Pearson, Longman, 1999)

Southcombe, George, Grant Tapsell, *Restoration Politics, Religion and Culture* (Basingstoke: Palgrave Macmillan, 2010)

Speck, W. A., 'James II and VII', *Oxford Dictionary of National Biography*

Spurr, John, 'England 1649–1750: differences contained?', in Steven N. Zwicker (ed.), *The Cambridge Companion to English Literature 1650–1740* (Cambridge: Cambridge University Press, 1998)

Swatland, Andrew, *The House of Lords in the Reign of Charles II* (Cambridge: Cambridge University Press, 1996)

Szechi, Daniel, 'A Blueprint for Tyranny? Sir Edward Hales and the Catholic Jacobite Response to the Revolution of 1688', *English Historical Review*, 116 (2001)

'T Hart, Marjolein, '"The devil or the Dutch": Holland's impact on the financial revolution in England, 1643–1694', *Parliaments, Estates and Representation*, 11 (1991)

Trim, David, 'Calvinist Internationalism and the Shaping of Jacobean Foreign Policy', in Timothy Wilks (ed.), *Prince Henry Revived: Image and Exemplarity in Early Modern England* (Southampton: Southampton Solent University Press, 2007)

Wanklyn, Malcolm, Frank Jones, *A Military History of the English Civil War: Strategy and Tactics* (Harlow: Pearson, Longman, 2005)

Wanklyn, Malcolm, *The Warrior Generals: Winning the British Civil Wars* (New Haven, Conn.: Yale University Press, 2010)

Wauchope, Piers, 'Talbot, Richard, first earl of Tyrconnell and Jacobite duke of Tyrconnell', *Oxford Dictionary of National Biography*

Wheeler, James Scott, *The Making of a World Power: War and the Military Revolution in Seventeenth-Century England* (Stroud: Sutton, 1999)

Wood, Jeremy, 'Dyck, Sir Anthony [*formerly* Antoon] Van', *Oxford Dictionary of National Biography*

Wormald, Jenny, 'James VI and I', *Oxford Dictionary of National Biography*
—— (ed.), *The Seventeenth Century* (Oxford: Oxford University Press, 2008)

Wynne, S. M., 'Palmer [*née* Villiers], Barbara, countess of Castlemaine', *Oxford Dictionary of National Biography*

Britain and Ireland, 1714–83

Allan, David, *Making British Culture: English Readers and the Scottish Enlightenment* (Abingdon: Routledge, 2008)

Allen, Robert C., *The British Industrial Revolution in Global Perspective* (Cambridge: Cambridge University Press, 2009)

Anderson, M. S., *The War of the Austrian Succession, 1740–1748* (Harlow: Pearson, Longman, 1999)

Barker-Benfield, G. J., *The Culture of Sensibility: Sex and Society in Eighteenth-Century Britain* (Chicago: University of Chicago Press, 1992)

Battestin, Martin C., 'Fielding, Henry', *Oxford Dictionary of National Biography*

Baugh, Daniel, *The Global Seven Years War 1754–1763: Britain and France in a Great Power Contest* (Harlow: Pearson, Longman, 2011)

Berg, Maxine, 'In Pursuit of Luxury: Global History and British Consumer Goods in the Eighteenth Century', *Past and Present*, 182 (2004)
——, *Luxury and Pleasure in Eighteenth-Century Britain* (Oxford: Oxford University Press, 2005)

Berry, Helen, 'Polite Consumption in Eighteenth-Century England', *Transactions of the Royal Historical Society*, sixth series, 12 (2002)

Bindman, David, 'Hogarth, William', *Oxford Dictionary of National Biography*

Black, Jeremy, 'Hanover and British Foreign Policy 1714–1760', *English Historical Review*, 120 (2005)

Brewer, John, *The Pleasures of the Imagination: English Culture in the Eighteenth Century* (London: HarperCollins, 2004)

Broadie, Alexander, *The Cambridge Companion to the Scottish Enlightenment* (Cambridge: Cambridge University Press, 2003)

Browning, Reed, *The War of the Austrian Succession* (New York: St Martin's Press, 1993)

——, 'Holles, Thomas Pelham-, duke of Newcastle upon Tyne and first duke of Newcastle under Lyme', *Oxford Dictionary of National Biography*

Cannon, John, *Samuel Johnson and the Politics of Hanoverian England* (Oxford: Oxford University Press, 1994)

——, 'George II', *Oxford Dictionary of National Biography*

——, 'George III', *Oxford Dictionary of National Biography*

Carter, Philip, 'Polite "Persons": Character, Biography and the Gentleman', *Transactions of the Royal Historical Society*, sixth series, 12 (2002)

Clark, Jonathan, Howard Erskine-Hill (eds), *Samuel Johnson in Historical Context* (Basingstoke: Palgrave Macmillan, 2002)

Clayton, T. R., 'The Duke of Newcastle, the Earl of Halifax, and the American Origins of the Seven Years' War', *Historical Journal*, 24 (1981)

Clingham, Greg (ed.), *The Cambridge Companion to Samuel Johnson* (Cambridge: Cambridge University Press, 1997)

Colley, Linda, *Britons: Forging the Nation 1707–1837* (New Haven, Conn.: Yale University Press, 2005 edn)

Connolly, William W., 'Christian Johnson and Pagan Hume', *Hume Studies*, 27 (2001)

Conway, Stephen, *The British Isles and the War of American Independence* (Oxford: Oxford University Press, 2002)

——, 'Continental Connections: Britain and Europe in the Eighteenth Century', *History*, 90 (2005)

——, *War, State, and Society in Mid-Eighteenth-Century Britain and Ireland* (Oxford: Oxford University Press, 2006)

——, 'Christians, Catholics, Protestants: the Religious Links of Britain and Ireland with Continental Europe, c.1689–1800', *English Historical Review*, 124 (2009)

——, *Britain, Ireland and Continental Europe in the Eighteenth Century: Similarities, Connections, Identities* (Oxford: Oxford University Press, 2011)

Dickinson, H. T., 'Wyvill, Christopher', *Oxford Dictionary of National Biography*

—— (ed.), *Blackwell Companion to Eighteenth-Century Britain* (Oxford: Blackwell, 2002)

Donald, Diana, Frank O'Gorman (eds), *Ordering the World in the Eighteenth Century* (Basingstoke: Palgrave Macmillan, 2006)

Eger, Elizabeth, 'Bluestocking circle [bluestockings] *(act. c.1755–c.1795)*', *Oxford Dictionary of National Biography*

Frey, Linda, Marsha Frey, 'Townshend, Charles, second Viscount Townshend', *Oxford Dictionary of National Biography*

Gibbs, G. C., 'George I', *Oxford Dictionary of National Biography*

Goldie, Mark, 'The English system of liberty', in Goldie, Robert Wokler (eds), *The Cambridge History of Eighteenth-Century Political Thought* (Cambridge: Cambridge University Press, 2006)

Goldsmith, M. M., 'Mandeville, Bernard', *Oxford Dictionary of National Biography*

Greene, Jack P., 'Competing Authorities: the Debate over Parliamentary Imperial Jurisdiction, 1763–1776', *Parliamentary History*, 14 (1995)

Gregg, Edward, 'James Francis Edward [James Francis Edward Stuart; styled James VIII and III; *known as* Chevalier de St George, Pretender, Old Pretender]', *Oxford Dictionary of National Biography*

Griffin, Emma, *A Short History of the British Industrial Revolution* (London: Palgrave Macmillan, 2010)

Hanham, A. A., 'Stanhope, James, first Earl Stanhope', *Oxford Dictionary of National Biography*

Harris, Bob, '"American Idols": Empire, War and the Middling Ranks in Mid-Eighteenth-Century Britain', *Past and Present*, 150 (1996)

——, *Politics and the Nation: Britain in the Mid-Eighteenth Century* (Oxford: Oxford University Press, 2002)

Harris, Ron, 'The Bubble Act: its Passage and its Effects on Business Organization', *Journal of Economic History*, 54 (1994)

Holmes, Geoffrey, Daniel Szechi, *The Age of Oligarchy: Pre-industrial Britain* (London: Longman, 1993)

Hoppit, Julian, 'The Myths of the South Sea Bubble', *Transactions of the Royal Historical Society*, sixth series, 12 (2002)

Hundert, E. J., *The Enlightenment's Fable: Bernard Mandeville and the Discovery of Society* (Cambridge: Cambridge University Press, 2nd edn 2005)

Jarrett, Derek, *England in the Age of Hogarth* (New Haven, Conn.: Yale University Press, 1986)

Langford, Paul, *A Polite and Commercial People: England 1727–1783* (Oxford: Oxford University Press, 1989)

—— (ed.), *The Eighteenth Century 1688–1815* (Oxford: Oxford University Press, 2002)

——, 'The Uses of Eighteenth-Century Politeness', *Transactions of the Royal Historical Society*, sixth series, 12 (2002)

Maples, Thomas, 'Gin and Georgian London', *History Today*, 41 (1991)

McJimsey, Robert, 'Crisis Management: Parliament and Political Stability, 1692–1719', *Albion*, 31 (1999)

Monod, Paul Kléber, *Jacobitism and the English People, 1688–1788* (Cambridge: Cambridge University Press, 1989)

Mullan, John, *Sentiment and Sociability: The Language of Feeling in the Eighteenth Century* (Oxford: Oxford University Press, 1990)

Peters, Marie, 'Pitt, William, first earl of Chatham [*known as* Pitt the elder]', *Oxford Dictionary of National Biography*

Pittock, Murray G. H., 'Charles Edward [Charles Edward Stuart; styled Charles III; *known as* the Young Pretender, Bonnie Prince Charlie]', *Oxford Dictionary of National Biography*

Potkay, Adam, *The Passion for Happiness: Samuel Johnson and David Hume* (Ithaca, NY: Cornell University Press, 2000)

Rack, Henry D., 'Wesley [Westley], John', *Oxford Dictionary of National Biography*

Reilly, Robin, 'Wedgwood, Josiah', *Oxford Dictionary of National Biography*

Roberts, Clayton, 'The Growth of Political Stability Reconsidered', *Albion*, 25 (1993)

Robertson, John, 'Hume, David', *Oxford Dictionary of National Biography*

Rogers, Nicholas, *Crowds, Culture, and Politics in Georgian Britain* (Oxford: Oxford University Press, 1998)

Schochet, Gordon J. (ed.), *Politics, Politeness, and Patriotism* (Washington, DC: Folger Institute, 1993)

Schweizer, Karl Wolfgang, 'Stuart, John, third earl of Bute', *Oxford Dictionary of National Biography*

Sheehan, Michael, 'Balance of power intervention: Britain's decisions for or against war, 1733–56', *Diplomacy & Statecraft*, 7 (1996)

——, 'The Sincerity of the British Commitment to the Maintenance of the Balance of Power 1714–1763', *Diplomacy & Statecraft*, 15 (2004)

Simms, Brendan, *Three Victories and a Defeat: The Rise and Fall of the First British Empire, 1714–1783* (London: Allen Lane, Penguin, 2007)

Smith, Hannah, 'The Court in England, 1714–1760: a Declining Political Institution?', *History*, 90 (2005)

——, *Georgian Monarchy: Politics and Culture, 1714–1760* (Cambridge: Cambridge University Press, 2006)

Speck, W. A., Matthew Kilburn, 'Promoters of the South Sea Bubble (*act.* 1720)', *Oxford Dictionary of National Biography*

Stockley, Andrew, *Britain and France at the Birth of America: The European Powers and the Peace Negotiations of 1782–1783* (Exeter: University of Exeter Press, 2001)

Sweet, R. H., 'Topographies of Politeness', *Transactions of the Royal Historical Society*, sixth series, 12 (2002)

Szabo, Franz A. J., *The Seven Years War in Europe, 1756–1763* (Harlow: Pearson, Longman, 2008)

Taylor, Stephen, 'Walpole, Robert, first earl of Orford', *Oxford Dictionary of National Biography*

Thomas, Peter D. G., 'North, Frederick, second earl of Guilford [*known as* Lord North]', *Oxford Dictionary of National Biography*

——, 'Wilkes, John', *Oxford Dictionary of National Biography*

Thompson, Andrew C., *George II: King and Elector* (New Haven, Conn.: Yale University Press, 2011)

Thomson, Peter, 'Garrick, David', *Oxford Dictionary of National Biography*

Uglow, Jenny, 'Lunar Society of Birmingham (*act. c.*1765–*c.*1800)', *Oxford Dictionary of National Biography*

White, Jonathan, 'The "Slow but Sure Poyson": the Representation of Gin and Its Drinkers, 1736–1751', *Journal of British Studies*, 42 (2003)

Williams, Abigail, 'The poetry of the un-enlightened: politics and literary enthusiasm in the early eighteenth century', *History of European Ideas*, 31 (2005)

Wilson, Kathleen, *The Sense of the People: Politics, Culture, and Imperialism in England, 1715–1785* (Cambridge: Cambridge University Press, 1998)

Woodfine, Philip, *Britannia's Glories: The Walpole Ministry and the 1739 War with Spain* (Woodbridge: Boydell, 1998)

Colonies and Empire, 1500–1783

Allen, Thomas B., *Tories: Fighting for the King in America's First Civil War* (New York: HarperCollins, 2010)

Allison, Robert J., *The American Revolution: A Concise History* (Oxford: Oxford University Press, 2011)

Anderson, Fred, *The Crucible of War: The Seven Years' War and the Fate of Empire in British North America, 1764–1766* (London: Faber and Faber, 2000)

Andrews, Charles M., 'British Committees, Commissions, and Councils of Trade and Plantations, 1622–1675', *Johns Hopkins University Studies in Historical and Political Science*, series 26 (Baltimore: The Johns Hopkins Press, 1908)

Appleby, John C., 'An Association for the West Indies?: English Plans for a West India Company 1621–29', *Journal of Imperial and Commonwealth History*, 15 (1987)

Armitage, David, 'The Cromwellian Protectorate and the Languages of Empire', *Historical Journal*, 35 (1992)

——, 'Making the Empire British: Scotland in the Atlantic World 1542–1707', *Past and Present*, 155 (1997)

——, *The Ideological Origins of the British Empire* (Cambridge: Cambridge University Press, 2000)

——, Michael J. Braddick (eds), *The British Atlantic World, 1500–1800* (London: Palgrave Macmillan, 2002)

Bangs, Jeremy Dupertuis, 'Pilgrim Fathers (*act.* 1620)', *Oxford Dictionary of National Biography*

Bayly, C. A., Katherine Prior, 'Cornwallis, Charles, first Marquess Cornwallis', *Oxford Dictionary of National Biography*

Bliss, Robert M., *Revolution and Empire: English Politics and the American Colonies in the Seventeenth Century* (Manchester: Manchester University Press, 1990)

Block, Kristen, 'Cultivating Inner and Outer Plantations: Property, Industry, and Slavery in Early Quaker Migration to the New World', *Early American Studies*, 8 (2010)

Bowen, H. V., 'British conceptions of global empire, 1756–83', *Journal of Imperial and Commonwealth History*, 26 (1998)

——, M. Lincoln and N. Rigby (eds), *The Worlds of the East India Company* (Woodbridge: Boydell, 2002)

——, *The Business of Empire: The East India Company and Imperial Britain, 1756–1833* (Cambridge: Cambridge University Press, 2005)

Breen, T. H., 'An Empire of Goods: The Anglicization of Colonial America, 1690–1776', *Journal of British Studies*, 25 (1986)

Canny, Nicholas (ed.), *The Oxford History of the British Empire*, vol. I, *The Origins of Empire: British Overseas Enterprise to the Close of the Seventeenth Century* (Oxford: Oxford University Press, 1998)

Clement, Alain, 'English and French mercantilist thought and the matter of colonies during the 17th century', *Scandinavian Economic History Review*, 54 (2006)

Cogswell, Thomas, '"In the Power of the State": Mr Anys's Project and the Tobacco Colonies, 1626–1628', *English Historical Review*, 123 (2008)

Donoghue, John, 'Radical Republicanism in England, America, and the Imperial Atlantic, 1624–1661' (University of Pittsburgh Ph.D. thesis 2006)

——, '"Out of the Land of Bondage": the English Revolution and the Atlantic Origins of Abolition', *American Historical Review*, 115 (2010)

Eltis, David, 'The Volume and Structure of the Transatlantic Slave Trade: a Reassessment', *William and Mary Quarterly*, third series, 58 (2001)

Engerman, Stanley L., Robert E. Gallman, *The Cambridge Economic History of the United States*, vol. 1, *The Colonial Era* (Cambridge: Cambridge University Press, 1996)

Farnell, J. E., 'The Navigation Act of 1651, the First Dutch War, and the London Merchant Community', *Economic History Review*, 16 (1964)

Fausz, J. Frederick, 'An "Abundance of Blood Shed on Both Sides": England's First Indian War, 1609–1614', *Virginia Magazine of History and Biography*, 98 (1990)

Ferguson, Niall, *Empire: How Britain Made the Modern World* (London: Allen Lane, Penguin, 2004)

Ferling, John, *Almost a Miracle: The American Victory in the War of Independence* (Oxford: Oxford University Press, 2009)

Fitzmaurice, Andrew, 'The Commercial Ideology of Colonization in Jacobean England: Robert Johnson, Giovanni Botero, and the Pursuit of Greatness', *William and Mary Quarterly*, third series, 64 (2007)

Games, Alison, *The Web of Empire: English Cosmopolitans in an Age of Expansion 1560–1660* (Oxford: Oxford University Press, 2008)

Gruber, Ira D., 'Howe, William, fifth Viscount Howe', *Oxford Dictionary of National Biography*

Harrington, Matthew Craig, "'The Worke wee may doe in the World": the Western Design and the Anglo-Spanish Struggle for the Caribbean, 1654–1655' (Florida State University MA thesis 2004)

Higman, B. W., 'The sugar revolution', *Economic History Review*, 53 (2000)

Jasanoff, Maya, 'The Other Side of Revolution: Loyalists in the British Empire', *William and Mary Quarterly*, third series, 65 (2008)

Johnson, Richard R., "'Parliamentary Egotisms": the Clash of Legislatures in the Making of the American Revolution', *Journal of American History*, 74 (1987)

Kupperman, Karen Ordahl, 'Errand to the Indies: Puritan Colonization from Providence Island through the Western Design', *William and Mary Quarterly*, third series, 45 (1988)

Lawson, Philip, *The East India Company: A History* (Harlow: Longman, 1993)

Leng, Thomas, "'A Potent Plantation well armed and Policeed": Huguenots, the Hartlib Circle, and British Colonization in the 1640s', *William and Mary Quarterly*, third series, 66 (2009)

Lenman, Bruce, *England's Colonial Wars 1550–1688* (Harlow: Pearson, Longman, 2001)

——, *Britain's Colonial Wars 1688–1783* (Harlow: Pearson, Longman, 2001)

Lepore, Jill, 'Metacom [Philip; *called* King Philip]', *Oxford Dictionary of National Biography*

Linebaugh, Peter, Marcus Rediker, *The Many-Headed Hydra: The Hidden History of the Revolutionary Atlantic* (London: Verso, 2000)

Lorimer, Joyce, 'The failure of the English Guiana ventures 1595–1667 and James I's foreign policy', *Journal of Imperial and Commonwealth History*, 21 (1993)

Mackillop, Andrew, 'A Union for Empire?: Scotland, the English East India Company and the British Union', *Scottish Historical Review*, 87 (2008)

MacMillan, Ken, 'Common *and* Civil Law? Taking Possession of the English Empire in America, 1575–1630', *Canadian Journal of History*, 38 (2003)

Marshall, P. J. (ed.), *The Oxford History of the British Empire*, vol. II, *The Eighteenth Century* (Oxford: Oxford University Press, 1998)

——, *The Making and Unmaking of Empires: Britain, India, and America c.1750–1783* (Oxford: Oxford University Press, 2005)

McConville, Brendan, *The King's Three Faces: The Rise & Fall of Royal*

America, 1688–1776 (Chapel Hill, NC: The University of North Carolina Press, 2006)

Milobar, David, 'Quebec Reform, the British Constitution and the Atlantic Empire: 1774–1775', *Parliamentary History*, 14 (1995)

Murison, Barbara Cresswell, 'William Blathwayt's Empire: Politics and Administration in England and the Atlantic Colonies, 1668–1710' (University of Western Ontario Ph.D. thesis 1981)

Nash, Gary B., 'Slaves and Slaveowners in Colonial Philadelphia', *William and Mary Quarterly*, third series, 30 (1973)

Onuf, P. S., 'Jefferson, Thomas', *Oxford Dictionary of National Biography*

Peters, Marie, 'Early Hanoverian Consciousness: Empire or Europe?', *English Historical Review*, 122 (2007)

Pincus, Steve, 'England and the World in the 1650s', in John Morrill (ed.), *Revolution and Restoration: England in the 1650s* (London: Collins & Brown, 1992)

Rankin, Stuart, 'White, Samuel [*called* Siamese White]', *Oxford Dictionary of National Biography*

Richter, Daniel K., 'War and Culture: the Iroquois Experience', *William and Mary Quarterly*, third series, 40 (1983)

Roper, L. H., 'Charles I, Virginia, and the Idea of Atlantic History', *Itinerario*, 30 (2006)

Royster, Charles, 'Washington, George', *Oxford Dictionary of National Biography*

Sarson, Steven, *British America 1500–1800: Creating Colonies, Imagining an Empire* (London: Hodder Arnold, 2005)

Schlenther, Boyd Stanley, 'Whitefield, George', *Oxford Dictionary of National Biography*

Smith, S. D., 'British Exports to Colonial North America and the Mercantilist Fallacy', *Business History*, 37 (1995)

Steele, Ian K., 'The British Parliament and the Atlantic Colonies to 1760: New Approaches to Enduring Questions', *Parliamentary History*, 14 (1995)

Stern, Philip J., '"A Politie of Civill & Military Power": Political Thought and the Late Seventeenth-Century Foundations of the East India Company-State', *Journal of British Studies*, 47 (2008)

——, *The Company-State: Corporate Sovereignty and the Early Modern Foundations of the British Empire in India* (Oxford: Oxford University Press, 2011)

Taylor, Stephen, Richard Connors and Clyve Jones (eds), *Hanoverian*

Britain and Empire: Essays in Memory of Philip Lawson (Woodbridge: Boydell, 1998)

Valeri, Mark, 'William Petty in Boston: Political Economy, Religion, and Money in Provincial New England', *Early American Studies*, 8 (2010)

Waldstreicher, David, 'Capitalism, Slavery, and Benjamin Franklin's American Revolution', in Cathy D. Matson (ed.), *The Economy of Early America: Historical Perspectives and New Directions* (University Park, PA: Pennsylvania State University Press, 2006)

Webb, Stephen Saunders, *1676: The End of American Independence* (Syracuse, NY: Syracuse University Press, 1995)

Winship, M. P., 'Godly republicanism and the origins of the Massachusetts polity', *William and Mary Quarterly*, third series, 63 (2006)

Wood, Peter H., 'Teach [Thatch], Edward [*known as* Blackbeard]', *Oxford Dictionary of National Biography*

Zahedieh, Nuala, *The Capital and the Colonies: London and the Atlantic Economy 1660–1700* (Cambridge: Cambridge University Press, 2010)

NOTES

Preface

1 Matthew Hodgart (ed.), *Horace Walpole: Memoirs and Portraits* (London: B. T. Batsford, 1963), p. 37.
2 Giovanni Botero, *The Travellers Breviat* (London, 1601), pp. 15–16.
3 *Remarks on the Letter addressed to two great men* (Dublin, 1760), p. 10 (the writer's emphasis). Cited, in part, in Stephen Conway, 'Continental Connections: Britain and Europe in the Eighteenth Century', *History*, 90 (2005), p. 373.

1 Lost Kingdoms, 1485–1526

1 Sir Henry Ellis (ed.), *Three Books of Polydore Vergil's English History* (Camden Society, old series, vol. xxix, 1844), p. 224.
2 Shakespeare, *Richard III*, act 5, scene 5.
3 Denys Hay (ed.), *The Anglica Historia of Polydore Vergil, A.D. 1485–1537* (Camden Society, third series, vol. lxxiv, 1950), p. 3.
4 *Rutland Papers. Original Documents Illustrative of the Courts and Times of Henry VII and Henry VIII* (Camden Society, old series, vol. xxi, 1842), pp. 14–15.
5 Hay (ed.), *The Anglica Historia of Polydore Vergil*, p. 79.
6 *State Papers Published under the Authority of His Majesty's Commission. King Henry the Eighth*, vol. 2, part 3: 1515–38, p. 1.
7 Brian Vickers (ed.), *Francis Bacon. The History of the Reign of King Henry VII* (Cambridge: Cambridge University Press, 1998), p. 50.
8 Andrew Hadfield, Willy Maley (eds), *Edmund Spenser. A View of the Present State of Ireland* (Oxford: Blackwell, 1997), p. 21.
9 British Library [BL], Harleian MS 3364, fo. 7.
10 Hay (ed.), *The Anglica Historia of Polydore Vergil*, pp. 145, 147.
11 ibid., p. 23.
12 Vickers (ed.), *Francis Bacon. The History of the Reign of King Henry VII*, p. 96.
13 Shakespeare, *Henry V*, act 5, scene 2.
14 Cited in John M. Currin, '"To Traffic with War"? Henry VII and the French campaign of 1492', in David Grummitt (ed.), *The English Experience in France c.1450–1558: War, Diplomacy and Cultural Exchange* (Aldershot: Ashgate, 2002), p. 109.
15 Cited in C. J. Harrison, 'The petition of Edmund Dudley', *English Historical Review*, 87 (1972), p. 86.
16 Botero, *The Travellers Breviat*, p. 18.
17 Cited in Maurice Keen, 'Chivalry', in Raluca Radulescu, Alison Truelove (eds), *Gentry Culture in Late Medieval England* (Manchester: Manchester University Press, 2005), p. 47.

18 Cited in Steven G. Ellis, 'Fitzgerald, Gerald, eighth earl of Kildare', *Oxford Dictionary of National Biography*.

19 Vickers (ed.), *Francis Bacon. The History of the Reign of King Henry VII*, p. 202.

20 ibid., p. 95.

21 Hay (ed.), *The Anglica Historia of Polydore Vergil*, p. 127.

22 *Calendar of State Papers, Spanish, 1485–1509*, p. 163.

23 Cited in Thomas Penn, *Winter King: The Dawn of Tudor England* (London: Allen Lane, Penguin, 2012), p. 169.

24 *Calendar of State Papers, Spanish, 1485–1509*, p. 178.

25 Cited in David Potter, *A History of France, 1460–1560: The Emergence of a Nation State* (London: Macmillan, 1995), pp. 143–4.

26 Cited in Sybil M. Jack, 'Wolsey, Thomas', *Oxford Dictionary of National Biography*.

27 Vickers (ed.), *Francis Bacon. The History of the Reign of King Henry VII*, p. 130.

28 ibid., pp. 175, 177.

29 I am grateful to John Adamson for sharing his observations on Richmond Palace and its chapel.

30 John Fisher, *This Sermon Folowynge* (London, 1509), unpag.

31 C. H. Miller, L. Bradner, C. A. Lynch (eds), *The Complete Works of St. Thomas More* (New Haven, Conn.: Yale University Press, 1984), vol. 3, part 2, pp. 100–13.

32 J. S. Brewer (ed.), *Letters and Papers, Foreign and Domestic, of the Reign of Henry VIII* (London, 1864), vol. 2, part 1: 1515–16, p. 395.

33 J. S. Brewer (ed.), *Letters and Papers, Foreign and Domestic, of the Reign of Henry VIII* (London, 1867), vol. 3, part 1: 1519–21, p. 350.

34 *Calendar of State Papers, Venetian, 1509–19*, p. 400.

35 ibid., p. 242.

36 Cited in John Hale, *The Civilisation of Europe in the Renaissance* (London: HarperCollins, 2005), p. 62.

37 Sir Walter Ralegh, *The History of the World* (London, 1614), preface, sig. Bv.

38 Richard Standish Sylvester, Davis P. Harding (eds), *Two Early Tudor Lives* (New Haven, Conn.: Yale University Press, 1962), pp. 12–13.

39 Cited in Michael Riordan, 'Henry VIII, privy chamber of', *Oxford Dictionary of National Biography*.

40 Hay (ed.), *The Anglica Historia of Polydore Vergil*, p. 197.

41 Ralegh, *The History of the World*, preface, sig. Bv.

42 *Nicholas Machiavel's Prince* (London, 1640), p. 179.

43 Cited in Peter R. Roberts, 'Henry VIII, Francis I and the Reformation Parliament', *Parliaments, Estates and Representation*, 27 (2007), pp. 135–6.

44 John Fisher, *Here After Ensueth Two Fruytfull Sermons* (1532), unpag.

45 *Calendar of State Papers, Venetian, 1520–6*, p. 82.

46 Hay (ed.), *The Anglica Historia of Polydore Vergil*, p. 269.

47 Cited in John Matusiak, 'Puissance and Poverty: Henry VIII and the Conquest of France', *History Review*, 64 (2009), p. 41.

48 *State Papers Published under the Authority of His Majesty's Commission. King Henry the Eighth*, vol. 2, part 3: 1515–38, p. 90.

49 J. S. Brewer (ed.), *Letters and Papers, Foreign and Domestic, of the Reign of Henry VIII* (London, 1872), vol. 4, part 2: 1526–8, p. 1077.

50 Cited in Ellis, 'Fitzgerald, Gerald, ninth earl of Kildare'.

51 Cited in C. S. L. Davies, John Edwards, 'Katherine [Catalina, Catherine, Katherine of Aragon]', *Oxford Dictionary of National Biography*.

2 The Protestant Cause, 1527–1603

1 Cited in G. W. Bernard, *The King's Reformation: Henry VIII and the Remaking of the English Church* (New Haven, Conn.: Yale University Press, 2005), p. 244.
2 *Calendar of State Papers, Venetian, 1527–33*, p. 365.
3 Cited in Michael A. R. Graves, *Henry VIII: A Study in Kingship* (Harlow: Pearson, Longman, 2003), p. 135.
4 William Tyndale, *The Obedience of a Christen Man* (1528), fos lv, lxxviii (verso).
5 Cited in Ives, 'Henry VIII'.
6 Cited in John Guy, *Tudor England* (Oxford: Oxford University Press, 1988), p. 155.
7 The Act of Supremacy, 1534.
8 Cited in Alec Ryrie, *The Age of Reformation: The Tudor and Stewart Realms 1485–1603* (Harlow: Pearson, Longman, 2009), p. 137.
9 Cited in Glenn Burgess, *British Political Thought, 1500–1660: The Politics of the Post-Reformation* (Basingstoke: Palgrave Macmillan, 2009), p. 18.
10 James Gairdner, R. H. Brodie (eds), *Letters and Papers, Foreign and Domestic, of the Reign of Henry VIII* (London, 1896), vol. 15: 1540, p. 423.
11 Cited in Guy, *Tudor England*, p. 189.
12 Cited in Howard Leithead, 'Thomas Cromwell, earl of Essex', *Oxford Dictionary of National Biography*.
13 It was in leading the English navy against the French invasion fleet, at the battle of the Solent, that the *Mary Rose* broached and sank, in full view of Henry. It seems that her crew had been negligent in not closing the lower gun ports after firing on the French ships, so that when she heeled over in a sudden gust of wind she quickly shipped water and sank.
14 Cited in Paul E. J. Hammer, *Elizabeth's Wars: War, Government and Society in Tudor England, 1544–1604* (Basingstoke: Palgrave Macmillan, 2003), p. 29.
15 Barrett L. Beer, Sybil M. Jack (eds), *The Letters of William, Lord Paget of Beaudesert, 1547–63* (Camden Society, fourth series, vol. xiii, 1974), p. 23.
16 Cited in Eamon Duffy, *The Stripping of the Altars: Traditional Religion in England 1400–1580* (New Haven, Conn.: Yale University Press, 2nd edn 2005), p. 462.
17 Cited in Ian W. Archer, 'Wyatt, Sir Thomas', *Oxford Dictionary of National Biography*.
18 Cited in David Potter, 'Mid-Tudor Foreign Policy and Diplomacy: 1547–63', in Susan Doran, Glenn Richardson (eds), *Tudor England and its Neighbours* (Basingstoke: Palgrave Macmillan, 2005), p. 108.
19 Cited in Susan Wabuda, 'Latimer, Hugh', *Oxford Dictionary of National Biography*.
20 Cited in Hammer, *Elizabeth's Wars*, p. 236.
21 Cited in David Potter, 'Britain and the Wider World', in Tittler, Jones (eds), *Blackwell Companion to Tudor Britain*, p. 189.
22 Preamble to the Act in Restraint of Appeals, 1533.
23 Cited in Ryrie, *The Age of Reformation*, p. 299.
24 ibid., p. 307.
25 *Calendar of State Papers, Spain, 1529–30*, p. 734.
26 Cited in Roberts, 'Henry VIII, Francis I, and the Reformation Parliament', p. 135.
27 Cited in David Daniell, 'Tyndale, William', *Oxford Dictionary of National Biography*.
28 Cited in Patrick Collinson, *The Elizabethan Puritan Movement* (London: Jonathan Cape, 1967), p. 64.

29 John Field, *An Admonition to the Parliament* (1572), unpag. (STC 10847).

30 Cited in Michael Graham, 'The Scottish Reformation', in Tittler, Jones (eds), *Blackwell Companion to Tudor Britain*, p. 289.

31 'An Homily against Peril of Idolatry and Superfluous Decking of Churches'.

32 Phillip Stubbes, *A Motive to Good Workes* (London, 1593), pp. 80–1.

33 Cited in Graham Parry, *The Arts of the Anglican Counter-Reformation: Glory, Laud and Honour* (Woodbridge: Boydell, 2006), p. 181.

34 Cited in Kenneth Fincham, Nicholas Tyacke, *Altars Restored: The Changing Face of English Religious Worship, 1547–c.1700* (Oxford: Oxford University Press, 2007), p. 65.

35 Cited in Jessica Warner, 'The naturalisation of beer and gin in early modern England', *Contemporary Drug Problems*, 24 (1997), p. 382.

36 John Stockwood, *A Sermon Preached at Paules Crosse on Barthelmew Day, being the 24. of August. 1578* (London, 1578), pp. 23–4, 135.

37 Thomas White, *A Sermo[n] Preached at Pawles Crosse on Sunday the Thirde of November 1577* (London, 1578), p. 47.

38 Stockwood, *A Sermon Preached at Paules Crosse*, pp. 134–5.

39 Cited in Glynne Wickham, Herbert Berry and William Ingram (eds), *Theatre in Europe, a Documentary History: English Professional Theatre, 1530–1660* (Cambridge: Cambridge University Press, 2000), p. 177.

40 Christopher Marlowe, *The Jew of Malta* (c.1590), prologue.

41 Botero, *The Travellers Breviat*, pp. 16, 17.

42 British Library, Cotton MS Titus B XIII, fo. 105.

43 Cited in N. A. M. Rodger, 'Queen Elizabeth and the Myth of Sea-power in English History', *Transactions of the Royal Historical Society*, sixth series, 14 (2004), p. 155.

44 Cited in James McDermott, *England & the Spanish Armada: The Necessary Quarrel* (New Haven, Conn.: Yale University Press, 2005), p. 153.

45 Sir Walter Ralegh, *Discoverie of the Large, Rich, and Bewtiful Empire of Guiana* (London, 1596), sig. ¶3v.

46 Victoria and Albert Museum, London, Forster MS 185: Drake to Lord Burghley, aboard the *Elizabeth Bonaventure*, 27 Apr. 1587.

47 Sir Robert Naunton, *Fragmenta Regalia* (1641), p. 17.

48 Cited in Blair Worden, *The Sound of Virtue: Philip Sidney's Arcadia and Elizabethan Politics* (New Haven, Conn.: Yale University Press, 1996), p. 73.

49 Cited in David Dean, 'Wentworth, Paul', *Oxford Dictionary of National Biography*.

50 Cited in Gerald Bowler, '"An axe or an acte": the Parliament of 1572 and resistance theory in early Elizabethan England', *Canadian Journal of History*, 19 (1984), p. 355.

51 Thomas Churchyard, *A Generall Rehearsall of Warres* (London, 1579), p. 75.

52 Cited in Hiram Morgan, '"Never any realm worse governed": Queen Elizabeth and Ireland', *Transactions of the Royal Historical Society*, sixth series, 14 (2004), p. 301.

53 Cited in Neil Hanson, *The Confident Hope of a Miracle: The True History of the Spanish Armada* (London: Doubleday, 2004), p. 30.

54 Cited in Geoffrey Parker, *The Grand Strategy of Philip II* (New Haven, Conn.: Yale University Press, 2000), p. 174.

55 Cited in McDermott, *England & the Spanish Armada*, p. 166.

56 Cited in Susan Brigden, *New Worlds, Lost Worlds: The Rule of the Tudors*

1485–1603 (London: Allen Lane, Penguin, 2000), p. 294.

57 Cited in Hammer, *Elizabeth's Wars*, p. 128.

58 Cited in Parker, *Grand Strategy*, p. 287.

59 Cited in McDermott, *England & the Spanish Armada*, p. 367.

60 Cited in Guy, *Tudor England*, p. 400.

61 John Bruce (ed.), *Correspondence of King James VI. of Scotland with Sir Robert Cecil and Others in England* (Camden Society, vol. lxxviii, 1860–1), p. 59.

62 Cited in Lawrence Stone, *The Crisis of the Aristocracy, 1558–1641* (Oxford: Oxford University Press, 1965), p. 206. I should like to thank John Adamson for this reference.

63 Bruce (ed.), *Correspondence of King James VI*, p. 59.

64 James Spedding, Robert Leslie Ellis and Douglas Denon Heath (eds), *The Works of Francis Bacon* (London: Longmans, Green, Reader, and Dyer, 1858), vol. 6, p. 317.

65 William Camden, *The History of the Princess Elizabeth, Late Queen of England* (London, 4th edn 1688), p. 624.

66 Cited in Alexandra Gajda, *The Earl of Essex and Late Elizabethan Political Culture* (Oxford: Oxford University Press, 2012), pp. 67, 69.

67 Cited in Christopher Haigh, *Elizabeth I* (Harlow: Pearson, Longman, 3rd edn 2001), p. 171.

68 ibid., p. 91.

69 Cited in Peter Lake, '"The Monarchical Republic of Queen Elizabeth I" (and the Fall of Archbishop Grindal) Revisited', in John F. McDiarmid (ed.), *The Monarchical Republic of Early Modern England: Essays in Response to Patrick Collinson* (Aldershot: Ashgate, 2007), p. 137.

70 Cited in Nicholas W. S. Cranfield, 'Bancroft, Richard', *Oxford Dictionary of National Biography*.

71 *An Apologie of the Earl of Essex* (London, 1600), sig. C3.

72 Cited in Paul E. J. Hammer, *The Polarisation of Elizabethan Politics: The Political Career of Robert Devereux, 2nd Earl of Essex, 1585–1597* (Cambridge: Cambridge University Press, 1999), p. 243.

73 Cited in Hammer, 'The Use of Scholarship: the Secretariat of Robert Devereux, Second Earl of Essex, c.1585–1601', *English Historical Review*, 109 (1994), p. 30.

74 Sir John Hayward, *The First Part of the Life and Raigne of King Henrie the IIII* (London, 1599), sig. A3.

75 Cited in Guy, *Tudor England*, p. 396.

76 David Starkey (ed.), *Lives and Letters of the Great Tudor Dynasties: Rivals in Power* (London: Macmillan, 1990), p. 276.

77 Cited in Paul Slack, *From Reformation to Improvement: Public Welfare in Early Modern England* (Oxford: Oxford University Press, 1999), p. 11.

78 Cited in *The Earl of Essex*, p. 30.

79 Cited in Maureen Claire King, '"Essex, that could Vary himself into all shapes for a time": the Second Earl of Essex in Jacobean England' (University of Alberta Ph.D thesis 2000), p. 1.

80 [?Arthur Wilson], *The Five Years of King Iames* (London, 1643), p. 2.

3 Free Monarchy, 1603–37

1 Louis A. Knafla, *Law and Politics in Jacobean England: The Tracts of Lord Chancellor Ellesmere* (Cambridge: Cambridge University Press, 1977), p. 254.

2 Neil Rhodes, Jennifer Richards and Joseph Marshall (eds), *King James VI and I: Selected Writings* (Aldershot: Ashgate, 2003), pp. 143–4.

3 *The Essayes or Morall, Politike and Millitarie Discourses of Lo: Michaell de Montaigne* (London, 1603), p. 52.

4 *Calendar of State Papers, Venetian, 1603–7*, p. 353.

5 Cited in *Letters to King James the Sixth* (Edinburgh, 1835), p. xxii.

6 James I, *A Counterblaste to Tobacco* (London, 1604), sig. B3.

7 Cited in J. Duncan Mackie, "A loyall subiectes advertisment" as to the Unpopularity of James I's Government in England, 1603–4', *Scottish Historical Review*, 23 (1925), p. 3.

8 Arthur Wilson, *The History of Great Britain Being the Life and Reign of King James the First* (London, 1653), p. 13.

9 Cited in Mackie, "A loyall subiectes advertisment"', p. 3.

10 James Orchard Halliwell (ed.), *The Autobiography of Sir Simonds D'Ewes* (London: Richard Bentley, 1845), vol. 1, p. 170.

11 Cited in Jenny Wormald, 'James VI and I', *Oxford Dictionary of National Biography*.

12 ibid.

13 Cited in Burgess, *British Political Thought*, p. 89.

14 Cited in Hugh Trevor-Roper, *Europe's Physician: The Various Life of Sir Thomas Mayerne* (New Haven, Conn.: Yale University Press, 2006), p. 191.

15 Charles Howard McIlwain (ed.), *The Political Works of James I: Reprinted from the Edition of 1616* (Cambridge, Mass.: Harvard University Press, 1918), pp. 333, 340.

16 Wilson, *The History of Great Britain*, p. 202.

17 McIlwain (ed.), *The Political Works of James I*, p. 63.

18 Samuel Rawson Gardiner (ed.), *Debates in the House of Commons in 1625* (Camden Society, new series, vol. vi, 1873), p. 31.

19 Knafla, *Law and Politics*, p. 247.

20 ibid., pp. 244–5.

21 ibid., pp. 79, 258.

22 [Sir Anthony Weldon], *A Discription of Scotland* (1626 edn), p. 3.

23 The Gunpowder plotters included a number of Catholics who had been closely associated with the earl of Essex. Their hopes of religious toleration had been raised to unrealistic heights by Essex, and therefore their disappointment with the new king was all the more acute: Gajda, *Earl of Essex*, pp. 138, 140, 255–6.

24 Wilson, *The History of Great Britain*, p. 17.

25 ibid., p. 25.

26 Barnabe Rich, *Opinion Deified* (London, 1613), pp. 7, 8.

27 National Archives of Scotland, Edinburgh (NAS), RH2/8/12, fos 9v–10v.

28 Cited in John McCavitt, 'Chichester, Arthur, Baron Chichester', *Oxford Dictionary of National Biography*.

29 Cited in Ben Kiernan, *Blood and Soil: A World History of Genocide and Extermination from Sparta to Darfur* (New Haven, Conn.: Yale University Press, 2007), p. 210.

30 Lawrence Kemys, *A Relation of the Second Voyage to Guiana* (London, 1596), sig. A4r.

31 Cited in C. A. Patrides (ed.), *Sir Walter Raleigh: History of the World* (London: Macmillan, 1971), p. 8.

32 BL, Additional MS 63854B, fos 46, 99.

33 Cited in Anthony Pagden, 'The Struggle for Legitimacy and the Image of Empire in the Atlantic to c.1700', in Nicholas Canny (ed.), *The Origins of Empire: British Overseas Enterprise to the Close of the Seventeenth Century* (Oxford: Oxford University Press, 1998), p. 52.

34 Cited in Thomas Cogswell, "In the Power of the State": Mr Anys's Project and the Tobacco Colonies,

1626–1628', *English Historical Review*, 123 (2008), p. 56.

35 Cited in Peter C. Mancall, 'Native Americans and Europeans in English America, 1500–1700', in Canny (ed.), *The Origins of Empire*, p. 341.

36 John Underhill, *Newes from America* (London, 1638), p. 40.

37 Cited in Andrew Thrush, 'The Personal Rule of James I, 1611–1620', in Thomas Cogswell, Richard Cust, Peter Lake (eds), *Politics, Religion and Popularity in Early Stuart Britain: Early Stuart Essays in Honour of Conrad Russell* (Cambridge: Cambridge University Press, 2002), p. 94.

38 Greville, *The Five Years of King James*, p. 7.

39 Halliwell (ed.), *The Autobiography of Sir Simonds D'Ewes*, vol. 1, pp. 166–7.

40 Cited in Roger Lockyer, *Buckingham: The Life and Political Career of George Villiers, First Duke of Buckingham 1592–1628* (London: Longman, 1981), p. 43. When James made this remark he was perhaps thinking of a passage in the New Testament (John 13:23): 'Now there was leaning on Jesus' bosom one of his disciples [John], whom Jesus loved.'

41 Wilson, *The History of Great Britain*, p. 25.

42 *A Record of Some Worthy Proceedings in the Honourable, Wise, and Faithfull Howse of Commons in the late Parliament* (?Amsterdam, 1611), pp. 30, 32.

43 Samuel Rawson Gardiner (ed.), *Parliamentary Debates in 1610* (Camden Society, old series, vol. lxxxi, 1862), pp. 175, 177.

44 Cited in John Cramsie, *Kingship and Crown Finance under James VI and I 1603–1625* (Woodbridge: Boydell, 2002), p. 121.

45 Cited in Thrush, 'The Personal Rule of James I', p. 90.

46 Cited in Lockyer, *Buckingham*, p. 101.

47 Cited in Robert Zaller, 'Parliament and the Crisis of European Liberty', in J. H. Hexter (ed.), *Parliaments and Liberty, from the Reign of Elizabeth to the English Civil War* (Stanford, CA: Stanford University Press, 1992), p. 210.

48 Cited in Thrush, 'The Personal Rule of James I', p. 84.

49 *Proceedings in Parliament 1628: Commons Debates 1628, 17 March–19 April 1628* (New Haven, Conn.: Yale University Press, 1977), vol. 2, p. 58.

50 Wilson, *The History of Great Britain*, p. 268.

51 Willson Havelock Coates (ed.), *The Journal of Sir Simonds D'Ewes* (New Haven, Conn.: Yale University Press, 1942), p. 185.

52 Scott, *The Belgicke Pismire*, p. 72.

53 Warwick's man-of-business John Pym probably favoured introducing an excise tax – or he did by 1641 at the very latest. The courtiers Philip Earl of Montgomery (the 4th earl of Pembroke from 1630) and his friend Sir Henry Vane senior put much thought into how royal revenues could be improved, and may well have weighed up the financial pros and the political cons of a general sales tax.

54 BL, Stowe MS 326, fos 39v, 72v.

55 *An Apologie of the Earl of Essex* (London, 1600), sig. A2.

56 *Historical Manuscripts Commission: Report on the Manuscripts of Viscount De L'Isle*, vol. 5, pp. 319–20, 321, 324.

57 James Spedding (ed.), *The Letters and the Life of Francis Bacon* (London: Longman, Green, Longman, and Roberts, 1872), vol. 6, p. 159.

58 Wilson, *The History of Great Britain*, p. 161. Though familiar with the

events he was describing, Wilson was a client of the earl of Warwick and was writing in the 1640s: Graham Parry, 'Wilson, Arthur', *Oxford Dictionary of National Biography*.

59 *Cabala: Sive Scrinia Sacra* (London, 1691), p. 257.

60 Wilson, *The History of Great Britain*, p. 148; Greville, *The Five Years of King Iames*, p. 3.

61 Francis Bacon, *The Essayes, or Counsels, Civill and Morall* (London, 1625), p. 79.

62 Vincentio Saviolo, *Vincentio Saviolo, his Practise, in Two Bookes* (London, 1595), sigs Y3v, Y31v.

63 *Tom Tell Troath or a Free Discourse touching the Manners of the Tyme* (?Holland, *c.*1630), p. 1.

64 James I, *A Proclamation Against Excesse of Lauish and Licentious Speech of Matters of State* (London, 1620).

65 Wilson, *The History of Great Britain*, p. 150.

66 Cited in Robert Cross, 'Pretense and Perception in the Spanish Match, or History in a Fake Beard', *Journal of Interdisciplinary History*, 37 (2007), p. 581.

67 W. Dunn Macray (ed.), *The History of the Rebellion and Civil Wars in England . . . by Edward, Earl of Clarendon* (Oxford: Oxford University Press, 1888), vol. 1, p. 29.

68 Although styled 'Henrietta Maria' by modern historians, she signed herself 'Henriette Marie', as one would expect of a French princess, and was known in England as Queen Mary.

69 John Rushworth, *Historical Collections of private Passages of State* (London, 1721), vol. 1, p. 356.

70 William Knowler (ed.), *The Earl of Strafforde's Letters and Dispatches* (London, 1739), vol. 1, p. 42.

71 Macray (ed.), *The History of the Rebellion and Civil Wars in England*, vol. 1, p. 37.

72 Samuel Rawson Gardiner (ed.), *The Constitutional Documents of the Puritan Revolution 1625–1660* (Oxford: Oxford University Press, 3rd edn 1906), p. 95.

73 Cited in John Adamson, review of Kevin Sharpe, *Criticism and Compliment*, in *English Historical Review*, 105 (1990), p. 132.

74 *Proceedings in Parliament 1628: Commons Debates 1628, 28 May–26 June 1628* (New Haven, Conn.: Yale University Press, 1978), vol. 3, p. 6.

75 Cited in Jeremy Wood, 'Dyck, Sir Anthony', *Oxford Dictionary of National Biography*.

76 Cited in Alison Plowden, *Henrietta Maria: Charles I's Indomitable Queen* (Stroud: Sutton Publishing, 2001), p. 168.

77 St Paul's Cathedral, Monumental inscription on Van Dyck's tomb (translated from the Latin).

78 Ruth Spalding (ed.), *The Diary of Bulstrode Whitelocke 1605–1675* (Oxford: Oxford University Press, 1990), pp. 101–5.

79 Cited in Neil Cuddy, 'Reinventing a Monarchy: the Changing Structure and Political Function of the Stuart Court, 1603–88', in Eveline Cruickshanks (ed.), *The Stuart Courts* (Stroud: The History Press, 2009), p. 65.

80 James F. Larkin (ed.), *Stuart Royal Proclamation: Royal Proclamations of King Charles I* (Oxford: Oxford University Press, 1983), p. 34.

81 James Sutherland (ed.), *Lucy Hutchinson: Memoirs of the Life of Colonel Hutchinson* (London: Oxford University Press, 1973), p. 46.

82 Cited in David Lindley, 'The Stuart masque and its makers', in Jane Milling, Peter Thomson (eds), *The Cambridge History of the British*

Theatre, vol. 1, *Origins to 1660* (Cambridge: Cambridge University Press, 2004), p. 401.

83 Cited in Ian Donaldson, 'Jonson, Benjamin', *Oxford Dictionary of National Biography*.

84 ibid.

85 *Mr. William Shakespeares Comedies, Histories, & Tragedies Published According to the True Originall Copies* (London, 1623), preface.

86 Halliwell (ed.), *The Autobiography of Sir Simonds D'Ewes*, vol. 1, p. 402.

87 Larkin (ed.), *Royal Proclamations of King Charles I*, p. 228.

88 *Calendar of State Papers, Venetian, 1625–6*, p. 508.

89 Johann P. Sommerville (ed.), *Sir Robert Filmer: Patriarcha and Other Writings* (Cambridge: Cambridge University Press, 1991), p. 5.

90 Cited in Wormald, 'James VI and I'.

91 Esther S. Cope, Willson H. Coates (eds), *Proceedings of the Short Parliament of 1640* (Camden Society, fourth series, vol. xix, 1977), p. 204.

92 Thomas Hooker, *The Danger of Desertion* (London, 1641), p. 15.

93 James Welwood, *Memoirs of the Most Material Transactions in England for the Last Hundred Years* (London, 1700), pp. 75, 78.

94 Halliwell (ed.), *The Autobiography of Sir Simonds D'Ewes*, vol. 2, p. 100.

95 Welwood, *Memoirs*, p. 77.

96 Cited in Kevin Sharpe, *The Personal Rule of Charles I* (New Haven, Conn.: Yale University Press, 1992), p. 646.

97 Bodleian Library, Oxford, MS Clarendon 9, fo. 23v. For evidence to suggest that recovering the Palatinate was still very much in Charles's mind, see Glenn Richardson (ed.), *The Contending Kingdoms: France and England, 1420–1700* (Aldershot: Ashgate, 2008), pp. 141–2.

98 Cited in E. C. Legh, Lady Newton,

The House of Lyme: from its Foundation to the End of the Eighteenth Century (New York: G. P. Putnam's Sons, 1917), p. 135.

99 Cited in David Scott, 'Counsel and Cabal in the King's Party, 1642–6', in Jason McElligott and David L. Smith (eds), *Royalists and Royalism during the English Civil Wars* (Cambridge: Cambridge University Press, 2007), p. 132.

100 Cited in M. Perceval-Maxwell, 'Sir Robert Southwell and the duke of Ormond's reflections on the 1640s', in Micheál Ó Siochrú (ed.), *Kingdoms in Crisis: Ireland in the 1640s: Essays in Honour of Dónal Cregan* (Dublin: Four Courts Press, 2001), p. 238.

101 *Calendar of State Papers, Venetian, 1636–9*, p. 125.

4 Behemoth and Leviathan, 1637–60

1 Gilbert Burnet, *The Memoires of the Lives and Actions of James and William Dukes of Hamilton* (London, 1677), p. 60.

2 James Howell, *Mercurius Hibernicus* (Bristol, 1644), p. 4.

3 Knowler (ed.), *Strafforde's Letters*, vol. 2, p. 119.

4 Welwood, *Memoirs*, p. 38.

5 Gardiner (ed.), *Constitutional Documents of the Puritan Revolution*, pp. 124–34.

6 Larkin (ed.), *Royal Proclamations of King Charles I*, p. 633.

7 *Historical Manuscripts Commission: Third Report* (London, 1872), p. 3.

8 Huntington Library, California, Ellesmere MSS, EL 7849.

9 Howell, *Mercurius Hibernicus*, p. 2.

10 *A Discourse Discovering Some Mysteries of Our New State* (Oxford, 1645), p. 15.

11 Maija Jansson (ed.), *Proceedings in the Opening Session of the Long Parliament: House of Commons and*

the *Strafford Trial, 22 March–17 April 1641* (New Haven, Conn.: Yale University Press, 2001), vol. 3, p. 112.

12 Richard Tuck (ed.), *Thomas Hobbes: Leviathan* (Cambridge: Cambridge University Press, 1996), p. 88.

13 BL, Additional MS 70002, fo. 313.

14 *Information for the Ignorant* (1640), sigs B2v, B3.

15 *Englands Complaint to Iesus Christ* (1640), p. 8.

16 Cited in John Adamson, *The Noble Revolt: The Overthrow of Charles I* (London: Phoenix, 2009), p. 298.

17 James Bliss (ed.), *The Works of William Laud* (Oxford: Oxford University Press, 1853), vol. 3, p. 443. Parliament had Laud beheaded in January 1645 as a sop to the Scottish Covenanters.

18 Richard Scrope (ed.), *State Papers Collected by Edward, Earl of Clarendon* (Oxford, 1773), vol. 2, p. 296.

19 Cited in Andrew Hopper, '*Black Tom*': *Sir Thomas Fairfax and the English Revolution* (Manchester: Manchester University Press, 2007), p. 139.

20 Sir Thomas Aston, *A Petition Delivered in to the Lords Spirituall and Temporall, by Sir Thomas Aston* (1641).

21 Thomas Carte, *The Life of James Duke of Ormond* (Oxford: Oxford University Press, 1851), vol. 5, p. 281.

22 *Calendar of State Papers, Domestic, 1641–3*, pp. 217–18, 242–3.

23 John Digby, earl of Bristol, *An Apologie of John Earl of Bristol* (London, 1656), p. 56.

24 Cited in Richard Cust, 'Charles I and popularity', in Cogswell, Cust and Lake (eds), *Politics, Religion and Popularity in Early Stuart Britain*, p. 253.

25 *A Declaration, or Resolution of the County of Hereford* (London, 1642).

26 ibid.

27 Staffordshire Record Office, D868/2/32 (Leveson correspondence).

28 Cited in Glenn Burgess, 'Royalism and Liberty of Conscience in the English Revolution', in John Morrow and Jonathan Scott (eds), *Liberty, Authority, Formality: Political Ideas and Culture, 1600–1900* (Exeter: Imprint Academic, 2008), p. 20.

29 C. H. Firth (ed.), *The Narrative of General Venables* (Camden Society, new series, vol. lx, 1900), p. 1.

30 Mary Anne Everett Green (ed.), *Letters of Queen Henrietta Maria* (London: Richard Bentley, 1857), pp. 174–5.

31 BL, Harleian MS 164, fo. 122v.

32 Sir Philip Warwick, *Memoires of the Reigne of King Charles I* (London, 1701), pp. 247–8.

33 David Laing (ed.), *The Letters and Journals of Robert Baillie* (Edinburgh: Robert Ogle, 1841), vol. 2, p. 229.

34 C. H. Firth (ed.), *The Life of William Cavendish Duke of Newcastle* (London: Routledge, 1886), p. 40.

35 Rushworth, *Historical Collections*, vol. 5, p. 703.

36 *Mercurius Aulicus*, no. 35 (25–31 Aug. 1644), p. 1142.

37 Hull City Archives, Hull Letters, L383.

38 David Underdown, 'The Parliamentary Diary of John Boys, 1647–8', *Bulletin of the Institute of Historical Research*, 39 (1966), p. 156.

39 Carte, *Life of Ormond*, vol. 6, pp. 311–12.

40 Cited in Micheál Ó Siochrú, *Confederate Ireland 1642–1649: A Constitutional and Political Analysis* (Dublin: Four Courts Press, 1999), p. 96.

41 Bodleian Library, MS Clarendon 25, fo. 162.

42 NAS, Clerk of Penicuik Manuscripts, GD18/3110. I am grateful to Sir John Clerk of Penicuik for permission to publish extracts from this manuscript.

43 Scrope (ed.), *Clarendon State Papers*, vol. 2, p. 411.

44 ibid., p. 243.

45 National Library of Wales, Aberystwyth (NLW), Wynnstay manuscripts, 90/16. I am grateful to Lloyd Bowen for this reference.

46 ibid.

47 *Journal of the House of Lords*, vol. 9, p. 115.

48 J. R. Powell and E. K. Timmings (eds), *Documents Relating to the Civil War 1642–1648* (Navy Records Society, 1963), p. 354.

49 Clement Walker, *Compleat History of Independencie* (London, 1661), part 1, pp. 141, 145.

50 Bodleian Library, MS Clarendon 30, fo. 310.

51 William Allen, *A Faithful Memorial of that Remarkable Meeting of Many Officers of the Army of England, at Windsor Castle* (London, 1659), p. 5.

52 Wilbur Cortez Abbott, *The Writings and Speeches of Oliver Cromwell* (Cambridge, Mass.: Harvard University Press, 1937), vol. 1, p. 691.

53 BL, Additional MS 78303, fo. 34; *King Charls his Speech Made upon the Scaffold at Whitehall-Gate* (London, 1649), pp. 6–7.

54 Daly, 'Cosmic Harmony', p. 15.

55 Cope, Coates (eds), *Proceedings of the Short Parliament*, p. 185.

56 Cited in Adamson, *The Noble Revolt*, p. 21.

57 M. J. Braddick, M. Greengrass (eds), 'The Letters of Sir Cheney Culpeper (1641–1657)', in *Seventeenth-Century Political and Financial Papers* (Camden Society, seventh series, vol. vii, 1996), p. 328.

58 Thomas Chaloner, *An Answer to the Scotch Papers . . . Concerning the Disposal of the King's Person* (London, 1646), p. 14.

59 *King Charls his Speech Made upon the Scaffold at Whitehall-Gate*, pp. 9–10.

60 Clement Walker, *Anarchia Anglicana: or the History of Independency, the Second Part* (London, 1649), p. 2.

61 Revelation 21:1.

62 John Milton, *Areopagitica* (London, 1644), p. 17.

63 Cited in Steve Pincus, 'Neither Machiavellian Moment nor Possessive Individualism: Commercial Society and the Defenders of the English Commonwealth', *The American Historical Review*, 103 (1998), p. 727.

64 Cited in Nicholas Von Maltzahn, 'From pillar to post: Milton and the attack on republican humanism at the Restoration', in Ian Gentles, John Morrill and Blair Worden (eds), *Soldiers, Writers and Statesmen of the English Revolution* (Cambridge: Cambridge University Press, 1998), p. 269.

65 Cited in Quentin Skinner, *Reason and Rhetoric in the Philosophy of Thomas Hobbes* (Cambridge: Cambridge University Press, 1996), p. 315.

66 Thomas Hobbes, *Philosophicall Rudiments Concerning Government and Society* (London, 1651), p. 177 [*De Cive*, chapter 12, section 3]; Tuck (ed.), *Leviathan*, p. 226.

67 Sir William Molesworth (ed.), *The English Works of Thomas Hobbes* (London, 1839), p. ix.

68 Tuck (ed.), *Leviathan*, p. 89.

69 ibid., p. 88.

70 Cited in John Morrill, Philip Baker, 'Oliver Cromwell and the Sons of Zeruiah', in Jason Peacey (ed.), *The Regicides and the Execution of Charles I* (Basingstoke: Palgrave Macmillan, 2001), p. 14.

71 *Complete Prose Works of John Milton*, vol. 7, p. 423.

72 Sir Henry Vane, *A Healing Question* (London, 1656), p. 2.

73 Bodleian Library, MS Eng. hist. b.205, fo. 87. I am grateful to Grant Tapsell for this reference.

74 *A Speech Made by Alderman Garroway* (Oxford, 1643), p. 9.

75 For example, Algernon Percy 10th earl of Northumberland, William Fiennes 1st Viscount Saye and Sele, Philip 4th Baron Wharton, Sir Henry Vane senior and junior, Sir John Evelyn of Wiltshire, Oliver St John, William Pierrepont etc. (it would be hard to describe Northumberland, Vane senior, Evelyn, St John or Pierrepont as Puritans in the early 1640s).

76 Scrope (ed.), *Clarendon State Papers*, vol. 2, p. 307.

77 *Mercurius Pragmaticus*, no. 24 (5–12 Sept. 1648), sig. Gg2v.

78 David Buchanan, *An Explanation of Some Truths* (London, 1646), pp. 53, 55–6.

79 Clement Walker, *The Mysterie of the Two Juntos* (London, 1647), p. 7.

80 *Mercurius Pragmaticus*, no. 18 (25 July–1 Aug. 1648), sigs S4, S6v.

81 Jack R. McMichael, Barbara Taft (eds), *The Writings of William Walwyn* (Athens, GA: University of Georgia Press, 1989), pp. 299, 301.

82 Samuel Pepys, *Diary*, entries for 12 March 1662, and 27 February 1667.

83 Cited in Jonathan Scott, '"Good Night Amsterdam". Sir George Downing and Anglo-Dutch Statebuilding', *English Historical Review*, 118 (2003), p. 349.

84 The navy during James I's reign had possessed just two small, and ineffectual, frigates; and though it had over a dozen ships called 'frigates' during Charles I's reign, most of these were slower and less nimble than enemy privateers operating in the Channel. The seven new frigates built by Parliament during the 1640s were small – about 120 feet long and 30 feet wide – carried 30 guns, and were designed for 'the scattring and surprisall' of enemy privateers: TNA, ADM 7/673, pp. 201, 215, 385, 400.

85 Yet even a 32-pound shot – usually the heaviest fired by a seventeenth-century warship – did no major structural damage. Enemy vessels were rarely sunk by gunfire alone. More often they surrendered when casualties reached unacceptable levels, or when they could no longer manoeuvre: Geoffrey Parker, 'Ships of the Line', in Parker (ed.), *The Cambridge History of Warfare* (Cambridge: Cambridge University Press, 2005), p. 125.

86 Cited in N. A. M. Rodger, *The Command of the Ocean: A Naval History of Britain 1649–1815* (London: Penguin, 2005), p. 17.

87 Shakespeare, *Julius Caesar*, act 3, scene 1.

88 Cited in Ronald Hutton, 'The Triple-crowned Islands', in Lionel K. J. Glassey (ed.), *The Reigns of Charles II and James VII & II* (Basingstoke: Palgrave Macmillan, 1997), p. 72.

89 The phrase appears in John Milton's *Paradise Lost*, book 11, line 672.

90 Document in the Osborn Collection, Beinecke Rare Book and Manuscript Library, Yale University. Cited in Sheffield University Library, Hartlib Papers, YAL/10.

91 Abbott, *The Writings and Speeches of Oliver Cromwell*, vol. 2, p. 642.

92 British Library, Additional MS 78221, fo. 61v.

93 Macray (ed.), *History of the Rebellion*, vol. 6, p. 94.

94 Welwood, *Memoirs*, pp. 104–5.

95 Cited in David L. Smith, 'Oliver Cromwell and the Protectorate Parliaments', in Patrick Little (ed.),

The Cromwellian Protectorate (Woodbridge: Boydell, 2007), p. 20.

96 Thomas Birch (ed.), *A Collection of the State Papers of John Thurloe* (London, 1752), volume 4, p. 187.

97 Cited in John Morrill, 'Cromwell, Oliver', *Oxford Dictionary of National Biography*.

98 James D. Ogilvie (ed.), *Diary of Sir Archibald Johnston of Wariston*, volume III, *1655–1660* (Scottish History Society, third series, vol. xxxiv, 1940), p. 162.

99 C. H. Firth (ed.), *The Clarke Papers* (Camden Society, new series, vol. lxii, 1901), p. 153.

100 John Taylor, *The World Turn'd Upside Down* (London, 1647), p. 3.

101 Ferdinand Tönnies (ed.), *Behemoth or The Long Parliament* (London: Simpkin, Marshall, 1889), p. 26.

5 The French Connection, 1660–1714

1 Cited in Julia Cartwright, *Madame: A Life of Henrietta, Daughter of Charles I* (London: Seeley and Co., 1894), pp. 332–3.

2 Cited in N. H. Keeble, *The Restoration: England in the 1660s* (Oxford: Blackwell, 2002), p. 179.

3 ibid., p. 42.

4 Cited in Bob Bushaway, 'Popular Culture', in H. T. Dickinson (ed.), *Blackwell Companion to Eighteenth-Century Britain* (Oxford: Blackwell, 2002), p. 353.

5 Cited in Tim Harris, *Restoration: Charles II and His Kingdoms* (London: Penguin, 2006), p. 105.

6 David Lloyd, *Memoires of the Lives, Actions, Sufferings & Deaths of those . . . Excellent Personages that Suffered . . . for the Protestant Religion* (London, 1668), p. 585.

7 Cited in Glassey (ed.), *The Reigns of Charles II and James VII & II*, p. 90.

8 Pepys, *Diary*, entry for 13 October 1660.

9 Cited in Jonathan Scott, *England's Troubles: Seventeenth-Century English Political Instability in European Context* (Cambridge: Cambridge University Press, 2002), p. 162.

10 Cited in Mark Knights, '"Meer religion" and the "church-state" of Restoration England: the impact and ideology of James II's declarations of indulgence', in Alan Houston, Steve Pincus (eds), *A Nation Transformed: England after the Restoration* (Cambridge: Cambridge University Press, 2001), p. 45.

11 Cited in Paul D. Halliday, *Dismembering the Body Politic: Partisan Politics in England's Towns 1650–1730* (Cambridge: Cambridge University Press, 1998), p. 343.

12 Cited in Paul Seaward, 'Charles II', *Oxford Dictionary of National Biography*.

13 Welwood, *Memoirs*, p. 126.

14 Lewis Walpole Library, Yale (LWL), MS 101, part xix ('History of the times of Charles II'), fo. 15; Welwood, *Memoirs*, p. 144.

15 Cited in George Southcombe, Grant Tapsell, *Restoration Politics, Religion and Culture* (Basingstoke: Palgrave Macmillan, 2010), p. 136.

16 ibid., p. 151.

17 Cited in Keeble, *Restoration*, p. 176.

18 LWL, MS 101, part xix, fo. 15.

19 Huntington Library, Ellesmere MSS, EL 8092.

20 Cited in Keeble, *Restoration*, p. 178.

21 ibid.

22 *Complete Prose Works of John Milton*, vol. 7, p. 426.

23 *The Life of Edward Earl of Clarendon* (Oxford: Oxford University Press, 1857), vol. 2, p. 301.

24 Cited in S. M. Wynne, 'Gwyn,

Eleanor [Nell]', *Oxford Dictionary of National Biography*.

25 Cited in Southcombe, Tapsell, *Restoration Politics*, p. 156.

26 Cited in Steve Pincus, 'Popery, Trade and Universal Monarchy: the Ideological Context of the Outbreak of the Second Anglo-Dutch War', *English Historical Review*, 107 (1992), pp. 24, 25.

27 Pepys, *Diary*, entry for 21 June 1667.

28 Cited in Steve Pincus, 'From Butterboxes to Wooden Shoes: the Shift in English Popular Sentiment from Anti-Dutch to Anti-French in the 1670s', *Historical Journal*, 38 (1995), p. 359.

29 Cited in Scott, *England's Troubles*, p. 436.

30 Cited in Southcombe, Tapsell, *Restoration Politics*, p. 44.

31 *England's Appeal from the Private Cabal at White-Hall* (1673), p. 30.

32 Cited in Mark Knights, 'Osborne, Thomas, first duke of Leeds', *Oxford Dictionary of National Biography*.

33 Cited in Pincus, 'From Butterboxes to Wooden Shoes', p. 359.

34 George Savile, marquess of Halifax, *A Character of King Charles the Second* (London, 1750), p. 28.

35 Cited in S. M. Wynne, 'Palmer [née Villiers], Barbara, countess of Castlemaine', *Oxford Dictionary of National Biography*.

36 This is what Nell Gwyn called Portsmouth: Wynne, 'Gwyn, Eleanor [Nell]'.

37 Cited in Nancy Klein Maguire, 'The duchess of Portsmouth: English royal consort and French politician, 1670–85', in Malcolm Smuts (ed.), *The Stuart Court and Europe: Essays in Politics and Political Culture* (Cambridge: Cambridge University Press, 1996), pp. 250, 251.

38 ibid., p. 264.

39 Andrew Marvell, *An Account of the Growth of Popery and Arbitrary Government in England* (Amsterdam, 1677), p. 3.

40 John Locke, *A Letter from a Person of Quality* (London, 1675), pp. 27, 29.

41 Cited in Scott, *England's Troubles*, p. 188.

42 ibid., p. 440.

43 Cited in Harris, *Restoration*, p. 143.

44 Stephen Parks (ed.), *A Newly Discovered Burlesque by John Wilmot Earl of Rochester* (New Haven, Conn.: Yale University Press, 1997), lines 14–20.

45 Cited in Scott, *England's Troubles*, p. 440.

46 Roger L'Estrange, *Toleration Discuss'd* (London, 1663), p. 102.

47 Cited in Scott, *England's Troubles*, p. 438.

48 *The Epilogue written by Mr. [Thomas] Otway to his Play call'd Venice Preserv'd or, A Plot Discover'd, Spoken upon His Royal Highness the Duke of York's Coming to the Theatre, Friday, April 21 1682*.

49 Cited in Harris, *Restoration*, p. 189.

50 Welwood, *Memoirs*, p. 133.

51 Cited in Southcombe, Tapsell, *Restoration Politics*, p. 56.

52 D. Jones, *The Life of James II* (London, 1702), p. 413.

53 Cited in Tim Harris, *Revolution: The Great Crisis of the British Monarchy, 1685–1720* (London: Penguin, 2007), p. 9.

54 ibid., p. 45.

55 Cited in Southcombe, Tapsell, *Restoration Politics*, p. 78.

56 Cited in Steve Pincus, 'The Making of a Great Power? Universal Monarchy, Political Economy, and the Transformation of English Political Culture', *The European Legacy*, 5 (2000), p. 533.

57 Cited in Daniel Szechi, 'A Blueprint for Tyranny? Sir Edward Hales and the Catholic Jacobite Response to the Revolution of 1688', *English Historical Review*, 116 (2001), p. 362.

58 *By the King a Proclamation* (1687).

59 George Savile, marquess of Halifax, *A Letter to a Dissenter, upon Occasion of His Majesties Late Gracious Declaration of Indulgence* (London, 1687), p. 3.

60 Jones, *Life of James II*, p. 412.

61 T. B. Howell (ed.), *A Complete Collection of State Trials* (London, 1816), vol. 12, p. 279.

62 Cited in Harris, *Revolution*, pp. 271–2.

63 Pepys, *Diary*, entry for 4 June 1664.

64 Cited in Szechi, 'A Blueprint for Tyranny?', p. 352.

65 John Trenchard, *A Short History of Standing Armies in England* (London, 1698), p. 19.

66 Cited in Steve Pincus, *1688: The First Modern Revolution* (New Haven, Conn.: Yale University Press, 2009), p. 262.

67 *Journal of the House of Lords*, vol. 14, p. 125.

68 Cited in Linda Colley, *Britons: Forging the Nation 1707–1837* (New Haven, Conn.: Yale University Press, 2005 edn), p. 47.

69 Cited in Harris, *Revolution*, pp. 402–3.

70 *Journal of the House of Commons*, vol. 10, p. 36.

71 Cited in Scott, *England's Troubles*, p. 471.

72 *An Apologie of the Earl of Essex* (London, 1600), sig. A3.

73 *Journal of the House of Commons*, vol. 10, p. 94.

74 Cited in Rodger, *The Command of the Ocean*, p. 147.

75 Charles Davenant, *An Essay upon the Ways and Means of Supplying the War* (London, 1695), p. 152.

76 Cited in Harris, *Restoration*, p. 36.

77 Jonathan Swift, *The Conduct of the Allies and of the Late Ministry* (London, 2nd edn 1711), p. 25.

78 Cited in M. Sheehan, 'The Development of British Theory and Practice of the Balance of Power before 1714', *History*, 73 (1988), p. 31.

79 Daniel Defoe, *A True Collection of the Writings of the Author of The True-Born English-man* (London, 1703), An Explanatory Preface.

80 Cited in Gregg, 'Anne (1665–1714)'.

81 Cited in Hussey, *Marlborough: John Churchill, Duke of Marlborough, Hero of Blenheim* (London: Weidenfeld & Nicolson, 2004), pp. 158–9.

82 Cited in Gregg, 'Anne (1665–1714)'.

83 Jonathan Swift, *Journal to Stella*, letter 11: 14 Dec. 1710.

84 Cited in D. W. Hayton, *The History of Parliament: The House of Commons 1690–1715* (Cambridge: Cambridge University Press, 2002), vol. 1, p. 469.

85 Cited in John Spurr, 'England 1649–1750: differences contained?', in Steven N. Zwicker (ed.), *The Cambridge Companion to English Literature 1650–1740* (Cambridge: Cambridge University Press, 1998), p. 22.

86 *The Examiner*, no. 31 (8 March 1710).

87 ibid.

88 Swift, *Conduct of the Allies*, sig. A2, pp. 7, 18–19.

89 John Houghton, *England's Great Happiness* (London, 1677), p. 8.

90 I have taken 'urban' to apply to those communities with a population of at least 2,500 – a sizeable town in early modern Britain.

91 Daniel Defoe, *A Tour Thro' the Whole Island of Great Britain, Divided into Circuits or Journies* (London, 1724), vol. 1, preface, p. vi.

92 Nicholas Barbon, *A Discourse of Trade* (London, 1690), p. 29.

93 Cited in Pincus, *1688*, p. 73.

94 Cited in Maxine Berg, 'French Fancy and Cool Britannia: the Fashion Markets of Early Modern Europe', *Proceedings of the Istituto*

Internazionale di Storia Economica, 32 (2001), pp. 38–9.

95 Cited in Helen Berry, 'Polite Consumption in Eighteenth-Century England', *Transactions of the Royal Historical Society,* sixth series, 12 (2002), p. 382.

96 Cited in Julian Hoppit, *A Land of Liberty?: England 1689–1727* (Oxford: Oxford University Press, 2000), p. 427.

97 Cited in Colin Franklin, *Lord Chesterfield: His Character and Characters* (Aldershot: Scolar Press, c.1993), p. 91.

98 Cited in R. O. Bucholz, '"Nothing but Ceremony": Queen Anne and the Limitations of Royal Ritual', *Journal of British Studies,* 30 (1991), p. 312.

99 Cited in Steve Pincus, '"Coffee Politicians Does Create": Coffeehouses and Restoration Political Culture', *Journal of Modern History,* 67 (1995), p. 833.

100 ibid., p. 819.

101 W. D. Christie (ed.), *Letters Addressed from London to Sir Joseph Williamson* (Camden Society, new series, vol. ix, 1874), p. 68.

102 Cited in Pat Rogers, 'Addison, Joseph', *Oxford Dictionary of National Biography.*

103 *The Tatler,* no. 264 (16 Dec. 1710).

104 Cited in Spurr, 'England 1649–1750', p. 27.

105 Cited in Lawrence E. Klein, *Shaftesbury and the Culture of Politeness: Moral Discourse and Cultural Politics in Early Eighteenth-Century England* (Cambridge: Cambridge University Press, 1994), p. 164.

106 Cited in Burgess, 'Royalism and Liberty of Conscience', p. 26.

107 Milton, *Paradise Lost,* book 12, lines 546–7.

108 Cited in Hoppit, *A Land of Liberty?,* p. 220.

109 ibid., p. 237.

110 Cited in Shelley Burtt, 'The Societies for the Reformation of Manners: between John Locke and the devil in Augustan England', in Roger D. Lund (ed.), *The Margins of Orthodoxy: Heterodox Writing and Cultural Response, 1660–1750* (Cambridge: Cambridge University Press, 1995), p. 153.

111 *The Works of the Most Reverend Dr. John Tillotson* (London, 8th edn 1720), p. 180.

112 Cited in Houston, Pincus (eds), *A Nation Transformed,* p. 32.

113 Thomas Sprat, *The History of the Royal-Society of London* (London, 1667), p. 53.

114 Cited in G. R. Cragg, *From Puritanism to the Age of Reason* (Cambridge: Cambridge University Press, 1957), p. 100.

115 Cited in James E. Force, 'Providence and Newton's *Pantokrator*: Natural Law, Miracles, and Newtonian Science', in J. E. Force, S. Hutton (eds), *Newton and Newtonianism: New Ideas* (Dordrecht: Kluwer, 2004), p. 74.

116 Cited in Mark Knights, 'Politics after the Glorious Revolution', in Barry Coward (ed.), *Blackwell Companion to Stuart Britain* (Oxford: Blackwell, 2003), p. 469.

117 Cited in Berg, 'French Fancy and Cool Britannia', p. 30.

118 Cited in Pincus, 'From Butterboxes to Wooden Shoes', p. 359.

119 *The Tatler,* no. 207 (5 August 1710).

120 Cited in Hoppit, *A Land of Liberty?,* p. 369.

6 The Balance of Europe, 1714–54

1 LWL, MS vol. 59, p. 1. Although the duke of Newcastle has been credited as the author of this manuscript, it is in fact critical of

the duke at one point (p. 18). From internal evidence the writer was most probably a Lowland Scot of Whiggish sympathies.

2 Verse from 'The Vicar of Bray', *The British Musical Miscellany* (London, 1734), vol. 1, p. 31.

3 Cited in David Eastwood, 'Local Government and Local Society', in Dickinson (ed.), *Blackwell Companion to Eighteenth-Century Britain*, p. 41.

4 Daniel Defoe, *A Hymn to the Mob* (London, 1715), p. iii.

5 John Toland, *An Account of the Courts of Prussia and Hanover* (London, 1705), p. 70.

6 Cited in Franklin, *Lord Chesterfield*, p. 91.

7 ibid.

8 ibid., pp. 91, 92.

9 Francis Atterbury, *English Advice to the Freeholders of England* (1714), p. 29.

10 ibid., p. 27.

11 Cited in Kathleen Wilson, *The Sense of the People: Politics, Culture, and Imperialism in England, 1715–1785* (Cambridge: Cambridge University Press, 1998), p. 104; Brendan Simms, *Three Victories and a Defeat: The Rise and Fall of the First British Empire, 1714–1783* (London: Allen Lane, Penguin, 2007), p. 85.

12 *Journal of the House of Lords*, vol. 20, p. 150.

13 Cited in Hoppit, *Land of Liberty?*, p. 394.

14 ibid., p. 398.

15 Cited in Simms, *Three Victories and a Defeat*, p. 186.

16 Cited in Tony Claydon, *Europe and the Making of England, 1660–1760* (Cambridge: Cambridge University Press, 2007), p. 195. For official use of the phrase 'a just balance of power', see W. S. Lewis (ed.), *Horace Walpole Correspondence* (New Haven, Conn.: Yale University Press, 1954), vol. 17, p. 400.

17 Cited in Philip Woodfine, *Britannia's Glories: The Walpole Ministry and the 1739 War with Spain* (Woodbridge: Boydell, 1998), p. 188.

18 Cited in Simms, *Three Victories and a Defeat*, p. 124.

19 Cited in Franklin, *Lord Chesterfield*, p. 101.

20 Cited in Stephen Taylor, 'Walpole, Robert, first earl of Orford', *Oxford Dictionary of National Biography*.

21 Cited in Anon., *The South Sea Bubble, and the Numerous Fraudulent Projects to which it Gave Rise in 1720* (London, 2nd edn 1825), p. 10.

22 Cited in Hoppit, *Land of Liberty?*, p. 335.

23 ibid.

24 *Cato's Letters*, no. 16 (11 Feb. 1721).

25 ibid., no. 6 (10 Dec. 1720).

26 Cited in Stuart Handley, 'Aislabie, John', *Oxford Dictionary of National Biography*.

27 Cited in Simms, *Three Victories and a Defeat*, p. 171.

28 Cited in Franklin, *Lord Chesterfield*, p. 114.

29 ibid., p. 115.

30 James Ralph, *A Critical History of the Administration of Sr. Robert Walpole* (London, 1743), p. 342.

31 Cited in Simms, *Three Victories and a Defeat*, p. 165.

32 ibid., p. 186.

33 ibid., p. 191.

34 LWL, MS 101 (History of the Seven Years' War, 1756–1762), pt viii, fo. 177.

35 Cited in Paul Langford, *A Polite and Commercial People: England 1727–1783* (Oxford: Oxford University Press, 1989), p. 14.

36 William Coxe, *Memoirs of the Life and Administration of Sir Robert Walpole* (London, 1798), vol. 2, p. 492.

37 *The Groans of Germany* (London, 3rd edn 1741), p. 21.
38 ibid., pp. 15, 30.
39 ibid., p. 26.
40 Cited in Simms, *Three Victories and a Defeat*, p. 234.
41 ibid., p. 243.
42 ibid., p. 269.
43 Cited in Woodfine, *Britannia's Glories*, p. 116.
44 ibid., p. 130.
45 ibid., p. 176.
46 Cited in Mark Goldie, 'The English system of liberty', in Goldie, Robert Wokler (eds), *The Cambridge History of Eighteenth-Century Political Thought* (Cambridge: Cambridge University Press, 2006), p. 41.
47 Cited in Woodfine, *Britannia's Glories*, p. 201.
48 Hogarth painted himself into the left of the tableau – in the act of being arrested as he sketches the gate.
49 John Ireland, *Hogarth Illustrated* (London, 2nd edn 1793), vol. 1, p. 219.
50 Cited in Woodfine, *Britannia's Glories*, p. 203.
51 Cited in Pincus, *1688*, p. 17.
52 Cited in David Womersley, 'Introduction: the Cultures of Whiggism', in Womersley (ed.), *'Cultures of Whiggism': New Essays on English Literature and Culture in the Long Eighteenth Century* (Cranbury, New Jersey: Rosemont, 2005), p. 24.
53 *The Parliamentary History of England* (London, 1812), vol. 10, p. 444.
54 Cited in Woodfine, *Britannia's Glories*, p. 234.
55 Cited A. S. Foord, *His Majesty's Opposition, 1714–1830* (Oxford: Oxford University Press, 1964), p. 1.
56 Cited in Spurr, 'England 1649–1750', p. 19.
57 *A Series of Wisdom and Policy* (London, 1735), p. 8.
58 Cited in Gerd Mischler, 'English Political Sermons 1714–1742: A Case Study in the Theory of the "Divine Right of Governors" and the Ideology of Order', *British Journal for Eighteenth-Century Studies*, 24 (2001), p. 45.
59 Cited in Goldie, 'The English system of liberty', p. 77.
60 *The Parliamentary History of England*, vol. 11, p. 1256.
61 Cited in Hoppit, *Land of Liberty?*, p. 408.
62 ibid.
63 Cited in Wilson, *The Sense of the People*, p. 125.
64 Cited in G. A. Cranfield, 'The "London Evening-Post" and the Jew Bill of 1753', *Historical Journal*, 8 (1965), p. 22.
65 *The Parliamentary History of England*, vol. 10, p. 448.
66 Cited in Michael T. Davis, 'Meres [Meeres], John', *Oxford Dictionary of National Biography*.
67 Cited in Woodfine, *Britannia's Glories*, p. 60; Jerry C. Beasley, 'Portraits of a Monster: Robert Walpole and Early English Prose Fiction', *Eighteenth-Century Studies*, 14 (1981), p. 406.
68 Cited in Hoppit, *Land of Liberty?*, p. 486.
69 ibid., p. 415.
70 ibid., p. 416.
71 Bernard Mandeville, *The Fable of the Bees: or, Private Vices Publick Benefits* (London, 1714), pp. 2, 19.
72 Cited in E. J. Hundert, *The Enlightenment's Fable: Bernard Mandeville and the Discovery of Society* (Cambridge: Cambridge University Press, 2nd edn 2005), p. 203.
73 Mandeville, *The Fable of the Bees*, p. 98.
74 Mandeville, *The Fable of the Bees* (London, 4th edn 1725), p. 69.
75 Cited in Hundert, *The Enlightenment's Fable*, p. 144.

76 Henry Fielding, *The History of the Adventures of Joseph Andrews* (Dublin, 1743), vol. 2, p. 49.

77 Swift's fictional alter ego, Lemuel Gulliver, had this to say about the Georgian nobility: 'That our Young Noblemen are bred from their Childhood in Idleness and Luxury; that as soon as Years will permit, they consume their Vigour, and contract odious Diseases among lewd Females; and when their Fortunes are almost ruined, they marry some Woman of mean Birth, disagreeable Person, and unsound Constitution, merely for the Sake of Money, whom they hate and despise': Robert Demaria (ed.), *Jonathan Swift: Gulliver's Travels* (London: Penguin, 2003 edn), p. 236.

78 Cited in Taylor, 'Walpole, Robert'.

79 ibid.

80 Cited in Geoffrey Holmes, Daniel Szechi, *The Age of Oligarchy: Pre-industrial Britain* (London: Longman, 1993), p. 145.

81 Daniel Defoe, *The life and strange surprizing adventures of Robinson Crusoe* (London, 1719), p. 3.

82 Daniel Defoe, *A Plan of the English Commerce* (London, 1728), p. 79.

83 Cited in Langford, *A Polite and Commercial People*, p. 65.

84 ibid., p. 96.

85 John Brown, *An Estimate of the Manners and Principles of the Times* (London, 1757), pp. 42–3.

86 Thomas Wilson, *Distilled Spirituous Liquors the Bane of the Nation* (London, 1736), p. 7.

87 Cited in Warner, 'The naturalisation of beer and gin in early modern England', p. 377.

88 Wilson, *Distilled Spirituous Liquors*, p. 31.

89 ibid., p. 4.

90 Cited in Jonathan White, 'The "Slow but Sure Poyson": The Representation of Gin and Its

Drinkers, 1736–1751', *Journal of British Studies*, 42 (2003), p. 49.

91 Daniel Defoe, *The Complete English Tradesman, in Familiar Letters* (London, 1726), pp. 318–19.

92 Defoe, *A Tour Thro' the Whole Island of Great Britain*, vol. 1, p. 6.

93 Cited in Woodfine, *Britannia's Glories*, p. 128.

94 Hodgart (ed.), *Horace Walpole: Memoirs and Portraits*, p. 108.

95 Cited in Derek Jarrett, *England in the Age of Hogarth* (New Haven, Conn.: Yale University Press, 1986), p. 185.

96 Cited in Langford, *A Polite and Commercial People*, p. 244.

97 Cited in Jarrett, *England in the Age of Hogarth*, p. 184.

98 Cited in Simms, *Three Victories and a Defeat*, p. 275.

99 *Historical Manuscripts Commission 14th Report* (London: Eyre and Spottiswoode, 1895), vol. 9, p. 54.

100 Cited in M. S. Anderson, *The War of the Austrian Succession, 1740–1748* (Harlow: Pearson, Longman, 1999), p. 61.

101 Cited in Simms, *Three Victories and a Defeat*, p. 299.

102 Coxe, *Memoirs of the Life and Administration of Sir Robert Walpole*, vol. 1, p. 695.

103 Cited in Langford, *A Polite and Commercial People*, p. 185.

104 Cited in Simms, *Three Victories and a Defeat*, p. 317. There was also outrage that George had worn a Hanoverian yellow sash at Dettingen, rather than British colours.

105 Cited in John Cannon, 'George II', *Oxford Dictionary of National Biography*.

106 Cited in Anderson, *War of the Austrian Succession*, p. 144.

107 Cited in Simms, *Three Victories and a Defeat*, p. 340.

108 Cited in Reed Browning, *The War*

of the Austrian Succession (New York: St Martin's Press, 1993), p. 241.

109 Cited in Simms, *Three Victories and a Defeat*, p. 341.

110 ibid., p. 344.

111 Cited in Anderson, *War of the Austrian Succession*, p. 190.

112 Cited in Robin Eagles, '"The Only Disagreeable Thing in the whole": the Selection and Experience of the British Hostages for the Delivery of Cape Breton in Paris, 1748–49', in Kathleên Hardesty Doig, Dorothy Medlin (eds), *British–French Exchanges in the Eighteenth Century* (Newcastle: Cambridge Scholars Publishing, 2007), p. 101.

113 Cited in Anderson, *War of the Austrian Succession*, p. 210.

114 ibid., pp. 210–11.

115 LWL, MS vol. 59, p. 76.

116 Cited in Simms, *Three Victories and a Defeat*, p. 369.

7 Greatness of Empire

1 Pepys, *Diary*, entry for 29 September 1665.

2 London Metropolitan Archives, CLA/002/02/01/0500.

3 *The Spectator*, no. 69 (19 May 1711).

4 Pepys, *Diary*, entry for 8 October 1665.

5 Cited in Joyce Lorimer, 'The failure of the English Guiana ventures 1595–1667 and James I's foreign policy', *Journal of Imperial and Commonwealth History*, 21 (1993), p. 16.

6 *A Declaration of His Highnes, by the Advice of his Council* (London, 1656), p. 4.

7 Cited in Karen Ordahl Kupperman, 'Errand to the Indies: Puritan Colonization from Providence Island through the Western Design', *William and Mary Quarterly*, third series, 45 (1988), p. 87.

8 The National Archives (TNA), CO 1/19, fo. 144; *Calendar of State Papers, Colonial Series, 1574–1660*, pp. 257–8.

9 Defoe, *A Plan of the English Commerce*, pp. 304–5.

10 Cited in Robert M. Bliss, *Revolution and Empire: English Politics and the American Colonies in the Seventeenth Century* (Manchester: Manchester University Press, 1990), p. 19. Charles also tried to establish a 'generall Governem[en]t' in New England in the mid-1630s, to put a stop to the 'many inconveniences and misscheifs' among the colonists there. Couched in similarly high-flown language, that scheme too came to nothing: TNA, CO 1/9, fo. 143; *Calendar of State Papers, Colonial Series, 1574–1660*, pp. 178, 191–2, 200, 204–5, 256–7.

11 C. H. Firth (ed.), *The Clarke Papers: Selections from the Papers of William Clarke* (Camden Society, new series, vol. lxi, 1899), pp. 203–4.

12 BL, Egerton MS 2395, fo. 110.

13 Cited in David Armitage, 'The Cromwellian Protectorate and the Languages of Empire', *Historical Journal*, 35 (1992), p. 541.

14 Benjamin Worsley, *The Advocate* (London, 1652), p. 12.

15 ibid., p. 1.

16 John Houghton, *England's Great Happiness, or, a Dialogue between Content and Complaint* (London, 1677), p. 19.

17 Sir Frederic Madden (ed.), 'A Relation of Some Abuses which are Committed Against the Commonwealth . . . 1629' (Camden Society, old series, vol. lxi, 1855), p. 23.

18 Cited in Pincus, *1688*, p. 84.

19 Cited in Nuala Zahedieh, 'Overseas Expansion and Trade in the Seventeenth Century', in Canny (ed.), *The Origins of Empire*, p. 410.

20 Pepys, *Diary*, entries for 1 July 1661, and 5 Sept. and 21 Nov. 1663.

21 George Villiers, 2nd duke of Buckingham, *A Letter to Sir Thomas Osborn* (London, 1672), p. 11.

22 Defoe, *A Plan of the English Commerce*, pp. 143–4.

23 BL, Additional MS 11411, fos 11v–12v; Egerton MS 2395, fos 270–5.

24 Cited in Jill Lepore, 'Metacom [Philip; *called* King Philip]', *Oxford Dictionary of National Biography*.

25 Cited in Steven Sarson, *British America 1500–1800: Creating Colonies, Imagining an Empire* (London: Hodder Arnold, 2005), p. 59.

26 Cited in Richard R. Johnson, 'The Revolution of 1688–9 in the American colonies', in Jonathan I. Israel (ed.), *The Anglo-Dutch Moment: Essays on the Glorious Revolution and its World Impact* (Cambridge: Cambridge University Press, 1991), 220.

27 Cited in Richard R. Johnson, 'Andros, Sir Edmund', *Oxford Dictionary of National Biography*.

28 Cited in Barbara Cresswell Murison, 'William Blathwayt's Empire: Politics and Administration in England and the Atlantic Colonies, 1668–1710' (University of Western Ontario Ph.D. thesis 1981), p. 83.

29 *Historical Manuscripts Commission: House of Lords, New Series* (London: H.M.S.O., 1953), vol. 10, p. 154.

30 Cited in Edward Pearce, *Pitt the Elder: Man of War* (London: Pimlico, 2011), p. 50.

31 *Historical Manuscripts Commission: The Manuscripts of the Duke of Buccleuch* (London: Eyre and Spottiswoode, 1897), vol. 2, p. 119.

32 Beinecke Library, Yale, Osborn fb 237. I would like to thank Paul Grant-Costa for this reference.

33 Cited in Daniel K. Richter, 'War and Culture: the Iroquois Experience', *William and Mary Quarterly*, third series, 40 (1983), p. 548.

34 Charles Johnson, *A General History of the Pyrates* (London, 2nd edn 1724), p. 88.

35 *Calendar of State Papers, Colonial Series, America and West Indies, 1712–1714* (London: H.M.S.O., 1926), p. 29.

36 Henry Stevens (ed.), *The Dawn of British Trade to the East Indies* (London: Henry Stevens & Son, 1886), p. 199.

37 John Skinner, *A True Relation of the Uniust, Cruell, and Barbarous Proceedings against the English at Amboyna* (London, 1624), pp. 7–11.

38 Cited in Philip J. Stern, '"A Politie of Civill & Military Power": Political Thought and the Late Seventeenth-Century Foundations of the East India Company-State', *Journal of British Studies*, 47 (2008), pp. 280, 282.

39 Pepys, *Diary*, entry for 25 Sept. 1660.

40 *The Craftsman*, no. 11 (6–9 Jan. 1727).

41 Cited in Holmes, Szechi, *The Age of Oligarchy*, p. 254.

42 Carl Theo Eben (ed.), *Gottlieb Mittelberger's Journey to Pennsylvania in the Year 1750* (Philadelphia: John Jos. McVey, 1898), p. 19.

43 ibid., pp. 20–4.

44 There is some doubt surrounding whether Equiano was born in Africa, as he claims in his published life story, or was the son of a slave in South Carolina. Either way, he was intimately acquainted with the experiences of enslaved Africans: James Walvin, 'Equiano, Olaudah', *Oxford Dictionary of National Biography*.

45 Olaudah Equiano, *The Interesting Narrative of the Life of Olaudah Equiano* (London, 1789), vol. 1, pp. 78–9.

46 Cited in Kristen Block, 'Cultivating Inner and Outer Plantations: Property, Industry, and Slavery in Early Quaker Migration to the New World', *Early American Studies*, 8 (2010), p. 524.

47 Cited in Ruth Paley, Cristina Malcolmson and Michael Hunter, 'Parliament and Slavery, 1660–c.1710', *Slavery and Abolition*, 31 (2010), p. 258.

48 Richard Hall (ed.), *Acts, Passed in the Island of Barbados from 1643 to 1762* (London, 1764), p. 130.

49 M. Postlethwayt, *The African Trade, the Great Pillar and Support of the British Plantation Trade in America* (London, 1745), p. 14.

50 John Towill Rutt (ed.), *Diary of Thomas Burton* (London, 1828), vol. 4, pp. 255–9.

51 Cited in James Horn, 'British Diaspora: Emigration from Britain, 1680–1815', in P. J. Marshall (ed.), *The Eighteenth Century* (Oxford: Oxford University Press, 1998), p. 43.

52 ibid., p. 41.

53 Postlethwayt, *The African Trade*, p. 2.

54 ibid., pp. 6, 34.

55 TNA, CO 1/9, fo. 46.

56 Cited in Sarson, *British America*, p. 127.

57 Mather, *Magnalia Christi Americana*, book 1, p. 15.

58 Cited in Sarson, *British America*, p. 140.

59 ibid., p. 159.

60 Cited in Block, 'Cultivating Inner and Outer Plantations', p. 536.

61 Cited in Gary B. Nash, 'Slaves and Slaveowners in Colonial Philadelphia', *William and Mary Quarterly*, third series, 30 (1973), p. 225.

62 Cited in Peter Linebaugh, Marcus Rediker, *The Many-Headed Hydra: The Hidden History of the*

Revolutionary Atlantic (London: Verso, 2000), p. 201.

63 Cited in John Donoghue, '"Out of the Land of Bondage": the English Revolution and the Atlantic Origins of Abolition', *American Historical Review*, 115 (2010), p. 953.

64 Cited in Alison Games, *The Web of Empire: English Cosmopolitans in an Age of Expansion 1560–1660* (Oxford: Oxford University Press, 2008), p. 146.

65 Cited in Sarson, *British America*, p. 178.

66 ibid., p. 94.

67 Cited in Nuala Zahedieh, 'Economy', in David Armitage, Michael J. Braddick (eds), *The British Atlantic World, 1500–1800* (London: Palgrave Macmillan, 2002), p. 57.

68 Cited in Linebaugh, Rediker, *The Many-Headed Hydra*, p. 195.

69 ibid., p. 193.

70 ibid., p. 105.

71 Cited in Sarson, *British America*, p. 113.

72 Carl Bridenbaugh (ed.), *Gentleman's Progress: The Itinerarium of Dr. Alexander Hamilton, 1744* (Chapel Hill, NC: The University of North Carolina Press, 1948), pp. 13–14.

73 Eben (ed.), *Gottlieb Mittelberger's Journey to Pennsylvania*, pp. 54–5.

74 Cited in Boyd Stanley Schlenther, 'Whitefield, George', *Oxford Dictionary of National Biography*.

75 ibid.

76 ibid.

77 Worsley, *The Advocate*, p. 1.

78 *The Country Journal: or, The Craftsman*, no. 649 (9 Dec. 1738); no. 650 (16 Dec. 1738).

79 *Historical Manuscripts Commission 14th Report*, vol. 9, p. 58.

80 Cited in Simms, *Three Victories and a Defeat*, p. 94.

81 ibid., p. 246.

82 ibid.

83 Cited in Langford, *A Polite and*

Commercial People, p. 172. Voltaire thought it would be better for France if Canada was 'at the bottom of the Arctic Sea': Holmes, Szechi, *The Age of Oligarchy*, p. 254.

84 Cited in Wilson, *The Sense of the People*, p. 154.

85 *Considerations upon the Present State of Our Affairs* (London, 2nd edn 1739), p. 9.

86 Cited in J. K. Laughton, rev. Richard Harding, 'Jenkins, Robert', *Oxford Dictionary of National Biography*.

87 *Gentleman's Magazine*, no. 9 (Feb. 1739), p. 103.

88 Cited in Simms, *Three Victories and a Defeat*, p. 345.

89 Cited in Sarson, *British America*, p. 193.

90 ibid., p. 202.

91 Cited in Niall Ferguson, *Empire: How Britain Made the Modern World* (London: Allen Lane, Penguin, 2004), p. 90.

92 Cited in P. J. Marshall, *The Making and Unmaking of Empires: Britain, India, and America c.1750–1783* (Oxford: Oxford University Press, 2005), p. 77.

93 Cited in W. A. Speck, 'Dunk, George Montagu, second earl of Halifax', *Oxford Dictionary of National Biography*.

94 Cited in Marshall, *The Making and Unmaking of Empires*, p. 75.

8 New World Order, 1754–83

1 John Mitchell, *Contest in America between Great Britain and France* (London, 1757), p. ix.

2 Ralph Griffiths, 'The progress of the French, in their views of universal monarchy', *The Monthly Review*, 14 (Mar. 1756), pp. 265–6.

3 BL, Additional MS 32850, fos 218v–219.

4 Cited in T. R. Clayton, 'The Duke of Newcastle, the Earl of Halifax, and the American origins of the Seven Years War', *Historical Journal*, 24 (1981), p. 598.

5 Cited in Marie Peters, 'Pitt, William, first earl of Chatham [*known as* Pitt the elder]', *Oxford Dictionary of National Biography*.

6 Cited in Peter D. G. Thomas, 'Townshend, Charles', *Oxford Dictionary of National Biography*.

7 Mitchell, *Contest in America*, p. xxi.

8 Cited in Beckles Willson, *The Life and Letters of James Wolfe* (London: William Heinemann, 1909), p. 392.

9 LWL, MS vol. 101, pt iii, fos 69r, 69v.

10 ibid., pt iii, fo. 52.

11 Seven French warships were destroyed in or soon after the battle, and a further nine never made it back out of the Vilaine River, where they had fled for safety.

12 LWL, MS vol. 101, pt iv, fos 86–7.

13 Cited in Simms, *Three Victories and a Defeat*, p. 484. Pitt's speech in the Commons in which he made this boast lasted 'near two hours', and was clearly a major social event, for the House was 'so crowded with ladies, as well as gentlemen' that an order had to be passed 'prohibiting any person to appear there for the future, except the members [i.e. MPs] themselves': LWL, MS vol. 101, pt xiii, fo. 81.

14 ibid., pt iv, fo. 93; pt v, fos 96–7.

15 ibid., pt v, fos 95–6.

16 Cited in Peters, 'Pitt, William'.

17 LWL, MS vol. 101, pt viii, fo. 183.

18 ibid., pt ix, fo. 184. Clearly George VI (1895–1952) was not the first British monarch to receive elocution lessons for his inaugural speech.

19 Cited in John Cannon, 'George III', *Oxford Dictionary of National Biography*.

20 Cited in Simms, *Three Victories and a Defeat*, p. 475.

21 Cited in Cannon, 'George III'.

22 LWL, MS vol. 101, pt ix, fo. 192.

23 Cited in Peters, 'Pitt, William'.

24 Cited in Jarrett, *England in the Age of Hogarth*, p. 27.

25 Cited in Simms, *Three Victories and a Defeat*, p. 502.

26 Cited in John Brewer, 'The Misfortunes of Lord Bute: a Case-Study in Eighteenth-Century Political Argument and Public Opinion', *Historical Journal*, 16 (1973), p. 4.

27 Edmund Burke, *A letter from Edmund Burke, Esq. One of the Representatives in Parliament for the city of Bristol* (Dublin, 1777), p. 41.

28 Cited in Marshall, *The Making and Unmaking of Empires*, p. 163.

29 Cited in H. V. Bowen, *The Business of Empire: The East India Company and Imperial Britain, 1756–1833* (Cambridge: Cambridge University Press, 2005), p. 8.

30 John Cartwright, *Take Your Choice!* (London, 1776), p. xxi.

31 Some historians put the figure at nearer £150 million.

32 Cited in Fred Anderson, *The Crucible of War: The Seven Years' War and the Fate of Empire in British North America, 1764–1766* (London: Faber and Faber, 2000), p. 642.

33 Cited in John Phillip Reid, *Authority to Legislate: Constitutional History of the American Revolution* (Madison: University of Wisconsin Press, 1991), p. 75.

34 Cited in Marshall, *The Making and Unmaking of Empires*, p. 167.

35 ibid., p. 168.

36 *The Charters of the Following Provinces of North America* (London, 1766), p. 18.

37 ibid., p. 5.

38 Cited in Bruce Lenman, *England's Colonial Wars 1550–1688* (Harlow: Pearson, Longman, 2001), p. 265.

39 Cited in Anderson, *Crucible of War*, p. 683.

40 *Vox Populi, Vox Dei. A Providence Gazette Extraordinary* (24 Aug. 1765), front page.

41 Cited in John Ferling, *Almost a Miracle: The American Victory in the War of Independence* (Oxford: Oxford University Press, 2009), p. 91; Robert J. Allison, *The American Revolution: A Concise History* (Oxford: Oxford University Press, 2011), p. 16.

42 D. O. Thomas (ed.), *Richard Price: Political Writings* (Cambridge, Cambridge University Press, 1991), p. 42.

43 Cited in Cannon, 'George III'.

44 *Letters from the Year 1774 to 1796 of John Wilkes* (London: Longman, Hurst, Rees, and Orme, 2nd edn 1805), vol. 1, p. 72.

45 Cited in Holmes, Szechi, *The Age of Oligarchy*, p. 212.

46 John Brown, *An Estimate of the Manners and Principles of the Times* (London, 2nd edn 1757), pp. 67, 74, 157.

47 ibid., p. 182.

48 Cited in Wilson, *The Sense of the People*, p. 72.

49 Cited in Bob Harris, *Politics and the Nation: Britain in the Mid-Eighteenth Century* (Oxford: Oxford University Press, 2002), p. 74.

50 Cited in Wilson, *The Sense of the People*, p. 224.

51 Mary Wollstonecraft, *A Vindication of the Rights of Woman* (London, 1792), p. 451.

52 Cited in Langford, *A Polite and Commercial People*, p. 157.

53 Cited in John Rule, 'The Labouring Poor', in Dickinson (ed.), *Blackwell Companion to Eighteenth-Century Britain*, p. 191.

54 Cited in Jarrett, *England in the Age of Hogarth*, p. 48.

55 LWL, MS vol. 101, pt iii, fo. 69.

56 Cited in Holmes, Szechi, *The Age of Oligarchy*, p. 221.

57 Cited in Simms, *Three Victories and a Defeat*, p. 584.

58 *Speeches of the Governors of Massachusetts from 1765 to 1775* (Boston, Mass., 1818), p. 218.

59 Hodgart (ed.), *Horace Walpole Memoirs*, p. 225.

60 Douglass Adair, John A. Schutz (eds), *Peter Oliver's Origin and Progress of the American Rebellion: A Tory View* (Stanford, CA: Stanford University Press, 1961), pp. 115, 116.

61 Cited in Brendan McConville, *The King's Three Faces: The Rise & Fall of Royal America, 1688–1776* (Chapel Hill, NC: The University of North Carolina Press, 2006), p. 290.

62 Cited in Richard R. Johnson, '"Parliamentary Egotisms": the Clash of Legislatures in the Making of the American Revolution', *Journal of American History*, 74 (1987), p. 356.

63 Cited in Simms, *Three Victories and a Defeat*, p. 589.

64 Adair, Schutz (eds), *Peter Oliver's Origin and Progress of the American Rebellion*, p. 118.

65 Cited in Bruce Lenman, *Britain's Colonial Wars 1688–1783* (Harlow: Pearson, Longman, 2001), p. 202.

66 Cited in Ferling, *Almost a Miracle*, p. 26.

67 Cited in Marshall, *The Making and Unmaking of Empires*, p. 169.

68 The accusation that Howe had effectively 'murdered' the redcoats at Bunker Hill was made by one of his own officers: Ferling, *Almost a Miracle*, p. 60.

69 Cited in Charles Royster, 'Washington, George', *Oxford Dictionary of National Biography*.

70 Cited in Simms, *Three Victories and a Defeat*, p. 597.

71 Cited in Thomas B. Allen, *Tories: Fighting for the King in America's First Civil War* (New York: HarperCollins, 2010), p. 203.

72 ibid.

73 Cited in Ferling, *Almost a Miracle*, p. 298.

74 Cited in Cannon, 'George III'.

75 Cited in Ferling, *Almost a Miracle*, p. 118.

76 Samuel Johnson, *Taxation no Tyranny* (London, 1775), p. 89.

77 George Birkbeck Hill (ed.), *Boswell's Life of Johnson* (Oxford: Clarendon Press, 1887), vol. 3, p. 69.

78 ibid., p. 79.

79 ibid., vol. 2, p. 121; vol. 3, p. 77.

80 Samuel Johnson, *The Patriot* (London, 1774), p. 22.

81 Samuel Johnson, *A Dictionary of the English Language* (London, 1775), vol. 2, p. 332.

82 Hill (ed.), *Boswell's Life of Johnson*, vol. 4, p. 221.

83 I have based my definition of the Enlightenment primarily on the best recent study of the movement: John Robertson, *The Case for the Enlightenment: Scotland and Naples, 1680–1760* (Cambridge: Cambridge University Press, 2005), pp. 8, 29–32, and chapter 1 generally.

84 David Hume, *Essays, Moral and Political* (Edinburgh, 1741), p. 89.

85 Hodgart (ed.), *Walpole Memoirs*, p. 79.

86 Cited in Langford, *A Polite and Commercial People*, p. 469.

87 Cited in John Robertson, 'Hume, David', *Oxford Dictionary of National Biography*.

88 Cited in John Mullan, *Sentiment and Sociability: The Language of Feeling in the Eighteenth Century* (Oxford: Oxford University Press, 1990), pp. 24, 28.

89 ibid., p. 231.

90 ibid., pp. 203, 204.

91 *The London Review of English and Foreign Literature*, 1 (1775), p. 101.

92 Cited in Philip Carter, 'Polite "persons": Character, Biography and the Gentleman', *Transactions of the*

Royal Historical Society, sixth series, 12 (2002), p. 345.

93 Cited in Langford, *A Polite and Commercial People*, p. 471.

94 Anna Laetitia Barbauld (ed.), *The Correspondence of Samuel Richardson* (London: Richard Phillips, 1804), vol. 4, pp. 240–1.

95 Cited in Langford, *A Polite and Commercial People*, pp. 610–11.

96 Cited in Peter Thomson, 'Garrick, David', *Oxford Dictionary of National Biography*.

97 Defoe, *A Tour Thro' the Whole Island of Great Britain*, vol. 3, p. 223.

98 Cited in Clement Hawes, 'Johnson's Cosmopolitan Nationalism', in Philip Smallwood (ed.), *Johnson Re-Visioned: Looking Before and After* (Cranbury, NJ: Rosemont Publishing, 2009), p. 52.

99 Cited in G. J. Barker-Benfield, *The Culture of Sensibility: Sex and Society in Eighteenth-Century Britain* (Chicago: Chicago University Press, 1996), p. 213.

100 Cited in John Mullan, 'Sentimental novels', in John Richetti (ed.), *The Cambridge Companion to the Eighteenth Century Novel* (Cambridge: Cambridge University Press, 1996), p. 236.

101 Cited in Robin Reilly, 'Wedgwood, Josiah', *Oxford Dictionary of National Biography*.

102 Cited in Langford, *A Polite and Commercial People*, p. 674.

103 Goldsmith, *The Deserted Village*, lines 309, 326.

104 Cited in L. H. Butterfield, Marc Friedlaender and Mary-Jo Kline (eds), *The Book of Abigail and John: Selected Letters of the Adams Family, 1762–1784* (Cambridge,

Mass.: Harvard University Press, 1975), p. 142.

105 BL, Additional MS 35912, fo. 237.

106 Cited in Simms, *Three Victories and a Defeat*, p. 628.

107 ibid., p. 629.

108 ibid., p. 644.

109 Cited in Ferling, *Almost a Miracle*, 349.

110 Cited in Wilson, *The Sense of the People*, p. 249.

111 Cited in Marshall, *The Making and Unmaking of Empires*, p. 358.

112 ibid., p. 339.

113 Cited in Allen, *Tories*, p. 139.

114 Cited in Nicholas Rogers, *Crowds, Culture, and Politics in Georgian Britain* (Oxford: Oxford University Press, 1998), p. 152.

115 Cited in Ferling, *Almost a Miracle*, p. 466.

116 ibid., p. 510.

117 Cited in C. A. Bayley, Katherine Prior, 'Cornwallis, Charles, first Marquess Cornwallis', *Oxford Dictionary of National Biography*.

118 Cited in Ferling, *Almost a Miracle*, p. 516.

119 Cited in Peter D. G. Thomas, 'North, Frederick, second earl of Guilford [*known as* Lord North]', *Oxford Dictionary of National Biography*.

120 Cited in Cannon, 'George III'.

121 Cited in Lord Edmond Fitzmaurice, *Life of William, Earl of Shelburne* (London: Macmillan, 1876), vol. 3, pp. 297–8.

Epilogue

1 Marchamont Nedham, *Mercurius Pragmaticus*, no. 24 (5–12 Sept. 1648), sig. Gg2v.

ACKNOWLEDGEMENTS

I would like to thank the following scholars for reading and commenting on one or more of my draft chapters: John Adamson, Robin Eagles, Ian Gentles, Aaron Graham, Simon Healy, Hannes Kleineke, Noel Malcolm, Sarah Mortimer, Stephen Roberts, Philip Salmon, Arthur Williamson, and Brian Young. I am particularly grateful to John Adamson for inspiring and encouraging me, and to Arabella Pike for her advice and patience. My thanks must also go to Paul Seaward and Stephen Roberts at the History of Parliament Trust; to Paul Grant-Costa and Toby Glaza at the Yale Indian Papers Project; and to the wonderfully helpful staff at the Lewis Walpole Library. This book would have been impossible without the support of my father. But it is dedicated to my wife, for all her love and kindness.

INDEX